MW00951739

Advertising & Marketing Law: Cases and Materials: Volume 1

Third Edition • October 2016

Rebecca Tushnet
Georgetown Law

&

Eric Goldman
Santa Clara University School of Law

CONTENTS

i

CHAPTER 6: SPECIAL TOPICS IN COMPETITOR LAWSUITS

CHAPTER 16: THE ADVERTISING INDUSTRY ECOSYSTEM—INTERMEDIARIES AND THEIR REGULATION 1205

PREFACE TO THE THIRD EDITION

Portions © 2012–2016 Rebecca Tushnet and Eric Goldman

To make this book as accessible and easy-to-use for readers as possible, we have deliberately priced this casebook low and provided a DRM-free e-book. If you think your friends and colleagues would like their own copies, we'd appreciate it if you encouraged them to buy their own low-cost copies rather than sharing your copy with them.

About the Authors

Eric Goldman is a professor of law and Co-Director of the High Tech Law Institute at Santa Clara University School of Law. Before he became a full-time academic in 2002, he practiced Internet law for eight years in the Silicon Valley. His research and teaching focuses on Internet, intellectual property and advertising law topics, and he blogs on those topics at the Technology & Marketing Law Blog, http://blog.ericgoldman.org. Email: egoldman@gmail.com.

Rebecca Tushnet is a professor of law at Georgetown University Law Center. She clerked for Associate Justice David H. Souter and worked on intellectual property and advertising litigation before beginning teaching. Her academic work focuses on copyright, trademark and advertising law. Her blog is at http://tushnet.blogspot.com. Email: rlt26@law.georgetown.edu.

A Note to Professors

If you are adopting this book for your course, please email us. We can provide you with a variety of support materials, including our course notes and PowerPoint decks as well as access to a database of case-related props. We are also working on a teacher's manual.

A Note to Students

If you are interested in more information, consider the following resources:

- Professor Tushnet's blog at http://tushnet.blogspot.com or Twitter account at http://twitter.com/rtushnet.
- Professor Goldman's blog at http://blog.ericgoldman.org and Twitter account at http://twitter.com/ericgoldman.
- The ABA Antitrust Section's Advertising Disputes & Litigation Committee (at http://www.abanet.org/dch/committee.cfm?com=AT311570) has a number of useful resources as well, including an email list. They also put on teleconferences about careers in advertising law.

You may also want to check out Professor Goldman's blog post on Pursuing a Career in Advertising Law, http://blog.ericgoldman.org/personal/archives/2012/07/careers_in_adv e.html. The post includes course recommendations too.

We are slowly developing a complementary website for the book. Check out our in-process efforts at http://www.advertisinglawbook.com/.

Please email us with your corrections to this casebook and any suggestions for improvement!

If You Bought a Hard Copy of the Book

If you bought a hard copy of this book: While we've done our best to make the hard copy version of the book useful to you, the hard copy is missing some features, such as color images, clickable links and keyword searching. You may find a PDF version of the book helpful to complement your hard copy version. Please email Prof. Goldman (**egoldman@gmail.com**) your hard copy purchase receipt and he will happily email you a PDF at no extra cost to you.

A Note about International Advertising Law

On occasion, this book discusses international advertising laws and perspectives. However, we have deliberately chosen to focus on U.S. law. International advertising laws differ from U.S. law in many important ways, so it would be hard to address all of these major differences sufficiently. For more information about international advertising legal issues, you might check out the resources at http://www.galalaw.com/.

Editing Practices

Some notes about our editing practices:

- Textual omissions are noted with ellipses.
- Omitted footnotes are not indicated, but all footnote numbers are original.
- In-text citations are omitted without indication (including parenthetical explanations and some parallel citations).
- Although we usually preserved the original formatting (such as italics, bold and block quotes), some of this formatting may have changed or been lost in the conversion.

To improve readability, we have aggressively stripped out case citations and parenthetical explanations (more so than most casebooks). If you are interested in the case's/author's full text or intend to quote or cite any republished materials in the book, we *strongly* recommend that you obtain and reference a copy of the original materials.

To make the book more functional for you, we've liberally provided hyperlinks to underlying source materials throughout the book. You'll see these as blue text in the PDF. Not all sources are linked, and of course links are likely to rot. Still, we hope you find them helpful.

Acknowledgements

Thanks are due to many people, including students in Professor Goldman's and Professor Tushnet's respective classes who provided feedback on drafts. Tamara Piety of the University of Tulsa organized a 2011 conference on the casebook, and participants were thoughtful and generous in their responses. Special thanks to James Grimmelmann, Sam Halabi and Brant Harrell for their comments. The authors also would like to extend special thanks to Susanna McCrea, Georgetown Law's manuscript editor, for her work.

1. Why Study Advertising Law?

You've made an excellent choice studying advertising and marketing law! Some reasons why:

A Horizontal Course

Many of the courses you study in law school examine a single legal doctrine in some depth, such as contracts or criminal law. This course is structured differently. Instead of a deep "vertical" look at one legal doctrine, this course will survey a lot of disparate topics "horizontally." This course addresses material that may touch on other law school courses—contracts, trademarks, copyrights, an intellectual property survey course, Internet law, constitutional law, consumer law, professional responsibility (especially with respect to attorney advertising), business torts/advanced torts, entertainment/sports law and many others.

Horizontal evaluation of legal issues is a skill most lawyers use daily, and this course will give you a sense of how to do so. Because of its realism, students often find this doctrinal heterogeneity liberating. However, if you've never taken a horizontal course before, it will require some adjustment on your part. We'll cover a lot of doctrines relatively superficially. You should not expect to master the nuances of each doctrine covered in this course. Instead, you should focus on how the various legal doctrines interact with each other.

An Industry-Specific Course

This course focuses on a single industry: the advertising and marketing industry. You will get to know that industry in depth, including the business practices and lingo used by industry insiders.

Relevance to Your Practice

Advertising legal issues are ubiquitous. Every for-profit business needs to generate consumer demand, and even nonprofits advertise. Your clients will be pursuing advertising and marketing from the moment they launch their enterprises—and they will need legal help doing so. Whether or not you "like" advertising personally, your clients need to know what ads they can run. If you become an in-house attorney, it is even more likely that legal questions on advertising and marketing will hit your desk. You will have to consider law as well as ethics: What kinds of businesses are you willing to represent? What kinds of claims are you willing to approve?

Unlike consumer law courses, this course also covers lawsuits by competitors, rather than just consumer lawsuits and concomitant regulation. Nonetheless, consumer lawsuits are an important part of civil litigation (one consumer law scholar reports 120 appellate-level cases a year in Texas alone), creating substantial demand for both plaintiff and defense attorneys in this area.

Fun

Because you've been exposed to advertising all of your life, you already have first-hand experience with many of the issues we explore in this course. In fact, you may have seen or heard some of the ads spawning the litigation covered in this book. Even if not, advertising is an integral part of pop culture, and this is a rare course where enjoying television or the radio can improve your understanding of the course material—but only if you *don't* skip the ads!

Jobs?!

One report estimated that over a half-million employees work in the advertising industry. *Economic Impact of Advertising in the United States*, IHS.com, March 2015. You might join them, or you might find work providing legal support to them.

2. A Few Words About the History of Advertising

Advertising is as old as commerce. For as long as vendors have sought to sell goods and services, they have needed to inform and persuade consumers to transact with them.

Advertisers' ability to reach consumer audiences has depended, and continues to depend, on technology. Before printing was widely available, businesses principally relied on advertising techniques that could only reach local audiences, such as criers in the town square and signage. Location also played a key role in generating consumer demand. Numerous 19th century "unfair competition" cases involved a new competitor that opened shop close to an existing well-known business and used ambiguous or confusing signage, hoping that consumers would get misdirected to the competitor's location.

Many manufacturers branded their goods with unique identifiers such as symbols. These symbols acted as signals of quality to future buyers—after all, manufacturers depended on their reputation for quality, and poor-quality goods would degrade that reputation. The symbol also acted simultaneously as a form of advertising. Consumers who encountered the goods in the marketplace even after they had been purchased by someone else could learn where to procure goods of a similar quality. Manufacturers' use of identifiers on their goods gave rise to trademark law and the law of geographic indications of origin.

7

Technological innovations have created new ways to reach consumers, which have spurred changes in advertising. For example, proliferation of the printing press allowed advertisers to cost-effectively print handbills to give to consumers. The printing press led to print periodicals such as newspapers and magazines, and periodicals started running print advertising in the early 1700s. Among his many contributions to society, Ben Franklin was an important early innovator of print advertising.

The second half of the 1800s saw several interrelated technological innovations that spawned the modern advertising industry. First, industrialization improved manufacturing economies of scale, allowing manufacturers to cost-effectively produce mass identical copies of their goods. Manufacturers producing a high volume of goods concomitantly needed to reach increasingly larger consumer populations. Second, railroads reduced manufacturers' distribution costs, enabling them to spread their mass-produced goods to larger geographic areas and increasing their potential consumer population. However, this broadened geographic reach also meant that manufacturers could not rely exclusively on local advertising to build consumer awareness of their goods. Manufacturers needed efficient ways to reach larger consumer audiences, and this fueled demand for mass-media advertising—first print, then postal mail, radio and TV advertising, and more recently Internet advertising.

Iconic Ad Campaigns

Occasionally, an advertising campaign transcends into popular culture. In many cases, iconic ads are generation-specific because the ad campaigns only run for a limited period of time and are therefore unknown to people who weren't around or were too young to remember them. The 1970s and 1980s produced many iconic ads because of media concentration—a small number of media outlets could reach large segments of consumers—meaning that most consumers saw the same ads.

In 1999, *Advertising Age* ranked the top ten advertising characters of the 20th century. How many are you familiar with?

#10: Elsie, Borden dairy products
#9: Tony the Tiger, Kellogg's Sugar Frosted Flakes
#8: The Michelin Man, Michelin tires
#7: Aunt Jemima, Aunt Jemima pancake mixes and syrup
#6: The Pillsbury Doughboy, assorted Pillsbury foods
#5: The Energizer Bunny, Eveready Energizer batteries
#4: Betty Crocker, Betty Crocker food products
#3: The Green Giant, Green Giant vegetables
#2: Ronald McDonald, McDonald's restaurants
#1: The Marlboro Man, Marlboro cigarettes

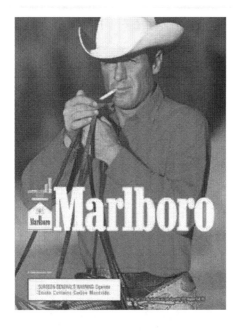

In 1999, *Advertising Age* also ranked the top 100 advertising campaigns. How many of the top ten do you recognize?

#10: Avis, "We try harder" (1963)
#9: Clairol, "Does she . . . or doesn't she?" (1957)
#8: Miller Lite beer, "Tastes great, less filling" (1974)
#7: Absolut Vodka, the Absolut Bottle (1981)
#6: DeBeers, "A diamond is forever" (1948)
#5: McDonald's, "You deserve a break today" (1971)
#4: Nike, "Just do it" (1988)
#3: Marlboro, the Marlboro Man (1955)
#2: Coca-Cola, "The pause that refreshes" (1929)
#1: Volkswagen, "Think Small" (1959)

Occasionally, specific ads have become iconic. For example, the line "Where's the Beef?" from a Wendy's TV advertisement spawned countless parodies and played a key role in the 1984 presidential campaign, when Walter Mondale ridiculed his Democratic primary opponent Gary Hart by asking "Where's the beef?" in response to Gary Hart's promise of "new ideas."

Over the past three decades, reaching a majority of consumers in a single ad campaign has become increasingly challenging. Consumers have more media choices, which fragment consumer audiences. Further, technology that makes it easier to skip ads, such as digital video recorders, has reduced the odds that numerous consumers will see any given TV ad. Meanwhile, marketers are producing more specialized products targeted for ever-smaller consumer niches, so many advertisers no longer want a specific ad to reach large groups of consumers.

Even so, a truly fresh ad concept can still achieve wide recognition among most consumers. A more recent example is the "Old Spice Guy," who had a huge hit with his first TV ad (plus millions of

YouTube views). He followed up the TV ads in 2010 on Twitter and YouTube, responding by speaking directly to consumers who submitted comments and questions.

3. Advertising Pervasiveness

Advertisers spend around $300 billion a year on advertising. *Economic Impact of Advertising in the United States*, IHS.com, March 2015. This constitutes over 2% of the United States' gross domestic product (GDP).* In 2008, U.S. census data recorded advertising expenditures of over $270 billion as follows:

Medium	Dollars Spent (millions)
Direct Mail	$59,622
Broadcast TV	43,734
Newspapers	35,788
Cable TV	27,544
Radio	17,535
Yellow Pages	13,844
Magazines	12,960
Internet (excluding search)	11,371
"Out-of-home" (billboards, buses, kiosks, etc.)	7,562
Business papers	4,111
Miscellaneous	36,696

---

* In a different study, it was estimated that "US advertisers will spend nearly $565 on paid media, on average, to reach each consumer in the country in 2014." eMarketer, Global Ad Spending Growth to Double This Year, July 9, 2014, http://www.emarketer.com/Article/Global-Ad-Spending-Growth-Double-This-Year/1010997.

The allocation of revenues among the various media, and to emerging media, has changed substantially over time. For example, Google reported about $35 billion in domestic revenues in 2015, much of which was derived from search advertising. Given the relative size of other ad media, it's easy to see how search ads have shaken up the advertising world. Mobile advertising is producing a similarly important shift in advertising budgets.

These amounts only include the out-of-pocket expenditures of advertisers; they don't include the salary costs of marketing employees and may not include other costs of preparing ad copy, such as licensing intellectual property or retaining freelancers. As a result, the total economic scope of the advertising and marketing industry is probably higher than these numbers indicate.

Advertising-Saturated Society

Wherever people go, advertisements now follow. There are ads on eggs, subway turnstiles, motion sickness bags on airplanes, bins in airport security lines, and other previously ad-free spaces. *See* Louise Story, *Anywhere the Eye Can See, It's Likely to See an Ad*, N.Y. TIMES, Jan. 15, 2007. Ads can be tattooed onto people (sometimes called "skinvertising"), placed on panhandler signs (sometimes called "bumvertising") and placed in men's urinals. What's the most striking place you've ever seen an ad?

Collectively, we are exposed to a huge number of ads every day. No one knows exactly how many, and this quantity is often subject to hyperbole. David Shenk, author of the book *Data Smog* (1997), estimated that the average American encountered 560 daily advertising messages in 1971 and over 3,000 messages per day in 1997. Other estimates from around the same time were that the average American was exposed to 245 commercial messages each day.

Even at the lower estimate, the average person would still encounter over 15 commercial messages every waking hour.

4. Consumers Often Dislike Advertising

We all have examples of advertising we like: Ads that saved us money or time. Ads that made us laugh out loud. Ads that evoke a special time in our lives or made us nostalgic. Some ads may even move us to tears. Sometimes, we go out of our way to seek out advertising—some folks arrive at the movie theater early to catch the previews, or we may search Google hoping to see who advertises.

Yet, no matter how you personally feel about advertising, if you are considering a career in advertising law, you need to accept a simple and incontrovertible truth: most consumers dislike most advertising most of the time, even if every consumer has favorite ads they really like. This general anti-ad sentiment holds true in every historical period, demographic segment, geography and culture. This means that consumers try to avoid advertising in general, regardless of whether they'd like a particular ad if they saw it.

Thus, with respect to any particular advertisement, the odds are in fact very high that most people will dislike that ad. Many advertisers—even those who understand that most consumers dislike most ads—believe that *their* ads are the exception. They are almost always mistaken.

Eric Goldman, *A Coasean Analysis of Marketing*, 2006 WIS. L. REV. 1151 (excerpt)

Consumers hate spam. They hate pop-up ads, junk faxes, and telemarketing. Pick any marketing method, and consumers probably say they hate it. In extreme cases, unwanted marketing can cause consumers to experience "spam rage."

There are many reasons for consumers' deep antipathy toward marketing, but a principal cause is that consumers get too much of it. According to a 2004 Yankelovich study, "61% feel the amount of marketing and advertising is out of control; and 65% feel constantly bombarded with too much marketing and advertising."

Worse, the volume of marketing probably will increase as technology continues to lower marketing distribution costs and marketers seek out new ways to reach consumers. As one commentator has said, "marketers all over the world soak up every square inch of space, every extra second of time . . . . Every idle moment you possess is seen by some business somewhere as an opportunity to interrupt you and demand more of your attention." Because human attention is a scarce and largely fixed resource, continued growth in marketing volume creates a seemingly unavoidable crisis. Eventually, consumers may experience information overload, where their attention will be overrun by too much marketing. Some might feel that they have reached this point already.

NOTES AND QUESTIONS

The Medium is the Message. Consumers' attitudes towards ads partially depend on the delivery medium. Empirical studies repeatedly show that consumers overwhelmingly hate telemarketing more than any other form of advertising. (Door-to-door sales also historically garnered massive consumer antipathy, but the practice is relatively rare nowadays). Spam is also heavily reviled, although the improvement of anti-spam technologies has softened this attitude a bit. In contrast, while consumers dislike broadcast advertising, this hatred falls into percentages far below the hatred for telemarketing. So consider this: The exact same ad copy could be broadcast on radio and used as a telemarketing recording, yet it would produce a much stronger negative reaction in the latter form. Why does consumer response vary based on the advertising medium? *See* Eric Goldman, *Where's the Beef? Dissecting Spam's Purported Harms*, 22 J. MARSHALL J. COMPUTER & INFO. L. 13 (2003).

Why do consumers dislike advertising in general so much? Do *you* dislike most ads? Try a thought experiment: Imagine a world where advertising simply did not exist. Would you prefer that world over our current situation? What, if anything, would be lost? If you had a magic wand and could eliminate some or all ads, what kinds of ads would you allow, and where would you allow them? *See generally* Eric Goldman, *Fantasize About A World Without Advertising? Try Cuba*, FORBES TERTIUM QUID, Aug. 22, 2013.

Advertising as a Negative Externality. Advertising critics often characterize advertising as a negative externality similar to pollution. They argue that advertisers create uninternalized social costs—such as consumer annoyance—by "overproducing" ads (i.e., exceeding socially optimal levels of advertising). Based on this premise, critics sometimes argue that advertising should be treated like an environmental pollutant. *See, e.g.*, Dennis Hirsch, *Protecting the Inner Environment: What Privacy Regulation Can Learn from Environmental Law*, 41 GA. L. REV. 1 (2006). Are advertisers equivalent to smoke-belching factories? Why or why not? *See* Eric Goldman, *A Coasean Analysis of Marketing*, 2006 WIS. L. REV. 1151.

Advertising as the "Cost" of Content. Many publishers provide valuable editorial content to consumers via advertiser support, without making the consumers pay directly for the content. Instead, consumers "pay" for the content by consuming the associated advertising. Often, the ads are presented as what marketing guru Seth Godin has called "interruption marketing." The ads are interspersed in the editorial content in a way that interrupts enjoyment of the content itself.

Publishers often justify ads as the "price" of enjoying free editorial content. For example, Jamie Kellner, the CEO and chairman of Turner Broadcasting, responded in 2002 to the proliferation of DVRs (which make it easy to fast-forward through TV ads) by saying: "It's theft. Your contract with the network when you get the show is you're going to watch the [ad] spots. Otherwise you couldn't get the show on an ad-supported basis. Any time you skip a commercial … you're actually stealing the programming." He did acknowledge that "there's a certain amount of tolerance for going to the bathroom." Do you agree with Kellner's characterizations?

If advertising is a "cost" to consumers, naturally consumers will try to minimize their "costs" by avoiding the ads. This manifests itself in a variety of ways: the impulse to switch radio stations when ads come on; the development of "banner ad blindness," where consumers instinctively look past banner advertisements on web pages; and skipping television ads by fast-forwarding through them or doing other tasks (getting a snack or going to the bathroom) during the commercial breaks. What steps do you take to ignore advertising? When do you pay attention? How did you learn these coping mechanisms?

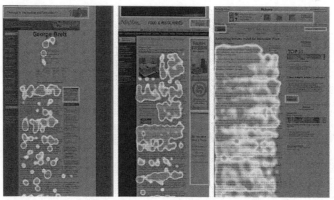

[Figure: three eye-tracking studies showing that web visitors ignore banner ads (shown in the yellow highlighted boxes). Used with permission of Jakob Nielsen, http://www.useit.com.]

In a sense, when advertisers treat ads as a "cost," they teach consumers to avoid ads. Ads succeed best when they help consumers make their lives better, in which case consumers *want* the ads. Achieving this degree of relevance to consumers has proven exceptionally hard in practice.

See generally Daniel G. Goldstein et al, *The Economic and Cognitive Costs of Annoying Display Advertisements*, 51 J. MKTG. RES. 742 (2014).

Consumer Distrust. Consumers say that they distrust advertising, generally ranking it toward the lower end of believability. *See Advertising Age*, March 5, 1984, at 1, col. 1. Yet most people accept that advertising has a major effect on consumer behavior. For example, a 2007 study that found that children were more likely to choose items in McDonald's packaging over identical food items contained in plain, unmarked packaging. *See* Thomas N. Robinson et al., *Effects of Fast Food Branding on Young Children's Taste Preferences*, 161 ARCHIVES PEDIATRIC & ADOLESCENT MED. 792 (2007). And consumers do enjoy particular ad campaigns, even turning them into cultural touchstones, as Section 2 indicated. Do you have any thoughts about how we might reconcile this apparent paradox? See the first few sections of Chapter 2.

But Does Advertising Actually Work? One well-known quote, attributed to retail mogul John Wanamaker, is "Half the money I spend on advertising is wasted; the trouble is I don't know which half." The eye-tracking images above don't represent a situation unique to online advertising. Even highly informational banner ads, presented to consumers searching for specific terms, may not have much effect, at least for brands that are already well known. *See* Tom Blake et al., *Consumer Heterogeneity and Paid Search Effectiveness: A Large Scale Field Experiment*, 83 ECONOMETRICA 155 (2015).

Consumer behavior is so erratic that it is hard to say what works even when a marketer has massive amounts of data at its disposal. *See* Randall A. Lewis & Justin M. Rao, *On the Near Impossibility of Measuring the Returns to Advertising* (Apr. 23, 2013) (research by Google and Yahoo! data scientists). *But see* Randall A. Lewis & David H. Reiley, *Does Retail Advertising Work? Measuring the Effects of Advertising on Sales via a Controlled Experiment on Yahoo!* (June 8, 2011) (research by data scientists at Google finding that display ads on Yahoo! led to more purchases in stores).

5. A Few Key Issues

Throughout the semester, keep your eye on the following key issues:

The Advertising/Non-Advertising Divide

In theory, it should be easy to classify the world into "advertising" and "everything else." In practice, sorting information into tidy buckets is incredibly hard. First, the term "advertising" doesn't have only one universally accepted definition. Second, advertisers and publishers are constantly developing new ways of delivering their advertising messages. These ongoing innovations put substantial pressure on a legal system that doesn't handle the categorization issue well. And it puts substantial pressure on lawyers to recognize when their clients are advertising and what issues might arise.

Telling the Truth

The top-line objective of false advertising law is simple: advertisers must tell consumers the truth. But we trust your time in law school has taught you that determining "the truth" is rarely simple. Typically, false advertising law is interested in how consumers perceive an advertiser's claims. But groups of consumers may evaluate or understand claims differently, and we have to consider both the express claims advanced by the advertiser as well as any implied claims that consumers might derive from the information they receive. So complying with the basic tenet of advertising law— tell the truth—turns out to be much more nuanced than you might anticipate.

As Jean Wegman Burns has written,

> Most areas of life lack the precision of mathematics, and the search for a single, unchanging, and ascertainable "truth" is a near impossible quest. To choose just one example, a court has determined that it is misleading to label a vegetable-based food product as "gelatin," despite the fact that the general public has no clear idea of whether gelatin is an animal- or vegetable-derived product. Compounding the problem of discerning the "truth" of an advertising claim, courts are often faced with advertising claims based on highly technical areas of science, medicine, or engineering in which they have no expertise. In addition . . . courts must often determine the truth or falsity of advertising jargon written in "catchy" phrases containing broad claims that do not lend themselves to precise analysis.

Jean Wegman Burns, *Confused Jurisprudence: False Advertising Under the Lanham Act*, 79 B.U.L. REV. 807 (1999) (footnotes omitted).

The reality that truth isn't binary poses constant ethical challenges for advertising lawyers. Even if an advertisement is "truthful" (or, at least, truthful enough) in the legal sense, can advertising lawyers still object to it as unethical? Throughout the course, constantly ask yourself whether you would have approved the advertisement in question if you had been the advertiser's lawyer. If not, why not? And do you think you could express your position strongly enough to resist the pressures of one or more marketing folks who really, *really* want to make the claim?

You might also self-reflect whether your internal ethical standards towards advertising become more (or less) flexible as you study the materials this semester. After seeing so many egregious examples of advertisements, does it make you more tolerant of ads that merely stretch the truth? If you're an advertising lawyer dealing with clients who, every day, are asking you to approve ads filled with puffery and not-exactly-deceptive-but-not-exactly-truthful claims, will you become desensitized to the grey areas between truthful and deceptive?

Who Regulates Advertising?

Advertising is subject to a complex mosaic of regulators and regulations, including federal, state and local requirements. There are also many self-regulatory efforts, both across all industries (such as the National Advertising Division, "NAD," discussed in Chapter 3) and within individual industries.

Advertisers face numerous potential plaintiffs, including:

- *Government agencies*, especially consumer protection agencies such as the Federal Trade Commission and state analogues. Other agencies may have enforcement powers against advertisers in specific media or specific fields, such as the Federal Communications Commission and the Food and Drug Administration. Indeed, most major federal agencies have some advertising-related regulations in their regulatory domain.
- *Competitors*. Government agencies tend to focus on the most severe advertising abuses. For everything else, we rely heavily on businesses to monitor and contest the errors of their competitors.

- *Consumers*. Individual consumers can and do sue advertisers, but most consumer lawsuits against advertisers involve aggregated claims in the form of class action lawsuits. Because class action lawsuits are a key part of advertising regulation, new developments in class action procedures and practices may have significant implications for advertising law.
- *Rightsowners*, including copyright owners, trademark owners and individuals asserting their personality rights.

Partially reflecting this array of plaintiffs, this book can be divided into four major parts and a coda:

- Chapters 1 and 2 provide an overview and define our terms.
- Chapters 3 through 8 explore false advertising claims, including claims by government agencies, competitors and consumers.
- Chapters 9 through 14 discuss legal restrictions on advertising other than regulations of truth/falsity, including intellectual property rights, privacy, and antitrust law.
- Chapters 15 and 16 address recurring issues that apply across advertising and marketing campaigns.
- Chapter 17 explores a potpourri of the regulations applicable to marketing in specific industries or targeted to specific groups.

As you go through, you should think about who is the *best* enforcer to stop advertiser misstatements or misdeeds. Each option has pros and cons. As you review the material this semester, consider how you might design better a more effective regulatory scheme.

Who Is Liable for a Problematic Ad?

As you review this casebook's materials, take note of the defendants' identity. Typically the advertiser is responsible for its choices, but a variety of other players are potentially liable as well, including company executives, ad agencies, publishers and more. Think about how that legal exposure affects the behavior of these secondary actors.

CHAPTER 2: WHAT IS AN ADVERTISEMENT?

What is an advertisement? In many cases, we know it when we see it. However, translating our intuition into legally precise language is difficult.

Advertising is more heavily regulated than other types of speech and receives reduced constitutional protection. Yet, we sometimes struggle to explain why we regulate advertising differently than other means of human communication. This chapter will attempt to define advertising for purposes of legal regulation and explore some justifications for developing advertising-specific regulations.

1. Definitions

The advertising industry is filled with jargon, not all of which has precise definitions. Before we get to legal definitions in Section 3 of this chapter, we'll start with a survey of the key terminology and concepts.

Advertising vs. Marketing vs. Sales

Advertising. Communications scholars often characterize "advertising" as paid persuasive communication that has an identified sponsor and occurs via mass media. They are also interested in "marketing communications"/"commercial persuasion," which may be considered a broader category that includes special events, stealth marketing (where sponsorship isn't disclosed), public relations, and corporate communications that might appear in news stories rather than in paid ads.

Lawyers' definitions of advertising rarely track the definition used by theorists. Our focus will not be limited to mass media because legal regulation of promotional communication extends beyond that—but how far beyond is often uncertain.

Marketing. Marketing experts often define "marketing" using the "Four Ps of Marketing": product, place, price and promotion. *Product* refers to designing commercial offerings that consumers want. *Place* stands for the distribution channels used to deliver the offering to consumers. *Price* is price-setting, such as using a low price to beat the competition or a high price to signal the product's status as a luxury good. *Promotion* includes advertising, press relations and sales.

Each "P" offers options for vendors to differentiate themselves from their competition. For example, some vendors compete principally based on price; others compete by developing non-traditional distribution channels (e.g., selling products via in-home parties instead of retail stores). Advertising and sales are other ways for competitors to differentiate themselves.

Advertising v. Sales. Although both are housed under the promotion category, advertising is often distinguished from sales both in content and in the personnel responsible for carrying them out. Typically, advertising stimulates general consumer interest in the advertiser's offerings. *See, e.g.,* the Merriam-Webster dictionary definition of advertising ("the action of calling something to the attention of the public especially by paid announcements"). Some types of transactions are complicated enough that buyers benefit from individual counseling about their purchase. "Sales" are this individual counseling by salespeople.

Consider how the process works in automobile transactions. Auto manufacturers advertise to get consumers to consider their models. Auto retailers ("dealers") advertise to get consumers to select them instead of other dealers. Even in the relatively rare cases where the advertising efforts "make the sale" (i.e., convince consumers to purchase a car without any further persuasion), many consumers need individual counseling to decide about specific models, customizable options, financing, trade-ins, etc. Thus, typically, good auto advertising gets consumers interested enough to show up at the dealer; the salesperson takes over from there to close the deal.

Advertising Can Have Different Purposes

To make things more complicated, advertising can have different objectives. Advertising by for-profit enterprises (to distinguish from cause advertising and political advertising) can be organized into at least four categories:

- *Direct response advertising* (sometimes called "direct marketing"): This type of advertising seeks to get an immediate response (such as a sale) from consumers. Examples include telemarketing and infomercials (imploring viewers to "CALL NOW!").

- *Brand or image advertising*: Brand advertising has the opposite intent from direct response advertising. Instead of trying to get consumers to act now, brand advertising seeks to define and reinforce the brand in consumers' minds. If successful, brand advertising establishes and increases consumer loyalty when consumers are subsequently faced with making a consumer decision. Examples include Nike's television advertising and the advertising for most luxury goods. The slogan "GE brings good things to life" is an example of corporate image advertising.

- *Informational advertising*: Another type of advertising is designed simply to get the facts—product specifications, product availability, price—out to consumers. An example: grocery store circulars showing products and prices.

- *Ideological or issue advertising*: Advertising can also have political or public service objectives, and publishers regularly accept payment for such ads (or "donate" time and space for them). Phillip Morris ads touting freedom of choice are examples of issue advertising.

2. Why Does Advertising Exist?

Advertising plays several roles in our society. This part highlights three complementary explanations for the existence of advertisers: (1) advertising helps vendors maximize profits; (2) advertising helps competition; and (3) advertising influences consumer behavior. We'll begin to discuss some of the socially disadvantageous consequences associated with these motivating forces.

A.   Advertising and Profit Maximization

If consumers were omniscient, advertising would not be necessary; consumers would know all of the competitive offerings and each vendor's trustworthiness, so there would not be any educational or informational benefits from ads. Of course, the real world looks quite different. It takes time for consumers to research product availability, pricing information and vendor trustworthiness. Advertising can fill these information gaps for consumers. (Some critics complain that advertising exacerbates consumers' information management problems rather than solving them; we'll address those complaints later).

From an advertiser's standpoint, advertising is a necessary cost of doing business. Although some commercial offerings become successful solely by word-of-mouth (for example, for many years Google did minimal advertising) or based on other factors like customer foot traffic from a prime physical location, many advertisers need to inform consumers of their availability and competitive superiority.

When calculating how much to spend on advertising, the answer is simple: advertisers should invest in advertising so long as it is profitable. In economic terms, the advertiser should advertise until the marginal dollar of advertising (marginal cost) produces only one dollar of incremental profit (the marginal benefit). So long as $1 of advertising produces more than $1 of profit, the advertiser should do more advertising.

You can see how an advertiser might optimize advertising through a highly stylized example involving search engine advertisers. Search engines pit companies against each other in a bidding war over keywords. When users enter a keyword into the search engine, the highest bidder's advertisement is prominently displayed at the top of the page; lower bidders go below, and predictably get fewer consumer clicks. Assume that for every 100 clicks, the advertiser makes one sale with an average gross profit of $10 (meaning that each click has an expected gross profit of $0.10).* Further assume that for the keyword, the advertiser anticipates the following results:

---

* A special note for economics geeks: Advertisers in a perfectly competitive market should not make any "profit" at all after internalizing the cost of capital. If so, the $10 "profit" represents the return on capital.

Bid Per Click	Anticipated Clicks	Gross Profit	Click Costs	Net Profit
$0.10	1,200	$120	$120	$0
$0.09	1,000	$100	$90	$10
$0.08	800	$80	$64	$16
$0.07	600	$60	$42	$18
$0.06	400	$40	$24	$16
$0.05	200	$20	$10	$10
$0	0	$0	$0	$0

You can visualize net profits in this diagram:

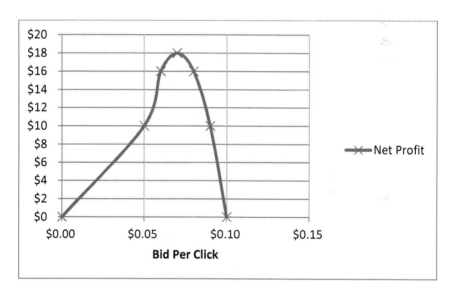

As the diagram shows, the advertiser maximizes net profits by bidding 7 cents per click. Bidding 8 or 9 cents will increase the number of anticipated clicks and gross profit, but those extra clicks cost more than they generate in revenue and therefore drag down net profit.

Note: Google tells advertisers how many clicks they can anticipate based on different bid prices, but its estimates aren't always reliable.

While the math may look elegant, unfortunately this example is unrealistic. Many advertisers—even large advertisers you might assume are fairly sophisticated—do not know such basic details as their profits and losses from product sales or how to attribute sales to any particular advertising source. This is true even in contexts such as keyword advertising, where in theory profits-per-click are seemingly computable. So while the theory predicts that advertisers will advertise so long as it's profitable, the advertiser's lack of data often makes such decisions more like guess-work. And many ads, such as brand advertisements, aren't meant to lead directly to sales at all, making the calculation of their profitability virtually impossible.

B.   Advertising and Competitive Markets

The economics of information begins with this proposition: efficient markets require that consumers have information about products and services to inform their decision-making. Price, quality, safety, and so on are attributes, each of which can be transmitted as information. If information is perfect and consumers are rational, consumers can satisfy their preferences as well as possible by weighing the various offerings. Meanwhile, producers have an incentive to improve their products across the attributes consumers want, because consumers will recognize the improvements and reward them. However, if information is imperfect, producers will have less incentive to compete on price and quality, and consumers as a whole may end up worse off.

As Lillian BeVier has explained, in the early and mid-twentieth century, many theorists thought advertising harmed competition by creating barriers to entry for new competitors, by distorting tastes (convincing people that identical products were different just because of their branding) and by manipulating demand.

Economists responded to these critiques in several ways. As to competition, they argued that advertising actually encourages new entrants and makes markets more efficient: a company with a good product can explain to consumers why they should switch.

Restraints on price advertising, by contrast, correlated with increased prices. For example, in a classic study, Lee Benham showed that consumers paid higher prices in markets with restrictions on advertising eyeglass prices than in markets where such price advertising was permitted. Lee Benham, *The Effect of Advertising on the Price of Eyeglasses*, 15 J. L. & ECON. 337 (1972). Subsequently, Benham and his coauthor reported that the benefits of advertising were strongest for the least educated consumers. Lee Benham & Alexandra Benham, *Regulating through the Professions: A Perspective on Information Control*, 18 J.L. & ECON. 421 (1975).

Benham's studies focused on ads where prices were mentioned. The pro-competitive results from advertising pricing information do not necessarily translate to other types of advertising.

A comprehensive study of legal fees and attorney advertising found that advertising appeared to drive down the price of wills, personal bankruptcies, and uncontested divorces, but lawyers who advertised personal injury legal services charged higher prices than their non-advertising counterparts. WILLIAM W. JACOBS ET AL., CLEVELAND REG'L OFFICE & BUREAU OF ECON., FTC, IMPROVING CONSUMER ACCESS TO LEGAL SERVICES: THE CASE FOR REMOVING RESTRICTIONS ON TRUTHFUL ADVERTISING (Nov. 1984). Consider possible explanations for this result: contingent fees may complicate consumers' ability to compare prices; personal injury lawyers may be able to increase demand for their services via advertising more than divorce lawyers can; the personal injury lawyers' ad copy didn't mention price; etc.

Another study found that Quebec's ban on television advertising to children raised the price of children's cereals in Quebec compared to other provinces, while prices for other cereals, which were still allowed to advertise, were no higher in Quebec. C. Robert Clark, *Advertising Restrictions and Competition in the Children's Breakfast Cereal Industry*, 50 J.L & ECON. 757, 759-60 (2007). This result is particularly interesting given that such ads rarely include price information—yet advertising still apparently lowered children's cereal prices, perhaps by increasing competition.

In other situations, advertising causes consumers to spend money on things they don't need and may not necessarily "want." For example, decades of cigarette advertising, including showing widely admired movie stars smoking in glamorous situations, helped establish the "coolness" of cigarettes. *See* ALLAN M. BRANDT, THE CIGARETTE CENTURY: THE RISE, FALL, AND DEADLY PERSISTENCE OF THE PRODUCT THAT DEFINED AMERICA (2007).

Advertising critics further point to the cumulative effect of advertising. By definition, most advertising seeks to point out how the advertiser's offering can satisfy consumers' preferences or otherwise improve their lives. However, an advertising-pervasive society means that consumers are constantly being reminded that they have unmet needs and told that buying more consumer products is the cure-all solution. The critics argue that collectively this leaves consumers feeling perpetually inadequate and feeling that they need to spend more money—money they often don't have—in a Sisyphean quest to fix those inadequacies. *See* BARRY SCHWARTZ, THE PARADOX OF CHOICE (2004).

C.   Advertising and Consumer Persuasion

We will occasionally discuss psychological and economic theories that try to explain what advertising does, why it works (when it works), whether and when advertisers might make false claims, and how advertisers and consumers are likely to react to particular forms of regulation. Economists talk about advertising as a means of conveying information, whereas psychologists and marketers are more likely to talk in terms of persuasion than of information. (Robert Cialdini's *Influence: The Psychology of Persuasion* provides an excellent overview from the psychological/marketing side.) What's the difference? If we focus on what kind of persuasion is misleading or otherwise unfair, are we likely to get different regulations than if we focus on what kind of information is false or misleading?

The legal literature on advertising regulation has tilted more toward the economics side. This section draws heavily on some key law-and-economics articles and responses thereto: Howard Beales et al., *The Efficient Regulation of Consumer Information*, 24 J. L. & ECON. 491 (1981); Lillian R. BeVier, *Competitor Suits for False Advertising under Section 43(a) of the Lanham Act: A Puzzle in the Law of Deception*, 78 VA. L. REV. 1 (1992); Fred S. McChesney, *Deception, Trademark Infringement and the Lanham Act: A Property-Rights Reconciliation*, 78 VA. L. REV. 49 (1992); Roger E. Schechter, *Additional Pieces of the Deception Puzzle: Some Reactions to Professor Bevier*, 78 VA. L. REV. 57 (1992); and Lee Goldman, *The World's Best Article on Competitor Suits for False Advertising*, 45 FLA. L. REV. 487 (1993).

Satisfying Consumer Preferences…or Changing Them?

An economic defense of ads treats brand preferences as neutral or even positive. If people feel better about buying Tide than about buying the store's generic detergent, then they may be better off paying a brand premium even if both products clean equally well. Brand loyalty reflects satisfaction, not deception.

But changes in consumer preferences can happen both for legitimate and less legitimate reasons. Advertising may educate consumers why a particular offering is superior to substitutes/alternatives, which can promote consumers to spend their dollars on the best option. (In economic terms, advertising changes the cross-elasticity of demand between the rival offerings).

Perhaps less legitimately, advertising can create consumer demand for offerings where the demand did not exist before. A prime example might be the Listerine brand's campaign based on the "disease" of "chronic halitosis" (basically, the ordinary condition of bad breath) and marketing of Listerine as a cure for this faux disease. The demand for Listerine grew because Listerine defined a problem and then offered itself as a solution. *See* GARY CROSS, AN ALL-CONSUMING CENTURY: WHY COMMERCIALISM WON IN MODERN AMERICA 35 (2000); *see also* SUSAN STRASSER, SATISFACTION GUARANTEED: THE MAKING OF THE AMERICAN MASS MARKET (1989) (providing a historical overview); Carl Elliott, *How to Brand a Disease—and Sell a Cure,* CNN.com, Oct. 11, 2010 (describing how pharmaceutical marketers engage in marketing to make consumers aware of diseases; the demand for drugs to cure those diseases follows). However, advertising's defenders argue that encouraging demand is neutral: if consumers now prefer to consume more, then ads simply enable them to satisfy their new preferences.

Advertisers often seek to change consumer preferences to create marketplace opportunities for themselves. Most "image" advertising/brand advertising is designed to sell a lifestyle such that consumers are trying to construct their own identities when they buy the product. Further, advertisers in many fashion-driven industries are dependent on finding ways to distinguish themselves from their peers. At its most insidious, advertising seeks to change consumer preferences by changing the consumers' subconscious—perhaps the nadir of free will/informed consumer choices assumed by neo-classical economists. (There is little evidence that classic "subliminal" advertising directly triggers purchases, but there is substantial evidence that simply repeating exposure to brands can increase preferences for those brands even though consumers don't understand that this has occurred and offer alternate explanations for their preferences when asked.)

Advertising law generally defines certain kinds of preference-changing as inherently non-deceptive (e.g., making people feel good about a car by showing it associated with beautiful people) and ignores the potential for preference-changing when consumers are objectively harmed in some way. For example, as a policy matter we try to stop consumers from deciding that the risk of a horrible smoking-related death is less important to them than the cool image of smoking and the temporary high it provides. This second response, ignoring potential changes in preferences, often involves arguments that preference changes only occurred because of deception. Consider the cigarette example, where cigarette companies have been charged with minimizing the actual risks and distracting consumers from the truth about addiction.

3. Legal Definitions of Advertising

We now turn to the legal question: What kinds of communications are legally defined as "advertising," and how are those communications regulated?

Introduction to the Central Hudson *Case*

Typically, courts apply one of three levels of scrutiny when evaluating if a legal regulation of speech comports with the First Amendment: strict scrutiny, intermediate scrutiny and rational basis scrutiny.

Presumptively, restrictions on speech are subject to strict scrutiny, which (almost) invariably means courts will find the restriction violates the First Amendment.

However, some categories of speech get lower levels of scrutiny. "Content-neutral" speech restrictions, such as "time/place/manner" restrictions, are typically subject to intermediate scrutiny. Certain categories of harmful speech, including obscenity, imminent threats of violence and (importantly for our purposes) false advertising, are not protected by the First Amendment at all, so restrictions of those speech categories are effectively subject to rational basis review, which means they are rarely if ever found to violate the First Amendment.

The following case established that regulations of truthful commercial speech are subject to an intermediate level of First Amendment scrutiny, and it has become a seminal citation for that proposition. As you read the case, also think about how the advertising at issue could benefit or harm society.

Central Hudson Gas & Elec. Corp. v. Public Service Commission of New York, 447 U.S. 557 (1980)

POWELL, J., delivered the opinion of the Court.

This case presents the question whether a regulation of the Public Service Commission of the State of New York violates the First and Fourteenth Amendments because it completely bans promotional advertising by an electrical utility.

I

In December 1973, the Commission, appellee here, ordered electric utilities in New York State to cease all advertising that "promot[es] the use of electricity." The order was based on the Commission's finding that "the interconnected utility system in New York State does not have sufficient fuel stocks or sources of supply to continue furnishing all customer demands for the 1973–1974 winter."*

Three years later, when the fuel shortage had eased, . . . the Commission extended the prohibition in a Policy Statement issued on February 25, 1977.

. . . The Commission declared all promotional advertising contrary to the national policy of conserving energy. It acknowledged that the ban is not a perfect vehicle for conserving energy. . . . [S]ince oil dealers are not under the Commission's jurisdiction and thus remain free to advertise, it was recognized that the ban can achieve only "piecemeal conservationism." Still, the Commission adopted the restriction because it was deemed likely to "result in some dampening of unnecessary growth" in energy consumption.

The Commission's order explicitly permitted "informational" advertising designed to encourage "*shifts* of consumption" from peak demand times to periods of low electricity demand. (emphasis in original). . . .

When it rejected requests for rehearing on the Policy Statement, the Commission supplemented its rationale for the advertising ban. The agency observed that additional electricity probably would be more expensive to produce than existing output. . . . This additional electricity would be subsidized by all consumers through generally

---

* [Editor's note: In 1973, OPEC (a cartel of mostly Arab, oil-producing countries) embargoed oil sales to the United States as punishment for the United States' military assistance to Israel in the Yom Kippur War. The resulting oil undersupply contributed to a brief but severe economic crisis. OPEC lifted the embargo in March 1974.]

higher rates. The state agency also thought that promotional advertising would give "misleading signals" to the public by appearing to encourage energy consumption at a time when conservation is needed. . . .

II

The Commission's order restricts only commercial speech, that is, expression related solely to the economic interests of the speaker and its audience. The First Amendment, as applied to the States through the Fourteenth Amendment, protects commercial speech from unwarranted governmental regulation. Commercial expression not only serves the economic interest of the speaker, but also assists consumers and furthers the societal interest in the fullest possible dissemination of information. In applying the First Amendment to this area, we have rejected the "highly paternalistic" view that government has complete power to suppress or regulate commercial speech. "[P]eople will perceive their own best interests if only they are well enough informed, and . . . the best means to that end is to open the channels of communication rather than to close them. . . ." Even when advertising communicates only an incomplete version of the relevant facts, the First Amendment presumes that some accurate information is better than no information at all.

Nevertheless, our decisions have recognized "the 'commonsense' distinction between speech proposing a commercial transaction, which occurs in an area traditionally subject to government regulation, and other varieties of speech."[5] The Constitution therefore

---

[5] . . . This Court's decisions on commercial expression have rested on the premise that such speech, although meriting some protection, is of less constitutional moment than other forms of speech. As we stated in *Ohralik*, the failure to distinguish between commercial and noncommercial speech

accords a lesser protection to commercial speech than to other constitutionally guaranteed expression. The protection available for particular commercial expression turns on the nature both of the expression and of the governmental interests served by its regulation.

The First Amendment's concern for commercial speech is based on the informational function of advertising. Consequently, there can be no constitutional objection to the suppression of commercial messages that do not accurately inform the public about lawful activity. The government may ban forms of communication more likely to deceive the public than to inform it, or commercial speech related to illegal activity.[6]. . .

In commercial speech cases, then, a four-part analysis has developed. At the outset, we must determine whether the expression is protected by the First Amendment. For commercial speech to come within that provision, it at least must concern lawful activity and not be misleading. Next, we ask whether the asserted governmental interest is substantial. If both inquiries yield positive answers, we must determine whether the regulation directly advances the governmental interest asserted, and whether it is not more extensive than is necessary to serve that interest.

"could invite dilution, simply by a leveling process, of the force of the [First] Amendment's guarantee with respect to the latter kind of speech."

[6] In most other contexts, the First Amendment prohibits regulation based on the content of the message. Two features of commercial speech permit regulation of its content. First, commercial speakers have extensive knowledge of both the market and their products. Thus, they are well situated to evaluate the accuracy of their messages and the lawfulness of the underlying activity. In addition, commercial speech, the offspring of economic self-interest, is a hardy breed of expression that is not "particularly susceptible to being crushed by overbroad regulation."

III

We now apply this four-step analysis for commercial speech to the Commission's arguments in support of its ban on promotional advertising.

A

. . . Because appellant holds a monopoly over the sale of electricity in its service area, the state court suggested that the Commission's order restricts no commercial speech of any worth. . . .

Even in monopoly markets, the suppression of advertising reduces the information available for consumer decisions and thereby defeats the purpose of the First Amendment. . . . Indeed, a monopoly enterprise legitimately may wish to inform the public that it has developed new services or terms of doing business. A consumer may need information to aid his decision whether or not to use the monopoly service at all, or how much of the service he should purchase. In the absence of factors that would distort the decision to advertise, we may assume that the willingness of a business to promote its products reflects a belief that consumers are interested in the advertising. Since no such extraordinary conditions have been identified in this case, appellant's monopoly position does not alter the First Amendment's protection for its commercial speech.

B

The Commission offers two state interests as justifications for the ban on promotional advertising. The first concerns energy conservation. Any increase in demand for electricity—during peak or off-peak periods—means greater consumption of energy. The Commission argues, and the New York court agreed, that the State's interest in conserving energy is sufficient to support suppression of advertising designed to increase consumption of electricity. In view of our country's dependence on energy resources beyond our control, no one can doubt the importance of energy conservation. Plainly, therefore, the state interest asserted is substantial.

The Commission also argues that promotional advertising will aggravate inequities caused by the failure to base the utilities' rates on marginal cost. . . . If peak demand were to rise, . . . the extra costs would be borne by all consumers through higher overall rates. Without promotional advertising, the Commission stated, this inequitable turn of events would be less likely to occur. The choice among rate structures involves difficult and important questions of economic supply and distributional fairness. The State's concern that rates be fair and efficient represents a clear and substantial governmental interest.

C

Next, we focus on the relationship between the State's interests and the advertising ban. Under this criterion, the Commission's laudable concern over the equity and efficiency of appellant's rates does not provide a constitutionally adequate reason for restricting protected speech. The link between the advertising prohibition and appellant's rate structure is, at most, tenuous. The impact of promotional advertising on the equity of appellant's rates is highly speculative. Advertising to increase off-peak usage would have to increase peak usage, while other factors that directly affect the fairness and efficiency of appellant's rates remained constant. Such conditional and remote eventualities simply cannot justify silencing appellant's promotional advertising.

In contrast, the State's interest in energy conservation is directly advanced by the Commission order at issue here. There is an immediate connection between advertising and demand for electricity. Central Hudson would not contest the advertising ban unless it believed that promotion would increase its sales. Thus, we find a direct link between the state interest in conservation and the Commission's order.

D

We come finally to the critical inquiry in this case: whether the Commission's complete suppression of speech ordinarily protected by the First Amendment is no more extensive than necessary to further the State's interest in energy conservation. The Commission's order reaches all promotional advertising, regardless of the impact of the touted service on overall energy use. But the energy conservation rationale, as important as it is, cannot justify suppressing information about electric devices or services that would cause no net increase in total energy use. In addition, no showing has been made that a more limited restriction on the content of promotional advertising would not serve adequately the State's interests. Appellant insists that but for the ban, it would advertise products and services that use energy efficiently. These include the "heat pump," which both parties acknowledge to be a major improvement in electric heating, and the use of electric heat as a "backup" to solar and other heat sources. . . . In the absence of authoritative findings to the contrary, we must credit as within the realm of possibility the claim that electric heat can be an efficient alternative in some circumstances.

. . . . To the extent that the Commission's order suppresses speech that in no way impairs the State's interest in energy conservation, the Commission's order violates the First and Fourteenth Amendments and must be invalidated.

The Commission also has not demonstrated that its interest in conservation cannot be protected adequately by more limited regulation of appellant's commercial expression. To further its policy of conservation, the Commission could attempt to restrict the format and content of Central Hudson's advertising. It might, for example, require that the advertisements include information about the relative efficiency and expense of the offered service, both under current conditions and for the foreseeable future.[13] In the absence of a showing that more limited speech regulation would be ineffective, we cannot approve the complete suppression of Central Hudson's advertising. . . .

[Justices Brennan's and Blackmun's concurrences in the judgment, and Justice Rehnquist's dissent, omitted]

JUSTICE STEVENS, concurring in the judgment.

Because "commercial speech" is afforded less constitutional protection than other forms of speech, it is important that the commercial speech concept not be defined too broadly lest speech deserving of greater constitutional protection be inadvertently suppressed. The issue in this case is whether New York's prohibition on the promotion of the use of electricity through advertising is a ban on nothing but commercial speech.

In my judgment one of the two definitions the Court uses in addressing that issue is too broad and the other may be somewhat too

---

[13] The Commission also might consider a system of previewing advertising campaigns to insure that they will not defeat conservation policy. It has instituted such a program for approving "informational" advertising under the Policy Statement challenged in this case. We have observed that commercial speech is such a sturdy brand of expression that traditional prior restraint doctrine may not apply to it. . . .

narrow. The Court first describes commercial speech as "expression related solely to the economic interests of the speaker and its audience." Although it is not entirely clear whether this definition uses the subject matter of the speech or the motivation of the speaker as the limiting factor, it seems clear to me that it encompasses speech that is entitled to the maximum protection afforded by the First Amendment. Neither a labor leader's exhortation to strike, nor an economist's dissertation on the money supply, should receive any lesser protection because the subject matter concerns only the economic interests of the audience. Nor should the economic motivation of a speaker qualify his constitutional protection; even Shakespeare may have been motivated by the prospect of pecuniary reward. Thus, the Court's first definition of commercial speech is unquestionably too broad.

The Court's second definition refers to "'speech proposing a commercial transaction.'" A salesman's solicitation, a broker's offer, and a manufacturer's publication of a price list or the terms of his standard warranty would unquestionably fit within this concept. Presumably, the definition is intended to encompass advertising that advises possible buyers of the availability of specific products at specific prices and describes the advantages of purchasing such items. Perhaps it also extends to other communications that do little more than make the name of a product or a service more familiar to the general public. Whatever the precise contours of the concept, and perhaps it is too early to enunciate an exact formulation, I am persuaded that it should not include the entire range of communication that is embraced within the term "promotional advertising."

This case involves a governmental regulation that completely bans promotional advertising by an electric utility. This ban encompasses a great deal more than mere proposals to engage in certain kinds of commercial transactions. It prohibits all advocacy of the immediate or future use of electricity. . . . The breadth of the ban thus exceeds the boundaries of the commercial speech concept, however that concept may be defined.

The justification for the regulation is nothing more than the expressed fear that the audience may find the utility's message persuasive. Without the aid of any coercion, deception, or misinformation, truthful communication may persuade some citizens to consume more electricity than they otherwise would. I assume that such a consequence would be undesirable and that government may therefore prohibit and punish the unnecessary or excessive use of electricity. But if the perceived harm associated with greater electrical usage is not sufficiently serious to justify direct regulation, surely it does not constitute the kind of clear and present danger that can justify the suppression of speech. . . .

In sum, I concur in the result because I do not consider this to be a "commercial speech" case. . . .

NOTES AND QUESTIONS

Advertising as a Social Good. If society might benefit from certain advertising, such as increasing awareness of heat pumps or encouraging conservation, maybe the government should undertake the consumer education function itself rather than relying on a profit-maximizing private company to do it?

For the majority, advertising's informational function provides the basis for First Amendment protection for advertising. However, advertising doesn't always convey factual information. In particular, brand advertising is designed to generate emotional responses from consumers, not educate them. Consider what information is imparted by this advertisement for a Belgian electricity company: https://www.youtube.com/watch?v=3hrH09KmPTY.

What is Commercial Speech? As Justice Stevens indicates in his *Central Hudson* concurrence, the court articulated multiple definitions of "commercial speech" which have different First Amendment implications.

Frequently, commercial speech is defined as "speech that proposes a commercial transaction." However, another definition of commercial speech is "expression related solely to the economic interests of the speaker and its audience." Justice Stevens fears this broader definition could allow the restriction of speech that deserves the highest level of First Amendment scrutiny (i.e., strict scrutiny). Consider whether subsequent cases validate his concern, or whether courts have basically gotten it right as new forms of advertising have emerged.

Central Hudson's *Four Factor Test*: *Central Hudson* is generally understood to establish a four-factor test for commercial speech regulation:

(1) the First Amendment protects non-misleading commercial speech about lawful activity; if the commercial speech is protected and the government seeks to regulate it,
(2) the asserted governmental interest must be substantial,
(3) the regulation must directly advance the governmental interest asserted, and
(4) the regulation must not be more extensive than is necessary to serve that interest.

Notice the possible inherent tension between factors three and four: a regulation that directly advances the government's interest (by going after most or all of the speech that causes harm) is likely to be fairly broad, while a narrow regulation may be unlikely to do much to advance the asserted interest.

Subsequent Case Law. The Supreme Court has generally been hostile to the regulation of truthful commercial speech in recent years, regularly finding that a given regulation fails to satisfy one of the last three *Central Hudson* factors.

Citizens United v. Federal Election Commission, 558 U.S. 50 (2010) made it nearly impossible to regulate corporation-funded political speech. However, the ruling did not itself purport to change *Central Hudson*'s legal test as applied to conventional product/service advertising.

In *Sorrell v. IMS Health Inc.,* 131 S. Ct. 2653 (2011), the Supreme Court suggested that regulation of commercial speech was content-based and subject to heightened scrutiny, though the majority did not revisit the first *Central Hudson* factor, which takes as a given that false and misleading commercial speech receives *no* First Amendment protection. As a result, some courts now treat *Sorrell* as having superseded *Central Hudson*'s four-factor test for the regulation of truthful, nonmisleading commercial speech. *See, e.g.,* Retail Digital Network, LLC v. Appelsmith, 810 F.3d 638 (9th Cir. 2016) (holding that strict scrutiny applies to content-or speaker-based restrictions on nonmisleading commercial speech regarding lawful goods or services); United States v. Caronia, 703 F.3d 149 (2d Cir. 2012) (same).

The Eighth Circuit, taking a slightly different approach, held that *Sorrell* "devised a new two-part test for assessing restrictions on commercial speech." 1-800-411-Pain Referral Serv., LLC v. Otto, 744 F.3d 1045, 1054 (8th Cir. 2014). According to the Eight Circuit, because *Sorrell* "did not define what 'heightened scrutiny' means, ... [t]he upshot is that when a court determines commercial speech restrictions are content- or speaker-based, it should then assess their constitutionality under *Central Hudson.*" *Id.* at 1055. *See also* King v. Governor of the State of N.J., 767 F.3d 216, 236 (3d Cir. 2014), *cert.*

denied sub nom. King v. Christie, 135 S. Ct. 2048 (2015) (suggesting that strict scrutiny might apply to some commercial speech regulations but declining to apply strict scrutiny to the challenged content- and speaker-based restriction on "professional speech" because the court found that the law did not "discriminat[e] on the basis of content [or speaker] in an impermissible manner"). How could any regulation targeting commercial speech not be content-based?

In *U.S. v. Alvarez*, 132 S. Ct. 2537 (2012), regarding a statute criminalizing falsely claiming military honors, the Court indicated that the First Amendment can protect false speech if the speech didn't cause any harm (e.g., if the falsity supported a fraudulent transaction). Ordinarily, false commercial speech receives no First Amendment protection, but the *Alvarez* court's protection of non-commercial false speech raises questions about whether that rule is still categorically true.

4. Distinguishing Between Advertising and Editorial Content

If regulations could easily sort between advertising and editorial content, we might be less concerned about the First Amendment implications of regulating advertising. But case after case shows us that there is a potentially big overlap in the Venn diagrams depicting advertising and editorial content, so regulations of advertising routinely pose some risk of unintentionally covering—and chilling—editorial content that ought to receive unqualified First Amendment protection.

A.   Kasky v. Nike

Introduction to the Case

Kasky v. Nike, Inc., 27 Cal. 4th 939 (Cal. 2002), is a flagship case involving commercial speech regulation, but it produced such a complicated and long-winded set of opinions that (based on strong student feedback) we have chosen to summarize it. If you are still confused about particular issues after reading to the end of our notes on the case, you may wish to look up the full opinion.

The case involves what we might call corporate speech: speech that doesn't propose an immediate commercial transaction but still might financially benefit the speaker. Furthermore, the plaintiff wasn't Nike's competitor or consumer, but was an activist seeking to use false advertising laws to attack a social issue. The interplay between false advertising law and political discourse often flummoxes judges, and balancing the various interests fractured the judges.

As you read the case summary, focus on two key issues:

1) Under the court's holding, is material disseminated by a for-profit company always "commercial" speech?

2) What makes commercial speech more appropriate to regulate than non-commercial speech?

Case Summary

In 1997, Nike reported $9.2 billion of revenues from selling shoes and sports apparel, and spent about $1 billion on advertising and marketing. Most of Nike's products were made in China, Vietnam and Indonesia by subcontractor manufacturers. The subcontractors' labor practices were the subject of substantial public scrutiny. Activists repeatedly charged that subcontractors violated local labor and safety laws and provided unacceptable working conditions.

Nike publicly responded to the criticism in several ways, including full-page ads in newspapers. An example:

"It is my sincere belief that Nike is doing a good job... but Nike can and should do better."

Ambassador Andrew Young
GoodWorks International, LLC

After six months of investigation, visiting twelve Asian factories and interviewing hundreds of workers in Indonesia, China, and Vietnam about Nike's overseas labor practices, this was how Andrew Young concluded his independent 75-page report, released yesterday.

Nike agrees. Good isn't good enough in anything we do. We can and will do better.

For details on exactly how — and for a complete copy of Ambassador Young's report and recommendations — please call 1-800-501-6295, go to www.nike.com/report, or go directly to GoodWorks at www.digitalrelease.com and enter the keyword: GoodWorks

Nike also sent a letter to many university administrators claiming innocence in the matter of the working conditions of its subcontractors' employees:*

June 18, 1996

Dear President and Director of Athletes,

As most of you have probably read, heard or seen, NIKE Inc. has recently came under attack from the Made in the USA Foundation, and other labor organizers, who claim that child labor is used in the production of its goods. While you may also be aware that NIKE has gone on the record to categorically deny these allegations as completely false and irresponsible, I would like to extend the courtesy of providing you with many of the facts that have been absent from the media discourse on this issue. I hope you will find this information useful in discussions with faculty and students who may be equally disturbed by these charges.

First and foremost, wherever NIKE operates around the globe, it is guided by principles set forth in a code of conduct that binds its production subcontractors to a signed Memorandum of Understanding. The Memorandum strictly prohibits child labor, and certifies compliance with applicable government regulations regarding minimum wage and overtime, as well as occupational health and safety,

---

* [Text retyped for clarity].

environmental regulations, worker insurance and equal opportunity provinces.

NIKE enforces its standards through daily observation by staff members who are responsible for monitoring adherence to the Memorandum. NIKE currently employs approximately 100 staff members in Asia alone to oversee operations. Every NIKE subcontractor knows that the enforcement of the Memorandum includes systematic, evaluation by third-party auditors. These thorough reviews include interviews with workers, examination of safety equipment and procedures, review of free health-care facilities, investigation of worker grievances and audits of payroll records.

Furthermore, over the past 20 years we have established long-term relationships with select subcontractors, and we believe that our sense of corporate responsibility has influenced the way they conduct their business. After all, it is incumbent upon leaders like NIKE to ensure that these violations do not occur in our subcontractor's factories.

We have found over the years that, given the vast area of our operations and the difficulty of policies such a network, some violations occur. However, we have been proud that in all material respects the code of conduct is complied with. The code is not just word. We live by it. NIKE is proud of its contribution in helping to build economies, provide skills, and create a brighter future for millions of workers around the world.

As a former Director of Athletes, and currently the Director of Sports Marketing at NIKE, I am indeed sensitive to these issues. I would be more than happy to make myself available to either discuss that issues and/or receive any opinions or insights you may have. We are committed to the world of sports and all that it stands for. I remain at your disposal.

Kindest regards,

Steve Miller

Steve Miller
Director
NIKE Sports Marketing

SM:en

cc: Philip H. Knight
        Donna Gibbs
        Kit Morris
        Erin Patton

The plaintiff asserted that Nike's public communications were false and therefore violated California's false advertising and unfair competition laws.

Justice Kennard wrote the majority opinion, joined by 3 other judges. The majority opinion summarized its conclusion:

> Because the messages in question were directed by a commercial speaker to a commercial audience, and because they made representations of fact about the speaker's own business operations for the purpose of promoting sales of its products, we conclude that these messages are commercial speech for purposes of applying state laws barring false and misleading commercial messages.

Summarizing U.S. Supreme Court precedent, the majority opinion identified three reasons for denying First Amendment protection for false advertising: (1) the speaker can more easily verify the accuracy of commercial speech, (2) commercial speech is "hardier" than noncommercial speech because the speaker wants to make a profit, and (3) the regulation of commercial speech may be intertwined with the government's authority to regulate the underlying commercial transaction.

The majority wrote:

> The United States Supreme Court has not adopted an all-purpose test to distinguish commercial from noncommercial speech under the First Amendment, nor has this court adopted such a test under the state Constitution, nor do we propose to do so here.

The majority examined the U.S. Supreme Court's ruling in *Bolger v. Youngs Drug Products Corp.*, 463 U.S. 60 (1983), which involved the dissemination of educational pamphlets about contraceptives. The *Bolger* opinion identified three factors that can be used to gauge if speech is commercial: the message's "advertising format, product references, and economic motivation." *Bolger* did not provide any bright lines. The presence of all three factors at the same time isn't *necessary* for speech to be commercial, but the combination of all three factors might render some speech commercial even in circumstances in which the presence of only one or two factors wouldn't be sufficient. The *Kasky* opinion explained that *Bolger* held that

> statements may properly be categorized as commercial "notwithstanding the fact that they contain discussions of important public issues," and that "advertising which 'links a product to a current public debate' is not thereby entitled to the constitutional protection afforded noncommercial speech," explaining further that "[a]dvertisers should not be permitted to immunize false or misleading product information from government regulation simply by including references to public issues."

Based on the *Bolger* factors but not using them directly, the majority adopted a different set of factors to distinguish commercial from noncommercial speech:

> categorizing a particular statement as commercial or noncommercial speech requires consideration of three elements: the speaker, the intended audience, and the content of the message.

The majority explained about the speaker and intended audience factors:

> the speaker is likely to be someone engaged in commerce— that is, generally, the production, distribution, or sale of goods or services—or someone acting on behalf of a person so engaged, and the intended audience is likely to be actual or potential buyers or customers of the speaker's goods or services, or persons acting for actual or potential buyers or customers, or persons (such as reporters or reviewers) likely to repeat the message to or otherwise influence actual or potential buyers or customers.

(In dissent, Justice Brown objected to conditioning the status of speech on a speaker's identity, saying that speaker-neutrality is "a fundamental tenet of First Amendment jurisprudence.")

The majority also defined the message content:

> [Commercial] speech consists of representations of fact about the business operations, products, or services of the speaker (or the individual or company that the speaker represents), made for the purpose of promoting sales of, or other

commercial transactions in, the speaker's products or services.

The majority then applied those factors to Nike's public messages about its labor practices, as follows:

Factor one (commercial speaker): Nike was a commercial speaker because it is "engaged in commerce."

Factor two (intended audience of purchasers/people who would act for or communicate to purchasers). University administrators were a commercial audience for Nike's letters because they buy lots of shoes and athletic apparel. Nike's press releases and letters to the editor, even though not communicated directly to consumers, were nevertheless intended to influence the buying public; and Nike desired "to maintain and/or increase its sales and profits."

Factor three (factual content promoting sales). Nike made factual representations about the labor conditions in its subcontracting manufacturers' facilities, and "Nike was in a position to readily verify the truth of any factual assertions it made on these topics." The majority continued:

> Nike engaged in speech that is particularly hardy or durable. Because Nike's purpose in making these statements, at least as alleged in the first amended complaint, was to maintain its sales and profits, regulation aimed at preventing false and actually or inherently misleading speech is unlikely to deter Nike from speaking truthfully or at all about the conditions in its factories. To the extent that application of these laws may make Nike more cautious, and cause it to make greater efforts to verify the truth of its statements, these laws will serve the purpose of commercial speech protection by

"insuring that the stream of commercial information flow[s] cleanly as well as freely."

The majority categorically rejected Nike's argument that its speech wasn't commercial because it addressed an issue "of intense public interest."

In dissent, Justice Brown argued that "Nike's commercial statements about its labor practices cannot be separated from its noncommercial statements about a public issue, because its labor practices are the public issue." Plainly, if globalization leads to children being beaten in factories, one might have a different perspective on globalization than if it improves those children's lives. So, the dissents contended, chilling Nike's factual claims would make its broader argument harder or impossible to convey. (Previous Supreme Court cases had used strict scrutiny where commercial elements were "inextricably intertwined" with noncommercial speech, such as fundraising for nonprofits by paid fundraisers, so the idea of inextricability could have had constitutional significance.)

The majority responded that commercial speech regularly addresses matters of public interest, even if it is "inextricably intertwined" with noncommercial speech. To take the speech at issue in *Bolger* as an example, condom ads inherently relate to political debates about contraception; they're still ads.

The majority also wasn't concerned about foregone commercial speech because of its hardiness and verifiability. The majority did, however, concede:

> To the extent Nike's press releases and letters discuss policy questions such as the degree to which domestic companies should be responsible for working conditions in factories located in other countries, or what standards domestic

companies ought to observe in such factories, or the merits and effects of economic "globalization" generally, Nike's statements are noncommercial speech. Any content-based regulation of these noncommercial messages would be subject to the strict scrutiny test for fully protected speech.

Nike argued that the false advertising laws constituted a viewpoint-based restriction (which would be subject to strict scrutiny) because they favored the speech of Nike's critics over Nike's own speech. The majority responded that the laws simply restrict false factual claims.

Justices Chin and Brown, in their dissents, objected to holding Nike to the equivalent of strict liability for any false statements it made about its labor practices, while Nike's activist critics—disseminating noncommercial speech when criticizing Nike—typically would be liable for factual errors only if they had "actual malice" about those errors. The majority didn't find that perturbing, saying this outcome was the logical consequence of the Supreme Court's jurisprudence and was defensible because of the hardiness and verifiability of commercial speech.

In dissent, Justice Brown objected:

> The majority ... creates an overbroad test that, taken to its logical conclusion, renders all corporate speech commercial speech. As defined, the test makes any public representation of fact by a speaker engaged in commerce about that speaker's products made for the purpose of promoting that speaker's products commercial speech....Because all corporate speech about a public issue reflects on the corporate image and therefore affects the corporation's business goodwill and sale value, the majority's test makes all such speech commercial notwithstanding the majority's assertions to the contrary....

By subjecting all corporate speech about business operations, products and services to the strict liability provisions of [California's false advertising and unfair competition laws], the majority's limited-purpose test unconstitutionally chills a corporation's ability to participate in the debate over matters of public concern.

Justice Brown's dissent argued that the Supreme Court should revisit *Central Hudson* and give full constitutional protection to much commercial speech. She suggested that some, but not all, false advertising regulation would survive higher scrutiny: For efficacy, quality, value, or safety, "the governmental interest in protecting consumers from fraud is especially strong because these representations address the fundamental questions asked by every consumer when he or she makes a buying decision." But "the governmental interest in protecting against consumer fraud is less strong if the [advertiser's] representations are unrelated to the characteristics of the product or service," as they were here. Do you agree? If the advertiser chooses to tell consumers about the conditions under which their products are made, what does that communicate about the importance of that information?

NOTES AND QUESTIONS

Subsequent Proceedings. In response to the California Supreme Court ruling, the U.S. Supreme Court granted certiorari in this case, but later dismissed the grant as improvidently granted. Nike, Inc. v. Kasky, 539 U.S. 654 (2003). Three justices dissented from the dismissal. Shortly after the Supreme Court's non-ruling, the parties settled the case, with Nike paying $1.5 million to a non-profit organization. *See* Adam Liptak, *Nike Move Ends Case Over Firms' Free Speech*, N.Y. TIMES, Sept. 13, 2003.

In 2004, California voters enacted Proposition 64, which requires that a plaintiff suffer an injury in fact and have "lost money or property" to bring a claim under California's unfair competition law and false advertising laws (the provisions used by Kasky). Prop. 64 doesn't change the case's holding about the characterization of corporate speech, but it prevents similar lawsuits from labor activists like Kasky because they have not lost money or property due to Nike's labor practices.

Distinguishing Commercial from Non-Commercial Speech. In the *Bolger* case, the U.S. Supreme Court indicated that commercial and non-commercial speech could be distinguished by considering the "advertising format, product references, and economic motivation." The majority's opinion reinterprets these factors, saying that courts should consider "the speaker, the intended audience, and the content of the message" to determine if speech is commercial or non-commercial. Pursuant to the majority's test, commercial speech will generally have:

- As a speaker: "someone engaged in commerce" or their representative.
- As the intended audience: "actual or potential buyers or customers" or their representative. Consumer influencers, such as reporters or product reviewers, are included.
- As message content: "representations of fact about the business operations, products, or services of the speaker (or the individual or company that the speaker represents), made for the purpose of promoting sales of, or other commercial transactions in, the speaker's products or services."

While these factors may be helpful considerations, you should not rely on this articulation too heavily. Although this opinion remains the governing law in California, courts routinely use various tests and factors inconsistently.

Can you think of any ways to better distinguish between commercial and non-commercial speech than those offered by the majority or Justice Brown? Or is this a situation where border cases always will be confounding?

Is Justice Brown correct that all corporate speech is commercial speech under the majority's test? *Compare* Citizens United v. FEC, 558 U.S. 310 (2010). As long as only factual statements in commercial speech can be challenged in court, and value claims like "globalization is a good idea" remain protected speech, would such a result be undesirable? (Return to this question once you've learned what kinds of claims are factual rather than puffery or opinion).

Consider the following example: a "counseling organization" represented that it could "cure" homosexuality—for a fee, of course. Former clients sued the organization for false advertising, claiming that the organization falsely advertised that homosexuality was a mental illness or disorder and that its therapy program was effective in changing the sexual orientation of clients. Commercial speech? *See* Ferguson v. JONAH (Jews Offering New Alternatives for Healing F/K/A Jews Offering New Alternatives to Homosexuality), No. HUD-L-5473-12 (N.J. Super. Ct. Feb. 5, 2015) (New Jersey Consumer Fraud Act claim).

Justifying Differential Treatment of Commercial Speech. The majority opinion lays out three reasons for protecting commercial speech less than non-commercial speech under the First Amendment:

1) The disseminator can more easily verify the commercial speech's veracity because the disseminator knows its products better than anyone else.

2) Commercial speech is "hardier" than much other speech because the profit motive helps trump any chilling effects from regulation.

3) The government's power to prevent commercial harms extends to speech that is "linked inextricably" to those harms.

How persuasive do you find these rationales? Would they apply to non-commercial speech as well?

Alex Kozinski and Stuart Banner, in their article, *Who's Afraid of Commercial Speech?*, 76 VA. L. REV. 627 (1990), make several retorts. First, they note that the words of the First Amendment do not distinguish between commercial and non-commercial speech. Then, they show how the various arguments in support of the commercial speech doctrine are both under- and over-inclusive. For example, much commercial speech, just like non-commercial speech, is not easily objectively verifiable, and much editorial content, such as newspapers, is produced with a profit motive, just like commercial speech. Finally, as illustrated by cases like *Kasky*, they show that efforts to define commercial speech are also under- and over-inclusive.

Focusing on this case in particular, do you think that the speech at issue—Nike's responses to criticisms about its labor practices—is "hardy"? As Justice Chin's dissent explains, the First Amendment will likely excuse most errors made by Nike's non-competitor critics because they can be liable only if their errors are made with actual malice. In contrast, due to the reduced First Amendment protection for commercial speech, Nike can be liable for its errors on the same topics with a lower level of scienter. As Nike's counsel, knowing your potential liability exposure, what would you advise your client to say when you are less than 100% certain about the facts?

Can you imagine circumstances where you, as Nike's counsel, might authorize factual claims despite the liability exposure? Would the market provide adequate incentives for companies to produce this information despite potential liability? As an analogy, note that vendors still produce goods and services in the face of tort liability (sometimes even strict liability) for those offerings.

Conflicting Norms. It's easy to see why this case baffled the judges. On the one hand, for the market to function properly, we need companies to publish accurate content. Notice that Nike was effectively litigating for the right to publish inaccurate content, which is an awkward position to defend. *See* Tamara R. Piety, *Grounding Nike: Exposing Nike's Quest for a Constitutional Right to Lie*, 78 TEMPLE L. REV. 151 (2005). Furthermore, Nike had a profit incentive to misstate the facts. If Nike's labor practices were dissuading potential customers from buying Nike's products, then providing more favorable characterizations of its labor practices should help boost/preserve sales.

On the other hand, labor practices are a major social issue. Nike's practices tied in to broader public debates about offshoring U.S. jobs to less costly labor markets and the ethical implications of companies taking advantage of foreign laws that provide less protection to employees than United States labor laws. Further, U.S.-based Nike executives may have trouble confirming the accuracy of reports coming from Nike's foreign offices. Finally, a ruling against Nike could prompt Nike to emphasize (more than they already do) ads that do not disseminate any factual information, engaging consumers' emotions instead of their reason. If Nike reallocated its consumer-facing efforts that way, are consumers really better off?

B.   Other Examples

Commercial speech regulation manifests itself in so many ways that the considerations relevant in one situation may appear useless in others. Does *Nike* help in determining whether commercial speech is involved in the following cases?

Signage Regulation. Wag More Dogs, LLC v. Artman, 795 F. Supp. 2d 377 (E.D. Va. 2011), involved a county zoning ordinance that restricted "business signs" to 60 square feet total. Wag More Dogs was a local store providing services to pets. The store's building faced a local park popular with dog owners, so on the park-side exterior, the business commissioned a large mural (16 feet x 60 feet, or nearly 1,000 square feet):

This mural is both an artistic expression and brand advertising for the store's offerings. The store admitted as much, saying that the mural was commissioned, in part, to "create goodwill with the people who frequented the dog park, many of whom were potential Wag More Dogs customers." Furthermore, the dogs depicted in the mural resembled the dogs in the store's logo:

63

The county zoning enforcement authorities deemed the mural an illegal business sign. The court upheld the business sign restrictions against the store's constitutional challenge, holding that the zoning regulation was content-neutral and should be evaluated using intermediate scrutiny. The court said that a mural depicting "generic images of waterfalls, meadows, flowers, or some other object or scenery wholly unrelated to" the store's business wouldn't violate the zoning restriction, nor would "a County informational mural that included images of dogs but said 'Welcome to Shirlington Park's Community Canine Area.'" Later, the court upheld the zoning enforcer's position that the business signs restriction applies to any mural whose subject had "any relationship" to the store's business. Does it seem odd that the zoning restriction restricts a dog-themed mural in a dog park, but only when paid for by a pet-oriented business? If the result of this zoning requirement is that the wall never gets painted, is that a net win for consumers?

Blog Posts. A private defense attorney writes a blog, mostly about his cases (though only about the ones he's won). The blog is part of his firm's website and contains information about how to hire him; it does not allow comments, but has a "contact us" link. He says his

motivation is partly marketing, partly educational—to make the
point that not everyone who's arrested is guilty. The state bar
attempts to sanction him for advertising without the required
disclaimers that all cases are unique and that past results don't
guarantee future successes. Is his blog commercial speech? *See* Va.
State Bar, *ex rel.* Third Dist. Comm., 744 S.E.2d 611 (Va. 2013) (the
majority says yes; the dissent would have characterized posts about
the criminal justice system, even those discussing specific cases, as
political speech because the attorney "uses the outcome of his cases to
illustrate his views of the system").

Company Press Releases. As the *Nike* ruling did, cases often treat
companies' press releases as advertising, even when the press
releases do not expressly promote a commercial offering. *See, e.g.,*
Yeager v. Cingular Wireless LLC, 673 F. Supp. 2d 1089 (E.D. Cal.
2009) (determining that a Cingular press release touting its disaster
preparedness equipment, called MACH 1 and MACH 2, and invoking
legendary pilot Chuck Yeager's accomplishment of flying at Mach 1
speed made a commercial use of Yeager's identity); *see also* Tamara
R. Piety, *Free Advertising: The Case for Public Relations as
Commercial Speech*, 10 LEWIS & CLARK L. REV. 367 (2006).

*What Would Advertising Regulation Look Like Without the First
Amendment?* We will occasionally contrast U.S. regulation with the
regimes of other countries. In the U.K., for example, the Advertising
Standards Authority (ASA) oversees all sorts of advertising, including
what we would call political or issue advertising. And it regulates for
far more than truthfulness. For example, the ASA recently ordered
one advertiser to stop advertising labial plastic surgery which offered
"a more natural appearance" and claimed to be appropriate for
"enlarged labia." The ad violated the ASA's requirement that
advertising be socially responsible by encouraging women to be
dissatisfied with their bodies and by implying that any part of a
person's body was not natural in appearance. This kind of

advertising, by contrast, would be considered nonmisleading in the U.S.

A few other examples: The ASA ordered that this ad not be repeated because the player depicted was 24 years old, and it was socially irresponsible to feature a person under 25 in a gambling ad, as it might encourage other young people to gamble.

This ad was condemned for showing a child in an unsafe position:

This ad was irresponsibly sexualized:

Other repeat topics at the ASA in recent years have included disputes over what part of Jerusalem can be attributed to Israel; disputes over what people for and against wind farms in Scotland can say; and disputes over what people advocating for a planned airport expansion can say.

Needless to say, the First Amendment leads US regulation down a different path. Regulators cannot restrict truthful advertising based on moral norms or other considerations about how society should function; and some of the ASA's examples involve obvious political speech that would be unregulable in the United States. Do you like the ASA's, or the First Amendment's, approach to advertising regulation better?

C. Advertising Masquerading as Editorial Content

Consumers frequently treat advertising as less credible than editorial content. A 2005 study by Jansen and Resnick illustrates this phenomenon. *See* Bernard J. Jansen & Marc Resnick, *Examining Searcher Perceptions of and Interactions with Sponsored Results*, June 2005. Consumers were shown multiple sets of Internet search results, some of which were labeled as advertising. "While study participants rated 52 percent of the organic results as 'relevant,' searchers described 42 percent of sponsored links as 'relevant' even though both sets of results were identical." *See* Press Release, Penn State University, *Consumers Suspicious of Sponsored Links* (June 10, 2005). In other words, the label "advertising" itself caused consumers to think the content was less relevant.

Thus, advertisers have incentives to make ads look like editorial content, sometimes by mimicking a publication's font and layout. Some call these ads "advertorials." An advertorial example:

Some print publishers have internal policies that limit ad mimicry and label the ad as "advertising" when the mimicry is too close. These rules often trace back to the Post Office Appropriation Act of 1912, which gave cheaper postal rates to periodical publishers that labeled editorial-like advertising. *See* Lewis Publ'g Co. v. Morgan, 229 U.S. 288 (1913) (upholding the statute).

"Video news releases," or VNRs, are another example of ads mimicking editorial content. *See* Ellen P. Goodman, *Stealth Marketing and Editorial Integrity*, 85 TEX. L. REV. 83 (2006). VNRs promote a product or service but are designed to look like regular news reports, often including canned interviews into which shots of the local reporter can be inserted so it looks like he or she is asking the questions. The television station makes the ultimate decision to run a VNR, and it is not paid for doing so (but saves on costs of production). Are VNRs commercial speech?

Growing in popularity are "native advertisements," a variation of the advertorial where the advertiser pays to publish promotional content that looks like editorial content. In some cases, a publication's staff writers prepare the content rather than the advertiser's marketing team or ad agency, ensuring the content is in the publication's editorial voice. *See, e.g.*, Michael Sebastian, *Native Ad Production Values Keep Growing With 'Orange is the New Black' Promo*, AD. AGE, June 13, 2014, http://adage.com/article/media/york-times-runs-native-ad-orange-black/293713/ (Netflix promoted the TV series *Orange Is the New Black* by hiring a New York Times native ad team to publish a story about women in prison).

A case brought by the NAD (a self-regulatory body we will consider in more detail in Chapter 3) concerned a story in *Shape* magazine and on the *Shape* website. The article bore the caption "News," discussed the importance of staying hydrated, and recommended SHAPE Water Boosters: "The obvious solution is to stick with water, but about 20 percent of Americans reportedly don't like the taste. If that sounds like you, check out the new SHAPE Water Boosters . . . Just a single squeeze . . . adds delicious flavor—but not calories—along with a concentrated punch of nutrients that offer some important bonus benefits."

The NAD "was concerned that consumers may give more credence to the advertiser's objective claims about the product's attributes because of the context in which the claims appeared." Unlike standard product placement (see below), the ad made specific and objective claims about the product. It might be true that the connection between the content and the magazine was obvious to consumers, but the NAD noted that "consumers can reasonably attach different weight to recommendations made in an editorial context than recommendations made in an advertising context. Put another way, consumers may reasonably believe that editorial recommendations in *SHAPE* magazine are independent of the influence of a sponsoring advertiser." American Media, Inc. (Shape Water Boosters), NAD Case #5665 (Dec. 18, 2013).

One recent study found that many common forms of disclosure of sponsored or "native" advertising were ineffective. Only one form—disclosure within the content itself—resulted in more than half of readers recognizing that the content was an ad. The following page layouts were tested, with the disclosures located in the areas marked in orange:

See Ricardo Bilton, *Which Native Ad Disclosed Itself Best?*, DigiDay, Sept. 17, 2014 (discussing a study by Nudge, an analytics company).

How often do you encounter native advertising? How do you know?

Ads Intermixed With Editorial Content. In *Stewart v. Rolling Stone LLC,* 181 Cal. App. 4th 664 (Cal. Ct. App. 2010), *Rolling Stone* magazine had run an editorial feature, called "Indie Rock Universe," on pages that folded out of the magazine. The editorial feature referenced numerous band names and musicians presented in a cartoonish manner. Foldout pages at the beginning and end of the feature included music-themed ads for Camel Cigarettes drawn in a similar (but not identical) cartoonish style. One of the ads said "COMMITTED TO SUPPORTING & PROMOTING INDEPENDENT RECORD LABELS" and contained the text:

The world of independent music is constantly changing. New styles and sounds emerge daily. That's why we're bringing you The FARM. A collaboration between Camel and independent artists and record labels. It's our way of supporting these innovators as they rise up to bring their sounds to the surface. We give them more opportunities to be heard through online music and countless events across the nation. [¶] Visit THEFARMROCKS.COM* [¶] Free shows, great bands and more!

[Beginning of the feature]

[Editor's note: The Camel ad spanning the editorial feature. Each page folds open.]

[Editor's note: the feature's 4 interior pages]

[Editor's note: ad on the back page of the feature.]

Some musicians sued for publicity rights violations and related claims. As discussed more in Chapter 13, publicity rights limit the commercial use of a person's name, so the dispositive question was whether Rolling Stone made a commercial use of the musicians' names included in the editorial feature. The court explained:

> Plaintiffs claim "It is hard to tell where, if at all, the Camel cigarettes advertisement begins and ends." We have examined the pages at issue and do not perceive . . . the distinction between the ad and the Feature to be as close as plaintiffs allege. The graphic designs of the ad and the Feature are quite different, one being based on hand-drawn cartoons and the other being based on collages of photographs. The background of the Feature is white college-

ruled paper, not a grassy rural landscape. It is undisputed that, standing alone, the Feature itself is completely devoid of any commercial message. In fact, the only nexus between the ad and the Feature is the mutual references to independent music. None of the band names in the Feature appear in the Camel ad, and none of the language or elements of the Camel ad appear in the Feature....plaintiffs have not cited us to a case, and our research has disclosed none, in which a magazine's editorial content has been deemed transformed into commercial speech merely because of its proximity to advertisements touching on the same subject matter....

The court also noted that "the cigarette company had no role in the design of the Feature itself." As a result, the court said that the editorial feature was noncommercial speech (and the musicians' publicity rights claim failed).

Later in the opinion, the *Stewart* court observes:

We also note that the November 15, 2007 issue of *Rolling Stone* magazine is replete with full-page advertisements, many of which appear to target the magazine's readership. These ads are primarily for alcoholic beverages, automobiles, personal grooming devices, fashion items, and cellular telephones. Out of the magazine's 215 pages, including the cover pages, no fewer than 108 pages are devoted to full-page advertisements, including several multipage ads. Thus, all of the editorial content of the magazine is, in a sense, "embedded" with advertising. It is true that the gatefold layout may intensify the readers' exposure to the ads because the pages run more or less contiguously and because the format requires readers to lift the advertising pages to the left and to the right, instead of just mindlessly turning them. But we see no principled legal distinction between a page of editorial content that is preceded and followed by full-page ads, and the gatefold format, in which the ads appear only on the reverse side of a feature's pages.

Would it have made a difference if the *Rolling Stone* graphic designers had known that R.J. Reynolds had bought the advertising spots around the feature?

Article Reprints. A newspaper or magazine article—a paradigmatic example of "editorial" content—can become commercial speech when distributed verbatim by a company with an economic interest in the article's contents. *See* Gordon & Breach Sci. Publishers S.A. v. Am. Inst. of Physics, 859 F. Supp. 1521 (S.D.N.Y. 1994); United Fabricare Supply, Inc. v. 3Hanger Supply Co., Inc., No. CV 12-03755-MWF (C.D. Cal. 2012). Is this consistent with the First Amendment?

Corporate Newsletters. Many companies publish newsletters filled only with editorial content as a way of building relationships with customers. For example, many law firms publish "news alerts" about recent legal developments. Not infrequently, the clear implication is that the new development requires the reader to find an expert who can help the reader with his/her specific situation; but in many cases that sales pitch is only by implication.

Nevertheless, courts know what's going on and are likely to treat these corporate-published editorial newsletters as advertising. For example, in *Holtzman v. Turza*, 08 C 2014 (N.D. Ill. Oct. 19, 2010), an attorney sent repeated unsolicited one-page junk faxes, of which about 75% was a single editorial article and the remainder of the page had various ways to identify and contact the attorney.

The court concluded that the newsletter was an "advertisement" for purposes of the federal anti-junk-fax law. The court said it was clear the attorney's goal was to "generate awareness of defendant's services and build his client base. . . . [There were] no facts to show that his genuine, primary motivation . . . was to educate CPAs and his business contacts on various industry-related topics rather than to build brand recognition and solicit business referrals for his law practice." It also didn't help that the attorney didn't write the editorial content himself; instead, the marketer who also delivered junk faxes wrote the content.

Product Placement. Product placement is the paid inclusion of products in editorial content, such as TV or movie characters using a branded product or a product reference in song lyrics. A famous early product placement was the inclusion of Reese's Pieces in the movie *E.T.*, which contributed to a huge sales growth for the candy. *See Taking It E.T.*, Snopes, May 11, 2011.

Product placement may be most familiar in TV shows and movies, but many other media have taken advantage of the phenomenon. In one initiative, DC Comics featured six different Pontiacs on its comic covers, and used a storyline about a man who had become one with his Pontiac.

Even novelists are in on the act: for example, Amazon sponsored a Kindle-only novella by Stephen King focusing on the company's e-reader. *See generally* Zahr K. Said, *Mandated Disclosure in Literary Hybrid Speech*, 88 WASH. L. REV. 419 (2013). The producers of the artificial sweetener Sweet 'N Low invested $400,000 in an e-book romance novel whose heroine loves Sweet 'N Low. In one scene, a friend asks her "isn't it bad for you?" The heroine "replies that she has researched the claims online and found studies showing that the product is safe: 'They fed lab rats twenty-five hundred packets of Sweet 'N' Low a day ... And still the F.D.A. or E.P.A., or whatevs agency, couldn't connect the dots from any kind of cancer in humans to my party in a packet.'" "To help shape the scene," the sponsor showed the author some of the research the heroine cites. Alexandra

Alter, *E-Book Mingles Love and Product Placement*, N.Y. TIMES, Nov. 2, 2014. What legal issues might you, as counsel to the company, have considered? What about legal issues for the author?

A 2011 report estimated the global market for product placement at $14 billion. *See* Ben Rooney, *Digital Technology and the Re-Birth of Product Placement*, WALL ST. J., Aug. 16, 2011. There are good reasons for this success. Product placements can take advantage of the higher cognitive credit that consumers assign to editorial content instead of advertising. Consumers may implicitly assume that the publishers editorially chose to include the product because it is the most popular, the "best," or the most noteworthy. In this sense, consumers may interpret a product's inclusion as an implicit product endorsement by the publisher.

The endorsement effect may be magnified when the characters extol the product's attributes. For example, consider the joyous reaction of contestants on the TV show *Survivor* whenever they receive a branded food item as part of a product placement deal. The contestants are so hungry that they would be overjoyed to get any food, but their response makes the placed product seem even more attractive and desirable. Similarly, when TV show hosts like Oprah or Ellen give away freebies to their audience, audience members inevitably respond with glee about getting a freebie.

In addition, consumers cannot "skip" the product placement advertising because it is embedded in the editorial content. In this sense, product placements are "DVR-proof" from consumers fast-forwarding through the commercials. Therefore, some television advertisers—fearful that no one is watching any TV ads anymore—are shifting their ad dollars to product placements.

Regulators have struggled with developing sensible policies toward product placements. By definition, product placements are integrated into editorial content, so regulators have a tough time isolating the "ad" for special regulatory treatment without also regulating the editorial content, which may trigger strict scrutiny of the regulation. How should product placement be treated under the First Amendment? Does it matter how much editorial control the sponsor exerts over the artists—for example, whether the artists are required to describe the product in favorable terms, or barred from associating it with villainous characters or poor performance?

We're also seeing "reverse" product placement, where fictional products depicted in fictional materials are turned into real products that consumers can buy. Examples include the Bubba Gump Shrimp Restaurants inspired by the movie *Forrest Gump*, Wonka Candy inspired by the movie *Willy Wonka and the Chocolate Factory*, Buzz Cola inspired by the TV show *The Simpsons*, and Dunder Mifflin copy paper inspired by the TV show *The Office*. *See* Stuart Elliott, *Expanding Line of Dunder Mifflin Products Shows Success in Reverse Product Placement*, N.Y. TIMES, Nov. 23, 2012.

"Astroturfing." Astroturfing occurs when an advertiser publishes online content, such as a blog, designed to look like a consumer's genuine opinion. For example, a website in 2006 called "All I Want for Xmas is a PSP" featured "amateur" videos and a "fansite" blog raving about the PSP. The content, in fact, was created by an ad agency of Sony Computer Entertainment America (makers of PSP). Although there are no specific anti-astroturfing laws, it is difficult or impossible for the advertiser to deny that such content is, in fact, advertising; and the failure to disclose the advertiser's role in creating the content can support both private claims as well as government enforcement actions such as, for example, enforcement pursuant to the FTC's endorsement and testimonials guidelines. *See In re* Reverb Communications, F.T.C. No. 092-3199 (settlement announced Aug. 26, 2010). We will discuss disclosure issues surrounding endorsements in greater detail in subsequent chapters.

Advertising Hyperlinks in Editorial Content. Some major newspapers, such as the *Los Angeles Times* and the *Chicago Tribune*, display key phrases in their editorial articles as paid hypertext link ads. *See* Kate Kaye, *LA Times Follows Chicago Tribune's Paid Link Lead*, Clickz News, April 28, 2010. An example is depicted in the screenshot below.

[Screenshot taken on August 8, 2010. The words *Sigur Ros* and *"Go"* are green-colored, hyperlinked ads (you can see the alt text "Click to Shop" when the word *"Go"* is moused over). Both links went to topically relevant pages on Amazon.com.]

Without the link ads, the articles are almost certainly non-commercial content that receives the highest level of First Amendment protection. With the text ads, does the content's character morph into commercial speech? Does it make a difference if the online newspaper sometimes embeds links in articles as an editorial decision (i.e., without being compensated)?

Several screens below the top, the blog has the following disclosure in its right hand navigation list:

Affiliate links disclaimer:

> Clicking on the green links will direct you to a third-party Web site. Bloggers and staff writers are in no way affiliated with these links that are placed by an e-commerce specialist only after stories and posts have been published.

Does adequate disclosure of the paid nature of the links to readers, whatever "adequate" means, ameliorate any of your concerns? Do you consider this adequate disclosure?

Does the purported wall between editorial and the e-commerce specialist change your feelings about the practice?

Content as Advertising. Just like advertising, "pure" editorial content can call attention to commercial offerings and create a demand for them. For example:

- Despite the impressive box office revenue for the *Star Wars* movie franchise, the gross revenues from *Star Wars*–themed merchandise dwarfs the box office returns. In effect, the movies (the "editorial content") create and drive demand for the merchandise. (So what? What, if anything, might advertising regulators want to regulate in the films?)
- Talk show interviews with recent book authors—a standard feature of an author's "book tour"—can help drive demand for the author's books. For example, former President Bill Clinton's interview with Oprah, timed with the release of his memoirs, helped the book achieve sales records. Similarly, television show performances (such as on *Saturday Night*

Live) increase bands' sales of their recorded music and live performances.

Due to this demand-creating property of editorial content, some advertisers would gladly pay for inclusion in editorial content. For example, in the 1950s "payola scandal," some record companies paid radio DJs money to play their songs, which boosted the popularity of the songs and increased sales of those songs. In response, Congress enacted anti-payola laws requiring "sponsorship identification"—if the publisher (in this case, the radio station) accepts payment for publishing content (in this case, playing songs on the radio), then the publisher is required to disclose this fact to consumers. This concept has been extended to television broadcasts as well.

Sponsorship identification laws attempt to solve one sort of problem: consumers' perceived desire to want to know when content is advertising. *See* Ellen Goodman, *Stealth Marketing and Editorial Integrity*, 85 TEX. L. REV. 83 (2006); Eric Goldman, *Stealth Risks of Regulating Stealth Marketing*, 85 TEX. L. REV. *see also* 11 (2006). However, it does not solve the underlying problem that regulatory distinctions between "content" and "advertising" can become nonsensical when editorial content performs the same function as advertising.

This chapter provides an overview of the various laws and institutions that regulate advertising for its truth. Broadly speaking, there is a tripartite regulatory structure: (1) government regulators at the federal and state level, acting as enforcers of the public interest; (2) competitors, who pursue their own interests against unfair competition and, we hope, thereby protect the public from the same; and (3) consumers, often in class actions based on state consumer protection law, asserting that they have been deceived or harmed by advertising. All three modes interact; each tends to have its own emphasis, and an advertiser must take each into account. We will get into the substantive rules of false advertising in Chapter 4.

1. The Federal Trade Commission (FTC)

A.   Statutory Background

The FTC is an independent agency created in 1914 that administers a wide variety of consumer protection laws. In early years, courts confined the FTC's power to antitrust, requiring the FTC to prove injury to competitors; injury to consumers was insufficient. Over time, the FTC's mission broadened. In 1938, an amendment to the FTC Act (FTCA) added the prohibition of "unfair or deceptive acts or practices" to the FTC's mandate. 15 U.S.C. § 45. The amendment also specifically prohibited false advertising in the areas of food, drugs, devices and cosmetics.

There are a number of highly specialized laws regulating specific industries and behaviors under which the FTC has the authority to regulate everything from widespread credit practices (e.g., the Truth in Lending Act, 15 U.S.C. §§ 1601–1667f) to collectible coins and political items (Hobby Protection Act, 15 U.S.C. §§ 2101–2106) to petroleum marketing (Petroleum Marketing Practices Act, 15 U.S.C.

§§ 2801–2841) to "dolphin-safe" tuna labeling (Dolphin Protection Consumer Information Act, 15 U.S.C. § 1385). But Section 45 is at the core of the FTC's consumer protection powers. Unfair or deceptive methods, acts, or practices "in or affecting commerce" are within the scope of the law, and courts have interpreted this broadly.[*] The recently created Consumer Financial Protection Bureau is also changing the regulatory landscape, though the FTC works closely with it and the agencies are still figuring out how to coordinate with each other.

Deceptiveness

Under 15 U.S.C. §45(a), "deceptive acts or practices in or affecting commerce" are unlawful. The FTCA also has special provisions for food, drug, medical device, service, and cosmetic advertising, reflecting the traditional division in responsibility between the FTC and the Food and Drug Administration in responsibility for regulating such things. 15 U.S.C. §52. The language of the FTCA is often quite broad, with much room for interpretation.[1]

---

[*] Certain institutions are exempt from the FTC's regulation, usually because some other industry-specific regulations exist. Banks, savings and loan institutions, and federal credit unions are probably the most significant. Common carriers, air carriers, and businesses that are subject to the Packers and Stockyards Act of 1921 are some other examples.

[1] Not everything is delegated to the FTC's discretion. Section 55(a)(2), for example, is a highly specific provision prohibiting producers of margarine from indicating in any way in ads that margarine is a dairy product. The presence of this provision suggests some of the political considerations that might lead to particular bans alongside general false advertising provisions (here, successful lobbying by powerful interests, in this case producers of dairy products such as butter, to give themselves advantages against competitors). It is also an indicator of the place of advertising law in the rise of the regulatory state. Historically, regulation of margarine provoked numerous constitutional challenges, ultimately resulting in rulings that

Unfairness

Although the FTC primarily relies upon its authority to enforce against deceptive trade acts, the FTCA also provides the FTC with the authority to enforce against "unfair" trade acts.

After a variety of controversies during the 1970s, many politicians concluded that the FTC was overreaching itself by trying to regulate too much of the economy, for example by sharply restricting advertising to children. "Unfair" had not previously been defined in the FTCA, and Congress codified a definition designed to limit the FTC's authority: unfairness requires that "the act or practice causes or is likely to cause substantial injury to consumers which is not reasonably avoidable by consumers themselves and not outweighed by countervailing benefits to consumers or to competition." § 45(n). Public policy cannot serve as a primary basis for a determination of unfairness. For the next three decades, the FTC rarely relied on its unfairness jurisdiction in the absence of an element of deception.

Increased attention to privacy and changing technologies have reinvigorated the FTC's interest in using its unfairness jurisdiction. For a detailed history of the FTC and its regulatory context and future, with special attention to privacy, see CHRIS JAY HOOFNAGLE, FEDERAL TRADE COMMISSION PRIVACY LAW AND POLICY (2016). We will discuss privacy in greater detail in Chapter 14, but by way of example, the FTC has successfully pursued a commercial site that

---

expanded the power of state and federal governments to regulate in the interest of the general welfare even when that interfered with the liberty of willing sellers (and occasionally of willing buyers). This was true, the courts ruled, even when the government might have been mistaken about the harms of, for example, margarine being substituted for butter.

posted sexually explicit pictures of women without their consent (e.g., "revenge porn") for unfairness.

Perhaps a more mainstream application of unfairness enforcement targeted Apple's policy of allowing in-app purchases, which were particularly popular in apps often used by children, such as "Tiny Zoo Friends." For an extended period, Apple treated a single authorization (for example, a parent entering her password to download an app) as valid for fifteen minutes. This period allowed many children to incur charges that they didn't understand and that were a surprise to their parents. Some of these charges were quite large, from $500 to $2600. The FTC alleged that billing parents and other iTunes account holders for children's activities in apps that are likely to be used by children without having obtained the account holders' express informed consent was an unfair billing practice. Apple agreed to provide full refunds of at least $32.5 million. In re Apple Inc., FTC File No. 112-3108 (Jan. 15, 2014).

Unfairness can also play something of a catchall role in dealing with bad behavior by advertisers, as long as it falls within the statutory definition. *See, e.g.,* FTC v. Roca Labs, Inc., No. 15-cv-02231 (M.D. Fla, Oct. 29, 2015) (enjoining a contractual prohibition on truthful and nondefamatory but "disparaging" reviews as unfair, and barring defendant from seeking to collect extra money from those who published such reviews).

Despite Congress' efforts to rein in the FTC's discretion to apply its unfairness authority, some FTC critics still question how the FTC uses it.

Structure of the Commission

The president appoints, with Senate confirmation, five commissioners to manage the FTC's activities. Appointments are for seven-year terms. No more than three commissioners may be members of the president's political party. Within the FTC, the Bureau of Competition administers antitrust law, the Bureau of Economics provides economic analysis and supports investigations and rulemakings, and the Bureau of Consumer Protection enforces the laws and rules on which we will focus.

Crucially, the FTCA does not provide for a private cause of action. *See, e.g.*, Carlson v. Coca-Cola Co., 483 F.2d 279 (9th Cir. 1973). The FTC is the exclusive enforcer of the FTCA.

The FTC has a number of avenues for exercising its broad regulatory mandate:

- Federal court litigation against a specific advertiser
- Adversarial administrative proceedings to require a specific advertiser to cease and desist unfair or deceptive practices, resulting in consent decrees or opinions pursuant to a final cease-and-desist order
- Rulemaking and public statements of enforcement policies to guide advertisers as a group
- Formal and informal advisory opinions for specific advertisers

This section will look more closely at each of these options.

B.   Enforcement of FTC Advertising Regulations

There are two pillars of truth in advertising according to the FTC: First, advertising must be truthful and not misleading. Second, advertisers must have adequate substantiation for all product claims before disseminating their advertising. Advertising Substantiation Policy Statement, 49 Fed. Reg. 30999, Aug. 2, 1984.

The FTC does not, of course, pursue every instance of misleading advertising. The factors that guide its enforcement discretion include:

- *Purchase frequency and price.* When a product is relatively inexpensive and purchased often, *and* the characteristic at issue is relatively easy for consumers to evaluate, the FTC assumes that sellers have little incentive to misrepresent themselves. Consumers can stop buying a product if they're unhappy with it, and the market can be trusted. As we'll discuss in Chapter 4, there are reasons why the market might not correct problems of this sort, given consumers' vulnerability to certain kinds of manipulations. Nonetheless, the FTC usually follows this rule.

- *Deterrence of widespread deceptive conduct.* The FTC is more interested in national and regional advertising than purely local matters, in order to protect the maximum number of consumers. The rise of the Internet, however, has made it possible for many more small businesses to reach national audiences. The FTC is also interested in objective claims that are difficult for consumers to evaluate, such as scientific claims about product performance.

- *Risk of physical or economic injury.* Health and safety claims are, for obvious reasons, traditional areas of FTC interest. Diet schemes and health supplements have been repeated targets over the past decade. Economic injury also matters: with economic downturns, the FTC focuses more attention on business opportunity and credit repair schemes targeting consumers who are already at financial risk.

In the 1970s and early 1980s, the FTC was especially willing to act against inexpensive products making health claims: Kraft Singles claiming to have more calcium than imitation cheese slices; Listerine claiming to prevent colds; various headache medicines claiming various kinds of superiority. Notice that these claims are difficult for consumers to verify, even though the products are inexpensive. Recently, the FTC has taken similar actions against mainstream advertisers, such as Kellogg when it made claims that its Frosted Mini-Wheats were "clinically shown to improve kids' attentiveness by nearly 20%" (as compared to an empty stomach, it turned out—and Kellogg cherry-picked the evidence even for that claim), and when it advertised that Rice Krispies "now helps support your child's immunity."

The FTC also accepts consumer complaints and may act on them. Of the over 1.8 million consumer complaints during calendar year 2011, 55% were fraud complaints, 15% identity theft complaints, and 30% other types of complaints. Other top categories: debt collection (10%); prizes, sweepstakes and lotteries (6%); shop-at-home and catalog sales (5%); banks and lenders (5%); Internet services (5%); auto related complaints (4%); impostor scams (4%); telephone and mobile services (4%); and advance-fee loans and credit protection/repair (3%). FEDERAL TRADE COMMISSION, CONSUMER SENTINEL NETWORK DATA BOOK FOR JANUARY-DECEMBER 2011 4 (2012). As both the variety of this list and the substantial percentage of complaints not falling within these categories indicate, the possibilities for deception are as infinite as the products and services available in the marketplace.

Competitors also may make complaints, but this is less likely. Once the FTC starts investigating a matter, the FTC might broaden its inquiry—potentially including looking at the complaining competitor's practices. As a result, a competitor must be confident that its own affairs are in order before complaining to the FTC, and even then, it cannot be certain that the FTC will take favorable action. In most cases, to retain control over the complaint, competitors will choose options discussed in the following sections:

suing its competitor directly or initiating a proceeding with the National Advertising Division of the Better Business Bureau.

Once it has decided to act, whether in response to a third-party complaint or on its own initiative, the FTC can go after deception at the industry-wide level or in relation to individual companies. When a deceptive practice is widespread, an industry-wide investigation may result in numerous actions against specific companies, which also has an educational effect on responsible competitors in the same field. In "Operation Waistline," for example, the FTC brought multiple actions against the providers of an entire spectrum of weight loss devices, products and programs—including supplements, diet programs, and shoe inserts that promised to burn calories for the wearer. The FTC also runs Internet sweeps and "surf days," targeting websites that offer products and services that are often associated with fraud, such as jewelry, healthcare, auctions, scholarship services and get-rich-quick schemes.

The FTC can issue civil investigative demands (CIDs) to investigate potential deception or unfairness. A CID is like a subpoena in that it can compel document production or oral testimony. The FTC may require the recipient to file written reports or responses to questions.

In the Undertaking Spam, Spyware, and Fraud Enforcement with Enforcers beyond Borders Act of 2006 (US SAFE WEB Act of 2006 or SAFE WEB), Congress further broadened the FTC's investigation and enforcement powers. SAFE WEB allows the FTC to share information with foreign agencies tasked with consumer protection; to use its civil investigative demand power to obtain information for a foreign consumer protection agency; and to share data with any foreign agency "vested with law enforcement or investigative authority in civil, criminal, or administrative matters" as long as the matter being investigated is "substantially similar" to practices prohibited by the FTC Act or other laws administered by the FTC.

Administrative Trials

Once a specific target has been identified, the FTC may use internal administrative trials to obtain cease-and-desist orders, which can then be enforced in federal court. 15 U.S.C. § 45(b). When the FTC first files an administrative complaint, the respondent may sign a consent agreement consenting to the entry of a final order. If the commission accepts the agreement, it will post the order in the Federal Register for public comment before making the order final.

If the respondent instead contests the charges, FTC staff will argue the case before an independent administrative law judge ("ALJ"). The FTC staff acts as complaint counsel. The FTC's rules govern the proceedings, but those rules are derived from the Federal Rules of Civil Procedure and the Federal Rules of Evidence, and the FTC has stated that the federal rules, and interpretations of them, can be consulted for guidance on the FTC's rules of practice. Discovery is allowed at the discretion and under the control of the ALJ. 16 C.F.R. § 3.43(b). The proponent of a factual assertion bears the burden of proof, and the findings and order must be based on competent and substantial evidence in order to be upheld in court in any subsequent appeal. 5 U.S.C. § 706(2)(E).

The ALJ holds a hearing and issues a decision that sets forth findings of fact and conclusions of law and recommends either a cease-and-desist order or dismissal. Either the complaint counsel or respondent (or both) may appeal the ALJ's decision to the full commission (i.e., the five FTC Commissioners). The Commissioners will hear the appeal, also in a trial-type proceeding with briefing, oral argument, and ultimately a final decision and order. A final decision is appealable by any respondent against whom it is issued, in any court of appeals within whose jurisdiction respondent "resides or carries on business or where the challenged practice was employed." A party dissatisfied with a court of appeals ruling may, as in other cases, petition for certiorari to the Supreme Court.

Federal Court Litigation

The FTC goes to federal court in two classes of cases. The first type is an enforcement proceeding. An FTC order becomes final in sixty days. A respondent who violates a final order may be sued in federal district court. The penalty can range up to $11,000 per violation, along with injunctive relief and "other further equitable relief" as the court deems appropriate. 15 U.S.C. § 45(1).

The second type of FTC proceeding in federal court is direct action against unfair and deceptive practices. When the FTC has "reason to believe" that a person or entity "is violating, or is about to violate" a law that the commission is charged with enforcing, it may proceed directly in district court. While courts increasingly hold competitor and consumer plaintiffs to Rule 9(b)'s rigorous standards for pleading with particularity in false advertising cases on the theory that false advertising is the same as fraud, they have been more forgiving with the FTC. *See* FTC v. AFD Advisors, LLC, No. 13 CV 6420, 2014 WL 274097 (N.D. Ill. Jan. 24, 2014) (finding that Rule 9(b) did not apply to a complaint for violation of the FTC Act because neither fraud nor mistake are elements of such a claim).

The FTC can ask for an injunction against the allegedly unlawful conduct while the FTC investigation is pending. 15 U.S.C. § 53(b), also known as § 13(b) of the FTC Act. This provision, added in the 1970s, expanded the FTC's power to go to federal court, which previously only existed in cases involving false advertising for food, drugs, medical devices or cosmetics. The initial intent of § 53(b) was to expand antitrust enforcement authority, but the FTC began to use injunctions to challenge false advertising in the 1980s. The FTC has obtained other relief in federal courts as well. Asset freezes are a particularly powerful tool. *See, e.g.*, FTC v. Southwest Sunsites, Inc., 665 F.2d 711 (5th Cir. 1982) (freezing assets and sending notifications to potentially injured consumers); FTC v. Equinox Int'l Corp., 1999-2 CCH Trade Cas. ¶ 72,704 (D. Nev. 1999) (appointing receiver).

The FTC may also seek redress for consumer injury and disgorgement of ill-gotten gains. This can lead to substantial awards to the FTC, which will disburse money to harmed consumers. The FTC may decide to forego restitution and disgorgement, however, if it believes that private actions or criminal proceedings will bring complete relief for consumers. In recent years, the FTC has taken an increased interest in private class action lawsuits, occasionally intervening to ensure that settlements are large enough to make deceived consumers whole.

Because the FTC has a choice of whether to sue in its internal administrative proceeding or in federal court, it is important to understand the costs and benefits of each approach. Starting with federal court can be more efficient because injunctive and monetary relief are available together; whereas when the FTC wins an administrative proceeding, it must still bring a later federal court action to get consumer redress. Moreover, an administrative cease-and-desist order is not final and effective until sixty days have passed, unlike an injunction.

So why would the FTC ever choose the administrative route? When it starts in federal court, it must prove the facts as any plaintiff must. A federal court reviewing an FTC administrative action, however, must affirm the commission's findings of fact if they are supported by "substantial evidence" and must give "substantial deference" to the FTC's constructions of the FTC Act as articulated in both adjudication and rulemaking. *See* 15 U.S.C. § 45(c) ("if supported by evidence, [FTC findings of fact] shall be conclusive"); Hospital Corp. of Am. v. FTC, 807 F.2d 1381 (7th Cir.1986) ("Our only function is to determine whether the Commission's analysis of the [evidence] is so implausible, so feebly supported by the record, that it flunks even the deferential test of substantial evidence."). A court may, however, examine the FTC's findings more closely where they differ from those of the ALJ. Thiret v. FTC, 512 F.2d 176 (10th Cir. 1975). The FTC receives some deference as to its informed judgment that a particular commercial practice violates the FTC Act, but courts resolve issues of law on their own merits. *See* FTC v. Ind. Fed'n of Dentists, 476 U.S. 447 (1986).

Reviewing the years 1978–1988, Ross D. Petty found 125 FTC administrative proceedings and 13 federal district court actions related to false advertising. Sixty percent settled by consent order during investigation, and nearly half of those litigated also settled. The FTC won almost every remaining case, losing only one ALJ trial and one of 12 cases appealed to a court of appeals. Ross D. Petty, *FTC Advertising Regulation: Survivor or Casualty of the Reagan Revolution?*, 30 AMER. BUS. L.J. 1 (1992).

According to the FTC, "[f]rom April 2010 through March 15, 2011, the Commission filed 38 actions in federal district court and obtained 82 judgments and orders requiring the defendants to pay nearly $368 million in consumer redress or disgorgement of ill-gotten gains. Cases referred to the Department of Justice resulted in eight civil penalty orders and over $5 million in assessed civil penalties. In addition, the Commission gave final approval to 14 administrative orders." Federal Trade Commission, *The FTC in 2011* (Apr. 2011). (As these numbers indicate, the volume of FTC action has increased in recent years).

Older studies have found that FTC deceptive advertising complaints are correlated with stock market losses. Alan Mathios & Mark Plummer, *The Regulation of Advertising by the FTC: Capital Market Effects*, 12 RES. L. & ECON. 77 (1989); Sam Peltzman, *The Effects of FTC Advertising Regulation*, 24 J.L & ECON. 403, 419 (1981) ("[T]he overall message of the results is that the salary of the copywriter or lawyer who avoids entanglement with the FTC in the first place is a bargain."). Some critics of the FTC's pursuit of monetary remedies have used these results to suggest that additional penalties are unnecessary to deter major, publicly traded companies from making false claims, especially given the likelihood that an FTC complaint will trigger a follow-on class action asserting the same claims on behalf of consumers. Others defend consumer redress measures as important ways to protect consumers who have suffered losses, especially given the increasing barriers to successful consumer class actions that we will discuss over the course of these materials.

Non-litigation Activity

The agency engages in substantial consumer and business education efforts, most of which are available on its website. Its activities for children provide a useful introduction to the types of consumer education the FTC has offered in recent years. Business guidance focuses on advice intelligible to non-lawyers. *See, e.g.*, Federal Trade Comm'n, Advertising FAQ's: A Guide for Small Business.

The FTC may also offer formal and informal advisory opinions. Parties may "request advice from the Commission with respect to a course of action which the requesting party proposes to pursue." 16 C.F.R. § 1.1(a). Although the FTC is under no obligation to answer an inquiry, it will consider the inquiry and issue an advisory opinion "where practicable," when (1) the matter involves a substantial or novel question of fact or law and there is no clear FTC or court precedent; and (2) the subject matter of the request and consequent publication of FTC advice is of significant public interest. 16 C.F.R. § 1.1(a)(1)–(2).

The FTC will not consider hypothetical questions and will generally decline to consider requests that are already the subject of rulemaking, industry guidelines, or enforcement proceedings against other parties. Advisory opinions are not binding, and the FTC expressly reserves the right to reconsider the question and rescind its opinion. However, good faith reliance on a commission opinion will preclude an enforcement action provided that all the relevant facts and circumstances were disclosed. The FTC's informal advice also is not binding; however, the FTC reserves the right not only to rescind informal advice, but also to commence an enforcement proceeding "where appropriate."

In addition, the FTC has rulemaking authority to deal with persistent problems, but its authority is extremely limited compared to most federal agencies. For example, it cannot make rules according to the notice-and-comment procedure that is governed by the Administrative Procedure Act. Instead, it must go through a significantly more complex and burdensome process—another consequence of the perception in the late 1970s and early 1980s that the FTC was trying to exercise too much control over the economy.

Rulemaking must begin with a determination that the practice at issue is "prevalent." 15 U.S.C. § 57a(b)(3). It therefore often follows a series of individual actions against specific advertisers. The FTC staff engages in a preliminary investigation, after which the Federal Register publishes an advanced notice of proposed rulemaking. Interested parties are invited to comment on whether a rulemaking should occur. If the FTC decides to initiate formal rulemaking, the Federal Register publishes a notice of the proposed rule and the FTC holds public hearings. Interested parties have limited rights of cross-examination. After a period for rebuttal comments, the staff publishes a recommended decision and invites further public comment. At that point, the full commission decides whether or not to promulgate the rule. The rule, if any, is subject to appeal. Knowingly violating FTC rules may result in a civil penalty of up to $11,000.

Given how extensive this process is, an investigation often results in some other action, such as a staff report, a policy statement or a report to Congress. These don't have the force of law or of rules, but advertisers should pay attention to them. Because rules are so hard for the FTC to make and therefore so rare, policy statements and guides are often the best indicators of what sorts of ads will trigger FTC action. The FTC typically conducts workshops and solicits public comment on proposed guides or policy statements. It is also likely to survey consumers to gather evidence about their understanding about particular terms, practices or claims. The result, even in the absence of a formal rule, is often a policy that is easy to find and more easily generalized than the results of individual enforcement actions, and it has had the benefit of input from various constituencies.

One common form of FTC policy is the "Industry Guide," a statement of enforcement policy with respect to a practice common to many industries or to specific practices of a particular industry. Some industry guides are sector-specific, targeting sellers of automobiles, jewelry, leather and tires, among others. Other guides apply to specific types of advertising, including "free" merchandise, price comparisons, and warranties. A guide typically consists of numbered definitions and rules, followed by hypothetical examples. If the FTC alleges a violation of a guide, the respondent may still argue that its conduct does not violate the FTC Act, and it is entitled to a full adjudicatory hearing on the matter. *See* FTC v. Mary Carter Paint Co., 382 U.S. 46 (1965). Without voluntary compliance, then, a guide may be toothless. In practice, however, the guides are a good preview of the FTC's perspectives about the law. As a result, advertisers—especially large advertisers that can more readily comply with the guides—have strong incentives to comply voluntarily to avoid being subject to an FTC investigation.

NOTES AND QUESTIONS

Degree of Judicial Deference to FTC Pronouncements. Given that
guides and policy statements don't have the force of formally enacted
rules, what sort of deference should a reviewing court give them? In a
case involving enforcement of a cease-and-desist order against one
dental organization's policy designed to give member dentists
leverage in dealing with insurers, the Supreme Court stated that
"courts are to give some deference to the Commission's informed
judgment that a particular commercial practice is to be condemned as
'unfair.'" FTC v. Ind. Fed'n of Dentists, 476 U.S. 447 (1986).

If the FTC is entitled to deference in particular cases, do the same
rationales apply to its general guidelines? In *Miller v. Herman*, 600
F.3d 726 (7th Cir. 2010), the court noted that FTC actions not rising
to the level of substantive rules are not entitled to the deference given
to government agencies under *Chevron U.S.A., Inc. v. Natural
Resources Defense Council*, Inc., 467 U.S. 837 (1984), which upholds
agency determinations if they are based on a permissible construction
of the governing statute. However, it continued, an agency
interpretation may be entitled to some deference "whatever its form,
given the specialized experience and broader investigations and
information available to the agency, and given the value of uniformity
in its administrative and judicial understandings of what a national
law requires." The amount of deference given depends on factors such
as the thoroughness with which the FTC developed the policy, the
agency's expertise in the area, the persuasiveness of its reasoning,
and its consistency with other FTC pronouncements.

The FTC typically wins its cases, in part because of careful selection
and the resulting credibility the agency has developed. Given the
FTC's role as a primary consumer watchdog, courts often defer to the
FTC's position even if not legally required to do so.

What role should FTC policy statements play in cases that are not brought by the FTC? In other words, if a court finds that a defendant has engaged in conduct that a guide declares deceptive, should that suffice to show that the defendant has in fact engaged in deceptive conduct? What if defendant's conduct matches an example a guide approves as nondeceptive? Should the plaintiff necessarily lose? *See* B. Sanfield, Inc. v. Finlay Fine Jewelry Corp., 168 F.3d 967 (7th Cir. 1999) (finding in a Lanham Act case about deceptive pricing that the FTC Guides Against Deceptive Pricing "should serve as the starting, if not the ending, point of the court's analysis").

Should the FTC have the same rulemaking authority as other agencies under the Administrative Procedure Act? Is the FTC more troublesome than the EPA, OSHA, or other agencies?

The FTC can use its rules to create easier-to-win legal questions than proving consumer deception. For example, *Federal Trade Commission v. Tashman*, 318 F.3d 1273 (11th Cir. 2003), involved an interpretation of the FTC's Franchise Rules, which regulate advertising for certain types of business opportunities. The district court held that the franchisor didn't mislead franchisees under Section 5 of the FTC Act. The appeals court rejected that finding, but also ruled that the franchisor didn't comply with the Franchise Rule's requirement that the franchisor have a documented and disclosed "reasonable basis" for its predictions about franchisees' revenues or profits. Proof that the predictions are reasonable is obviously related to whether the predictions are misleading, but it is often easier to identify whether the franchisor has maintained and disclosed its evidence than to prove consumer deception. The FTC thus succeeded in its enforcement action by showing that the franchisor hadn't followed the proper procedure. In *Tashman*, the franchisor apparently couldn't do so because the proof didn't exist; the more common such situations are, the more reasonable it seems to use FTC rules mandating recordkeeping and disclosure to replace the consumer deception standard of Section 5. We'll revisit similar issues when we discuss the FTC's substantiation requirements.

Rulemaking vs. Other Enforcement Methods. Pom Wonderful, facing an enforcement action using the ALJ method, argued that the FTC had unlawfully required a new, higher level of substantiation for health claims than mandated by the existing rules. The FTC was allegedly imposing this new standard by requiring all consent orders to include an agreement to make only advertising claims that would satisfy the FDA's stringent requirements (two well-controlled double-blinded clinical studies supporting the claims). Pom Wonderful alleged that this new standard had been imposed both in violation of the Administrative Procedure Act and the Constitution. After the full Commission upheld a finding that Pom had violated the FTCA, the D.C. Circuit affirmed Pom's liability. POM Wonderful LLC v. FTC, 777 F.3d 478 (D.C. Cir. 2015). The Court of Appeals stated that it "is well settled that an agency 'is not precluded from announcing new principles in an adjudicative proceeding,'" and that "'the choice between rulemaking and adjudication lies in the first instance within the agency's discretion.'" However, the court independently held that the FTC's proposed blanket requirement of *two* well-controlled clinical studies was too much, for First Amendment reasons; one study was all that could be required absent a more specific FTC showing of further need.

Presently, in any enforcement action against a health claim, the FTC still has to prove that advertising violated the general prohibition on deceptive or unfair conduct under § 5, since there is no more specific formal rule that an advertiser could be charged with violating. But, if the FTC announces that it will proceed under § 5 against companies making certain specific claims, does the potential chilling effect of such an announcement justify judicial review even if there is no governing language other than § 5 in place?

Individual Liability. The FTC can and often does sue corporate officers and executives personally. *See* Paul D. Rubin & Smitha G. Stansbury, *FTC Enforcement Against Individuals*, Patton Boggs LLP, April 2011. The individuals can be liable if the company violates the FTC Act and "the individual defendants participated directly in the practices or acts or had the authority to control them." *See* FTC v. Amy Travel Serv., Inc., 875 F.2d 564 (7th Cir. 1989). In this respect, the FTC is not constrained by traditional limits on piercing the corporate veil.

The FTC also can pursue "relief defendants" who did not violate the FTC Act themselves but nevertheless possess ill-gotten gains. An example might be the spouse of an individual who violated the FTC Act.

The Consumer Financial Protection Bureau. Banks and other financial institutions (aside from debt collectors) were statutorily excluded from the FTC's authority. For a long time, there was no entity specifically charged with protecting consumers from deceptive and unfair conduct by banks, mortgage lenders, and the like. The CFPB was, amid much controversy, created to fill that regulatory gap. The new agency has rulemaking, supervision, and enforcement authority over "an extremely broad swath of the consumer financial services industry." Adam J. Levitin, *The Consumer Financial Protection Bureau: An Introduction*, 32 REV. BANKING & FIN. L. 321 (2013) (providing an overview of the CFPB's powers and limitations).

Its first public enforcement action was a major settlement with Capital One over charges of deceptive marketing of credit card "add-on" products, such as payment protection and credit monitoring. Capital One agreed to pay a total of between $140 million and $150 million in restitution to 2 million customers, along with $60 million in penalties. CFPB Probe into Capital One Credit Card Marketing Results in $140 Million Consumer Refund, July 18, 2012. Other big-dollar settlements have followed. *See* Brian Wolfman, *CFPB Obtains Massive Credit-Card Deception Consent Order from Bank of America*, Consumer L. & Pol'y Blog, Apr. 9, 2014 (discussing settlement involving $727 million in consumer refunds and $20 million penalty based on deceptive marketing of credit card protection services and unfair billing practices). The CFPB has also issued numerous rules, mostly on various aspects of mortgage lending. CFPB, *Regulations*.

While both the CFPB and the FTC have authority to stop unfair and deceptive conduct, the CFPB can also regulate "abusive" conduct. An "abusive" practice is one that

> (1) materially interferes with the ability of a consumer to understand a term or condition of a consumer financial product or service; or
> (2) takes unreasonable advantage of—
>> (A) a lack of understanding on the part of the consumer of the material risks, costs, or conditions of the product or service;
>> (B) the inability of the consumer to protect the interests of the consumer in selecting or using a consumer financial product or service; or
>> (C) the reasonable reliance by the consumer on a covered person to act in the interests of the consumer.

Consumer Financial Protection Act § 1031(d)(2). Is there "abusive" conduct that wouldn't also be "unfair" or "deceptive"? One writer has suggested that conduct is abusive when it "exploit[s] certain predictable consumer behaviors, even when those behaviors are not economically rational." Benedict J. Schweigert, *The CFPB's "Abusiveness" Standard and Consumer Irrationality* (2012). That is, the CFPB has authority to act on the insights of behavioral economics, which identifies systematic and predictable cognitive errors made by many people, such as overestimating their future ability to pay when borrowing or underestimating how often they will overdraft their accounts. "Unlike the 'unfair' and 'deceptive' standards, this provision places the burden of reasonableness on the lender and employs an empirical model of consumer behavior." Schweigert argues that, by contrast, the FTC has focused on injury to consumers acting rationally. (Recall that the definition of unfair conduct is conduct that causes "substantial injury to consumers which is not reasonably avoidable by consumers themselves and not outweighed by countervailing benefits to consumers or to competition." § 45(n).) Is abusiveness a good additional legal standard for government enforcement agencies?

How Other Countries Do It. Consumer protection agencies exist worldwide. Japan's consumer protection law, for example, was adopted in 1968. In the UK, comprehensive fair trading legislation supplemented more targeted consumer protection measures in 1973, creating the Office of Fair Trading. *See* IAIN RAMSEY, CONSUMER LAW AND POLICY: TEXT AND MATERIALS ON REGULATING CONSUMER MARKETS (2007). Canada's consumer protection regime has the same basic provisions as the FTCA, imposing both a nonmisleadingness and a substantiation requirement. Section 74.01(1)(a) of the Canadian Competition Act (R.S.C. 1985, c. C-34) prohibits any "representation to the public that is false or misleading in a material respect," while section 74.01(1)(b) prohibits any "representation to the public ... of the performance, efficacy, or length of life of the product that is not based on an adequate and proper test thereof." Among other remedies, the law authorizes administrative penalties of up to $10 million for the first violation and $15 million per violation thereafter.

Some jurisdictions, including the U.S., UK and Australia, combine consumer protection and competition (antitrust) regulation into the same agencies. Others separate the two functions. The Nordic countries have separate consumer ombudsmen. *See* Kjersti Graver, *A*

Study of the Consumer Ombudsman Institution in Norway with Some References to the Other Nordic Countries I: Background and Description, 9 J. CONSUMER POL'Y 1 (1986). How do you think housing antitrust and consumer protection objectives within a single agency affects regulators' views of what helps consumers? From a business point of view, is there any downside to having regulation concentrated in a single agency?

In the European Community, Directive 2005/29/EC Article 2(e) (the Directive on Unfair Commercial Practices) prohibits misleading practices, defined as practices that are likely to mislead the average consumer and thereby likely to cause him or her to take a transactional decision he or she would not have taken otherwise. The Directive sets both a floor and a ceiling: in order to further the free movement of goods and services, Member States can't implement stricter—or looser—rules.

However, the Directive doesn't specify enforcement tools, and nations can choose from public or private enforcement as well as from civil, administrative, or criminal penalties. Many choose combinations of the options, though few allow anything like the American class action. Nongovernmental organizations commonly help enforce consumer protection law. In the United Kingdom, for example, designated consumer bodies can file complaints with the competition authority and other regulators. By law, the regulators must respond expediently. *See* Colin Scott, *Enforcing Consumer Protection Laws*, in HANDBOOK OF RESEARCH ON INTERNATIONAL CONSUMER LAW (Howells et al. eds., 2010).

Other private parties can sometimes take action on their own. The Australian Trade Practices Act 1974, for example, allows consumers, competitors and consumer organizations to enforce the prohibition on misleading and deceptive practices. Most other countries, however, do not allow class action suits or embrace the distinctly American litigation culture that makes class actions so significant in the U.S.

2. Competitors: The Lanham Act and Self-Regulation

Although false advertising lawsuits between competitors often involve claims under state law, including common law unfair competition and statutory consumer protection violations, the main law used by competitors is the federal Lanham Act, which covers both trademark and false advertising. The major alternative to litigation for national advertisers is voluntary arbitration by the National Advertising Division (NAD) of the Better Business Bureau. Choosing between a lawsuit and an NAD proceeding can be complicated, as we will see.

A.   The Lanham Act

This overview is brief, because the next few chapters will review the various elements of a Lanham Act false advertising claim in detail. For now, it will be useful to survey the broad contours of a Lanham Act claim to help contextualize the other legal mechanisms available to challenge advertising.

History

The initial version of § 43(a) of the Lanham Act, as enacted in 1946, provided that

> [a]ny person who shall . . . use in connection with any goods or services . . . any false description or representation, including words or other symbols tending falsely to describe or represent the same, and shall cause such goods or services to enter into commerce, . . . shall be liable to a civil action by any

person . . . who believes that he is or is likely to be damaged by the use of any such false description or representation.

At first, because the Lanham Act was primarily known as a trademark statute, courts required something akin to trademark infringement, also known as "passing off" or "palming off"— misleading consumers into thinking that the defendant's goods came from the plaintiff. Over time, courts began to generalize further, allowing plaintiffs to sue when defendants were making other false claims about their products. This transition was eased by cases that involved facts similar to passing off. So, when a retailer advertised a picture of plaintiff's dress—which was not protected by any intellectual property rights, and was thus free for copying—but actually sold an "inferior" and "notably different" dress, the facts supported a § 43(a) claim. L'Aiglon Apparel, Inc. v. Lana Lobell, Inc., 214 F.2d 649 (3d Cir. 1954).

As one might expect, plaintiffs pushed the boundaries of the law, and courts went along, until many recognized a general cause of action for false advertising in § 43(a). However, a significant minority of courts held that the only false advertising claims actionable under the Lanham Act were those the defendant made about its own products or services, not those made about the plaintiff's competing products or services. See, e.g., Clamp-All Corp. v. Cast Iron Soil Pipe Inst., 851 F.2d 478 (1st Cir. 1988) (declining to disturb older law that § 43(a) covered only source confusion).

Other cases required falsity about an "inherent quality or characteristic" of the good or service advertised, even when the defendant was making false claims that could be expected to influence consumers' decisions. For example, an ad for imitation fur claiming that it spared the lives of tigers and leopards was false because federal law already banned the use of tiger and leopard fur for clothing. The court, however, dismissed the claim because the advertiser said nothing false about the imitation furs themselves. *See* Fur Info. & Fashion Council, Inc. v. E.F. Timme & Son, Inc., 501 F.2d 1048 (2d Cir. 1974). The doctrine requiring misrepresentation about an "inherent quality" of the product or service enabled courts to dismiss claims when the relevant consumers cared about features that the court didn't think were really part of the advertised product. So, in *Hertz Corp. v. Avis, Inc.*, 725 F. Supp. 170 (S.D.N.Y. 1989), the court found that a car rental company's ad targeting travel agencies, which focused on the speed with which commissions were paid, did not pertain to an inherent quality of the service of car renting. Today, by contrast, courts are likely to find that an "inherent quality" is any quality likely to influence a consumer decision.

Present Form

The Trademark Law Revision Act of 1988 ("TLRA"), which became effective in November 1989, split § 43(a) (15 U.S.C. § 1125(a)) into two parts. Section 43(a)(1)(A) deals with source/origin claims and confers federal jurisdiction for trademark infringement claims when the plaintiff lacks a federally registered trademark. Section 43(a)(1)(B) now bars the "use in commerce" of

> any word, term, name, symbol, or device, or any combination thereof, or any false designation of origin, false or misleading description of fact, or false or misleading representation of fact, which . . . in commercial advertising or promotion, misrepresents the nature, characteristics, qualities, or geographic origin of his or her or another person's goods, services, or commercial activities.

This language codifies the older majority rule that § 43(a) did prohibit false advertising, whether the falsity concerned the plaintiff's products and services or the defendant's. Because false claims about anyone's products are actionable, false advertising claims under the

Lanham Act substitute for or complement common law causes of action for commercial defamation, commercial disparagement, or trade libel. The TLRA also broadened the Lanham Act language to clarify that virtually any type of false advertising or promotional claim may be actionable.

According to the statute, "any person who believes that he or she is or is likely to be damaged by" false advertising may sue in federal court. Courts do not allow consumers to sue under the Lanham Act, reasoning that, despite the breadth of this language, Congress was targeting competitive harm rather than direct harm to consumers. The Supreme Court ultimately clarified the scope of this provision and endorsed the rule that consumers can't sue, as we will discuss in Chapter 6.

Otherwise, courts have often given broad effect to § 43(a)'s sweeping language. For example, because the law prohibits misrepresentations about "commercial activities" as well as "goods" and "services," falsehoods about the general way in which a plaintiff conducts business are actionable. Proctor & Gamble, Co. v. Haugen, 222 F.3d 1262 (10th Cir. 2000) (allegations that plaintiff's profits were used to fund a Satanic cult were actionable); *see also* Fuente Cigar, Ltd. v. Opus One, 985 F. Supp. 1448 (M.D. Fla. 1997) (statements made by competitor in trade publication interview that cigar manufacturer was trying to "trade on" reputation of winemaker and had "effectively appropriated" winemaker's mark were statements about manufacturer's commercial activities). For convenience, we generally refer only to goods and services, but keep in mind that commercial activities are also covered.

Today, many courts use a six-factor inquiry to determine a Lanham Act violation. A plaintiff will prevail when there is:

1) a false or misleading statement of fact,
2) in interstate commerce (this element is almost always satisfied and rarely even contested),
3) in connection with commercial advertising or promotion,
4) that actually deceives or has the tendency to deceive an appreciable number of consumers in the intended audience,
5) that is material, and
6) that is likely to cause injury to the plaintiff.

A key point, on which we will elaborate in the next chapter, is that the case law distinguishes between *false messages*—claims that are simply untrue on their face—and *misleading messages*—claims that are technically or literally true, but whose ambiguities lead reasonable consumers to draw mistaken inferences. A plaintiff has a substantially easier time prevailing against a false statement than a misleading one, in large part because courts require evidence that consumers are actually deceived by misleading statements, usually with a consumer survey.

Critics of the Lanham Act's expansion of false advertising law argue that false advertising cases brought by competitors are more wasteful than most litigation. They often require judges to decide highly technical claims in which they have no background. The parties are often wealthy companies that can afford to litigate every aspect of the case to death. The claims often are more likely to change market share allocation (i.e., reallocate consumer dollars between competitors) than improve consumer welfare (i.e., drive consumers to alternative products or stop shopping altogether). *See* Lillian R. BeVier, *Competitor Suits for False Advertising under Section 43(a) of the Lanham Act: A Puzzle in the Law of Deception*, 78 VA. L. REV. 1 (1992).

NOTES AND QUESTIONS

Even if courts aren't perfect at determining the truth, how should we evaluate the risks of false positives (wrongly enjoining true claims) and false negatives (wrongly failing to enjoin false claims)? Are competitors likely to be worse advocates for the truth than other potential challengers such as consumers, the FTC, or state attorneys general? As it happens, critics of competitor suits often dislike consumer class actions and government lawsuits as well.

Remedies. Both monetary and equitable remedies are available in Lanham Act cases. Damages (but not punitive damages) are available, though most courts require a plaintiff to show actual consumer confusion or intentional deception before awarding them. Damages may be trebled if needed to compensate the plaintiff, if the harm "can neither be dismissed as speculative nor precisely calculated." ALPO Petfoods, Inc. v. Ralston-Purina Co., 997 F.2d 949 (D.C. Cir. 1993).

Equitable remedies include a temporary restraining order or preliminary injunction upon a showing that satisfies the general requirements for equitable relief. A plaintiff who succeeds at trial may also receive a permanent injunction against continuing false advertising. In extraordinary cases, recall and destruction of advertising materials or corrective advertising may be ordered, though such outcomes are extremely rare. In exceptional cases, courts can also award attorneys' fees.

A few multi-million-dollar-damage verdicts have been awarded in false advertising cases, but by far the most common outcome is injunctive relief. In fact, many false advertising cases are decided on motions for preliminary injunctions, and settlement regularly follows

the grant or denial of a preliminary injunction. We will discuss
remedies in further detail in Chapter 8.

The Relationship between the Lanham Act and the FTC. Courts in
Lanham Act cases occasionally draw on FTC standards for guidance,
but in general, private parties receive much less deference, and
plaintiffs have the burden of showing falsity, whereas the FTC puts
the burden of substantiation on the advertiser.

Structurally, the existence of the Lanham Act complements the FTC's
endeavors. Competitors have different incentives than the FTC: they
may not sue when it's in every competitor's interest to make a certain
set of false claims, such as cigarette companies' toleration for claims
about the health effects of particular brands of cigarettes. Similar
patterns exist in the supplement and weight-loss industries, where
extravagant claims are common and competition is so intense that
most advertisers benefit more from being able to make shaky claims
of their own than from suppressing any one competitor's shaky
claims. The Lanham Act is unlikely to be useful, or used much, in
those industries.

In other words, enforcement actions against false commercial speech
have a "public goods" aspect—there may be benefits from the
enforcement that do not accrue to any individual competitor, in which
case governments or consumers are appropriate plaintiffs. Thus, the
Lanham Act alone is unlikely to keep ads truthful.

However, where the benefits of enforcement will sufficiently
concentrate with a single competitor, that competitor has enough
private incentive to bring the enforcement action even if other
competitors or the public will also derive benefit from the
enforcement. Indeed, competitors are likely to police some kinds of
claims much more carefully than the FTC or other regulators can. For
one thing, competitors may be well-placed to evaluate highly

technical claims. They are likely to routinely test both their own products and their competition's, and they may detect falsity or misleadingness invisible to non-experts.

Moreover, the existence of competitor lawsuits allows the FTC to devote its resources elsewhere. Because competitors can and do sue, the FTC may be able to give low priority to false comparative claims and false claims in fields like shaving, antacids, and analgesics, where false representations can affect market share. The FTC's tendency to avoid intervening in markets for cheap, repeat-purchase goods may make sense in part because competitor suits exist to police falsity and protect consumers in such markets. Though correlation is not causation, the explosion in competitor suits happened in the 1990s—after the FTC stopped pushing the limits of its authority to regulate truth in advertising.

B.   BBB/ASRC/NAD

The Advertising Self-Regulatory Council (ASRC), a creation of the Better Business Bureau (BBB), oversees the National Advertising Division (NAD) and other divisions focusing on children's advertising and direct-response advertising. The National Advertising Review Board (NARB) hears appeals from decisions by the other divisions.

ASRC defines its mission as (1) minimizing governmental involvement in the advertising business, (2) maintaining a level playing field for settling disputes among competing advertisers, and (3) fostering brand loyalty by increasing public trust in the credibility of advertising. *See* About the National Advertising Review Council (note that not all references have made the change from the former acronym, NARC). In effect, the NAD provides a venue to adjudicate competitor disputes as an alternative to Lanham Act lawsuits in court.

The NAD was founded in 1971, though advertisers' use of it to resolve disputes increased substantially in recent decades, especially as Lanham Act litigation became more expensive and court dockets more crowded. The deregulatory impulses of the 1980s and 1990s also meant that the FTC was more hesitant to challenge advertising except in extreme circumstances, increasing demand for self-regulation.

As a self-regulatory body, the NAD can be both more aggressive in its inquiries and more limited in its powers than a court proceeding. Like the FTC and state attorneys general, the NAD monitors advertising, accepts consumer complaints, and engages in its own investigations. Competitors can also bring challenges, which make up the bulk of the NAD's activities. A competitor challenge is less likely to occur when industries are subject to common problems of substantiation, such as claims made by diet or vitamin supplement companies. In such cases, the NAD may act on its own initiative when it becomes aware of troublesome claims. The NAD currently adjudicates around 200 to 300 disputes a year, though the backlog is growing. It has rendered more than 5,000 decisions to date.

Because NAD's staff attorneys have substantial experience reviewing advertising, advertisers tend to take their rulings seriously. Like the FTC, the NAD requires substantiation from advertisers, contrasting with litigation under the Lanham Act, where the burden is on the plaintiff to prove the falsity of challenged advertising. Moreover, like the FTC, NAD staff attorneys are willing to rely on their own expertise to determine that an ad is likely to deceive consumers; consumer surveys are not required, nor is discovery available. Thus, the NAD can be a substantially cheaper and quicker route than litigation in federal court.

As a national body, the NAD also attempts to create uniform nationwide precedents. Federal and state courts can't do the same, at least in the absence of a ruling from the Supreme Court, which is a rarity in advertising law–related matters. The NAD publishes its decisions, creating a body of "jurisprudence" that is relatively coherent and reliable.

Unlike the FTC or a court, the NAD lacks power to compel participation in its adjudicative process or compliance with its decisions. If an advertiser declines to participate, or refuses to change its advertising after an adverse decision, the NAD simply closes the case and the challenger must seek redress elsewhere, often by filing a lawsuit. The NAD, however, tells the FTC when a business refuses to participate in its proceedings, and the FTC has stated that it takes these referrals very seriously as a means of supporting the self-regulatory enterprise.

Advertisers ignore NAD proceedings at their peril. One such NAD referral resulted in an $83 million FTC judgment against a weight-loss company. *See* Seth Stevenson, *How New Is "New"? How Improved Is "Improved"? The People Who Keep Advertisers Honest*, SLATE, July 13, 2009.

In another case, the maker of "Cholestaway," a chewable tablet that promised a variety of health benefits including lower cholesterol, lower blood pressure, and weight loss, refused to comply with the NAD's findings that its claims were largely unsubstantiated. Bogdana Corp., NAD Case No. 3215 (closed 7/10/95). After the matter was referred to the FTC, the advertiser and its advertising agency were ultimately subject to a consent decree barring the claims, requiring adequate substantiation in the future, and mandating regular compliance reports to the FTC. FTC Press Release, *Dietary Supplement Advertiser Settles FTC Charges of Deceptive Health Claims*, May 12, 1998 ("[A]s this case illustrates, when self-regulation fails, we are prepared to take action.").

116

Companies and/or competitors who make challenges must pay the BBB to offset some of the costs of the process. As of 2015, these charges range from $10,000 to $25,000.

The NAD will only accept challenges to "national" advertising, "those ads disseminated on a nationwide or broadly regional basis. The advertising may be placed on broadcast or cable television, in radio, magazines and newspapers, on the Internet or commercial on-line services, or provided direct to the home or office." About NAD. Local campaigns, no matter how misleading, are not within its jurisdiction. The NAD advises: "If a complaint involves local advertising or local business practices, such as payment and refund problems, delays in delivery, or 'bait and switch' tactics, the best qualified self-regulatory organization to contact is the Better Business Bureau (BBB) located nearest to the advertiser's address."

In general, however, the NAD defines "advertising" broadly, including product labels. It will evaluate challenges even when an advertiser argues that some federal agency already regulates the claim at issue: the NAD does not recognize a general "preemption" principle. *See* Intervet, Inc., NAD Case No. 3625 (closed Feb. 25, 2000) ("The fact that a government agency regulates a particular industry does not relieve NAD of its responsibility to ensure the truthfulness and accuracy of the advertising claims made by members of that industry. To avoid inconsistency, however, NAD strives to harmonize its analysis and decisions with any related regulations.").

The NAD might not accept jurisdiction for other reasons. The NAD bars participants who use the process from touting it "for any advertising and/or promotional purposes." NAD/CARU/NARB Procedures 2.2B. Thus, participants cannot issue press releases about bringing or winning challenges. If they do, the NAD will terminate their challenges. The idea is to avoid bringing the NAD into public relations wars. In addition, the NAD will not act while litigation between the parties is pending (see below for more on the interaction between the NAD and the courts).

If the NAD decides to pursue a matter, the challenge is forwarded to the advertiser, who has fifteen business days to respond with evidence and argument. There is no discovery for either side. The timeline is much faster than a court timeline and the time for response is measured in days. Submissions are not released to the public, and the advertiser has the right to submit confidential materials (such as product tests) without sharing them with the opponent. Proceedings may or may not involve an in-person hearing.

The NAD produces a written decision. The advertiser may add an Advertiser's Statement to the decision, indicating whether the advertiser will comply with the decision or appeal to the NARB. The final decision, including the Advertiser's Statement, is then published, along with a press release available on the NAD's website. Decisions ideally take only a few months, but as the case load has increased at the NAD, some resolution times have stretched further.

Because the NAD has no enforcement power, it can only find advertising substantiated or recommend that it be changed. In a typical successful challenge, (1) the NAD will recommend the advertiser change some or all of the challenged claims, and (2) the advertiser, for its part, will announce that it disagrees with the NAD's decision but, because the ad campaign at issue has run its course, it is discontinuing the claims at issue.

If the advertiser feels that the claims are competitively valuable, however, it may decide to appeal to the NARB. Each NARB panel consists of five members—three who work in national advertising, one from an advertising agency, and one from the "public" (academics and former members of the public sector). Panel hearings include representatives of the NAD, the advertiser, and the complainant.

Participants regularly include outside counsel, research and development employees, and marketers. The NARB reports that it is not unusual to have 20–25 people attending a hearing. The NARB's review is on the record, without new evidence, and it rarely reverses NAD determinations.

The NAD claims a compliance rate of over 95% (including compliance after an appeal). The NAD categorizes outcomes as follows:

- "Advertising Substantiated": The NAD is satisfied that the advertiser has a "reasonable basis" for the challenged claims.
- "Advertising Modified or Discontinued": The NAD determined that the advertising lacks a reasonable basis, and the advertiser agreed to modify or discontinue it.
- "Advertising Referred to Government Agency": The NAD could not resolve the dispute, whether because the advertiser failed to comply with its decision, declined to state whether it would comply, or declined to participate in the process entirely. In rare cases, the NAD may refer a case to the FTC for guidance. *See, e.g.*, J.C. Penney Co., NAD Case No. 3564G (closed July 31, 2000) (determining that jewelry advertiser's "modified advertising is not in compliance," but, "[g]iven the impact that this decision could have on J.C. Penney as well as many other advertisers," referring the matter to the FTC and requesting its determination on the same issue).

The NAD is relatively cheap and moderately fast. The decision to use the NAD instead of litigation, however, can be a complex one.

If the advertising at issue is central to an advertiser's image, the advertiser may need faster relief than the NAD can provide, and may also need to take advantage of public relations during the pendency of the dispute, which the NAD does not allow. Jenny Craig began an advertising campaign in early January 2010—New Year's resolution time—claiming that a major clinical trial had found that Jenny Craig clients lost on average over twice as much weight as lost via the leading competitor, Weight Watchers. Weight Watchers immediately sought a temporary restraining order (TRO), and Weight Watchers was able to announce the TRO on television when it was granted on January 20. The need for discovery, the likelihood that the advertiser won't comply with the NAD, or the prospect of substantial damages from a favorable verdict, can also counsel in favor of going straight to litigation.

NOTES AND QUESTIONS

Self-Regulation v. Government Regulation. Angela Campbell has summarized the arguments for and against industry self-regulation as compared to government regulation. *See* Angela J. Campbell, *Self-Regulation and the Media*, 51 FED. COMM. L.J. 711 (1999).

In favor of self-regulation: (1) efficiency, especially in terms of industry participants' superior knowledge (here, of how advertising works on consumers and also of substantiation of particular claims); (2) flexibility, in that voluntary bodies can recognize when change is necessary (when, for example, new claims like "carbon neutral" become popular) and adopt new standards swiftly compared to staid government rulemaking; (3) better compliance, because industry participants perceive self-regulation as more reasonable and less intrusive; (4) lower costs to government; and (5) fewer constitutional constraints, such as First Amendment limits on government controls of advertising.

Against self-regulation: (1) expertise may be used to benefit industry rather than the public by approving tactics that sell products but that don't help consumers; (2) self-regulation is often under-regulation, because industries may not invest sufficient resources in the self-regulatory body or give it any bite, which in turn makes the self-regulatory body more cautious in finding violations for fear of triggering open defiance; (3) bad actors can easily ignore industry self-regulation; (4) on the other side, enforcement might be biased, and discretionary decisions might be hard to review; and (5) relatedly, self-regulation might be anticompetitive, if it supports the aims of established companies against upstarts who might be using unusual or aggressive tactics to attract consumers' attention.

Can you see how NAD demonstrates many of these pros and cons?

Antitrust Concerns. Although the FTC has been highly supportive of the NAD, self-regulation in other contexts is sometimes challenged by the FTC on antitrust grounds. The National Association of Broadcasters, for example, at one time adopted provisions limiting the number of minutes per hour of commercials, the number of commercials per hour, and the number of products advertised in a commercial for radio and television stations. These measures had the actual purpose and effect of reducing the supply of commercial television time, which naturally raised prices to advertisers. We will discuss antitrust considerations further in Chapter 12.

Claim substantiation is designed to benefit consumers, but it imposes real costs on advertisers. Any legal rule that raises advertisers' costs will discourage marketplace entry and favor established incumbent players. Thus, even a seemingly laudable requirement like substantiation potentially affects the market's competitiveness.

Relationship between the NAD and the Courts. As indicated previously, the NAD will stop a proceeding if either party sues in court. In *Russian Standard Vodka (USA), Inc. v. Allied Domecq Spirits & Wine USA, Inc.*, 523 F. Supp. 2d 376 (S.D.N.Y. 2007), the NAD respondents initiated a lawsuit after an NAD proceeding had already started. The court granted a thirty-day stay to allow the NAD to complete its proceeding because "allowing the NAD, a highly reputable institution, to provide its expert view on Stoli's authenticity as a Russian vodka would be extremely useful in resolving remaining claims in the complaint."

Other courts have reached an opposite conclusion. Expedia, Inc. v. Priceline.com Inc., 2009 WL 4110851 (W.D. Wash. Nov. 23, 2009) (no stay in part because it wasn't clear that a final NAD decision would be admissible evidence); Rexall Sundown, Inc. v. Perrigo Co., 651 F. Supp. 2d 9, 36–37 (E.D.N.Y. 2009) (NAD findings are "inadmissible hearsay").

A competitor who tries a NAD proceeding before suing is less likely to be denied a preliminary injunction for delaying the lawsuit. *See* Millennium Imp. Co. v. Sidney Frank Importing Co., 2004 WL 1447915 (D. Minn. Jun. 11, 2004). Given that injunctive relief often contemplates further disputes between the parties, it may also be tempting to order them to resolve their differences in a NAD proceeding instead of going back to court. *See* Bracco Diagnostics, Inc. v. Amersham Health, Inc., 627 F. Supp. 2d 384 (D.N.J. 2009) (ordering that the parties must submit disputes about future advertising to an arbitrator such as the NAD; the defendant would bear the costs of arbitration if the ads were found to be false, and the plaintiff would do so if the ads were not found to be false, which is not the usual rule in NAD proceedings).

3. State Law: Consumers (and Occasionally Others)

A. Common Law Claims

Contracts (a Historical Perspective)

From the buyer's perspective, a false ad is a broken promise. The advertiser has offered one thing, but has delivered something else, and the difference is significant to the plaintiff.

This should sound familiar: a breach of contract is also a broken promise. Sometimes, a broken promise can support both a false advertising claim and a breach of contract claim; in other cases, it can support only one of the two claims and sometimes none of the above.

To sort through the interactions between contracts and false advertising, we start with the classic Carbolic Smoke Ball case, an early example of how courts used contract law to fix a false advertisement.

Carlill v. Carbolic Smoke Ball Company [1892] EWCA Civ 1 (English Court of Appeal)

LORD JUSTICE LINDLEY: . . . The first observation I will make is that we are not dealing with any inference of fact. We are dealing with an express promise to pay £100 in certain events. Read the advertisement how you will, and twist it about as you will, here is a distinct promise expressed in language which is perfectly unmistakable—

> £100 reward will be paid by the Carbolic Smoke Ball Company to any person who contracts the influenza after having used the ball three times daily for two weeks according to the printed directions supplied with each ball.

We must first consider whether this was intended to be a promise at all, or whether it was a mere puff which meant nothing. Was it a mere puff? My answer to that question is No, and I base my answer upon this passage:

> £1000 is deposited with the Alliance Bank, shewing our sincerity in the matter.

Now, for what was that money deposited or that statement made except to negative the suggestion that this was a mere puff and meant nothing at all? The deposit is called in aid by the advertiser as proof of his sincerity in the matter—that is, the sincerity of his promise to pay this £100 in the event which he has specified. . . .

It appears to me, therefore, that the defendants must perform their promise, and, if they have been so unwary as to expose themselves to a great many actions, so much the worse for them.

LORD JUSTICE BOWEN: I am of the same opinion. . . .

[T]he main point seems to be that the vagueness of the document shews that no contract whatever was intended. It seems to me that in order to arrive at a right conclusion we must read this advertisement in its plain meaning, as the public would understand it. It was intended to be issued to the public and to be read by the public. How would an ordinary person reading this document construe it?

. . . . And it seems to me that the way in which the public would read it would be this, that if anybody, after the advertisement was published, used three times daily for two weeks the carbolic smoke ball, and then caught cold, he would be entitled to the reward. Then again it was said:

> How long is this protection to endure? Is it to go on for ever, or for what limit of time?

. . . I think . . . it means that the smoke ball will be a protection while it is in use. That seems to me the way in which an ordinary person would understand an advertisement about medicine, and about a specific against influenza. It could not be supposed that after you have left off using it you are still to be protected for ever, as if there was to be a stamp set upon your forehead that you were never to catch influenza because you had once used the carbolic smoke ball. I think the immunity is to last during the use of the ball. . . .

But it was said there was no check on the part of the persons who issued the advertisement, and that it would be an insensate thing to promise £100 to a person who used the smoke ball unless you could check or superintend his manner of using it. The answer to that argument seems to me to be that if a person chooses to make extravagant promises of this kind he probably does so because it pays him to make them, and, if he has made them, the extravagance of the promises is no reason in law why he should not be bound by them.

It was also said that the contract is made with all the world—that is, with everybody; and that you cannot contract with everybody. It is not a contract made with all the world. There is the fallacy of the argument. It is an offer made to all the world; and why should not an offer be made to all the world which is to ripen into a contract with anybody who comes forward and performs the condition? . . . It is not like cases in which you offer to negotiate, or you issue advertisements that you have got a stock of books to sell, or houses to let, in which case there is no offer to be bound by any contract. Such advertisements are offers to negotiate—offers to receive offers . . . . If this is an offer to be bound, then it is a contract the moment the person fulfils the condition.

. . . If I advertise to the world that my dog is lost, and that anybody who brings the dog to a particular place will be paid some money, are all the police or other persons whose business it is to find lost dogs to be expected to sit down and write me a note saying that they have accepted my proposal? Why, of course, they at once look after the dog, and as soon as they find the dog they have performed the condition. The essence of the transaction is that the dog should be found, and it is not necessary under such circumstances, as it seems to me, that in order to make the contract binding there should be any notification of acceptance. It follows from the nature of the thing that the performance of the condition is sufficient acceptance without the notification of it, and a person who makes an offer in an advertisement of that kind makes an offer which must be read by the light of that common sense reflection. He does, therefore, in his offer impliedly indicate that he does not require notification of the acceptance of the offer. . . .

[The opinion of Lord Justice A.L. Smith, who agrees with the others, is omitted.]

NOTES AND QUESTIONS

Carbolic acid (Phenol) is a caustic acid and can affect the human nervous system (the Nazis used it to execute people). Basically, it's a poison.

At the time of the influenza pandemic of 1889–90, when the Carbolic Smoke Ball Company was advertising, no one knew what the flu was or how to prevent or cure it. The makers of the smoke ball, like many sellers of useless remedies, advertised heavily and successfully.

After the case, the company's founder formed a new company with limited liability and started up advertising again. In a new ad, the new Carbolic Smoke Ball Co., Ltd., described the previous ad and then claimed,

> Many thousand Carbolic Smoke Balls were sold on these advertisements, but only three people claimed the reward of £100, thus proving conclusively that this invaluable remedy will prevent and cure the above mentioned diseases. The CARBOLIC SMOKE BALL COMPANY LTD. now offer £200 REWARD to the person who purchases a Carbolic Smoke Ball and afterwards contracts any of the following diseases. . .

The fine print had some restrictive conditions, allowing three months to use the ball and present a claim.

Now, a number of additional statutory remedies would be available for a false advertisement of this type in the UK. *See* Consumer Protection from Unfair Trading Regulations 2008/1277 at § 5 (a commercial practice is misleading "if it contains false information and is therefore untruthful . . . or if it or its overall presentation in any way deceives or is likely to deceive the average consumer . . . even if the information is factually correct").

In addition, the modern regulatory response would likely focus on the fact that the carbolic smoke ball did not work, rather than on the reward. Why does the law now ban a claim in the form "Our product works, and if it doesn't work for you we'll pay you?" if the product doesn't actually work? Why isn't enforcement of that promise sufficient?

Ads as Contract Offers Today

Consider the following case. Shell service stations displayed this ad:

After buying ten gallons of fuel, a customer got a voucher with the receipt. But the voucher was a two-for-one coupon and couldn't be exchanged for a free lift ticket. The consumer could only get a free ticket by buying another at full price, and there were various other restrictions. (Note that this promotion would appear to violate FTC and similar state rules about "free" offers).

In response to a breach of contract claim, defendant Equilon argued that its ad lacked sufficient specificity to be an offer, and therefore there could be no acceptance or meeting of the minds. How would you evaluate this argument?

The *Equilon* court stated that the key issue was whether the recipient "reasonably might have concluded that by acting in accordance with the request a contract would be formed." Equilon, "in clear and positive terms, promised to render performance in exchange for the purchase of ten gallons of fuel." Plaintiffs sufficiently alleged consideration when they stated that they purchased ten gallons of fuel at a participating Shell station with the intention of participating in the "Ski Free" promotion. While the consumer protection claims were dismissed for failure to plead with sufficient particularity, the breach of contract claims therefore survived. Kearney v. Equilon Enters., LLC, 65 F. Supp. 3d 1033 (D. Or. 2014).

Recall Lord Justice Bowen's statement: "[W]e must read this advertisement in its plain meaning, as the public would understand it. It was intended to be issued to the public and to be read by the public. How would an ordinary person reading this document construe it?" If we take this idea as the foundation of advertising law, does the addition of the legal concepts of offer, acceptance, and consideration advance the analysis at all?

Modern consumer protection class actions often add a breach of warranty count to their breach of contract claims. State law requirements for breach of warranty claims vary; in Sandoval v. PharmaCare US, Inc., 145 F. Supp. 3d 986 (S.D. Cal. 2015), for example, the consumer plaintiff adequately pled breach of express warranty by identifying specific statements on a supplement product's packaging that promised increased sexual performance from consumption; alleging reasonable reliance on those statements; and alleging harm because the product didn't and couldn't provide its promised benefits. *Sandoval,* like many consumer cases asserting warranty claims, also claimed for breach of the implied warranty of merchantability, which in California "is breached when the goods do not conform to the promises or affirmations contained on the container or label or are not fit for the ordinary purposes for which the goods are used." Given the allegations that the product didn't work, the *Sandoval* plaintiff stated a claim under the former theory. Despite the plaintiff's successes in *Sandoval,* breach of warranty claims can be difficult to win.

Finally, some plaintiffs may be able to bring Magnuson–Moss Warranty Act (MMWA) claims. The MMWA regulates warranties on consumer goods. It applies to written warranties, which are defined as a written affirmation that "relates to the nature of the material or workmanship and affirms or promises that such material or workmanship is defect free or will meet a specific level of performance over a specific period of time." 15 U.S.C. § 2301(6)(A). Separately, it borrows state-law causes of action for breach of warranty and makes them enforceable in federal court.

One way to look at things is that, under modern consumer protection law, there is a space for liability between a promise serious enough to count as an offer (and thus a possible contract breach) or a warranty and promise-like assertions that no reasonable consumer would take seriously. The space in between—where a reasonable consumer would believe the claim but a court would not find an offer, warranty, or other actionable promise under contract law—is now the province of consumer protection law. Of course, a false or misleading offer might *also* violate a consumer protection statute.

Common Law Fraud or Deceit

Under a common law fraud or deceit action, a plaintiff must generally satisfy the following elements: (1) proof of a false, material

130

representation, (2) scienter, or knowledge or recklessness by defendant of its falsity with an intent to deceive, and (3) justifiable reliance by the purchaser upon the misrepresentation. Consider the following case, involving a sympathetic but deluded plaintiff. As you read, try to imagine how the plaintiff Audrey Vokes initially understood her relationship to the defendant dance studio (and perhaps to individual instructors), and also try to imagine how the defendants' employees thought about her.

Vokes v. Arthur Murray, Inc., 212 So. 2d 906 (Fla. Ct. App. 1968)

Defendant Arthur Murray, Inc., a corporation, authorizes the operation throughout the nation of dancing schools under the name of 'Arthur Murray School of Dancing' through local franchised operators, one of whom was defendant J. P. Davenport whose dancing establishment was in Clearwater.

Plaintiff Mrs. Audrey E. Vokes, a widow of 51 years and without family, had a yen to be 'an accomplished dancer' with the hopes of finding 'new interest in life'. So, on February 10, 1961, a dubious fate, with the assist of a motivated acquaintance, procured her to attend a 'dance party' at Davenport's 'School of Dancing' where she whiled away the pleasant hours, sometimes in a private room, absorbing his accomplished sales technique, during which her grace and poise were elaborated upon and her rosy future as 'an excellent dancer' was painted for her in vivid and glowing colors. As an incident to this interlude, he sold her eight 1/2-hour dance lessons to be utilized within one calendar month therefrom, for the sum of $14.50 cash in hand paid, obviously a baited 'comeon'.

Thus she embarked upon an almost endless pursuit of the terpsichorean art during which, over a period of less than sixteen months, she was sold fourteen 'dance courses' totalling in the aggregate 2302 hours of dancing lessons for a total cash outlay of $31,090.45, all at Davenport's dance emporium. . . .

These dance lesson contracts and the monetary consideration therefor of over $31,000 were procured from her by means and methods of Davenport and his associates which went beyond the unsavory, yet legally permissible, perimeter of 'sales puffing' and intruded well into the forbidden area of undue influence, the suggestion of falsehood, the suppression of truth, and the free exercise of rational judgment, if what plaintiff alleged in her complaint was true. From the time of her first contact with the dancing school in February, 1961, she was influenced unwittingly by a constant and continuous barrage of flattery, false praise, excessive compliments, and panegyric encomiums, to such extent that it would be not only inequitable, but unconscionable, for a Court exercising inherent chancery power to allow such contracts to stand.

She was incessantly subjected to overreaching blandishment and cajolery. She was assured she had 'grace and poise'; that she was 'rapidly improving and developing in her dancing skill'; that the additional lessons would 'make her a beautiful dancer, capable of dancing with the most accomplished dancers'; that she was 'rapidly progressing in the development of her dancing skill and gracefulness', etc., etc. She was given 'dance aptitude tests' for the ostensible purpose of 'determining' the number of remaining hours' instructions needed by her from time to time.

At one point she was sold 545 additional hours of dancing lessons to be entitled to award of the 'Bronze Medal' signifying that she had reached 'the Bronze Standard', a supposed designation of dance achievement by students of Arthur Murray, Inc.

Later she was sold an additional 926 hours in order to gain the 'Silver Medal', indicating she had reached 'the Silver Standard', at a cost of $12,501.35.

At one point, while she still had to her credit about 900 unused hours of instructions, she was induced to purchase an additional 24 hours of lessons to participate in a trip to Miami at her own expense, where she would be 'given the opportunity to dance with members of the Miami Studio'.

She was induced at another point to purchase an additional 123 hours of lessons in order to be not only eligible for the Miami trip but also to become 'a life member of the Arthur Murray Studio', carrying with it certain dubious emoluments, at a further cost of $1,752.30.

At another point, while she still had over 1,000 unused hours of instruction she was induced to buy 151 additional hours at a cost of $2,049.00 to be eligible for a 'Student Trip to Trinidad', at her own expense as she later learned.

Also, when she still had 1100 unused hours to her credit, she was prevailed upon to purchase an additional 347 hours at a cost of $4,235.74, to qualify her to receive a 'Gold Medal' for achievement, indicating she had advanced to 'the Gold Standard'.

On another occasion, while she still had over 1200 unused hours, she was induced to buy an additional 175 hours of instruction at a cost of $2,472.75 to be eligible 'to take a trip to Mexico'.

Finally, sandwiched in between other lesser sales promotions, she was influenced to buy an additional 481 hours of instruction at a cost of $6,523.81 in order to 'be classified as a Gold Bar Member, the ultimate achievement of the dancing studio'.

All the foregoing sales promotions, illustrative of the entire fourteen separate contracts, were procured by defendant Davenport and Arthur Murray, Inc., by false representations to her that she was improving in her dancing ability, that she had excellent potential, that she was responding to instructions in dancing grace, and that they were developing her into a beautiful dancer, whereas in truth and in fact she did not develop in her dancing ability, she had no 'dance aptitude', and in fact had difficulty in 'hearing that musical beat'. The complaint alleged that such representations to her 'were in fact false and known by the defendant to be false and contrary to the plaintiff's true ability, the truth of plaintiff's ability being fully known to the defendants, but withheld from the plaintiff for the sole and specific intent to deceive and defraud the plaintiff and to induce her in the purchasing of additional hours of dance lessons'. It was averred that the lessons were sold to her 'in total disregard to the true physical, rhythm, and mental ability of the plaintiff'. In other words, while she first exulted that she was entering the 'spring of her life', she finally was awakened to the fact there was 'spring' neither in her life nor in her feet. . . .

Defendants contend that contracts can only be rescinded for fraud or misrepresentation when the alleged misrepresentation is as to a material fact, rather than an opinion, prediction or expectation, and that the statements and representations set forth at length in the complaint were in the category of 'trade puffing', within its legal orbit.

It is true that 'generally a misrepresentation, to be actionable, must be one of fact rather than of opinion'. But this rule has significant qualifications, applicable here. It does not apply where there is a fiduciary relationship between the parties, or where there has been some artifice or trick employed by the representor, or where the parties do not in general deal at 'arm's length' as we understand the phrase, or where the representee does not have equal opportunity to become apprised of the truth or falsity of the fact represented. As stated by Judge Allen of this Court in *Ramel v. Chasebrook Construction Company*, Fla. App. 1961, 135 So.2d 876:

> . . . A statement of a party having . . . superior knowledge may be regarded as a statement of fact although it would be considered as opinion if the parties were dealing on equal terms.

It could be reasonably supposed here that defendants had 'superior knowledge' as to whether plaintiff had 'dance potential' and as to whether she was noticeably improving in the art of terpsichore. And it would be a reasonable inference from the undenied averments of the complaint that the flowery eulogiums heaped upon her by defendants as a prelude to her contracting for 1944 additional hours of instruction in order to attain the rank of the Bronze Standard, thence to the bracket of the Silver Standard, thence to the class of the Gold Bar Standard, and finally to the crowning plateau of a Life Member of the Studio, proceeded as much or more from the urge to 'ring the cash register' as from any honest or realistic appraisal of her dancing prowess or a factual representation of her progress.

Even in contractual situations where a party to a transaction owes no duty to disclose facts within his knowledge or to answer inquiries respecting such facts, the law is if he undertakes to do so he must disclose the Whole truth. From the face of the complaint, it should have been reasonably apparent to defendants that her vast outlay of cash for the many hundreds of additional hours of instruction was not justified by her slow and awkward progress, which she would have been made well aware of if they had spoken the 'whole truth'.

. . . We repeat that where parties are dealing on a contractual basis at arm's length with no inequities or inherently unfair practices employed, the Courts will in general 'leave the parties where they find themselves'. But in the case sub judice, from the allegations of the unanswered complaint, we cannot say that enough of the accompanying ingredients, as mentioned in the foregoing authorities, were not present which otherwise would have barred the equitable arm of the Court to her. In our view, from the showing made in her complaint, plaintiff is entitled to her day in Court.

NOTES AND QUESTIONS

Vokes purchased over 2,300 hours of training. If she did dance training for 40 hours a week (a remarkable physical endurance feat for anyone), it would take her about 14 straight months to use up her purchased hours. If she trained 7 hours a week—an hour a day, every day—it would take her over 6 years to use up her hours. Obviously, at some point, she was accumulating training hours that she was unlikely to use—ever.

As to Vokes' dancing potential, do you agree that it was reasonable for Vokes to rely on the claimed expertise of the defendants? Shouldn't she have been able to assess her progress for herself? If you think she was fooling herself with the eager assistance of the defendants, might you still think the defendants behaved badly?

The idea that people with special knowledge may have special duties is a common one. If a health professional falsely told Vokes that her treatment for cancer was going well, would we expect Vokes to be able to discern the truth? When one's own senses are not necessarily reliable, reliance on an apparent expert may be more reasonable.

Consider the role of gender stereotypes in the court's decision: was the court influenced by the idea that women, especially older single women, need special protection? In a time when women were routinely denied financial education and experience, was the court acting appropriately in assessing Vokes' capacities according to her pleadings? See Debora L. Threedy, *Dancing Around Gender: Lessons*

136

from Arthur Murray on Gender and Contracts, 45 WAKE FOREST L. REV. 749 (2010). What would a gender-neutral standard of reasonableness look like, and how would that differ from a standard of reasonableness that uses an unimpaired adult male as the model "reasonable person"?

The result in *Vokes* is not particularly common today. In fraud cases, the courts are often less solicitous of consumers who have let themselves be duped when they could have protected themselves. In many states, various doctrines require "reasonable" consumers to behave like suspicious lawyers, reading for ambiguity and disbelieving promises that aren't contained in a binding contract, even when a salesperson explicitly promises that the fine print is just meaningless legalese. *See* Debra Pogrund Stark & Jessica M. Choplin, *A License To Deceive: Enforcing Contractual Myths Despite Consumer Psychological Realities*, 5 N.Y.U. J. L. & BUS. 617 (2009).

In recent years, the trend has been to tighten reliance requirements, allowing sellers to disavow promises made by salespeople or in ads through contracts that consumers don't read or understand. Research, however, shows that people often fail to read written contracts that contradict oral promises, even when the contradictory terms are (1) highlighted in red, (2) in a larger font than other terms, (3) require the consumer to initial the terms, *and* (4) part of a single-page document. Even when people do read the contracts, they often accept the oral representations instead, because of social norms related to trusting the person with whom they're speaking. *See* Jessica M. Choplin et al., *A Psychological Investigation of Consumer Vulnerability to Fraud: Legal and Policy Implications*, 35 L. & PSYCH. REV. 61 (2011).

Under the modern Federal Rules of Civil Procedure, plaintiffs must plead fraud claims with particularity, which requires far more detail than other claims do. Consumer-plaintiffs often have difficulty fulfilling the heightened pleading requirements for a fraud claim and difficulty proving the scienter element. *See* Bell Atlantic Corp. v. Twombly, 550 U.S. 544 (2007) (raising the pleading standard in general).

Not every "lie" counts as "fraud," depending on what the defendant might have known or believed. Thus, consumer plaintiffs tend to emphasize statutory causes of action, though they may plead fraud in the alternative. The remainder of this chapter explains how state consumer protection laws operate, both for consumer-plaintiffs and for state attorneys general, who enforce the laws on behalf of their states' populations.

B.   Consumer Protection Laws

Overview

Every state has a consumer protection law that protects its own consumers—which means that national ads may be subject to differing state-by-state legal standards.

Many state consumer protection laws were enacted in the 1960s out of concern that the FTC and other agencies were under-enforcing the law. *See generally* RICHARD ALDERMAN & MARY DEE PRIDGEN, CONSUMER PROTECTION AND THE LAW § 2:10 (2008). Lawmakers were also concerned that traditional fraud causes of action imposed burdens too high for deceived plaintiffs to meet, and that even when a case could be made, the remedies were insufficient to deter deception. Traditional fraud doctrine, for example, presumed a one-on-one transaction, not a repeated campaign, and made prospective injunctive relief difficult to secure. The requirement of proving fraudulent intent also defeated many claims even when consumers had been deceived and harmed. As we saw earlier, contract theories had significant limits, as did breach of warranty claims. And regardless of the theory, without the ability to recover statutory damages or attorneys' fees, most losses due to deception were simply too small to sustain a lawsuit. The solution was to establish new laws aimed specifically at protecting consumers from false advertising and deceptive business techniques.

State consumer protection laws mirror the FTC Act's prohibition of *"unfair or deceptive acts or practices* in or affecting commerce," 15 U.S.C. § 45(a)(1), so they are often referred to as UDAP or "Little FTC" statutes. A critical difference between the FTCA and most UDAP statutes, however, is that the latter usually provide for private enforcement by consumer-plaintiffs, either because of an express provision in the statute or by judicial interpretation.

Consumers—or at least their lawyers—have taken up the invitation. According to one study of over 17,000 reported federal district and state appellate decisions, "[b]etween 2000 and 2007 the number of CPA [consumer protection act] decisions reported in federal district and state appellate courts increased by 119%. This large increase in CPA litigation far exceeds increases in tort litigation as well as overall litigation during the same period." Searle Civil Justice Institute, *State Consumer Protection Acts: An Empirical Investigation of Private Litigation Preliminary Report* (Dec. 2009).

There is a sometimes bewildering amount of variety in state UDAP laws. The amount of variation is indicated by the range in statutes of limitation: from one year in Arizona to six years in Maine. But that is far from the most important difference. This section sketches out generalities and indicates points of variation that are often significant.

Some UDAP statutes are based on the Uniform Deceptive Trade Practices Act (UDTPA), drafted in 1964 and rewritten in 1966. The UDTPA enumerates twelve specific deceptive practices, covering misleading trade identification (including passing off and trademark infringement), false advertising, deceptive advertising, and a final catchall ban on "any other conduct which similarly creates a likelihood of confusion or misunderstanding."* As the inclusion of trademark infringement and similar conduct indicates, the UDTPA prioritized competitive concerns.

Other state laws are based on the Model Unfair Trade Practices and Consumer Protection Law (UTPCPL), which was developed by the FTC, published in 1967, and amended in 1969 and 1970. *See* Unfair Trade Practices and Consumer Protection Law (Council of State Gov'ts 1970).

---

* The list: (1) passing off goods or services as those of another; (2) causing likelihood of confusion or of misunderstanding as to the source, sponsorship, approval, or certification of goods or services; (3) causing likelihood of confusion or of misunderstanding as to affiliation, connection, or association with, or certification by, another; (4) using deceptive representations or designations of geographic origin in connection with goods or services; (5) representing that goods or services have sponsorship, approval, characteristics, ingredients, uses, benefits, or qualities that they do not have or that a person has a sponsorship, approval, status, affiliation, or connection that he does not have; (6) representing that goods are original or new if they are deteriorated, altered, reconditioned, reclaimed, used, or secondhand; (7) representing that goods or services are of a particular standard, quality, or grade, or that goods are of a particular style or model, if they are of another; (8) disparaging the goods, services, or business of another by false or misleading representation of fact; (9) advertising goods or services with intent not to sell them as advertised; (10) advertising goods or services with intent not to supply reasonably expectable public demand, unless the advertisement discloses a limitation of quantity; (11) making false or misleading statements of fact concerning the reasons for, existence of, or amounts of price reductions; (12) engaging in any other conduct which similarly creates a likelihood of confusion or of misunderstanding.

The UTPCPL brought together many existing approaches in three subvariants: (1) tracking the FTCA almost verbatim and barring unfair methods of competition or unfair or deceptive acts in trade or commerce; (2) prohibiting false, misleading or deceptive acts or practices as the FTCA did, but not barring "unfair" practices; and (3) enumerating prohibited activities, including the "laundry list" from the UDTPA and adding a prohibition on acts or practices that were "unfair or deceptive to the consumer." In contrast to the UDTPA, the UTPCPL had a more consumer-directed orientation.

Today, most of the states using a list of prohibited practices also have a catchall provision covering deceptive practices. Some states, such as Hawaii, Georgia and Illinois, have adopted both the UTPCPL and the UDTPA. Moreover, the items on the basic laundry list vary substantially in specificity. This raises the statutory drafting question of why the laws include specific enumerated verboten practices as a supplement to the general catch-all prohibitions on false and misleading ads.

Many states, including California and New York, also allow claims for unfair trade practices based on the advertiser's violation of another governing law (including federal law). *See, e.g.*, People v. Ford Motor Co., 74 N.Y.2d 495 (1989). This may sound redundant, but it can be extremely important for creating causes of action based on laws that don't themselves allow private enforcement.

Some state laws explicitly include or exclude certain industries, such as real estate, franchising, insurance, or industries regulated by some other agency. States often exempt conduct specifically approved by a regulatory agency, though an agency's failure to regulate (yet) does not constitute approval of the practice.

UDAP laws also exclude suits over ordinary breach of contract claims and employment disputes. However, UDAP laws cover deceptive practices designed to induce a consumer to *enter into* a standard contract.

States also vary somewhat in the degree that their laws draw upon the FTCA's jurisprudence. Twenty-five state statutes explicitly instruct courts to draw on FTC decisions in deciding cases. The degree of deference due to the federal standard varies widely, from requiring that state courts give it "consideration" or "due consideration and great weight," to requirements that courts be "guided" by or "consistent" with federal decisions. Additional states direct that state enforcement policies, rules and regulations be "consistent" with their federal counterparts. Many state laws also direct courts to harmonize their decisions with those of other states.

It's worth elaborating further on the difference between consumer protection statutes and the common law. The absence of a reliance requirement can be important in situations where, for example, the fine print of a contract contradicts the message the consumer took away from the advertiser's claims. Under many state consumer protection laws, the consumer has a cause of action even if the parol evidence rule would defeat her fraud claim. *See* Victor E. Schwartz & Cary Silverman, *Common-Sense Construction of Consumer Protection Acts*, 54 KAN. L. REV. 1 (2005); Salisbury v. Chapman Realty, 465 N.E.2d 127 (Ill. App. Ct. 1984). Other traditional barriers to success in fraud cases, such as the Statute of Frauds, warranty disclaimers, the common law merger doctrine, and contractual limitations on liability or remedies—ways in which a seller can use a written contract to argue that the plaintiff agreed to accept what she got even though that may not have been what she was originally promised or what she thought she was getting—are also less likely to defeat consumer protection claims.

Nonetheless, there are substantial state-by-state variations in how far the consumer protection law deviates from the common law. The current trend is to tighten causation requirements, so that even if there is no explicit reliance element, a false or misleading representation must be directly connected to a plaintiff's harm, which is often the same thing as reliance. California achieved this result by amending its consumer protection laws to require actual injury.

There may be special limits on lawsuits by non-consumers. Massachusetts allows claims by people engaged in "trade or commerce" but specifically requires courts in such cases to be guided by antitrust principles, a requirement absent from the portion of the law allowing consumers to sue. MASS. GEN. LAWS, Chapter 93A § 11. In addition, Massachusetts requires that such claims can only be brought if the unfair or deceptive acts or practices "occurred primarily and substantially within" the state, whereas consumer suits are not subject to this requirement. Why make this distinction?

State Attorneys General

In virtually every state, the attorney general (AG) can enforce consumer protection laws on behalf of the public. Acting as a public representative, the AG in practice often receives greater deference from courts than private plaintiffs do.

AGs investigate possible violations. They have the authority to issue Civil Investigative Demands (CIDs) requesting documents or testimony from targets. Some AGs also promulgate rules and guidance, similar to the FTC. AGs may issue cease-and-desist orders; enter into consent decrees or voluntary assurances of compliance, which if breached may result in contempt charges; or file lawsuits on behalf of consumers, seeking prospective injunctive relief, restitution for deceived consumers and/or disgorgement of unlawfully acquired profits. Restitution goes directly to affected customers when they can be readily identified. When this is prohibitively difficult, it is generally given to relevant nonprofit organizations under the doctrine of *cy pres* (Law French for "as close as possible"). Both civil and criminal penalties are generally available to AGs. In some larger cities, the state attorney or district attorney may also have a consumer protection division enforcing state and local law.

State AGs are actively pursuing consumer protection cases and enlarging their enforcement departments, in part because of the general availability of fee awards to a prevailing AG. In recent years, the National Association of Attorneys General (NAAG) has helped AGs coordinate their activity, so multistate AG actions are increasingly common. Generally, one AG or a small group will take the lead, with the aim of obtaining a comprehensive nationwide resolution of the claims.

State attorneys general may also be increasingly willing to assert "unfairness" violations where statutorily authorized. In one Massachusetts case, *Commonwealth of Massachusetts v. Fremont Investment and Loan & Fremont General Corporation*, 123 Mass. L. Rep. 567 (2008), the state attorney general successfully obtained a preliminary injunction requiring a lender to submit its pending Massachusetts subprime mortgage foreclosures to the AG for prior review and approval. The AG argued that the subprime loans originated by Fremont should be presumed structurally unfair if they contained four specific attributes correlated with foreclosure. Unfairness jurisdiction was superior to deceptiveness jurisdiction for this purpose because there was no need to prove individual borrower injury or a deceptive pattern or practice—the AG could move for injunctive relief before too many consumers were injured, and was able to obtain loan modification as a remedy. Larry Kirsch, *The State Attorney General as Consumer Advocate: A Recent Effort to Tame Unfair Subprime Lending* (2010), http://www.law.columbia.edu/center_program/ag/policy/consumer/.

Although the procedure for bringing AG actions varies from state to state, New York is illustrative. New York's UDAP statute, GBL § 349, and its false advertising statute, § 350, give the attorney general statutory authority to seek an injunction, restitution and penalties when he or she believes anyone has engaged in deceptive acts and practices or false advertising, which includes advertising that is literally true but is likely to mislead consumers. The attorney general may act without awaiting actual consumer complaints or injury. Scienter, intent and good faith are immaterial. Voluntary discontinuance is also no defense. Additionally, New York Executive Law § 63(12) gives the attorney general authority, on five days' notice, to bring a special proceeding against persons or businesses who "engage in repeated fraudulent or illegal acts or otherwise demonstrate persistent fraud or illegality in the carrying on, conducting or transaction of business."

AGs' consumer protection divisions generally view themselves as experts, able to look at an ad and tell whether it's likely to deceive consumers. In cases brought under the Lanham Act, plaintiffs alleging that an ad is misleading must present extrinsic evidence of consumer deception, usually through survey evidence. Despite many defendants' attempts to argue for a similar requirement under state UDAP laws, courts have generally (but not always) rejected the analogy between UDAP laws and the Lanham Act. Extrinsic evidence is useful, but not required. As with the FTC, courts will often defer to the AGs' expertise.

As we proceed, consider the merits and costs of requiring extrinsic evidence of likely consumer deception and whether expertise in the area can substitute for such evidence. Just because a lawyer works in the consumer protection field, does that mean that she knows how consumers are likely to react to a particular claim? What does expertise mean in this context?

Consumer Lawsuits

The existence of a private cause of action is a key difference between the FTCA and the majority of state statutes. The private right evolved over time: the model UDTPA, for example, limited the remedy available to private parties to injunctive relief. As amended in 1966, the UDTPA authorized reasonable attorneys' fees for plaintiffs if the defendant's conduct was willful and knowing, and most UDTPA statutes ultimately amended their consumer protection law to allow monetary relief to consumers. Currently, all state consumer protection laws allow private parties to sue to enforce them, with Iowa at last joining the ranks in 2009. *See* Searle Civil Justice Institute, State Consumer Protection Acts, An Empirical Investigation of Private Litigation, Preliminary Report 10 (December 2009). Arkansas limits its private right of action to elderly and disabled persons. ARK. CODE § 4-88-204.

Class Actions

Lawsuits under state consumer protection/UDAP laws are often brought as class actions, which allow a plaintiff greater leverage against a defendant given the greater magnitude of a potential loss (which also includes any fee award) compared to an individual claim.

As the result of increasing concerns about abuses of class actions, Congress, in the Class Action Fairness Act (CAFA), and the courts have adopted various rules that make it harder to maintain many class actions. We will investigate this phenomenon in detail in Chapter 7.

Most prominently, questions about differences between various state laws can make it difficult to maintain a multistate class action. To get around this, plaintiffs in large consumer class-action lawsuits may create state-specific subclasses, at least for the more populous states.

Questions about individual reliance on deceptive statements can additionally make it difficult to maintain a class action at all, if each plaintiff will be required to show that she saw and relied on the deceptive statements at issue to prevail.

The following chart summarizes a few of the bigger variations between state UDAP laws.

	No	Yes
Intent to deceive or bad faith required?	Majority of states	Georgia, Kansas, New Jersey, New Mexico and Utah
Heightened pleading required under Rule 9(b) (cause of action "sounds in fraud")?	Historically not required	Increasingly required
Consumer reliance upon the claim required?	Majority of states: falsity or tendency to deceive is enough to get at least an injunction	Some states require actual consumer reliance on the claim (but not "reasonable" reliance)
Are only consumers protected?	Some states protect anyone harmed, including competitors	Some states protect only consumers or people engaged in consumer transactions
Public interest requirement?	Majority of states: no	Minority of states (including NY) require the practice at issue could harm the public
Class actions allowed?	Majority of states: yes	Minority: no; Ohio only allows in very

		limited circumstances
Statutory damages or treble damages available?	Majority: yes; New Jersey and North Carolina require trebling damages if a violation is established; a number of other states require bad faith, intent, or knowledge; some states provide a statutory minimum recovery, from $200 in Montana to $5,000 in Kansas	Minority (at least a dozen): no, only actual damages, restitution, or equitable relief
Class actions excluded from statutory minimum damages or damages capped in class action?	Majority of states: no	Minority approaches vary: Hawaii offers treble damages or $1,000, whichever is greater, in individual cases but not class actions; in Idaho, award per class member cannot exceed $1,000; Kansas excludes class actions from statutory damages of $5,000 available to individuals
Fee awards available?	Majority of states: yes; mandatory for	Approaches vary: in Florida, only

	successful plaintiff in many states Alabama, Maine, New Hampshire, New Jersey, Texas, Vermont, and Wisconsin	consumer plaintiffs can recover fees; in other states, such as Ohio, the defendant must have knowingly violated the statute before fees are available

Case Study: Law School Advertising

The following cases involve one-state consumer class actions about a topic that may be close to your heart. As you read, pay attention to the pleading standard as applied to the elements of the cause of action.

Gomez-Jimenez v. New York Law School, 943 N.Y.S.2d 834 (Sup. Ct. 2012)

This is a motion to dismiss a complaint brought by nine graduates of New York Law School (NYLS) who allege that data published by their school pertaining to the school's graduates' employment and salaries is misleading and, in fact, fraudulent. They assert that in having relied on this misleading information to make their decision to attend NYLS, they now find themselves in disadvantaged employment positions and, consequently, they seek damages equal to the difference between the alleged inflated tuition they paid because of the allegedly misleading statements and what they characterize as the "true value" of a NYLS degree, together with certain expenses they incurred.

Background

NYLS enrolls approximately 1,500 students. Tuition is $47,800 per annum. According to plaintiffs, NYLS has been able to attract a large number of applicants and charge an expensive price for its educational services because the school has disseminated this misleading information about its graduates' employment profiles. . . . Plaintiffs allege that many of the school's working graduates in the legal sector hold part-time or temporary employment, paying barely enough to service the debt incurred to finance their law school tuition and expenses. . . .

The allegedly misleading information was disseminated for the entering classes 2005–2010. According to the complaint, the NYLS data allegedly omitted facts which, in plaintiffs' view, would have given prospective students a more accurate picture of NYLS's post-graduation employment prospects. For example, plaintiffs allege the data consistently reported that approximately 90–92 percent of NYLS graduates secured employment within nine months of graduation, but did not report the percentage of graduates employed in part-time or temporary positions. According to plaintiffs, a graduate could be working part-time as a barista in Starbucks—or toiling away in any job—and be deemed employed in business, although such employment is temporary and does not require a law degree. A contract attorney, without permanent employment, working in document review projects in a law firm, would be deemed employed in private law practice under the NYLS profile.

The data allegedly inflated graduate mean salaries by reporting them based on a small, deliberately selected, intensely solicited, subset of graduates. . . .

Plaintiffs claim the employment and salary data reported by NYLS were at odds with national legal employment statistics reported and made available to the public by the National Association for Law Placement (NALP) and with the reality of NYLS's ranking by the U.S. News & World Report (US News).

. . . Plaintiffs assert three causes of action. They allege that NYLS's actions (i) constitute unlawful, unfair, deceptive and fraudulent practices under N.Y. General Business Law (GBL) 349, (ii) are fraudulent in that NYLS disseminated information which contained numerous false representations and omissions of material facts, and (iii) constitute negligent misrepresentation. . . .

GBL 349 Claim

To state a cause of action under GBL 349, a plaintiff must allege that the defendant's conduct was: (1) consumer oriented; (2) deceptive or misleading in a material way; and (3) that plaintiff suffered injury as a result. While the statute does not require an assertion of justifiable reliance, or the defendant's intent to deceive or mislead, a plaintiff must allege that defendant's consumer-oriented, deceptive acts or practices "resulted in actual injury to the plaintiff." . . .

Deceptive Acts and Practices: "The Reasonable Consumer"

The New York Court of Appeals, concerned about what it termed a "tidal wave of litigation against businesses that was not intended by the Legislature" pursuant to GBL 349, adopted "an objective definition of deceptive acts and practices, whether representations or omissions, limited to those likely to mislead a reasonable consumer acting reasonably under the circumstances." Therefore, plaintiffs must plead that NYLS has engaged "in an act or practice that is deceptive or misleading in a material way . . . to a reasonable consumer."

Also, to the extent that allegations are not fact supported, they fail to state a GBL 349 claim. Here, the only fact-supported, allegedly misleading statements are (1) NYLS's failure to differentiate among types of employment when publishing its employment statistics and (2) NYLS's publication of salary data based on a small group of students.

The NYLS employment statistics for each year show data based on the graduates reporting their employment information. NYLS reported that 92 percent of its 2005 and 2006 classes reporting their employment information were employed within nine months of graduation. For the classes of 2007, 2009, and 2010, NYLS reported employment rates of 92.3 percent, 89.7 percent and 91.9 percent, respectively, based on the graduates reporting their employment information. NYLS also disclosed that for the class of 2007, 96 percent of the graduates reported employment information; for the class of 2009, 94 percent of the graduates reported employment information; and for the class of 2010, 95 percent of the graduates reported employment information.

Plaintiffs allege that these statistics somehow deceptively make it appear that the jobs reported are all full-time permanent positions for which a law degree is required or preferred. They contend that in the circumstances where all applicants want a full-time law job, and are willing to take on in excess of $100,000 of debt to be eligible for one, any reasonable consumer would infer NYLS's data was reporting full-time, permanent employment for which a law degree was required or preferred, thus purporting to demonstrate success at finding employment. No such statement is made by NYLS in its marketing materials, however.

The court does not view these post-graduate employment statistics to be misleading in a material way for a reasonable consumer acting reasonably. By anyone's definition, reasonable consumers—college graduates—seriously considering law schools are a sophisticated subset of education consumers, capable of sifting through data and weighing alternatives before making a decision regarding their post-college options, such as applying for professional school. These reasonable consumers have available to them any number of sources of information to review when making their decisions.

Plaintiffs' own complaint confirms the court's view. Plaintiffs cite NALP's employment reports and various studies, initiatives and news articles. According to NALP, the percentage of graduates who found full-time legal employment on a national level is considerably more modest, i.e. 40 percent, than NYLS's allegedly misleading employment data for NYLS would suggest. That this statistic provides context for the reasonable consumer of a legal education also suggests that more detailed employment information is available to the law school consumer through NALP's reports. . . .

Plaintiffs' complaint also compares NYLS with its law school peers as reflected in the rankings of US News. Notwithstanding that plaintiffs do not challenge the quality of the education they received, the complaint asserts that because NYLS finds itself in the bottom tier of the US News law school rankings, "logic dictates that NYLS's true employment rate would be below the statistical mean of the bell curve." One would think that reasonable consumers, armed with the publicly available information from US News that plaintiffs cite, thus would avail themselves of plaintiffs' own logic as stated in their complaint when it comes to evaluating their chances of obtaining the full-time legal job of their choice within nine months post-graduation.

Indeed, the court takes judicial notice that US News, in addition to its general law school rankings to which plaintiffs themselves refer in their complaint, has published a plethora of information ranking law schools, including NYLS, in a number of job-related categories including: "Whose graduates are the most and least likely to land a job?," "Whose graduates earn the most? The Least?," "Where do graduates work?," "Who's the priciest? Who's the cheapest?," "Whose graduates have the most debt? The Least?." *See, e.g.,* Ultimate Guide to Law Schools, U.S. News and World, L.P. Report, 2d ed. (2006).

As to the salary data being misleading because it allegedly was based on a "deliberately selected" small sample of graduates, the relatively small percentage of responding students was disclosed whenever the salary data included the average salary statistic. . . . In addition, the materials cautioned that the highest reported salary for those years "is not the typical salary for most law school graduates—in New York City and nationwide." Finally, there is simply no representation in NYLS's marketing materials that the sample of the reported salaries is in any way representative of the salaries earned by all the employed graduates in a given year. The court thus finds that the documentary evidence of statements presenting salary data do not violate the prohibition against deceptive business practices as "there can be no [GBL 349] claim when the allegedly deceptive practice was fully disclosed."

. . . It is also difficult for the court to conceive that somehow lost on these plaintiffs is the fact that a goodly number of law school graduates toil (perhaps part-time) in drudgery or have less than hugely successful careers. NYLS applicants, as reasonable consumers of a legal education, would have to be wearing blinders not to be aware of these well-established facts of life in the world of legal employment.

The complaint also cites NYLS's statements on its website which address the fact that many students who have no intention of practicing law choose to attend law school and pay a significant sum to do so: "While the course of study leading to the Juris Doctorate degree is designed to prepare students to become practicing lawyers, the program is also ideal preparation for anyone whose work in other professions, in business, or in public service involves understanding law and lawyers."

The widely held perception that a law degree from a respectable, accredited institution opens innumerable career paths beyond solely the practice of law, and leads to advancement in other fields is thus also an integral part of defendant's marketing materials. Choosing to disregard their own documentary evidence from defendant's marketing materials in this respect, plaintiffs have selectively relied only on the relatively incomplete statistics of these materials and have mischaracterized them in their entirety as a deceptive enticement that makes it appear all jobs reported are full-time law jobs for which a law degree is required or preferred.

. . . . Given the impact of the 2008 Great Recession on the legal job market as described in plaintiffs' complaint, see discussion, *infra*, NYLS's statements could not have been materially misleading to a reasonable consumer acting reasonably under the circumstances, i.e. taking into account the obvious, dramatic changes in the economy as they began to impact the legal profession.

In sum, reasonable consumers would have considered and compared the NYLS statements on employment and compensation along with other decision factors such as other sources of data cited in the complaint, career preference cited in the complaint, i.e. obtaining a law degree for purposes other than practice of law, available financial resources, and economic circumstances in the law business cited in the complaint, all of which would have had to play an important part in reasonable consumers' investigation when deciding whether to commit to attend NYLS and to complete their legal education there. In that context, NYLS's acts and practices complained of by these plaintiffs do not fit the objective definition of "deceptive" when viewed through the lens of the "reasonable consumer acting reasonably under the circumstances."

Damages: Remote and Speculative

The court is also of the view that plaintiffs' GBL 349 claim fails to satisfy the statute's requirement that the actual injury each plaintiff sustained as a result of the misleading statements be identified. In their Opposition Memorandum, plaintiffs claim they "enrolled in NYLS to obtain full time, permanent employment in the legal industry." . . .

In their argument for damages, plaintiffs are essentially asking the court to "accept as true" their allegation that a[n] NYLS degree is worth less than what NYLS allegedly represented it to be in its marketing materials. Then, they purport to measure their damages as the difference in value between "a degree where a high paying, full-time, permanent job was highly likely and . . . [a] degree where full-time, permanent legal employment at any salary, let alone a high salary, is scarce, as is the case in the legal market." Accordingly, plaintiffs seek "restitution and disgorgement of all tuition monies remitted to NYLS, totaling $225 million, which is the difference between the inflated tuition paid by class members based on the material misrepresentations . . . and the true value of a[n] NYLS degree[.]" In addition, plaintiffs claim that NYLS's deceptive and misleading employment reports caused them to incur numerous "consequential costs" such as interest on loans, books, traveling and housing expenses.

As the court noted earlier, plaintiffs' sole objection to the degrees they earned at NYLS is purely in employment terms. To show that the value of a NYLS degree was inflated, plaintiffs allege that "many NYLS graduates are . . . working in dead-end jobs, doing document review and other menial, mindless drudgery, essentially functioning as glorified paralegals or secretaries with little control over their careers." This type of work is said not to provide compensation and a lifestyle worthy of the time, money and sacrifice plaintiffs invested in earning a NYLS degree.

. . . . [T]he complaint does not allege facts from which pecuniary damages can be inferred as a direct result of the alleged wrong. . . . On oral argument, plaintiffs emphasized:

> Your Honor, we're here today not talking about whether or not New York Law School guaranteed a job to our clients. That claim appears nowhere in the complaint. . . . This is a case about a product being mislabeled; and because that product is mislabeled, the law school can charge a premium for it. . . . We believe through expert testimony . . . you can measure the difference between a degree where you have a 40 percent or 30 percent chance of getting a job, and the degree that New York Law School misled . . . our clients in getting which was a degree where you have a 90 percent chance of a job[.]"

The starting point of any such measurement is beyond this court, and perhaps this is why plaintiffs fail to allege any method by which any theoretical damages ever could be calculated.

Measuring damages the way plaintiffs would have it would be speculative for another reason as well. As noted earlier, eight of the nine plaintiffs here graduated NYLS between 2008–2011, directly into the Great Recession and its aftermath with the exception of Ms. Gomez–Jimenez who graduated in 2007. Plaintiffs' own complaint acknowledges that one would have to "bury [his/her] head in the sand" to miss the "brutal reality of the current economic environment[,]" and that we are witnessing "one of the grimmest legal job markets in decades." . . .

In these new and troubling times, the reasonable consumer of legal education must realize that these omnipresent realities of the market obviously trump any allegedly overly optimistic claims in their law school's marketing materials. Under New York law, "[f]rustration and disappointed expectations do not of themselves give a rise to a cognizable cause of action." The alleged misstatements in NYLS's marketing materials themselves became obsolete statements as a result of the bleak prospects for legal employment as a result of the Great Recession. That such a widely-known, unanticipated "decimat[ion of] the legal industry" as portrayed in the complaint itself occurred after plaintiffs entered NYLS belies their argument for damages based on NYLS's marketing materials allegedly misrepresenting the likelihood of obtaining legal jobs that plaintiffs believe to be worthy of their investments. To measure damages based on the difference in value between a degree which guarantees a good legal job, as defined by plaintiffs, and one that does not, against the background of the remote, supervening impact of the Great Recession, would require the court to engage in naked speculation. This the court cannot do. . . .

[The court also dismissed fraud and negligent misrepresentation claims.]. . . Reliance must be reasonable. . . . Measuring reasonableness is done in the context of circumstances. Here, plaintiffs were among the select segment of students accepted into an American law school. They were making a substantial economic commitment, for which most of them would incur substantial debt, and they had ample opportunity to discover their realistic post-graduation employment prospects by consulting the many sources of information they cite in their complaint, and cannot claim that it was reasonable to confine their research and reliance solely on what amounts to just two sentences in NYLS's marketing materials. . . . It is simply not plausible that NYLS's data thus was the predicate on which plaintiffs relied to conclude they were guaranteed a job in the legal profession, commensurate with their education, within nine months of graduation. . . .

Harnish v. Widener University School of Law, 931 F.Supp.2d 641 (D.N.J. 2013)

. . . The New Jersey Consumer Fraud Act ("NJCFA") was intended to be one of the strongest in the country. It was designed to address "sharp practices and dealings in the marketing of merchandise and real estate whereby the consumer could be victimized by being lured into a purchase through fraudulent, deceptive or other similar kind of selling or advertising practices." At all times, as "remedial legislation," the NJCFA "should be construed liberally."

The NJCFA states:

> The act, use or employment by any person of any unconscionable commercial practice, deception, fraud, false pretense, false promise, misrepresentation, or the knowing, concealment, suppression, or omission of any material fact with intent that others rely upon such concealment, suppression or omission, in connection with the sale or advertisement of any merchandise or real estate, or with the subsequent performance of such person as aforesaid, whether or not any person has in fact been misled, deceived or damaged thereby, is declared to be an unlawful practice.

N.J. Stat. Ann. § 56:8-2.

To state a claim under the Act, Plaintiffs must allege sufficient facts to demonstrate: (1) unlawful conduct; (2) an ascertainable loss; and (3) a causal relationship between the unlawful conduct and the ascertainable loss. . . .

a.   Affirmative Acts

Plaintiffs allege Widener "stat[ed] false placement rates" and "disseminat[ed] false post-graduate employment data and salary information." These allegations are unsupported by specific facts. Yet, even though such claims of Defendant may not have been false, Plaintiffs' allegations of deception and misinterpretation are still plausible. The NJCFA recognizes "the fact that the [advertisements are] literally true does not mean they cannot be misleading to the average consumer."

. . . For example, the "Class of 2004 Profile" stated "Graduates of the Class of 2004 had a 90% employment rate within nine months of graduation." Plaintiffs allege that over the years the statements, as posted on Widener's website and disseminated to third party evaluators, of an "employment rate" between 90–95 percent misled prospective law students into believing that rate refers to legal employment.

Under somewhat similar facts about a different law school, two New York Supreme Courts, and a New York Appellate Court affirmance, concluded that no reasonable person could be misled to believe a statement referring to an employment rate refers to legal employment only. Gomez-Jimenez, et al. v. New York Law School, 943 N.Y.S.2d 834 (N.Y. Sup. Ct. 2012), aff'd, 956 N.Y.S.2d 54, 59 (2012) (despite being "troubled by the unquestionably less than candid and incomplete nature of defendant's disclosures" the Appellate court nevertheless concluded, the "disclosures were not materially deceptive or misleading."); Austin v. Albany Law School of Union Univ., 957 N.Y.S.2d 833, 840–843 (N.Y. Sup. Ct. 2013) (concluding under New York's consumer fraud law that as applied to "reasonably well-educated (though not necessarily sophisticated) . . . consumers", "ALS's publication of aggregated 'employment rates' cannot be considered deceptive or misleading"). This Court disagrees.

Perception is often affected by location of the object. Here, we have data displayed above the category of "Full Time Legal Employers." Why should a reasonable student looking to go to law school consider that data to include non law-related and part-time employment? Should that student think that going to Widener Law School would open employment as a public school teacher, full or part-time, or an administrative assistant, or a sales clerk, or a medical assistant?

The study of law is the learning of a profession. Widener's website promotes a professional school. Its function is to persuade a prospective law student to attend Widener in order to receive a degree in law. The employment rate was disseminated to third-party evaluators to establish Widener's standing among law schools. Within this context, it is not implausible that a prospective law student making the choice of whether or which law school to attend, would believe that the employment rate referred to law related employment. *See* Hallock v. University of San Francisco, No. CGC-12-517861, at *2 (Cal. Super. Ct. July 19, 2012) ("[T]here is nothing before me to suggest that any of the plaintiffs were not reasonable consumers of a law school education. Moreover, the statements attributed to defendant were allegedly made in a context (i.e. in materials designed to attract and retain law students to defendant's law school) where a reasonable prospective or current law student could reasonably believe that the statements pertained only to jobs for which a law school education is a requirement or preference and did not include jobs for which a law school education is irrelevant or of minimal utility. This issue . . . must await factual development by the parties.") . . .

Despite [information available from other sources such as NALP], "[u]nlike other states that require plaintiff to prove reliance under their consumer protection statutes, the proof requirements that the New Jersey statute places on its claimants is less burdensome." "The causes of action differ . . . in that common law fraud requires proof of reliance while consumer fraud requires only proof of a causal nexus between the concealment of the material fact and the loss."

The NJCFA is "aimed at more than the stereotypic con man." It is intended to "promote the disclosure of relevant information to enable the consumer to make intelligent decisions." Under the Act "[a] practice can be unlawful even if no person was in fact misled or deceived thereby."

Here, an employment rate upwards of 90 percent plausibly gave false assurance to prospective students regarding their legal employment opportunities upon investment in and attainment of a Widener degree. While the thread of plausibility may be slight, it is still a thread. At this motion to dismiss stage, under New Jersey's broad remedial statute, Plaintiffs have sufficiently pled an unlawful affirmative act under the NJCFA.

b. Omissions

To establish an act of omission under the NJCFA, "plaintiff must show that defendant (1) knowingly concealed (2) a material fact (3) with the intention that plaintiff rely upon the concealment."

Widener cursorily asserts that because Plaintiffs failed to plead Widener intended the omissions, Plaintiffs' claims fail as a matter of law. The "heightened pleading standard of Rule 9(b) allows essential elements of the omission under the NJCFA, such as intent, to be alleged generally." Plaintiffs plainly accuse Widener of "engag[ing] in a pattern and practice of knowingly and intentionally making numerous false representations and omissions of material facts, with the intent to deceive and fraudulently induce reliance by Plaintiffs and the members of the Class." Plaintiffs have sufficiently pled intent. Similarly, through the same statement, Plaintiffs pled knowing concealment since, like intent, "knowing" can be alleged generally under Rule 9(b).

Plaintiffs allege Widener made material omissions "concerning [Widener]'s reputation with potential employers . . . concerning the value of a [Widener] degree . . . concerning the rate at which recent graduates can obtain gainful employment in their chosen field and [c]ausing students to pay inflated tuition based on . . . omissions, including, specifically that approximately 90–95 percent of [Widener] graduates secure gainful employment." These omissions are plausibly material. What makes the posted and disseminated employment rate misleading is the failure to include notice that the employment rate refers to all types of employment, that it is not specifically referring to law-related employment, and that the rate may have been inflated by selectively disregarding employment data (as example, failure to count the graduate if she responded "not seeking work"). Without these additional facts, Plaintiffs may have been misled to believe the employment rate referred to their post-graduate employment prospects in the legal sector, and not to employment generally. Plaintiffs have sufficiently pled a knowing omission under the NJCFA.

2. Ascertainable Loss

Typically, "to demonstrate a loss, a victim must simply supply an estimate of damages, calculated within a reasonable degree of certainty." . . .

Widener claims Plaintiffs allege their ascertainable loss is an "inability to obtain a fulltime legal job having their benchmark salary of $92,000." But this is a mischaracterization. Plaintiffs' Amended Complaint in fact seeks a remedy for "the difference between the inflated tuition paid by Class members based on the material representations that approximately 90–95 percent of graduates are employed within nine months of graduation and the true value of a WLS degree." Each Plaintiff asserts they "would not have paid the amount in tuition" had they "been aware of WLS's true job placement rate and salary statistics."

These pleadings are sufficient to meet NJCFA's broad standard for ascertainable loss. *See* Miller v. American Family Publishers, 663 A.2d 643 (N.J. Super. Ct. Ch. Div.1995) ("[F]or their money, they received something less than, and different from, what they reasonably expected in view of defendant's presentations. That is all that is required to establish 'ascertainable loss'"); Talalai v. Cooper Tire & Rubber Co., 823 A.2d 888 (N.J. Super. Ct. Law Div.2001) ("[O]ne has suffered an ascertainable loss under the New Jersey Consumer Fraud Act where that loss is measurable—even though the precise amount is not known.").

3. Causal Nexus

The "'causal nexus' . . . is one of proximate cause." "Plaintiffs are required to prove only that defendant's conduct was a cause of damages." And Plaintiffs "need not prove that [defendant's] conduct was the sole cause of damages."

. . . The claimed causal connection is between the allegedly misleading statements and Plaintiffs' inducement to buy legal education from Widener, not whether Plaintiffs received a legal job. Plaintiffs argue "they would not have paid over $30,000 a year in tuition had they known that merely 56% of Widener graduates were employed in jobs that require or use a Widener law degree." Plaintiffs have sufficiently pled a casual nexus to satisfy the NJCFA.

The NJCFA is a broad remedial act. "[T]o counteract newly devised stratagems undermining the integrity of the marketplace, 'the history of the [NJCFA] [has been] one of constant expansion of consumer

164

protection.'" Under this expansive reach, Plaintiffs have pled a cognizable claim under the NJCFA.

[The court reached the same result under the "virtually identical" Delaware CFA.]

NOTES AND QUESTIONS

Which case is more persuasive? (How does your own educational experience affect your determination of plausibility?)

Macdonald v. Thomas M. Cooley Law School, 724 F.3d 654 (6th Cir. 2013), reached a similar result as *Gomez-Jimenez* on fraud and misrepresentation claims, though it held that Michigan's Consumer Protection Act (CPA) didn't apply to the purchase of legal education to obtain employment, since, like many state consumer protection laws, the MCPA didn't cover purchases for business or commercial purposes. Because the complaint alleged that the graduates attended law school in order to obtain full-time legal employment, they weren't covered. In 2016, a jury rejected similar claims against Thomas Jefferson School of Law in San Diego, applying California Law.

Procedural Considerations. The courts all considered the contents of the various schools' websites on a motion to dismiss. The rule that a court may consider concededly authentic documents integral to a complaint without converting a motion to dismiss to a motion for summary judgment is an important one in advertising cases, because it allows the court to look at any tangible advertising materials on which the plaintiff seeks to base its case.

Iqbal and *Twombly* were significant for all types of cases, but they pose special challenges for advertising cases. Many defendants seek to get rid of advertising cases on motions to dismiss, before (expensive) discovery. *Iqbal* and *Twombly* required facially plausible allegations of liability. How much should a judge be able to rely on his or her own reaction to an ad in assessing the plausibility of a claim that consumers were deceived by that ad?

Consider the following cases. Can you glean a consistent rule from them? In *Tseng v. Marukai Corp. U.S.A.*, 2009 WL 3841933 (C.D. Cal. 2009), the court found this allegation insufficient: "defendants falsely advertised their infringing goods as genuine and authorized products by imprinting [the number of plaintiff's patent]" on the goods. False advertising is a legal conclusion that requires allegation of underlying facts. The plaintiff needed to offer facts indicating what kind of advertising defendants engaged in, what they said and why it was false.

By contrast, the complaint in *Gates Corp. v. Dorman Products, Inc.*, 2009 WL 5126556 (D. Colo. 2009), survived. The complaint alleged that the defendant's ads falsely claimed that certain of its auto parts met all the specifications of a particular standard-setting organization and that this claim was important to customers. Gates included representative ads with the complaint, showing that the claims had been made, and the court concluded that it had alleged facts sufficient to show falsity or misleadingness. It is reasonable to assume that quality influences purchase decisions. The court commented that the plaintiff "cannot be expected to present detailed evidence in its Complaint on the nuances of consumer confusion, such as survey evidence, when [the Lanham Act] only requires a 'tendency to deceive.'" Discovery was the place for exploration of the evidence.

In *Wright v. General Mills, Inc.*, 2009 WL 3247148 (S.D. Cal. 2009), the complaint at issue challenged the "100% Natural" label on Nature Valley cereal and cereal bars as false and misleading because the products actually were made with high fructose corn syrup, a substance that was allegedly not "natural." To the court, this complaint contained little more than conclusory and speculative allegations. For example, it was insufficient simply to allege that members of the public were likely to have been deceived and to have made purchases because they believed that a "100% natural" product would not have high fructose corn syrup.

Does your assessment of plausibility differ from that of the *Wright* court's? Does it matter that different people often have different ideas of what counts as "common sense"? *See* Dan M. Kahan, David A. Hoffman & Donald Braman, *Whose Eyes Are You Going to Believe?* Scott v. Harris *and the Perils of Cognitive Illiberalism*, 122 HARV. L. REV. 838 (2009) (reporting on a study showing that demographic variables profoundly affected the interpretation of videotape evidence, even though a majority of Supreme Court justices determined that the tape could only bear one reasonable interpretation); Terry A. Maroney, *Emotional Common Sense as Constitutional Law*, 62 VAND. L. REV. 851 (2009). What about when "common sense" is the same thing as a stereotype about how people—women, low-income consumers, elderly people, or even Americans in general—think and behave? *See* Linda Hamilton Krieger & Susan T. Fiske, *Behavioral Realism in Employment Discrimination Law: Implicit Bias and Disparate Treatment*, 94 CAL. L. REV. 997 (2006).

Choice of Law. Whereas the Lanham Act is a federal statute and applies nationwide (despite circuit-by-circuit differences in some details), the state laws applicable to consumer protection claims vary enough that most courts consider them to present a conflict of laws. If a putative class action plaintiff cannot succeed in convincing a court that the law of one state (usually, but not always, the defendant's home state) covers all claims, it may be impossible to maintain the class action. We will return to this topic in Chapter 7.

Traditional Fraud Claims. What benefits did the NJCFA offer plaintiffs that traditional fraud claims did not? The NJCFA, like other state consumer protection laws, was designed to offer broader relief for consumers than the common law. Are the changes from common law fraud sufficient? Too much?

The Private Lawsuit and Public Purposes of the Law. Some argue that litigation under state consumer protection acts leads to overenforcement, given that private plaintiffs bring lawsuits that the FTC would not. *See* Henry N. Butler & Joshua D. Wright, *Are State Consumer Protection Acts Really Little-FTC Acts?*, 63 FLA. L. REV. 163 (2011). What do you think plaintiffs' attorneys would say in response to this criticism? Are there reasons the FTC might underenforce the prohibition on deceptive advertising? Why would a legislature have decided to provide for class actions while also relaxing the standards for relief compared to the common law of fraud? How hard *should* it be to recover in court against advertising that a fact finder, whether judge or jury, determines to be false or misleading?

Marketplace Discipline. Assume for a moment that the law school statistics were overblown. Would marketplace forces punish the law schools for exaggerating/falsifying their statistics? In other words, would the prospect of unhappy customers be enough to make sellers in this market compete on advertising accuracy?

Buyer Sophistication. Do the courts treat these buyers as naïve, completely capable of protecting their interests, or somewhere in between? How does each court justify the level of sophistication it attributes to the buyers?

4. Comparing the Types of Regulation

The relationship between the FTC, the Lanham Act, and state-law actions is complicated. See generally Arthur Best, Controlling False Advertising: A Comparative Study of Public Regulation, Industry Self-Policing, and Private Litigation, 20 GA. L. REV. 1 (1985). The FTC is a political agency, and will generally move in the direction of the political position of the executive branch. The Reagan years, for example, brought a real cutback in activism. States may have different political orientations. New York, for example, has been known for its aggressive consumer protection positions (and not incidentally, perhaps, the political ambitions of its enforcers) in recent years, taking action against everything from the financial sector to restrictive contracts that purport to prohibit software buyers from writing critical reviews about that software.

The FTC, like most other institutions, is also motivated to succeed: it wants to win the cases that it brings, especially when, by virtue of its status as a major federal agency, it can expect publicity for its wins and losses. A few representative cases may have a profound educational effect on at least the major national advertisers, whose lawyers and ad agencies are more likely to be paying attention to what the FTC is doing. To the extent that the FTC gets to make the rules, it makes rules favoring itself, as revealed by its rules as to who has the burden of providing substantiation (the advertiser) and whether the FTC needs to conduct a consumer survey to show deception (no). The FTC does not design its rules with the idea that they'll be enforced by multiple plaintiffs.

Given these factors, it might not make sense to apply the same standards to private enforcers. Moreover, the FTC's resource constraints mean that it can only choose a limited number of cases. Private plaintiffs, whether competitors or consumers, have different incentives. Whether this is likely to lead to overenforcement of the law by private plaintiffs seizing on minor and irrelevant inaccuracies, or to correction of the inevitable underenforcement that comes from a resource-constrained government, or both, is a matter for debate. Proponents of the overenforcement concern point to allegedly distorted incentives for competitors who might be trying to shut down legitimate competition (or at least might be indifferent to whether or not they deter the competition from truthful advertising) and for class action lawyers looking for easy settlements with large fee awards. Proponents of the underenforcement view note, for example, that the increase in the number of FTC employees over the past few decades did not come close to keeping pace with the expansion of the economy; the FTC's budget of roughly $250 million is dwarfed by the amount of advertising in the United States.

The FTC and state AGs are also likely to leave some cases alone by choice: comparative advertising, for example, where the targeted competitor is able to object if it believes that it is being falsely denigrated. But even where there is a plausible private plaintiff, the FTC may still act if the fraud is sufficiently blatant and harmful to consumers.

In 2010, for example, the FTC sued defendants who falsely claimed ties to Google Inc. in ads claiming that their customers could earn $100,000 in 6 months. Defendants got account information supposedly to pay for shipping a work-from-home kit, and then charged customers over $72 per month until they cancelled. The FTC secured a $29.5 million dollar judgment against the defendants for restitution to consumers (a remedy that would have been unavailable to Google in a trademark infringement action). FTC v. Infusion Media, Inc., Civil Action No. 09-CV-01112, F.T.C. File No. 092 3060 (D. Nev.).

However, when the issue is one of market share as between competitors who are roughly equal in their ability to fight—in the marketplace, before the NAD, and in court—it makes less sense for regulators to allocate their resources to investigating it.

Private plaintiffs also differ among themselves. Competitor suits can serve to protect consumers from deception, when the competitor's interest aligns with the public interest. But sometimes consumers may be harmed, and no competitor may be likely to act. When a problem is industry-wide, for example, competitors are unlikely to have an interest in shutting down false claims that help everyone— the decades of obfuscation of the health effects of cigarettes and the lack of substantiation of many types of diet and health claims are obvious examples. (Arguably the law school cases in the previous section fall into this category).

Likewise, when the market is so competitive that a single business wouldn't get enough out of suing one of its hundreds of competitors, false claims may go uncorrected by competitors (and, of course, marginal entities are particularly unlikely to participate in self-regulatory measures such as the NAD). Consumers and government regulators are the likely enforcers in such cases.

Government involvement is especially likely when both conditions apply—when industries are full of small players and extravagant claims, only the government may have the necessary resources and perseverance to discipline fraudsters.

Consumer plaintiffs, by contrast, may be motivated to go after larger players, especially national advertisers, whose deep pockets may make settlement more attractive even with a relatively weak case. As many critics of the plaintiffs' bar have argued, this dynamic is encouraged by the fact that consumer protection cases often involve large fees for the lawyers and minimal recovery for individual plaintiffs, leading to potentially distorted incentives for plaintiffs' lawyers. Defenders of class actions, however, respond that this pattern is precisely what the class action is for: joining claims that are too small to justify litigation on their own but, in the aggregate, represent substantial social harm despite small individual recoveries.

There are also cases where competitors have greater incentives than consumers to act against false claims, and even a greater ability to succeed. Consider a mass-market ad campaign for a common product.

Consumers are often unlikely to remember which ads they saw or keep records about what they bought. Even if the relevant UDAP laws don't require reliance, they will usually be interpreted to require some sort of causation linking the false ads to purchases, and this may be hard to establish, especially at the wholesale level necessary to maintain a class action. Courts increasingly reject class actions that will require an individualized showing of deception or harm for each member of the class. Thus, the competitor—who need only show that a substantial percentage of consumers are likely to be deceived to prevail—can succeed with a probabilistic showing of harm, where a consumer class action predicated on the exact same deception might well fail. In such cases, the competitor is serving as a stand-in for consumers whose injury is hard to show. On the other hand, if the problem is industry-wide (as with cigarettes, alcohol, or other products with substantial negative externalities) and if consumers can't win and competitors won't sue, then a regulatory response is the only alternative.

Private plaintiffs face more evidentiary problems than the government, providing a potential constraint. Even if a private lawyer is willing to spearhead a lawsuit (which can be essential for consumer class actions), that lawyer needs a willing plaintiff and adequate evidence—some of which may not be functionally available until after discovery—but the lawsuit might be foreclosed by *Twombly/Iqbal*. In contrast, government entities can open investigations that will lead to CIDs or voluntary provisioning of information by the investigatory target even if the government actor lacks enough evidence initially to survive a *Twombly/Iqbal* motion to dismiss.

Private lawsuits may also move faster than government investigations, which generally have multiple layers of procedural constraints, including requirements that a high-level official approve any resulting lawsuit. If a competitor is willing to spend the money to prepare a case, it can seek a temporary restraining order (TRO) a few days after an ad starts to run. Government agencies, by contrast, are much more likely to rely on the general deterrent effect of large penalties, imposed long after the fact. This is not unrelated to the fact that the FTC and the AGs generally wish to send messages to entire industries in their enforcement actions, whereas an advertiser who sues under the Lanham Act is much more likely to want one specific ad to stop (and in fact may prefer a certain freedom to operate in its own advertising).

The following chart, though far from comprehensive, offers a few comparisons:

	FTC	AG	Competitor	Consumer
Source of Authority	FTCA	State law	Lanham Act; some state laws; NAD (voluntary)	State law (both common & statutory)
Standard	Unfair or misleading; burden on advertiser to substantiate	Various; burden usually on AG to show violation of law	False or deceptive (Lanham Act); burden on competitor to show falsity/ deceptiveness (but NAD requires substantiation)	Various; burden on consumer to show violation of law
Key Constraints	Resources; politics	Resources; politics	Time; resources; interest in preserving own freedom to make claims	Low recovery usually means only class actions are sustainable; barriers to class actions
Key Remedies	Full range, including consumer redress	Full range, including consumer redress	Injunction usually a priority; damages possible	Damages; fees for counsel in class actions

Another way to compare and contrast the various options is from a policy standpoint:

	Pros	Cons
FTC	* Broad authority * Broad remedies * Enhanced discovery powers	* Small agency + national scope = selective enforcement * Political
State AGs	* Similar to FTC	* Power restricted to state * Not uniform * Political
Competitor– NAD	* Quick (but slower than TRO) * High expertise * Cheap (no discovery) * Confidential submissions * Uniform rules nationally * Rules can evolve flexibly	* "Voluntary" * Only for national campaigns * Limited remedies
Competitor– Court	* Incentive to call out competitive overclaims * Don't need to prove consumer reliance	* Litigation over market allocation, not consumer interest * Enforcement is public good * Won't sue over bad industry practices *Judges lack expertise * Expensive * Litigation duration > ad campaign
Consumer Litigation	* Can challenge industry-wide practices * Can overcome the public goods problem	* Expensive * Self-interested attorneys *_Twombly_/ _Iqbal_ lead to quick dismissals

CHAPTER 4: DECEPTION

It is very easy to say that the law requires truth, and much harder to say what is true or false. This chapter covers the key elements of the law of falsity.

We start with an overview of the ways false advertising harms consumers and society. We then turn to the boundary question: what kinds of statements can be considered true or false? Though a legal regime could theoretically limit advertisers only to claims that they can prove to be truthful, the United States has instead generally chosen to regulate only falsity. Thus, non-falsifiable claims, often categorized as mere opinion or puffery, are outside the scope of false advertising law.

With those foundations, we turn to claims that are concededly factual and examine how decision makers deem them truthful or false. We consider the substantiation requirement imposed by the Federal Trade Commission (and the NAD), as well as various subtypes of factual claims.

If we are ultimately concerned with harm to consumers, then we also need to examine how those consumers think. We consider how courts identify the reasonable target consumer for an ad and assess what kinds of responses to ads are expected or out of bounds. We then turn to a related, and increasingly important, component of the falsity inquiry, materiality. Not every detail in an ad is necessarily important to consumers. If a falsehood would not affect a reasonable consumer's purchasing decision, then judicial intervention to suppress that falsehood may not be justified.

1. The Harms of False Advertising*

Truthful informational advertising is generally conceded to be
socially beneficial. Reciprocally, false advertising is generally
considered to be unequivocally bad for society. It causes consumers to
misallocate their dollars, and consumers can suffer irreparable harm
because of it—such as a consumer who takes medicine falsely
advertised to help her medical condition, and who foregoes other
treatments that might have helped.

False advertising can also cause economic loss to society if consumers
spend money on a product that doesn't work. As Professor Lee
Goldman explains, "[I]f Excedrin does not relieve headache pain fast,
not only will there be many cranky consumers, but too much capital
and labor will be employed to produce a worthless product rather
than a more effective pain reliever or some other socially useful good."

Many people additionally believe that it is morally wrong to deceive
consumers, even if they suffer no identifiable physical or economic
harm as a result. False advertising also harms competitors, both
through sales they don't get and by undermining the general
trustworthiness of advertising, a point we take up in greater detail in
the next section.

Deception: An Introduction

Information can be deceptive if it makes a false claim about
something that consumers care about—a material fact. But because
people make inferences, we can't confine the definition of deception to
claims that are explicitly false. Beales et al. use the example of a
product that truthfully but misleadingly claims that "no product is

---

* [Note: consult Chapter 2 for citations to several of the sources discussed in
these first two parts.]

more effective" in curing an incurable condition. This claim is deceptive because it *implies* effectiveness.

We could try again: perhaps a claim is deceptive if it produces in consumers a false belief about a material fact. But omitting information can also be deceptive—for example, failing to disclose that a book is an abridged version or failing to disclose that a used product isn't new. So failing to correct a preexisting belief may be deceptive under some circumstances. As Beales et al. note, consumers have standard expectations for things that are advertised as "books," as products *not* marked as used, and so on. Failure to disclose implies compliance with those expectations. These expectations are so standard that consumers probably don't even think about them consciously unless prompted to do so. This can lead to deception by omission.

Taking these expectations into account, we could say that an ad is deceptive if it fails to disclose material information (i.e., information that would change consumers' behavior). But that's clearly unworkable, because most ads can't disclose all material information, and if they did, consumers wouldn't read them (consider the overwhelmingly long disclosures in ads for prescription drugs or car leases). Information is costly to provide and to process, so perfect information will never be possible. We could say that an ad is deceptive if it fails to disclose the optimal amount of information—but the devil is in the details.

A Note on Implicature

Much advertising relies not on the strict logical meanings of the words it uses, but on the contextual meaning of the information actually presented. Philosopher Paul Grice attempted to explain how conversation generally works with his cooperative principle, which states that contributions to a conversation must be guided by the accepted purpose or direction of that conversation. PAUL GRICE, LOGIC AND CONVERSATION, SYNTAX AND SEMANTICS, 3: SPEECH ACTS (P. Cole & J. Morgan ed. 1975).

In other words, people have to cooperate in order to have a conversation. Grice proposed four "maxims of conversation" that people generally assume are being followed by other people. The maxims are:

(1) *Relevance*: What you say should have something to do with the topic of the conversation.

(2) *Quantity*: Say neither more nor less than required: enough to get your meaning across, but not so much information that meaning is lost.

(3) *Manner*: Be brief and orderly; avoid ambiguity and obscurity. In particular, don't be so vague that the other person can't figure out why you're saying something. If you say "Paul is either in Los Angeles or Boston," you actually should be uncertain where Paul is. If you know that Paul is in Los Angeles, you have violated the maxim of manner.

(4) *Quality*: Do not lie; do not make unsupported claims.

Because of the cooperative principle, when someone obviously violates one of these maxims, we ordinarily presume that he or she is doing it for a reason, and we try to relate the statement to the conversation. This is known as *implicature*. For example, when someone asks her dinner companion, "Could you pass the salt?," he's unlikely to interpret this as a literal inquiry into whether he's physically able to pass the salt. Using the maxim of relevance, he infers that she wants the salt and he passes it.

Another example from personal relationships would be this exchange: Q: "What's Doug like? Is he nice?" A: "He's very tall." The answer here violates the maxim of quantity, failing to say enough to answer the questions. We infer that the speaker has done so for some reason, and it's probably because he thinks Doug is not nice at all.

Grice's maxims are not the only tool for parsing grammatical constructions, but they can provide a helpful tool for understanding the ways that advertisers can sway, and possibly manipulate, consumers.

For example, when an advertiser prominently claims some feature for its product, we are likely to assume that the feature is relevant and desirable. The advertiser is using the cooperative principle of relevance to *imply* these things without stating them directly. The only direct statement is that the feature exists. Researchers have studied irrelevant claims used to tout brands, such as claims that instant coffee has flaked crystals. When some consumers saw ads featuring relevant attributes and others saw ads featuring irrelevant attributes, the latter group preferred the product more. Even when the researchers told consumers which attributes were irrelevant in advance, consumers still preferred the product more when shown ads using the irrelevant attribute. *See* Gregory S. Carpenter et al., *Meaningful Brands From Meaningless Differentiation: The Dependence on Irrelevant Attributes*, 31 J. MKTG. RES. 339 (1994).

The maxims are not separate. While it might seem that the maxim of quality (don't lie) is the basic foundation of truth in advertising, distracting or overwhelming a consumer with too much information or with irrelevant information—violating the maxim of quantity—can also fool the consumer. And devices common in advertising, such as humor, may play with several maxims at once. Human communication ordinarily presupposes cooperation in making and interpreting meaning, and advertisers can exploit this cooperation.

The law often recognizes implicature. If a prospectus advertises that a piece of property is five miles from the waterfront, readers will have good cause to cry foul if the five miles are measured as the crow flies, while the driving distance is actually fifteen to forty miles. *See* Lustiger v. United States, 386 F.2d 132 (9th Cir. 1967). The statement "five miles from the waterfront" in a real estate prospectus ordinarily implies that humans could reach the water by traveling that distance. Otherwise, the information is irrelevant and unhelpful.

Similarly, if Kraft advertises that its cheese slices are made with five ounces of milk, an ordinary consumer may infer that the benefits of those five ounces—especially the calcium, milk's best-known nutrient—are retained in the slices, not dissipated in the processing. Otherwise, the information about the *number* of ounces involved is irrelevant to an ordinary purchasing decision. *See* Kraft, Inc. v. FTC, 970 F.2d 311 (7th Cir. 1992) (affirming the decision that Kraft's ads made a misleading and material claim); Richard Craswell, *Taking Information Seriously: Misrepresentation and Nondisclosure in Contract Law and Elsewhere*, 92 VA. L. REV. 565 (2006).

Are reasonable consumers entitled to assume that advertisers are following the maxims? Are they entitled to do so under some circumstances—such as when the advertiser makes a claim that could be scientifically proven—but not others?

How Much Information?

If publishing information were costless, sellers would have an incentive to disclose it all. The better products on the market would benefit from full disclosure, and incomplete disclosure would signal some relative defect. But publishing information is not costless, so advertisers don't always disclose optimally.

Moreover, information is a public good. It benefits people who don't pay for it. For example, consider how pomegranate products gained popularity after Pom Wonderful invested millions of dollars in research on the benefits of pomegranates and more millions on ads disseminating that research. Competitors' ability to piggyback on the new consumer demand decreases the advertiser's incentive to provide positive information—though obviously not enough to destroy it altogether. Still, an advertiser like Pom Wonderful wants consumers to believe that it delivers more pomegranate-related benefits than its piggybacking competitors.

When Can Law Help?

To answer the question "when should law intervene to govern ads?," we can start by evaluating consumers' disparate information sources.

Consumers can examine some products or product characteristics for themselves ("search" characteristics, like the color of a car). They can rely on their own prior experience ("experience" characteristics, like the taste of a soda or the quality of a cable company's service). They can get information from other sources—friends, product reviews on the Internet or from *Consumer Reports*, home inspectors, and so on. They can even get information from industry competitors—though note that competitors typically only make comparative claims. For example, cigarette manufacturers will not claim that their competitor's products cause cancer. To the extent that consumers are relying on expert claims such as "studies prove that this drug effectively treats high blood pressure"—whether from third parties or from the advertisers themselves—they are relying on "credence" claims, since consumers cannot themselves verify whether a drug works better than a placebo or whether a car model has a better overall performance record than a different model.

Categorizing advertising into search, experience or credence characteristics can help identify where advertisers are most likely to deceive consumers. Advertisers are unlikely to misrepresent search characteristics. After all, a consumer can easily determine whether or not a car is red and can punish the seller for a misrepresentation by publicizing an instance of obvious deception—especially in the Internet age. Thus, we could argue that regulators shouldn't worry too much about claims relating to search characteristics. *See* Gary T. Ford et al., *Consumer Skepticism of Advertising Claims: Testing Hypotheses from Economics of Information*, 16 J. CONSUMER RES. 433 (1990). As Lillian BeVier writes, consumers "should be understood as capable of punishing false advertisers both by spreading the word about the offending product and by not repurchasing it." Indeed, you've probably publicly shared your opinions about marketplace offerings.

Despite the possibility of punishment in the market, advertisers can and do misrepresent search characteristics. Counterfeiting brand names is one example. A consumer looking for, say, actual Eveready batteries can be deceived by counterfeits, because the "search" characteristic—the brand name—acts as a proxy for other quality features.

Sellers also may misrepresent search characteristics if they're engaging in bait-and-switch tactics, such as claiming to have a particular product in stock but then trying to sell consumers something more expensive once the consumers show up. Will dissatisfied consumers adequately punish sellers for bait-and-switch tactics? Perhaps, but only if the business intends to remain in business in the same place or under the same name for a long time.

Bait and switch can benefit even long-term market participants. For example, a buyer is promised a low car payment, but just before the contract is signed, the seller reveals that the price is actually substantially higher. The buyer often feels committed and willing to pay more to be able to drive off the lot with "her" car. *See* Philip Reed & Nick James, *Confessions of an Auto Finance Manager*, Edmunds.com, updated Apr. 30, 2009. Even if some buyers walk away in disgust, the ones who stay may be profitable enough to more than cover the loss. *See* GORKAN AHMETOGLU ET AL., PRICING PRACTICES: THEIR EFFECTS ON CONSUMER BEHAVIOUR AND WELFARE 4 (Mar. 2010) ("One large scale study suggests that the bait-and-switch practice may have a substantial (negative) impact on consumers. Moreover, consumers are drawn in to promotions and where the item is out of stock, they predominantly switch to another item within the same store, due to lowered search intentions."); *id.* at 23 (noting that older consumers are particularly likely to stick with earlier decisions and thus may be particularly vulnerable).

What about false claims about experience characteristics, such as "our frozen pizza tastes freshly made"? Advertisers can succeed with those claims even if they are untrue, especially if consumers' negative experiences take time to accumulate.

False claims about credence qualities are even more likely to be effective (if consumers believe them) because consumers may never know they've been fooled—and may even go on to provide testimonials to other consumers. For example, if a consumer takes an ineffective headache relief remedy and then his headache goes away, as it naturally would have done no matter what he did, then he may falsely believe that the remedy worked.

One view, articulated well by Lillian BeVier, is that because experience and credence claims can deceive consumers, rational consumers will know better than to trust such claims, and rational advertisers will therefore avoid making such claims. BeVier says, "[t]he rational advertisers' reaction to consumer skepticism, moreover, will be not to waste resources making direct, inherently unbelievable quality claims at all—either true or false. Such a reaction further protects consumers." Indeed, consumers routinely say they don't trust ad claims very much.

Still, think back to the ads you've seen recently: did they make experience or credence claims? Doesn't that disprove the theory? BeVier acknowledges that, in practice, there are plenty of credence claims in the market. Drawing on work by Philip Nelson, however, BeVier argues that advertising is not primarily about specific factual claims. Instead, advertising signals to consumers—regardless of the ad copy—that the advertiser is investing in its brand. Consumers can infer that an advertiser intends to reap the returns from advertising over time, which will happen only if the advertiser delivers quality goods that actually satisfy consumer preferences. Thus, advertising can improve consumers' trust in the advertiser's intentions. *See* Phillip Nelson, *Advertising as Information*, 82 J. POL. ECON. 729, 730 (1974); Phillip Nelson, *The Economic Consequences of Advertising*, 48 J. BUS. L. 213 (1975). According to this theory, ads offer a general quality signal rather than a specific claim, no matter what claims the ads *seem* to make. Is that what you think ads are doing?

Trust and Rationality: Do Consumers Follow the Search-Experience-Credence Model?

BeVier's argument does not satisfactorily resolve the problem of generalized mistrust, also known as the "market for lemons" problem. Assume consumers understand that credence claims are unverifiable and therefore disbelieve or discount them. If so, a producer who has a product that really does what it says—cures headaches faster, for example—can't reap the full benefits of its investment in creating and advertising that product. The level of investment in products that really cure headaches will drop, and consumers will lose out. In this account, regulations that promote the flow of truthful information— such as subjecting credence claims to verification by the Food & Drug

Administration or other authority—prevents a destructive cycle of consumer cynicism and lower investment in truthful claims. *See* George A. Akerlof, *The Market for 'Lemons': Quality Uncertainty and the Market Mechanism*, 84 Q. J. ECON. 488 (1970).

Advertisers can try to overcome consumer cynicism by offering warranties and money-back guarantees to consumers. Beales et al. point out that these trust-enhancing moves pose significant information and enforcement problems of their own. Especially for low-cost products where pre-purchase research or post-purchase enforcement aren't cost-justified, consumers may end up unable to take advantage of such guarantees as a practical matter, and thus consumers will either ignore them (rendering them incapable of performing their desired function of making claims credible) or be deceived by them.

Certification by nongovernmental third-party entities can also combat consumers' distrust of experience or credence claims, but the consumer still needs to trust that the certifier is really independent and actually certified the advertiser's product. Beales et al. also caution that verification is expensive: the headache remedy may actually work, but proving it to the FDA's satisfaction (or the satisfaction of some other independent authority) is likely to be extremely resource-intensive, so strong verification requirements can also decrease the number of effective products available to consumers.

Furthermore, consumers may rely on observable attributes (like price) or potential signals of quality (like celebrity endorsements) more than on quality itself. As Beales et al. write, "If consumers cannot easily obtain information about a product's safety (but can easily observe its price), price competition may reward those who cut price by offering a less safe product." In markets where quality information is hard to come by, consumers may use low price as a signal of low quality, even though price isn't a reliable signal.

As Beales et al. also point out, consumers might not know why they need to know more; or they might make errors of judgment or submit to sales pressure to buy now without finding out more. They might take a chance that the claim is true and then stick to the brand out of habit. Thus, advertisers may make a false claim hoping that consumers will not discount it enough. Consider shopping for funeral homes—bereaved consumers may not have enough time or energy to do full research, and prices may be needlessly high and quality needlessly low. Indeed, the FTC and state regulators specifically regulate funeral and casket providers to prevent them from exploiting consumers' relative inability to do comparison shopping.

Lee Goldman also notes how consumers may fail to test claims that are testable in theory. Suppose a competitor falsely claims superiority to another competitor and the consumer buys the first product. If the consumer is satisfied, even if he would have been happier with the competing product, he may stick with what he knows (especially given widespread habits of brand inertia). If he's dissatisfied, he may well assume that the competitor is no better, given the initial superiority claim.

In empirical research, Ford et al. tested the prediction that "consumers will be most skeptical of advertising claims they can never verify and least skeptical of claims they can easily and inexpensively verify prior to purchase," as well as the prediction that consumers are more likely to believe experience claims about cheap goods than about expensive ones. Their results were only somewhat consistent with the predictions made by the search-experience-credence model. Consumers were relatively less skeptical of search claims, trusting them because they were easily verified, but they were not more skeptical of credence claims than of experience claims. They were not more skeptical of experience claims for high-priced goods than of experience claims for low-priced goods. In other words, they were skeptical of claims that the Nelson model said they ought to trust (experience claims for low-priced goods), and not especially skeptical of credence claims that the model predicted they ought to distrust. As Roger Schechter explains, "[a]s long as consumers put at least some stock in credence claims, advertisers have an incentive to make such claims, and ultimately, to exaggerate them."

Consumers may believe that there is some government regulation of advertising claims, such that a producer would not be allowed to make such a claim if it weren't true. For example, research has shown that consumers do believe that the FDA is actively evaluating claims for nutritional supplements. Does that belief itself justify government intervention to protect consumers?

Do you believe some ad claims more readily than others? When was the last time you consciously relied on a search quality of a good or service you were considering buying? Did you trust the advertiser's claims or did you verify the quality yourself, and how hard was it to do so? When was the last time you relied on an experience claim in choosing a good or service? When was the last time you consciously relied on a credence claim in choosing a good or service? When you consider friends' recommendations or reviews, what kinds of information do they offer, and why do you trust or distrust them?

Recall that one part of Nelson's argument, taken up by BeVier, is that advertising is about signaling general quality (ability to invest in advertising, which implies that the seller has a product in whose quality the seller is confident and for which consumers have proven willing to pay) rather than about making specific claims. But advertisers may overinvest in the signal and compete until they destroy its information value. For example, "lead generation" companies have outspent traditional locksmiths in Internet advertising. Local locksmiths generally have more expertise and may often cost consumers less, but because they can't take advantage of economies of scale in advertising, consumers can't find them among advertisers who falsely claim to operate locally and who spend their resources on "search optimization." *See* David Segal, *Picking the Lock of Google's Search*, N.Y. TIMES, July 9, 2011.

No Free Lunch: When Is Intervention Worth Its Costs?

Ultimately, the law-and-economics approach discourages regulatory intervention in the market for advertising. Just as strict product liability raises the cost of production, strict liability for deceptive advertising may limit the production of truthful information. If, as BeVier argues, consumers can cheaply protect themselves from deception, legal intervention may be more trouble than it's worth. At least the law should focus on instances in which it is difficult for consumers to protect themselves.

BeVier argues that courts should be particularly cautious because consumers may receive multiple messages from ads, only some of which are deceptive. She gives an example of an ad for a shampoo that claimed that 900 women like the model in the ad preferred the shampoo to three major competitors. One of those competitors sued, successfully arguing that the survey on which this claim was based was so flawed as to be unreliable. But, BeVier argues, many consumers probably got only truthful messages from the ad—that the shampoo was available for purchase, that it competed with the leading brands, that the model in the ad liked the shampoo, that the shampoo would produce similar results for the consumer as for the model, and so on. Only a small fraction might have paid attention to the specifics of the survey claim, and an even smaller fraction would have believed and relied on that claim. And, if they tried the shampoo and didn't like it, they could quickly punish the advertiser. Therefore, allowing the competitor to sue was wasteful at best and suppressed all these true messages at worst.

But couldn't the advertiser have communicated the truthful messages BeVier identified without communicating the false claims about the survey? If so, wouldn't it be better to require the advertiser to use that ad instead?

2. The Psychology of Advertising

Advertising's Powerful Effects

Though consumers don't like to believe that ads influence them, and though some ads plainly don't work, advertising works in ways that don't fit well with the model of the perfectly rational consumer.

For example, ads can distort memory and perception, even when consumers have direct experience with a product. Researchers showed people a false claim of "no bitterness" in coffee and then had them taste coffee made bitter by deliberate over-brewing. Consumers who'd seen the ad and tasted the coffee rated the coffee as less bitter than consumers who had only tasted the coffee. Even though the tasting had some effect on the first group's opinions, they still ended up being affected by the ad in the face of directly contradictory experience. Jerry C. Olson & Philip A. Dover, *Cognitive Effects of Deceptive Advertising*, 15 J. MKTG. RES. 29 (1978). This result—that ads can change memories, even memories of direct experiences—has been confirmed in numerous other contexts by other researchers. *See, e.g.*, Kathryn A. Braun, *Postexperience Advertising Effects on Consumer Memory*, 25 J. CONSUMER RES. 319 (1999) (finding that advertising can induce consumers to change taste judgments from negative to positive). As one researcher comments, "From an advertising and marketing perspective, this is a major breakthrough: the work showed that exposure to advertising can transform 'objective' sensory information, such as taste, in a consumer's memory, prior to the judgment process, and after the consumer [has] tasted the product." Bruce F. Hall, *A New Model for Measuring Advertising Effectiveness*, J. ADVERT. RES., Mar.–Apr. 2002, at 25. These results provide evidence of a confirmation bias, i.e., people want to avoid feeling like a dupe who believed an untrue claim.

Simple repetition of advertising also improves its credibility. *See, e.g.,* Scott A. Hawkins et al., *Low-Involvement Learning: Repetition and Coherence in Familiarity and Belief*, 11 J. CONSUMER PSYCHOL. 1 (2001). As Sarah Haan has explained, the "truth effect" means that the more familiar a claim appears to a consumer, the more likely the consumer is to believe that the claim is true. Thus, repeated advertising can wear down consumers' skepticism. *See* Sarah C. Haan, Note, *The "Persuasion Route" of the Law: Advertising and Legal Persuasion*, 100 COLUM. L. REV. 1281 (2000).

The effects of repeated exposures occur even when consumers initially rate the claim as low in credibility. Ian Skurnik et al. elaborate:

> [S]uppose the claim "shark cartilage will help your arthritis" feels familiar to consumers because they have encountered it recently. They might trust it less if they remember reading it in a tabloid headline than if they remember hearing it as advice from their physician. A weakness of this strategy is that memory for prior exposure to a claim is often much better than, and can be wholly independent of, memory for the context in which the claim appeared. And, when people find a claim familiar because of prior exposure but do not recall the original context or source of the claim, they tend to think that the claim is true.

Ian Skurnik et al., *How Warnings about False Claims Become Recommendations*, 31 J. CONSUMER RES. 713 (2005).

191

Skurnik et al. also found that warnings that claims are false can be counterproductive. Their research showed that "after 3 days had passed, the more times older adults had been warned that a claim was false, the more likely they were to misremember the claim as true," and that "trying to discredit claims after making them familiar to older adults backfired and increased their tendency to call those claims true." As a result, "merely identifying a given claim as unsubstantiated or false" may actually increase belief in the claim.

Other psychological evidence suggests that consumers tend to default to assuming that statements are true. It can be very hard to resist advertising claims, especially when consumers don't have a lot of time to devote to consciously debunking them. The ads are, after all, designed to persuade. *See* DAVID M. BOUSH, DECEPTION IN THE MARKETPLACE: THE PSYCHOLOGY OF DECEPTIVE PERSUASION AND CONSUMER SELF-PROTECTION 17 (2009) ("Deception self-protection among high school friends or in everyday work environments is not the same as effective self-protection against professional marketers' ploys."). And, unfortunately, falsity detection skills we learn in one context may not transfer easily to new contexts. *See id.* at 189 ("[S]omeone who has become wary of television ads in which actors are falsely portrayed as 'experts' about a product may not be as suspicious and discerning when he or she first encounters people masquerading as 'experts' in, say, Internet chat rooms or Web site visits, blogs, telemarketing calls or service relationships. The change of media and context put a person out of touch with deception protection skills they have developed in other situations.").

What lessons does this empirical evidence suggest for advertising regulation? Do the results about repetition and counterspeech provide justification for banning certain claims entirely? Is repetition all about persuasion, or can it cross the line into deception?

The Example of Price

Consumers' reactions to various claims can be counterintuitive. For example, research by Baba Shiv et al. found that pricing can actually change the physical effects of products. Apparently, price triggers unconscious expectations about efficacy. Researchers told some study participants that the researchers had bought the energy drink being studied at a steep discount, and told other participants that the researchers had paid the regular price. The first group rated their workouts as less intense and rated themselves as more fatigued than the second group. The participants didn't, however, *believe* that price had influenced their perceptions.

In another study, consumers who paid a discounted price for an energy drink that they were told was supposed to increase mental acuity were able to solve fewer puzzles compared to consumers who paid the regular price—and even compared to consumers who didn't drink anything. And the detrimental effect was worsened by greater expectations for the product. However, study participants who bought the drink at its regular price and heard strong advertising claims about the drink's effectiveness solved more puzzles than those in the control condition. In other words, the price affected not just the perceived quality of the product, but its objective effectiveness. Baba Shiv et al., *Placebo Effects of Marketing Actions: Consumers May Get What They Pay For*, 42 J. MKTG. RES. 383 (2005); *see also* Emir Kamenica et al., *Advertisements Impact the Physiological Efficacy of a Branded Drug*, Proceedings of the National Academy of Scientists (June 6, 2013) (finding that ads for Zyrtec decreased the physiological effect of Claritin by over 90% for subjects not familiar with antihistamines; subjects familiar with antihistamines didn't differ in their responses).

These results are consistent with earlier research finding that consumers often believe and judge lower priced items to be of lower quality, even when objective testing finds no quality differences or advantages for the lower-priced versions. In one case, an advertiser carefully priced its instant coffee sold in single-serving pods just below the price of brand-name Keurig ground coffee, which contributed to consumers' beliefs that the advertiser's product couldn't be instant coffee. "This had the dual benefit of reaping a high profit and forestalling consumer suspicions. As one executive admitted candidly, 'If you actually got the price too low, people would perceive it as poor quality.'" Suchanek v. Sturm Foods, Inc., 764 F.3d 750 (7th Cir. 2014).

Price effects may be an instance of framing effects, in which how a product is presented affects how consumers evaluate it. For example, meat labeled "25% fat" tastes better than the same meat that is labeled "75% fat free." I.P. Levin & J.G. Gaeth, *How Consumers Are Affected by the Framing of Attribute Information Before and After Consuming the Product*, 15 J. CONSUMER RES. 374 (1988); *see also, e.g.,* Dirkjan Joor et al., *The Emperor's Clothes in High Resolution: An Experimental Study of the Framing Effect and the Diffusion of HDTV*, 7 ACM COMPUTERS IN ENT., No. 3, Article 40 (September 2009) (telling consumers that they were watching HDTV led them to report that the picture quality was higher).

A different framing effect is found in presentations of options. Advertisers know that consumers are wary of extremes. But the advertisers themselves can control what the "middle" options are. So presenting a 36-inch TV, a 42-inch TV and a 50-inch TV together predictably drives up sales of the 42-inch version, and putting a high-priced entrée on a menu leads diners to buy the second-highest-priced entrée, indulging themselves without feeling like they're going too far. *See* DAN ARIELY, PREDICTABLY IRRATIONAL 2–10 (rev. ed. 2010). The advertiser can then make sure its profit margin is highest on the middle options.

Price can be used to manipulate choices in other ways. What if an advertiser claims that it's offering a new, lower price? If it charges the "new" price, would it matter that there was never an old, higher price? As one group of researchers explains,

> [t]here is a large body of evidence to show that the presence of an advertised *reference price* increases consumers' valuations of a deal and purchase intentions, and can lower their search intentions. Reference prices can have a significant impact *even* when these are disproportionally large and when consumers are skeptical of their truthfulness. The effects of reference prices are stronger when consumers are not readily able to compare them to an industry price, such as with unbranded, or retailers' "own brand" goods, and with less frequently purchased and more expensive items.

GORKAN AHMETOGLU ET AL., PRICING PRACTICES: THEIR EFFECTS ON CONSUMER BEHAVIOUR AND WELFARE 3 (MAR. 2010).

Is deliberate framing of this sort deceptive? The practice undeniably induces people to choose more expensive options for reasons they don't understand and couldn't accurately explain, but does that differ from ordinary persuasion? Does it matter if consumers hold false *conscious* beliefs, instead of unconscious ones?

Images and Words

Advertising regulation focuses a lot on claims communicated via words. However, advertisers make heavy use of images as well, and images don't always work the same way as words do. To what extent, if any, should the law treat images (or other nonverbal forms of advertising) differently?

Edward F. McQuarrie and Barbara J. Phillips point out that "[i]t is rare to find a magazine ad that makes a straightforward claim like 'Tide gets clothes clean.' Instead, detergent ads claim to make your clothes 'as fresh and clean as sunshine,' or show a picture of a measuring cup filled with blue sky." They argue that using images as metaphors makes consumers more likely to pay attention to an ad, encouraging them to use their imaginations to interpret the image, which is more fun than just getting explicit information.

One benefit for advertisers is that this process is more convincing: "Consumers are less likely to argue against associations they came up with themselves, and more likely to remember and act on them." But depending on how consumers use their imaginations, they might draw truthful or misleading conclusions. McQuarrie and Phillips found in their empirical research that when comparing ads using straightforward claims, verbal metaphors or visual metaphors, all three ads communicated the same basic message. Nonetheless, the metaphors left consumers with more positive thoughts toward the product—they even reported receiving factual claims not explicitly present in the ad—and visual metaphors did better than verbal metaphors. Moreover, the visual metaphors worked immediately, whereas verbal metaphors required further prompting.

These researchers conclude that

> legal protections may need to evolve beyond a focus on whether a claim made in words is true or false. . . . [I]t is not reasonable to infer from a picture of a cleaning product next to a grenade that this brand is more powerful than others. Nonetheless, based on the evidence of this study, it is an empirical fact that such thoughts do occur when consumers are exposed to visual metaphors. Whether the legal system can evolve to address the possibility of misleading claims delivered through pictures remains to be seen.

Edward F. McQuarrie & Barbara J. Phillips, *Indirect Persuasion in Advertising: How Consumers Process Metaphors Presented in Pictures and Words*, 34 J. ADVER. 7 (2005).

Persuasion happens in other subtle ways. Putting an antiperspirant in a box, for example, may lead people to think it's stronger than an identical unboxed version. *See* Jack Neff, *Wanting Less But Buying More*, ADVERTISING AGE, March 3, 2008. More generally, packaging sends a variety of powerful messages that affect consumers' choices. In one experiment, researchers sent subjects an identical deodorant in three differently colored packages and asked them to rate the three. With one color scheme, subjects "praised its pleasant yet unobtrusive fragrance and its ability to stop wetness and odor for as many as twelve hours." The second color scheme "was found to have a strong aroma, but not really very much effectiveness." The third "was downright threatening. Several users developed skin rashes after using it, and three had severe enough problems to consult dermatologists." THOMAS HINE, THE TOTAL PACKAGE: THE SECRET HISTORY AND HIDDEN MEANINGS OF BOXES, BOTTLES, CANS, AND OTHER PERSUASIVE CONTAINERS 212 (1997).

Trademark law recognizes the communicative power of packaging by providing trademark rights for distinctive packaging. What about advertising law generally? If antiperspirant in a box isn't actually stronger, should we deem the practice of putting it in the box misleading? Does it matter that packaging creates additional social costs, like manufacturing and disposing of the packaging?

3. Facts and Non-facts: Puffery and Related Doctrines

No matter who the challenger is and no matter what the forum, the basic target of false advertising law is the same: deception that tends to make consumers more likely to buy what the advertiser is selling, or less likely to buy the competitors' products or services.

But U.S. law has also determined that, as a rule, only false statements of *fact* are actionable. We know that nonfactual atmospherics in an ad, such as the presence of attractive people, drive sales. Nonetheless, we have chosen not to regulate such atmospherics. The FTC or states with unfair practices laws can find particular nonfactual sales techniques to be *unfair* because of their effects on consumers' reasoning. However, as a matter of doctrine, only ad elements that convey factual claims can be *false or misleading*.

As you read the materials in this section, consider whether this result is sound as a matter of policy. Even if consumers are affected by nonfactual claims, perhaps the fact that they're open to all competitors is sufficient to justify a hands-off approach, especially given the costs of litigation. Without a specific factual claim that can be falsified, it may simply be too hard to determine which ads take persuasion too far. Or does our tolerance for puffery reflect an unwarranted confidence in consumers' ability to apply careful logic to every ad claim they see?

Fact vs. Opinion

Courts in advertising cases sometimes use the construct "fact v. opinion" instead of "fact v. puffery," depending on the parties' arguments and the particular statements at issue. An ad that quotes a third-party review, such as *"Toaster Magazine raves: 'This is the best toaster on the market!' "* could be deemed Toaster Magazine's opinion about toasters, though "best" is also considered puffery (note that the ad makes a separate fact claim that Toaster Magazine actually said those words). In general, think of opinion and puffery as two similar but distinct ways for courts to say that the statements aren't factual enough to be actionable.

A statement of fact is a "specific and measurable claim, capable of being proved false or of being reasonably interpreted as a statement of objective fact." Coastal Abstract Serv. Inc. v. First Am. Title Ins. Co., 173 F.3d 725 (9th Cir. 1999). By contrast, when a statement is "obviously a statement of opinion," it cannot "reasonably be seen as stating or implying provable facts." Groden v. Random House, 61 F.3d 1045 (2d Cir. 1995). The fact/opinion divide grows out of defamation law—only facts can be defamatory, not opinions in themselves.

The distinction between fact and opinion can be elusive. Some states' consumer protection laws have explicitly been interpreted to cover opinions, as long as they're accompanied by failure to disclose facts that would lead a reasonable person to question the opinion. *See, e.g.,* Canady v. Mann, 419 S.E.2d 597 (N.C. Ct. App. 1992) (upholding claim based on agent's statement that properties were good investments and suitable for building where agent knew or had reason to know that representations were false because wetlands precluded development), *review dismissed,* 429 S.E.2d 348 (N.C. 1993). More generally, the *Restatement (Third) of Unfair Competition* points out that "[i]n many circumstances prospective purchasers may reasonably understand a statement of opinion to be more than a mere assertion as to the seller's state of mind. Some representations of opinion may imply the existence of facts that justify the opinion, or at least that there are no facts known to the speaker that are substantially incompatible with the stated opinion." § 3 cmt. d (1995). (Compare the *Vokes* fraud case from Chapter 3.)

Thus, statements in the form of opinions may be actionable when it would be reasonable for a consumer, under the circumstances, to treat the opinion as a factual representation, for example when the speaker purportedly possesses special expertise unavailable to the consumer. FTC Policy Statement on Deception, § III (Oct. 14, 1983) ("Claims phrased as opinions are actionable . . . if they are not honestly held, if they misrepresent the qualifications of the holder or the basis of his opinion or if the recipient reasonably interprets them as implied statements of fact. . . . [R]epresentations of expert opinions will generally be regarded as representations of fact."); FTC v. Sec. Rare Coin & Bullion Corp., 931 F.2d 1312 (9th Cir. 1991) (upholding injunction against representations that coins were good investment vehicles with high profit potential and low risk). This rule is similar to the rule for defamation law, which also holds that statements with the semantic form of opinion may assert defamatory facts, or imply the existence of undisclosed defamatory facts. Milkovich v. Lorain Journal Co., 497 U.S. 1 (1990).

In the ordinary case, however, where reasonable consumers should understand that a statement is no more than a prediction and might not be accurate, there can be no liability. *See, e.g.*, Ameritox, Ltd. v. Millennium Labs., Inc., 2014 WL 1456347 (M.D. Fla. 2014) (layperson's claims about the legality of a billing practice under federal statutes and rules were non-actionable opinion, because no court or agency had yet found the billing practice to be unlawful; a clear and unambiguous judicial or agency holding is required for falsity of statements about law); Koagel v. Ryan Homes, Inc., 562 N.Y.S.2d 312 (N.Y. App. Div. 1990) (defendant not liable for statement regarding property taxes because statement was merely estimate and tax rates and assessments are volatile); Opsahl v. Pinehurst, Inc., 380 S.E.2d 796 (N.C. Ct. App. 1989), *review dismissed*, 385 S.E.2d 400 (N.C. 1987) (defendant not liable for statement that utilities would be available to rural lot by a certain date, because it is common knowledge that projected completion dates in construction industry are frequently missed). As the case law indicates, courts are more likely to treat individualized sales pitches as presenting fact/opinion questions, because the more blanket statements made in general advertising are harder to understand as opinions—though they may still be non-actionable puffery.

Sometimes, courts find that a statement is opinion even when the defendant explicitly tries to get people to rely on it. In *ZL Technologies, Inc. v. Gartner, Inc.*, 2009 WL 3706821 (N.D. Cal. 2009), the defendant sold its research reports on business software, claiming to have the "combined brainpower of 1,200 research analysts and consultants who advise executives in 80 countries every day," "tens of thousands of pages of original research annually," "highly discerning research that is objective, defensible, and credible to help [customers] do their job better," "relevant experience and institutional knowledge [that] prevent[s] costly and avoidable errors," and an ability to "show you how to buy, what to buy, and how to get the best return on your technology investment." The court found that all the challenged statements were not factually verifiable, despite the use of words such as "objective." Gartner's "sophisticated readers"—corporate and government executives and professionals—would not infer that Gartner's rankings were anything other than opinion. But if all of these statements were opinion, why did Gartner try so hard to convince customers that it was using accurate, objective, reliable criteria?

When should the question of whether a statement is fact or opinion be left to a finder of fact? This determination is highly dependent on the circumstances, and it can be difficult to predict. Courts may send the matter to the jury if they aren't sure whether a statement is fact or opinion, but they may also make this determination as a matter of law.

Science

Is a scientific conclusion a fact? You might think that the answer is yes, and most false advertising cases accept that without hesitation.

The following case explores why a court might refuse to treat a scientific conclusion as a fact for purposes of false advertising law.

ONY, Inc. v. Cornerstone Therapeutics, Inc., 720 F.3d 490 (2d Cir. 2013)

This case asks us to decide when a statement in a scientific article reporting research results can give rise to claims of false advertising under the Lanham Act, deceptive practices under New York General Business Law § 349, and the common-law torts of injurious falsehood and interference with prospective economic advantage. We conclude that, as a matter of law, statements of scientific conclusions about unsettled matters of scientific debate cannot give rise to liability for damages sounding in defamation. We further conclude that the secondary distribution of excerpts of such an article cannot give rise to liability, so long as the excerpts do not mislead a reader about the conclusions of the article.

BACKGROUND

. . . Plaintiff ONY, Inc. ("ONY") and defendant Chiesi Farmaceutici, S.p.A. ("Chiesi") are two of the biggest producers of surfactants, biological substances that line the surface of human lungs. Surfactants are critical to lung function: they facilitate the transfer of oxygen from inhaled air into the blood stream. Although the human body naturally produces surfactants, prematurely born infants often produce inadequate surfactant levels. Infants with such a deficiency are at a higher risk for lung collapse and Respiratory Distress Syndrome ("RDS"), a condition that can result in respiratory failure and death. The non-human surfactants produced and sold by, among others, ONY and Chiesi are the primary treatment for RDS. . . . ONY produces one derived from bovine lung surfactant that bears the trade name "Infasurf." Chiesi produces a competing surfactant derived from porcine lung mince that goes by "Curosurf." Chiesi, an

202

Italian pharmaceutical firm, contracts with its co-defendant Cornerstone Therapeutics, Inc. ("Cornerstone") to distribute and market Curosurf in the United States.

The parties vigorously contest the relative effectiveness of their products—in the marketplace, in the scientific literature, and in the instant lawsuit. The parties agree that two variables are particularly relevant to this comparison: mortality rate and length of stay. Mortality rate means the percentage of infants treated with a particular surfactant who do not survive. Length of stay refers to the amount of time an infant remains in the hospital for treatment. These two variables are not entirely independent: in some cases the length of stay is shortened by death, which is reflected in the mortality rate. Put differently, some of the same causes of increased mortality rate (low birth weight, shorter gestational period) also cause shorter lengths of stay. Conversely, infants with shorter hospitalization might have had less serious medical conditions from the beginning, independent of treatment variables. At the same time, a particularly effective drug may both reduce mortality rate and shorten length of stay.

In 2006, as part of its effort to promote and sell Curosurf, Chiesi hired defendant Premier, Inc. ("Premier") to build a database and conduct a study of the relative effectiveness of the different surfactants. . . . Chiesi then hired several medical doctors, including defendants Rangasamy Ramanathan, Jatinder J. Bhatia, and Krishnamurthy Sekar (the "physician defendants"), to present findings based on Premier's database at various medical conferences. . . .

In 2011, the physician defendants [along with a Chiesi employee] eventually decided to publish some of the findings from the same data set in a peer-reviewed journal. They submitted their article to the *Journal of Perinatology*, the leading journal in the field of neonatology, which is the study of newborn infants. The article was published in the September 1, 2011 volume of the journal after being peer reviewed by two anonymous referees.

According to ONY, the article contains five distinct incorrect statements of fact about the relative effectiveness of Curosurf versus Infasurf: (1) that Infasurf "was associated with a 49.6% greater likelihood of death than" Curosurf; (2) that Curosurf "treatment for RDS was associated with a significantly reduced likelihood of death when compared with" Infasurf; (3) that the authors' "model found [Infasurf] to be associated with a significantly greater likelihood of death than" Curosurf; (4) that the authors' study showed "a significant greater likelihood of death with" Infasurf than Curosurf; and (5) the summary concluding sentence:

> In conclusion, this large retrospective study of preterm infants with RDS found lower mortality among infants who received [Curosurf], compared with infants who received either [Infasurf] or [a third competitor's product], even after adjusting for patient characteristics such as gestational age and [birth weight], and after accounting for hospital characteristics and center effects.

Plaintiff also alleges that the circumstances surrounding the article's publication were unusual: Bhatia is an Associate Editor, and Sekar is a member of the editorial board, of the *Journal of Perinatology*. Plaintiff alleged in its complaint that one of the two peer reviewers objected to its publication, but the other peer reviewer recommended the article for publication, and the Editor-in-Chief broke the tie. Plaintiff does not allege, however, that the publication of the article based on the affirmative opinions of one reviewer and the Editor-in-Chief was a departure from accepted or customary procedure. Further, the article was published in an "open access" format, which allows it to be viewed electronically by the general public without paying the typically applicable fee or ordering a subscription; the fees associated with such publication were paid by Chiesi and Cornerstone.

The article's conclusions were not unqualified. The authors considered the objection that the retrospective nature of the study might cause a disparity between the groups included in the study. More specifically, the authors noted that the article's finding may "most likely . . . be due to different surfactant doses administered to the infants included in the database," because Curosurf was, on average, prescribed in higher doses than its competitors. Finally, the authors disclosed that the study was sponsored by Chiesi, that Ernst was an employee of Premier, that Chiesi hired Premier to conduct the study, and that all three physician defendants had served as consultants to Chiesi.

Plaintiff's primary objection to the substance of the article's scientific methodology is that the authors omitted any mention of the length-of-stay data . . . . Because an important determinant of mortality rate is the pre-treatment health of the infants in the sample, plaintiff contends that the omission of length-of-stay data was intentional and designed to mask the fact that the neonatal infants treated with Curosurf had a greater ex ante chance of survival than did the group treated with Infasurf. If the length-of-stay data had been included, plaintiff alleges, "it would be obvious to readers that the differences in the results were a result of differences in the groups of patients treated, not of any differences in the effect of the particular lung surfactant administered." Plaintiff also objects to the authors' failure to cite articles with different primary conclusions, although such contradictory authority was known to them, and to the use of retrospective data, which was allegedly improper because it rendered the data subject to "selective distortion." Finally, plaintiff contends that Chiesi and Cornerstone paid Premier to collect data that supported their own product's effectiveness.

After the article's publication, Chiesi and Cornerstone issued a press release touting its conclusions and distributed promotional materials that cited the article's findings. Since the article's publication, meanwhile, plaintiff has, through its corporate officers—themselves pediatricians—written letters to the *Journal of Perinatology* rebutting the article's conclusions, objecting to its methods, and asking that it be retracted. We take judicial notice of the fact that several of those letters were eventually published by the journal, although they did not appear in print until after the district court dismissed the complaint. The authors were given, and took, the opportunity to respond to those letters. . . .

DISCUSSION

. . . The Lanham Act generally prohibits false advertising. In particular, it provides a civil cause of action against "any person" who, in interstate commerce, "uses . . . any . . . false or misleading description of fact, or false or misleading representation of fact." 15 U.S.C. § 1125(a)(1). Because the Act proscribes conduct that, but for its false or misleading character, would be protected by the First Amendment, free speech principles inform our interpretation of the Act. Indeed, "we have been careful not to permit overextension of the Lanham Act to intrude on First Amendment values." We have been especially careful when applying defamation and related causes of action to academic works, because academic freedom is "a special concern of the First Amendment."

Generally, statements of pure opinion—that is, statements incapable of being proven false—are protected under the First Amendment. Milkovich v. Lorain Journal Co., 497 U.S. 1, 19-20 (1990). But the line between fact and opinion is not always a clear one. In *Milkovich*, the Supreme Court declined to carve out an absolute privilege for statements of opinion and reaffirmed that the test for whether a

206

statement is actionable does not simply boil down to whether a
statement is falsifiable. To illustrate the difficulty, the Court provided
the example of a statement of fact phrased as a statement of opinion:
stating that "in my opinion John Jones is a liar" is no different from
merely asserting that John Jones is a liar. Thus, the question of
whether a statement is actionable admits of few easy distinctions.

In this case, plaintiff claims that the article made statements about
scientific findings that were intentionally deceptive and misleading,
and that it therefore constituted false advertising. Plaintiff's theory is
that scientific claims made in print purport to be statements of fact
that are falsifiable, and such statements can be defamatory or
represent false advertising if known to be false when made. . . .

Scientific academic discourse poses several problems for the fact-
opinion paradigm of First Amendment jurisprudence. Most
conclusions contained in a scientific journal article are, in principle,
"capable of verification or refutation by means of objective proof."
Indeed, it is the very premise of the scientific enterprise that it
engages with empirically verifiable facts about the universe. At the
same time, however, it is the essence of the scientific method that the
conclusions of empirical research are tentative and subject to
revision, because they represent inferences about the nature of reality
based on the results of experimentation and observation.
Importantly, those conclusions are presented in publications directed
to the relevant scientific community, ideally in peer-reviewed
academic journals that warrant that research approved for
publication demonstrates at least some degree of basic scientific
competence. These conclusions are then available to other scientists
who may respond by attempting to replicate the described
experiments, conducting their own experiments, or analyzing or
refuting the soundness of the experimental design or the validity of
the inferences drawn from the results. In a sufficiently novel area of
research, propositions of empirical "fact" advanced in the literature

may be highly controversial and subject to rigorous debate by qualified experts. Needless to say, courts are ill-equipped to undertake to referee such controversies. Instead, the trial of ideas plays out in the pages of peer-reviewed journals, and the scientific public sits as the jury.

. . . The Seventh Circuit has also declined to allow suits based on claims of false conclusions in matters of scientific controversy to proceed. *See* Underwager v. Salter, 22 F.3d 730, 736 (7th Cir.1994) ("Scientific controversies must be settled by the methods of science rather than by the methods of litigation. . . . More papers, more discussion, better data, and more satisfactory models—not larger awards of damages—mark the path toward superior understanding of the world around us."). District courts presented with controversial scientific questions have also declined to find them actionable. *See* Arthur v. Offit, 2010 WL 883745, at *6 (E.D. Va. March 10, 2010) ("Plaintiff's claim . . . threatens to ensnare the Court in [a] thorny and extremely contentious debate over . . . which side of this debate has 'truth' on their side. That is hardly the sort of issue that would be subject to verification based upon a core of objective evidence." (internal quotation marks omitted)); *cf.* Padnes v. Scios Nova Inc., 1996 WL 539711 (N.D. Cal. 1996) ("Medical researchers may well differ with respect to what constitutes acceptable testing procedures, as well as how best to interpret data garnered under various protocols. The securities laws do not impose a requirement that companies report only information from optimal studies, even if scientists could agree on what is optimal." (internal citation omitted)).

Where, as here, a statement is made as part of an ongoing scientific discourse about which there is considerable disagreement, the traditional dividing line between fact and opinion is not entirely helpful. It is clear to us, however, that while statements about contested and contestable scientific hypotheses constitute assertions about the world that are in principle matters of verifiable "fact," for purposes of the First Amendment and the laws relating to fair competition and defamation, they are more closely akin to matters of opinion, and are so understood by the relevant scientific communities. In that regard, it is relevant that plaintiff does not allege that the data presented in the article were fabricated or fraudulently created. If the data were falsified, the fraud would not be easily detectable by even the most informed members of the relevant scientific community. Rather, plaintiff alleges that the inferences drawn from those data were the wrong ones, and that competent scientists would have included variables that were available to the defendant authors but that were not taken into account in their analysis. But when the conclusions reached by experiments are presented alongside an accurate description of the data taken into account and the methods used, the validity of the authors' conclusions may be assessed on their face by other members of the relevant discipline or specialty.

We therefore conclude that, to the extent a speaker or author draws conclusions from non-fraudulent data, based on accurate descriptions of the data and methodology underlying those conclusions, on subjects about which there is legitimate ongoing scientific disagreement, those statements are not grounds for a claim of false advertising under the Lanham Act [or under state law]. Here, ONY has alleged false advertising not because any of the data presented were incorrect but because the way they were presented and the conclusions drawn from them were allegedly misleading. Even if the conclusions authors draw from the results of their data could be actionable, such claims would be weakest when, as here, the authors readily disclosed the potential shortcomings of their methodology and their potential conflicts of interest. . . .

NOTES AND QUESTIONS

Taken seriously, *ONY* would seem to prohibit most of what the Food and Drug Administration (FDA) does with respect to pharmaceuticals: the FDA evaluates scientific studies and determines whether they support the health-related claims the manufacturer wishes to make for the drug. If the FDA finds the study insufficient, the claim may not legally be made, no matter what the manufacturer believes or is willing to disclose about the study's limitations. Is this materially distinguishable from what the *ONY* court said the government—in the form of a court—could not do? (Some pharmaceutical companies are beginning to make precisely this argument, and the Second Circuit has proven highly receptive.)

Should we let the claim "this paint will last up to twenty years even in tough weather conditions" be "settled by the methods of science rather than by the methods of litigation"? Most courts treat scientific claims as run-of-the-mill falsity claims, even if the actual facts are hard to discern because the science is complicated. In *Eastman Chemical Co. v. Plastipure, Inc.*, 775 F.3d 230 (5th Cir. 2014), the Fifth Circuit explicitly rejected the argument that *ONY* required it to remain agnostic on a disputed question of scientific proof.

Eastman alleged that Plastipure disparaged Eastman's plastic resin, Tritan, by falsely stating that it could leach chemicals capable of harming humans. A jury found in Eastman's favor. Defendants sought to overturn the verdict, arguing that they didn't make empirically falsifiable factual statements about Tritan, but rather participated in a scientific debate protected by the First Amendment.

The *Plastipure* court reasoned that the *ONY* plaintiff sought to enjoin statements "within the academic literature and directed at the scientific community." Here, Eastman didn't sue Plastipure for publishing in a scientific journal, but for ads directed at nonscientist customers without the full scientific context, including a description of the data, the methodology, conflicts of interest, and divergences between raw data and the experimenter's conclusions. "In this commercial context, the First Amendment is no obstacle to enforcement of the Lanham Act":

Advertisements do not become immune from Lanham Act scrutiny simply because their claims are open to scientific or public debate. Otherwise, the Lanham Act would hardly ever be enforceable— "many, if not most, products may be tied to public concerns with the environment, energy, economic policy, or individual health and safety." [*Central Hudson*.] ... The First Amendment ensures a robust discourse in the pages of academic journals, but it does not immunize false or misleading commercial claims.

Does the court succeed in distinguishing *ONY*? Why couldn't a jury have resolved the battle of the experts in that case as well? Wasn't the defendant in *ONY* using the scientific paper to tout itself to the relevant consumers as well, who just happened to be doctors who read journals? (As you can see, the concept of the reasonable consumer, to be discussed later in the chapter, may inform the concept of what is falsifiable.)

What about a business that advertised that it could "cure" gay men and lesbians and turn them heterosexual? Should such claims be subject to false advertising laws, given the consensus of counselors and healthcare professionals that such therapies are ineffective and harmful? *See* Ferguson v. JONAH, No. L-5473-12 (N.J. Super. Ct. July 19, 2013) (denying "cure" organization's motion to dismiss New Jersey false advertising claims).

4. Puffery

Some advertising is just bluster. Vague superlatives such as "best," "finest," "brightest," "most delicious," and the like are so common that reasonable consumers are presumed to treat them as unverifiable, unquantifiable, subjective, and unreliable. This conclusion is normative—it is about how consumers should behave, not about what advertisers should say. As Learned Hand wrote in *Vulcan Metals Co. v. Simmons Mfg. Co.*, 248 F. 853 (2d Cir. 1918), "There are some kinds of talk which no sensible man takes seriously, and if he does he suffers from his own credulity." The result is that an advertiser has a privilege "to lie his head off, so long as he says nothing specific." W. Page Keeton et al., *Prosser & Keeton on The Law of Torts* § 109, at 756–57 (5th ed. 1984). Thus, the slogan "You're in good hands with Allstate" was puffery, as was a claim that the advertiser's baby food was the "most nutritious." The law treats these as vague and nebulous claims, meaningless sales patter.

Puffery generally constitutes claims about the advertiser's own product. However, courts have also held that vague derogatory claims can be puffery. *See, e.g.*, U.S. Healthcare, Inc. v. Blue Cross, 898 F.2d 914 (3d Cir. 1990) ("Better than HMO. So good, it's Blue Cross and Blue Shield" tag line was "the most innocuous kind of 'puffing'"). *Compare* Tempur Seal Int'l, Inc. v. Wondergel, LLC, 2016 WL 1305155 (E.D. Ky. Apr. 1, 2016) (statement "Looking for some shoulder pain? Try a hard mattress. It may feel like a rock and put pressure on your hips, but it's the perfect way to tell your partner: 'Hey baby, want some arthritis?'" wasn't puffery, "as these statements regarding potential negative health effects clearly cross the line beyond what is permissible advertising").

The line between puffery and an actionable factual claim can be fuzzy, and we will consider various types of puffery below, from opinion to humor to meaningless statements. Puffery tends to center around four characteristics: (1) it is general and vague, not specific; (2) it makes a claim that is unmeasurable or unverifiable; (3) it is presented as a subjective statement; and therefore (4) it is the kind of claim upon which consumers are unlikely to rely.[2] A determination that a claim is simply puffery usually involves a combination of these factors, with the core issue being consumers' likely reliance on a falsifiable claim.

What about statements that a racehorse with a heart murmur was "truly outstanding," "bound to run," a "fine athlete," in "very good condition," the "leader of the pack," "one of the best yearlings in the state," and had "great prospects to win"? Travis v. Washington Horse Breeders Ass'n, 734 P.2d 956 (Wash. Ct. App. 1987), *rev'd on other grounds*, 759 P.2d 418 (Wash. 1988). What if the seller had no actual knowledge of the horse's condition? In that case, should it have been making those statements?

Claims that might in theory be verifiable can be deemed puffery because they're too exaggerated or superlative to be believable. *See* Imagine Medispa, LLC v. Transformations, Inc., 2014 WL 770810, No. 2:13-26923 (S.D. W. Va. Feb. 26, 2014) ("West Virginia's Lowest Price Weight Loss and Skin Care Clinic" and "Lowest Prices in WV!" didn't refer to any specific services or products, and drew no direct comparisons but instead were "broad, vague exaggerations or boasts on which no reasonable consumer would rely"). What about claims to

---

[2] This exact wording is not used as a test in any circuit; it is generalized from the cases. *Cf., e.g.*, Pizza Hut, Inc. v. Papa John's Int'l, Inc., 227 F.3d 489 (5th Cir. 2000) ("[W]e think that non-actionable 'puffery' comes in at least two possible forms: (1) an exaggerated, blustering, and boasting statement upon which no reasonable buyer would be justified in relying; or (2) a general claim of superiority over comparable products that is so vague that it can be understood as nothing more than a mere expression of opinion."); C&H Sugar Co., 119 F.T.C. 39, 44 (1995) ("The term 'puffery' as used by the Commission here generally includes representations that ordinary consumers do not take literally, expressions of opinion not made as a representation of fact, subjective claims (taste, feel, appearance, smell) and hyperbole that are not capable of objective measurement.").

have won awards, where the nature of the award isn't specified? *See* General Steel Domestic Sales, LLC v. Chumley, 129 F. Supp. 3d 1158 (D. Colo. 2015) (boast "Awarded Best in the Industry" was puffery, "as no reasonable consumer would rely on such an assertion without first inquiring further into the nature and credibility of the entity granting the award"); Hackett v. Feeney, 2011 WL 4007531 (D. Nev. 2011) (a boast that a particular theatrical performance was "Voted #1 Best Show in Vegas," when no such "vote" ever occurred, was puffery).

The cases involve widely diverging factual situations, with no clear patterns distinguishing different states or circuits, and you may find yourself dissatisfied by the gap between the general principles stated above and the highly specific claims found to be puffery or fact. In reviewing these materials, you should aim to train your judgment and to be able to liken new claims to previous cases, even though certainty may be impossible.

A.　　Verifiable or Merely Puff?

Sometimes the vagueness of a claim precludes it from being verifiable. Courts and the NAD have found the following claims unverifiable: "anything closer could be too close for comfort," used as a tagline for a shaver; a claim that a computer chess game was "like playing [a grand master] as your opponent"; claims that the advertiser would "make every effort," offer "exhaustive planning, careful attention," and use "common sense and good judgment"; and "the most advanced home gaming system in the universe."

By contrast, these claims have been deemed verifiable: a claim that one credit card was "preferred"; a claim that one type of grass required "50% less mowing"; a claim that a motor oil provided "longer engine life and better engine protection"; claims that customers for a biographical directory were "nominated" and that the number of memberships was "limited"; claims to have "official" approval; claims

214

that the advertiser employs "seasoned professionals who have experience in all types of hardware and software environments," "it is highly unlikely for us to be presented with an application or problem to which we have had no exposure," "firm adherence to control standards," and "[t]he end product of [our] services has almost always been an operating computer program or software system designed to conform to the requirement of each specific client"; and the statement that "The hospital my HMO sent me to just wasn't enough."

When performance on the advertised attribute is bad enough, even vague claims can be false. The FTC prevailed against a defendant who advertised the opportunity to buy high-quality cars at below-market prices, where the evidence established that the cars were actually in poor condition and, in the unusual case where the cars were in good condition, they sold for market price. Likewise, advertising for a cruise ship touting "a very special kind of luxury" with "impeccable taste, in the design and furnishings of the beautifully appointed lounges, dining room and cabins," combined with pictures and other representations that the cabins would be "beautiful" and "luxurious," supported a consumer fraud claim where the plaintiffs' cabin was actually dirty and furnished with broken, damaged, and outworn furniture. Vallery v. Bermuda Star Line, Inc., 532 N.Y.S.2d 965 (City Civ. Ct. 1988); see also In re Countrywide Financial Corp. Secs. Litig., 588 F. Supp. 2d 1132, 1144 (C.D. Cal. 2008) ("[T]he [complaint] adequately alleges that [the defendant's] practices so departed from its public statements that even 'high quality' became materially false or misleading; and that to apply the puffery rule to such allegations would deny that 'high quality' has any meaning."). But see Intertape Polymer Corp. v. Inspired Techs., Inc., 2010 WL 2776562 (M.D. Fla. 2010) (finding vague superiority claims to be puffery despite internal testing evidence suggesting that the advertiser knew that its product performed worse than that of the challenger).

In the absence of extremely poor quality, what causes a claim to cross the line to verifiability? Context matters, whether that's the context of the ad or the larger competitive context, just as both extrinsic and intrinsic evidence can be relevant to contract interpretation. For an example of a larger regulatory context, consider *Bruton v. Gerber Products Co.*, No. 12-CV-02412, 2013 WL 4833413 (N.D. Cal. Sept. 6, 2013). Bruton challenged Gerber's "As Healthy As Fresh" tagline for its baby food. Gerber defended this as puffery, but the word "healthy" is regulated by the FDA when used on food products. Unlike ordinary puffery cases, "the products at issue here are covered by federal regulations which impose specific labeling requirements and which appear to assume that consumers in fact do rely on health-related claims on labels." Even if they didn't originally do so, consumers might now rely on the fact that "healthy" can only be used on foods that meet certain standards.

Government definition of terms isn't necessary to provide relevant context. When an insurer told its clients that the replacement parts it used in car repairs were of "like kind or quality" as the original parts, and that the parts would restore insured clients' cars to their "pre-loss condition," an Illinois court rejected a puffery defense, upholding most of a $1.18 billion judgment. The court concluded that a reasonable policyholder would have interpreted the representations as factual. *Avery v. State Farm Mut. Auto. Ins. Co.*, 2001 WL 346308 (Ill. Ct. App. 2001) (unpublished portion). Other cases involving "like new" claims had found such statements to be puffery. But the *Avery* plaintiffs established that industry standards existed for replacement parts, that the defendant's parts were inferior by any reasonable measure, and that the defendant knew this. Thus, subjective knowledge might do more than make the defendant look bad: it might indicate that the matter at issue is factual enough for reasonable people to consider it true or false. *See also* U.S. Bank Nat'l Ass'n v. PHL Variable Ins. Co., 2013 WL 791462, No. 12 Civ. 6811 (S.D.N.Y. March 5, 2013) (magistrate judge) (holding that statements that insurance policies were "flexible" and allowed lower payments, while not absolute or "measurable," described such fundamental characteristics of the policies that they weren't necessarily puffery when taken in context of other claims); Ram Int'l, Inc. v. ADT Sec. Serv., Inc., No. 12-2023, 2014 WL 446824 (6th Cir. Feb. 4, 2014) (when a provider of security services, which require constant and uninterrupted monitoring, made representations that it would "be there for its clients '24 hours a day, 7 days a week' " and that it offered "24-hour monitoring by ADT trained professionals," false advertising claims couldn't be dismissed as puffery as a matter of law).

Moreover, ads are not to be dissected into their component words. Other parts of an ad can give specific meaning to otherwise vague words. Thus, a claim that a product was "economical," which standing alone has been found too general to support a false advertising claim, was false because of its context: the advertiser claimed that its de-icing product was economical because users need only use half as much as a competitor's, but the prices made the advertiser's product four times more expensive per unit of coverage. *See* Performance Indus. Inc v. Koos Inc., 18 U.S.P.Q.2d 1767 (E.D. Pa. 1990). Though "the world's best aspirin" was puffery standing alone, it was false when it appeared "in a context which invites the viewer to conclude that Bayer is therapeutically superior to any other aspirin." Sterling Drug Inc., 102 F.T.C. 395 (1983).

The FTC generally does not seek empirical evidence of consumer reaction before calling a claim puffery. In private plaintiff cases, the courts are not in agreement on whether puffery is a matter of law or a factual question that can be answered by showing that a claim is in fact material to consumers. Sometimes, courts decide for themselves. *See, e.g.*, Perkiss & Liehe v. Northern Cal. Collection Serv., Inc., 911 F.2d 242 (9th Cir. 1990) (puffery determinations are for court as matter of law), *and In re* Century 21–RE/MAX Real Estate Advert.

Claims Litig., 882 F. Supp. 915 (C.D. Cal. 1994) (refusing to consider plaintiff's evidence that public could be misled by claim because statement was puffery as matter of law).

But in *Federal Express Corporation v. United States Postal Service,* 40 F. Supp. 2d 943 (W.D. Tenn. 1999), the court reached a different result. FedEx alleged that the USPS violated the Lanham Act by falsely advertising itself as a private commercial entity that offers delivery service "around the world." The USPS argued that calling itself a "company" and claiming delivery around the world was puffery.

On a motion to dismiss, the court ruled that the USPS's "representation of itself as a company" shouldn't be characterized as puffery. FedEx argued that the term "company" evoked images of a private, commercial enterprise in the minds of the buying public and misled them into comparing the USPS and FedEx as two private companies. (Editors' question: so what?) The use of "company" was not an example of "exaggerated advertising, blustering and boasting" or "claims of general superiority." Nor was it so vague and exaggerated that no reasonable person could have relied upon it.

The USPS argued that common sense knowledge about the Postal Service and its governmental nature would prevent any reasonable reliance on the implication that a "company" is private. The court rejected this argument:

> While it may be true that no consumer construed or was likely to construe Defendant's description of itself as a company, those considerations are not relevant to the inquiry at hand. In a motion to dismiss for failure to state a claim, a court addresses a very narrow question: has the Plaintiff pled facts respecting all material elements of the claim in question? . . . Furthermore, it would not be appropriate for

218

this court to rely upon such ambiguous concepts as "common sense" or its own intuitive notions of how an advertising statement should have been interpreted to conclude that Defendant's statement is not actionable because no one could have relied upon it. The relevant barometer is the opinion of the consumer, not that of a court.

Likewise, the court refused to dismiss claims relating to the USPS's "around the world" advertising:

On its face, the phrase "around the world" does seem to be the type of vague, general exaggeration which no reasonable person would rely upon in making a purchasing decision. . . . [But w]here the context of an advertising statement may lend greater specificity to an otherwise vague representation, the court should not succumb to the temptation to hastily rule a phrase to be inactionable under the Lanham Act. To do so would insulate from liability some of the misleading advertising which the Lanham Act was intended to prohibit.

In the context of the mail/package delivery industry, the proper rule was to evaluate "around the world" against the backdrop of industry norms. Norms can establish consumer expectations and make terms that are "vague in a vacuum" specific enough to be actionable. But, on a motion to dismiss, the court didn't have enough information to analyze industry norms. Thus, it declined to dismiss the claim.

Is the court's reasoning persuasive? When, if ever, *should* a court seek consumer perception evidence before determining that a claim is or is not puffery? The issue is that puffery may give consumers a favorable image of a product or service—otherwise it is hard to understand why advertisers would bother to puff—but they do not actually give consumers a specific reason to act. Thus, such claims may be effective in influencing purchases without being either provable or falsifiable. And it may be beyond the desirable reach of the law to combat advertising that changes consumers' preferences for no good reason. Thus, a determination that a claim is pure puffery should arguably trump evidence that it actually influences consumers.

On the other hand, an essential justification for excusing puffery is that reasonable consumers are unlikely to rely on it. If a significant number of consumers actually *would* rely on a claim, then that justification has been shown to be inapplicable. This may explain why some courts consider the advertiser's intent in evaluating puffery defenses. *See, e.g.,* People v. Maclean Hunter Pub'g Corp., 457 N.E.2d 480 (Ill. Ct. App. 1983) ("It is true that a bare and naked statement as to value is ordinarily deemed the opinion of the party making the representation . . . [but] such statement may be a positive affirmation of a fact, intended as such by the party making it, and reasonably regarded as such by the party to whom it is made. When it is such, it is like any other representation of fact . . . ").

How should a court consider different parts of an ad? Can specifics in one part of an ad convert a general claim like "best" into non-puffery? Consider the following case assessing a jury verdict that found Papa John's liable for false advertising:

Pizza Hut, Inc. v. Papa John's International, Inc., 227 F.3d 489 (5th Cir. 2000)

This appeal presents a false advertising claim under section 43(a) of the Lanham Act, resulting in a jury verdict for the plaintiff, Pizza Hut. At the center of this appeal is Papa John's four word slogan "Better Ingredients. Better Pizza."

... We conclude that (1) the slogan, standing alone, is not an [objectively verifiable] statement of fact upon which consumers would be justified in relying, and thus not actionable under section 43(a); and (2) ... the slogan, when utilized in connection with some of the post–May 1997 comparative advertising—specifically, the sauce and dough campaigns—conveyed objectifiable and misleading facts ...

I

... Since 1995, Papa John's has invested over $300 million building customer goodwill in its trademark "Better Ingredients. Better Pizza." The slogan has appeared on millions of signs, shirts, menus, pizza boxes, napkins and other items, and has regularly appeared as the "tag line" at the end of Papa John's radio and television ads, or with the company logo in printed advertising.

... In early May 1997, Papa John's launched its first national ad campaign. The campaign was directed towards Pizza Hut, and its "Totally New Pizza" campaign. . . . The ad campaign was remarkably successful. During May 1997, Papa John's sales increased 11.7

percent over May 1996 sales, while Pizza Hut's sales were down 8 percent.

. . . Papa John's ran a series of ads comparing specific ingredients used in its pizzas with those used by its "competitors." During the course of these ads, Papa John's touted the superiority of its sauce and its dough. During the sauce campaign, Papa John's asserted that its sauce was made from "fresh, vine-ripened tomatoes," which were canned through a process called "fresh pack," while its competitors— including Pizza Hut—make their sauce from remanufactured tomato paste. During the dough campaign, Papa John's stated that it used "clear filtered water" to make its pizza dough, while the "biggest chain" uses "whatever comes out of the tap." Additionally, Papa John's asserted that it gives its yeast "several days to work its magic," while "some folks" use "frozen dough or dough made the same day." At or near the close of each of these ads, Papa John's punctuated its ingredient comparisons with the slogan "Better Ingredients. Better Pizza." [Pizza Hut sued.] . . . .

On November 17, 1999, the jury returned its responses to the special issues finding that Papa John's slogan, and its "sauce claims" and "dough claims" were false or misleading and deceptive or likely to deceive consumers.

The court concluded that the "Better Ingredients. Better Pizza." slogan was "consistent with the legal definition of non-actionable puffery" from its introduction in 1995 until May 1997. However, the slogan "became tainted . . . in light of the entirety of Papa John's post–May 1997 advertising." Based on this conclusion, the magistrate judge permanently enjoined Papa John's from "using any slogan in the future that constitutes a recognizable variation of the phrase 'Better Ingredients. Better Pizza.' or which uses the adjective 'Better' to modify the terms 'ingredients' and/or 'pizza'." . . .

Essential to any claim under section 43(a) of the Lanham Act is a determination of whether the challenged statement is one of fact—actionable under section 43(a)—or one of general opinion—not actionable under section 43(a). Bald assertions of superiority or general statements of opinion cannot form the basis of Lanham Act liability. Rather the statements at issue must be a "specific and measurable claim, capable of being proved false or of being reasonably interpreted as a statement of objective fact." . . .

(b)

. . . Drawing guidance from the writings of our sister circuits and the leading commentators, we think that non-actionable "puffery" comes in at least two possible forms: (1) an exaggerated, blustering, and boasting statement upon which no reasonable buyer would be justified in relying; or (2) a general claim of superiority over comparable products that is so vague that it can be understood as nothing more than a mere expression of opinion. . . .

Bisecting the slogan "Better Ingredients. Better Pizza.," it is clear that the assertion by Papa John's that it makes a "Better Pizza." is a general statement of opinion regarding the superiority of its product over all others. This simple statement, "Better Pizza.," epitomizes the exaggerated advertising, blustering, and boasting by a manufacturer upon which no consumer would reasonably rely. Consequently, it appears indisputable that Papa John's assertion "Better Pizza." is non-actionable puffery.[8]

---

[8] It should be noted that Pizza Hut uses the slogan "The Best Pizza Under One Roof." Similarly, other nationwide pizza chains employ slogans touting their pizza as the "best": (1) Domino's Pizza uses the slogan "Nobody Delivers Better."; (2) Danato's uses the slogan "Best Pizza on the Block."; (3) Mr. Gatti's uses the slogan "Best Pizza in Town: Honest!"; and (4) Pizza Inn uses the slogans "Best Pizza Ever." and "The Best Tasting Pizza."

Moving next to consider separately the phrase "Better Ingredients.," the same conclusion holds true. Like "Better Pizza.," it is typical puffery. The word "better," when used in this context is unquantifiable. What makes one food ingredient "better" than another comparable ingredient, without further description, is wholly a matter of individual taste or preference not subject to scientific quantification. Indeed, it is difficult to think of any product, or any component of any product, to which the term "better," without more, is quantifiable. As our court stated in *Presidio*:

> The law recognizes that a vendor is allowed some latitude in claiming merits of his wares by way of an opinion rather than an absolute guarantee, so long as he hews to the line of rectitude in matters of fact. Opinions are not only the lifestyle of democracy, they are the brag in advertising that has made for the wide dissemination of products that otherwise would never have reached the households of our citizens. If we were to accept the thesis set forth by the appellees, [that all statements by advertisers were statements of fact actionable under the Lanham Act,] the advertising industry would have to be liquidated in short order.

. . . . Finally, turning to the combination of the two non-actionable phrases as the slogan "Better Ingredients. Better Pizza.," we fail to see how the mere joining of these two statements of opinion could create an actionable statement of fact. . . .

B

. . . [T]here is sufficient evidence to support the jury's conclusion that the sauce and dough ads were misleading statements of fact actionable under the Lanham Act. [The court reviews and accepts

224

Pizza Hut's evidence that there are no "demonstrable" or "quantifiable" differences between the parties' sauces and doughs.]

. . . Consequently, the district court was correct in concluding that: "Without any scientific support or properly conducted taste preference test, by the written and/or oral negative connotations conveyed that pizza made from tomato paste concentrate is inferior to the 'fresh pack' method used by Papa John's, its sauce advertisements conveyed an impression which is misleading. . . ." . . .

(3)

. . . . In support of the district court's conclusion that the slogan was transformed, Pizza Hut argues that "in construing any advertising statement, the statement must be considered in the overall context in which it appears." . . .

We agree that the message communicated by the slogan "Better Ingredients. Better Pizza." is expanded and given additional meaning when it is used as the tag line in the misleading sauce and dough ads. . . . [A] reasonable consumer would understand the slogan, when considered in the context of the comparison ads, as conveying the following message: Papa John's uses "better ingredients," which produces a "better pizza" because Papa John's uses "fresh-pack" tomatoes, fresh dough, and filtered water. In short, Papa John's has given definition to the word "better." Thus, when the slogan is used in this context, it is no longer mere opinion, but rather takes on the characteristics of a statement of fact. When used in the context of the sauce and dough ads, the slogan is misleading for the same reasons we have earlier discussed in connection with the sauce and dough ads.[11]

---

[11] . . . . Our review of the record convinces us that there is simply no evidence to support the district court's conclusion that the slogan was irreparably

NOTES AND QUESTIONS

Do you have a working definition of puffery now? Compare *Pizza Hut* with the *FedEx* case, *supra*. What paths do they take to figure out whether a claim is mere puffing, and what role does the extrinsic evidence of consumers' reactions play in each?

What is the role of context in evaluating puffery? Should statements like "best" simply be removed from consideration and any more specific claims be evaluated on their own terms? Or should a fact finder consider the interplay between specific claims and general evaluative claims? What else—besides specific claims made in the same ad—counts as relevant "context" when determining what is mere puffery? The *FedEx* court emphasizes consumer understanding and industry norms, but how are these to be proven?

---

tainted as a result of its use in the misleading comparison sauce and dough ads. At issue in this case were some 249 print ads and 29 television commercials. After a thorough review of the record, we liberally construe eight print ads to be sauce ads, six print ads to be dough ads, and six print ads to be both sauce and dough ads. Further, we liberally construe nine television commercials to be sauce ads and two television commercials to be dough ads. Consequently, out of a total of 278 print and television ads, the slogan appeared in only 31 ads that could be liberally construed to be misleading sauce or dough ads.

We find simply no evidence, survey or otherwise, to support the district court's conclusion that the advertisements that the jury found misleading— ads that constituted only a small fraction of Papa John's use of the slogan— somehow had become encoded in the minds of consumers such that the mention of the slogan reflectively brought to mind the misleading statements conveyed by the sauce and dough ads. Thus, based on the record before us, Pizza Hut has failed to offer sufficient evidence to support the district court's conclusion that the slogan had become forever "tainted" by its use as the tag line in the handful of misleading comparison ads.

Who's "Best"? In FN8 of the *Pizza Hut* opinion, the court recounts how many industry competitors all claim to be "best." Does this overusage imply that the word "best" is meaningless to consumers, or does its prevalence suggest that the competitors believe the word has selling power, in which case perhaps it should be subject to regulation?

Common Sense? The *Federal Express* court says "it would not be appropriate for this court to rely upon such ambiguous concepts as 'common sense' or its own intuitive notions . . . ." Isn't that what common law courts do all the time? Isn't that what *Iqbal* (decided after *Federal Express*) now requires? The *Federal Express* opinion continued: "The relevant barometer is the opinion of the consumer, not that of a court." What steps will (or should) the court take to ascertain the opinions of consumers?

Applying the Standard. Consider the following case. In *Procter & Gamble Co. v. Kimberly-Clark Corp.*, 569 F. Supp. 2d 796 (E.D. Wis. 2008), P&G challenged the advertising of Huggies Natural Fit diapers, whose sides were contoured toward the center. Kimberly-Clark ads suggested that other diapers would fit bricks well, but not babies:

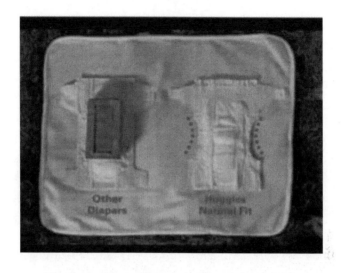

The ads claimed that Huggies were designed for "babies of the human variety" and that a Huggies diaper "fits more naturally." Huggies' own study concluded that the ad was very persuasive.

The court found that "natural fit" and "fits more naturally" were puffery, "so vague and subjective that they are neither provable nor disprovable." Neither of the parties were able to identify "a fixed set of criteria" for what "fit more naturally" might mean. The court asked: "which garment fits a woman more 'naturally'—a tailored English business suit, a Japanese kimono, or an Indian sari?" Indeed, testimony before the court suggested that consumers' standards for measuring fit vary widely because fit is subjective, and even depends on the diapers' appearance.

As the court pointed out, despite extensive testing, P&G still doesn't know how consumers decide that a given product "fits naturally." In fact, P&G's designers were once convinced, after using quantifiable measures, that a particular diaper would be an excellent fit, but consumers disagreed. Given that the benchmark concept is incapable of concrete definition, the court continued, "fits more naturally" and "natural fit" could neither be proved nor disproved, and thus they could not be falsified. In fact, even if we could all agree on what it meant for a diaper to "fit more naturally," our individual conclusions on which diaper did so "would be based on purely subjective judgments." Such "opinion puffery" can't be proved.

P&G argued that because consumer testing can substantiate a diaper fit claim, such claims are verifiable through consumer tests. But the court concluded that even if consumer testing provides companies with useful market information, that doesn't make it a legitimate way of assessing truth or falsity for Lanham Act purposes. The court held that, just as it's impossible to prove which pizza is better (as in *Pizza Hut*), it's impossible to demonstrate "conclusively" whether one diaper "fits more naturally." "[A]n assertion whose truth depends solely on consumer opinion is an inactionable one." Thus, taste tests showing that Pizza Hut was preferred by 75% of consumers over Papa John's still wouldn't have disproved the "Better Pizza" claim.

Would the same conclusion apply to superlatives other than "better"? Imagine, for example, if the diaper claim had been "gentler"—could the effects on a baby's skin be measured? What about "safer"?

The court continued that "[w]henever subjective preference is the arbiter of a claim—whether of pizza or natural fitting diapers—resort to consumer studies is of limited value in the Lanham Act context and only underscores the inherent difficulty in disproving such claims." In fact, the court held, the study results presented to it demonstrated that consumers couldn't agree on which diapers fit more naturally. For several sizes, 51% of consumers found that Pampers fit more naturally, while 45% preferred Huggies and 4% had no preference. The court called this a "coin toss" based on individual preference, not objective truth.

Is the Huggies case an application of *Pizza Hut*, or an extension of it? Do you agree that taste tests could not have disproved "Better Ingredients. Better Pizza"?

B.   The Advertiser's Special Knowledge and Puffery

The amount of authority possessed by the advertiser can indicate that claims are merely subjective. For example, one court found that disparaging oral statements by salespeople to individual customers were claims that "an ordinary listener would recognize as personal opinion as opposed to representations of hard definable facts, such as product descriptions." Licata & Co. v. Goldberg, 812 F. Supp. 403 (S.D.N.Y. 1993). What if the statement were contained in a published ad? Would consumers be more likely to believe that the statement had been made by a more authoritative source, vetted and verified?

Not all individual salespersons' statements are subjective puffery. Drug sales representatives are supposed to be well-trained, and courts have held drug manufacturers liable for individual statements when the representatives' training encouraged (or failed to discourage) false or unsubstantiated claims. If individual salespeople are supposed to be experts on their products or services compared to consumers, then their statements are less likely to be taken as opinion.

There are important limitations to the principle that subjective claims are mere puffery. If the source of the subjective statement presents his or her experience as typical when in fact it is not, then the fact that the statement describes a subjective state will not prevent it from being labeled false advertising. As an application of that principle, taste tests may be subjective as to each individual taster, but a superiority or equivalence claim based on taste tests may be shown to be false.

More generally, simply couching an advertisement in terms of the advertiser's opinion will not insulate it from challenge if the statement is one that is, in fact, verifiable. In *National Commission on Egg Nutrition v. Federal Trade Commission*, 570 F.2d 157 (7th Cir. 1977), the Commission on Egg Nutrition argued that its statement that there was "no scientific evidence" that eating eggs increased the risk of heart and circulatory disease was merely an expression of opinion. The Seventh Circuit agreed with the FTC that the phrase "is also, and perhaps more reasonably subject to the interpretation" that no such reliable scientific evidence existed. If a claim is of the type that can be confirmed or disconfirmed, the claim will be treated as factual.

Ivan Preston, whose views are discussed in more detail in the next section, argues that, in the modern economy, consumers are likely to see advertisers as experts with special access to the facts, including facts about competing products. Moreover, if the advertiser is communicating in a mass medium, consumers are likely to believe that its claims are valid across a large group of consumers. As a result, he argues, consumers will give greater deference to their statements—treating them as inherently less subjective and more verifiable—than they would to the statements of a single individual.

Some courts, however, have reasoned to the contrary: broad advertising is more likely to be puffery. *See, e.g.*, Guidance Endodontics, LLC v. Dentsply Int'l, Inc., 2010 WL 1608949 (D. N.M. 2010) ("[T]he larger the audience the more likely it is that the statement is puffery"; in marketing materials, "a seller is expected to cast his wares in the best possible light to tempt consumers to buy his product rather than any other."). Is this more plausible? When would an individualized pitch be more credible than a mass advertising campaign, and when would it be less so? If a salesperson says, "This mortgage is the best fit for you," should we accept a puffery defense, given that "best mortgage" would clearly be puffery in a newspaper ad? Consider how the generalized/individualized comparison relates to the difference between fact and opinion discussed above. Should it matter if the salesperson and the prospective customer have one or more social connections beyond the vendor-vendee relationship? For example, if they have occasionally dined together in social settings, or if a person hosts a party at their house to sell to his or her friends?

C.   What If Puffery Works?

The powerful effect of puffery, as well as the law's refusal to regulate it, can be seen in the FTC's response to requests to modify consent orders against advertisers. Firestone had been ordered not to make unsubstantiated safety claims. *See Firestone Tire & Rubber Co.*, 81 F.T.C. 398 (1972). It successfully asked the FTC to exclude "generalized safety claims." Thus, Firestone could, without substantiation, make claims such as "quality you can trust." *See* Clarification of Three Provisions of a 1972 Order Concerning Safety Claims for its Tires, 112 F.T.C. 609, 610 (1989) (advisory opinion). A dissent argued that such claims were capable of being substantiated.

Similarly, C&H Sugar was ordered in 1977 not to call its brand "superior" to or otherwise different from other granulated sugars without substantiation. *See* C&H Sugar Co., 119 F.T.C. 39 (1995) (rehearing), *rev'g* 89 F.T.C. 15 (1977). In 1995, it claimed that it was barred from using ads such as "I love C&H the best" or "C&H tastes best," which harmed it because its competition was free to make similar unsubstantiated claims. The FTC granted the modification, because competing ad campaigns were able to "take advantage of C&H's inability to counter claims that either constitute puffery or relate to the source or origin of the product . . . ." The underlying problem was that

> [t]he homogeneous nature of the product means that there are few truthful, nondeceptive comparisons that can be made

among competing products. In order to promote their brands, sugar refiners must rely on . . . subjective endorsement claims . . . or objective product source and origin claims which are precisely the kinds of claims prohibited by the existing order. . . . The order against C&H was intended to protect consumers from misleading claims about the alleged superiority or difference of C&H sugar, not to stifle the respondent's ability to participate in healthy competition on the basis of truthful, nondeceptive advertising. We are persuaded, therefore, that modification to permit puffery is warranted.

The FTC, however, then suggested that "I love C&H the best" or "C&H tastes best" are capable of being substantiated. (In light of the *Pizza Hut* case, do you agree? How would you disprove the statement?) But then it went on to say that claims not relating to "health, safety, nutritional quality, or purity . . . will not be deemed to contain an implied comparison under this order." Thus, taste claims would be allowed.

Ivan Preston has characterized this as a finding of fact, as a matter of law, that such claims are meaningless: that consumers don't understand "C&H tastes better" as a factual claim. He argues that this conclusion is both paradoxical—the better taste claim is concededly capable of being substantiated—and wrong. Ivan L. Preston, *Puffery and Other "Loophole" Claims: How The Law's "Don't Ask, Don't Tell" Policy Condones Fraudulent Falsity in Advertising*, 18 J.L. & COM. 49 (1998).

Separately, C&H is only at a competitive disadvantage if puffery *works*: that is, if consumers are influenced by puffery to think that competitors' products are better than C&H's. But if that is so, what happened to the definition of puffery as vague and unverifiable claims on which reasonable consumers wouldn't rely? Doesn't this decision show that it's a mistake to have a category of puffery distinct from actual consumer reaction? As Preston points out, the president of the American Advertising Federation said that without puffery, advertisers "would, in effect, be denied the ability to compete on anything other than factual grounds. Thousands of products do not compete on factual grounds because they are essentially the same." If that's true, do we really want them claiming to be different?

Preston argues that current puffery doctrine is a mistaken evolution from nineteenth-century cases involving individual buyers and sellers that held that buyers couldn't sue for fraud based on statements that they could easily have verified or disproved themselves. When buyers were unable to verify the claims, however, the law provided them redress. But as the puffery doctrine developed, it turned into a rule that consumers treated certain claims as meaningless and therefore rejected them at the outset.

In fact, Preston argues, marketing research demonstrates that, with many claims that the law calls puffery, consumers receive messages containing factual, verifiable, and reliable claims, so failure to regulate puffery subjects consumers to a substantial risk of deception. He argues that courts and regulators should ask what messages consumers actually receive rather than presuming that puffery is meaningless.

Preston points to consumer research asking respondents whether ad claims were "completely true," "partly true," or "not true at all." Twenty-two percent said that "State Farm is all you need to know about life insurance" was completely true, and 36% said it was partly true. Even higher percentages found Pan Am's claim to be "the world's most experienced airline" completely or partly true; Texaco's "you can trust your car to the man who wears the star" obtained similar levels of agreement. Preston claims that, if consumers were responding to puffery in the way the law presumes, they would have answered "not true at all." Do you agree? Does it matter that the researchers didn't give consumers the option of responding "neither true nor false"?

In another study cited by Preston, a researcher used different versions of a car ad, one using facts such as "27 miles per gallon" and the other using puffery such as "truly excellent gas mileage." Consumers rated the importance and credibility of these claims essentially the same, though courts would usually call the latter claim puffery. *See* Morris B. Holbrook, *Beyond Attitude Structure: Toward the Informational Determinants of Attitude*, 15 J. MARKETING RES. 545 (1978). More generally, Preston argues, while one can criticize various aspects of these studies, there is no empirical evidence supporting the law's assumption that consumers typically see puffery as meaningless. (What about consumers' general skepticism about ads, discussed in the first section of this chapter? Does that have any bearing on puffery?)

Preston concludes that, since puffs generally imply facts, and since advertisers could benefit even more from adding explicit truthful statements if they could do so, a puff without an accompanying fact claim is likely to be fraudulent. That is, an advertiser who has safety tests (or some other tests) showing its tires to be the best should logically advertise that it has conducted such tests rather than simply claim to be the best. If it makes only the weaker puff, then it is trying to fool people into thinking that some kind of superiority exists. Do you agree?

Consider *Daugherty v. Sony Electronics, Inc.*, 2006 WL 197090 (Tenn. Ct. App. 2006). The court of appeals allowed a Tennessee Consumer Protection Act claim to survive on appeal. The complaint named several Sony ads touting Sony's product quality, including statements that "the company has earned a solid reputation for quality, reliability, innovation and stylish design." As to DVD players specifically, Sony's ads claimed that its DVD players "set[] the standard" and were "superior." The court decided to leave the issue of puffery to the jury: the key issue was whether the buyer reasonably understood that he or she was getting some kind of assurance about specific facts. Echoing Preston's reasoning, the court refused to find as a matter of law that, "notwithstanding the amount of money that Sony spends on advertising its DVD players, Sony never intended for Plaintiff or any consumer actually to rely on so much as even one of these advertisements and, if there was such reliance by a consumer, it was altogether unjustified." Do you agree with the result?

D.   Are Incomprehensible Claims Puffery?

In *Date v. Sony Electronics Inc.*, 2009 WL 435289 (E.D. Mich. 2009), Sony advertised its television as offering "Full HDTV," the "World's Greatest High Definition Television," "new display technology . . . to meet and exceed the demands of a High Definition Image at its full 1080 line resolution," and the ability to display digitally transmitted high definition signals without interlacing. Sony also stated in the specifications sheet that the televisions' native video resolution was "1080p" (the best available technology). The TVs, however, could not display a 1080p signal. Instead, at best they could display an upconverted 1080i (interlaced) signal from a 1080p device. The upconversion process results in undesirable artifacts like feathering that make the viewing experience worse.

Sony argued that its claims were puffery, based on a prior similar case. In *Johnson v. Mitsubishi Digital Electronics America, Inc.*, 578 F. Supp. 2d 1229 (C.D. Cal. 2008), the court concluded that, although Mitsubishi designated its television set as a 1080p television set, the phrase 1080p "does not convey a specific claim that is recognizable to the targeted customer." The *Johnson* court thought 1080p only had meaning for engineering professionals, and that all that the plaintiff wanted was a top-of-the-line set. Because he didn't understand what 1080p meant, the claim was puffery to him.

The *Date* court found that at least some plaintiffs had an idea of what 1080p meant, and pointed out that Sony put the term on its specification sheet addressed to consumers, suggesting that it wasn't puffery. Which court's reasoning makes more sense? Does a consumer have to be able to define the term in order for us to conclude that she received a specific message? That is, if a consumer receives a message that she thinks is factual, credible and material, is anything more needed?

That information is of marginal value to the buying public does not make it false. In *OPA (Overseas Publishing Association) Amsterdam BV v. American Inst. of Physics*, 973 F. Supp. 414 (S.D.N.Y. 1997), a federal district court dismissed claims that a publisher of physics journals engaged in false advertising when it touted its journals as more "cost-effective" than others, even though cost-effectiveness might be a bad measure for academic journals. Similarly, another court found that an idiosyncratic "formula" concocted by a vacuum cleaner manufacturer to measure the cleaning power of its vacuum cleaners was not very useful, but not false in that all the components of the rating were accurate. Royal Appliance Mfg. Co. v. Hoover Co., 845 F. Supp. 469 (N.D. Ohio 1994).

E.   Humor and Parody

An ad may be humorous and yet still make believable claims, in which case those claims will be tested using the same standards as those applied to any other claims. However, humor can make clear to reasonable consumers that an exaggerated claim is not meant to be believed. As a result, humor can take a claim or representation out of the realm of falsifiable fact.

One ad for Alamo rental cars showed a family trying to drive "all the miles in Alamo territory," only to be frustrated as, over the years,

Alamo added more and more miles for the family to drive. At the end,
a sign reads "Over 20,000,000 locations World Wide." Because at the
time of the commercial Alamo did not have "world wide" locations,
Hertz challenged the advertising. The NAD agreed with Alamo that
the claim was unlikely to be taken as a literal statement about
Alamo's current capability, but cautioned:

> Humor and hyperbole do not necessarily shield a commercial
> from making implied claims, but each case must be judged on
> its own particular facts and context. . . . The issue here is
> what claims are reasonably being made on the face of this
> commercial?

The standard rules on misleadingness apply, sometimes filtered
through the recognition that humor can change the message
consumers take away from the ad. A humorous ad showing
outrageously exaggerated product comparisons in which the
competitor's product comes off badly might be challenged by a party
arguing that consumers are likely to believe that the ad is
representing reality. Consider whether what follows is such a case.

S.C. Johnson & Son, Inc. v. Clorox Co., 241 F.3d 232 (2d Cir. 2001)

This case involves a Lanham Act challenge to the truthfulness of a
television commercial and print advertisement depicting the plight of
an animated goldfish in a Ziploc Slide-Loc bag that is being held
upside down and is leaking water. Plaintiff-appellee S.C. Johnson &
Son manufactures the Ziploc bags targeted by the advertisements. In
an Order dated April 6, 2000, the United States District Court for the
Southern District of New York (Griesa, J.) permanently enjoined the
defendant-appellant, The Clorox Company, manufacturer of Ziploc's
rival Glad-Lock resealable storage bags, from using these

advertisements. We conclude that the district court did not abuse its discretion in entering this injunction and accordingly affirm.

BACKGROUND

In August 1999, Clorox introduced a 15-second and a 30-second television commercial ("Goldfish I"), each depicting an S.C. Johnson Ziploc Slide-Loc resealable storage bag side-by-side with a Clorox Glad-Lock bag. The bags are identified in the commercials by brand name. Both commercials show an animated, talking goldfish in water inside each of the bags. In the commercials, the bags are turned upside-down, and the Slide-Loc bag leaks rapidly while the Glad-Lock bag does not leak at all. In both the 15- and 30-second Goldfish I commercials, the Slide-Loc goldfish says, in clear distress, "My Ziploc Slider is dripping. Wait a minute!," while the Slide Loc bag is shown leaking at a rate of approximately one drop per one to two seconds. In the 30-second Goldfish I commercial only, the Slide-Loc bag is shown leaking while the Slide-Loc goldfish says, "Excuse me, a little help here," and then, "Oh, dripping, dripping." At the end of both commercials, the Slide Loc goldfish exclaims, "Can I borrow a cup of water!!!"

On November 4, 1999, S.C. Johnson brought an action against Clorox under section 43(a) of the Lanham Act, 15 U.S.C. § 1125(a), for false advertising in the Goldfish I commercials. . . .

Dr. Phillip DeLassus, an outside expert retained by S.C. Johnson, conducted "torture testing," in which Slide-Loc bags were filled with water, rotated for 10 seconds, and held upside-down for an additional 20 seconds. He testified about the results of the tests he performed, emphasizing that 37 percent of all Slide-Loc bags tested did not leak at all. Of the remaining 63 percent that did leak, only a small percentage leaked at the rate depicted in the Goldfish I television commercials. The vast majority leaked at a rate between two and twenty times slower than that depicted in the Goldfish I commercials.

On January 7, 2000, the district court entered findings of fact and conclusions of law on the record in support of an Order permanently enjoining Clorox from disseminating the Goldfish I television commercials. . . .

The court found that "the commercial impermissibly exaggerates the facts in respect to the flow of water or the leaking of water out of a Slide-Loc bag." The court further found that:

> [t]he commercial shows drops of water coming out of the bag at what appears to be a rapid rate. In fact, the rate is about one fairly large drop per second. Moreover, there is a depiction of the water level in the bag undergoing a substantial and rapid decline. Finally, there is an image of bubbles going through the water.

The district court found that "the overall depiction in the commercial itself is of a rapid and substantial leakage and flow of water out of the Slide-Loc bag." The court noted that "[t]his is rendered even more graphic by the fact that there is a goldfish depicted in the bag which is shown to be in jeopardy because the water is running out at such a rate."

The district court found "that when these bags are subjected to the same kind of quality control test as used by Clorox for the Glad bags, there is some leakage in about two-thirds of the cases." However, the court found "that the great majority of those leaks are very small and at a very slow rate." The court found that "[o]nly in about 10 percent of these bags is there leakage at the rate shown in the commercial, that is, one drop per second." The district court further found that "[t]he problem with the commercial is that there is no depiction in the

240

visual images to indicate anything else than the fact that the type of fairly rapid and substantial leakage shown in the commercial is simply characteristic of that kind of bag." . . .

In February 2000, Clorox released a modified version of the Goldfish I television commercials as well as a related print advertisement ("Goldfish II"). In the 15 second Goldfish II television commercial, a Ziploc Slide-Loc bag and Glad-Lock bag are again shown side-by-side, filled with water and containing an animated, talking goldfish. The bags are then rotated, and a drop is shown forming and dropping in about a second from the Slide-Loc bag. During the approximately additional two seconds that it is shown, the Slide-Loc goldfish says, "My Ziploc slider is dripping. Wait a minute." The two bags are then off-screen for approximately eight seconds before the Slide-Loc bag is again shown, with a drop forming and falling in approximately one second. During this latter depiction of the Slide-Loc bag, the Slide-Loc goldfish says, "Hey, I'm gonna need a little help here." Both bags are identified by brand name, and the Glad-Lock bag does not leak at all. The second-to-last frame shows three puddles on an orange background that includes the phrase "Don't Get Mad."

In the print advertisement, a large drop is shown forming and about to fall from an upside-down Slide-Loc bag in which a goldfish is partially out of the water. Bubbles are shown rising from the point of the leak in the Slide-Loc bag. Next to the Slide-Loc bag is a Glad-Lock bag that is not leaking and contains a goldfish that is completely submerged. Under the Slide-Loc bag appears: "Yikes! My Ziploc® Slide-Loc™ is dripping!" Under the Glad-Lock bag is printed: "My Glad is tight, tight, tight." On a third panel, three puddles and the words "Don't Get Mad" are depicted on a red background. In a fourth panel, the advertisement recites: "Only Glad has the Double-Lock™ green seal. That's why you'll be glad you got Glad. Especially if you're a goldfish."

After these advertisements appeared, S.C. Johnson moved to enlarge the January 7 injunction to enjoin the airing and distribution of the Goldfish II advertisements. On April 6, 2000, after hearing oral argument, the district court entered another order on the record, setting forth further findings of fact and conclusions of law in support of an Order permanently enjoining the distribution of the Goldfish II television commercial and print advertisement. . . .

The court then addressed the Goldfish II print advertisement, which, it found "is, if anything, worse," because "[i]t has a single image of a Slide-Loc bag with a large drop about to fall away and a goldfish in danger of suffocating because the water is as portrayed disappearing from the bag." The district court concluded that the Goldfish II print advertisement "is literally false." The court also found that the inability of a Ziploc Slide-Loc bag to prevent leakage is portrayed as an inherent quality or characteristic of that product. Accordingly, the court found that the Goldfish II television commercial and print advertisement "portray[ ] the leakage as simply an ever-present characteristic of the Slide-Loc bags."

. . . Clorox now appeals from this April 6, 2000 Order permanently enjoining the use of the Goldfish II television commercial and print advertisement.

DISCUSSION

. . . "[T]he district judge's determination of the meaning of the advertisement [is] a finding of fact that 'shall not be set aside unless clearly erroneous.' "

. . . In considering a false advertising claim, "[f]undamental to any task of interpretation is the principle that text must yield to context."

> Thus, we have emphasized that in reviewing FTC actions prohibiting unfair advertising practices under the Federal Trade Commission Act a court must "consider the advertisement in its entirety and not . . . engage in disputatious dissection. The entire mosaic should be viewed rather than each tile separately." . . .

I. The district court's findings of fact are not clearly erroneous.

Clorox argues that the district court committed clear error in finding that its Goldfish II television commercial and print advertisement contain literal falsehoods. We find no clear error in the district court's findings of fact in support of its conclusion that the Goldfish II television commercial and print advertisement are literally false as a factual matter. We note that the court made its finding of literal falsity after a seven-day bench trial. The evidence presented at trial clearly indicates that, as the court found, only slightly more than one out of ten Slide-Loc bags tested dripped at a rate of one drop per second or faster, while more than one-third of the Slide-Loc bags tested leaked at a rate of less than one drop per five seconds. Over half of the Slide-Loc bags tested either did not leak at all or leaked at a rate no faster than one drop per 20 seconds. Moreover, less than two-thirds, or 63 percent, of Slide-Loc bags tested showed any leakage at all when subjected to the testing on which Clorox based its Goldfish I and II advertisements.

The only Slide-Loc bag depicted in each of the two Goldfish II advertisements, on the other hand, is shown leaking and, when shown, is always leaking. Moreover, each time the Slide-Loc bag is on-screen, the Goldfish II television commercial shows a drop forming immediately and then falling from the Slide-Loc bag, all over a period of approximately two seconds. Accordingly, the commercial falsely depicts the risk of leakage for the vast majority of Slide-Loc bags tested.

Clorox argues that, because approximately eight seconds pass between the images of the drops forming and falling in the Goldfish II television commercial, the commercial depicts an accurate rate of leakage. However, the commercial does not continuously show the condition of the Slide-Loc bag because the Slide-Loc bag is off-screen for eight seconds. Likewise, the print ad does not depict any rate of leakage at all, other than to indicate that the Slide-Loc bag is "dripping." . . .

II. The district court committed no error of law.

. . . [T]he Goldfish II advertisement depicts a literal falsity . . . : that Slide-Loc bags always leak when filled with water and held upside down. . . .

244

. . . [I]f Clorox wants to portray water leakage from Slide-Loc bags, it must portray the rate of leakage accurately and indicate that only a certain percentage of bags leak, even when subjected to an extreme water "torture" test.

NOTES AND QUESTIONS

Why doesn't the court directly address the humor of the ads? Is the humor irrelevant to the falsity at issue, or did the court ignore an important aspect of the case? Could you make an argument that the offending image should be deemed puffery?

Why doesn't it matter that, as far as the record shows, Clorox's bags outperform Johnson's when it comes to leakage? How easy will it be to create a good ad that is more precise about the extent of Clorox's comparative advantage?

What happens if reasonable consumers would believe that the claim is exaggerated, but also believe that the claim is true to some degree, and they mistake the degree? Should this be actionable false advertising? Consider the famous Wendy's "Where's the Beef?" commercial. If a Wendy's burger is 5% bigger than a McDonald's burger, but a substantial number of consumers take away the message that the Wendy's burger is at least 25% bigger, then isn't the ad both funny and deceptive?

In *SmithKline Beecham Consumer Healthcare, L.P. v. Johnson & Johnson-Merck Consumer Pharmaceuticals Co.*, 19 Fed. Appx. 17 (2d Cir. 2001), SmithKline sued J&J for an ad comparing J&J's Pepcid Complete to Tums as heartburn treatments. Pepcid Complete, an acid blocker, decreases the production of acid in the stomach and can last for nine hours, while Tums, an antacid, neutralizes acid in the stomach and leaves the stomach in an hour or two. Many people receive complete relief from this because their acid production is time-limited, but some sufferers need to re-dose, and for them Pepcid Complete can provide superior relief.

The Pepcid Complete ad depicted

> a rumpled, slobby man vacuuming out his car. His car dashboard is littered with Tums tablets, food and other debris. The man picks up an old slice of pizza from among the trash and begins to eat it. The announcer asks, "Ever notice how many Tums you have around because your heartburn keeps coming back?" There is a pause in the vacuuming as the man looks quizzically down the vacuum hose, at which point the vacuum explodes, coating the man and the car with white powder. The Commercial then cuts to a shot of the Pepcid complete box, with the words "fast" and "seven times longer" superimposed on top. The announcer states, "There's a neater idea. New Pepcid Complete. It works as fast as Tums, but lasts seven times longer all in a chewable tablet." The Commercial returns to the slobby man, shown sitting in the front seat of his car, covered in white powder and attempting to vacuum himself. It closes with the announcer saying, "New Pepcid Complete. Just one and heartburn's done."

SmithKline argued that only a small percentage of Tums users actually needed to re-dose, and argued that the *S.C. Johnson* case supported its claim of literal falsity through exaggeration. The court of appeals disagreed, because the Leaky Goldfish ad

> targeted all consumers interested in the product by showcasing a flaw found only in a small percentage of the product. Here, the Commercial targets a small segment of consumers who may suffer continuing heartburn symptoms as a result of a characteristic common to all antacids: they work for less time than acid blockers do. There is no

246

showcasing of a product flaw, as both parties agree the effect of antacids lasts for only an hour or two. That all consumers may not need the extended period of protection offered by acid blockers does not render the Commercial literally false.

Is the court's distinction between the facts of this case and those of *S.C. Johnson* sensible? Are consumers more likely to know whether they fall into the class that needs to re-dose than they are to know whether Slide-Loc bags are risky for them? Could a reasonable consumer who was presently satisfied with Tums have been affected by the ad?

Other Exaggeration Cases. The law sometimes presumes that consumers are unlikely to accept vague or hyperbolic claims at face value. *See* Hansen Beverage Co. v. Vital Pharm., Inc., 2010 WL 1734960 (S.D. Cal. 2010) (the claim that an energy beverage "will leave you 'amped' to the max in minutes, ready to tear apart the weights and wear out the treadmill like a tiger released from its cage!" was puffery); Blue Cross v. Corcoran, 558 N.Y.S.2d 404 (App. Div. 1990) ("Remember, if you don't have Blue Cross, you're not covered" so obviously false that it was neither intended nor likely to be taken literally by people of average education and intelligence). Where an ad for a dry shaver portrayed wet shavers as snakes biting, bees stinging, and flamethrowers burning, a court concluded that these derogatory exaggerations were based on colloquialisms used to describe the actual pain of wet shaving, and that it was not deceptive to exaggerate their underlying meaning "beyond the point of believability, in order to ensure that that underlying message is conveyed." *See* Gillette Co. v. Norelco Consumer Prods. Co., 946 F. Supp. 115 (D. Mass. 1996). What makes the claims in *Clorox* any different from the exaggerated representations of the pain of wet shaving?

In *Time Warner Cable, Inc. v. DirecTV, Inc.*, 497 F.3d 144 (2nd Cir. 2007), Time Warner offered both analog and digital signals, but its competitor DirecTV had only digital service. Both offered high-definition (HD) service on a limited number of channels. The parties agreed that the HD services were equivalent in picture quality. For non-HD channels, digital is generally better than analog, because it resists interference. But Time Warner's analog service met FCC requirements for a signal that provides "enjoyable viewing with barely perceptible impairments."

DirecTV began an ad campaign to educate consumers that, even with an HD TV set, one must also receive HD programming from the TV service provider in order to enjoy an HD picture. Among other things, it ran Internet ads showing unwatchable TV images contrasted to sharp and clear images, labeled "Other TV" and "DirecTV," and inviting consumers to "Find out why DirecTV's picture beats Cable."

DirecTV didn't dispute that the highly pixelated images it used in its Internet ads were inaccurate depictions of cable picture quality, whether digital or analog. Thus, the Internet ads were explicitly and literally false. But DirecTV argued that they were also so exaggerated that no reasonable buyer would believe them—negative puffery. But, according to Time Warner, DirecTV's own rationale for running the ads—that consumers were highly confused about HD technology and needed to be educated that both digital equipment and digital signals were required to experience HD quality—was reason to think that consumers might rely on the ads.

The court of appeals observed that prior puffery cases didn't offer good principles for evaluating images. "Unlike words, images cannot be vague or broad." While one standard definition of puffery—general claims of superiority that are so vague as to be meaningless—fits images badly, the other—"an exaggerated, blustering, and boasting statement upon which no reasonable buyer would be justified in relying," could be applied.

The court of appeals found that the district court clearly erred in accepting Time Warner's argument about consumer uncertainty. The "other TV" images in the Internet ads were extremely bad— "unwatchably blurry, distorted, and pixelated, and . . . nothing like the images a customer would ordinarily see using Time Warner Cable's cable service," according to Time Warner's senior network engineer. Indeed, the pixelation was "not the type of disruption[] that could naturally happen to an analog or non-HD digital cable picture." Thus, the ads were not even remotely realistic, and the court found it difficult to imagine that any consumer, no matter how unsophisticated, could be fooled into thinking cable's picture quality would be that bad. The court accepted DirecTV's argument that even a person who didn't know anything about cable would know that Time Warner couldn't supply an unwatchable signal and still survive in the market. The comparison of DirecTV picture quality to basic cable picture quality was so "obviously hyperbolic" that no reasonable buyer would be justified in relying on it.

Was the district court clearly erroneous to accept Time Warner's argument about the transitioning market? A new HD customer might know that "ordinarily" her cable wouldn't be anything near that bad. But would she have been confident about what cable would look like when she attached an analog cable feed to her new HD TV?

Should courts treat negative puffery differently than positive puffery, or are the justifications for discounting both equally persuasive?

With the Time Warner case in mind, consider the following images from McDonald's and Burger King ads paired with pictures of actual burgers. Do you think the ads are puffery because everyone knows fast food burgers don't look like that? Or actionable because it is possible for burgers to look like that, but these companies' burgers don't? (Credit Dario D.)

[Burger King Whopper]

[McDonald's Angus Deluxe Third Pounder]

McDonald's freely acknowledges the discrepancy between its ads and the food delivered in its stores. In New Zealand, it provided the following graphic:

...and explanation (from
http://yourquestions.mcdonalds.co.nz/questions/20842):

> ...when we prepare a Macca's burger for its moment in front
> of the camera, there's a lot of time spent getting it looking
> picture-perfect.
>
> Just like a family portrait, we want our burgers presented at
> their very best. So while the burgers seen in the images are
> the same size with the same ingredients, it's important to
> note that they've been slowly assembled, expertly lit and
> professionally photographed over a lengthy period of time.
>
> When it comes to a burger we serve up in our restaurants, we
> want the choice ingredients assembled and served up quickly
> to ensure it stays warm and ready for you to eat, which is why
> you might find that it's not identical to the one you see in our
> advertisements.

We also encourage you to watch the short YouTube video "Behind the scenes at a McDonald's photo shoot," June 19, 2012.

When McDonald's admits that the ad images are "not identical" to the in-store delivery, has it conceded that its ads are false? Or, by educating consumers that the ads are dramatized depictions, is McDonald's actually improving a potential puffery defense?

Finally, consider that very subtle tweaks in ads may have profound effects. Could they still be puffery? When researchers tested the images below, 60% of consumers thought that a paid spokesperson was a medical expert when she was shown with a background image of blue products versus 23% when she was shown with a white background. Is the background misleading? *See* Chris Jay Hoofnagle & Eduard Meleshinsky, Native Advertising and Endorsement: Schema, Source-Based Misleadingness, and Omission of Material Facts, Technology Science, Dec. 15, 2015.

5. Falsity

We arrive now at the core of advertising regulation: falsity. But how do we know what claims are false? Context—both general social knowledge and other information conveyed by the ad—is often vital, as is the substantiation possessed by the advertiser for its claims. As we will discuss, certain types of factual claims pose particular challenges for the law. For example, we will consider whether claims based on the placebo effect—real, but created solely by the claim itself—can be true.

A basic tenet of modern advertising law is that falsity and misleadingness are actionable, even if the advertiser did not intend to deceive. In that sense, liability for false advertising is strict. Bad intent may be relevant to trigger various presumptions or increase damages, but it is not required. Here, American law is consistent with European law. *See* CHS Tour Serv. GmbH v. Team4 Travel GmbH, Case C-435/11 (E.C.J. 2013) (holding that the advertiser's exercise of due diligence didn't protect against a determination that a claim was false or misleading).

A.   Advertising Claims in the Context of the Ad

Advertising claims must always be interpreted with reference to the other elements—the context—of the ad in which they appear. "Fundamental to any task of interpretation is the principle that text must yield to context, and that a court must view the 'entire mosaic' of the advertisement rather than 'each tile separately.' " Avis Rent-A-Car Sys., Inc. v. Hertz Corp., 782 F.2d 381 (2d Cir. 1986). The context of the ad may modify the explicit message of the ad as a whole (as is the case with a sufficiently prominent and effective disclaimer, see Chapter 5), or it may change the implicit message.

In the context of an ad for a headache remedy, then, the claim that "nothing is better than Advil" does not mean that (1) Advil is better than everything else in the world or (2) it is better to use nothing than to use Advil. Rather, it means that nothing beats Advil at treating headaches.[3] The fact that the ad is about headaches provides interpretive guidance, as in contract law. Likewise, when Avis challenged the statement that "Hertz has more new cars than Avis has cars," Avis initially won an injunction when it was able to show that it *owned* as many cars as Hertz did, if cars in its corporate fleet and cars it had put up for sale were counted. But on appeal, the Second Circuit reversed: in context, the ad was a claim about the number of new cars *available for rental*. The ad was targeted to potential renters, rather than car buyers or financial analysts; it showed a rental lot; and the text three times referred to rentals.

Avis is an example of truth in context. But context can also show falsity. When an international pharmacy advertised "FDA guidelines let you import drugs for your personal use. . . . If a drug you use is on our list, order today," the first statement was true standing alone but false combined with the second statement, because the FDA did not in fact allow importation of certain drugs on the pharmacy's list. Syntex (U.S.A.), Inc. v. Interpharm, Inc., 1993 WL 643372 (N.D. Ga. 1993). Proximity of claims to each other can often affect whether the claims are false. For example, ads for Anacin appeared to claim that it had a unique pain-killing formula that was proven superior to all other over-the-counter analgesics. If "read with sedulous attention," however, the challenged advertising actually claimed only that Anacin was (1) **as** effective as the leading prescription analgesic and

---

[3] One of the casebook's authors suggested rewording this statement as "Advil is the best way to treat headaches." Note the success of the advertiser's implication even with this highly ad-savvy and careful lawyer: the *formal* logical meaning of "nothing beats Advil" is not that Advil is the best, but that it has no superior. Other methods of treatment could be equal, and the explicit claim would still be true. However, the advertiser wants the audience to believe that Advil is the *best*—and seems to have succeeded! If other treatments are in fact equal, then the explicit claim is true but the implicit message is false. Recall this example when we consider implication.

(2) had more pain reliever than other over-the-counter analgesics. Am. Home Prod. Corp. v. FTC, 695 F.2d 681 (3d Cir. 1982). The court of appeals declined to parse the claims with lawyerly precision. Instead, it noted that the ad was "designed to resemble a clipping from a medical journal" that gave the impression of clinical accuracy, and that, by claiming equivalence to prescription medicine, the ad appeared to claim superiority to other over-the-counter medicines. A magistrate judge reached a similar conclusion with the juxtaposition of two claims on the following package:

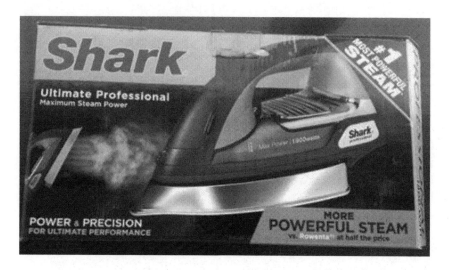

The "#1 Most Powerful Steam*" claim was qualified by additional information about the models to which the advertiser was comparing its product, while "More Powerful Steam vs. Rowenta*† at half the price" was qualified by *different* additional information comparing different Rowenta models. This juxtaposition was literally false. Moreover, the court used the definition of "power" set forth in the packaging's footnote, because "[w]hen a product's packaging includes an advertising claim and unambiguously defines a claim term, the packaging's definition of the claim term applies to the claim's explicit message." Grpe. SEB USA, Inc. v. Euro-Pro Operating LLC, 774 F.3d 192 (3d Cir. 2014). As you will see in Chapter 5, fine print can't redefine a term that is misleading on its own, but the problem here was different: the defendant made a claim based on a particular kind of evidence, and then when its evidence was proven false, said that it didn't mean to rely on that kind of evidence.

B.   Literally False Claims, also Known as Explicitly False Claims

Explicitly or literally false statements violate the Lanham Act without further proof of consumer deception: courts presume that consumers receive the false message. In many circuits, showing that a claim is literally false also entitles a plaintiff to various other presumptions in its favor. But the biggest advantage for a Lanham Act plaintiff in arguing literal falsity is the avoidance of an expensive and no doubt hotly contested consumer survey showing what consumers actually perceive the message of the ad to be. For this reason, Lanham Act cases focus intensely on the difference between literally false and implicitly false (misleading) claims. We will spend more time on this distinction in Chapter 6. For other types of cases, the distinction is less vital; the FTC, state attorneys general and the NAD all consider themselves capable of determining misleadingness without consumer reaction evidence. Still, the more expressly a false claim is made, the less likely a court is to be sympathetic to the advertiser, so even in non–Lanham Act cases the distinction is worth keeping in mind.

Express claims are stated literally in an ad. They may be verbal or visual. An example of a visually deceptive ad featured images of two identical gas pumps or airline tickets with varying prices accompanied by the slogan "Which one would you choose?" This was literally false because it made a claim that, like the gas and the tickets, the advertised drug was completely equivalent to the competitor. Rhone-Poulenc Rorer Pharms., Inc. v. Marion Merrell Dow, Inc., 93 F.3d 511 (8th Cir. 1996). In another case, an ad showing an orange being squeezed directly into a carton was literally false because the juice was actually made from pasteurized, and occasionally frozen, oranges. *Coca Cola Co. v. Tropicana Prods., Inc.*, 690 F.2d 312 (2nd Cir. 1982). How good do you think courts are at translating images into express word claims? Do you agree that showing two tickets is a claim of complete equivalence, or that consumers would perceive the juice ad as a representation that the oranges didn't undergo any processing?

Literally false claims come in many flavors; scientific testing (or its absence) isn't always required to establish falsity. The following are some examples:

- A claim that a dictionary was "The Authentic Webster's"
- Claims to offer the "same," "identical," and "duplicate" cigars as more expensive makers, where the defendant made no attempt to duplicate the origin or regional conditions of the tobacco used in the expensive cigars
- Claims that dog food was "specially formulated" into twelve varieties targeted toward particular dog types, when in fact the manufacturer simply repackaged a few types of kibble into those varieties

Would you have found any of these to be puffery?

Claims of *uniqueness* can be particularly troublesome. Doan's advertised itself as the "back specialist" of analgesics, but it didn't do any better with back pain than other analgesics. Thus, its claim of specialization was false. *In re* Novartis Corp., No. 9279, 1999 WL 353248 (F.T.C. May 13, 1999), *aff'd*, 223 F.3d 783 (D.C. Cir. 2000). In an attempt to avoid negative associations with aspirin, other analgesic manufacturers touted their products as "unique," having a "unique formula," or "uniquely effective"; these were all false because the products were all essentially aspirin. *See, e.g.*, Sterling Drug, Inc. v. Federal Trade Comm'n, 741 F.2d 1146 (9th Cir. 1984). Similarly, it was false for a maker of hemorrhoid medication to claim to offer a "new medication" and a "major advance" when the only new aspect of the product was its suppository form. *See* Am. Home Prods. Corp. v. Abbott Labs., 522 F. Supp. 1035 (S.D.N.Y. 1981).

Other *individual words* can be false. In *Kraft General Foods, Inc. v. Del Monte Corp.*, 28 U.S.P.Q.2d 1457 (S.D.N.Y. 1993), the court found the use of the word "gelatin" literally false to describe snacks made from carageenan, a substance derived from seaweed, reserving use of the term to traditional animal-based "gelatin." Another court found the name BreathAsure literally false for a capsule that did nothing to produce or sustain fresh breath. Warner-Lambert Co. v. BreathAsure, Inc., 204 F.3d 87 (3d Cir. 2000).

Some kinds of *exaggerations* have been treated as expressly false, perhaps because the context makes exaggeration seem real. This occurred in the *S.C. Johnson* "leaky goldfish" case, excerpted above, where the court interpreted the defendant's ads to claim that the competitor's bags would "always leak," rather than leak sixty-three percent of the time (compared to a much lower percentage for the advertiser's bags). Similarly, the First Circuit found that a claim that "whiter is not possible" than the results achieved with "Ace con Blanqueador" detergent might be literally false if, as the plaintiff alleged, tests proved that chlorine bleach produced better results. Clorox Co. Puerto Rico v. Proctor & Gamble Commercial Co., 228 F.3d 24 (1st Cir. 2000). But exaggeration may also be puffery, or perhaps at most implicit falsehood—consider the classic Wendy's "Where's the Beef?" campaign mocking the size of other chain restaurants' burgers. The ambiguity of the exaggerations and the likelihood that reasonable consumers would perceive the exaggeration to be truthful are key to drawing the line between an unacceptable exaggeration and one that may survive scrutiny.

Overgeneralizations can also be literally false. An advertisement claiming that one manufacturer's tractors had "approximately three times as many failures" as the advertiser's was literally false because the language was "overinclusive, drawing no distinction between mowing and garden tractors, and offering no specificity as to the kinds of tractors that [defendant's] engineers tested." Garden Way Inc. v. The Home Depot Inc., 94 F. Supp. 2d 276 (N.D.N.Y. 2000). The advertiser tested only three units of a single model. Vastly overclaiming the scope of its test constituted falsity.

Slight qualifications, however, unrelated to the core advertising claim, are unlikely to make an advertisement literally false. For example, a computer manufacturer alleged that a competing advertiser's claims to be "100% compatible" and "fully compatible" with the manufacturer's products were false, because the advertiser's products would give prefailure warnings at different times than the manufacturer's products and were slightly different physically. The court determined that "compatibility" meant that the products would work or function with the manufacturer's products, and dismissed the manufacturer's claims because they did not refute the core advertising promise. *See* Compaq Comput. Corp. v. Procom Tech., Inc., 908 F. Supp. 1409 (S.D. Tex. 1995).

Situations of this sort may also be handled under the heading of puffery or materiality (whether it would make a difference to consumers). If a court finds a claim to be puffery, it will not accept evidence of consumer confusion. If the court instead thinks that the qualification means that the claim is not literally false but still potentially misleading, then extrinsic evidence of confusion becomes relevant, and even required in a Lanham Act case. When the qualification is one that may be immaterial, courts have not been entirely clear about the standard they are applying. One court found that a claim that a miter saw offered "4,000 RPM" was not false because, although a test found the actual speed to be 3,650 RPM, this was "an acceptable variance speed." Black & Decker (U.S.) Inc. v. Pro-Tech Power Inc., 26 F. Supp. 2d 834, 863 (E.D. Va. 1998). How should the fact finder determine what sort of variance is "acceptable"?

For an example that may hit closer to home, consider the results of empirical testing finding that, in fact, Double Stuf Oreos only contain roughly 1.9 times the "stuf" of regular Oreos. Dan Anderson, *Oreo Verification*, http://blog.recursiveprocess.com/2013/08/20/oreo-verification/, Aug. 20, 2013. Is "Double Stuf" a literally false claim?

Even unavoidable falsity may be deemed literally false. In *Playtex Prods., LLC v. Munchkin, Inc.*, 2016 WL 1276450 (S.D.N.Y. Mar. 29, 2016), Munchkin made bags to refill Playtex's diaper pail, the Diaper Genie. When it redesigned the Diaper Genie, Playtex informed Munchkin that its refills wouldn't fit the redesigned products. When Playtex began selling the redesigned versions, Munchkin responded that, beginning on March 17, 2014, it would put an orange sticker on its refills that said that the refills were guaranteed to fit all Diaper Genie pails bought before March 1, 2014, and that new refills would be coming soon to fit the new Diaper Genies.

The court found that, between March 1 and March 17, 2014, Munchkin's fit claims were literally false because they failed to disclose that the refills wouldn't fit the newly released redesigned Diaper Genies. The fit claims were also material and caused harm to Playtex, so Playtex won summary judgment as to Munchkin's liability for this period. Query: what, if anything, could Munchkin have done to avoid this result on liability? Pulled the product entirely? Pre-stickered with an open-ended date, which might be more confusing? Limited its guarantee to pails sold before 2014, even though it could indeed guarantee fit for pails sold in the first three months of 2014?

C.   Constraining the Boundaries of Literal Falsity?

Sometimes courts just don't think one side deserves to win, and they may create new rules that explain why. In *Schering-Plough Healthcare Products, Inc. v. Schwarz Pharma, Inc.*, 586 F.3d 500 (7th Cir. 2009), plaintiff Schering had FDA approval to sell a laxative over the counter (OTC). Defendant Schwarz sold a generic version of the same laxative, but only had approval to sell it as a prescription drug. This created a problem under FDA rules, which require generics to have the exact same labels as the original drug. The label on Schwarz's version of the laxative differed from Schering's label in two ways: it contained the prescription-only warning, and it omitted a warning to "use [for] no more than 7 days" that the FDA had required as part of the Schering's OTC approval.

Under FDA rules, it seemed that Schwarz was both required to use an identical label and barred from doing so (since its product was still prescription-only and the additional warning was not approved for its label). The FDA was looking into the matter, but Schering decided to litigate under the Lanham Act, perhaps because the FDA was likely to take a long time to act. Schering argued that Schwarz's labels were false, because the drug was not "prescription only," and because patients wouldn't realize that, if their conditions changed and they didn't need to use the drug for more than seven days, they could buy the OTC version.

[defendants' labels]

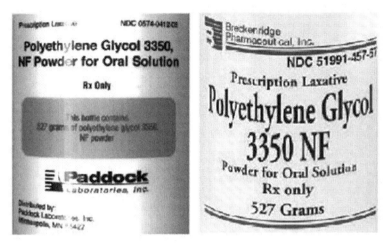

[defendants' patient information inserts]

PATIENT INFORMATION

Polyethylene Glycol 3350, NF Powder for Oral Solution is a prescription only laxative which has been prescribed by your physician to treat constipation.

PATIENT INFORMATION
Polyethylene Glycol 3350 NF (Polyethylene Glycol 3350 Powder for Oral Solution) is a prescription only laxative which has been prescribed by your physician to treat constipation. This product should only be used by the person for whom it was prescribed.

Writing for the court of appeals, Judge Posner ruled that Schering was mistaken to argue that all it needed to show was "literal falsity":

> The purpose of the false-advertising provisions of the Lanham Act is to protect sellers from having their customers lured away from them by deceptive ads (or labels, or other promotional materials). Many literally false statements are

263

not deceptive. When the Soviet Union in the 1930s declared that "2 + 2 = 5," it was not deceiving anyone; it was announcing a slogan designed to spur workers to complete the Five-Year Plan in four years. If one opened the *New York Times* "literally" at random one might find an ad that calls Graff Diamonds "The Most Fabulous Jewels in the World." That is literally false because the jewels sold by Graff are no more fabulous than, say, the Crown Jewels of England, or the Hope Diamond. But no one is deceived, so there is no injury, and a suit by a competitor of Graff would fail. The cases that reject liability do so in the name of "puffery"—meaningless superlatives—but the principle cuts deeper; if no one is or could be fooled, no one is or could be hurt.

The other side of this coin is that a representation may be so obviously misleading that there is no need to gather evidence that anyone was confused. And it is often clearer that a claim is misleading than that it is literally false, because what is "literally" false is often a semantic question.

What the cases mean when they say that proof of literal falsity allows the plaintiff to dispense with evidence that anyone was misled or likely to be misled is that the seller who places an indisputably false statement in his advertising or labeling probably did so for a malign purpose, namely to sell his product by lies, and if the statement is false probably at least some people were misled, and since it was a lie why waste time on costly consumer surveys? When this is stated as the doctrine of "literal falsity," "literal" must be understood in the common colloquial sense in which Americans . . . say things like "I am literally out of my mind." A "literal" falsehood is bald-faced, egregious, undeniable, over the top.

We know this is what the cases are driving at because they add to "literal falsity" such qualifiers as that the meaning of the alleged literal falsehood must be considered in context and with reference to the audience to which the statement is addressed. That is how one obtains an understanding of the real meaning of "2 + 2 = 5" in Soviet propaganda.

The proper domain of "literal falsity" as a doctrine that dispenses with proof that anyone was misled or likely to be misled is the patently false statement that means what it says to any linguistically competent person, unlike the examples we have given. So suppose the labels on the defendants' products stated: "All polyethylene glycol 3350, by whomever made, can be sold only by prescription; there is no over-the-counter version of this drug." That would be false and misleading per se; there would be no need to consider context or audience.

But that is not what the labels say. There is no statement in the ordinary sense, because there is no verb. There is the manufacturer's name at the top, the name of the active ingredient, the symbol "Rx only," and some other information. Obviously this product, the product of the named manufacturer, is prescription only, but it is not obvious . . . that every other product containing polyethylene glycol 3350 is prescription only. Schering cannot just intone "literal falsity" and by doing so prove a violation of the Lanham Act. . . .

Does the opinion import a fault requirement into the Lanham Act? Are many of the literal falsehoods described in this chapter "bald-faced, egregious, undeniable, [or] over the top"? Is it enough that they are, on the weight of the evidence, wrong? Consider the line of cases, to be discussed below, about claims that "tests prove" that a product works. If the tests on which the advertiser relies don't actually prove that the product works, because the plaintiff shows the tests to be unreliable or insufficient even if reliable, the defendant loses. How would Judge Posner analyze such cases?

Similarly, should a false ad require a "statement in the ordinary sense," including a verb? Could "55 MPG" be a false representation on a car ad? How would Posner deal with an allegedly false image, such as two identical gas pumps used to indicate that two drugs were equivalent?

Another example of creative reinterpretation of the concept of "literal falsity" came from In re *GNC Corp.*, 789 F.3d 505 (4th Cir. 2015), in which the court held that "marketing statements that accurately describe the findings of duly qualified and reasonable scientific experts are not literally false," and that a plaintiff must plead that *no* reasonable scientist would agree with defendant's claims in order to plead literal falsity. This was a class action case purporting to borrow Lanham Act standards, though you should be able to see that it was in fact a serious reinterpretation (not to say misreading) of them.

D.   Substantiation

FTC Substantiation Policy

The FTC takes the position that advertisers are "required to have substantiation not just for express statements but for all reasonable interpretations of their advertisements," and courts have followed its lead. *See* Fed. Trade Comm'n v. Lights of Am., Inc., No. 10-1333 (C.D. Cal. Sept. 17, 2013). Here, the FTC explains its general thinking on substantiation.

FTC Policy Statement Regarding Advertising Substantiation, appended to Thompson Medical Co., 104 F.T.C. 648, 839 (1984), aff'd, 791 F.2d 189 (D.C. Cir. 1986)

. . . The Reasonable Basis Requirement

First, we reaffirm our commitment to the underlying legal requirement of advertising substantiation—that advertisers and ad agencies have a reasonable basis for advertising claims before they are disseminated.

The Commission intends to continue vigorous enforcement of this existing legal requirement that advertisers substantiate express and implied claims, however conveyed, that make objective assertions about the item or service advertised. Objective claims for products or services represent explicitly or by implication that the advertiser has a reasonable basis supporting these claims. These representations of substantiation are material to consumers. That is, consumers would be less likely to rely on claims for products and services if they knew the advertiser did not have a reasonable basis for believing them to be true.[2] Therefore, a firm's failure to possess and rely upon a reasonable basis for objective claims constitutes an unfair and deceptive act or practice in violation of Section 5 of the Federal Trade Commission Act.

Standards for Prior Substantiation

Many ads contain express or implied statements regarding the amount of support the advertiser has for the product claim. When the substantiation claim is express (e.g., "tests prove", "doctors recommend", and "studies show"), the Commission expects the firm to

---

[2] Nor presumably would an advertiser have made such claims unless the advertiser thought they would be material to consumers.

have at least the advertised level of substantiation. Of course, an ad may imply more substantiation than it expressly claims or may imply to consumers that the firm has a certain type of support; in such cases, the advertiser must possess the amount and type of substantiation the ad actually communicates to consumers.

Absent an express or implied reference to a certain level of support, and absent other evidence indicating what consumer expectations would be, the Commission assumes that consumers expect a "reasonable basis" for claims. The Commission's determination of what constitutes a reasonable basis depends, as it does in an unfairness analysis, on a number of factors relevant to the benefits and costs of substantiating a particular claim. These factors include: the type of claim, the product, the consequences of a false claim, the benefits of a truthful claim, the cost of developing substantiation for the claim, and the amount of substantiation experts in the field believe is reasonable. Extrinsic evidence, such as expert testimony or consumer surveys, is useful to determine what level of substantiation consumers expect to support a particular product claim and the adequacy of evidence an advertiser possesses.

One issue the Commission examined was substantiation for implied claims. Although firms are unlikely to possess substantiation for implied claims they do not believe the ad makes, they should generally be aware of reasonable interpretations and will be expected to have prior substantiation for such claims. The Commission will take care to assure that it only challenges reasonable interpretations of advertising claims. . . .

NOTES AND QUESTIONS

Ex Post and Ex Ante Regulations. The substantiation requirement is broader than the no-falsity rule in a variety of ways. How will advertisers' behavior differ when substantiation is added to the no-falsity rule? For an economic model suggesting that, even setting aside enforcement cost issues, a substantiation requirement will improve the quality of information in the marketplace by encouraging marketers to invest in testing and to reveal information about their products, see Kenneth S. Cortsa, *Prohibitions on False and Unsubstantiated Claims: Inducing the Acquisition and Revelation of Information Through Competition Policy*, 56 J.L. & ECON. 453 (2013). A study by John Samuel Healey found mixed results: the substantiation policy reduced ambiguous statements where the consumer was expected to fill in the details and led instead to claims that "were either 'pure pap' or very factual in nature." Healy found that advertisers made fewer claims after the substantiation policy came into effect, but not that the studied products were advertised in a more informative way overall. John Samuel Healey, The Federal Trade Commission Advertising Substantiation Program and Changes in the Content of Advertising in Selected Industries (1978) (Ph.D. dissertation, University of California, Los Angeles, CA).

The Relationship between Testimonials and Substantiation. The FTC has more specific statements about certain types of substantiation. At one time, the FTC took the position that, while all ads needed to be assessed on their own merits, it would generally regard a clear "results not typical" disclaimer as sufficient when the advertiser was touting a testimonial by a consumer who'd achieved spectacular results. Research accumulated that this disclaimer simply did not work, however, and the FTC issued a revised guide in 2009.

FTC Guides Concerning the Use of Endorsements and Testimonials in Advertising, § 255.2 Consumer Endorsements

(a) An advertisement employing endorsements by one or more consumers about the performance of an advertised product or service will be interpreted as representing that the product or service is effective for the purpose depicted in the advertisement. Therefore, the advertiser must possess and rely upon adequate substantiation, including, when appropriate, competent and reliable scientific evidence, to support such claims made through endorsements in the same manner the advertiser would be required to do if it had made the representation directly, i.e., without using endorsements. Consumer endorsements themselves are not competent and reliable scientific evidence.

(b) An advertisement containing an endorsement relating the experience of one or more consumers on a central or key attribute of the product or service also will likely be interpreted as representing that the endorser's experience is representative of what consumers will generally achieve with the advertised product or service in actual, albeit variable, conditions of use. Therefore, an advertiser should possess and rely upon adequate substantiation for this representation. If the advertiser does not have substantiation that the endorser's experience is representative of what consumers will generally achieve, the advertisement should clearly and conspicuously disclose the generally expected performance in the depicted circumstances, and the advertiser must possess and rely on adequate substantiation for that representation.[1] . . .

---

[1] The Commission tested the communication of advertisements containing testimonials that clearly and prominently disclosed either "Results not typical" or the stronger "These testimonials are based on the experiences of a few people and you are not likely to have similar results." Neither disclosure adequately reduced the communication that the experiences depicted are generally representative. Based upon this research, the Commission believes that similar disclaimers regarding the limited applicability of an endorser's experience to what consumers may generally expect to achieve are unlikely to be effective.

Nonetheless, the Commission cannot rule out the possibility that a strong disclaimer of typicality could be effective in the context of a particular advertisement. Although the Commission would have the burden of proof in a law enforcement action, the Commission notes that an advertiser possessing reliable empirical testing demonstrating that the net impression of its

Example 1: A brochure for a baldness treatment consists entirely of testimonials from satisfied customers who say that after using the product, they had amazing hair growth and their hair is as thick and strong as it was when they were teenagers. The advertiser must have competent and reliable scientific evidence that its product is effective in producing new hair growth.

The ad will also likely communicate that the endorsers' experiences are representative of what new users of the product can generally expect. Therefore, even if the advertiser includes a disclaimer such as, "Notice: These testimonials do not prove our product works. You should not expect to have similar results," the ad is likely to be deceptive unless the advertiser has adequate substantiation that new users typically will experience results similar to those experienced by the testimonialists.

Example 2: An advertisement disseminated by a company that sells heat pumps presents endorsements from three individuals who state that after installing the company's heat pump in their homes, their monthly utility bills went down by $100, $125, and $150, respectively. The ad will likely be interpreted as conveying that such savings are representative of what consumers who buy the company's heat pump can generally expect. The advertiser does not have substantiation for that representation because, in fact, less than 20% of purchasers will save $100 or more. A disclosure such as, "Results not typical" or, "These testimonials are based on the experiences of a few people and you are not likely to have similar results" is insufficient to prevent this ad from being deceptive because consumers will still interpret the ad as conveying that the specified savings are representative of what consumers can generally expect. The ad is less likely to be

---

advertisement with such a disclaimer is non-deceptive will avoid the risk of the initiation of such an action in the first instance.

deceptive if it clearly and conspicuously discloses the generally expected savings and the advertiser has adequate substantiation that homeowners can achieve those results. There are multiple ways that such a disclosure could be phrased, e.g., "the average homeowner saves $35 per month," "the typical family saves $50 per month during cold months and $20 per month in warm months," or "most families save 10% on their utility bills." . . .

Example 7: An advertisement for a recently released motion picture shows three individuals coming out of a theater, each of whom gives a positive statement about the movie. These individuals are actual consumers expressing their personal views about the movie. The advertiser does not need to have substantiation that their views are representative of the opinions that most consumers will have about the movie. Because the consumers' statements would be understood to be the subjective opinions of only three people, this advertisement is not likely to convey a typicality message.

NOTES AND QUESTIONS

FTC Guidance. Given the two documents above, how would you think about clearing proposed ads for a client? For example, suppose your client wanted to advertise a new sneaker with the claim, "The construction is built for support and enhanced agility in your workout, on the track or off." What kinds of claims are being made? Is the client making a representation about performance? About the risk of injury? What sort of substantiation would you ask for? How, if at all, would the concept of puffery fit into your analysis? What kind of substantiation would you ask for if the client wanted to run a TV ad showing a model wearing the sneakers outside, who says, "These sneakers give me great support, and I've never had an easier workout!" A lawyer reviewing an ad should always think about ethical and attractive alternatives; your job is not simply to say yes or no, but to assist in developing a truthful message. This can require you to discuss alternative possible claims with your clients.

Substantiation of Scientific Claims—What Is the Appropriate Standard?

The FTC and courts have been willing to require a significant amount of evidence for strong claims. For example, "[w]here an advertiser makes claims using specific figures or facts, a high level of substantiation, such as scientific or engineering tests, is required." Fed. Trade Comm'n v. Lights of Am., Inc., No. 10-1333 (C.D. Cal. Sept. 17, 2013).

In several consent decrees for advertisers who had made insufficiently substantiated health claims for their products, such as claims that drinking "probiotic" yogurt would reduce the chances of getting a cold or the flu, the FTC articulated a high substantiation standard for future health claims. *See, e.g.,* Federal Trade Commission, File No. 082 3158, The Dannon Company, Inc.; Analysis of Proposed Consent Order to Aid Public Comment, Federal Register/Vol. 75, No. 244, December 21, 2010, p. 80051.

In the probiotic yogurt case, for example, Dannon was prohibited from claiming "that a covered product [yogurt products identified in the order] reduces the likelihood of getting a cold or the flu unless the FDA has issued a regulation authorizing the claim based on a finding that there is significant scientific agreement among experts qualified by scientific training and experience to evaluate such claims, considering the totality of publicly available scientific evidence."

Dannon *could* make a claim "characterizing limited scientific evidence supporting the relationship between a covered product and a reduced likelihood of getting a cold or the flu." But Dannon did so at substantial risk: "[I]f the net impression of that advertising is that the covered product reduces the likelihood of getting a cold or the flu, and not merely that there is limited scientific evidence supporting the claim," the advertisement would violate the consent decree. Thus, if consumers interpreted limited claims as making broader claims about the evidence, Dannon could suffer potentially severe sanctions.

The day after the FTC settlement was publicly announced, a Dannon spokesperson said, "After 3 rigorous reviews, we continue to market the products as per usual." He also emphasized that Dannon admitted no wrongdoing in connection with the settlement, and noted that only $1 million had been claimed out of a potential fund of $35 million that was established in a 2009 class action settlement, although the remainder of the fund would be remitted to charities. However, Dannon also entered into a $21 million settlement with 39 states, which added a periodic compliance monitoring requirement. What factors might have convinced Dannon to enter into the FTC and state settlements?

As Dannon's lawyer, how would you work to ensure compliance? Under these circumstances, what sort of scientific evidence would you require before allowing your client to make such claims? Aside from the scientific evidence, would you also require copy testing to make sure consumers understand the limitations of the claims before authorizing a large-scale ad campaign? Given the costs of these tests, would you expect your client to make many health claims?

The FTC also attempted to give more precision to the substantiation requirement in an administrative proceeding against Pom Wonderful (Pom), which had long made aggressive claims about the health benefits of its pomegranate products, with ads like this one:

With respect to a number of ads, the FTC found that reasonable consumers would indeed receive an implied claim that the Pom products treated, prevented, or reduced the risk of heart disease, prostate cancer, or erectile dysfunction, and some of the ads falsely conveyed the further message that these effects were clinically proven. The ad's references to the described studies as "promising," "initial" or "preliminary," in context, were insufficient to neutralize the otherwise unequivocally positive claims of specific results. As the FTC held, the "use of one or two adjectives does not alter the net impression," especially "when the chosen adjectives" (such as "promising") "provide a positive spin on the studies rather than a substantive disclaimer."

The FTC complaint counsel argued that two double-blind, placebo-controlled, randomized clinical trials—the kind of evidence required by the FDA before approving a prescription drug—were required to substantiate health claims of the sort made by Pom. A majority of the commissioners agreed, but the D.C. Circuit modified the relief ordered. Under *Central Hudson*, a requirement that Pom have at least one well-conducted randomized clinical trial supporting any health claim that it made was justified, but not a two-trial requirement. POM Wonderful, LLC v. Fed. Trade Comm'n, 777 F.3d

478 (D.C. Cir. 2015). If two randomized clinical trials were required, consumers might be "denied useful, truthful information about products with a demonstrated capacity to treat or prevent serious disease." A single trial that was good enough, and supported by other evidence, might justify a disease-related claim. The court noted that two-trial requirements had been upheld in the past, but found them limited to specific situations where experts agreed that replication was necessary given the limitations of the data.

In general, in order to determine the appropriate level of substantiation required for a claim, the FTC considers (1) the amount of substantiation experts in the field would consider to be sufficient, (2) the products involved, (3) the type of claim, (4) the benefits of a truthful claim, (5) the ease of developing substantiation for the claim, and (6) the consequences of a false claim. In *POM*, the Commission reasoned, although Pom's product was a well-known food generally known to be safe, it was making a health claim, which justified a high standard. With or without explicit "clinically proven" language, Pom's claims weren't sufficiently substantiated, since experts in the relevant scientific communities would require the same level of substantiation for the claim in either form. The economic injury was also significant, since consuming pomegranate products at the level suggested by Pom would cost a consumer hundreds of dollars per year.

Pom argued that randomized clinical trials are expensive, which is true, but the Court of Appeals emphasized that POM could choose to specify a lower level of substantiation with an effective disclaimer.

NOTES AND QUESTIONS

The *POM Wonderful* decision appears to accept that in the modern world, consumers are likely to perceive some types of claims—health claims prominent among them—as based on scientific evidence even if there aren't explicit statements to that effect. Is that a reasonable conclusion?

If consumers do in fact receive disease prevention/treatment messages from health claims made by food or supplement producers, why *not* require those claims to meet the same standards as would be required if a drug manufacturer made the exact same claims about a drug? Otherwise, drug manufacturers are at a perhaps unwarranted competitive disadvantage to food producers, just because the food has other characteristics than a claimed health benefit. We discuss the laws specific to drugs and supplements in Chapter 17.

Requiring advertisers to meet FDA standards in order to make certain claims may in practice deter them from making such claims at all. This may prevent consumers from getting potentially useful information, and may encourage advertisers to use more puffery, or make claims that are more easily substantiated but less valuable to consumers. Are consumers better off if producers differentiate their products using, say, celebrity endorsers instead of potentially but not definitely true health claims? What if producers instead make their products taste better at the expense of nutrition because it's too hard—for them *and* for the competition that would otherwise keep them in check—to make nutrition claims? Is there any way to avoid disincentivizing truthful health claims while also maintaining a high standard of substantiation? Can you draft a disclaimer that, as the D.C. Circuit suggested, explains a lesser level of substantiation? (See Chapter 5.)

One reason for the FTC's attempt to define acceptable substantiation more precisely is to avoid disputes over whether particular evidence suffices as substantiation. *See* F.T.C. v. Garden of Life, Inc., 516 Fed.Appx. 852 (11th Cir. 2013) (where consent decree only required advertiser to have "competent and reliable scientific evidence substantiating its claims," court of appeals largely upheld district court's refusal to find a violation of the consent decree based on a "battle of the experts").

Substantiation and Private Claims. The FTC and the states require advertisers to possess substantiation for their factual claims; unsubstantiated claims are treated like false claims. (Is this consistent with the First Amendment? Would we tolerate a similar presumption for defamation, so that speakers would have to possess substantiation for any negative statement they made about other people?) The NAD also applies a substantiation requirement.

In a private action, however, the burden is on the plaintiff—whether a competitor or a consumer—to show that the defendant's statements were false or misleading. The Third Circuit has recognized an exception to this rule in Lanham Act cases, however: where an advertiser makes a claim with no reason to believe that it is true— pulls the claim out of a hat, essentially—that utter lack of substantiation violates the Lanham Act. *See* Novartis Consumer Health, Inc. v. Johnson & Johnson-Merck Consumer Pharms. Co., 290 F.3d 578 (3d Cir. 2002) (antacid's claim of nighttime superiority made with no evidence of such superiority was literally false). Should all courts adopt this rule for private plaintiff actions? Should we put at least the burden of production on an advertiser whose factual claim is challenged in court, even if we leave the burden of proof with the plaintiff? *See* Grpe. SEB USA, Inc v. Euro-Pro Operating LLC, 2014 WL 2002126, No. 14-137 (W.D. Pa. May 15, 2014) (magistrate judge) (applying *Novartis* where defendant claimed superiority to plaintiff's steam iron "based on independent comparative steam burst testing" but did not produce such testing to the court or to its expert).

6. False Establishment Claims

An establishment claim conveys an explicit or implicit message that "tests prove that X cleans better," "studies show that Y lasts longer," or some similar message indicating to the consumer that scientific or experimental evidence supports an advertising claim. Establishment claims are not limited to claims about laboratory tests; a claim about consumer preferences ("surveys show . . .") or another kind of quantitative claim can be an establishment claim. Establishment claims can be implicit as well as explicit. The impression that scientific studies lie behind a claim can be created by an actor in a lab coat, by pictures of scientific reports, or by showing graphs or diagrams. *See* Sterling Drug, Inc. v. F.T.C., 741 F.2d 1146 (9th Cir. 1984) (establishment claim made because of visual aspects of ad, including "pictures of medical and scientific reports from which consumers could infer that Bayer's effectiveness had been objectively evaluated" and "serious tone" and "scientific aura" of ads). As in *POM Wonderful*, sufficiently scientific language may inherently make an establishment claim. Smithkline Beecham Consumer Healthcare, L.P. v. Merck Consumer Pharms. Co., 906 F. Supp. 178 (S.D.N.Y. 1995) (treating the claim "based on pH data of stomach acidity" as an establishment claim); W.L. Gore & Assoc., Inc. v. Totes Inc., 788 F. Supp. 800 (D. Del. 1992) (finding that the statement that advertiser's golf suit allowed "seven times more air and sweat vapor" to pass through than competitor's product falsely indicated that advertiser had run independent tests when no such tests existed). These results may be an application of the "necessary implication" doctrine, discussed in Chapter 6, where implications that would be understood by any reasonable consumer are considered as if they'd been explicitly stated.

Establishment claims may be more persuasive, but that also means that advertising law subjects them to special scrutiny:

> We live in [a] society that values quantification. You can read about the 100 "top" colleges in *U.S. News & World Report*, or the ten "best" cars in *Consumer Reports*. But comparative advertising confers on advertisers a serious responsibility to

the public and competitors. If Defendants wish to secure the undoubted advantage of numerical comparisons, then they should get them right.

Garden Way Inc. v. The Home Depot Inc., 94 F. Supp. 2d 276 (N.D.N.Y. 2000). In other contexts, courts have in recent years expressed concerns over "junk science" used to convince juries that products are dangerous when they aren't. But junk science can be found everywhere, not least in the hands of advertisers with every incentive to claim superiority.

Courts applying the Lanham Act have developed the rule that an establishment claim may be proven false by showing that the studies on which the ad relies are not sufficiently reliable to support with reasonable certainty the claim made by the ad. This may be shown by demonstrating either (1) that the tests, even if valid, do not establish the claim actually made by an ad, or (2) that the tests are invalid and objectively unreliable. Similarly, the NAD has stated that when tests or surveys are cited in advertising as support for a claim, the advertising is false if the test or survey is "inadequate to support the claim." *In re* Visa U.S.A., Inc. NAD Case No. 3426 (closed 11/6/97).

Courts consider "all relevant circumstances, including the state of the testing art, the existence and feasibility of superior procedures, the objectivity and skill of the persons conducting the tests, the accuracy of their reports, and the results of other pertinent tests." Proctor & Gamble Co. v. Chesebrough-Pond's, Inc., 747 F.2d 114 (2d Cir. 1984). One court has suggested in dicta that, where the relevant consumers are sophisticated and the advertiser provides them with abstracts of the tests on which a claim is founded, the consumers are in a position to decide for themselves whether the tests are sufficiently reliable. *See* Pfizer, Inc. v. Miles, Inc., 868 F. Supp. 437 (D. Conn. 1994); *cf. ONY, supra.*

The flaws in the supporting test must be substantial in order for the advertising to be false. A plaintiff cannot win merely by exposing methodological imperfections. If the defendant's tests were, at the time they were conducted, the best-known way to measure the tested characteristic, later developments, and even doubts about the reliability of the conclusions on the part of the defendant's own employees, are insufficient to show that the tests were not reasonably reliable. *See* Omega Eng'g, Inc. v. Eastman Kodak Co., 30 F. Supp. 2d 226 (D. Conn. 1998). In general, "[t]o ensure vigorous competition and to protect legitimate commercial speech, courts applying [the sufficient reliability] standard should give advertisers a fair amount of leeway, at least in the absence of a clear intent to deceive or substantial consumer confusion." Rhone-Poulenc Rorer Pharms., Inc. v. Marion Merrell Dow, Inc., 93 F.3d 511 (8th Cir. 1996). As a result, two competing advertisers may be able to make contradictory establishment claims, if each relies on weak but not worthless tests. *See* Proctor & Gamble Co. v. Chesebrough-Pond's, Inc., 747 F.2d 114 (2d Cir. 1984) (allowing competing lotions to make diametrically opposed claims because neither party's tests could be proven scientifically invalid).

Advertisers should nonetheless make establishment claims carefully. Even if tests support a superiority claim, an establishment claim that quantitatively overstates the amount of superiority shown by the tests may be found false. In addition, a single "tests prove" claim about one aspect of the product may, depending on its context within an advertisement, be attributed to other claims about the same product, especially when the claims are closely related, resulting in liability when the tests do not prove those other claims. *See* Porter & Dietsch, Inc. v. F.T.C., 605 F.2d 294 (7th Cir. 1979) (where ad generally created impression that most users of diet pill would lose significant amounts of weight, claims that pill was "clinic tested" and "medically recognized" were treated as establishment claims that users would lose significant weight).

The burden of challenging a non-establishment claim has sometimes been labeled "greater" than the burden of challenging an establishment claim, because, in establishment cases, a plaintiff need only show that the underlying statement about the product lacks support from the evidence on which the defendant relies, not that it is affirmatively untrue. However, a plaintiff's demonstration that "tests *don't* show X" disproves the defendant's "tests show X" claim. In other words, the burden of showing falsity is the same, but the claim at issue is different: it is the "tests prove" claim that the plaintiff alleges is false and not the substantive claim that the "tests" supposedly "prove" to be true. Is such a falsehood as likely to be important to consumers as the underlying factual claim? See the discussion of materiality *infra*.

If an ad simply asserts a fact without stating (or implying) that tests back up the claim, then it generally is not enough for a Lanham Act plaintiff to show that the claim was unsubstantiated. *See, e.g.*, C.B. Fleet Co. v. SmithKline Beecham Consumer Healthcare, L.P., 131 F.3d 430 (4th Cir. 1997). Moreover, even if an advertisement is based on tests, if it makes no establishment claims, it is not subject to establishment claim standards.

But what should happen if a competitor shows with credible evidence that consumers expect that a particular claim is only made because it is substantiated? Logically, the claim should be treated as an implicit establishment claim, like a claim made while showing a chart or graph. *See* C.B. Fleet Co. v. SmithKline Beecham Consumer Healthcare, L.P., 131 F.3d 430 (4th Cir. 1997) (whether claim implies survey or tests is question of fact); Sandoz Pharms. Corp. v. Richardson-Vicks, Inc., 902 F.2d 222 (3d Cir. 1990) ("[A] plaintiff must produce consumer surveys or some surrogate therefore to prove whether consumers expect an advertising claim to be substantiated and whether they expect the level of substantiation to be greater than that which the defendant has performed.").

The FTC has adopted the view that scientific substantiation is required for certain classes of products, such as drugs. American Home Prods. Corp. v. F.T.C., 695 F.2d 681 (3d Cir. 1982) (approving FTC's reasoning that consumers are likely to believe that statements about drug efficacy are supported by scientific evidence, though the existence of such evidence is neither stated nor otherwise implied); *In re* Pfizer, Inc., 81 F.T.C. 23 (1972) ("[T]here may be some types of claims for some types of products for which the only reasonable basis, in fairness and in the expectations of consumers, would be a valid scientific or medical basis.").

Should courts deciding cases brought by private plaintiffs accept the FTC's reasoning? *Compare* Upjohn Co. v. Riahom Corp., 641 F. Supp. 1209 (D. Del. 1986) (representation that product had been clinically tested was misleading because "American consumers who see a product claiming that clinical tests have shown it safe for use expect that the product has gone through extensive and rigorous testing by the manufacturer, the government or both before its general sale," and minimal tests were insufficient to make claim true), *with* Glaxo-Warner Lambert OTC G.P. v. Johnson & Johnson-Merck Consumer Pharms. Co., 935 F. Supp. 327 (S.D.N.Y. 1996) (rejecting the argument that statements about the equivalency of two over-the-counter drugs inherently suggested that tests supported the claims).

The Placebo Effect

What happens when a product only "works" because consumers believe it helps them? Is it misleading to advertise that the product will help them? The following case uses economic reasoning, but is it ultimately enforcing a moral distaste?

Federal Trade Commission v. QT, Inc., 512 F.3d 858 (7th Cir. 2008)

WIRED Magazine recently put the Q-Ray Ionized Bracelet on its list of the top ten Snake-Oil Gadgets.

[the "Gold Deluxe" Q-Ray Ionized Bracelet]

The Federal Trade Commission has an even less honorable title for the bracelet's promotional campaign: fraud. In this action under 15 U.S.C. §§ 45(a), 52, 53, a magistrate judge, presiding by the parties' consent, concluded after a bench trial that the bracelet's promotion has been thoroughly dishonest. The court enjoined the promotional claims and required defendants to disgorge some $16 million (plus interest) for the FTC to distribute to consumers who have been taken in.

According to the district court's findings, almost everything that defendants have said about the bracelet is false. Here are some highlights:

- Defendants promoted the bracelet as a miraculous cure for chronic pain, but it has no therapeutic effect.
- Defendants told consumers that claims of "immediate, significant or complete pain relief" had been "test-proven"; they hadn't.
- The bracelet does not emit "Q-Rays" (there are no such things) and is not ionized (the bracelet is an

electric conductor, and any net charge dissipates swiftly). The bracelet's chief promoter chose these labels because they are simple and easily remembered—and because Polaroid Corp. blocked him from calling the bangle "polarized".

- The bracelet is touted as "enhancing the flow of bio-energy" or "balancing the flow of positive and negative energies"; these empty phrases have no connection to any medical or scientific effect. Every other claim made about the mechanism of the bracelet's therapeutic effect likewise is techno-babble.

- Defendants represented that the therapeutic effect wears off in a year or two, despite knowing that the bracelet's properties do not change. This assertion is designed to lead customers to buy new bracelets. Likewise the false statement that the bracelet has a "memory cycle specific to each individual wearer" so that only the bracelet's original wearer can experience pain relief is designed to increase sales by eliminating the second-hand market and "explaining" the otherwise-embarrassing fact that the buyer's friends and neighbors can't perceive any effect.

- Even statements about the bracelet's physical composition are false. It is sold in "gold" and "silver" varieties but is made of brass.

The magistrate judge did not commit a clear error, or abuse his discretion, in concluding that the defendants set out to bilk unsophisticated persons who found themselves in pain from arthritis and other chronic conditions.

Defendants maintain that the magistrate judge subjected their statements to an excessively rigorous standard of proof. Some passages in the opinion could be read to imply that any statement about a product's therapeutic effects must be deemed false unless the claim has been verified in a placebo-controlled, double-blind study: that is, a study in which some persons are given the product whose effects are being investigated while others are given a placebo (with the allocation made at random), and neither the person who distributes the product nor the person who measures the effects knows which received the real product. Such studies are expensive, not only because of the need for placebos and keeping the experimenters in the dark, but also because they require large numbers of participants to achieve statistically significant results. Defendants observe that requiring vendors to bear such heavy costs may keep useful products off the market (this has been a problem for drugs that are subject to the FDA's testing protocols) and prevent vendors from making truthful statements that will help consumers locate products that will do them good.

Nothing in the Federal Trade Commission Act, the foundation of this litigation, requires placebo-controlled, double-blind studies. The Act forbids false and misleading statements, and a statement that is plausible but has not been tested in the most reliable way cannot be condemned out of hand. The burden is on the Commission to prove that the statements are false. (This is one way in which the Federal Trade Commission Act differs from the Food and Drug Act.) Think about the seller of an adhesive bandage treated with a disinfectant such as iodine. The seller does not need to conduct tests before asserting that this product reduces the risk of infection from cuts. The bandage keeps foreign materials out of the cuts and kills some bacteria. It may be debatable how much the risk of infection falls, but the direction of the effect would be known, and the claim could not be condemned as false. Placebo-controlled, double-blind testing is not a legal requirement for consumer products.

But how could this conclusion assist defendants? In our example the therapeutic claim is based on scientific principles. For the Q-Ray

Ionized Bracelet, by contrast, all statements about how the product works—Q-Rays, ionization, enhancing the flow of bio-energy, and the like—are blather. Defendants might as well have said: "Beneficent creatures from the 17th Dimension use this bracelet as a beacon to locate people who need pain relief, and whisk them off to their homeworld every night to provide help in ways unknown to our science."

Although it is true, as Arthur C. Clarke said, that "[a]ny sufficiently advanced technology is indistinguishable from magic" by those who don't understand its principles, a person who promotes a product that contemporary technology does not understand must establish that this "magic" actually works. Proof is what separates an effect new to science from a swindle. Defendants themselves told customers that the bracelet's efficacy had been "test-proven"; that statement was misleading unless a reliable test had been used and statistically significant results achieved. A placebo-controlled, double-blind study is the best test; something less may do (for there is no point in spending $1 million to verify a claim worth only $10,000 if true); but defendants have no proof of the Q-Ray Ionized Bracelet's efficacy. The "tests" on which they relied were bunk. (We need not repeat the magistrate judge's exhaustive evaluation of this subject.) What remain are testimonials, which are not a form of proof because most testimonials represent a logical fallacy: post hoc ergo propter hoc. (A person who experiences a reduction in pain after donning the bracelet may have enjoyed the same reduction without it. That's why the "testimonial" of someone who keeps elephants off the streets of a large city by snapping his fingers is the basis of a joke rather than proof of cause and effect.)

To this defendants respond that one study shows that the Q-Ray Ionized Bracelet does reduce pain. This study, which the district court's opinion describes in detail, compared the effects of "active" and "inactive" bracelets (defendants told the experimenter which was which), with the "inactive" bracelet serving as a control. The study found that both "active" and "inactive" bracelets had a modest—and identical—effect on patients' reported levels of pain. In other words, the Q-Ray Ionized Bracelet exhibits the placebo effect. Like a sugar pill, it alleviates symptoms even though there is no apparent medical reason. The placebo effect is well established. Defendants insist that the placebo effect vindicates their claims, even though they are false-indeed, especially because they are false, as the placebo effect depends on deceit. Tell the patient that the pill contains nothing but sugar, and there is no pain relief; tell him (falsely) that it contains a powerful analgesic, and the perceived level of pain falls. A product that confers this benefit cannot be excluded from the market, defendants insist, just because they told the lies necessary to bring the effect about.

Yet the Federal Trade Commission Act condemns material falsehoods in promoting consumer products; the statute lacks an exception for "beneficial deceit." We appreciate the possibility that a vague claim— along the lines of "this bracelet will reduce your pain without the side effects of drugs"—could be rendered true by the placebo effect. To this extent we are skeptical about language in *FTC v. Pantron I Corp.*, 33 F.3d 1088 (9th Cir. 1994), suggesting that placebo effects always are worthless to consumers. But our defendants advanced claims beyond those that could be supported by a placebo effect. They made statements about Q-Rays, ionization, and bio-energy that they knew to be poppycock; they stated that the bracelet remembers its first owner and won't work for anyone else; the list is extensive.

One important reason for requiring truth is so that competition in the market will lead to appropriate prices. Selling brass as gold harms consumers independent of any effect on pain. Since the placebo effect can be obtained from sugar pills, charging $200 for a device that is represented as a miracle cure but works no better than a dummy pill is a form of fraud. That's not all. A placebo is necessary when scientists are searching for the marginal effect of a new drug or device, but once the study is over a reputable professional will recommend whatever works best.

Medicine aims to do better than the placebo effect, which any medieval physician could achieve by draining off a little of the patient's blood. If no one knows how to cure or ameliorate a given condition, then a placebo is the best thing going. Far better a placebo that causes no harm (the Q-Ray Ionized Bracelet is inert) than the sort of nostrums peddled from the back of a wagon 100 years ago and based on alcohol, opium, and wormwood. But if a condition responds to treatment, then selling a placebo as if it had therapeutic effect directly injures the consumer.

Physicians know how to treat pain. Why pay $200 for a Q-Ray Ionized Bracelet when you can get relief from an aspirin tablet that costs 1¢? Some painful conditions do not respond to analgesics (or the stronger drugs in the pharmacopeia) or to surgery, but it does not follow that a placebo at any price is better. Deceit such as the tall tales that defendants told about the Q-Ray Ionized Bracelet will lead some consumers to avoid treatments that cost less and do more; the lies will lead others to pay too much for pain relief or otherwise interfere with the matching of remedies to medical conditions. That's why the placebo effect cannot justify fraud in promoting a product. . . .

NOTES AND QUESTIONS

A double-blinded, placebo-controlled test failed to find any benefit from these bracelets. See Stewart J. Richmond et al., Copper Bracelets and Magnetic Wrist Straps for Rheumatoid Arthritis— Analgesic and Anti-Inflammatory Effects: A Randomised Double-Blind Placebo Controlled Crossover Trial, PLoS ONE (2013), doi:10.1371/journal.pone.0071529.

A False Distinction? Judge Easterbrook says that the $200 bracelet and a one-cent aspirin tablet will yield the same result. What if the defendant could show that by spending the extra money, the buyers experienced a more pronounced placebo effect? What if the difference is statistically significant but small (such that, for example, one out of thirty sufferers will benefit from the enhanced pain relief, while the other twenty-nine will not)?

Why do people buy worthless products? Are health (or weight loss or beauty) claims areas where hope beats out experience? Don't consumers really know, deep down, that they're buying snake oil, and, if so, why protect them against such claims?

7. False Demonstrations and Dramatizations

Even if an advertiser possesses substantiation that a product or service is capable of achieving a certain result, it is false to advertise it by using a rigged demonstration. A famous case involves a shaving cream that actually could "shave" sandpaper. On TV, however, real sandpaper looked like nothing but colored paper. The advertiser, therefore, rigged a demonstration using simulated "sandpaper" made of plexiglass covered with sand. The Supreme Court upheld the FTC's order barring the ad. FTC v. Colgate-Palmolive Co., 380 U.S. 374 (1965). The Court agreed with the FTC's conclusion that "even if an advertiser has himself conducted a test, experiment or demonstration which he honestly believes will prove a certain product claim, he may not convey to television viewers the false impression that they are seeing the test, experiment or demonstration for themselves, when they are not because of the undisclosed use of mock-ups."

In another case, a commercial advertising the strength of a Volvo automobile showed a "monster truck" crushing a row of conventional cars, leaving the Volvo unharmed. The Volvo, unlike the other cars, had been reinforced to make it stronger. The FTC found that this dramatization was false and fined the company $150,000. *See In re Volvo North America Corp.*, F.T.C. File No. 912-3032 (June 12, 1991).

Recently, the UK advertising regulator has challenged post-production editing on ads for beauty products, leading major companies to withdraw some ads. Likewise, the NAD opened an investigation on its own initiative into Procter & Gamble's ads for CoverGirl mascara, suggesting that the ads could convey the implied messages that consumers who use the product would get lashes like those depicted and that the lashes depicted were achieved solely by using the CoverGirl product, even though the ads bore the legend "lashes enhanced in post-production." Competitors in the beauty market have not challenged each others' use of such editing techniques, even when they make the advertised products look more effective than they are. Why would a competitor refrain from such a challenge? Is there good reason for regulatory intervention into this market? Suzanne Grayson, a beauty consultant, offered one perspective: " 'Everybody does it,' said Ms. Grayson, . . . adding that retouching of lashes in mascara advertising has become particularly aggressive in recent years. 'It's been more aggressive by manufacturers, because they see what other people are getting away with, and it becomes, "Can you top this?"' Ms. Grayson said." Jack Neff, *National Ad Division Goes After Retouching of Beauty Ads*, ADVERTISINGAGE, Dec. 15, 2011.

The NAD has also examined similar mascara ads where there was an explicit disclosure that the model was "styled with lash inserts," which make the lash fringe look thicker. The NAD did not see a reason to distinguish postproduction editing from physically adding volume to lashes. Makeup ads are not exempt from the general rules about false demonstrations and dramatizations, even though makeup sells a fantasy more blatantly than some other products. The NAD reached this conclusion despite the advertiser's consumer survey, which the advertiser claimed indicated that consumers did not expect their lashes to look like the model's even if they used the mascara: even if consumers didn't take away the message that they'd achieve the *same* results as the model, the false demonstration nonetheless enhanced the credibility of the key claim that the mascara would make the user's lashes thicker and lusher. But because the photo didn't depict the volume that could be achieved using the mascara alone, even on an unusually beautiful woman, it was literally false. *See* L'Oréal U.S.A., Inc., NAD Case No. 5628 (Sept. 6, 2013). The NAD recommended discontinuing the ad or putting in the main message that the product touted was mascara plus lash inserts.

However, the NAD did agree with the advertiser about a different photograph, where the advertiser explained that lash inserts were only used to recreate the model's natural lash line, where her lashes had been thinned by frequent heavy makeup application and removal. (The advertiser is currently appealing to NARB.)

Demonstrations and dramatizations may be legitimate if they sufficiently replicate all the significant aspects of the testing environment and carry a sufficient disclaimer, as discussed in Chapter 5. In addition, using undisclosed props is not necessarily false. Falsity arises when consumers are told to rely on their own perceptions to verify the advertiser's claim. The Supreme Court gave the example of a scoop of mashed potatoes used to stand in for ice cream under hot studio lights. If the potatoes are not used to prove a product claim, there is no problem. But if "the focus of the commercial becomes the undisclosed potato prop and the viewer is invited, explicitly or by implication, to see for himself the truth of the claims about the ice cream's rich texture and full color, and perhaps compare it to a 'rival product,'" it would become false.

As you read the following case, recall the drowning goldfish from the *S.C. Johnson* case, *supra*. Consider when dramatizations count as "factual"—how would you direct an ad agency to animate the claim at issue?

Schick Manufacturing, Inc. v. Gillette Company, 372 F. Supp. 2d 273 (D. Conn. 2005)

The plaintiff, Schick Manufacturing Company ("Schick"), seeks a preliminary injunction enjoining the defendant, The Gillette Company ("Gillette"), from making certain claims about its M3 Power razor system ("M3 Power"). Schick contends that Gillette has made various false claims in violation of section 43(a) of the Lanham Act, 15 U.S.C. § 1125(a) and the Connecticut Unfair Trade Practices Act ("CUTPA"), Conn. Gen. Stat. § 42-110a, *et seq.*

. . . Gillette's original advertising for the M3 Power centered on the claim that "micropulses raise hair up and away from skin," thus allowing a consumer to achieve a closer shave. This "hair-raising" or hair extension claim was advertised in various media, including the internet, television, print media, point of sale materials, and product packaging. . . . Of Gillette's expenditures on advertising, 85% is spent on television advertising. At the time of the launch, the television advertising stated, "turn on the first micro-power shaving system from Gillette and turn on the amazing new power-glide blades. Micro-pulses raise the hair, so you shave closer in one power stroke." The advertisement also included a 1.8 second-long animated dramatization of hairs growing. In the animated cartoon, the oscillation produced by the M3 Power is shown as green waves moving over hairs. In response, the hairs shown extended in length in the direction of growth and changed angle towards a more vertical position.

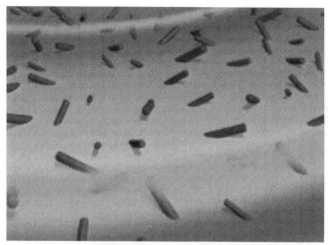

[screenshot from first ad]

. . . In late January of 2005, Gillette revised its television commercials for the M3 Power in the United States. . . . The animated product demonstration in the television commercials was revised so that the hairs in the demonstration no longer changed angle, and some of the hairs are shown to remain static. The voice-over was changed to say, "Turn it on and micropulses raise the hair so the blades can shave closer." The product demonstration in the revised advertisements depicts the oscillations to lengthen many hairs significantly. The depiction in the revised advertisements of how much the hair lengthens—the magnitude of the extension—is not consistent with Gillette's own studies regarding the effect of micropulses on hair. The animated product demonstration depicts many hairs extending, in many instances, multiple times the original length. . . .

Gillette conceded during the hearing that the M3 Power's oscillations do not cause hair to change angle on the face. Its original advertisements depicting such an angle change are both

294

unsubstantiated and inaccurate. Gillette also concedes that the animated portion of its television advertisement is not physiologically exact insofar as the hairs and skin do not appear as they would at such a level of magnification and the hair extension effect is "somewhat exaggerated." The court finds that the hair "extension" in the commercial is greatly exaggerated. Gillette does contend, however, that the M3 Power's oscillations cause beard hairs to be raised out of the skin. Gillette contends that the animated product demonstration showing hair extension in its revised commercials is predicated on its testing showing that oscillations cause "trapped" facial hairs to lengthen from the follicle so that more of these hairs' length is exposed. . . .

[Gillette's theory of why the razor would raise hairs was unsupported by scientific evidence; the parties both submitted studies that were small, uncontrolled, and otherwise unreliable.]

The flaws in testing conducted by both parties prevent the court from concluding whether, as a matter of fact, the M3 Power raises beard hairs.

II. ANALYSIS
. . . B. False Advertising

. . . Where, . . . as here, the accused advertising does not allege that tests or clinical studies have proven a particular fact, the plaintiff's burden to come forward with affirmative evidence of falsity is qualitatively different. "To prove that an advertising claim is literally false, a plaintiff must do more than show that the tests supporting the challenged claim are unpersuasive." The plaintiff must prove falsity by a preponderance of the evidence, either using its own scientific testing or that of the defendant. If a plaintiff is to prevail by relying on the defendant's own studies, it cannot do so simply by criticizing the defendant's studies. It must prove either that "such tests 'are not sufficiently reliable to permit one to conclude with reasonable certainty that they established' the claim made" or that the defendant's studies establish that the defendant's claims are false.

The challenged advertising consists of two basic components: an animated representation of the effect of the M3 Power razor on hair and skin and a voice-over that describes that effect. . . . Schick asserts that this M3 Power advertising is false in three ways: first, it asserts the razor changes the angle of beard hairs; second, it portrays a false amount of extension; and third, it asserts that the razor raises or extends the beard hair.

With regard to the first claim of falsity, if the voiceover means that the razor changes the angle of hairs on the face, the claim is false. . . .

With regard to the second asserted basis of falsity, the animation, Gillette concedes that the animation exaggerates the effect that the razor's vibration has on hair. Its own tests show hairs extending approximately 10% on average, when the animation shows a significantly greater extension. The animation is not even a "reasonable approximation," which Gillette claims is the legal standard for non-falsity. Here, Schick can point to Gillette's own studies to prove that the animation is false.

Gillette argues that such exaggeration does not constitute falsity. However, case law in this circuit indicates that a defendant cannot argue that a television advertisement is "approximately" correct or, alternatively, simply a representation in order to excuse a television ad or segment thereof that is literally false. Indeed, "[the Court of Appeals has] explicitly looked to the visual images in a commercial to assess whether it is literally false."

. . . . Clearly, a cartoon will not exactly depict a real-life situation, here, *e.g.*, the actual uneven surface of a hair or the details of a hair plug. However, a party may not distort an inherent quality of its product in either graphics or animation. Gillette acknowledges that the magnitude of beard hair extension in the animation is false. The court finds, therefore, that any claims with respect to changes in angle and the animated portion of Gillette's current advertisement are literally false.

The court does not make such a finding with respect to Schick's third falsity ground, Gillette's hair extension theory generally. Gillette claims that the razor's vibrations raise some hairs trapped under the skin to come out of the skin. While its own studies are insufficient to establish the truth of this claim, the burden is on Schick to prove falsity. Neither Schick's nor Gillette's testing can support a finding of falsity.

While there can be no finding of literal falsity with respect to Gillette's hair extension claim at this stage in the instant litigation, the court expresses doubt about that claim. . . .

Nevertheless, putting forth credible evidence that there is no known biological mechanism to support Gillette's contention that the M3 Power raises hairs is insufficient to meet Schick's burden. Such evidence is not affirmative evidence of falsity. . . . [H]ere Gillette's own tests do not prove hair extension does not occur. Schick merely proved that Gillette's testing is inadequate to prove it does occur.

NOTES AND QUESTIONS

Schick sued Gillette for false advertising around the world. Courts in France, Belgium, and the Netherlands refused to enjoin the disputed advertising, but courts in Germany and Australia, along with the district court whose opinion is excerpted here, issued preliminary injunctions. After extensive U.S. discovery, Gillette and Schick reached a worldwide settlement. But class action litigation followed in several states and Canadian jurisdictions. All the state cases were removed and all the federal cases were transferred to the Massachusetts district court and consolidated. The district court gave preliminary approval to a proposed settlement, discussed in Chapter 7. *In re* M3 Power Razor Sys. Mktg. & Sales Practice Litig., 2010 WL 3082198 (D. Mass. 2010).

8. False Implied Claims

A claim that is literally true but nonetheless deceives or misleads consumers by its implications also constitutes false advertising. Otherwise, "clever use of innuendo, indirect intimations, and ambiguous suggestions could shield the advertisement from scrutiny precisely when protection against such sophisticated deception is most needed." Am. Home Prods. Corp. v. Johnson & Johnson, 577 F.2d 160 (2d Cir. 1978).

In Lanham Act cases, plaintiffs usually need to show evidence from consumer surveys indicating that a not insubstantial number of consumers understood the implied message. However, some circuits have ruled that survey evidence of consumer deception may not be necessary if a plaintiff can show that the defendant intended to deceive consumers with the implicit message, though this rule is stated far more often than it is applied in a plaintiff's favor. *See, e.g.,* Cashmere & Camel Hair Mfrs. Inst. v. Sacks Fifth Ave., 284 F.3d 302 (1st Cir. 2002). The general rule: without a survey, plaintiff loses.

By contrast, both the FTC and the NAD have sufficient advertising expertise to judge an ad's implied claims for themselves regardless of intent, and survey evidence is unnecessary (though potentially helpful) in FTC and NAD proceedings. Indeed, courts often give the FTC substantial deference. FTC v. Lights of Am., Inc., No. 10-1333

(C.D. Cal. Sept. 17, 2013) ("The FTC is not required to show that every reasonable consumer would have been, or in fact was, misled," and ads "that are capable of being interpreted in a misleading way should be construed against the advertiser"). This flexibility increases the FTC's freedom to act and allows it to invest fewer resources in proving each case.

In the following case, the Seventh Circuit rejected Kraft's argument that the FTC should be required to follow an explicit/implicit distinction in determining what claims Kraft had made about the superiority of its processed cheese slices to imitation cheese slices.

Kraft, Inc. v. Federal Trade Commission, 970 F.2d 311 (7th Cir. 1992)

. . . In determining what claims are conveyed by a challenged advertisement, the Commission relies on two sources of information: its own viewing of the ad and extrinsic evidence. Its practice is to view the ad first and, if it is unable on its own to determine with confidence what claims are conveyed in a challenged ad, to turn to extrinsic evidence. The most convincing extrinsic evidence is a survey "of what consumers thought upon reading the advertisement in question," but the Commission also relies on other forms of extrinsic evidence including consumer testimony, expert opinion, and copy tests of ads.

Kraft has no quarrel with this approach when it comes to determining whether an ad conveys express claims, but contends that the FTC should be required, as a matter of law, to rely on extrinsic evidence rather than its own subjective analysis in all cases involving allegedly implied claims. The basis for this argument is that implied claims, by definition, are not self-evident from the face of an ad. This, combined with the fact that consumer perceptions are shaped by a host of external variables—including their social and educational backgrounds, the environment in which they view the ad, and prior experiences with the product advertised, makes review of implied claims by a five-member commission inherently unreliable. The Commissioners, Kraft argues, are simply incapable of determining what implicit messages consumers are likely to perceive in an ad. Making matters worse, Kraft asserts that the Commissioners are predisposed to find implied claims because the claims have been identified in the complaint, rendering it virtually impossible for them to reflect the perceptions of unbiased consumers. *See* Comment, *The Use and Reliability of Survey Evidence in Deceptive Advertising Cases*, 62 OR. L. REV. 561, 572 (1983) ("since the commissioners are highly trained attorneys with very specialized views of advertising, they lack the perspective to accurately identify the meaning given an advertisement by the general public").

Kraft buttresses its argument by pointing to the use of extrinsic evidence in an analogous context: cases brought under § 43(a) of the Lanham Act. Courts hearing deceptive advertising claims under that Act, which provides a private right of action for deceptive advertising, generally require extrinsic proof that an advertisement conveys an implied claim. Were this a Lanham Act case, a reviewing court in all likelihood would have relied on extrinsic evidence of consumer perceptions. While this disparity is sometimes justified on grounds of advertising "expertise"—the FTC presumably possesses more of it than courts—Kraft maintains this justification is an illusory one in that the FTC has no special expertise in discerning consumer perceptions. Indeed, proof of the FTC's inexpertise abounds: false advertising cases makes up a small part of the Commission's workload, most commissioners have little prior experience in advertising, and the average tenure of commissioners is very brief. That evidence aside, no amount of expertise in Kraft's view can replace the myriad of external variables affecting consumer perceptions. Here, the Commission found implied claims based solely on its own intuitive reading of the ads (although it did reinforce that conclusion by examining the proffered extrinsic evidence). . . .

While Kraft's arguments may have some force as a matter of policy, they are unavailing as a matter of law. Courts, including the Supreme Court, have uniformly rejected imposing such a requirement on the FTC, and we decline to do so as well. We hold that the Commission may rely on its own reasoned analysis to determine what claims, including implied ones, are conveyed in a challenged advertisement, so long as those claims are reasonably clear from the face of the advertisement.

Kraft's case for a per se rule has two flaws. First, it rests on the faulty premise that implied claims are inescapably subjective and unpredictable. In fact, implied claims fall on a continuum, ranging from the obvious to the barely discernible. The Commission does not have license to go on a fishing expedition to pin liability on advertisers for barely imaginable claims falling at the end of this spectrum. However, when confronted with claims that are implied, yet conspicuous, extrinsic evidence is unnecessary because common sense and administrative experience provide the Commission with adequate tools to make[ ] its findings. . . .

Second, Kraft's reliance on Lanham Act decisions is misplaced. For one, not all courts applying the Lanham Act rely on extrinsic evidence when confronted with implied claims, but more importantly, when they do, it is because they are ill equipped—unlike the Commission— to detect deceptive advertising. And the Commission's expertise in deceptive advertising cases, Kraft's protestations notwithstanding, undoubtedly exceeds that of courts as a general matter. That false advertising cases constitute a small percentage of the FTC's overall workload does not negate the fact that significant resources are devoted to such cases in absolute terms, nor does it account for the institutional expertise the FTC gains through investigations, rulemakings, and consent orders. The Commissioners' personal experiences quite obviously affect their perceptions, but it does not follow that they are incapable of predicting whether a particular claim is likely to be perceived by a reasonable number of consumers.

. . . Kraft contends that by relying on its own subjective judgment that an ad, while literally true, implies a false message, the FTC chills nonmisleading, protected speech because advertisers are unable to predict whether the FTC will find a particular ad misleading. Advertisers can run sophisticated pre-dissemination consumer surveys and find no implied claims present, only to have the Commission determine in its own subjective view that consumers would perceive an implied claim. Indeed, Kraft maintains that is precisely what happened here. Even more troubling, Kraft maintains that the ads most vulnerable to this chilling effect are factual, comparative ads, . . . of greatest benefit to consumers. The net result of the Commission's subjective approach will be an influx of soft "feel good" ads designed to avoid unpredictable FTC decisions. The way to avoid this chilling effect, according to Kraft, is to require the Commission to rely on objective indicia of consumer perceptions in finding implied claims.

Kraft's first amendment challenge is doomed by the Supreme Court's holding in *Zauderer*, which established that no first amendment concerns are raised when facially apparent implied claims are found without resort to extrinsic evidence. In *Zauderer*, a lawyer advertised that clients who retained him on a contingent-fee basis would not have to pay legal fees if their lawsuits were unsuccessful, without disclosing that these clients would be charged for costs, even though these are terms of art unknown to most laypersons; thus, the ad implied that hiring this lawyer was a no-lose proposition to potential clients. The state sanctioned Zauderer for engaging in misleading advertising, and he challenged that sanction on first amendment grounds. In approving the state's action, the Supreme Court declared,

"When the possibility of deception is as self-evident as it is in this case, we need not require the State to 'conduct a survey of the . . . public before it [may] determine that the [advertisement] had a tendency to mislead.'"

Thus, *Zauderer* teaches that consumer surveys are not compelled by the first amendment when the alleged deception although implied, is conspicuous. . .

Our holding does not diminish the force of Kraft's argument as a policy matter, and, indeed, the extensive body of commentary on the subject makes a compelling argument that reliance on extrinsic evidence should be the rule rather than the exception. . . .

NOTES AND QUESTIONS

A concurring opinion by Judge Manion emphasized that "neither this case nor *Zauderer* gives the FTC leave to ignore extrinsic evidence in every case." When, under *Kraft* (or under the First Amendment), should the FTC be required to submit consumer survey evidence?

The *Kraft* court leans heavily on precedent in upholding the FTC's ability to determine how consumers would respond to an implicit claim without a survey. If the court were writing on a blank slate, how should it decide? Kraft's arguments for requiring a survey are well articulated in the opinion; are there any countervailing considerations?

The Variety of Implicit Claims. Examples of false implicit claims are as numerous as there are products and services to advertise:

- An ad portraying a broken, hard-to-find toy being replaced because the toy had been purchased with a particular credit card, when the credit card company did

not replace broken goods but merely refunded the
purchase price

- An advertisement for windshield wipers including an
order form that asked for the make and model of the
buyer's car, implying that the wipers were customized to
fit certain cars when in fact the buyer had to alter them to
fit his or her car

- Advertisements for a pain reliever that, in claiming to
have twice as much pain reliever as the leading analgesic,
implied that it had twice as much pain reliever as all
commonly available pain relievers

- A claim that hospitals recommend "acetaminophen, the
aspirin-free pain reliever in Anacin-3, more than any
other pain reliever," when hospitals were actually
recommending Tylenol (which contains acetaminophen),
but consumers received the message that hospitals were
recommending Anacin-3

- Claims that Geritol would cure tiredness caused by "iron
deficiency anemia," when most tired people have no such
deficiency

As that last example suggests, misleadingness can be a matter of
failing to disclose material facts that change the import of the explicit
claim. The FTC and NAD have been particularly attentive to
"biodegradable" and "recyclable" claims. In the former case, most
waste goes to landfills where no biodegradation takes place; in the
latter, local variation may determine whether recycling is available.
Thus, reasonable consumers may misunderstand how "green" their
purchases are.

To take another example, the FTC found that an ad showing Baggies
brand sandwich bags compared to the "other brand" was deceptive
when it showed the Baggies bag resisting submersion in water while
the other brand leaked. Because most people don't submerge their

sandwiches, the ad falsely implied superiority in ordinary use. In re Colgate-Palmolive Co., 77 F.T.C. 150 (1970). Is this case consistent with the Ziploc Goldfish case, decided under the Lanham Act, *supra*? *See also* BP Lubricants USA, Inc. (Castrol EDGE), NAD Report No. 5674 (Jan. 14, 2014) (ad showed a "torture test" of motor oil with two cars running at 75 miles per hour on a 7% grade, fully loaded with 1600 pounds; on day 5 of the test, the engine using the competitor's motor oil failed while the advertiser's engine continued to run; while ad accurately depicted the test conditions, no real consumer's vehicle would ever be subjected to these conditions; the NAD determined that torture tests can only be used to support product claims when they represent conditions with real-world relevance).

If the situation is properly described and the extreme or unusual circumstances are important to consumers, however, such statements may not be misleading. Thus, when an advertisement for residential heat detectors promoted the products as useful additions to smoke detectors for home fire safety, the FTC did not find the advertisement deceptive even though heat detectors would rarely improve safety. Figgie Int'l, Inc., 107 F.T.C. 313 (1986). "Even a very small amount of additional protection from death or serious injury caused by fire would no doubt be considered significant by some consumers."

Implication often arises out of context, such as the contrast between the words of an advertisement, which may be literally true, and the accompanying images. For instance, an advertisement for an allergy drug showed consumers of a competitor's product falling asleep in all sorts of unlikely situations, creating two misleading impressions: (1) that the competitor's drug caused irresistible drowsiness, and (2) that the advertiser's drug did not cause drowsiness. *See* Warner-Lambert Co. v. Schering-Plough Corp., 1991 WL 221107 (S.D.N.Y. 1991). In another case, the defendant claimed that its new anti-irritation strip was six times smoother than the rival razor's strip. The visuals in the commercial, however, focused on the smoothness of the resulting shave, and a survey revealed that 37% of consumers thought the commercial meant that the *shave* was smoother. As a result, the rival won an injunction and an award of damages. Gillette Co. v. Wilkinson Sword, Inc., 1992 WL 30938 (S.D.N.Y. 1992).

Consumers may also blur separate ad claims together if an advertisement does not clearly distinguish them. *See* Telebrands Corp. v. Media Grp., Inc, 1997 WL 790576 (S.D.N.Y. 1997) (advertisement for a can opener that touted the smoothness of the opened lid deceived consumers into thinking that the opened edge of the can was also smooth and safe).

What about when consumers don't know the meaning of a word? *Suchanek v. Sturm Foods, Inc.*, 764 F.3d 750 (7th Cir. 2014), involved an advertiser who wished to make generic single-serving coffee pods for Keurig's expensive coffee brewing machine. However, for patent reasons it couldn't use a filter in the pods, and so it decided to use instant coffee instead—coffee crystals that dissolve in water. Sturm's consultants warned that "use of the word 'instant' is a real no-no" and should be avoided "if at all possible" in marketing the product to Keurig owners. The packaging displayed roasted coffee beans next to images of a pod, but stated in small font that it contained "naturally roasted soluble and microground Arabica coffee." Sturm did not use the better-known name for soluble coffee: instant coffee. The contents were over 95% instant coffee with only a tiny bit of microground coffee mixed in.

Other parts of the package offered a Coffee Lover's Bill of Rights promising "highest quality Arabica beans, roasted and ground to ensure peak flavor" and evoked the narrative of a neighborhood coffee shop.

In one survey, only 14% of participants who looked at the packages said the product contained instant coffee. Another survey found that essentially all consumers expected ground coffee in the pods, not instant coffee. Sturm's own expert found that only one in 151 test participants equated the term "soluble and microground" with the term "instant and microground." The district court ruled that no reasonable consumer could have been confused because the packages were clearly marked "soluble." As it pointed out, the lead plaintiff admitted that she understood the word "soluble" to mean that something is capable of dissolving.

In reversing, the court of appeals commented:

> But the fact that Suchanek correctly understood the definition of that English word is not enough to throw out her entire consumer-fraud claim. Did she know that soluble coffee is instant coffee? Did she understand that the [Sturm] product was over 95% instant? Suchanek says not. As she stated, "Keurig brews coffee.... If I was going to buy a k-cup of instant coffee, I would have used my hot water tap that has boiling water at the sink instead of buying an expensive Keurig machine." Taking all disputed facts in the light most favorable to Suchanek, a reasonable juror could conclude that Suchanek was deceived.

Here, consumers apparently failed to grasp the significance of the term "soluble" even though they knew what it meant in the abstract. Was the court of appeals correct to find sufficient evidence of misleadingness? Does Sturm's intent matter?

Ideally, and often in practice, the advertiser will be aware of the material claims implied by its ad. A lawyer reviewing an ad should begin by asking the advertiser what it intends to convey, and what it expects reasonable consumers will take away from the ad. From there, for a sufficiently large campaign, consumer testing may further elucidate what the ad implies. In all cases, the advertiser must possess substantiation for claims reasonably implied by the ad. If the advertiser says that it can only substantiate the explicit claims but intends a broader implicit claim, a good lawyer will insist that the ad go back to the drawing board, perhaps for a better disclosure or disclaimer (*see* Chapter 5).

What happens when context creates implications? Researchers found that consumers visiting hospitals with McDonald's restaurants on-site believed that McDonald's food was healthier than consumers visiting hospitals without such restaurants. Hannah B. Sahud et al., *Marketing Fast Food: Impact of Fast Food Restaurants in Children's Hospitals*, 118 PEDIATRICS 2290 (2006). What kind of regulation, if any, is appropriate for implications such as this?

In another case, a court found that it couldn't be false advertising for Wal-Mart to market two headache remedies with identical ingredients, where one was in a box with a red background and was two to three times more expensive than the other, which was sold in a box with a green background. The consumer plaintiffs alleged that the differences deceived consumers into thinking that the more expensive product was stronger and more effective. They contended that "no reasonable consumer would pay more than $9 for Equate Migraine when he or she could pay less than $3 for Equate ES [Extra strength] unless he or she believed Equate Migraine was more effective than Equate ES." But the court ruled that Wal-Mart hadn't engaged in any relevant "act, statement, or omission" as required by the relevant consumer protection law and that a consumer's assumptions couldn't establish liability.

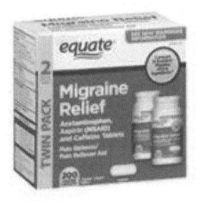 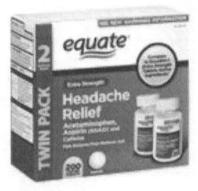

Boris v. Wal-Mart Stores, Inc., No. CV 13-7090 2014 WL 1477404 (C.D. Cal. Apr. 9, 2014). Why can't price and color be "acts" or even "statements" that imply comparative strength? Recall the discussion of price as a quality signal earlier in this chapter.

9. The Target Consumer

Consumers' inattention to the details of ads is a problem of long standing. In 1759, Samuel Johnson noted that "advertisements are now so numerous that they are very negligently perused." Samuel Johnson, The Works of Samuel Johnson, LL.D 159 (Luke Hansard & Sons 1810). On whom should the burden of any resulting misunderstanding or deception fall?

If the Ad Is Misleading, Who Is Being (Mis)led?

The standard applied under all false advertising laws asks whether an advertisement is "likely to mislead" consumers. For FTC and most state law purposes, no proof of actual deception is required; even an unsuccessful advertisement may be prohibited. *See, e.g.,* Novartis Corp. v. FTC, 223 F.3d 783 (D.C. Cir. 2000). Similarly, under the Lanham Act, once a plaintiff shows that an ad contains an explicit or implicit falsehood, injunctive relief has traditionally been available without proof that the falsehood actually convinced consumers to buy the advertised product or service.

"Misleading" is not, however, the same as "confusing." If consumers do not understand what message is being conveyed, as when they are presented with a "rating" that means nothing to them, there is no deception. *See* Royal Appliance Mfg. Co. v. Hoover Co., 845 F. Supp. 469 (N.D. Ohio 1994) ("While one might independently question the wisdom and effectiveness of a marketing campaign that leaves consumers shaking their heads in confusion, the Lanham Act does not speak to masochism.").

Traditionally, though not with perfect consistency, courts have held that consumers do not need to accept the false message as true in order to qualify as deceived. All that is required is that they perceive the false message—that is, understand that the advertiser wants them to believe the message. *See* Castrol, Inc. v. Pennzoil Quaker State Co., 2000 WL 1556019 (D.N.J. 2000) (finding false and enjoining a radio advertisement that was "not only inane, but insult[ed] the intelligence of the average consumer"); Am. Home Prods. Corp. v. Abbott Labs., 522 F. Supp. 1035 (S.D.N.Y. 1981) (enjoining claim interpreted by consumers to have false meaning, though "most consumers appear to discount or disregard this intended meaning"; "skepticism . . . does not affect the meaning itself or the fact that the meaning was conveyed").

If consumers instead understand something else—for example, that the advertiser is joking—then they haven't been deceived. In *Ebsco Industries, Inc. v. LMN Enterprises, Inc.*, 89 F. Supp. 2d 1248 (N.D. Ala. 2000), a manufacturer of fishing lures included on its packaging stories about "Boomer Wells," said to be a professional fisherman, including stories of his winning a trip to Finland and a trip to "the slammer" after winning a fishing tournament. Purchasers had stated "that they either love the funny stories about Boomer Wells, or wish the defendants' brand would be more serious." Under the circumstances, the court found no evidence of likely deception.

Why require only evidence of *reception* and not the extra step of evidence of *deception*? First, if an express claim is falsely made, the law presumes that consumers are likely to be deceived by it. Once it has been demonstrated that consumers receive a message, it is the same as if the message had been explicitly stated. Second, consumers may be better judges of what messages they receive from ads than of what ultimately influences their purchasing decisions. If a claim is false and is being received, there is no justification for allowing it to influence consumers, even subliminally. Third, even if many consumers apply an automatic discount to most advertising claims, the law can still keep advertisers from calculated exploitation of consumer cynicism. Otherwise, there would be a classic problem of the market for lemons. True claims would be indistinguishable from a welter of false claims. As a result, courts generally only require that consumers receive a false message, not that they believe it, before granting relief.

What should happen if a defendant provides a properly conducted, convincing survey demonstrating that consumers overwhelmingly don't believe the message they receive? Is that proof that the message is puffery, even if it has the form of fact?

The Credulous Consumer: The Consumer Who Believes Too Readily

Courts have long construed the prohibition on "deceptive" conduct in the FTCA broadly. At a minimum, "deceptive" meant that a practice had a tendency to deceive a significant number of consumers, even unsophisticated ones. When Charles of the Ritz advertised that Rejuvenescence skin cream would "restore natural moisture necessary for a live, healthy skin" and produce a skin that would "know no drought years," the FTC alleged that this was a deceptive promise that the cream would actually reverse the aging process. Charles of the Ritz responded that no reasonable person would believe such a thing, but the court of appeals found the "reasonable" person irrelevant. The "law was not made for the protection of experts, but for the public—that vast multitude which includes the ignorant, the unthinking and the credulous." Charles of the Ritz Dist. Corp. v. FTC, 143 F.2d 676 (2d Cir. 1944).

This standard was broad enough to engender significant criticism and uncertainty. The FTC staff even brought a complaint against the maker of a bathing garment (to be worn under a bathing suit) advertised as "invisible." The commission dismissed the case, reasoning that

> An advertiser cannot be charged with liability in respect of every conceivable misconception, however outlandish, to which his representations might be subject among the foolish or feeble-minded. . . . Perhaps a few misguided souls believe, for example, that all "Danish pastry" is made in Denmark. Is it therefore an actionable deception to advertise "Danish pastry" when it is made in this country? Of course not.

Heinz W. Kirchner, 63 F.T.C. 1282 (1963).

Even though the FTC has abandoned this standard, and many states have followed, the "credulous consumer" concept remains in some state consumer protection statute cases. *See, e.g.*, Weinberg v. Sun Co., 740 A.2d 1152 (Pa. 1999) (Pennsylvania Unfair Trade Practices and Consumer Protection Law); Doe v. Boys Clubs, Inc., 907 S.W.2d 472 (Tex. 1995) (Texas Deceptive Trade Practices Act). Unless a state has recent precedent applying this standard, however, it may be unwise for a plaintiff to rely on it even if there is case law using this language, given the modern trend.

The original formulation of the standard can be read as an empirical claim: the vast multitude of the public includes those who are ignorant, unthinking, and/or credulous. If, as some tort cases hold, "[a] drunken man is as much entitled to a safe street as a sober one, and much more in need of it," Robinson v. Pioche, Bayerque & Co., 5 Cal. 460 (1855), then doesn't the same reasoning hold for advertising?

Or should we worry more about discouraging wariness? Do we want the ignorant, unthinking and credulous to take more care, and *can* we make them do so? In other words, would a few bad experiences with believing ad claims really encourage them to become more educated, thoughtful and skeptical? Marketers tend to identify certain groups as having a generally high or generally low skepticism about ads, suggesting that it might be hard for the legal regime to have significant effects on consumers' default level of wariness. *See, e.g.,* Prendergast et al., *A Hong Kong Study of Advertising Credibility,* 26 J. CONSUMER MKTG. 320 (2009) (skeptical consumers tend to be older and more educated than credulous ones, and to have more self-esteem).

Recall the facts of *Vokes v. Arthur Murray, Inc.,* 212 So. 2d 906 (Fla. Ct. App. 1968), from Chapter 3. Was Audrey Vokes a credulous consumer? A reasonable consumer? What standard did the court use to protect her?

The Reasonable Consumer

In 1983, in response to Congressional directives to revisit its policies, the FTC issued a new Policy Statement. *See* FTC Policy Statement on Deception, Appended to Cliffdale Associates, Inc., 103 F.T.C. 110, 174 (1984). First, the FTC took the position that a practice is deceptive if it is "likely to mislead," rather than having a "tendency to mislead." Second, the FTC would examine the practice from "the perspective of a consumer acting reasonably in the circumstances. If the representation or practice affects or is directed primarily to a particular group, the commission examines reasonableness from the perspective of that group." And finally, the practice would have to be material—"likely to affect the consumer's conduct or decision with regard to a product or service." Courts applying the Lanham Act also use these standards. In general, European regulators also use the concept of the average or reasonable consumer, though they are likely to be more concerned with vulnerable consumers in a mixed population.

If a practice is "likely to mislead" the relevant consumers, then is anything additional gained by asking if they are acting reasonably? Can you imagine a situation where a practice would be likely to mislead a substantial number of consumers who were not acting reasonably under the circumstances? In practice, regulators and courts are likely to interpret these two requirements in tandem *if*— and it is a big if—they have not already deemed the representation at issue to be puffery.

The reasonable consumer standard is flexible. Because the focus is on the relevant consumers, an ad targeted at children will be evaluated from their perspective. Children are presumed to have less experience sorting truth from untruth. *See, e.g.*, ITT Continental Baking Co. v. FTC, 532 F.2d 207 (upholding FTC's determination that advertising for Wonder Bread was deceptive as to children, who were targeted). Similarly, if an advertisement is targeted at another vulnerable population (people in search of magical charms or cures for serious illnesses), it will be evaluated from their perspectives. *See* Gottlieb v. Schaffer, 141 F. Supp. 7 (S.D.N.Y. 1956) (claims that "magical or necromantic articles" would produce good luck and romantic success constituted mail fraud; products were targeted "only to the ignorant, superstitious and credulous, who by reason of the representations might rely upon the worthless articles"); FTC Policy Statement on Deception § III ("[T]erminally ill consumers might be particularly susceptible to exaggerated cure claims.").

According to the FTC Policy Statement, "[t]o be considered reasonable, the interpretation or reaction does not have to be the only one. When a seller's representation conveys more than one meaning to reasonable consumers, one of which is false, the seller is liable for the misleading interpretation." In addition, if an advertiser intends a meaning, that interpretation will be presumed reasonable. And reasonability is not necessarily the same thing as rationality; predictable cognitive failures can be taken into account (as advertisers are surely doing when they run ads). *See* Porter & Dietsch, 90 F.T.C. 770 (1977) ("[M]any people who need or want to lose weight regard dieting as bitter medicine. To these corpulent consumers the promises of weight loss without dieting are the Siren's call, and advertising that heralds unrestrained consumption while muting the inevitable need for temperance, if not abstinence, simply does not pass muster."), *aff'd*, 605 F.2d 294 (7th Cir. 1979).

Courts sometimes determine a reasonable consumer's understanding as a matter of law, even without evidence. *See* Oswego Laborers' Local 214 Pension Fund v. Marine Midland Bank, 647 N.E.2d 741 (N.Y. 1995). Depending on the situation, a reasonable consumer might have to consult other available information rather than relying solely on the advertiser's claims. (Recall the *New York Law School* case from Chapter 3.) Moreover, a reasonable consumer isn't necessarily entitled to rely on a slogan or catchphrase, especially where it should be clear that individual results may vary. A consumer who failed to amass "True Savings" as a result of a telephone company's "True Savings" slogan had no remedy under the "reasonable consumer" standard. Marcus v. AT&T Corp., 938 F. Supp. 1158 (S.D.N.Y. 1996). Another court held that a reasonable consumer would use common sense and would not expect a telephone company's billing to be calculated in seconds. Porr v. NYNEX Corp., 230 A.D.2d 564 (2d Dep't 1997). (Is the factual, commonsense basis for this conclusion still valid?)

Like New York, many other states have followed the FTC's shift to the reasonable consumer standard. *See, e.g.*, Freeman v. Time, Inc., 68 F.3d 285 (9th Cir. 1995) (interpreting California statutes to protect a person of ordinary intelligence, unless particularly gullible consumers are targeted).

In fact, the difference between the "reasonable" and "credulous" standards may not be that significant in the majority of cases. The "reasonable consumer" is in fact an average target consumer. An ad violates the FTC Act if it misleads a substantial number of consumers, even if the majority are not misled. FTC Policy Statement on Deception, § III (Oct. 14, 1983) n. 20. Especially if an advertiser exploits the credulity of its target consumers, it can't rely on *caveat emptor*—the rule that the FTC Act and similar state laws were enacted precisely to reverse. *See* FTC v. Standard Educ. Soc., 302 U.S. 112 (1937) ("There is no duty resting upon a citizen to suspect the honesty of those with whom he transacts business. Laws are made to protect the trusting as well as the suspicious.").

The modern sales context also makes a difference. Given how many products and services are on the market, it would be impossible, and indeed unreasonable, for even the most prudent consumer to learn all the necessary information to evaluate them all. Thus, for example, an average consumer is not likely to know that 30% of the calcium in milk is lost in the process of making cheese. *See* Kraft, Inc. v. FTC, 970 F.2d 311 (7th Cir. 1992).

A reasonable consumer takes at least some factual claims at face value, even if he or she knows that a certain percentage are unreliable. The costs of sorting the false from the true are too great. For smaller purchases, it's even reasonable not to think much about ad claims at all. *See* Sterling Drug, Inc. v. FTC, 741 F.2d 1146 (9th Cir. 1984) (approving FTC's reliance on testimony that "consumers did not devote mental energy to interpreting [analgesic] advertisements and would not 'rationally process advertising communications' " to show that "given a broad general representation of 'quality,' consumers would not attempt to analyze the components of quality").

Even if the subject matter is expensive or important, a reasonable consumer who lacks the specialized information necessary to evaluate a claim is allowed to rely on the advertiser's apparent authority because he or she has no practical alternative. Thus, for example, an average consumer acting reasonably won't know much about credit insurance. *See* Card v. Chase Manhattan Bank, 669 N.Y.S.2d 117 (Civil Ct., City of N.Y. 1996). Consumers may also reasonably rely on "the representations of an apparently reputable firm staffed by experts and specializing in" the market for rare and valuable coins. FTC v. Sec. Rare Coin & Bullion Corp., 931 F.2d 1312 (9th Cir. 1991).

The Sophisticated Consumer

The law generally presumes that a sophisticated audience—usually, one composed of people with experience in the topic at hand—is less likely to be fooled. This is especially true when the issue is misleadingness rather than pure falsity. Sophisticated groups include:

- doctors, FTC Policy Statement § III;
- veterinarians, Pfizer, Inc. v. Merial, Ltd., 2000 WL 640669 (S.D.N.Y. 2000);
- hospitals, First Health Gp. Corp. v. United Payors & United Providers Inc., 95 F. Supp. 2d 845 (N.D. Ill. 2000);
- advertising buyers, San Juan Star v. Casiano Communic., Inc., 85 F. Supp. 2d 89 (D.P.R. 2000); and
- retailers, Plough, Inc. v. Johnson & Johnson Baby Prods. Co., 532 F. Supp. 714 (D. Del. 1982).

These groups are sophisticated as to particular claims within the scope of their expertise, such as the meaning of drug studies for doctors and veterinarians or the meaning of particular terms to the retail trade. Similarly, where the defendant showed a catalog to retailers at a toy fair, and it was well known in the industry that not all exhibited toys are ultimately manufactured, the presence of a toy in the catalog was not a false representation that the toy would definitely be available. *See* FASA Corp. v. Playmates Toys, Inc., 912

F. Supp. 1124 (N.D. Ill. 1996), *aff'd in relevant part*, 107 F.3d 140 (1997).

Sophistication won't always confer protection. Specialized training in medicine or another field, for example, may not confer special ability to ferret out linguistic ambiguities and uncertainties in advertising claims. *Cf.* CARL ELLIOTT, WHITE COAT, BLACK HAT: ADVENTURES ON THE DARK SIDE OF MEDICINE (2010) ("The best mark is often a person to whom the possibility of a con never occurs, simply because he thinks he is too smart to be tricked. . . . Many doctors know nothing about advertising, salesmanship, or public relations. They believe these are jobs for people who could not get into medical school. This is probably why doctors are so easily fooled."). Sophistication also can't protect against hard-to-verify false claims, such as misrepresentations about product ingredients. *See* Genderm Corp. v. Biozone Labs., 1992 WL 220638 (N.D. Ill. Sept. 3, 1992) (finding actionable falsehood in misrepresentation of a drug's active ingredient to physicians and pharmacists).

In close cases, the principle that all audiences are entitled to truth in advertising may control. *See* JR Tobacco, Inc. v. Davidoff of Geneva (CT), Inc., 957 F. Supp. 426 (S.D.N.Y. 1997) ("Regardless of the sophistication JR attributes to its audience [of cigar buyers], purchasers are entitled to truthful statements. . . . "). So an advertiser who touted its legal directory as "official" gave it an "imprimatur of state authority," and, even though the audience of lawyers might have been unlikely to regard the directory as state-sponsored, the term was still found to be literally false. Skinder-Strauss Assoc. v. Mass. Continuing Legal Educ., 914 F. Supp. 665 (D. Mass. 1995).

In addition, a statement that specialists would understand correctly may mislead a general audience. *See* Zauderer v. Office of Disciplinary Counsel of Supreme Court of Ohio, 471 U.S. 626 (1985) (lawyer's statements to public that clients would not have to pay "legal fees" if their lawsuits were unsuccessful were likely to deceive without disclosure that clients would have to pay costs of action; "it is a commonplace that members of the public are often unaware of the technical meanings of such terms as 'fees' and 'costs'—terms that, in ordinary usage, might well be virtually interchangeable").

A "Not Insubstantial Number" of Consumers

An ad only violates the law if it's *likely* to deceive consumers. Minimal deception resulting from unusual carelessness or idiosyncratic interpretations is insufficient to show false advertising. Thus, to justify relief, a "not insubstantial number" (the general phrase used in Lanham Act cases) or a "substantial number" (the standard adopted by the FTC) of consumers must be likely to be deceived.

The different wording doesn't seem to make a difference in result. Recall that the FTC doesn't need to provide consumer surveys, so it will less often need to speak in percentage terms than Lanham Act plaintiffs. (The FTC and NAD will, however, consider consumer evidence when it's available, and generally react similarly to surveys as courts applying the Lanham Act.) Even with the Lanham Act, if a statement is false on its face, courts won't require independent proof that a substantial number of consumers are actually deceived.

When numbers are present, the percentage considered "substantial" varies depending on the circumstances. Unsurprisingly, the FTC takes the position that, where deception is likely to cause very serious harm, the advertiser will be held to a very high standard, and Lanham Act courts have reasoned similarly when products involve human safety. *See, e.g.*, Firestone Tire & Rubber Co., 81 F.T.C. 429 (1972), *aff'd*, 481 F.2d 246 (6th Cir. 1973); Am. Home Prods. Corp. v. Johnson & Johnson, 654 F. Supp. 568 (S.D.N.Y. 1987).

320

But what litigants and courts really want to know is: what percentage of deceived consumers is sufficient to enjoin an ad? The case law here comes from the Lanham Act, and because false advertising sits side by side with trademark infringement in the Lanham Act, courts have drawn freely from both bodies of law in evaluating survey evidence, including the percentage of deception that will suffice to show likely deception/confusion.

We will consider surveys in more detail later, but a good rule of thumb is that a good, well-controlled survey that shows net 20% or greater deception will be highly persuasive for the plaintiff, and that one that shows 10% or less will be highly persuasive for the defendant. *Compare* McNeilab, Inc. v. Am. Home Prods. Corp., 675 F. Supp. 819 (S.D.N.Y. 1987), *aff'd*, 848 F.2d 34 (2d Cir. 1988) (21–34% was not insignificant); *and* R.J. Reynolds Tobacco Co. v. Loew's Theatres, Inc. 522 F. Supp. 867 (S.D.N.Y. 1980) (20–33% was not insignificant) *with In Re* Campbell Soup Co., NAD Case No. 3302 (closed May 21, 1996) (survey finding of slightly above 10% confusion "insufficient to warrant a finding that people are being misled"). For the substantial number of cases in which survey numbers fall in the middle of that range, other factors (specifically, the court's own assessment of likely deception), will probably determine the outcome. *See* Johnson & Johnson v. Carter-Wallace, Inc., 487 F. Supp. 740 (S.D.N.Y. 1979) (15% was not insubstantial).

There are always outliers, however. One court found 27% confusion not to be substantial enough. Borden, Inc. v. Kraft, Inc., 224 U.S.P.Q. 811 (N.D. Ill. 1984). Lower percentages will be more persuasive when that still means a large absolute number of consumers. *See* James Burrough, Ltd. v. Sign of the Beefeater, Inc., 540 F.2d 266 (7th Cir. 1976) (court "cannot agree that 15% is 'small' " percentage of deception, given the size of the restaurant-going community); Humble

Oil & Refining Co. v. Am. Oil Co., 405 F.2d 803 ("11% of a [consumer population] figure in the millions is a high number").

10. Materiality

Not all false claims actually change consumer behavior. Rather than worrying about inconsequential false claims, the plaintiff must show that the false claim is "material."

> ### A. Introduction (adapted from Rebecca Tushnet, *Running the Gamut from A to B: Federal Trademark and False Advertising Law*, 159 U. PENN. L. REV. 1305 (2010))

To be actionable under § 43(a)(1)(B), a falsehood must be material: it must be likely to affect a reasonable consumer's purchasing decision, because not all deceptions affect consumer decisions. Materiality, among other concepts, allows courts to exonerate certain ad claims on their face as non-actionable puffery, because consumers allegedly don't rely on general superiority claims or other puffing. Consumers are irrebuttably presumed not to rely on sufficiently vague or exaggerated claims.

Until the late twentieth century, the test for false advertising under the Lanham Act could be simply stated: a plaintiff only needed to show falsity plus harm to prevail. Materiality is intuitively part of harm, because harm only comes when there is a causal link between the falsehood and consumers' behavior. Materiality is now generally split out into a separate requirement in the more elaborate modern multifactor test for false advertising. Some courts applying the Lanham Act have demanded a showing that an advertiser "misrepresented an 'inherent quality or characteristic' " of a product or service, but this requirement is essentially equivalent to materiality.

Given the variety of products and services on the market, the number of possible material claims is almost infinite. A few litigated examples: a mixer's speed and efficiency; a tax preparer's claim to offer instant "refunds" rather than instant loans against anticipated refunds; and a representation that a product was EPA-approved. Still, not every divergence between claim and reality is material: courts have denied false advertising claims based on overstatements of the number of the defendant's real estate transactions by 4%; statements about technical aspects of a product when those aspects were not generally understood by and were not a significant concern of purchasers; statements that reimbursements would be "two and a half times faster" than competitors' reimbursements; statements that sports scores were updated "from the arena" when they actually were taken from simultaneous broadcasts; and a letter that warned of three lawsuits against a competitor's product when there were only two lawsuits.

In general, courts have evaluated materiality by inquiring whether, as a matter of common sense and the intended uses of the product or service, a claim is likely to be relevant to a purchasing decision. Cases have often taken materiality for granted, especially when a claim is central to an advertising campaign or relates to health or safety. Courts have also developed various doctrines allowing them to presume materiality in cases of outright falsity or bad intent.

In rare cases, courts have used materiality to express uncertainty about the effects of advertising writ large: one court thought that a cough syrup's claim to work instantly was not likely to be material because "[p]arents buy what their pediatrician or their own experience tells them is most effective." Sandoz Pharm. Corp. v. Richardson-Vicks, Inc., 735 F. Supp. 597 (D. Del. 1989).

Materiality can also help explain the "#1 Choice of Doctors" case, *Mead Johnson & Co. v. Abbott Labs.*, 201 F.3d 883, modified by 209 F.3d 1032 (7th Cir. 2000). In that case, the Seventh Circuit rejected the relevance of a survey showing that many consumers believed that "#1 Choice of Doctors" meant that most doctors preferred Abbott's infant formula, when in fact most doctors thought the products were all basically the same. Because Abbott's formula was the first choice *of the doctors who had a preference* (a not insignificant number, though not a majority), the court held that the claim was literally true and that survey evidence was inappropriate. The Seventh Circuit distinguished between claims that are "misleading" and claims that are merely "misunderstood" by consumers. Only the former, the court ruled, can be found to violate the Lanham Act. One way to read this is that the Lanham Act requires intentional falsity; *misleading* can imply a knowing misstatement, whereas a consumer might misunderstand an innocent, well-meant claim.

A better way to think about the difference between misunderstood and misleading claims is to focus on materiality. One may misunderstand a fact in the abstract: I could be wrong about how big a computer's hard drive is. If I am misled, however, I am *led*: induced, or at least potentially induced, to change my position by my misunderstanding, as when I am more likely to buy the computer because of my misunderstanding. It is the combination of misunderstanding and likelihood of action—materiality—that produces misleadingness. Understood in that way, *Mead Johnson's* distinction makes some sense.

The Seventh Circuit's attempt to focus on materiality in this somewhat confusing way is consistent with a general judicial trend of greater attention to materiality, albeit without a standardized vocabulary. The case that triggered greater attention to materiality was *Pizza Hut v. Papa John's*, whose facts are introduced *supra*. In the following excerpt, the court of appeals reverses the jury finding of false advertising. Given what you've read in the introductory materials, why wouldn't "Better ingredients" and similar claims be presumptively material to consumers?

Pizza Hut, Inc. v. Papa John's Int'l, Inc., 227 F.3d 489, 503 (5th Cir. 2000)

[Review the facts from the Puffery section.] . . . Concluding that when the slogan ["Better Ingredients. Better Pizza."] was used as the tag line in the sauce and dough ads it became misleading, we must now determine whether reasonable consumers would have a tendency to rely on this misleading statement of fact in making their purchasing decisions. We conclude that Pizza Hut has failed to adduce evidence establishing that the misleading statement of fact conveyed by the ads and the slogan was material to the consumers to which the slogan was directed. Consequently, because such evidence of materiality is necessary to establish liability under the Lanham Act, the district court erred in denying Papa John's motion for judgment as a matter of law.

As previously discussed, none of the underlying facts supporting Papa John's claims of ingredient superiority made in connection with the slogan were literally false. Consequently, in order to satisfy its prima facie case, Pizza Hut was required to submit evidence establishing that the impliedly false or misleading statements were material to, that is, they had a tendency to influence the purchasing decisions of, the consumers to which they were directed. *See* American Council, 185 F.3d at 614 (stating that "a plaintiff relying upon statements that are literally true yet misleading cannot obtain relief by arguing how consumers could react; it must show how consumers actually do react"). We conclude that the evidence proffered by Pizza Hut fails to make an adequate showing.

. . . . Although Papa John's 1998 Awareness, Usage & Attitude Tracking Study showed that 48% of the respondents believe that "Papa John's has better ingredients than other national pizza chains," the study failed to indicate whether the conclusions resulted from the advertisements at issue, or from personal eating experiences, or from a combination of both. Consequently, the results of this study are not reliable or probative to test whether the slogan was material. Further, Pizza Hut provides no precedent, and we are aware of none, that stands for the proposition that the subjective intent of the defendant's corporate executives to convey a particular message is evidence of the fact that consumers in fact relied on the message to make their purchases. Thus, this evidence does not address the ultimate issue of materiality.

NOTES AND QUESTIONS

How could Pizza Hut have proved materiality, especially if many people have in fact eaten at Papa John's and thus have personal experience? What is the relevance of the evidence that advertising can affect how people report their own sensory experiences of a product, discussed earlier in this chapter?

Though survey evidence of materiality is unlikely to be required in other cases, the *Pizza Hut* case and others like it show an increased attention to particularized evidence of materiality, such as statements from consumers that they care about a specific product claim. Thus, in a case involving "100%" pomegranate juice that was in fact made mostly of other juices and added coloring, the court carefully went through evidence that consumers cared that a product whose name was "100% Pomegranate Juice" actually contained pomegranate juice. The common sense that consumers care about health, safety, and/or explicit product claims that are the focus of advertising is no longer enough to guarantee a victory for a Lanham Act plaintiff, though it will often suffice if unchallenged.

Depending on the evidence, materiality may be a question of fact for a jury. *See* Fed. Express Corp. v. USPS, 40 F. Supp. 2d 943 (W.D. Tenn. 1999) (finding that the question of whether claims to be a "company" and to offer "worldwide" service were material required further factual development regarding consumer perceptions); Oil Heat Inst. v. Nw. Nat'l Gas, 708 F. Supp. 1118 (D. Or. 1988) (holding that jury could reasonably conclude that claims regarding amount of maintenance required by natural gas equipment were material).

Extrinsic evidence about materiality. In *LG Electronics v. Whirlpool Corp.*, 2010 WL 2921633 (N.D. Ill. 2010), LG's basic claim was that Whirlpool used the term *steam* in its ads and in the name of its Duet Steam Dryer, but didn't truly use steam, instead using a mist of cold water sprayed into a warm dryer drum. Whirlpool allegedly falsely advertised a misting dryer that competed with LG's true steam dryer. Whirlpool's expert conducted a survey on materiality, and opined that "even if one assumes that a majority of the consumers were taking away a claim that the Whirlpool Dryer injects hot vapor onto clothes . . . , my survey shows no statistical difference in the intent to purchase as well as in product quality in comparison to a control ad that explicitly added the language stating that a mist of water is injected and is heated after it is sprayed into the dryer drum."

The court found that this testimony would be relevant and helpful as a rebuttal to LG's implied falsity theory. However, if LG ultimately won the argument that it was literally false to call Whirlpool's dryer a "steam" dryer under any reasonable definition of steam, then the testimony would not be relevant, because literally false claims can be enjoined without further evidence of consumer reaction.

In another opinion in the same case, the court noted that materiality can be "self-evident" when a claim goes to the inherent quality of a product or a defining feature. Consumer complaints about their disappointment with the inability to rely on the claims at issue can also show materiality. It can also be reasonable to infer materiality from a marketing strategy highlighting the claimed feature. The court concluded, however, that even though surveys and expert testimony on materiality are not necessary, they can still be helpful.

Materiality doesn't have to be rational. Regardless of how it is shown, materiality remains a matter of subjective consumer preference. "The public is entitled to get what it chooses, though the choice may be dictated by caprice or by fashion or perhaps by ignorance." FTC v. Algoma Lumber Co., 291 U.S. 67 (1934) (Cardozo, J.). Trademark law reasons similarly. Confusion over the source of goods, even if there is no objective difference between the products, interferes with consumers' ability to make decisions based on experience with the trademark and to get their goods from a particular source of their choosing. "[P]eople like to get what they think they are getting, and courts have steadfastly refused in this class of cases to demand justification for their preferences. Shoddy and petty motives may control those preferences; but if the buyers wish to be snobs, the law will protect them in their snobbery." Benton Announcements v. FTC, 130 F.2d 254 (1942) (per curiam).

Similarly, an affirmative misrepresentation of EPA approval was enjoined because consumers are likely to consider it significant. Performance Indust. Inc. v. Koos Inc., 18 U.SP.Q.2d 1767 (E.D. Pa. 1990). Environmental-sounding certifications ("conflict-free diamonds," "dolphin-safe tuna," "no bovine growth hormone," and the like) are also likely to be material because they address the clearly articulated concerns of a subclass of consumers who will not otherwise purchase the product. *See* Performance Indust., *supra* ("In today's environmentally conscious world, [false claims regarding environmental safety] are serious misrepresentations. Consumers these days seem to favor products that are environmentally benign and to disdain those that are environmentally harsh. Middlemen merchants would tend to fill their inventories with the former. Thus, the potential economic impact is pronounced.").

The Supreme Court has embraced the idea that materiality depends on consumers' subjective preferences. A seller may regard consumers' preferences for new goods instead of reprocessed ones, or for verified product claims, as "an annoying or irrational habit," and may reason that "when the habit is broken the buyer will be satisfied with the performance of the product he receives." Nonetheless, misrepresentation may not be used to break such bad habits. FTC v. Colgate-Palmolive Co., 380 U.S. 374 (1965).

Materiality and the NAD. The NAD takes the position that materiality is not relevant to NAD's inquiry, which is focused on determining whether the advertiser has provided a reasonable basis substantiating all messages reasonably conveyed by its advertising. Sprint Corp. (Sprint Wireless Services), NAD Case #5812 (02/18/15).

B.   Materiality and the FTC

The FTC applies a presumption of materiality to several types of claims: (1) express claims (since the advertiser's reason for making a claim is ordinarily that consumers would rely on it), (2) implied claims where the seller intended to make the claim, (3) omissions where the seller knew that an ordinary consumer would need the omitted information to evaluate the product or service, and (4) claims that significantly involve health, safety, or other matters with which reasonable consumers would be concerned. This last category includes claims that concern the purpose, safety, healthfulness, efficacy or cost of the product or service; its durability, performance, warranties or quality; or findings by another agency regarding the product. FTC Policy Statement on Deception, 103 F.T.C. 174, appended to Cliffdale Assocs., 103 F.T.C. 110 (1984).

In one case, the advertiser offered an ad agency executive's opinion that consumers didn't care about aspirin content for rub-on pain relievers such as the company's Aspercreme. The FTC rejected this opinion, given research showing that a substantial percentage of consumers preferred aspirin over non-aspirin pain relievers. Thus, it was material that consumers believed that Aspercreme contained aspirin. Thompson Med. Co., 104 F.T.C. 648 (1984), aff'd, 791 F.2d 189 (D.C. Cir. 1986). In addition, a price premium charged for the misleading product compared to the prices of nonmisleading products may be good extrinsic evidence that the misleading claim is material, since the advertiser expects consumers to be willing to pay extra for it. See Am. Home Prods., 98 F.T.C. 136 (1981), aff'd, 695 F.2d 681 (3d Cir. 1982). However, most FTC cases don't involve extrinsic evidence of materiality on either side. And, as the next case shows, an advertiser may face difficulty disavowing the materiality of a claim it has prominently made.

Kraft, Inc. v. Federal Trade Commission, 970 F.2d 311 (7th Cir. 1992)

Kraft, Inc. ("Kraft") asks us to review an order of the Federal Trade Commission ("FTC" or "Commission") finding that it violated §§ 5 and 12 of the Federal Trade Commission Act ("Act"). The FTC determined that Kraft, in an advertising campaign, had misrepresented information regarding the amount of calcium contained in Kraft Singles American Pasteurized Process Cheese Food ("Singles") relative to the calcium content in five ounces of milk and in imitation cheese slices. The FTC ordered Kraft to cease and desist from making these misrepresentations and Kraft filed this petition for review. We enforce the Commission's order.

I.

. . . Process cheese food slices, also known as "dairy slices," must contain at least 51% natural cheese by federal regulation. Imitation cheese slices, by contrast, contain little or no natural cheese and consist primarily of water, vegetable oil, flavoring agents, and fortifying agents. While imitation slices are as healthy as process cheese food slices in some nutrient categories, they are as a whole considered "nutritionally inferior" and must carry the label "imitation." . . .

Kraft Singles are process cheese food slices. In the early 1980s, Kraft began losing market share to an increasing number of imitation slices that were advertised as both less expens[ive] and equally nutritious as dairy slices like Singles. Kraft responded with a series of advertisements, collectively known as the "Five Ounces of Milk" campaign, designed to inform consumers that Kraft Singles cost more than imitation slices because they are made from five ounces of milk rather than less expensive ingredients. The ads also focused on the calcium content of Kraft Singles in an effort to capitalize on growing consumer interest in adequate calcium consumption.

The FTC filed a complaint against Kraft charging that this advertising campaign materially misrepresented the calcium content and relative calcium benefit of Kraft Singles. The FTC Act makes it unlawful to engage in unfair or deceptive commercial practices, 15 U.S.C. § 45, or to induce consumers to purchase certain products through advertising that is misleading in a material respect. Thus, an advertisement is deceptive under the Act if it is likely to mislead consumers, acting reasonably under the circumstances, in a material respect. In implementing this standard, the Commission examines the overall net impression of an ad and engages in a three-part inquiry: (1) what claims are conveyed in the ad; (2) are those claims false or misleading; and (3) are those claims material to prospective consumers.

Two facts are critical to understanding the allegations against Kraft. First, although Kraft does use five ounces of milk in making each Kraft Single, roughly 30% of the calcium contained in the milk is lost during processing. Second, the vast majority of imitation slices sold in the United States contain 15% of the U.S. Recommended Daily Allowance (RDA) of calcium per ounce, roughly the same amount contained in Kraft Singles. Specifically then, the FTC complaint alleged that the challenged advertisements made two implied claims, neither of which was true: (1) that a slice of Kraft Singles contains the same amount of calcium as five ounces of milk (the "milk equivalency" claim); and (2) that Kraft Singles contain more calcium than do most imitation cheese slices (the "imitation superiority" claim).

. . . The Skimp ads were designed to communicate the nutritional benefit of Kraft Singles by referring expressly to their milk and calcium content. The broadcast version of this ad on which the FTC focused contained the following audio copy:

> Lady (voice over): I admit it. I thought of skimping. Could you look into those big blue eyes and skimp on her? So I buy Kraft Singles. Imitation slices use hardly any milk. But Kraft has five ounces per slice. Five ounces. So her little bones get calcium they need to grow. No, she doesn't know what that big Kraft means. Good thing I do.

> Singers: Kraft Singles. More milk makes 'em . . . more milk makes 'em good.

> Lady (voice over): Skimp on her? No way.

The visual image corresponding to this copy shows, among other things, milk pouring into a glass until it reaches a mark on the glass denoted "five ounces." The commercial also shows milk pouring into a glass which bears the phrase "5 oz. milk slice" and which gradually becomes part of the label on a package of Singles. In January 1986, Kraft revised this ad, changing "Kraft has five ounces per slice" to "Kraft is made from five ounces per slice," and in March 1987, Kraft added the disclosure, "one 3/4 ounce slice has 70% of the calcium of five ounces of milk" as a subscript in the television commercial and as a footnote in the print ads. . . .

After a lengthy trial, the Administrative Law Judge (ALJ) concluded that [the Skimp ad and another ad violated the FTCA. The FTC affirmed the ALJ's decision, finding that the ad conveyed a milk equivalency claim and an imitation superiority claim].

. . . The FTC next found that the claims were material to consumers. It concluded that the milk equivalency claim is a health-related claim that reasonable consumers would find important and that Kraft believed that the claim induced consumers to purchase Singles. The FTC presumed that the imitation superiority claim was material because it found that Kraft intended to make that claim. It also found that the materiality of that claim was demonstrated by evidence that the challenged ads led to increased sales despite a substantially higher price for Singles than for imitation slices. . . .

II.

Our standard for reviewing FTC findings has been traditionally limited to the highly deferential, substantial evidence test. . . . Accordingly, we decline to review de novo the FTC's findings and, with the substantial evidence test in mind, turn to the facts of this case.

III.

. . . A claim is considered material if it "involves information that is important to consumers and, hence, likely to affect their choice of, or conduct regarding a product." The Commission is entitled to apply, within reason, a presumption of materiality, and it does so with three types of claims: (1) express claims; (2) implied claims where there is evidence that the seller intended to make the claim; and (3) claims that significantly involve health, safety, or other areas with which reasonable consumers would be concerned. Absent one of these situations, the Commission examines the record and makes a finding of materiality or immateriality.

Here, the ALJ concluded that both claims were presumptively material because calcium is a significant health concern to consumers. The Commission upheld this conclusion, although it applied a presumption of materiality only to the imitation superiority claim. Kraft asserts the Commission's determination is not supported by substantial evidence. We disagree.

In determining that the milk equivalency claim was material to consumers, the FTC cited Kraft surveys showing that 71% of respondents rated calcium content an extremely or very important factor in their decision to buy Kraft Singles, and that 52% of female, and 40% of all respondents, reported significant personal concerns about adequate calcium consumption. The FTC further noted that the ads were targeted to female homemakers with children and that the 60 milligram difference between the calcium contained in five ounces of milk and that contained in a Kraft Single would make up for most of the RDA calcium deficiency shown in girls aged 9–11. Finally, the FTC found evidence in the record that Kraft designed the ads with the intent to capitalize on consumer calcium deficiency concerns.

Significantly, the FTC found further evidence of materiality in Kraft's conduct: despite repeated warnings, Kraft persisted in running the challenged ads. Before the ads even ran, ABC television raised a red flag when it asked Kraft to substantiate the milk and calcium claims in the ads. Kraft's ad agency also warned Kraft in a legal memorandum to substantiate the claims before running the ads. Moreover, in October 1985, a consumer group warned Kraft that it believed the Skimp ads were potentially deceptive. Nonetheless, a high-level Kraft executive recommended that the ad copy remain unaltered because the "Singles business is growing for the first time in four years due in large part to the copy." Finally, the FTC and the California Attorney General's Office independently notified the company in early 1986 that investigations had been initiated to determine whether the ads conveyed the milk equivalency claims. Notwithstanding these warnings, Kraft continued to run the ads and even rejected proposed alternatives that would have allayed concerns over their deceptive nature. From this, the FTC inferred—we believe, reasonably—that Kraft thought the challenged milk equivalency claim induced consumers to purchase Singles and hence that the claim was material to consumers.

With regard to the imitation superiority claim, the Commission applied a presumption of materiality after finding evidence that Kraft intended the challenged ads to convey this message. It found this presumption buttressed by the fact that the challenged ad copy led to increased sales of Singles, even though they cost 40 percent more than imitation slices. Finally, the FTC determined that Kraft's consumer surveys were insufficient to rebut this inference and in particular criticized Kraft's survey methodology because it offered limited response options to consumers.

Kraft asserts that neither materiality finding is supported by substantial evidence. It contends that the survey evidence on which the Commission relied shows only that calcium, not milk equivalency, is important to consumers. Materiality, Kraft maintains, turns on whether the claim itself, rather than the subject matter of the claim, affects consumer decision-making; accordingly, the Commission had to show that consumers would have acted differently with knowledge that Singles contain 70% rather than 100% of the calcium in five ounces of milk. *See* FTC Policy Statement, 103 F.T.C. at 175 (claim is material if it is "likely to affect the consumer's conduct or decision with regard to a product"). With the inquiry defined in this manner, the only relevant evidence on point—a Kraft consumer survey showing that 1.7% of respondents would stop buying Singles if informed of the effect of processing on calcium content—definitively disproves materiality. With regard to its conduct, Kraft argues it persisted in running the ads because it thought the ads as a whole, not the milk equivalency claim per se, contributed to increased sales and that, in any event, it responded to warnings by making a good faith attempt to modify the ads. Kraft repeats these arguments in attacking the FTC's finding that imitation superiority claim was material to consumers, claiming the evidence adduced showed only that Kraft intended to use the ads to differentiate Singles from imitation slices based on milk content, and not on calcium content, and that sales increased as a result of this general theme; inferring that the imitation superiority claim contributed to increased sales is pure conjecture.

Kraft's arguments lack merit. The FTC found solid evidence that consumers placed great importance on calcium consumption and from this reasonably inferred that a claim quantifying the calcium in Kraft Singles would be material to consumers. It rationally concluded that a 30% exaggeration of calcium content was a nutritionally significant claim that would affect consumer purchasing decisions. This finding was supported by expert witnesses who agreed that consumers would prefer a slice of cheese with 100% of the calcium in five ounces of milk over one with only 70%. Likewise, the materiality presumption applied to the imitation superiority claim was supported by substantial evidence. This finding rested on internal company documents showing that Kraft designed the ads to deliver an imitation superiority message. Although Kraft produced a study refuting this finding, the Commission discounted that study after finding its methodology flawed. Kraft concedes that the Skimp ads increased sales of Singles, but contends that the Commission cannot carry its burden of demonstrating a linkage between the ads and the imitation superiority claim per se. However, this increase in sales corresponded directly with the ad campaign and indisputably reversed that sagging sales and market share of Kraft Singles that had been attributed to competition from imitation slices. Moreover, Kraft's increase in market share came at a time when Singles were priced roughly 40% higher than imitation slices. Thus, the Commission reasonably inferred that the imitation superiority message, as a central theme in the ads, contributed to increased sales and market share.

NOTES AND QUESTIONS

Which view of materiality is better: Kraft's contention that we should look specifically at the effect of *difference* between the truth and the misleading claim, or the FTC's more general view? If there isn't much difference between the truth and the misleading claim, why did Kraft choose to advertise the misleading claim?

In *Novartis Corporation v. Federal Trade Commission*, 223 F.3d 783 (D.C. Cir. 2000), Novartis contested a materiality finding by arguing that the market share of its product (a back-pain remedy) had not increased during the period in which misleading advertising touted its superior efficacy. The court was unimpressed. "The FTC's definition of materiality . . . embraces any claim that is 'likely to mislead a reasonable consumer.' There is no requirement of actual deceit. If a claim is material because likely to deceive, it is not rendered otherwise simply because it is unsuccessfully advertised."

How can something be both likely to affect a consumer's decision and unsuccessful?

The role of contextual factors in judging materiality. A statement's prominence (or lack thereof) in an advertisement may be relevant to its materiality:

> The statements as to the particular origin of game updates constitute nothing more than minutiae about SportsTrax, a reality demonstrated by their lack of prominence in the advertisement . . . . The insignificance of the statement "from the arena" is illustrated further by eliminating it entirely from the clause in which it is found. If that clause simply stated, "Nationwide game updates," I find it difficult to envision (and NBA has not shown otherwise) that consumers suddenly would reassess their decisions to purchase SportsTrax.

NBA v. Sports Team Analysis & Tracking Sys., Inc., 939 F. Supp. 1071 (S.D.N.Y. 1996), *aff'd in relevant part sub nom.* National Basketball Ass'n v. Motorola, Inc., 105 F.3d 841 (2d Cir. 1997). Prominence in an ad is certainly relevant to the advertiser's belief in the importance of the statement, which is often a good guide to consumer reactions.

In *Schick Manufacturing, Inc. v. Gillette Co.*, 372 F. Supp. 2d 273 (D. Conn. 2005), whose facts are set forth in the section on explicit falsity, the court noted that "[b]ecause of the expense of television advertising, companies have a very short period of time in which to create a 'reason to believe' and are generally forced to pitch only the key qualities and characteristics of the product advertised." The court thus concluded:

It is clear that whether the M3 Power raises hairs is material.
Gillette's employees testified that television advertising time is too
valuable to include things that are "unimportant." Furthermore, in
this case, hair extension is the "reason to believe" that the M3 Power
is a worthwhile product. The magnitude and frequency of that effect
are also, therefore, material. Whether a material element of a
product's performance happens very often and how often that element
happens are, in themselves, material. . . .

C.   Materiality in the Face of Consumer Reaction Evidence

Are there some claims so self-evidently material that evidence
purporting to show the contrary should be disregarded, as Kraft
argued against the FTC? Consider the following case.

IDT Telecom, Inc. v. CVT Prepaid Solutions, Inc., 2009 WL 5205968 (D. N.J. 2009)

Prepaid calling cards are sold in dollar denominations (e.g., $5, $10)
and can be used to dial numerous destinations. The number of
minutes available on a calling card is determined by the rate per
minute of talk time to the destination called minus any fees and
charges. Advertisements for prepaid phone cards focus solely on the
number of minutes to the key destinations for that card. For example,
a poster will emphasize that a card offers "250 minutes to the
Dominican Republic."

[Defendants] used a system of fees and charges that could vary
according to destination, length and duration of the call, and reduced
the number of minutes available for talk time. . . . [P]osters informed
consumers about the gross number of minutes of talk time. The
posters also contained a disclaimer that addressed specific fees and
charges as follows: "[a]pplication of surcharges and fees will have the

effect of reducing total minutes actually received on the card from the minutes announced . . . . Prices and fees . . . are subject to change without notice." The same disclaimer was also included on the packaging that accompanied the calling cards.

. . . In addition to being false or misleading, the Plaintiffs must also prove that the Defendants' misrepresentation is "material, in that it is likely to confuse the purchasing decision." Defendants argue that the number of advertised minutes is completely immaterial to purchasers of prepaid calling cards. Defendants state that "[a]mong the most important factors for consumers are: (a) the number of minutes actually delivered by a card, rather than the advertised minutes; (b) the clarity of the connection; and (c) the connectivity of the card." Plaintiffs conducted a survey of potential prepaid calling card consumers. In this survey, they found that only 2 of 401 respondents indicated that Advertising/Posters/Flyers are how they "generally decide" which card to buy. The Johnson Report further states that only 3% of the consumers surveyed "look at the printed material in the store" to tell how many minutes are available on their cards. Defendants argue that these low numbers, on their own, prove that the advertisements are not material to the purchasing decisions of consumers. The Court is not convinced that low polling numbers in the Johnson report mean that the number of advertised minutes are, by law, immaterial to consumers. Because the advertisements go so clearly to the purpose of the product—the amount of minutes of talk time that they deliver—the statements are material as a matter of law. *See* S.C. Johnson & Son, Inc. v. Clorox Co., 241 F.3d 232, 238 (2d Cir. 2001) (lack of leakage is an inherent quality or characteristic of Ziploc storage bags such that a claim was clearly material). Thus, summary judgment with relation to the allegedly false and misleading posters is denied.

NOTES AND QUESTIONS

Didn't the court find materiality in the face of strong evidence that consumers ignore the claims at issue? What is the justification for this?

Why was a materiality survey appropriate in the LG/Whirlpool case, but not important in *IDT*? Is the claim in *IDT* simply more central to the product?

The court in *Rexall Sundown, Inc. v. Perrigo Co.*, 651 F. Supp. 2d 9 (E.D.N.Y. 2009), a case about competing joint care supplements, considered, among other things, the alleged falsity of a claim that the key ingredient in Rexall's product was "ten times more concentrated" than in other supplements. Consumers who were shown a package making that claim and consumers who were shown the same package from which the claim had been deleted showed no statistically significant difference in purchase interest. Rexall argued that this disproved materiality. The court disagreed:

> [T]he survey's inability to find evidence that any confusion influenced the purchasing decision does not require a finding of immateriality as a matter of law. In other words, the fact that a portion of the survey may undermine Perrigo's position regarding materiality does not mean that materiality cannot be proven by other means. Unlike on the issue of consumer confusion, materiality need not be proven by extrinsic evidence such as consumer surveys. Moreover, . . . materiality may be proven by showing that the misrepresentation related to an inherent characteristic of the product . . . . In the instant case, a reasonable jury could conclude that the "10 Times More Concentrated" Statement relates to an inherent characteristic or quality of the product—namely, its composition (in terms of the quantity of its active ingredient)

and/or effectiveness—such that it would be material to any consumer.

What's the proper approach to claim-specific surveys of materiality? Is the courts' apparent willingness to presume materiality when a claim is central to a product rebuttable, and if so, by what evidence?

What about more generalized evidence? Some research suggests that "Made in the USA" is material to consumers. *See* C. Min Han, *The Role of Consumer Patriotism in the Choice of Domestic Versus Foreign Products*, 28 J. ADVERTISING RES. 25 (1988); Oliver St. John, *Made in USA makes comeback as a marketing tool*, USA Today, Jan. 21, 2013 ("Over 80% of Americans are willing to pay more for Made-in-USA products, 93% of whom say it's because they want to keep jobs in the USA, according to a survey . . . ."). In litigation, what would the proper role of such evidence be? It isn't specific to the challenged ad but does say something about consumer beliefs—and might be more credible insofar as it comes from a source not associated with a defendant or a plaintiff.

D.   Endorsements and Other Stamps of Approval

Claims that appear to give a stamp of approval are generally material. For example, claims that numbers in a reference book were "Chilton times," the industry standard for determining automotive repair time, when the numbers were different from the original Chilton times, were material because consumers had relied on and trusted the original. Hearst Bus. Pub'g, Inc. v. W.G. Nichols, Inc., 76 F. Supp. 2d 459 (S.D.N.Y. 1999).

Even the statement "as seen on TV" has been found material, where the plaintiff's products actually have been advertised on television and the defendant's misrepresentation likely piggybacks on the plaintiff's television campaign. *See* Telebrands Corp. v. Wilton Indus.,

Inc., 983 F. Supp. 471 (S.D.N.Y. 1997). A misstatement about
television advertising could be material even without potential source
confusion: consumers may be more likely to purchase a product that
is advertised on television, in the belief that the advertiser has a
successful product that justifies the substantial outlay of television
advertising. This is an implication of Nelson's signaling theory of
advertising, discussed earlier in this chapter.

Does this mean that a celebrity endorsement is material? What about
the mere presence of a celebrity's name or image in an ad? Even if the
celebrity has no reason to know any more than a random person on
the street about whether or not the product is good? The FTC has
addressed many issues surrounding endorsements in its guide to
endorsements and testimonials. What current doctrine cannot quite
explain is why the FTC requires celebrity endorsements to reflect
some actual experience with/opinion about the product, even when
the celebrity makes no factual claim other than her or his
preference—that is, makes a claim that seems like classic puffery. We
will return to this puzzle in the next Chapter.

E.   The Scope of Materiality/Bait and Switch

If the consumer learns the truth about a claim before making a
purchase and then buys anyway, the advertiser may protest that the
falsity didn't affect the consumer's decision. Courts have been
unsympathetic to this defense, on the theory that consumers may
have been brought into the decision-making process on false
pretenses. Once there, various cognitive habits may lead consumers
to stick with their choices instead of walking out; consumers may also
simply not have the energy to go through the search process again. At
the very least, if leaving the transaction is harder than clicking the
"back" button on a browser, courts are likely to find that the falsity is
a but-for cause of the consumer's decision to buy and that this is not
allowed.

As the FTC says, "it is well established that it is unfair to make an initial contact or impression through a false or misleading representation, even though before purchase the consumer is provided with the true facts." Chrysler Corp., 87 F.T.C. 719 (1976), *modified on other grounds*, 90 F.T.C. 606 (1977). The FTC bars advertisers from misrepresenting a product such that later, on disclosure of the true facts, the purchaser may be switched to a different purchase. If a car is depicted in an ad with a certain price, the model depicted must be available at that price. If the model is instead substantially more expensive, even a disclaimer will not avoid liability. Federal Trade Commission Regulations, 16 C.F.R. § 238.0, et seq. The NAD reasons similarly. BMW of North America LLC, NAD Case No. 4156 (Mar. 17, 2004) ("starting at" base price should reflect the automobile shown in advertisement). Otherwise, buyers might inquire about the car at the price listed, only to discover that they'd need to pay more to get the car in the ad.

Once the advertiser has the consumer's attention, it may not discourage the purchase of the advertised product or service (which is usually a precursor of touting a more expensive alternative, completing the "switch"). Under the FTC regulations, evidence of whether or not an offer is bona fide includes (a) the refusal to show, demonstrate or sell the product offered in accordance with the terms of the offer, (b) the disparagement of the advertised product or associated services, (c) the failure to have sufficient quantity of the advertised product to meet reasonably anticipated demands, (d) the refusal to take orders for timely delivery, (e) the showing of a product that is defective or inappropriate for the purpose advertised, or (f) a sales or incentive plan designed to prevent or discourage salespeople from selling the advertised product.

F.   Materiality in Class Action Lawsuits

Class actions present a unique challenge for materiality: if a court requires evidence that a claim influenced each consumer, then class action treatment is impossible. As a result, in some states, including California, a finding that a claim is deceptive leads to a presumption of materiality that can be invoked on a class-wide basis. Other states disagree, and many putative class actions have failed on materiality or causation grounds—courts conclude that the plaintiff hasn't shown that, but for the misrepresentations, the class wouldn't have bought the product or service at issue, or would have paid less for it. At times, only competitors can bring viable claims when a significant percentage, but not all, of the relevant consumers would have been affected by a false claim.

G.   A Final Note on the Relevance of Materiality: What Really Sells Products?

As the materials at the beginning of this chapter indicated, numerous factors can affect consumer decision making. For example, advertisers exploit our urge for reciprocity: free samples and other "gifts" trigger a feeling of responsibility, such that we buy more. Surprisingly, this tactic even works when we didn't want and didn't like the free "gift," if we were unable to avoid accepting it. Notably, regulators have attempted to control abuses of this practice, such as the FTC's guides on the use of "free" and various statutory provisions regarding receipt of unsolicited merchandise. But free samples and other reciprocity-triggering tactics, which can be as small as complimentary candy at a car dealership, remain powerful and unregulated. *See* David Adam Friedman, *Free Offers: A New Look*, 38 N.M. L. REV. 45 (2008).

To take another example, people are averse to extremes. Like Goldilocks, we tend to look for something that is "just right" in between choices. Thus, if an advertiser offers two options, one smaller and cheaper than the other, people will often choose the smaller, cheaper version. But if the advertiser adds a third, even larger and more expensive size, suddenly the sales of the now-middle size will go up. *See* Kelman et al., *Context Dependence in Legal Decision Making*, 25 J. LEGAL STUD. 287, 288 (1996).

More generally, modern advertising is not primarily, and sometimes not at all, directed at providing traditional information such as price. Research suggests that the amount of information per unit of advertising has declined substantially even as consumers' exposure to advertising has steadily increased. Ads have become shorter—from a 60-second standard for television ads in the 1960s to a substantial percentage presently that are only fifteen seconds long or even shorter. Facts have been replaced by ads designed to generate positive emotions about products and services. This is consistent with marketing researchers' conclusions that creation of positive affect is often the most effective way of persuading consumers to buy. Especially when consumers are distracted or overwhelmed by all the ads competing for their attention, they respond much more readily to non-informational cues such as humor. *See* Sarah C. Haan, Note, *The "Persuasion Route" of the Law: Advertising and Legal Persuasion*, 100 COLUM. L. REV. 1281 (2000).

Haan cites research showing that people are more likely to choose a brand and to pay more for it if it's easier to evaluate than other brands. Other researchers have found that ads containing more information are less persuasive. The more we like something, the more we discount the problems or risks it poses. Advertisers can therefore get us to ignore products' downsides by appealing to positive emotions. As a result, we get pictures and animation, humor and cuteness, and this impels us to buy, even though we are convinced that we are unaffected.

Occasionally, awareness of these techniques has an impact on ad regulation. Opponents of tobacco advertising argued that the attractive cartoon mascot Joe Camel was intentionally designed to appeal to known cognitive weaknesses and to override factual messages of the dangers of tobacco. Joe Camel is no longer Camel's mascot, and the tobacco industry has agreed to avoid the use of cartoons entirely in the U.S. *See* Jon D. Hanson & Douglas A. Kysar, *Taking Behaviorism Seriously: Some Evidence of Market Manipulation*, 112 HARV. L. REV. 1423 (1999).

Recently, the Ninth Circuit used empirical research to rebut a defendant's argument that allegedly false advertising of discounts didn't cause consumers any harm. California—like many states—specifically bans false claims of discounts, as the court explained:

> Most consumers have, at some point, purchased merchandise that was marketed as being "on sale" because the proffered discount seemed too good to pass up. Retailers, well aware of consumers' susceptibility to a bargain, therefore have an incentive to lie to their customers by falsely claiming that their products have previously sold at a far higher "original" price in order to induce customers to purchase merchandise at a purportedly marked-down "sale" price. Because such practices are misleading—and effective—the California legislature has prohibited them.

The defendants argued that, nonetheless, the consumer hadn't suffered any actionable harm, since he received the product at the advertised price. The court of appeals concluded that, to some consumers, "a product's 'regular' or 'original' price matters; it provides important information about the product's worth and the prestige that ownership of that product conveys." The court cited Dhruv Grewal & Larry D. Compeau, *Comparative Price Advertising: Informative or Deceptive?*, 11 J. PUB. POL'Y & MKTG. 52 (1992) ("By creating an impression of savings, the presence of a higher reference price enhances subjects' perceived value and willingness to buy the product."); *id.* at 56 ("[E]mpirical studies indicate that as discount size increases, consumers' perceptions of value and their willingness to buy the product increase, while their intention to search for a lower price decreases."). Indeed, this significance is exactly why retailers have an incentive to falsely advertise sales, and exactly why the California legislature barred the practice. Hinojos v. Kohl's Corp., No. 11-55793 (9th Cir. May 21, 2013).

But legal acknowledgement of the cognitive/behavioral background of marketing is in its infancy. And researchers are adding new nuances to our understanding of marketing all the time. In several recent experiments, for example, Juliano Laran et al. found that slogans (which tend to make explicit claims, though those claims may well be puffery) generated resistance among consumers. Consumers recognized that the slogans were designed to sell to them and automatically, without conscious thought, responded by reacting in the opposite direction from the slogan's point, whether that point was savings or luxury. By contrast, popular brand names/logos—to which similarly strong associations are attached, but which generally contain no explicit claims—primed consumers to behave in ways consistent with the brand's image. The brands, unlike the slogans, didn't trigger persuasion resistance. Julian Laran et al., *The Curious Case of Behavioral Backlash: Why Brands Produce Priming Effects and Slogans Produce Reverse Priming Effects*, 37 J. CONSUMER RES. 999 (Apr. 2011).

The effects of other ad components can also be tested separately. Marianne Bertrand et al. tested the effects of various marketing treatments on purchase decisions. A South African lender sent out over 53,000 letters to consumers who'd previously taken out loans with the lender, offering short-term loans at randomly chosen monthly interest rates ranging from 3.25% to 11.75%. The letters varied: some had detailed descriptions of loan terms, others had promotional giveaways, and others had pictures of a smiling, attractive woman in the corner. The picture of the attractive woman produced an increased response rate for men equivalent to dropping the monthly interest rate by 4.5% (that is, about 25% of the rate). By contrast, a large selection of example loans decreased responses compared to a single example loan, consistent with other research suggesting that proliferation of options makes consumers more hesitant to pick any one (the so-called paradox of choice). Marianne Bertrand et al., *What's Advertising Content Worth? Evidence from a Consumer Credit Marketing Field Experiment*, 125 Q. J. ECON. 263 (2010).

A special rate for you.

Congratulations! As a valued client, you are now eligible for a special interest rate on your next cash loan from   This is a limited time offer, so please come in by 31 October 2003

You can use this cash to buy an appliance, or for anything else you want.

Enjoy low monthly repayments with this offer! For example:

	4 Months	6 Months	12 Months
R500	R149.95	R108.28	R66.62
R1000	R299.90	R216.57	R133.23
R2000	R599.80	R433.13	R266.47
R4000	R1199.60	R866.27	R532.93

LOAN AVAILABILITY SUBJECT TO TERMS & CONDITIONS

Loans available in other amounts. There are no hidden costs. What you see is what you pay.

If you borrow elsewhere you will pay R280.14 more in total on a R350.00, 4 month loan.

How to apply:

Bring your ID book and latest payslip to your usual branch, by **31 October 2003** and ask for

Names of clients, employees and Lender suppressed to preserve confidentiality.

Customer Consultant

PS. Unfortunately, if you have already taken a loan since the date this letter was issued, you do not qualify for this offer. Comparison based on a competitor's interest rate of 25%.

What do these results suggest about materiality? About the relationship between the "reasonable" consumer and the average consumer? Which consumer should we protect? Should advertisers have to take consumers as they find them, even when they behave irrationally? More broadly: Given all this evidence that facts are at best a small part of what consumers respond to in ads, is the law's focus on facts a losing game? What would be the alternative?

CHAPTER 5: OMISSIONS AND DISCLOSURES

It is impossible for an ad to provide all the information that might help a consumer's decision making. An advertiser's obligation to disclose material information often turns on what else the advertiser has affirmatively said, though there are also many sector-specific regulations requiring certain types of disclosures. When some sort of disclosure is required, questions arise as to its presentation. Advertisers may be motivated to hide uncomfortable information; the FTC in particular has developed many guidelines for proper presentation of disclosures to make sure they actually convey information to consumers.

1. Omissions as False Claims

This section will explore situations in which failure to disclose could cause an advertisement to be misleading. The following section takes up the specifics of effective implementation once a disclosure is determined necessary to avoid misleading consumers.

The Lanham Act and the NAD

In connection with the 1988 amendment of Section 43(a), Congress considered including a section that explicitly made failure to disclose actionable. The Senate Report explains that the section was ultimately not included "to respond to concerns that it could be misread to require that all facts material to a consumer's decision to purchase a product or service be contained in each advertisement. . . . The committee does not through the deletion indicate that it condones deceptive advertising, whether by affirmative misrepresentation or material omission, and leaves to the courts the task of further developing [and] applying this principle under section 43(a)."

The upshot is that under the Lanham Act advertisers are generally not required to disclose all the information that consumers might find relevant to making a purchase decision. Advertisers can generally promote only their products' strengths without mentioning their weaknesses. An advertiser may therefore tout a tire as "better" than a cheaper tire because it has a better warranty without disclosing that in all physical respects the tires are the same. *See* Tire Kingdom, Inc. v. Morgan Tire & Auto, Inc., 915 F. Supp. 360 (S.D. Fla. 1996). A drug maker can advertise that "hospitals trust" its product and use ten times as much of it as the next four brands combined, without revealing that the reason is that the drug maker supplies it to hospitals at very low prices. Am. Home Prods. v. Johnson & Johnson, 654 F. Supp. 568 (S.D.N.Y. 1987).

Indeed, an advertiser may fail to correct a popular misconception unrelated to the claim it's actually advertising without fear of Lanham Act liability. *See, e.g.,* Avon Prods., Inc. v. S.C. Johnson & Son, Inc., 984 F. Supp. 768 (S.D.N.Y. 1997) (advertiser not liable for failing to state publicly that its skin lotion was not an insect repellent). *But see* Church & Dwight Co. v. SPD Swiss Precision Diagnostics, GMBH, 2016 WL 4708179 (2d Cir. Sept. 9, 2016) (taking advantage of well-known consumer lack of understanding about medical calculation of pregnancy duration was misleading); *accord* Simeon Mgmt. Corp. v. FTC, 579 F.2d 1137 (9th Cir. 1978) (advertiser may not capitalize on consumers' preexisting beliefs that claims of safety and effectiveness of medical treatments are evaluated by the FDA by failing to disclose that its particular treatment hasn't been so evaluated).

The NAD follows similar rules: disclosures are only required to avoid materially misleading consumers. In *Bayer Healthcare*, NAD Case # 5200 (2010), the NAD found, among other things, that ads for Bayer's flea, tick and mosquito control products K9 Advantix and Advantage for dogs and cats were not false or misleading merely because they failed to disclose the need to use a non-detergent shampoo on pets to preserve the benefits of the treatment. The NAD does feel free to recommend additional disclosures where there is some uncertainty, and it recommended that the advertiser inform consumers that, for best results, pets should be bathed with a non-detergent shampoo. The NAD also assumes that consumers follow product use directions. Thus, Bayer could advertise its product as "waterproof" without needing to inform consumers in its ads that they needed to wait for the product to disperse and dry before allowing their pets to get wet.

Typically, treating omissions as not actionable preserves advertisers' freedom and doesn't pose real threats to consumers. Consumers aren't likely to expect that an advertisement promising cheapness also promises highest quality. At some point, though, an omission may so change the message of an advertisement that the omission makes the overt claim false or misleading for Lanham Act purposes. *See, e.g.*, U-Haul Int'l, Inc v. Jartran, Inc., 601 F. Supp. 1140 (D. Ariz. 1984) (failure to reveal that advertised prices were "special prices" or did not include drop-off charges violated Lanham Act), *aff'd in relevant part*, 793 F.2d 1034 (9th Cir. 1986). In other words, an omission becomes actionable if it leads consumers to draw erroneous conclusions about the meaning of the explicit claims.

Consider the *S.C. Johnson* "leaky goldfish" case from the puffery section in this light: arguably, the affirmative representation of leakiness didn't disclose typical rates of leakage, which was so closely related to the affirmative representations in the ad that the overall ad was false. Similarly, the Second Circuit reasoned that eBay's failure to disclose that substantial amounts of counterfeit Tiffany jewelry were for sale on the auction site might make its ads misleading when they stated that Tiffany jewelry was available. *See* Tiffany v. eBay, 600 F.3d 93 (2d Cir. 2010) ("An online advertiser such as eBay need not cease its advertisements for a kind of goods only because it knows that not all of those goods are authentic. A disclaimer might suffice. But the law prohibits an advertisement that implies that all of the goods offered on a defendant's website are genuine when in fact, as here, a sizeable proportion of them are not.").

In NAD Case # 3879 (02/12/02), *Guinness UDV of North America, Inc. (Smirnoff Ice Malt Beverage)*, the NAD considered a complaint by Mike's Hard Lemonade against the Smirnoff Ice brand of citrus-flavored malt beverages. The complaint charged that the trade dress of Smirnoff Ice, which looked almost exactly like the trade dress of Smirnoff Vodka, misled consumers into thinking that Smirnoff vodka was a main ingredient and failed to make clear that the product did *not* contain vodka. The challenger submitted two surveys. The first found that, based on the label and packaging, 43% of respondents believed that Smirnoff Ice contained vodka. The second found that, based on Smirnoff Ice TV commercials, 25% of respondents believed that the product contained vodka. In both surveys, over 60% of respondents indicated that vodka content would be important to a purchase decision. Ultimately, however, Guinness declined to participate in the NAD proceeding, so all the NAD could do was refer the matter to the appropriate governmental agencies, which declined to act. What was the source of the alleged deception in the Smirnoff Ice advertising and labeling? Could any disclosure short of a name change have corrected this deception?

Often, false and misleading omissions arise in comparative advertising, where an advertiser selectively highlights its comparative advantages. This can be *literal falsity*: A claim that a product was "economical" compared to a competitor's product, backed up by a statement that consumers only needed a pound of the advertiser's product to match the effectiveness of two pounds of the competitor's product, was false because the advertiser neglected to disclose that its product was eight times more expensive per pound, and thus four times less "economical" than the competitor's product. *See* Performance Indus. Inc. v. Koos Inc., 18 U.S.P.Q.2d 1767 (E.D.

Pa. 1990). Likewise, where an ad for a new kind of can opener emphasized the smoothness of the resulting cut lid, but did not disclose that the edge of the can itself would be sharp, a court reasoned that consumers familiar with ordinary can openers that leave smooth can edges but sharp lids would believe that the new can opener made both the lid and can edges smooth. *See* Telebrands Corp. v. Media Grp., Inc., 1997 WL 790576 (S.D.N.Y. Dec. 24, 1997).

Omissions can also make a statement *misleading*, for example, a comparison of an advertiser's circulation with its competitor's, without revealing that the advertiser's newspaper circulated only weekly while the competitor's was daily. *See* San Juan Star v. Casiano Commc'ns, Inc., 85 F. Supp. 2d 89 (D.P.R. 2000). When a defendant advertised that its plastic building blocks connected to plaintiff's blocks, but the connection required the use of special adapter blocks, and a survey revealed that consumers were less likely to buy defendant's product knowing of the need for adapter blocks, the failure to disclose the need for adapter blocks was misleading. Tyco Indus., Inc. v. Lego Sys., Inc, 1987 WL 44363 (D.N.J. Aug. 26, 1987).

Sometimes an omission converts what looks to the consumer like an apples-to-apples comparison into an apples-to-oranges comparison. So, if an advertiser notes the side effects of a competitor's medication but neglects to disclose its own medication's side effects, a consumer is likely to believe that only the competitor's medication has such side effects. The ad prevents the consumer from making a true comparison. E.R. Squibb & Sons, Inc. v. Stuart Pharm., 1990 WL 159909 (D.N.J. Oct. 1990).

How significant is the advertiser's knowledge of what its consumers are likely to consider important? In *Gillette Co. v. Norelco Consumer Products Co.*, 946 F. Supp. 115 (D. Mass. 1996), Gillette, a leading maker of razors and blades (wet-shaving), sued Norelco, a leading seller of electric razors (dry-shaving). Norelco launched an ad campaign to convince consumers that its Reflex Action was less irritating than wet-shaving. The problem was that Norelco's ads omitted "a material caveat—that the shaver is less irritating only after an acclimation period of at least twenty-one days." There was extensive evidence that Norelco was aware that the acclimation period was vital. The first thing the consumer would see on opening the packaging (after purchase) would be a red sticker warning: "Stop! Before You Shave . . . If you've been shaving with a blade, it takes 30 days for your skin to gradually adjust to Norelco's closest shave. Once you do, you'll never go back!" The instructions devoted significant attention to acclimation, including the statement that "[a]t first you may not get as close a shave as you expect, or your face may even become slightly irritated. This is normal since your beard and skin will need time to adjust."

Norelco developed its ad campaign knowing that most consumers were not interested in a two- or three-week trial period to get used to an electric razor, because Norelco had been unable to convince them that the ultimate results were worth the initial discomfort. The court concluded that "Norelco has largely rejected the idea of casting the acclimation period in a positive light. Norelco has decided instead to cast no light at all on acclimation in much, if not most, of its advertisements—this despite abundant evidence, known to Norelco, that acclimation is essential to favorable results for the Reflex Action, with respect to the lessening of skin irritation." Thus, the court found that Gillette was likely to succeed in showing that Norelco's ads were misleading. The court did not require survey evidence, because "[t]he fact that Norelco has expressly and impliedly acknowledged the importance of acclimation to the success of the Reflex Action as a less irritating shaving system than wet shavers, but has withheld that information in some of its advertisements, is *in se* strong evidence that such advertisements are misleading." Gillette Co. v. Norelco Consumer Prods. Co., 96-12034-RCL (D. Mass. Nov. 27, 1996).

Country of Origin Disclosures

Federal law requires labeling to mark goods as foreign-made. *See* 19
U.S.C. § 1304(a) (2000) ("[E]very article of foreign origin . . . imported
into the United States shall be marked in a conspicuous place as
legibly, indelibly, and permanently as the nature of the article . . . in
such manner as to indicate to an ultimate purchaser in the United
States . . . the country of origin of the article."). Failure to satisfy the
country-of-origin labeling rule may be a "per se" material omission for
Lanham Act purposes. Without labeling, a consumer will likely
assume the goods are domestically produced and is therefore likely to
be deceived. *See, e.g.,* Alto Prods. Corp. v. Tri Component Prods.
Corp., 1994 WL 689418 (S.D.N.Y. Dec. 8, 1994). This legal construct
is a variant of falsity by necessary implication (to be addressed in
Chapter 6), because the mandatory labeling requirement sets the
expectations of reasonable consumers.

The FTC and Omissions

The FTC Act prohibits omissions that are "material in the light of
[affirmative] representations or material with respect to
consequences which may result from the use of the commodity to
which the advertisement relates under the conditions prescribed in
said advertisement, or under such conditions as are customary or
usual." 15 U.S.C. § 55(a)(1).

Interpreting this provision, the Ninth Circuit recognized that "no
single advertisement could possibly include every fact relevant to the
purchasing decision . . . . Advertisers need not disclose negative
aspects of their product, other than material consequences of normal
use. Otherwise, an advertisement is misleading only if it fails to
disclose facts necessary to dissipate false assumptions likely to arise
in light of the representations actually made." FTC v. Simeon Mgmt.

Corp., 532 F.2d 708 (9th Cir. 1976). The court therefore held that a weight-loss program had no obligation to disclose that the program involved treatment with a drug not approved by the FDA for such use: "The FTC presented no evidence that those seeing the advertisements formed a belief either that HCG was not used or that, if used, HCG had been approved by the FDA. This would be a different case if the respondents had advertised their use of HCG; one could plausibly suggest that the public would then assume that the drug was effective or approved by the FDA."

Therefore, the FTC Act and the Lanham Act similarly handle omissions that are material in light of affirmative representations. *See* MacMillan, Inc., 96 F.T.C. 208 (1980) (holding that failure to disclose the number of assignments in an educational course was deceptive, because students needed to know the number of assignments to calculate their tuition obligations). Significant omissions relating to the ordinary uses or central qualities of the product are also prohibited if consumers are likely to be misled. For example, the Seventh Circuit sustained an FTC ruling that ads for diet pills were deceptive because they failed to disclose that the pills were not safe for all potential consumers. In fact, obese consumers, at whom the ads were directed, were particularly at risk for the possible side effects. *See* Porter & Dietsch v. FTC, 605 F.2d 294 (7th Cir. 1979).

Debt Collection

The Fair Debt Collection Practices Act (FDCPA), 15 U.S.C. § 1692, bars debt collectors from making false and misleading representations. Is it misleading to omit that a debt is time-barred in a collection letter offering to "settle" the debt? Does it matter that voluntary acknowledgement of the debt will remove the time bar and make the debt enforceable again? *Compare* Fed. Trade Comm'n, The Structure and Practice of the Debt Buying Industry 47 (2013) (failing to disclose that a lawsuit is time-barred can deceive consumers who don't know their rights), *and* McMahon v. LVNV Funding, LLC, 744 F.3d 1010 (7th Cir. 2014) (using an "unsophisticated consumer" standard, a collection letter may be misleading without disclosure even if it does not explicitly threaten litigation), *with, e.g.,* Freyermuth v. Credit Bureau Servs., Inc., 248 F.3d 767, 771 (8th Cir. 2001) ("[I]n the absence of a threat of litigation or actual litigation, no violation of the FDCPA has occurred when a debt collector attempts to collect on a potentially time-barred debt that is otherwise valid.").

State Laws

Many state consumer fraud laws prohibit omissions of material facts, usually requiring intent that consumers rely on the omission (or concealment or suppression) whether or not the omissions relate to affirmative representations.* *See, e.g.,* Casper Sleep, Inc. v. Mitcham, 2016 WL 4574388 (S.D.N.Y. Sept. 1, 2016) (finding New York consumer protection law to be broader than the Lanham Act in requiring "clear and conspicuous" disclosures of advertiser affiliate status). While these provisions might seem broader than the Lanham Act, in practice they are often quite similar, except where some class of persons—such as realtors, or those in the relationship of a trustee to the consumer—has a duty to disclose *every* material fact regardless

---

* The wording varies, though this is unlikely to affect outcomes. States prohibiting intentional omissions of material fact include Arizona and South Dakota. Delaware and Texas bar omissions of material fact with intent that others rely. Alaska, Illinois, Missouri, New Jersey and West Virginia additionally bar concealment or suppression of material facts with intent that others rely. Arkansas bars concealment of material facts. South Dakota bans intentional concealment, suppression or omissions of material fact. New York, like the FTCA, bars failure to reveal facts in light of affirmative representations, and Maryland, Michigan, New Mexico, Pennsylvania and Vermont generally bar deceptive omissions.

of what the speaker affirmatively states. *See, e.g.*, Carter v. Gugliuzzi, 716 A.2d 17 (Vt. 1998) (finding violation of Vermont Consumer Fraud Act for real estate broker's failure to disclose material facts, relying upon statutory duty of brokers to disclose such facts). Moreover, California, the source of much significant consumer protection law, does not generally require disclosure of material information unless it relates to an affirmative statement by the advertiser or to product health and safety. *See* Hodsdon v. Mars, Inc., 162 F. Supp. 3d 1016 (N.D. Cal. 2016) (advertiser was not obligated to disclose that its chocolate was produced by child and slave labor).

Severely unequal access to knowledge can justify a finding that an omission was material. *See* Oswego Laborers' Local 214 Pension Fund v. Marine Midland Bank, N.A., 647 N.E.2d 741 (N.Y. 1995) ("[The New York consumer protection] statute surely does not require businesses to ascertain consumers' individual needs and guarantee that each consumer has all relevant information specific to its situation. The scenario is quite different, however, where the business alone possesses material information that is relevant to the consumer and fails to provide this information."); *but cf.* Super Glue Corp. v. Avis Rent A Car Sys., 557 N.Y.S.2d 959 (App. Div. 1990) (failure to tell car renters that renters' own automobile insurance might protect rental vehicles was not deceptive because renters were in better position to know the terms of their own insurance policies), *appeal denied*, 567 N.E.2d 980 (N.Y. 1991).

An advertiser's special expertise can therefore create heightened disclosure obligations, even when there's no fiduciary relationship and even when the consumer is relatively sophisticated (such as a business). An insurance company violated the law by failing to disclose that health insurance might not provide adequate coverage for the insured's employees, because it failed to fully disclose its method for calculating rates, which obscured the fact that lower

initial rates could result in future spikes. Woodworker's Supply, Inc.
v. Principal Mut. Life Ins. Co., 170 F.3d 985 (10th Cir. 1999).

When the advertiser knows that the consumer would not make the
purchase if he or she knew the omitted fact, that satisfies the
requirement in many states that omissions must be made with intent
that the consumer rely on the omission. *See, e.g.*, Mackinac v. Arcadia
Nat'l Life Ins. Co., 648 N.E.2d 237 (Ill. Ct. App. 1995) (omission need
not be made with intent to deceive, as long as it was intended to
induce reliance; failure to disclose lack of coverage for preexisting
conditions was not actionable because defendants had no basis to
suspect that preexisting coverage restriction was of concern to
plaintiff and thus could not have intended her to rely on failure to
disclose).

Although state laws generally require only that the omitted
information be "material," in practice, courts often require a fairly
high standard of materiality if an omission is unrelated to an
advertiser's affirmative statements. Courts will find liability only
when it is likely that the advertiser knew that the omitted facts were
important to many consumers and expected consumers to rely on the
nondisclosure. *Compare* Haisch v. Allstate Ins. Co., 5 P.3d 940 (Ariz.
Ct. App. 2000) (because consumers purchase insurance coverage for
protection from calamity, failing to disclose that insurance did not
provide for double recovery was not material omission under Arizona
law), *with* Connick v. Suzuki Motor Co., 675 N.E.2d 584 (Ill. 1996)
(allegation that car manufacturer omitted material fact that car
posed safety hazard stated claim under Illinois law), *and* Salmeron v.
Highlands Ford Sales, Inc., 271 F. Supp. 2d 1314 (D.N.M. 2003)
(failure to disclose that a used car had been used as a rental car
violated the law).

Thus, courts finding violations of state law often explain why a
particular omission was so unreasonable that the advertiser must

have known that consumers would rely on the omission, implicitly limiting the duty to disclose to facts glaringly in need of disclosure. *See* Williams-Ward v. Lorenzo Pitts, Inc., 908 F. Supp. 48 (D. Mass. 1995) (claim over a lease in which the defendant knew that the property contained lead paint). Conversely, where the omitted information is unlikely to make a difference to consumers, an advertiser may be able to show that it did not intend consumers to rely on the omission. *See* State *ex rel.* Brady v. 3-D Auto World, Inc., 2000 WL 140854 (Del. Super. Ct. 2000) (where car dealer misrepresented interest charge as "carrying charge," but buyers allegedly knew exact amount and payment schedule of charges, dealer could show that he did not intend consumers to rely on omission or concealment of fact that charge was actually "interest").

These principles can be applied to a common scenario: the absence of price terms in an ad. Though price is ordinarily material, states are unlikely to require its disclosure if advertising touts only non-price-related characteristics, unless some other law requires price disclosure. An advertiser's intent to get consumers to care more about quality than about cost does not constitute an intent to induce consumers to rely on the absence of price information. Omitting price information does not deceive consumers into thinking the product or service is free; a reasonable consumer realizes there will be a price and can ask about it. By contrast, advertising that implied cheapness, playing on consumers' existing price preferences, could be deceptive for omitting price information.

Many actionable omissions under state law involve one-on-one sales, particularly sales of expensive goods such as homes or cars, where the advertiser knows something about the consumer's particular requirements. In such individualized situations, complete silence on an important topic can more readily imply that the offered alternatives suit the buyer's already-understood requirements. By contrast, in the usual case, it would be difficult to find that an advertiser intended a consumer to rely on an omission merely by touting its mass-marketed product's desirable features in general, non-personalized advertising, unless it also made a *related* affirmative statement. *See* Commonwealth v. Bell Tel. Co., 551 A.2d 602 (Pa. Commw. Ct. 1988) (omission of material facts that made service less desirable was actionable in standardized sales pitch by telephone company, where pitch also included a number of falsehoods and high-pressure tactics that would enhance the deceptive effect of the material omissions).

2. Disclosures/Disclaimers and Their Effectiveness

Space and time limitations, as well as creative imperatives, all limit the amount of factual information that advertising can effectively communicate. These limits are fairly obvious in common ad format likes fifteen-second radio ads, thirty-second television commercials and even full-page newspaper ads. Advertisers try to overcome these limits by using disclaimers, usually in small type at the bottom of a print ad or rapid fire narrative at the end of a radio or television commercial. Familiar disclaimers include:

- Dramatization.
- Shipping and handling not included.
- Subject to credit approval.
- No purchase necessary.
- Use only as directed.
- Void where prohibited by law.
- Offer good while supplies last.
- Offer valid at participating dealers only.

Notwithstanding their prevalence, many disclaimers are ineffective at educating consumers—and, not coincidentally, are legally dubious.

To be effective, a disclaimer must be clearly written and prominent. Courts and the FTC accept that a clearly written footnote or a prominent on-screen super* can alert consumers to the availability of further information. Thus, disclaimers may be effective at clarifying an ad's claims (e.g., "shipping and handling not included"), providing additional information of interest to certain subgroups (e.g., "contains phenylalanine"), or offering ways to find out more information.

There are two key questions about disclaimers: First, absent the disclaimer, is the ad going to be materially incomplete or misleading? If the answer is "no," then the disclaimer is fine. The advertiser may even be using it for reasons having little to do with consumers. For example, fine print may signal to competitors or regulators that the advertiser possesses substantiation. Second, if the disclaimer *is* required to avoid misleadingness, will the disclaimer as it is actually presented correct the problem?

A. Guidelines for Effective Disclosures and Disclaimers

According to the FTC Deception Statement, "[w]ritten disclosures or fine print may be insufficient to correct a misleading representation." Among other things, "[o]ther practices of the company may direct consumers' attention away from the qualifying disclosures," and "[a]ccurate information in the text may not remedy a false headline because reasonable consumers may glance only at the headline." In many circumstances, the solution is to rewrite the main claim. *See, e.g.,* FTC, *.Com Disclosures: How to Make Effective Disclosures in Digital Advertising* (March 2013) ("Often, disclosures consist of a

---

* A "super" is information superimposed on TV ad copy, such as a disclaimer, logo or other information.

word or phrase that may be easily incorporated into the text, along with the claim.").

Advertisers should not rely too heavily on disclaimers. An effective disclaimer can modify an ambiguous claim that has the potential to mislead. But a disclaimer cannot remove the deceptive effect of a literally false claim. *See, e.g.,* Cont'l Wax Corp. v. FTC, 330 F.2d 475 (2d Cir. 1964) ("[T]he effectiveness of qualifying language is usually limited to situations where the deception sought to be eliminated is created by an ambiguity. . . . [W]here, as here . . . the offending deception is caused by a clear and unambiguous false representation . . . and, because of this, the addition of a qualifying phrase denying the truth of that representation would lead to a confusing contradiction in terms, no remedy short of complete excision . . . will suffice."); WebMiles.com Corp., NAD Case No. 3749 (closed Apr. 20, 2001) (claim that airline travel program had "absolutely no restrictions" could not be made truthful by disclaimer that revealed actual restrictions).

In one NAD case, Citibank aired a commercial in which a woman searched all over town to buy a specific, nearly impossible-to-find toy. After she found one and bought it with her Citibank credit card, her son promptly broke it. The ad claimed that because she used Citibank, "They'll take care of it. It's that simple." A small disclaimer read: "Cardmembers are reimbursed for cost and repair or replacement." Citicorp Credit Services, Inc., NAD Case No. 3235 (closed Sept. 14, 1995). Because the entire theme of the commercial was "the difficulty in obtaining the item that is broken as opposed to the cost of the item," however, the ad falsely communicated that Citibank would replace the broken toy, not simply give the woman the money to start the hunt all over again from the beginning.

Advertisers also can't use disclaimers to change the ordinary meaning of their claims. Advertising that a shopping website would "Pay Your

Debt to Uncle Sam or Match Your Refund" for visitors before April 15, could not be effectively qualified by a footnote that limited the offer to five customers and the payment to "under $1000 each." DealTime.com, NAD Case No. 3673 (closed July 28, 2000). And a claim that one manufacturer's nicotine patch was the "only" one that could be worn for twenty-four hours could not be qualified by a footnote limiting the claim just to "non-prescription patches." SmithKline Beecham Consumer Healthcare, L.P., NAD Case No. 3436 (closed Jan. 1, 1998). In each of these cases, the main message was so clear and unqualified that no amount of disclaiming could modify it.

This principle is often coupled with the general distrust of small print disclaimers for important qualifications. An oft-cited formulation is that a disclaimer that "purports to change the apparent meaning of the claims and render them literally truthful, but which is so inconspicuously located or in such fine print that readers tend to overlook it, . . . will not remedy the misleading nature of the claims." Am. Home Prods. Corp. v. Johnson & Johnson, 654 F. Supp. 568 (S.D.N.Y. 1987). In *DirecTV Inc. v. Comcast of Illinois III, Inc.*, 2007 WL 2808235 (N.D. Ill. 2007), DirecTV claimed that consumers preferred DirecTV's picture quality to that of cable, but the ad didn't disclose that they'd been comparing analog cable to a digital signal; failure to disclose this was "obviously" misleading. There was a disclaimer on the ad, but the court discounted it entirely. It was on the screen for four seconds, but "even if it were on the screen for 40 seconds, it wouldn't be legible enough or conspicuous enough for anyone to see it and to read it and to understand it."

Scholars have argued that many deceptive ads could be rewritten simply and easily. Preston and Richards tested ads that had been challenged by the FTC as misleading even though the falsity was not explicit, along with ads that had been rewritten to avoid the false implication. For example, the FTC charged that ads for Efficin pain

366

reliever falsely implied that "Efficin is not associated with most of the side effects and contraindications with which aspirin is associated" by stating that Efficin "contains no aspirin." The resulting consent order allowed the advertiser to compare Efficin's safety to aspirin only if it clearly and prominently stated that Efficin "has side effects similar to aspirin." Adria Labs., Inc., 103 F.T.C. 512 (1984).

Preston and Richards tested the original ad as well as an ad written to the specifications of the consent order. Rewriting prevented the vast majority of subjects from being deceived. Subjects who saw the rewritten version were much more likely to report the true message as true and reject the false message, without decreasing their comprehension of the other, concededly nondeceptive, messages in the ad. *See* Ivan L. Preston & Jef I. Richards, *Consumer Miscomprehension and Deceptive Advertising: A Response to Professor Craswell*, 68 B.U. L. REV. 431 (1988).

Clear and Conspicuous

The key principle is that disclaimers must be "clear and conspicuous." "Small and inconspicuous portions of lengthy descriptions" generally do not protect consumers, particularly where advertisements are "models of clarity" in presenting those aspects of the claims designed to attract consumers but "models of obscurity" in presenting the unpleasant details in small type, buried where none but the most meticulous reader would read and understand them. Donaldson v. Read Magazine, Inc., 333 U.S. 178 (1948).

Clear disclosures must be readily understood and use language appropriate to the targeted consumers. Thus, advertisers contemplating disclaimers must take into account the relative sophistication of their audiences. In general, audiences shopping for more expensive products are presumed to read claims carefully, understand fairly subtle distinctions, and therefore be more easily informed through the use of disclaimers. *See, e.g.*, Core-Vent Corp. v. Nobel Indus. Sweden A.B., 1998 U.S. App. LEXIS 22175 (9th Cir. 1998) (promotional materials and newsletters sent to dental offices using study and stating study's limits were not false). By contrast, advertising directed at children requires more disclosures and disclaimers than advertising to adults, including the fundamental disclosure that an advertisement *is* an advertisement.

The FTC has at times broken down the elements of clear and conspicuous disclosures into the Four Ps:

> (1) Prominence: Is it big/loud/etc. enough for consumers to notice and read/hear?
>
> (2) Presentation: Is the wording and format easy for consumers to understand both physically and conceptually, and presented without distracting consumers' attention elsewhere?
>
> (3) Placement: Is it in a place consumers will look and/or conveyed in a way consumers will hear?
>
> (4) Proximity: Is it near the claim it qualifies?

Here is an example of problematic disclosure:

See Network Solutions, Inc., F.T.C. File No. 132 3084 (Apr. 7, 2015) (consent order). Network Solutions offered a "30 Day Money Back Guarantee," but did not adequately disclose that it withheld part of the refund—up to 30 percent—from customers who cancelled. Network Solutions didn't disclose the cancellation fee in ads that touted the guarantee or on webpages that promoted it. Consumers had to scroll to the bottom of the screen to find this statement in comparatively tiny print: "* See Terms and Conditions for ... 30-Day Money Back Guarantee ..." The link sometimes appeared in blue on a black background and was usually sandwiched between other links. A consumer who did click on the link would see a pop-up in which Network Solutions began calling the offer a "30-Day Limited Money Back Guarantee" and revealed details of the cancellation fee. This, the FTC concluded, was a classic "too little, too late" disclosure.

Proximity and Placement

Disclaimers must be legible, meaningful, and of sufficient size, and (where appropriate) they must remain on screen long enough to allow viewers to easily read and understand them. Small print, by itself or combined with other features such as color, contrast and placement, is almost always deemed ineffective because consumers are unlikely to wade through a long paragraph of fine print in order to find significant information.

For online disclosures, the FTC has issued numerous types of guidance. For example, to support its Endorsement Guides, it has put out The FTC's Endorsement Guides: What People Are Asking, which addresses numerous practical disclosure issues, such as:

> **If I upload a video to YouTube and that video requires a disclosure, can I just put the disclosure in the description that I upload together with the video?**
>
> No, because it's easy for consumers to miss disclosures in the video description. Many people might watch the video without even seeing the description page, and those who do might not read the disclosure. The disclosure has the most chance of being effective if it is made clearly and prominently in the video itself. That's not to say that you couldn't have disclosures in both the video and the description.

Some statutes mandate different types of disclosures for different media. For warranties, the FTC mandates specific disclosures for video ads. 16 C.F.R. § 239.2(a) (mandating disclosure "simultaneously with or immediately following the warranty claim" in the audio portion or "on the screen for at least five seconds" in the video portion). Rules governing advertising for credit terms and leases distinguish between print and broadcast disclosure. 12 C.F.R. §

213.7(d) (print); § 213.7(f) (broadcast). The rules for prescription drug advertising are also changing because of Internet advertising and use of short-form media such as Twitter, where the usual ability to disclose in detail is absent. *See* Chapter 17. Some states also have specific regulations. New Jersey, for example, requires consumer contracts with terms that are invalid in New Jersey to specify exactly which terms don't apply to New Jersey residents, rather than simply having an additional general term that says that terms that are invalid in a given jurisdiction will not apply.

Disclosures generally have to be complete within their specific context. Where the product is particularly complex and consumers will naturally understand this, however, it may be acceptable to direct consumers to another source for more information. Thus, radio and TV ads for consumer leases are permitted to direct consumers to complete lease terms disclosed elsewhere in appropriate circumstances, and broadcast advertisements for prescription drugs must direct consumers to the package labeling. Even for these products, however, regulators may require significant disclosures in the ad copy.

Moreover, in an ordinary case, the FTC takes the position that if (1) a particular format makes disclosure impossible, and (2) disclosure is necessary to avoid misleadingness, then the advertiser must avoid that format, since not every affected consumer will seek out more information. Thus, if a message becomes misleading when it's compressed into 140 characters, then Twitter isn't an appropriate ad medium for that message. *See* Caroline McCarthy, *Yes, New FTC Guidelines Extend to Facebook Fan Pages*, CNET News.com, Oct. 5, 2009 ("'There are ways to abbreviate a disclosure that fit within 140 characters,' [the associate director of the FTC's advertising division] said. 'You may have to say a little bit of something else, but if you can't make the disclosure, you can't make the ad.'").

In one case, the NAD reviewed ads claiming that people with high serum cholesterol could eat "twelve Eggland's Best Eggs a week as part of a low fat diet" without raising their cholesterol levels. As substantiation, the advertiser directed the NAD to its "customer service 800 #, consumer Q&A brochures, large space print ads with extensive Q&As, and a medical/informational public relations program." The NAD found that the TV ads did not adequately address "the complexity of the nutritional issues involved":

> If the television commercial could ever contain all the information, disclosures and disclaimers that appear in the full-page Q&A ad, the correct message might be transmitted to consumers. To rely on a total communications program to make up for any possible lack in the television commercials is unacceptable. Each piece of advertising must stand on its own.

Eggland's Best Eggs, Inc., NAD Case No. 3016 (June 1, 1993); *see also* F.T.C. v. Colgate-Palmolive Co., 380 U.S. 374 (1965) ("If, however, it becomes impossible or impractical to show simulated demonstrations on television in a truthful manner, this indicates that television is not a medium that lends itself to this type of commercial, not that the commercial must survive at all costs.").

This principle is an application of general proximity/prominence requirements. In the absence of more specific mandates, the default rule is that a disclosure or disclaimer should be presented in the same space or time as the claim it modifies. In writing, clear and conspicuous disclosures are printed in type that is large enough for consumers to readily read it, with the same emphasis and contrast as the offer—not buried where consumers would not think to read. Oral disclosures should be at normal speed and in the same tone and volume as the sales offer. *See, e.g.,* Federal Trade Commission,

Complying with the Telemarketing Sales Rule: What Does the Rule Require Sellers and Telemarketers To Do?

Special disclosures required for auto sales and pharmaceuticals may, as a result, consume a substantial percentage of ad space and copy. Does this create its own problems in that consumers are likely to ignore all that verbiage?

Here is an example of what the FTC considers poor placement:

[Asterisk circled in red; arrow indicates placement of disclosure, "frozen yogurt and sorbet combinations"]

See Häagen-Dazs Co., 119 F.T.C. 762 (1995) (consent order).

The FTC's recommendations are intuitive, but they are also supported by consumer research. That research has revealed the following: Improving size and contrast of disclosures can increase consumers' recall. Bigger disclosures and disclosures that are more isolated from other material (rather than embedded in a paragraph of unrelated text) are more noticeable. By contrast, background noise and clutter reduce awareness of disclosures. "Peripheral cues" such as color, celebrities, or music can distract consumers from a disclosure.

Consumers are more likely to grasp a disclosure in the same mode (visual and/or audio) as the claim it qualifies. "Generally recognized marketing principles suggest that, given the distracting visual and audio elements [of the television ad at issue] and the brief appearance of the complex superscript in the middle of the commercial, it is unlikely that the visual disclosure is effective as a corrective measure." Kraft, Inc., 114 F.T.C. 40 (1991), *aff'd*, 970 F.2d 311 (7th Cir. 1992).

Despite this guidance, secondary literature reports that many disclaimers used over the years have failed these requirements. *See* Maria Grubbs Hoy & Michael J. Stankey, *Structural Characteristics of Televised Advertising Disclosures: A Comparison with the FTC Clear and Conspicuous Standard*, 22 J. ADVERT. 47 (1993) (finding that none of 157 commercial disclosures studied met all of the FTC clear and conspicuous standards). For example, while the FTC disfavors text-only disclosures when a TV ad's claims are made in the audio portion of the ad, 99.6% of the disclosures studied were text-only. Fifty-nine percent of the disclosures were also low-contrast, the classic example of which is white lettering on a medium or light background. Over 41% had a type size smaller than the suggested minimum; over 43% ignored the FTC's recommendations and used multiple background colors behind the disclosure.

374

For broadcast ads, required reading comprehension rates depend on the length of the disclosure and the amount of time the disclosure is presented. In the U.S., the upper range of reading comprehension is about 300 words per minute (wpm) and the lower range is 100 wpm, with 150 considered the average. In the study cited above, the average presentation rate was 181.4 wpm, above the 180 wpm upper bound the FTC had allowed in warranty disclosure cases. TV disclosures regularly blast past even the upper ranges. In an ad for Brink's Home Security, for example, the audio portion stated: "For over 135 years, Brink's has been protecting people and their valuables around the world without the loss of one single dollar." One disclosure appeared for 2 seconds: "Brink's Home Security, Inc. does not warrant against loss to covered premises. Three year monitoring contract required. $23.95 monthly monitoring fee. (In California a two-year monitoring contract is required. Total monitoring price $574.80)" plus 28 more words (1860 wpm).

Even very simple disclosures can whiz past at an unreasonable rate. Universal Studios ran a "No Line. No Wait." ad for its amusement park with a disclosure that repeated the initial claims and added a qualification: "Universal Studios No Line. No Wait. Ride access 1-877-Orlando Anticipated maximum wait 15 minutes. Restrictions apply." A consumer would have needed to read 540 words per minute to read these 18 words. Keith B. Murray, *Broadcast Disclosures and Communication Effectiveness: Required Reading Comprehension Rate.*

Sometimes courts will relax comprehension requirements substantially. *Time Warner Cable, Inc. v. DirecTV, Inc.*, 2007 WL 1138879 (S.D.N.Y. 2007), was another round in litigation over DirecTV's comparative advertising for its high-definition services versus cable. The ad touted DirecTV's HD channels, but used a graphic stating, "Starting at $29.99/mo. Everyday price." The small print stated that HD programming carried an additional fee on top of the quoted price. The court found the disclaimer sufficient because "starting at" indicated that higher prices were also part of the offer and "the existence of a disclaimer of some sort[] is clearly visible at the bottom of the screen." Given that the ad focused on HD channels, was this the right result? How much weight should a court give to "the existence of a disclaimer of some sort," where the consumer can't tell what the subject of the disclaimer is? Is the court applying a contract-style concept of "inquiry notice"?

Time Warner is an outlier. More typically, a disclaimer designed to make an ad non-misleading is in fact ineffective. An asterisk, dagger or other sign to direct readers to disclaimers located elsewhere simply won't work for important information, such as any disclosures that contradict or substantially change a claim's meaning.

In such cases, qualifications should appear in direct conjunction with the claim itself. In one NAD case, a department store advertisement prominently advertised "0% Interest for 1 Year." A footnote disclosed, "if payment of 1/12 of transaction amount is made for 12 consecutive months, then all finance charges assessed and paid will be refunded." In other words, interest *would* be charged, but could be refunded. The disclosure, however, "appear[ed] in a paragraph with other details in the same type size." The NAD recommended both clarifying that interest must be paid and may be refunded and putting the important disclaimer "in larger type size than the other details." Montgomery Ward & Co., NAD Case No. 3019 (June 1, 1993).

The FTC has stated that consumers should be able to evaluate all relevant information—including disclaimers—before deciding on a purchase. Disclaimers that appear only when a consumer has already taken affirmative steps toward purchasing a product or service are deemed ineffective. This is part of the prohibition on bait-and-switch sales practices. Guides Against "Bait" Advertising, 16 C.F.R. § 238. Once consumers have determined to make a purchase or have made substantial progress toward that end, they are likely to discount or ignore disclosures.

Some courts even regard a hard-to-find disclaimer as evidence of the advertiser's intent to deceive consumers. One example involved sweepstakes used to sell magazine subscriptions. Although no subscription purchase was necessary to enter the sweepstakes, the mailings did everything possible to avoid that conclusion. In one case, bold, red block letters announced that the recipient was in danger of being "dropped" if she did not "order now," the impression being that she would be "dropped" from the sweepstakes if she did not order magazines. A disclaimer announcing that "no purchase is necessary to enter or win" accompanied every mailing, but the disclaimer was "approximately one-quarter inch high . . . in blue, near other letters also in blue . . . at or near the bottom of the page." As the court observed, "[i]f it is not designed expressly for the purpose of minimizing its visibility, the overall layout of the literature certainly enhances that likelihood." Miller v. Am. Family Publishers, 663 A.2d 643 (N.J. Sup. Ct. Ch. Div. 1995). (For more on sweepstakes, see Chapter 15).

Disclaimers, Literal Falsity and Ambiguity

Occasionally, a disclaimer can make a claim ambiguous, thus requiring a consumer survey to prove that consumers miss the disclaimer or fail to understand it. In *PBM Products, LLC v. Mead Johnson Nutrition Co.*, 2009 WL 1684471 (E.D. Va. 2009), for example, Mead Johnson's Enfamil made superiority claims that it improved eye and brain development for infants—but its studies compared new Enfamil to the older formulation of Enfamil. The challenged ad stated, "It may be tempting to try a less expensive store brand, but only Enfamil LIPIL is clinically proven to improve brain and eye development." The small-print disclaimer said that the comparison was old Enfamil versus new Enfamil. The mailer also said, "En-Fact: Enfamil LIPIL's unique formulation is not available in any store brand." There was also a graphic in which one side of a picture of a duck is blurry and the other is clear, marked "without LIPIL" and "with LIPIL" respectively, again with disclaimer. The same disclaimer accompanied the claim, "Store brands may cost less, but Enfamil gives your baby more." So it appeared three times, always in small print.

The court rejected a preliminary injunction for failure to show literal falsity. The reference to clinical studies was not literally false. (Were the studies sufficiently reliable to establish the claim being made?) "Moreover, to the extent that a consumer could read the statement to mean that clinical studies have compared Mead Johnson's formula to other brands (which indubitably would be inaccurate), the Disclaimer clarifies the point . . . ." A subsequent jury verdict, however, found Mead Johnson liable for $13.5 million in damages based on this advertising. PBM Prods., LLC v. Mead Johnson & Co., 2010 WL 723739 (E.D. Va. 2010).

As *PBM* demonstrates, even when courts accept the argument that disclaimers avoid literal falsity, sufficiently good proof of actual deception will still justify relief. But it is important to note that the presence of the disclaimer may substantially change the litigation landscape, making it much harder for the plaintiff to prevail. Thus, a readable disclaimer may have a practical payoff for an advertiser (even if consumers don't actually read it).

B.   Online Disclosures

The FTC has provided extensive guidance for online disclosures. Disclosures should be near the triggering claim and, when possible, on the same screen (though advertisers should keep in mind that screen size varies, especially in the age of mobile devices). If that's not possible, text and visual cues should be labeled to clearly indicate that consumers should scroll or click to find out specific important information. "See below for details" is insufficient. Hyperlinks may be acceptable for lengthy disclosures or disclosures that need to be repeated, as long as they are properly labeled and clearly signaled as links, and as long as the click-through page presents the disclosure properly. Advertisers need to keep technical limitations in mind. Not all devices support pop-ups, for example, and thus disclosures and disclaimers in pop-ups are unlikely to be effective. They also must assume that consumers don't read an entire web page, just as they don't read every word on a printed page. The FTC's recommendation is simple: "Don't be subtle." And since advertisers can easily collect data on click-through rates, the FTC advises them to monitor click-through on disclaimers and change the form if the rate is low. *See* .Com Disclosures, *supra*. These principles suggest the challenges of regulating user interfaces, which change regularly, and frequently get smaller and harder to read.

C.   Duration and Repetition

Disclaimers that are stated only once or twice, while the underlying claim is repeated, are ineffective. This rule is particularly applicable to lengthier advertising such as websites and infomercials. In one infomercial, Hair Club for Men offered "free hair" and a "free round-trip" airline ticket to those who signed up for a one-year membership. The disclosure that the one-year membership was a necessary part of the offer was not made at the same time as the offer. The NAD held that "consumers viewing only this segment of the infomercial . . . would not understand the true cost of the offer." Hair Club for Men, NAD Case No. 3457 (closed May 1, 1998).

D.   Understandability

Consumers' ability levels (age, education, special product knowledge) will be considered in assessing a disclosure's effectiveness. Thus, for a toy advertised to children, the disclosure "some assembly required" is less helpful than "you have to put this together." Most consumers won't be able to do much math quickly. *See* Kraft, Inc., 114 F.T.C. at 124 (holding that complicated superscript—"one ¾-ounce slice has 70% of the calcium of five ounces of milk"—did not cure deceptive calcium content claim for cheese slices), *aff'd*, 970 F.2d 311 (7th Cir. 1992).

In general, shorter disclosures are easier for consumers to comprehend than longer ones. On the other hand, overly general statements, such as "read the label" or "consult your doctor," tend not to be understood as well as more specific information. Consumers may perceive these too-short phrases as further statements about product benefits rather than as cautions. This concern must, however, be balanced by length considerations. "Consult your doctor for important information about side effects and people who shouldn't use X" might improve understanding, but a full list of the side effects might just cause consumers to tune out.

A recent study found that the calorie labels now found on soda bottles were only slightly more effective than no labels at all at increasing consumer knowledge about the health effects of sugar-sweetened beverages or discouraging parents from choosing them for their children. Without a warning label, 60% of parents chose a sugar-sweetened beverage for their child. With a calorie label, 53% of parents did, and with various warning labels, 40% did. The warning label therefore reduced parents' choice of sugar-sweetened beverages by 1/3, but that reduction was from 60% to 40%. Is this a success or a failure? Christina A. Roberto et al., *The Influence of Sugar-Sweetened Beverage Health Warning Labels on Parents' Choices*, PEDIATRICS (Jan. 2016).

A   Calorie label

240
CALORIES
PER BOTTLE

B   California label

SAFETY WARNING: Drinking beverages with added sugar(s) contributes to obesity, diabetes, and tooth decay.

C   Weight gain label

SAFETY WARNING: Drinking beverages with added sugar(s) contributes to weight gain, diabetes, and tooth decay.

Three labels tested by Roberto et al.

Some research suggests that standard verbal disclosures often don't work. Instead, visual disclosures or simple grading schemes may be more easily comprehended by a wider range of consumers. The FTC's research found, for example, that the health claim disclaimers the FDA currently requires of dietary supplement makers don't give ordinary consumers a good sense of the reliability of the underlying scientific evidence. However, a "report card" format with grades from A to D, however, did better. *FTC Staff Comments on Assessing Consumer Perceptions of Health Claims*, January 17, 2006, available at http://www.ftc.gov/be/V060005.pdf. Traffic signal-style disclosures (red, yellow, green lights) have also proven effective for food. Christina A. Roberto et al., *Facts Up Front Versus Traffic Light Food Labels A Randomized Controlled Trial*, 43 AM. J. PREV. MED. 134 (2012); Tina Rosenberg, *Labeling the Danger in Soda*, N.Y. TIMES, Mar. 30, 2016 (in Ecuador, where traffic-light labeling for food is mandatory, consumers in 31% of households surveyed said they had stopped buying products because of the stoplight, most often soft drinks).

Perhaps the most promising recent results come from a study in which a sign explained to purchasers how long they'd have to exercise to work off the calories in a bottle of soda or juice. The presence of the sign was associated with fewer purchases of caloric drinks and smaller bottles when there was a purchase, and the effect persisted even after the sign was removed. Sara N. Bleich et al., *Reducing Sugar-Sweetened Beverage Consumption by Providing Caloric Information: How Black Adolescents Alter Their Purchases and Whether the Effects Persist*, 104 AM. J. PUB. HEALTH 2417 (2014).

Consider the following letter from the FDA's Division of Drug Marketing, Advertising, and Communications (DDMAC). What would be left of the ad if the advertiser removed all the elements the FDA identifies as distracting?

Department of Health & Human Services, Public Health Service, Food and Drug Administration, Re: NDA #21-544– Seasonale® (levonorgestrel/ethinyl estradiol) Tablets

. . . The Division of Drug Marketing, Advertising, and Communications (DDMAC) has reviewed a direct-to-consumer (DTC) television advertisement (TV ad) entitled "Yes" for Seasonale® Tablets. . . . The TV ad is false or misleading because it fails to reveal material facts about Seasonale and minimizes the risks associated with Seasonale, in violation of the Federal Food, Drug and Cosmetic Act ("Act") and FDA implementing regulations. By omitting and minimizing the risks associated with Seasonale, the TV ad misleadingly suggests that Seasonale is safer than has been demonstrated by substantial evidence or substantial clinical experience.

. . . Minimization of Risk

. . . Seasonale is associated with numerous risks, including the
potentially serious risks of thromboembolic events and hypertension.

In addition, the risk information that is presented in the ad is
minimized by the compelling visuals, fast-paced scene changes, and
other competing modalities, such as background music and SUPERs,
occurring simultaneously during the presentation of risk information
in the TV ad. This complex presentation distracts from and makes it
difficult for consumers to process and comprehend the important risk
disclosures. Specifically, during the approximately 17 seconds of
auditorily-presented risk information, the camera: pans multiple
faces; shows a billowy cloth floating across the screen; presents many
pink dots swirling quickly across the screen; cuts quickly to women's
faces, body parts, pink dots, and a woman walking across the screen;
and shows, again with quick cut camera work, two women throwing
pink dots. This frenetic activity sequence occurs with shifting camera
perspectives while complex contextual information and other
unrelated informational elements are presented in subtitled SUPERs.
Additionally, the SUPERs containing important contextual
information are presented in small type as two lines of text at the
bottom of the screen, rendering them extremely difficult to read
under normal conditions, much less conditions under which they are
presented against moving backgrounds and with overlying music. The
overall effect of the distracting visual elements and the competing
audio message is to obscure and undermine the communication of the
important risk information, minimizing these risks and misleadingly
suggesting that Seasonale is safer than has been demonstrated by
substantial evidence or substantial clinical experience. . . .

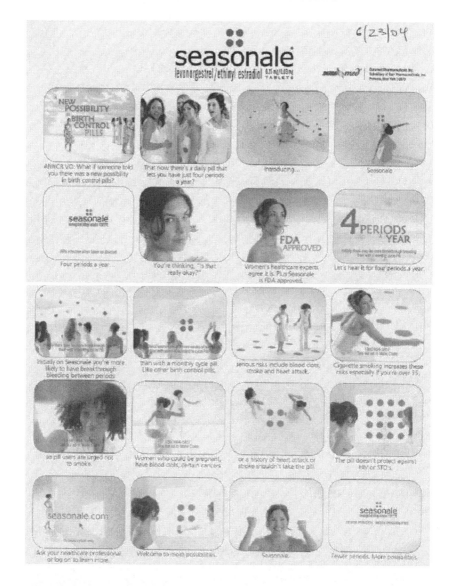

NOTES AND QUESTIONS

Why did the advertiser choose to present the risk information this way? How could it have made the ad attractive without distracting from the risk information? In response to this and similar

384

enforcement actions, drug advertisers may have pulled back on distractors, but shifted to dull, boring narration that also fails to inform consumers. As Dartmouth health policy researcher Adrienne Faerber says, "There's no requirement for [drug manufacturers] to present things in a way that's cognitively engaging." Megan Thielking, *How Drug Ad Narrators Take the Scariness out of Side Effects*, STAT, Feb. 18, 2016.

What happens if the main language of the ad is in Spanish, but the disclosures are in English? The FTC has increasingly taken the position that if disclosures are required to avoid misleadingness, then disclosures in a language other than that of the main ad do not help. *See, e.g.*, 16 C.F.R. 14.9 ("clear and conspicuous" disclosure must be made in the language of the target audience); 16 C.F.R. 610.4(a)(3)(ii) (in marketing free credit reports, mandatory disclosures must be made in the same language as that principally used in the advertisement).

Disclaimers are also subject to the usual rules for interpreting ad claims. They must use terms as they are commonly understood by consumers and not in themselves be misleading. A disclosure that refers to "basic rates" is inadequate if consumers do not understand what the term "basic rates" means. Ill. Bell Tel. Co. v. MCI Telecomms. Corp., 1996 WL 717466 (N.D. Ill. Dec. 9, 1996). Disclaimers are also inadequate if they are too vague. Report of NARB Panel No. 85, Disposition of Advertising Referred to NARB Regarding Advertising for 3M Company (Panel convened Mar. 23, 1995) (disclaimer that soap pads are appropriate for "many" kitchen surfaces was insufficient because it failed to specify how many surfaces it was inappropriate for).

3. Mandatory Disclosures and Their (Dis)contents

When policy makers conclude that a sales or commercial practice is troubling, they often decline to ban it, but rather attempt to make it less appealing by requiring certain disclosures of the more unattractive features of the relevant product or service. The most familiar example may be the warnings on cigarette packages and ads. Product- or service-specific regulations can make omission of required information unlawful without a separate showing of deceptiveness in any individual case. For example, the FTC has promulgated various rules and guides requiring specific disclosures for particular products and services or claims, including household appliances, textiles, jewelry and others, and states have their own rules, especially for contests and sweepstakes (as detailed in Chapter 15).

In general, when are such prophylactic disclosures justified?

A. Criticisms of Disclosure and Disclosure Creep

One might think that disclosures can't hurt, even if they don't always help. Tess Wilkinson-Ryan has criticized this argument from a psychological perspective. She argues that the presence of unread fine print can lead others—including legal decision makers—to blame consumers for any bad consequences they experience from a transaction, even as we all know that no one reads the fine print. In that case, disclosures could backfire, leaving consumers worse off. Tess Wilkinson-Ryan, *A Psychological Account of Consent to Fine Print*, 99 IOWA L. REV. 1745 (2014).

Furthermore, Omri Ben-Shahar and Carl E. Schneider argue that disclosures almost never work, because of the flawed incentives of the regulators and of the advertisers required to implement the disclosures, combined with the cognitive limitations that justified the FTC's detailed disclosure requirements in the first place. *See* Omri

Ben-Shahar and Carl E. Schneider, *The Failure of Mandated Disclosure*, 159 U. PENN. L. REV. 647 (2011); *see also* Kesten C. Green & J. Scott Armstrong, *Evidence on the Effects of Mandatory Disclaimers in Advertising*, 31 J. PUB. POL'Y & MARKETING, 293 (2012) (reviewing studies and concluding that mandatory disclaimers are useless or even counterproductive). Ben-Shahar & Schneider argue that disclosures are often more harmful than helpful—crowding out useful information, creating anticompetitive burdens, crowding out other consumer protection measures (since the advertiser can claim that no protection other than full disclosure is warranted), and helping only those who are already wealthy and educated enough to use disclosures.

Many times, consumers don't seem to pay attention to, much less understand, disclosures. For example, Ben-Shahar & Schneider cite studies showing that 90% of consumers don't understand how annual percentage rates (disclosed under the Truth in Lending Act) relate to simple annual interest rates.[*] There are too many disclosures for consumers to pay attention to, even if any given disclosure might be a good idea in the abstract. *See* Svetlana Bialkovaet al., *Standing Out in the Crowd: The Effect of Information Clutter on Consumer Attention for Front-of-Pack Nutrition Labels*, 41 FOOD POL'Y 65 (2013). In the worst-case scenario, disclosures can even backfire. *See* Molly Mercer & Ahmed E. Taha, *Unintended Consequences: An Experimental Investigation of the (In)Effectiveness of Mandatory*

---

[*] Unfortunately, many mandatory disclosures are wordy and hard to understand, but the Consumer Financial Protection Bureau has promulgated regulations allowing limited waivers of existing disclosure requirements for financial services in order to test other ways of conveying disclosures, seeking empirical data on which measures were effective and encouraging disclosures written in clear, succinct language. *See* Bureau of Consumer Financial Protection, Policy to Encourage Trial Disclosure Programs; Information Collection, 12 CFR Chapter X, 78 Fed. Reg. 64389 (Oct. 29, 2013).

Disclosures, 55 SANTA CLARA L. REV. 405 (2015) (finding that disclosures designed to warn consumers that most consumers don't actually redeem rebates, and that consumers overestimate their own probability of doing so, backfire; warnings *increase* willingness to buy products offering rebates and optimism about the consumer's own likelihood of actually redeeming the rebate); Yael Steinhart et al., *Warnings of Adverse Side Effects Can Backfire Over Time*, 24 PSYCHOL. SCI. 1842 (2013) (finding that when purchase of cigarettes, artificial sweeteners, and medication was delayed, warnings increased consumption because they made the advertisers' messages more trustworthy overall); *see also* D. Murphy et al., *Generic Copy Test of Food Health Claims in Advertising*, Federal Trade Commission Staff Report, Nov. 1998 (disclaimers must be very carefully and strongly worded; if not, they may have an effect opposite of that intended).

Even attempts to simplify disclosures may fail. In one study, simplification of terms and use of a short list of key features in a "Warning Label" helped only a little to inform consumers and didn't change their behavior, even when the "Warning Label" disclosed unpleasant practices:

Omri Ben-Shahar & Adam Chilton, *Simplification of Privacy Disclosures: An Experimental Test*, University of Chicago Coase-Sandor Institute for Law & Economics Research Paper No. 737 (2016). Would you have hesitated to share your personal information with a website that used these terms? (Note that, if you use Facebook, you already are subject to many of these practices).

Required calorie disclosure on fast-food menus provide another example of the information overload/effectiveness concern. So far, such disclosures have been upheld against First Amendment challenge. *See New York State Restaurant Ass'n v. New York City Board of Health*, 2008 WL 1752455 (S.D.N.Y. 2008). However, research suggests that they are basically ineffective. People, if asked, say they pay attention to the disclosures—then order almost exactly the same food. *See also* Nathaniel Good et al., *Stopping Spyware at the Gate: A User Study of Privacy, Notice and Spyware*, Symposium On Usable Privacy and Security (SOUPS) 2005 (even when orally told that P2P software contained unwanted adware bundled with it, users proceeded to download the bundle anyway). Do these findings suggest that mandatory disclosures will not help consumers make good marketplace choices for themselves? If so, what policy alternatives would do a better job?

Evidence from supplement labels also suggests that the wordy disclaimers common on health products simply don't work. Among other things, the disclosure, "This statement has not been evaluated by the Food and Drug Administration. This product is not intended to diagnose, treat, cure or prevent any disease" doesn't change consumers' perceptions about whether the FDA has evaluated the claims, much less whether the claims are likely to be true. Instead, consumers' level of trust in the government determines whether they believe that the government is evaluating dietary supplements, regardless of disclaimers. Disclaimers about the uncertainty of the underlying scientific evidence were also useless. Only consumers' preexisting level of education mattered: higher education led to greater skepticism about supplement claims. Karen Russo France & Paula Fitzgerald Bone, *Policy Makers' Paradigms and Evidence from Consumer Interpretations of Dietary Supplement Labels*, November 17, 2005 FDA Public Meeting: Assessing Consumers' Perception of Health Claims.

The "results not typical" language discussed in Chapter 4 is another example of failed disclosure. When an advertiser touts a particularly successful user, consumers disregard the advertiser's bias in choosing an exemplar, even when consumers explicitly acknowledge that the advertiser probably chose its best examples. This is related to the fact that concrete, vivid examples and easily remembered examples are misperceived as more common. *See* Ahmed E. Taha, *Selling the Outlier*, 41 J. CORP. L. 459 (2015); Jonathan J. Koehler & Molly Mercer, *Selection Neglect in Mutual Fund Advertisements*, 55 MGMT. SCI. 1107, 1110 (2009). In one study using a testimonial advertisement for a dietary supplement, "despite the presence of strongly worded, highly prominent disclaimers of typicality, between 44.1% and 70.5%" of the participants believed that the supplement would benefit "at least half of the people who try it." Manoj Hastak & Michael Mazis, *Effects of Consumer Testimonials in Weight Loss, Dietary Supplement and Business Opportunity Advertisements* (2004). What about requiring a disclosure of typical results alongside the testimonial? Sadly, that doesn't work very well either, in part because most consumers can't do math very well. So should atypical testimonials simply be banned?

Perhaps disclaimers fail because advertisers sabotage them. In a case involving multilevel marketing, the court noted that, "[i]n live presentations, when Vemma speakers include 'results not typical' disclaimers with income representations, they often follow the disclaimer with a statement such as, 'I hope you're not typical,' to weaken the disclaimer. As a result, the net impression is still that a

Vemma Affiliate is likely to earn substantial income, which is deceptive under the FTC Act." F.T.C. v. Vemma Nutrition Co., No. 15-cv-01578 (D. Ariz. Sept. 18, 2015).

There may be hope for properly formulated disclosures that focus on material attributes. Understanding why some disclosures fail can guide advertisers towards disclosures that succeed. For example, dieters who see a message focusing on the negative aspects of unhealthy food increase desire for and consumption of unhealthy foods, while dieters who see a two-sided message (focusing on both the negative and positive aspects of unhealthy food) are more likely to choose fewer unhealthy foods. Dieters interpret one-sided negative messages as a threat to their freedom, but two-sided messages such as "All dessert tastes good, but is bad for your health" provide more freedom of choice. Nguyen Pham et al., *Messages from the Food Police: How Food-Related Warnings Backfire among Dieters*, 1 J. ASSOC. CONSUMER RES. 175 (2016).

Likewise, Marianne Bertrand and Adair Morse studied payday loan borrowers and found that presenting certain information about the cost of payday borrowing—specifically information that made the long-term additive cost of payday loans salient—reduced the use of payday loans by about 10% for four months following exposure to the new information. The results were best with borrowers without a college education, those with higher self-control on self-reported measures, and those with lower borrowing-to-income ratios, suggesting that they were using the increased information about total costs of borrowing to satisfy their true preferences. Their results were consistent with other research finding that people shopping for new cars were much more likely to use the miles per gallon (MPG) information if it was presented as the expected total cost of gas for a year, instead of just "miles per gallon" in the abstract. Bertrand and Morse concluded that targeted disclosure can be effective when done right, though context is vital: disclosure at the point of on-the-spot decisions can serve to "de-bias" consumers away from typical mistakes. Marianne Bertrand & Adair Morse, *Information Disclosure, Cognitive Biases and Payday Borrowing*, 66 J. FIN. 1865 (2011); *see also* J. Michael Collins, *Protecting Mortgage Borrowers through Risk Awareness: Evidence from Variations in State Laws*, 48 J. CONSUMER AFF. 124 (2014) (loan applicants in states that mandated enhanced warnings about foreclosures were more likely to reject high-cost refinance mortgage loan offers from a lender compared to applicants in other states).

Responding to Ben-Shahar and Schneider's general criticism of disclosure, Richard Craswell makes several points. Richard Craswell, *Static Versus Dynamic Disclosures, and How Not to Judge Their Success or Failure*, 88 WASH. L. REV. 333 (2013). Briefly summarized, he distinguishes between static disclosures, which try to help consumers choose from a fixed set of options, and dynamic disclosures, which try to change the market. A disclosure that looks like a failure from the static perspective may still have dynamic effects.

Consider the example of mandatory fat labeling on food labels. Before the Nutritional Labeling Education Act (NLEA), makers of low-fat salad dressings often disclosed their calories and fat content voluntarily as a selling point. But after the NLEA required all sellers to disclose, the market share of high-fat dressings declined. Alan Mathios, *The Impact of Mandatory Disclosure Laws on Product Choices: An Analysis of the Salad Dressing Market*, 43 J. L. & ECON. 651 (2000). Craswell points out that consumers don't need to understand technical terms, whether it's the meaning of "net carbohydrates" or how "miles per gallon" is calculated, as long as they can compare products: this is the dynamic effect of disclosures. Mandatory disclosure therefore supports the voluntary disclosures of some advertisers—those that have a product that's superior on the relevant attribute.

And making the disclosure mandatory can create a commonly accepted metric, such as MPG, that is easier for consumers to understand and trust than multiple competing metrics. The mandatory nature of the disclosure may also signal to some consumers that the topic is important enough to consider in their decision making.

But even from a static perspective, Craswell argues that it's a mistake to say that disclosures "fail" without carefully defining "success." Recall that no ad is understood by 100% of viewers. It would be shocking if a disclosure could do better. The question is whether a disclosure requirement's marginal benefits justify the marginal costs. A safety-related disclosure might be worthwhile even if it only helped 10% of consumers, whereas a disclosure about a less important topic might not be. *Cf.* Joshua Mitts, *How Effective Is Mandatory Disclosure?, available at* http://papers.ssrn.com/sol3/papers.cfm?abstract_id=2404526 (finding that prominent disclosures deterred 20–30% of study respondents from accepting unusual contract terms, and increased understanding by 9–10%, though consumers tuned out if there were too many disclosures).

As an alternative, Lauren Willis has proposed performance-based measures: rather than mandating any particular disclosures, advertisers should be prepared to prove that their ads leave consumers with a correct understanding of key terms. This, she suggests, is the only way to overcome the otherwise inevitable incentives of advertisers to chip away at the effectiveness of disclaimers, and their nearly infinite creativity in doing so. (For example, when AT&T added a mandatory arbitration clause to its contract, "it designed the envelope, cover letter, and amended contract through extensive *anti-marketing* market testing to ensure that most consumers would not open the envelope, or if they did open it, would not read beyond the cover letter.") Lauren E. Willis, *The Consumer Financial Protection Bureau and the Quest for Consumer Comprehension, in* MICHAEL S. BARR, ED., FINANCIAL REFORM: PREVENTING THE NEXT CRISIS (2016). What do you think of a performance-based alternative to mandatory disclosures? How would performance be monitored?

B. Case Study: Distinguishing Ads from Editorial Content

The FTC's Campaign Against Undisclosed Ads

The FTC has led the regulatory efforts against surreptitious ads, such as advertising that looks like editorial content. The FTC's position is that such ads should be properly labeled to disclose their status as ads. In effect, the FTC treats the failure to disclose the advertiser's role behind non-obvious endorsements and testimonials as an omission that may be legally actionable.

For example, the FTC has been pushing search engines to make the distinction more clear between "organic" search results from their keyword ads. In 2013, it sent a letter to major search engine providers reminding them that it thinks paid keyword advertising is misleading if its nature as advertising was insufficiently disclosed. "[C]onsumers ordinarily expect that natural search results are included and ranked based on relevance to a search query, not based on payment from a third party. . . . In recent years, the features traditional search engines use to differentiate advertising from natural search results have become less noticeable to consumers, especially for advertising located immediately above the natural results ("top ads"). Indeed, a recent online survey by a search strategies company found that nearly half of searchers did not recognize top ads as distinct from natural search results and said the background shading used to distinguish the ads was white." FTC,

Sample Letter to General Purpose Search Engines, June 24, 2013. The
FTC suggested use of prominent visual cues, including clear shading
and borders, to distinguish ads, as well as text labels. How well does
the search engine you use comply with the FTC's advice?

Similarly, the FTC has fought against display ads that are presented
to consumers looking like editorial content. These ads have a variety
of names, including "advertorials" and "native ads," and the FTC
expects the advertisement to be accompanied by an effective
disclosure. In discussing online disclosures of native ads, the FTC
noted:

> Sometimes a focal point on a publisher site is something other
> than a headline or other written text – for example, images or
> graphics. Disclosures placed near focal points that are images,
> graphics, or other visually strong elements might not be
> sufficiently noticeable to consumers and disclosures might
> need to be placed on the focal points themselves. For example,
> in deciding which videos to watch on a video-sharing channel,
> consumers might pay little attention to written descriptions
> and instead look at thumbnail images of the videos. Under
> those circumstances, a disclosure placed directly on the
> thumbnail image itself is most likely to be effective.

FTC, Native Advertising: A Guide for Businesses. The evidence
suggests that consumers are not very aware of such "native
advertising"—and hard to educate about it. For example, in one
study, ads labeled "brand voice" or "presented by" were seven times
less likely to be identified as paid content than ads labeled
"advertising" or "sponsored content." Only 40% of readers noticed a
disclosure at the top of a page, while 90% noticed it if it appeared in
an outlined box in the middle of the story, and 60% noticed it at the
bottom. However, noticing a disclosure and understanding it are
different matters—only 18.3% of readers recognized the ad as an ad

when the term "sponsored content" was used. Bartosz W. Wojdynski & Nathaniel J. Evans, *Going Native: Effects of Disclosure Position and Language on the Recognition and Evaluation of Online Native Advertising*, 45 J. ADVERTISING 157 (2016). What could be done to fix this?

While perhaps search engine and display ads make sense for FTC intervention, the FTC has taken expansive and not-always-intuitive interpretations of what constitutes an "advertisement" and thus requires labeling. In particular, as we'll discuss more in Chapter 13, the FTC's Guides Concerning Use of Endorsements and Testimonials in Advertising take the position that when an advertiser gives online bloggers and social media influencers given free product samples, any resulting blog and social media posts are advertisements and need to be disclosed as such.

Lord & Taylor's Paisley Dress. Let's look more closely at an FTC enforcement action in this area. Lord & Taylor launched a new product line and decided to focus on one dress from that line. Lord & Taylor paid Nylon, an online fashion magazine, run an article (and Instagram post) about the clothing featuring a photo of the dress. Lord & Taylor reviewed and approved the resulting article and Instagram post, but didn't require Nylon to add a disclosure. In addition, Lord & Taylor recruited 50 "fashion influencers," who were paid to post photos of themselves in the dress on Instagram on one specified "product bomb" weekend, when the Nylon article appeared. Lord & Taylor preapproved each Instagram post to make sure the influencers included Lord & Taylor's chosen hashtags, and edited some of what the influencers planned to say, but didn't require them to disclose that they were paid.

The Instagram campaign reached 11.4 million users and led to 328,000 "brand engagements" (likes, comments, reposts, etc.) using Lord & Taylor's Instagram handle. The paisley dress sold out. The FTC complaint alleged three violations of the FTCA: (1) Lord & Taylor falsely represented that the 50 Instagram images and captions reflected the independent statements of impartial fashion influencers. (2) Lord & Taylor failed to disclose the material fact that the influencers were the company's paid endorsers. (3) Lord & Taylor falsely represented that the Nylon article and Instagram post reflected Nylon's independent opinion about the Design Lab line, when they were really paid ads. In re Lord & Taylor, LLC, No. 152 3181 (F.T.C. Mar. 15, 2016).

The Lord & Taylor campaign attempted to leverage both traditional media and social media. Are disclosure obligations equally justified for these types of communications? Were the "influencers" making material representations by posting images of themselves in the paisley dress without a disclosure? Would it have made a difference if the people who posted images of themselves in the dress weren't "influencers," but were just 50 people to whom Lord & Taylor had given the dress in return for posting about it? (Do you rely on user reviews on Amazon, Yelp, or other sites when you don't know the user leaving the review personally? Why or why not?)

As an exercise, can you draft a disclosure for an "influencer" that would have addressed the FTC's concerns? Can you make it fit in a single tweet?

Policy Justifications for Telling Consumers When Content is Advertising

Does the FTC's efforts to squash undisclosed ads make sense? Consider these two perspectives:

Rebecca Tushnet, *Attention Must Be Paid: Commercial Speech, User-Generated Ads, and the Challenge of Regulation* (excerpt)

[H]idden relationships may give advertisers excessive credibility by using apparently independent sources to confirm the advertiser's message.[81] Helen Norton summarizes:

> [E]vidence from cognitive psychology and related fields reveals that individuals often use a message's source as a mental shortcut, or heuristic, for evaluating its quality. Studies confirm that the more credible a speaker, the more likely her message will be effective, regardless of its content. Because speakers perceived as unpopular and/or unreliable will have more difficulty persuading listeners, they may be wise to seek the imprimatur of more trustworthy sources .... Moreover, the perception that a message is endorsed by such sources can help dispel onlookers' suspicion of perspectives understood to be in the speaker's own interest.[82]

---

[81] *See* Ellen Goodman, *Peer Promotions and False Advertising Law*, 58 S. CAR. L. REV. 683, 705 (2007) ("Marketing theory predicts ... that consumers will be more inclined to believe promotions when they are not clearly sourced by the brand owner. Marketing authorities instruct sponsors to keep a low profile in Web 2.0 promotions because speech that is or seems to be pure peer is more credible. If this is true, then peer promotions would seem to be highly credible and therefore potentially harmful if misrepresenting the facts. Even more so than traditional advertising, consumers would be at risk of 'uninformed acquiescence' to the advertiser's promotional scheme.") (footnotes omitted). . . .

[82] Helen Norton, *The Measure of Government Speech: Identifying Expression's Source*, 88 B.U. L. REV. 587, 592–93 (2008) (footnotes omitted); *see also* Shelly Chaiken & Durairaj Maheswaran, *Heuristic Processing Can Bias Systematic Processing: Effects of Source Credibility, Argument Ambiguity, and Task Importance on Attitude Judgment*, 66 J. PERSONALITY & SOC. PSYCHOL. 460, 464 (1994) (finding that, under many circumstances, product evaluations

. . . Studies of internet use in particular replicate this result. To take one significant example, consumers seek out and trust health information from other people (apparently) like them much more than they seek out and trust information from pharmaceutical companies.[84]

Advertisers can also take advantage of the phenomenon of social proof: people have a powerful tendency to put faith in the wisdom of crowds, which viral marketing can simulate.[85] Multiple sources

---

supposedly from *Consumer Reports* were more persuasive than the identical evaluations supposedly from a retailer); Roobina Ohanian, *The Impact of Celebrity Spokespersons' Perceived Image on Consumers' Intention to Purchase*, 31 J. ADVERT. RES. 46, 47, 52 (1991) (noting that friends are perceived as more trustworthy than sales personnel because of the potential conflict of interest, and that "the audience does not associate a high level of trustworthiness with individuals [such as celebrity endorsers] who get paid handsomely to promote a product"); Elaine Walster et al., *On Increasing the Persuasiveness of a Low Prestige Communicator*, 2 J. EXPERIMENTAL SOC. PSYCHOL. 325, 327 (1966) *available at* http://www2.hawaii.edu/~elaineh/14.pdf (stating that perceived self-interest decreases the credibility of a source, while perceived altruism increases it, whether the source is generally low in credibility (a criminal) or high in credibility (a prosecutor)).

[84] Noah Elkin, *How America Searches: Health and Wellness*, ICROSSING, Jan. 2008, *available at* http://www.icrossing.com/research/how-america-searches-health-and-wellness.php (showing substantial use of user-generated content and online social communities for health and wellness information); *id.* ("Consumers rank pharmaceutical companies and television as the two least trusted sources for information about health-related issues and questions, and place them in the bottom tier in terms of sources that influence their medication choices.").

[85] ROBERT B. CIALDINI, INFLUENCE: SCIENCE AND PRACTICE 99–102 (5th ed. Pearson 2009) (1985); Norton, *supra*, at 593 ("Some onlookers also rely on the public's reaction to a message as a shortcut for evaluating its content, using

endorsing the same product are more persuasive than a single source repeated multiple times.[86] Using apparently different sources is especially useful for strengthening initially less-plausible claims. Even better from the marketer's perspective, people don't understand why they find the repeated, multiple-source claim plausible. They attribute it to the inherent truth value of the claim rather than to the repetition, making them particularly vulnerable to manipulation of this type.[87]

With a wide swath of user-generated content, in the absence of disclosure a consumer can't tell whether a reviewer was compensated for the review or was simply sharing her opinion because she believed everyone is entitled to it. . . . Given that companies exist to sell their products and services, the default expectation is that the money has flowed from consumer to seller by the consumer's choice, and not the reverse. As a result, in the absence of disclosure, consumers will not assume that an apparently independent endorsement is in fact sponsored.

---

widespread acceptance or audience enthusiasm to gauge a message's quality.").

[86] Anne L. Roggeveen & Gita Venkataramani Johar, *Perceived Source Variability Versus Familiarity: Testing Competing Explanations for the Truth Effect*, 12 J. CONSUMER PSYCHOL. 81, 87 (2002) ("[B]elief in a claim is greater when it is perceived as coming from two different sources (vs. a single source).") . . . .

[87] *Id.* ("[T]he truth effect does occur for seemingly less plausible statements; however this occurs only under conditions where the multiple repetitions can be attributed to multiple sources. . . . [S]ubjects had no access to their use of number of sources in rating the truth value. Instead, subjects seized on the most likely explanation for their ratings—the plausibility of the claim. It appears that the use of source variability is an automatic process.").

Without regulation, a market for lemons will develop—a deterioration in the credibility of public discourse, because audiences won't be able to trust that a stated opinion is independent and sincerely held. . . .

A final matter of significant theoretical interest is the question of what, exactly, is false or misleading about undisclosed endorsement relationships. In the U.S., the law has rarely attempted to regulate "image" advertising—advertising that does not make factual representations but attempts to create a warm fuzzy glow or other feeling about a product or service. From a classic commercial speech perspective, regulation of image ads would be difficult to justify because such ads are not falsifiable, and thus can't be false. In false advertising doctrine, such claims are considered non-actionable puffery, on which no reasonable consumer would rely. The law has, in other words, equated non-falsifiability with unreliability, and irrebuttably presumed that consumers do not rely on that which is objectively unreliable.

But what about an endorser paid to puff? The regulatory theory is that an undisclosed sponsorship relationship could distort consumer decision making. Yet how could there be material deception if the endorser's positive but detail-free message was puffery? The endorsement guidelines implicitly recognize that, as advertising scholars have long maintained, image ads *do* affect consumer decisions—puffery *works*, which is why advertisers use it. Nonetheless, in the U.S., we usually do not try to regulate puffery because of the falsifiability problem. It is only when there is an undisclosed financial relationship that we can identify a specific element of the message that's deceptive.

It is still important to recognize that in an undisclosed sponsorship case where the speaker simply puffs, the deception can only be material if vague, fact-free claims made by a sufficiently credible source affect purchase decisions. And, it should be emphasized, this

403

paradox of material puffery is equally true in traditional ads, where the FTC has long required disclosure by endorsers where the endorsement relationship is not clear from context, regardless of whether an ad makes falsifiable factual claims.

The cool kid who tells her friends that a product is really awesome can get them to buy it. The cool kid's endorsement might even be performative, in that the endorsement *makes* the product cool. This is related to the problem of the placebo effect, where claiming that a product produces certain effects leads consumers to believe in (and even experience) those effects. The law has had little trouble finding that products that only work because of the placebo effect are falsely advertised. Regardless of how coolness is produced, it matters whether the cool kid is telling her friends voluntarily or for pay. This conclusion requires us to take even non-falsifiable claims seriously as claims that can distort a consumer's decisions.

Eric Goldman, *Stealth Risks of Regulating Stealth Marketing: A Comment on Ellen Goodman's Stealth Marketing and Editorial Integrity* (excerpt)

[C]onsumer distrust toward marketing is so strong that consumers often disregard marketing without assessing its actual utility to them. The "advertising" label is a powerful disclosure; it can single-handedly cause consumers to overlook content they would have otherwise found meritorious. A 2005 study by Jansen and Resnick illustrates this risk. Consumers were shown multiple sets of Internet search results, some of which were labeled advertising. Although the search results substantively were the same, consumers rated the unlabeled search results as more relevant than the labeled results. In other words, the advertising label single-handedly degraded the consumers' relevancy assessment even though the search results had the same level of relevancy.

The risk of consumer overresponse to marketing labels poses an interesting policy conundrum. Superficially, the populist approach would be to give consumers what they want (to know when content is marketing). Yet, this approach has the risk of counterproductively and systematically increasing consumers' erroneous content assessments, which in turn may hurt consumers' ability to get content they would find useful. At minimum, any cost–benefit analysis of sponsorship disclosure laws should account for the costs of these errors.

. . . [M]any consumers already suffer from information overload. Yet, noisy disclosures consume more of their already-strapped attention. Some consumers will feel that the disclosed information is valuable enough that they will not mind the "cost" of having their attention consumed, but others will resent the imposition. For the latter consumers, the mandated disclosure becomes another form of spam (unwanted content).

Ironically, mandated sponsorship disclosures could create a negative externality analogous to the one that [Ellen Goodman's] article attributes to stealth marketing. The article argues that stealth marketing degrades consumer trust in otherwise-trustworthy content. Similarly, to the extent that consumers do not find mandated sponsorship disclosures valuable to them, they will tune them out. Further, if consumers routinely find mandated disclosures unhelpful, they may be inclined to adopt an across-the-board heuristic to tune out mandated disclosures, even if those disclosures are socially valuable. Thus, as disclosures generally become noisier, consumers may increasingly become disinterested in all of them—a different negative externality than the one identified by the article, but problematic nonetheless.

Second, as discussed above, noisier disclosures should increase the number of consumers who see the disclosure and use it to make erroneous categorization judgments about the marketing. Indeed, this effect may support a self-reinforcing feedback loop. By mandating sponsorship disclosures, the government communicates to consumers that they should care about the distinctions between editorial and marketing content. Thus, consumers may care about the editorial–marketing divide because the government has mandated disclosure, while the government may mandate disclosure because consumers say they care about the divide.

NOTES AND QUESTIONS

Aren't so many things material that if we treated each one like sponsorship, we'd drown consumers in theoretically relevant—but functionally useless—information? *See* Sarah C. Haan, Note, *The 'Persuasion Route' of the Law: Advertising and Legal Persuasion*, 100 COLUM. L. REV. 1281 (2000) (discussing research indicating that consumers prefer not to face more than a few bits of information per advertisement). In any event, how can undisclosed sponsorship be material in cases where the only message conveyed is puffery?

Disclosure as Panacea? Research on disclosure of conflicts of interest sounds a cautionary note. Recipients of advice don't discount advice from biased advisors after disclosure as much as they should. *See* Daylian M. Cain et al., *The Dirt on Coming Clean: Perverse Effects of Disclosing Conflicts of Interest*, 34 J. LEGAL STUD. 1 (2005). This builds on other research (which you may have encountered in an evidence course) that people have difficulty ignoring information even when they're aware that it's inaccurate and/or that they should ignore it—the "curse of knowledge." Disclosure of a conflict of interest may increase trust unwarrantedly by making the audience feel that the speaker is being scrupulously honest. This is especially troubling because, as Cain et al. show, disclosure can increase advisors' bias, perhaps because they feel "morally licensed" by disclosure to pursue their own self-interest, and also perhaps because self-interest leads them to persuade themselves that their biased advice is best. While disclosures did lead listeners to discount the advice they received, that wasn't enough to offset the increase in the bias of the recommendations. The authors conclude that, while disclosure is not always counterproductive, it is far from a panacea. *But see* Genevieve Helleringer, *Trust Me, I Have a Conflict of Interest! Testing the Efficacy of Disclosure in Retail Investment Advice*, Oxford Legal Studies Research Paper No. 14/2016 (finding that disclosing that the disclosure is legally required, and clearly explaining the financial implications of the conflict of interest, could be effective when participants could compare advice and disclosures across multiple ads).

How might this research apply to disclosure of endorsements? Is a blogger who follows the disclosure rules even more likely to give a positive review of a product she got for free? On the other side, will consumers be more trusting after disclosure or less?

One recent study found that the disclosure "Brands are shown in this movie!" increased memories for brands, but not skepticism about brands. Eva A. van Reijmersdal et al., *The Effects of Brand Placement Disclosures on Skepticism and Brand Memory*, 38 COMM. 127 (2013). However, the researchers noted that there are conflicting studies on whether disclosure about persuasion triggers skepticism and resistance. In one study, for example, respondents perceived video news releases as less credible when accompanied by "video supplied by [sponsoring company]," but another found no effect on attitudes. Brand placement disclosures in particular may increase brand recall, which may be worthwhile to the advertiser, especially if it's not making any factual claims a regulator might target. Also, the wording may make a difference—"brands are shown" is a passive statement that might not trigger the same skepticism as "the advertiser paid to put this product in the movie."

B.   Legislative Definition of Terms?

Closely related to the issue of mandatory disclosures is the question of when, if ever, the government can establish by fiat that a word or phrase has a particular meaning, so that an advertiser who uses the word or phrase differently is engaged in false advertising. The following case considers this issue, against the backdrop of economic exploitation of Native Americans and the hope that Native American arts and crafts can provide economic benefits to Native American artisans. Being able to promise "authenticity," when non-American artisans can't, is apparently valuable, so non-Native American artisans have incentives to suggest that they too are offering "real" Native American art. How far can the government go in combating this free-riding?

Native American Arts, Inc. v. Waldron Corp., 399 F.3d 871 (7th Cir. 2005)

The Indian Arts and Crafts Act, 25 U.S.C. §§ 305 et seq., forbids (so far as bears on this case) selling a good "in a manner that falsely suggests it is . . . an Indian product." The principal plaintiff, Native American Arts (NAA), is a seller of goods produced by Indians. It brought this suit for damages against a non-Indian manufacturer of Indian-style jewelry that is advertised under such names as "Navajo," "Crow," "Southwest Tribes," and "Zuni Bear" and sold with tags that give information about the tribe. The ads identify the designer of the jewelry as Trisha Waldron, who is not an Indian. Neither the tags nor the ads contain any disclaimer of authenticity. The case was tried to a jury, the verdict was for the defendants, and the plaintiffs appeal.

Although the Indian Arts and Crafts Act dates back to 1935, this is—amazingly—the first reported appellate case under it. Until 1990, the only sanction for violating the false-advertising provision was criminal; and there were no prosecutions—zero. In 1990, Congress

authorized government and private civil suits, in which hefty
damages can be awarded. There have been some suits under the
amended statute, but none until this one that got beyond the district
court level.

The plaintiffs' principal argument is that the district judge should not
have held unconstitutional, and therefore refused to base an
instruction to the jury on, a regulation that provides that "the
unqualified use of the term 'Indian' or . . . of the name of an Indian
tribe . . . in connection with an art or craft product is interpreted to
mean . . . that the art or craft product is an Indian product." 25 C.F.R.
§ 309.24(a)(2). . . .

[The plaintiffs] challenge the soundness of Judge Der-Yeghiayan's
ruling that the "unqualified use" regulation infringes freedom of
speech and is also unconstitutionally vague and overbroad. He indeed
was wrong. If he were right, trademark law would be
unconstitutional. In effect the regulation makes "Indian" the
trademark denoting products made by Indians, just as "Roquefort"
denotes a cheese manufactured from sheep's milk cured in limestone
caves in the Roquefort region of France. A non-Indian maker of
jewelry designed to look like jewelry made by Indians is free to
advertise the similarity but if he uses the word "Indian" he must
qualify the usage so that consumers aren't confused and think they're
buying not only the kind of jewelry that Indians make, but jewelry
that Indians in fact made. There is no constitutional infirmity. But
this conclusion does less for the plaintiffs than they hoped.

The regulation is the work of a small office in the Department of
Interior called the Indian Arts and Crafts Board, and a more
substantial question than the constitutional questions that bedazzled
the district judge is whether a regulation that "interpret[s]" "the
unqualified use of the term 'Indian' . . . or the unqualified use of the
name of an Indian tribe" to denote "an Indian product" is authorized

409

by the Indian Arts and Crafts Act, which so far as relates to this issue merely authorizes the Department of the Interior to define the term "Indian product." That is not an authorization to determine what representations convey the impression that a work is such a product. There is no indication that Congress delegated to the Department authority to determine what constitutes sufficient proof of false advertising. The meaning of "Indian product" is plausibly within the scope of knowledge of an Indian Arts and Crafts Board—but not the requisites for proving consumer confusion, especially when it is not Indians, but non-Indians, who are the principal consumers of faux Indian products, and especially since the Board's enforcement role is extremely limited. The Board cannot conduct or initiate remedial proceedings; all it can do is refer complaints to the FBI for investigation, and to the Department of Justice for prosecution or civil action.

Well, it can do a little more; it can indicate the circumstances in which it will make such a reference. . . . The Board is certainly free to announce the policy that will guide it in deciding whether to refer matters to the Department of Justice for possible action. The "qualified use" regulation should be understood in this light rather than as an attempt to tell the courts how to decide whether consumers are likely to be confused.

But suppose we are wrong and the regulation governs suits to enforce the Indian Arts and Crafts Act; the next question would be the meaning of "unqualified use" and the bearing of that meaning on jury instructions, the closing arguments, and the jury's verdict. Perhaps the most natural meaning of "unqualified use of the term 'Indian' " or of the name of an Indian tribe is using the word or the name to denote an Indian product without including a disclaimer, such as "Indian style," or, more emphatically, if rather off-putting, "not manufactured by Indians." A common dictionary definition of "unqualified" is "not modified by reservations or restrictions."

. . . [T]he required qualification of the use of the name could consist of any pertinent contextual elements, such as the picture of Trisha Waldron that appears in some of the advertising or the type of store in which her jewelry is sold. [The court found that plaintiffs' proposed instruction related to the Board's rule would have been unhelpful to the jury.]

In any event the regulation (always assuming, contrary to our earlier ruling, that the regulation governs in litigation) would be pertinent only in a case in which there was no context: a case for example in which Waldron sold an unadvertised product labeled simply "Navajo Bracelet," with no mention of the manufacturer or even identification of the outlets in which the bracelet was sold—with nothing but the name and the price. There was plenty of context in this case. The question the jury had to answer was not what the names of the various items of jewelry meant but what the entire sales package, including advertising, labeling, and place of sale, suggested to the average consumer. In such a case, asking whether the defendant falsely suggested that it was selling Indian products, and asking whether it failed to qualify its use of the names of Indian tribes, come to the same thing.

So there was no error in the instructions. . . .

NOTES AND QUESTIONS

What is a reasonable consumer viewing Native American–style jewelry likely to think about its source? What about when the jewelry is coupled with names evoking Native American tribes? Should Congress enact the Board's rule into law? If it did, would that be constitutional?

How could "the picture of Trisha Waldron that appears in some of the advertising or the type of store in which her jewelry is sold" educate consumers about the true origin of the jewelry? Is the court making warranted assumptions about what Native Americans look like or where they sell their goods? If consumers use pictures and types of stores as proxies for authenticity, are they buying into stereotypes, and if so, could explicit labeling do anything to help?

C.   Disclosures and the First Amendment

The *Native American Arts* case involves a government attempt to define certain terms, but government control goes much farther. Sometimes, consumers might distinguish between products, but the government might want them to be labeled identically—or, contrariwise, the government might want to highlight differences that consumers wouldn't otherwise know or care about. Mandatory definitions and disclosures thus implicate important policy concerns—from what we should be consuming to how extensive commercial speakers' rights should be.

Consider the following case:

Am. Meat Inst. v. U.S. Dept. of Agriculture, 760 F.3d 18 (2014) (en banc)

Williams, Senior Circuit Judge:
Reviewing a regulation of the Secretary of Agriculture that mandates disclosure of country-of-origin information about meat products, a panel of this court rejected the plaintiffs' statutory and First Amendment challenges. The panel found the plaintiffs unlikely to succeed on the merits and affirmed the district court's denial of a preliminary injunction. On the First Amendment claim, the panel read *Zauderer v. Office of Disciplinary Counsel*, 471 U.S. 626, 651 (1985), to apply to disclosure mandates aimed at addressing problems

other than deception (which the mandate at issue in *Zauderer* had been designed to remedy). ... We now hold that *Zauderer* in fact does reach beyond problems of deception, sufficiently to encompass the disclosure mandates at issue here.

* * *

Congress has required country-of-origin labels on a variety of foods, including some meat products, and tasked the Secretary of Agriculture with implementation. ... For meat cuts, at least, the amended statute defined country of origin based on where the animal has been born, raised, and slaughtered—the three major production steps.

The Secretary, whom we refer to interchangeably with his delegate the Agricultural Marketing Service ("AMS"), first promulgated rules in 2009. The rules did not demand explicit identification of the production step(s) occurring in each listed country, but called more simply for labeling with a phrase starting "Product of," followed by mention of one or more countries. The 2009 rule also made allowance for a production practice known as "commingling." This made the labeling of meat cuts from animals of different origins processed together on a single production day relatively simple; the label could just name all the countries of origin for the commingled animals.

After the 2009 rule's adoption, Canada and Mexico filed a complaint with the Dispute Settlement Body of the World Trade Organization. In due course the WTO's Appellate Body found the rule to be in violation of the WTO Agreement on Technical Barriers to Trade. The gravamen of the WTO's decision appears to have been an objection to the relative imprecision of the information required by the 2009 rule. In a different section of its opinion, the Appellate Body seemed to agree with the United States that country-of-origin labeling in general can serve a legitimate objective in informing consumers. A

413

WTO arbitrator gave the United States a deadline to bring its requirements into compliance with the ruling.

The Secretary responded with a rule requiring more precise information—revealing the location of each production step. For example, meat derived from an animal born in Canada and raised and slaughtered in the United States, which formerly could have been labeled "Product of the United States and Canada," would now have to be labeled "Born in Canada, Raised and Slaughtered in the United States." In a matter of great concern to plaintiffs because of its cost implications, the 2013 rule also eliminated the flexibility allowed in labeling commingled animals.

The plaintiffs, a group of trade associations representing livestock producers, feedlot operators, and meat packers, whom we'll collectively call American Meat Institute ("AMI"), challenged the 2013 rule in district court as a violation of both the statute and the First Amendment. This led to the decisions summarized at the outset of this opinion.

AMI argues that the 2013 rule violates its First Amendment right to freedom of speech by requiring it to disclose country-of-origin information to retailers, who will ultimately provide the information to consumers. The question before us, framed in the order granting en banc review, is whether the test set forth in *Zauderer*, 471 U.S. at 651, applies to government interests beyond consumer deception. Instead, AMI says, we should apply the general test for commercial speech restrictions formulated in *Central Hudson*, 447 U.S. 557, 566, 100 S.Ct. 2343 (1980). ...

* * *

The starting point common to both parties is that *Zauderer* applies to government mandates requiring disclosure of "purely factual and

uncontroversial information" appropriate to prevent deception in the
regulated party's commercial speech. The key question for us is
whether the principles articulated in *Zauderer* apply more broadly to
factual and uncontroversial disclosures required to serve other
government interests. AMI also argues that even if *Zauderer* extends
beyond correction of deception, the government has no interest in
country-of-origin labeling substantial enough to sustain the
challenged rules.

Zauderer itself does not give a clear answer. Some of its language
suggests possible confinement to correcting deception. Having already
described the disclosure mandated there as limited to "purely factual
and uncontroversial information about the terms under which [the
transaction was proposed]," the Court said, "we hold that an
advertiser's rights are adequately protected as long as [such]
disclosure requirements are reasonably related to the State's interest
in preventing deception of consumers." 471 U.S. at 651. (It made no
finding that the advertiser's message was "more likely to deceive the
public than to inform it," which would constitutionally subject the
message to an outright ban. *See Central Hudson,* 447 U.S. at 563.)
The Court's own later application of *Zauderer* in *Milavetz, Gallop &
Milavetz, P.A. v. United States,* 559 U.S. 229 (2010), also focused on
remedying misleading advertisements, which was the sole interest
invoked by the government. Given the subject of both cases, it was
natural for the Court to express the rule in such terms. The language
could have been simply descriptive of the circumstances to which the
Court applied its new rule, or it could have aimed to preclude any
application beyond those circumstances.

The language with which *Zauderer* justified its approach, however,
sweeps far more broadly than the interest in remedying deception.
After recounting the elements of *Central Hudson, Zauderer* rejected
that test as unnecessary in light of the "material differences between
disclosure requirements and outright prohibitions on speech." Later

in the opinion, the Court observed that "the First Amendment interests implicated by disclosure requirements are substantially weaker than those at stake when speech is actually suppressed." After noting that the disclosure took the form of "purely factual and uncontroversial information about the terms under which [the] services will be available," the Court characterized the speaker's interest as "minimal": "Because the extension of First Amendment protection to commercial speech is justified principally by the value to consumers of the information such speech provides, appellant's constitutionally protected interest in *not* providing any particular factual information in his advertising is minimal." All told, *Zauderer*'s characterization of the speaker's interest in opposing forced disclosure of such information as "minimal" seems inherently applicable beyond the problem of deception, as other circuits have found. ....

In applying *Zauderer,* we first must assess the adequacy of the interest motivating the country-of-origin labeling scheme. AMI argues that, even assuming *Zauderer* applies here, the government has utterly failed to show an adequate interest in making country-of-origin information available to consumers. AMI disparages the government's interest as simply being that of satisfying consumers' "idle curiosity." Counsel for AMI acknowledged during oral argument that her theory would as a logical matter doom the statute, "if the only justification that Congress has offered is the justification that it offered here...."

Beyond the interest in correcting misleading or confusing commercial speech, *Zauderer* gives little indication of what type of interest might suffice. In particular, the Supreme Court has not made clear whether *Zauderer* would permit government reliance on interests that do not qualify as substantial under *Central Hudson*'s standard, a standard that itself seems elusive. But here we think several aspects of the government's interest in country-of-origin labeling for food combine to

416

make the interest substantial: the context and long history of country-of-origin disclosures to enable consumers to choose American-made products; the demonstrated consumer interest in extending country-of-origin labeling to food products; and the individual health concerns and market impacts that can arise in the event of a food-borne illness outbreak. Because the interest motivating the 2013 rule is a substantial one, we need not decide whether a lesser interest could suffice under *Zauderer*.

Country-of-origin information has an historical pedigree that lifts it well above "idle curiosity." History can be telling. In *Burson v. Freeman*, 504 U.S. 191, 211 (1992) (plurality opinion), for example, the Court, applying strict scrutiny to rules banning electioneering within a 100–foot zone around polling places, found an adequate justification in a "long history, a substantial consensus, and simple common sense." And country-of-origin label mandates indeed have a "long history." Congress has been imposing similar mandates since 1890, giving such rules a run just short of 125 years.

The history relied on in *Burson* was (as here) purely of legislative action, not First Amendment rulings by the judiciary. But just as in *Burson*, where "[t]he majority of [the] laws were adopted originally in the 1890s," the "time-tested consensus" that consumers want to know the geographical origin of potential purchases has material weight in and of itself. The Congress that extended country-of-origin mandates to food did so against a historical backdrop that has made the value of this particular product information to consumers a matter of common sense.

Supporting members of Congress identified the statute's purpose as enabling customers to make informed choices based on characteristics of the products they wished to purchase, including United States supervision of the entire production process for health and hygiene. Some expressed a belief that with information about meat's national

417

origin, many would choose American meat on the basis of a belief that it would in truth be better. Even though the production steps abroad for food imported into the United States are to a degree subject to U.S. government monitoring, it seems reasonable for Congress to anticipate that many consumers may prefer food that had been continuously under a particular government's direct scrutiny.

Some legislators also expressed the belief that people would have a special concern about the geographical origins of what they eat. This is manifest in anecdotes appearing in the legislative record, such as the collapse of the cantaloupe market when some imported cantaloupes proved to be contaminated and consumers were unable to determine whether the melons on the shelves had come from that country. Of course the anecdote more broadly suggests the utility of these disclosures in the event of any disease outbreak known to have a specific country of origin, foreign or domestic.

The record is further bolstered by surveys AMS reviewed, such as one indicating that 71–73 percent of consumers would be willing to pay for country-of-origin information about their food. The AMS quite properly noted the vulnerabilities in such data. Most obvious is the point that consumers tend to overstate their willingness to pay; after all, the data sound possibly useful, and giving a "Yes" answer on the survey doesn't cost a nickel. But such studies, combined with the many favorable comments the agency received during all of its rulemakings, reinforce the historical basis for treating such information as valuable....

Finally, agency statements (from prior rulemakings) claiming that country-of-origin labeling serves no food safety interest are not inconsistent with any of the government's litigation positions here. Simply because the agency believes it has other, superior means to protect food safety doesn't delegitimize a congressional decision to empower consumers to take possible country-specific differences in safety practices into account. Nor does such an agency belief undercut the economy-wide benefits of confining the market impact of a disease outbreak.

Having determined that the interest served by the disclosure mandate is adequate, what remains is to assess the relationship between the government's identified means and its chosen ends. Under *Central Hudson,* we would determine whether "the regulatory technique [is] in proportion to [the] interest," an inquiry comprised of assessing whether the chosen means "directly advance[s] the state interest involved" and whether it is narrowly tailored to serve that end. *Zauderer* 's method of evaluating fit differs in wording, though perhaps not significantly in substance, at least on these facts.

When the Supreme Court has analyzed *Central Hudson* 's "directly advance" requirement, it has commonly required evidence of a measure's effectiveness. But as the Court recognized in *Zauderer,* such evidentiary parsing is hardly necessary when the government uses a disclosure mandate to achieve a goal of informing consumers about a particular product trait, assuming of course that the reason for informing consumers qualifies as an adequate interest. 471 U.S. at 650; see also *Milavetz,* 559 U.S. at 249 (referring to *Zauderer* as providing for "less exacting scrutiny"). *Zauderer,* like the doctrine of *res ipsa loquitur,* identifies specific circumstances where a party carries part of its evidentiary burden in a way different from the customary one. There, a plaintiff proves negligence by meeting the specified criteria (such as proving the defendant's exclusive control over the agency causing the injury); here, by acting only through a reasonably crafted disclosure mandate, the government meets its burden of showing that the mandate advances its interest in making the "purely factual and uncontroversial information" accessible to the recipients. Of course to match *Zauderer* logically, the disclosure mandated must relate to the good or service offered by the regulated party, a link that in *Zauderer* itself was inherent in the facts, as the

419

disclosure mandate necessarily related to such goods or services. For purposes of this case, we need not decide on the precise scope or character of that relationship.

The self-evident tendency of a disclosure mandate to assure that recipients get the mandated information may in part explain why, where that is the goal, many such mandates have persisted for decades without anyone questioning their constitutionality. In this long-lived group have been not only country-of-origin labels but also many other routine disclosure mandates about product attributes, including, for instance, disclosures of fiber content, care instructions for clothing items, and listing of ingredients.

Notwithstanding the reference to "narrow tailoring," the Court has made clear that the government's burden on the final *Central Hudson* factor is to show a "reasonable fit," or a "reasonable proportion," between means and ends. To the extent that the government's interest is in assuring that consumers receive particular information (as it plainly is when mandating disclosures that correct deception), the means-end fit is self-evidently satisfied when the government acts only through a reasonably crafted mandate to disclose "purely factual and uncontroversial information" about attributes of the product or service being offered. In other words, this particular method of achieving a government interest will almost always demonstrate a reasonable means-ends relationship, absent a showing that the disclosure is "unduly burdensome" in a way that "chill[s] protected commercial speech."

Thus, to the extent that the pre-conditions to application of *Zauderer* warrant inferences that the mandate will "directly advance" the government's interest and show a "reasonable fit" between means and ends, one could think of *Zauderer* largely as "an *application* of *Central Hudson,* where several of *Central Hudson's* elements have already been established."

420

In this case, the criteria triggering the application of *Zauderer* are either unchallenged or substantially unchallenged. The decision requires the disclosures to be of "purely factual and uncontroversial information" about the good or service being offered. AMI does not contest that country-of-origin labeling qualifies as factual, and the facts conveyed are directly informative of intrinsic characteristics of the product AMI is selling.

As to whether it is "controversial," AMI objected to the word "slaughter" in its reply brief. Though it seems a plain, blunt word for a plain, blunt action, we can understand a claim that "slaughter," used on a product of any origin, might convey a certain innuendo. But we need not address such a claim because the 2013 rule allows retailers to use the term "harvested" instead, and AMI has posed no objection to that. And AMI does not disagree with the truth of the facts required to be disclosed, so there is no claim that they are controversial in that sense.

We also do not understand country-of-origin labeling to be controversial in the sense that it communicates a message that is controversial for some reason other than dispute about simple factual accuracy. Leaving aside the possibility that some required factual disclosures could be so one-sided or incomplete that they would not qualify as "factual and uncontroversial," country-of-origin facts are not of that type. AMI does not suggest anything controversial about the message that its members are required to express.

Nor does the mandate run afoul of the Court's warning that *Zauderer* does not leave the state "free to require corporations to carry the messages of third parties, where the messages themselves are biased against or are expressly contrary to the corporation's views."

Finally, though it may be obvious, we note that *Zauderer* cannot justify a disclosure so burdensome that it essentially operates as a restriction on constitutionally protected speech, as in *Ibanez v. Florida Department of Business and Professional Regulation*, 512 U.S. 136, 146–47 (1994), where a required disclaimer was so detailed that it "effectively rule[d] out notation of the 'specialist' designation on a business card or letterhead, or in a yellow pages listing." Nor can it sustain mandates that "chill[ ] protected commercial speech." AMI has made no claim of either of these consequences.

Accordingly we answer affirmatively the general question of whether "government interests in addition to correcting deception," can be invoked to sustain a disclosure mandate under *Zauderer*, and specifically find the interests invoked here to be sufficient. ...

So ordered.

[Judge Rogers concurred in part, arguing that *Central Hudson* and *Zauderer* were in fact separate standards and that thinking of *Zauderer* as a mere application of *Central Hudson* to the mandatory disclosure situation blurred the tests. Specifically, *Zauderer* does not put the burden on the government to show that a disclosure requirement directly advances its interest. Because commercial speakers have minimal interests in avoiding truthful, relevant disclosures,, and such disclosures promote the free flow of truthful information, disclosure requirements need only be reasonably related to the State's interest in preventing deception of consumers. *Zauderer* explained that "disclosure requirements trench much more narrowly on an advertiser's interests than do flat prohibitions on speech," and Judge Rogers concluded that "the Court was not tracing a shortcut through *Central Hudson* but defining a category in which the interests at stake were less threatened."]

Kavanaugh, Circuit Judge, concurring in the judgment:

May the U.S. Government require an imported Chinese-made product to be labeled "Made in China"? For many readers, the question probably answers itself: Yes. This case requires us to explain why that is so, in particular why such a requirement passes muster under the First Amendment. The precise First Amendment issue before us concerns a federal law that requires country-of-origin labels for meat and other food products. Country-of-origin labels are of course familiar to American consumers. Made in America. Made in Mexico. Made in China. And so on. For many decades, Congress has mandated such country-of-origin labels for a variety of products. I agree with the majority opinion that the First Amendment does not bar those longstanding and commonplace country-of-origin labeling requirements.

As a starting point, all agree that the First Amendment imposes stringent limits on the Government's authority to either restrict or compel speech by private citizens and organizations. This case involves commercial speech. The First Amendment protects commercial speech, and regulations of commercial speech are analyzed under the Supreme Court's *Central Hudson* framework. To justify laws regulating commercial speech, the Government must (i) identify a substantial governmental interest and (ii) demonstrate a sufficient fit between the law's requirements and that substantial governmental interest.

I will address in turn how those two basic *Central Hudson* requirements apply to this case.

First, under *Central Hudson,* the Government must identify a substantial governmental interest that is served by the law in question. Since its decision in *Central Hudson,* the Supreme Court has not stated that something less than a "substantial" governmental interest would justify either a restriction on commercial speech or a compelled commercial disclosure. And likewise, the majority opinion today does not say that a governmental interest that is less than substantial would suffice to justify a compelled commercial disclosure.

What interests qualify as sufficiently substantial to justify the infringement on the speaker's First Amendment autonomy that results from a compelled commercial disclosure? Here, as elsewhere in First Amendment free-speech law, history and tradition are reliable guides. ...

[T]he Government cannot advance a traditional anti-deception, health, or safety interest in this case because a country-of-origin disclosure requirement obviously does not serve those interests. Rather, the Government broadly contends that it has a substantial interest in "providing consumers with information." For *Central Hudson* purposes, however, it is plainly not enough for the Government to say simply that it has a substantial interest in giving consumers information. After all, that would be true of any and all disclosure requirements. That circular formulation would drain the *Central Hudson* test of any meaning in the context of compelled commercial disclosures. Not surprisingly, governments (federal, state, and local) would love to have such a free pass to spread their preferred messages on the backs of others. But as the Second Circuit has stated, "Were consumer interest alone sufficient, there is no end to the information that states could require manufacturers to disclose about their production methods." *International Dairy Foods Association v. Amestoy,* 92 F.3d 67, 74 (2d Cir.1996). Some consumers might want to know whether their U.S.-made product was made by U.S. citizens and not by illegal immigrants. Some consumers might want to know whether a doctor has ever performed an abortion. Some consumers might want to know the political affiliation of a business's owners. These are not far-fetched hypotheticals, particularly at the state or local level. Do such consumer desires suffice to justify compelled commercial disclosures of such information on a product or in an advertisement? I think not, and history and tradition provide no support for that kind of free-wheeling government power to mandate compelled commercial disclosures. ...

Although the Government's broad argument is meritless, country-of-origin labeling is justified by the Government's historically rooted interest in supporting American manufacturers, farmers, and ranchers as they compete with foreign manufacturers, farmers, and ranchers. Since the early days of the Republic, numerous U.S. laws have sought to further that interest, sometimes overtly and sometimes subtly. Although economists debate whether various kinds of protectionist legislation help U.S. consumers and the overall U.S. economy, there is no doubt that Congress has long sought to support and promote various U.S. industries against their foreign competition. How is that interest implicated by country-of-origin labeling? Country-of-origin labeling, it is widely understood, causes many American consumers (for a variety of reasons) to buy a higher percentage of American-made products, which in turn helps American manufacturers, farmers, and ranchers as compared to foreign manufacturers, farmers, and ranchers. That is why Congress has long mandated country-of-origin disclosures for certain products. *See, e.g., United States v. Ury,* 106 F.2d 28, 29 (2d Cir.1939) (purpose of early country-of-origin labeling requirements "was to apprise the public of the foreign origin and thus to confer an advantage on domestic producers of competing goods"). That historical pedigree is critical for First Amendment purposes and demonstrates that the Government's interest here is substantial. The majority opinion properly relies on the history of country-of-origin labeling laws as a basis for finding that the Government has a substantial interest in this case.

425

That said, one wrinkle in this case [is that] the Executive Branch has refrained during this litigation from expressly articulating its clear interest in supporting American farmers and ranchers in order to justify this law, apparently because of the international repercussions that might ensue. But the interest here is obvious, even if unarticulated by the Executive Branch for reasons of international comity. And more to the point for *Central Hudson* purposes, Members of Congress did articulate the interest in supporting American farmers and ranchers when Congress enacted this country-of-origin labeling law. And Congress's articulation of the interest suffices under *Central Hudson.*

In short, the Government has a substantial interest in this case in supporting American farmers and ranchers against their foreign competitors.

The second question under *Central Hudson* concerns the fit between the disclosure requirement and the Government's interest—as plaintiff AMI succinctly puts it, whether the disclosure requirement is "tailored in a reasonable manner."

As I read it, the Supreme Court's decision in *Zauderer* applied the *Central Hudson* "tailored in a reasonable manner" requirement to compelled commercial disclosures. ... In applying the teachings of *Central Hudson* to the state disclosure requirement, the *Zauderer* Court required that such mandatory disclosures be "purely factual," "uncontroversial," not "unduly burdensome," and "reasonably related to" the Government's interest. So *Zauderer* is best read simply as an application of *Central Hudson,* not a different test altogether. In other words, *Zauderer* tells us what *Central Hudson's* "tailored in a reasonable manner" standard means in the context of compelled commercial disclosures: The disclosure must be purely factual, uncontroversial, not unduly burdensome, and reasonably related to the Government's interest.

426

... *Zauderer* tightly limits mandatory disclosures to a very narrow class that meets the various *Zauderer* requirements. So to the extent that some courts, advocates, and commentators have portrayed a choice between the "tough *Central Hudson* standard" and the "lenient *Zauderer* standard," I see that as a false choice. ...

In this case, as the majority opinion properly concludes, those stringent *Zauderer* fit requirements are met. ...

[Judge Henderson's dissenting opinion is omitted.]

Brown, Circuit Judge, dissenting:
... The court holds "*Zauderer* ... reach[es] beyond problems of deception, sufficiently to encompass" factual and noncontroversial disclosure mandates aimed at providing more information to some consumers. As a result, the fundamental First Amendment right not to be coerced or compelled to say what one would not say voluntarily is now demoted to a mere tautology: "[B]y acting ... through a reasonably crafted disclosure mandate, the government meets its burden of showing that the mandate advances its interest in making the 'purely factual and uncontroversial information' accessible to the recipients." In other words, a business owner no longer has a constitutionally protected right to refrain from speaking, as long as the government wants to use the company's product to convey "purely factual and uncontroversial" information.

In so finding, the court today ignores the plain words of *Zauderer*'s text and disregards its historical context; both the text and history of the case emphasize the government's unique interest in preventing commercial deception....

In *Zauderer,* an attorney challenged Ohio's restrictions on lawyer advertising after he was disciplined for certain allegedly misleading newspaper advertisements. Specifically, when one advertisement promised clients would owe no legal fees in cases without a recovery, the disciplinary office complained the ad failed to follow regulations requiring disclosure that clients still may be liable for costs in unsuccessful claims.

First, the Supreme Court clarified both that the First Amendment protects commercial speech, and that it protects advertisers from compelled speech. However, the First Amendment does not shield deceptive, false, or fraudulent speech that proposes a commercial transaction. But, where that deceptive advertising could be cured by more speech, the government may choose between requiring disclosure and directly prohibiting the advertisement. While there are "material differences" between disclosure requirements and outright prohibitions, compelled speech "may be as violative of the First Amendment as [prohibited] speech," and the government faces a heavy burden to justify involuntary affirmation (being forced to carry the government's message). After reconfirming that the government may not attempt to "prescribe what shall be orthodox in politics, nationalism, religion, or other matters of opinion or force citizens" to conform to the state's assumptions, the Court then contrasted the imposition of orthodoxy—prohibited by the First Amendment—with Ohio's regulation of deceptive commercial advertising. When the purpose of compelling factual information is to cure deception, the advertiser's "constitutionally protected interest ... is minimal." To avoid any possible confusion, the court succinctly summarized: "[W]e hold that an *advertiser's rights* are adequately protected as long as disclosure requirements are reasonably related to the State's interest in preventing deception of consumers."

Crucial to the Court's analysis was not *just* the difference between disclosure and prohibition; it was also the difference between disclosure in advertising and that advertisement's outright prohibition, given the state's prerogative to prohibit misleading

428

commercial speech. The Court was absolutely clear: "[B]ecause disclosure requirements trench much more narrowly on an *advertiser's* interests than do flat prohibitions on speech, warnings or disclaimers might be appropriately required in order to dissipate *the possibility of consumer confusion or deception.*" In short, the state's option to require a curative disclosure cannot be disconnected from its right to entirely prohibit deceptive, fraudulent, or misleading commercial speech. Requiring an advertiser to provide "somewhat *more* information than they might otherwise be inclined to present," is thus constitutionally permissible when the government's available alternative is to completely ban that deceptive speech. Nowhere does *Zauderer* claim a commercial speaker can be *forced* to speak factual and noncontroversial information in the first instance. Instead, the text emphasizes the interests of advertisers, i.e., those who have already spoken.

Thus, even when the advertiser makes affirmative claims and the basis for a curative disclosure is self-evident, the advertiser still retains minimal First Amendment protections. Conversely, when the government is not curing deception, constitutional protections remain robust and undiminished. That the compelled information must be factual and noncontroversial is part of the government's burden. This characterization is not a trigger that transforms every seller's packaging into the government's billboard....

B

By parsing *Zauderer* in such a piecemeal fashion, this court robs the decision of its internal consistency and strips it of any historical context. The Framers resisted adding a Bill of Rights to the Constitution because they feared the elucidation of some rights would overshadow the *telos* inherent in the Constitution as a whole. The Constitution of liberty they conceived was premised on the natural law and conceded the immanence of the first principle of that law—

that an adult human being, as a free moral agent, cannot be coerced without good reason. At the same time, they understood James Wilson's observation that no one ever had a natural right to do wrong. This is precisely the balance the Supreme Court struck in its early opinions acknowledging protection for commercial speech.

When the Supreme Court extended formal constitutional protection to commercial speech, it emphasized that false or misleading commercial speech remained unprotected. ...

Zauderer ... does not offer a dispensation from *Central Hudson*'s intermediate scrutiny. Rather the government's burden under intermediate scrutiny is effectively met when the government commands purely factual and noncontroversial disclosures to prevent deceptive advertising. *Zauderer* is, in essence, a shortcut, "where several of *Central Hudson*'s elements have already been established."

To illustrate: Under *Central Hudson,* the government must first assert a substantial interest. Preventing inherent or actual deception in commercial advertising will always be such a substantial interest, so *Zauderer* satisfies the first element. Next, when a government's disclosure mandate is reasonably related to its deception interest—as *Zauderer* requires—we can be assured the disclosure will directly advance that interest; in other words, a reasonably related curative disclosure will necessarily make the deceptive advertisement less misleading. Finally, a disclosure requirement will be less restrictive than an outright ban, or no more extensive than necessary to cure the deception.

When the government's interest is not in curing deceptive advertising, however, *Zauderer* does not apply. The commercial speech "may be restricted only in the service of a substantial ... interest" articulated by the government, and "only through means that directly advance that interest." *Central Hudson*—without any

430

shortcuts—applies to disclosures that target interests other than deception.

... By holding the amorphous interests in today's case to be "substantial (and questioning whether any governmental interest could fail to be substantial, except those already found to be trivial, the court effectively absolves the government of any burden. Any interest that is not "trivial" will do....

The government's only asserted interest for the rule throughout this litigation—after abandoning its half-hearted post hoc deception rationale—has been a consistently vague one: "The government's interest is in providing consumers with information that those consumers can use to make choices about the food that they will ... purchase and serve to their families or eat themselves." Yet the government has never explained precisely *why* origin information assists with customer preferences, only suggesting "the production steps in each country *may* embody latent (hidden or unobservable) attributes, which *may* be important to individual consumers." The government never suggests, explains, or supports what those attributes might be. More importantly, the government never explains why coerced speech is the only solution.

The agency's stated ambiguous and amorphous interest in giving consumers more information is undoubtedly insufficient to survive even under an expanded-*Zauderer* regime. ...

Contrary to the court's assertions, the "long history" of country-of-origin labeling cannot support the government's interest here. The court claims the rule's "historical pedigree ... lifts it well above 'idle curiosity.'" However, in the First Amendment context, which has been steadily evolving since the late 1800s, history is not "telling," rather, it is an especially poor substitute for reasoned judgment. The Supreme Court's general reluctance to accept any free speech claims at the time country-of-origin labeling began certainly bears on the issue.

Modern "commercial speech" doctrine did not begin until the 1970s, when the Supreme Court formally extended First Amendment protection to commercial speech. That "Congress has been imposing [country-of-origin] mandates since 1890," eighty-six years before commercial speech received explicit protection, thus tells us very little about the practice's constitutionality. The Court's terminology in these early years was something of a self-fulfilling prophecy; what we now call "commercial speech," the court simply referred to as "commercial advertising" or some other business activity. This linguistic choice not only reflected the court's underlying thoughts and assumptions (i.e., that advertising was permissibly regulated as business conduct) but also likely influenced the litigating positions of parties. Litigants rarely raised First Amendment challenges to advertising restrictions—instead making substantive due process arguments by asserting restrictions affected their business rights.

For example, in 1907, when faced with the constitutional validity of a state law criminalizing the use of an American flag emblem on labels, the litigants and the Court "ignored potential free speech claims." Rather, the defendants attacked the statute as repugnant to the Equal Protection and Due Process Clauses, challenges rejected by the Court. ...

ii

The court concludes protectionism or patriotism is the true motive of the challenged country-of-origin labeling scheme, even if it is only acknowledged with a sly wink by the government. The court assumes—perhaps correctly—that absent the constraints of various trade treaties, Congress would have an interest in promoting American products. But, that interest would constitute a substantial justification for coercing speech only if the government had actually asserted it, and if voluntary action and direct government speech were obviously inadequate. ... Not only has the agency failed to raise or support any protectionist motive, it has, in fact, consistently denied one. *See, e.g.,* 2013 Rule, 78 Fed.Reg. at 31,376 ("The availability of [country-of-origin labeling] information does not imply that there will necessarily be any change in aggregate consumer demand or in demand for products of one origin versus others."); Mandatory Country of Origin Labeling, 68 Fed.Reg. 61,944, 61,955 (Oct. 30, 2003) [hereinafter "2003 Proposed Rule"] ("We find little evidence to support the notion that consumers' stated preferences for country of origin labeling will lead to increased demands for covered commodities bearing the U.S.-origin label."); 68 Fed.Reg. at 61,956 ("The lack of participation in government-provided programs for labeling products of U.S. origin provides evidence that consumers do not have a strong preference for country of origin labeling."); 68 Fed.Reg. at 61,956 ("The results from ... surveys indicate that the number of consumers with strong preferences for U.S.-origin labeled products is not sufficient for U.S. producers to benefit from labeling.").

iii

... [N]ot only has the government failed to raise or support any motive in consumer health and safety, it has, in fact, consistently eschewed that interest as supporting the rule. *See, e.g.,* 74 Fed.Reg. at 2683 (rejecting commenters' suggestions that country-of-origin labeling would provide "food safety benefits to consumers" because the program "does not address food safety issues"). This undercuts the court's claim that "it seems reasonable for Congress to anticipate that many consumers will prefer food that had been continuously under a particular government's direct scrutiny."

Even the anecdotes in the legislative record do not, as the court contends, "broadly suggest[ ] the utility of [country-of-origin] disclosures in the event of any disease outbreak known to have a

433

specific country of origin, foreign or domestic." Rather, the Agency also discredited this very purpose: "Appropriate preventative measures and effective mechanisms to recall products in the event of contamination incidents are the means used to protect the health of the consuming public...." ...

III

This case is really not about country-of-origin labeling. It is not even about patriotism or protectionism. And it is certainly not about health and safety. What is apparent from the record and the briefing is that this is a case about seeking competitive advantage. One need only look at the parties and amici to recognize this rule benefits one group of American farmers and producers, while interfering with the practices and profits of other American businesses who rely on imported meat to serve their customers. Even the court's citation to the congressional record underscores this point. Such a disproportionate burden "stands in sharp conflict with the First Amendment's command that government regulation of speech must be measured in minimums, not maximums."

Of course the victors today will be the victims tomorrow, because the standard created by this case will virtually ensure the producers supporting this labeling regime will one day be saddled with objectionable disclosure requirements (perhaps to disclose cattle feed practices; how their cattle are raised; whether their cattle were medically treated and with what; the environmental effects of beef production; or even the union status or wage levels of their employees). Only the fertile imaginations of activists will limit what disclosures successful efforts from vegetarian, animal rights, environmental, consumer protection, or other as-yet-unknown lobbies may compel.

If patriotism or protectionism would sell products, producers and sellers would happily festoon their products with Made in the USA or Product of the USA labels. Thus, any consumer's desire to buy American could be easily satisfied by voluntary action. Yet today this court offers to facilitate blatant rent-seeking behavior ....

By substantiating the government's nebulous interests, the court essentially permits the government to commandeer the speech of others. There is no limiting principle for such a flimsy interest as the government asserted in this case. More alarmingly, such self-referential interests can be marshalled in aid of any sort of crony capitalism or ideological arm-twisting. This labeling scheme is only one example.

The scheme is not designed to inform consumers; it is designed to take away the price advantage enjoyed by one segment of a domestic industry. The government's alleged interest in providing information that some consumers may desire will actually result in higher prices. Forcing meat packers to pay a premium for domestic beef will raise costs for consumers. Query whether the protections of the First Amendment should be abrogated for some businesses in order to benefit other businesses. That approach not only swallows important First Amendment protections, it does so in order to discriminate in favor of particular segments of particular industries. The First Amendment ought not be construed to allow the government to compel speech in the service of speculative or hypothetical interests for purely private benefits. Once we articulate such a principle of constitutional adjudication, there is really no limit to what government may compel. And if this example of cronyism is okay, who will balk at any other economic or ideological discrimination? The only limit the court seemed to recognize during the oral argument was labels that overtly promote invidious discrimination, but protectionism, patriotism, and environmentalism will be entirely permissible subjects for compelled labeling, especially where the motive can remain unspoken. A generous swath of protection the First Amendment once afforded to businesses against such encroachment has now been ceded to the government's allegedly good intentions....

There can be no right *not* to speak when the government may compel its citizens to act as mouthpieces for whatever it deems factual and non-controversial and the determination of what is and what is not is left to the subjective and ad hoc whims of government bureaucrats or judges. In a world in which the existence of truth and objective reality are daily denied, and unverifiable hypotheses are deemed indisputable, what is claimed as fact may owe more to faith than science, and what is or is not controversial will lie in the eye of the beholder....

NOTES AND QUESTIONS

Would any mandatory disclosures would be disallowed by the majority's analysis? Would any blanket mandatory disclosures (that is, disclosures that are mandatory based on the product, not based on anything in the advertising for the product, such as cigarette warnings) be allowed by the dissents'?

Subsequently, Congress repealed the country-of-origin labeling requirements after another adverse ruling by a trade panel. This decision, however, remains precedential.

Images. Graphic warnings have been found to be highly effective at getting people to quit cigarettes and discouraging them from starting. David Hammond, *Health Warning Messages on Tobacco Products: a Review*, Tobacco Control 2011; Christine Jolls, *Product Warnings, Debiasing, and Free Speech: The Case of Tobacco Regulation*, 169 J. INSTITUTIONAL & THEORETICAL ECON. 53 (2013) (reporting study results that images improved consumers' factual perceptions of smoking risks).

However, the graphic warnings proposed by the FDA have been held unconstitutional in the U.S. because they were too emotional and not "purely factual and uncontroversial." The graphic warnings were not "purely" factual because "they are primarily intended to evoke an emotional response, or, at most, shock the viewer into retaining the information in the text warning"; they were "unabashed attempts to evoke emotion (and perhaps embarrassment) and browbeat consumers into quitting," and thus could not satisfy *Zauderer*. Two of the images, a woman crying and a man wearing an "I QUIT" shirt, weren't even "accurate," since they didn't convey "information" about cigarettes. And "the image of a man smoking through a tracheotomy hole might be misinterpreted as suggesting that such a procedure is a common consequence of smoking—a more logical interpretation than FDA's contention that it symbolizes 'the addictive nature of cigarettes,' which requires significant extrapolation on the part of the consumers." R.J. Reynolds Tobacco Co. v. Food & Drug Admin., 696 F.3d 1205 (D.C. Cir. 2012).

Here are the warnings. Do you agree?

438

By contrast, the dissent accepted the FDA's argument that the emotions evoked by the images were appropriate because emotions assist people in making judgments, reasoning that "factually accurate, emotive, and persuasive are not mutually exclusive descriptions. While comprehending the facts about smoking "is likely to provoke emotional reactions," that's a natural consequence of the reality that the facts are grim. To the dissent, the warning text put the images in context, which made them factual and truthful. For example, the image accompanying the text "[c]igarettes are addictive" depicted a man smoking through a tracheotomy opening in his throat. "Viewed with the accompanying text, this image conveys the tenacity of nicotine addiction: even after under undergoing surgery for cancer, one might be unable to abstain from smoking." In fact, fifty percent of neck and head cancer patients continue to smoke—this image didn't depict an extreme or unusual situation. Similarly, the dissent concluded, images of an autopsy effectively symbolized death, while images of a baby enveloped in smoke and of a woman crying depicted the significant harms of secondhand smoke.

If vivid images are easier to remember and to act upon, is that sufficient reason to use them, even if consumers don't consciously understand that's why they're responding to the images and not to warning text? After Australia adopted similar graphic warnings, some Australians even reported that exposure to graphic warning labels made their cigarettes taste worse. Matt Siegel, *Labels Leave a Bad Taste*, N.Y. TIMES, July 11, 2013. Does that suggest that images are wrongfully manipulative?

Frankenfoods? In the midst of significant consumer concern over genetically modified foods, the FDA intervened in the debate in a way highly favorable to producers of such foods. FDA Draft Guidance for Industry: Voluntary Labeling Indicating Whether Food Has or Has Not Been Derived From Genetically Engineered Atlantic Salmon (Nov. 2015); Guidance for Industry: Voluntary Labeling Indicating Whether Foods Have or Have Not Been Derived from Genetically Engineered Plants (Nov. 2015).

First, the FDA concluded that there was no evidence that bioengineered foods differ from other foods in any material way. Even though comments overwhelmingly requested mandatory disclosure of the fact that food was produced using bioengineered ingredients, the FDA found such disclosure unnecessary. Further, the FDA concluded that the term "Non-GMO," short for non-genetically modified organisms, was inaccurate for food products, because most foods don't contain entire organisms. Instead, the FDA recommended "Not bioengineered" or "This oil is made from soybeans that were not genetically engineered." Does "bioengineered" have a different meaning from "GMO" to consumers, and if so, does either term communicate more accurately with consumers?

The FDA noted the need to consider the entire context. A claim that a product "does not contain bioengineered soybean oil" can be misleading if the product is made largely of flour derived from genetically engineered corn and only a small amount of soybean oil.

Instead, the FDA expressed hostility to producers who wished to label food as *not* being bioengineered. The FDA cautioned that statements that a food or its ingredients were not developed using bioengineering could be misleading by implying, contrary to the FDA's determination, that the food was therefore safer or of higher quality. "For example, the labeling of a bag of specific type of frozen vegetables that states they were 'not produced through modern biotechnology' could be misleading if, in addition to this statement, the labeling contains statements or [images] that suggest or imply that, as a result of not being produced through modern biotechnology, such vegetables are safer, more nutritious, or have different attributes than other foods solely because the food was not produced using modern biotechnology."

The FDA also warned that terms such as "GMO free" or "Non-GMO" could trigger false advertising challenges from consumers, and recommended that "manufacturers not use food labeling claims that indicate that a food is 'free' of ingredients derived through the use of biotechnology." In addition, a claim that "None of the ingredients in this food are genetically engineered" when some of the ingredients, like salt, are incapable of being processed through genetic engineering, could be misleading.

In the FDA's view, if a producer made bioengineering-free claims, sufficient disclaimers would have to be added to ensure that no such health or safety message was conveyed. *See, e.g.,* Joanna Sax & Neal Doran, *Food Labeling and Consumer Associations with Health, Safety and Environment,* J.L. MED. & ETHICS (forthcoming 2016) (finding that consumers consistently believed that foods labeled GMO were less healthy, safe and environmentally-friendly compared to all other labels). Given what you know about disclosures, how, if it all, could this be done? Under the FDA's guidance, producers can decide not to disclose the presence of bioengineered ingredients, or they can disclose, subject to the risks of having the disclosure deemed false or misleading. And a producer that wants to claim that it uses non-bioengineered ingredients as a selling point seems to face some serious risks. Is this deliberate shaping of the market legitimate? If it isn't, are other disclosure requirements any better?

If a state enacted the FDA's recommendations into law, would they violate the First Amendment?

Many consumer advocates believe that mandating the public production of information has a recursive effect on the production process. Once manufacturers know what information they must publicly disclose, they will try to manage that information to make themselves look better in the eyes of consumers, so they won't have to disclose anything embarrassing. Intermediaries may also put pressure on manufacturers once disclosure is mandatory. If labeling for the presence of GMO ingredients is mandatory, for example, some retailers might decide not to carry any GMO produce, just as some retailers won't carry video games with high ratings. As a result, required disclosures are likely to change the underlying level of activity.

If different groups are likely to be misled by disclosure and by nondisclosure, whom should we favor? Does it matter that consumers who might not spend extra money on fruit produced in ways that protect traditional farms *would* spend extra money on fruit that is less dangerous to their children? Some have argued that GMO-free labels deceive poor consumers into misallocating their scarce resources, believing that they are protecting their children from harmful chemicals. What do you think of this argument?

Congress passed a law regulating the labeling of GMO foods, and preempting contrary state laws. S. 764 (2016). The law defines "bioengineering," and any similar term, applied to food as meaning that the food "contains genetic material that has been modified through in vitro recombinant deoxyribonucleic acid (DNA) techniques; and for which the modification could not otherwise be obtained through conventional breeding or found in nature." The law directs the Secretary of Agriculture to establish a mandatory disclosure standard for bioengineered food and food that may be bioengineered. A food derived from an animal can't be considered bioengineered only because the animal consumed bioengineered feed. The Secretary has authority to establish how much of a bioengineered substance has to appear in food for the food to be considered "bioengineered."

The food manufacturer can choose how to disclose, whether by text, symbol, or digital or electronic link, though the Secretary can regulate the form of the disclosure. The law provides that it is sufficient disclosure to provide a digital or electronic link that says only "Scan here for more food information" or equivalent language, or a phone number that says only "Call for more food information." The bioengineering disclosure has to be on the first page accessed by a digital link, and manufacturers using the digital link can't collect, analyze, or sell information generated by consumers accessing the link. The Secretary is also supposed to "provide alternative reasonable disclosure options for food contained in small or very small packages." Small food manufacturers can also choose to disclose a phone number "accompanied by appropriate language to indicate that the phone number provides access to additional information" or an internet website. Restaurants aren't required to disclose.

The Secretary is also required to study the effects of digital disclosure; if the Secretary concludes that the study shows that "consumers, while shopping, would not have sufficient access to the bioengineering disclosure through electronic or digital disclosure methods," then new options must be implemented. Consider how this study should proceed: what questions should it ask, to whom, and in what contexts? Given what you know about disclosures, how likely is "scan here for more food information" to inform consumers about GMO content? Consider also how detailed the regulatory apparatus around the disclosure requirement is—suddenly privacy concerns are involved, as well as other design considerations. Is the game worth the candle?

Finally, the law provides that "[a] food may not be considered to be 'not bioengineered,' 'non-GMO,' or any other similar claim describing the absence of bioengineering in the food solely because the food is not required to bear a disclosure that the food is bioengineered under this subtitle." (However, organic certification is deemed sufficient as a matter of law to make a "non-GMO" claim; we take up organic certification in Chapter 17.) Does this make any sense? How do the FDA's earlier conclusions bear on this provision of the law? Does this part of the law pass First Amendment scrutiny? What about the rest of it?

For an excellent discussion of the issues arising from attempts to prohibit or limit disclosures about processes of production such as use of GMOs, see Douglas A. Kysar, *Preferences for Processes: The Process/Product Distinction and the Regulation of Consumer Choice*, 118 HARV. L. REV. 525 (2004). Kysar argues that consumer preferences are not stable and depend on what gets disclosed to them. Disclosure at the point of purchase makes conditions of production (child labor, GMOs, and so on) more salient and removes "moral wiggle room." As a result, we face a choice between a vision of a marketplace in which "consumers satisfy their personal interests unimpeded by concern for the welfare of others" and one in which consumers behave in accordance with more "altruistic" ideals held by the norm entrepreneurs who focus on particular conditions of production. These ideals may involve animal welfare, union labor, foreign production, or something else. Kysar concludes that neither set of behaviors reveal "true" preferences. Rather, context and the ability to see how one's choices affect others will determine behavior, meaning that the choice of a disclosure regime is fundamentally normative.

Slave Labor. California's Transparency in Supply Chains Act requires retailers and manufactures to "develop, maintain, and implement a policy setting forth its efforts to comply with state and federal law regarding the eradication of slavery and human trafficking from its supply chain" and post the policy on companies' websites. Does this requirement violate the First Amendment? Does it bear out disclosure opponents' concern for an infinite number of burdensome disclosures being imposed by busybody legislatures?

Competitor lawsuits present a number of specific challenges. Courts have articulated the following elements for liability under the Lanham Act, 15 U.S.C. §1125(a) (commonly known as §43(a)):

> (1) the defendant made a false or misleading description of fact or representation of fact in a commercial advertisement about his own or another's product; (2) the misrepresentation is material, in that it is likely to influence the purchasing decision; (3) the misrepresentation actually deceives or has the tendency to deceive a substantial segment of its audience; (4) the defendant placed the false or misleading statement in interstate commerce; and (5) the plaintiff has been or is likely to be injured as a result of the misrepresentation ....

Cashmere & Camel Hair Mfrs. Inst. v. Saks Fifth Ave., 284 F.3d 302 (1st Cir. 2002). The "interstate commerce" requirement is easily satisfied and rarely contested.

Lanham Act liability is strict; an advertiser's good-faith belief in the truth of its claims is no defense. In recent cases, courts have held that even a claim that was true when initially made can be rendered instantly false by a change in circumstances, such as a competitor's launch of a new product that makes a comparative claim false. Liability attaches at the moment the claim becomes false, without a grace period for the advertiser to remove the claim from the market. (This rule is mitigated by the fact that it might be extremely hard to prove damages based only on the period after the claim became false.) One court summarized as follows:

> The language of the statute is compulsory, and it includes no exceptions for cases in which a manufacturer undertakes good faith, commercially reasonable efforts to remove a false claim

446

from the marketplace upon learning of its falsity. Good faith is simply not a defense to a false advertising claim under the Lanham Act. Thus, the case law and the statute seem to appropriately establish that an advertiser that puts a claim into the marketplace bears all of the risk of the claim being false or becoming stale. An approach that allowed such an advertiser to continue to benefit from false or stale claims, so long as reasonably commercial efforts were undertaken to remove the advertising, would not adequately disincentivize the behavior prohibited by the Lanham Act or foster vigilance about the accuracy of advertising claims. Further, it would unfairly shift the cost of stale or inaccurate claims from the sponsor of such claims to its competitors, as long as the sponsor made reasonable efforts to remove those claims.

SharkNinja Operating LLC v. Dyson Inc., No. 14-cv-13720 (D. Mass. Aug. 3, 2016).

How does this work in practice? Competitors often sue over comparative statements, so first we will examine the law governing comparative claims, with representative examples.

We will then turn to a key Lanham Act issue: distinguishing between explicit and implicit falsity. This distinction is often outcome-determinative and at a minimum will establish the complexity, expense and length of the litigation. We will then cover surveys, which essentially always provide the required extrinsic evidence for a successful implied falsity Lanham Act claim. Finally, we will consider the question of standing in Lanham Act cases.

1. False Comparative Claims

Comparative claims are of two sorts: superiority claims and parity claims. Statements that consumers "prefer" a product or that it is "more effective" than its competitors are comparative superiority claims, which can be proven false by showing that the competitor's product is superior or equivalent to the advertiser's product on the relevant measure. A claim that consumers think that a product is "as good as" a competitor, or that "nothing is more effective," by contrast, are comparative parity (or equivalence) claims that can only be proven false by showing that the competitor's product is superior. Are consumers likely to understand this difference, especially when the claim is in the form "nothing is more effective"?

Preference claims must be based on an adequate study or survey of the relevant market. For example, ads claiming that VISA was the "preferred lodging card" were found to be false because VISA's evidence showed only that consumers *use* VISA more, but did not prove that consumers *like* VISA more. *In re* Visa USA, Inc., 28 NAD Case Rep. #3506NFY (closed Dec. 7, 1998), *aff'd*, Panel No. 101 (NARB, May 1999).

Generally, comparative preference claims are more likely to be found false (or, where substantiation is required, inadequately substantiated) if they are based on "monadic" testing, in which one group rates one product and a second group rates another. Use of two separately conducted studies to substantiate comparative claims is even more questionable. With some exceptions, courts have largely accepted the argument that comparisons should be based on head-to-head testing, not on separate tests or studies. Different studies may select differing populations, methodologies, endpoints and other factors that make comparison difficult if not inherently misleading.

Advertising claims should compare apples to apples. Even without changes in the market that make an existing true ad false, testing a product against an outdated or unavailable version of a competitor's product can produce false claims. As a result, when a competitor comes out with new versions, it is important for advertisers to reevaluate any comparative claims they may be making. One court found that a defendant's comparative "This Week's Eyewear Price Check" ad using its competitor's prices from weeks, and even months, before could be literally false, even with a small print disclosure of the actual survey dates. *See* LensCrafters, Inc. v. Vision World, Inc., 943 F. Supp. 1481 (D. Minn. 1996).

In addition, the "apples to apples" principle requires fairness in definition. Though the advertiser is generally free to choose the terms of its comparison, once those terms are chosen it must be consistent. In one case, a home pregnancy test claimed it was a "one-step" test, referring to the *chemical reaction* in the test. But the ad compared the test to competing products that allegedly required multiple manipulations by the user, counting the *number of manipulations* as "steps." Because the "one-step" test also required multiple manipulations by the user, the comparison was false. Tambrands Inc. v. Warner-Lambert Co., 673 F. Supp. 1190 (S.D.N.Y. 1987). Similarly, a bar chart that advertised "237 million prescriptions" for the advertiser's heartburn medications compared to a competitor's "36 million" was false because the former was spread out over eighteen years and the latter over only nine. *See* SmithKline Beecham Consumer Healthcare, L.P. v. Merck Consumer Pharms. Co., 906 F. Supp. 178 (S.D.N.Y. 1995).

One brand of bread claimed to have fewer calories than other brands, but the lower calorie content was achieved by making thinner slices out of loaves that had the same number of calories as other loaves. The comparison ignored significant nutritional differences, and consumers' consumption behaviors meant that slice-by-slice comparison was inappropriate. The FTC found that this comparison was therefore misleading. *See In re* Nat'l Bakers Servs., Inc., 62 F.T.C. 1115, *aff'd*, 329 F.2d 365 (7th Cir. 1964).

Visual claims must also be apples-to-apples. Consider the following image:

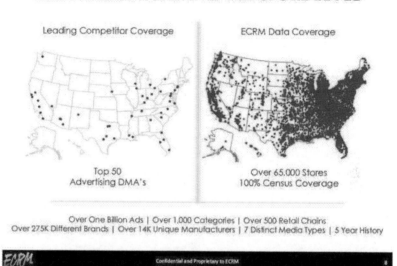

Here, the defendant, an ad tracking company, capped its competitor's markets at the top 50, but showed *all* of its coverage. It also consolidated all stores in any given area covered by its competitor into a single dot (representing up to 1500 stores), but didn't do the same for itself. Because each dot was identically sized, the defendant conveyed the literally false message that its data covered 1300 times the geographic area as its competitor did. Market Track, LLC v. Efficient Collaborative Retail Marketing, LLC, 2015 WL 3637740, No. 14 C 4957 (N.D. Ill. June 11, 2015).

Nonetheless, products need not be identical to be compared. If the basis of comparison is sensible in light of consumer uses of a product or service, then comparison is legitimate even though other types of comparisons are also possible. Thus, one advertiser compared two low-calorie breath mints on a per-mint basis. Its competitor claimed that the comparison should be by weight. The court found that there were no significant nutritional differences making a mint-by-mint comparison false, and also no evidence that there was a standard serving size by weight or that actual consumption habits depended on weight rather than number of mints. *Se*Ragold, Inc. v. Ferrero, U.S.A. Inc., 506 F. Supp. 117 (N.D. Ill. 1980). In other words, even if another comparison might be more useful to consumers, if an advertisement's comparison is truthful and non-misleading, it is legitimate.

So what counts as a comparative ad? A claim may be comparative if the competitor's identity is readily inferred from the advertisement. References to "the leading motor oils" have been treated as comparative, even though the leading motor oils were not named. Similarly, an ad using a readily identifiable product silhouette is likely to be understood by consumers as comparative. A claim that "Only PEPCID AC has proven that it can prevent heartburn and acid indigestion" was a false exclusivity claim that necessarily targeted competitors, whereas "PEPCID AC can actually prevent heartburn" is non-comparative. *See* SmithKline Beecham Consumer Healthcare, L.P. v. Johnson & Johnson-Merck Consumer Pharms. Co., 1996 U.S. Dist. LEXIS 7257 (S.D.N.Y. 1996).

Yet not all advertising using terms such as "better" or "stronger" is comparative. A competitor must be reasonably identifiable. One court refused to find that an ad referring to "most spill proof cups," with a picture of a cup that did not have any recognizable distinctiveness, compared the advertiser's product with the leading competitor. *See* Playtex Prods., Inc. v. Gerber Prods. Co., 981 F. Supp. 827 (S.D.N.Y. 1997). Particularly in a field with many contenders, such as analgesics, broad references to "better" performance are unlikely to be deemed comparative without a more specific identification of the targeted competitor.

Complexity and Counterclaims in Comparative Advertising Cases

In practice, advertising cases don't come neatly divided into specific issues. Falsity, substantiation and other concepts interact, as the following case illustrates. As you read it, keep in mind that in advertising law there is no substitute for understanding the relevant business. It is impossible to represent someone vigorously, or to regulate properly, without a grasp of the details.

In *Schering-Plough Healthcare Products, Inc. v. Neutrogena Corp.*, 2010 WL 960635 (D. Del. 2010), the plaintiff ("Coppertone" for convenience) made Coppertone Sport sunscreen, and defendant made Neutrogena Ultimate Sport sunscreen. UVA and UVB rays are both components of sunlight that can cause skin damage. The parties disagreed about whether a sunscreen's ability to protect against UVA rays was subsumed within the SPF (sun protection factor) measurement, but SPF definitely measures UVB protection. Another measurement, protection factor A (PFA), can be used to quantify protection against UVA rays.

Coppertone challenged a Neutrogena Ultimate Sport ad touting the "best line of sport sun protection" and claiming superiority based on "average" combined SPF and PFA scores across the parties' sport product lines. The ad compared Neutrogena and Coppertone Sport with the phrase "Best average UVA/UVB protection vs. leading sport lines" next to a chart.

[text in bottom left corner of chart box: "Best average UVA/UVB protection vs. leading sport lines"]

Was the Ad's Use of Averages False?

Coppertone's line included SPF 15 to SPF 70 products, whereas Neutrogena's line began at SPF 55, leading to very different averages. On the motion for preliminary injunction, the court had refused to find literal falsity for the differentials between the combined SPF and UVA bars. The average of Coppertone products' SPF was 38.5; the average of Neutrogena products' SPF was 64; and the difference across the lines was 40%. Because the SPF portion of the bars in the ad differed by about 40%, there was no literal falsehood. Likewise, the PFA scores across the entire product lines were approximately correct, showing a near 100% difference in relative heights based on a 30.2 average for Neutrogena and 16.7 for Coppertone.

Is it false to compare averages when no one would ever use an average Neutrogena or Coppertone product, but would always pick one particular level of protection? Would it matter that, in fact, very high levels of SPF offer no real additional protection to users?

Graphs as Establishment Claims

The court then found that the bar graphs constituted an implied establishment claim: a signal that numerical values for UVA and SPF were "derived from some manner of product testing." Neither party presented the court with enough evidence to analyze Neutrogena's PFA testing, so the court found that Coppertone hadn't met its burden to show that the tests were inappropriate or unreliable. Thus, notwithstanding "obvious deficiencies" in Neutrogena's substantiation, this claim failed.

Were the Graphs Properly Constructed?

The court found that the bar graph was literally false in other ways, such as wrongly using UVA and SPF as separate measures of protection. Due to the predominance of UVB in SPF measurements, SPF is commonly understood to refer to UVB, and the FDA has issued a statement to this effect. But at least 10% of SPF correlates to UVA. The ad was literally false because it provided a separate UVA quantification which is "neither an accurate description of protection nor completely independent of the SPF value." It conveys, by using different labels, that UVA and SPF are different measurements, and this is "indisputably not so." Though Coppertone and Neutrogena were both treated the same, the "absence of bias" caused by the double counting didn't eliminate the falsity.

Take a look at the graph. Do you agree with the court's conclusion?

Counterclaim: Coppertone's Comparative Establishment Ad

This case also illustrates an important practical principle: a competitor plaintiff who sues for false advertising can often expect a counterclaim. The marginal cost of bringing a counterclaim once the parties are in litigation is often lower than initiating suit, and even if it isn't, the defendant may want to make the case riskier for the plaintiff by threatening the plaintiff's own promotional strategies. Thus, a Lanham Act plaintiff should have some confidence that its own advertising house is in order, or it may end up worse off for having sued.

The counterclaim here dealt with a Coppertone Sport ad showing athletes running in the ocean, applying sunscreen, then running/swimming/biking. The voiceover said, "You give your sport 100%—so should your sunscreen. Coppertone Sport® spray and Neutrogena spray provide the same amount of sun protection. Coppertone Sport® gives you better coverage. Waterproof, sweatproof—Coppertone Sport®—100%."

Text: Among clear sprays.

better protective coverage.

Text: Use as directed.

Neutrogena is 28% chemical propellant.

"Better coverage" accompanies an image in which a Coppertone spray user is depicted covered by blue shading, while a Neutrogena spray user is covered by slightly lighter blue shading. Text at the bottom

456

says, "Simulated coverage study results. Among sprays with comparable SPF." One version of the ad also had a visual where the Coppertone user was labeled "100% sunscreen formula" and the Neutrogena user "28% chemical propellant," with a voiceover to the same effect.

The court agreed that "better coverage" was an establishment claim, and it was false because it was not supported by sufficiently reliable tests. Coppertone hadn't performed an in vivo coverage study on either spray featured in the ad, though it had tested other non-sport-branded products on living subjects. In that earlier test, Coppertone Ultra-Guard outperformed Neutrogena Fresh Cooling Mist in density, and there was testimony that density alone provides better coverage, as well as corroborating in vivo evidence.

The court disapproved of running a head-to-head comparative ad without testing the actual products. Coppertone argued that its in vivo study showed that its method of delivery provided better coverage than Neutrogena's aerosol, regardless of formulation. The court found this conclusion "too sweeping" to be based on a comparison of just one of each party's products. A Neutrogena scientist testified that formulation differences made extrapolation of test results impossible, and a consultant with experience in aerosol design made the same point about the design of the spray can. In fact, given the "generally accepted scientific principle that compositions of different molecular weights tend to have different properties," it was more likely than not that differently formulated sprays would differ in performance.

Even when Coppertone tested the right products, the in vivo test was insufficiently reliable to support a coverage claim. The test had no specific goals for substantiation; it looked at density, evenness and thoroughness. Coppertone chose density after the fact because Coppertone prevailed on density. But density doesn't equal "coverage." Ultimately, Coppertone used a non-standard protocol (there was no standard one) with no particular goal in mind, and the analysis "was driven by the results obtained by the tests."

In a footnote, the court stated that it didn't want to discourage novel protocols. The issue here was not novelty but overall unreliability, "a portion of which" was attributable to the lack of protocol or cited industry support for Coppertone's methods. How would you advise a client whose substantiation comes from a new protocol? Suppose your client runs a test and its product is superior on some attributes but not others: how would you advise it about touting that study?

Overall, there was no "true scientific basis" for attributing the Neutrogena Fresh Cooling Mist data to Neutrogena Ultimate Sport. Coppertone "elected not to test the competitive product at the heart of its advertisement and, instead, superimposed data from an in vivo test of another competitive product into its commercial. This type of unsubstantiated 'scientific' claim is precisely what the Lanham Act seeks to prevent."

The court also addressed the "28% chemical propellant" statement in one version of the ad. The court found that the "ultimate import" of the ad was that the Neutrogena sunscreen "as applied on the athlete" was 28% propellant. This was undisputedly false: though the can contains 28% propellant by weight, this mostly evaporates when the aerosol is used. The ad "contrasts two sunscreens, not two cans or delivery methods." The visual—overlaying the words "Neutrogena" and "28% propellant" on the bare chest of an athlete—reinforces the message that 28% is applied to the body. There was no qualifying statement or other clarifying language. This was a literally false message, unambiguously conveyed by necessary implication (a phrase we will examine in detail shortly).

In conclusion, the court commented that these ads were "essentially meaningless and, therefore, of no help to the consuming public who, finally, is paying attention to the health concerns presented by overexposure to the sun." Is meaninglessness the same thing as falsity?

Technical Deficiencies or False Advertising?

In later proceedings in the same case, the court ruled that another aspect of Neutrogena's advertising was literally false. The package and ads for one Neutrogena sunscreen claimed that it contained Helioplex, a proprietary photostabilizing agent. Helioplex is the term Neutrogena adopted for a patented combination of chemicals (known as DEHN) that prevented the sunscreen from breaking down when exposed to sunlight. The court relied on this definition, supplied by Neutrogena, at previous stages in this litigation, and Neutrogena used the same definition in § 43(a) litigation against L'Oréal. The problem was that one Neutrogena product, though Helioplex-branded, didn't contain DEHN until February 2010.

Neutrogena argued that Helioplex need not, by definition, contain DEHN. The court disagreed, because Neutrogena expressly defined Helioplex to include "DEHN (a stabilizer)" in its ads to the consuming public, stating that "stabilization prevents bond breakage, allowing avobenzone to continue providing high UVA protection." The public had no basis on which to perceive any flexibility in the formula. Because of the literal falsity, the court presumed confusion.

Do you expect the public to know what "Helioplex" is? Can you construct an argument in which consumers suffer harm from Neutrogena's falsity?

More generally: are there any lessons about appropriate strategy in the claims and counterclaims in this case? How would you counsel a client in terms of reviewing its own advertising before initiating suit?

2. Determining the Nature of the Claim

The line between implicitly false claims and explicitly or literally false claims can be difficult to draw. Nonetheless, the first step in a Lanham Act case must be to determine the literal claim being made by the advertisement. Only then can a fact finder decide whether the claim is explicitly false or implicitly false.

Courts have held that literally false claims are so likely to deceive consumers that no additional evidence of consumer reaction is required, unless no reasonable consumer would take them seriously (puffery, covered in Chapter 4). Claims that are not literally false, but are potentially misleading, lead to liability if there is evidence that they do in fact deceive consumers. However, courts will sometimes dispense with the requirement of extrinsic evidence if the misleadingness is obvious enough—a doctrine called falsity by necessary implication, which we will cover in the next section. The following chart provides an overview:

	Consumers receive false message	Consumers don't receive false message
Explicitly/literally false message	Liability (courts presume reception of false message without extrinsic evidence)	Puffery (usually as a matter of law, presumed without extrinsic evidence); no liability
Literally true message with	Liability if consumer reception of false implication	No liability

allegedly false implication	demonstrated (usually through survey). Courts may use doctrine of necessary implication to presume reception	

Whether a claim is explicitly or implicitly false affects many aspects of a case, including the cost of litigation and the choice of forum, because the NAD does not require consumer surveys and may be a better venue for an implicit falsity claim if the NAD is otherwise acceptable.

Courts may rely on their own logic and common sense to determine a claim's literal meaning. "The greater the degree to which a message relies upon the viewer or consumer to integrate its components and draw the apparent conclusion, . . . the less likely it is that a finding of literal falsity will be supported. Commercial claims that are implicit, attenuated, or merely suggestive usually cannot be characterized as literally false." United Indus. Corp. v. Clorox Co., 140 F.3d 1175 (8th Cir. 1998). Courts can also rely on advertisers' own definitions, when those definitions are not themselves misleading: when the advertiser of a steam iron chose to claim superior "power" to its main competition, and then defined how it measured power in fine print, the court found literal falsity when the competitor was actually superior according to that measurement. Grpe. SEB USA, Inc. v. Euro-Pro Operating LLC, 774 F.3d 192 (3d Cir. 2014) (finding this claim explicit and unambiguous, even if portions were in fine print).

Of course, all advertising requires consumers to apply their general beliefs, such as definitions of words and a basic understanding of society. Automobile advertising rarely explains why braking power is important. Courts thus increasingly invoke "ambiguity" in determining whether an ad is literally or implicitly false. If consumers could reasonably get either a false message or a truthful message from a particular ad, then the ad cannot be facially false, and must be evaluated under the standards for implied falsity. On the other hand, if the only message a reasonable consumer in the target audience could get from the ad is false, then the ad is explicitly and facially false.

Thus, an advertisement that Maxxatrax roach bait "kills roaches in 24 hours" was not *literally* false because it was literally true in one sense—roaches who came into contact with Maxxatrax died within twenty-four hours. Any other claim perceived in the phrase—such as the *implied* claim that it rids the entire home of roaches in twenty-four hours—would need a consumer survey to prove. United Indus. Corp. v. Clorox Co., 140 F.3d 1175 (8th Cir. 1998). Similarly, claims that computer equipment was "fully compatible" and "100% compatible" might be understood to mean that it would perform in exactly the same way, but might also mean something less. Actual consumer perception evidence was required in order to find the claim false. Compaq Computer Corp. v. Procom Technology, Inc., 908 F. Supp. 1409 (S.D. Tex. 1995).

There are at least two kinds of ambiguity. There are some claims, like "number one in the industry!" that might not have a specific meaning to consumers at all. In other words, they might be puffery. Other claims, such as "kills roaches in 24 hours," have a specific meaning, but a court might not be sure what that meaning is for large groups of consumers. In both cases, the plaintiff gets a chance to prove how consumers perceive the claim, though the difference might affect, among other things, how a survey should ask consumers about the claims they understand the ads at issue to be making.

Moreover, not every conceivable ambiguity removes a claim from the ambit of literal falsity. Rather, courts have found ambiguity sufficient to move a claim from explicit to implicit where an advertisement's claims are "equally open" to a true or a false interpretation, Coors Brewing Co. v. Anheuser-Busch Cos., Inc., 802 F. Supp. 965 (S.D.N.Y. 1992), or are "so balanced between several plausible meanings that the claim made by the advertisement is too uncertain to serve as the basis of a literal falsity claim," Clorox Co. Puerto Rico v. Proctor & Gamble Commercial Co., 228 F.3d 24 (1st Cir. 2000). If an advertiser's interpretation of a contested claim is strained, courts will ignore it. Thus, when an ad claimed that a competitor's product had experienced "catastrophic failure," the court accepted testimony that the phrase was generally understood in the relevant medical community to mean failure resulting in serious equipment damage or patient injury, and rejected the advertiser's proposed broader definition. Energy Four, Inc. v. Dornier Med. Sys., Inc., 765 F. Supp. 724 (N.D. Ga. 1991).

Context can also sweep away ambiguity: in one case, an advertiser claimed that its odor-absorbing product worked "five times better" than baking soda. The court examined the advertisements at issue, which showed visuals such as five puppies apparently urinating on a floor, reduced to three puppies, then to one, then to none, and also promoted the product "to keep your home smelling fresh and clean."

MAN SINGS: It's five times fresher.

ANNCR: New Glade Carpet
Potpourri, in a new Pet Formula
too,

for wet pet accidents.

AN SINGS: It's five times better

than baking soda.

ANNCR: Fresh from Glade, S.C.
Johnson Wax. (MUSIC OUT)

The court had no difficulty determining that the meaning of "five
times better" was that consumers would perceive a fivefold
improvement, not that the product reduced "odor particles" in a
laboratory five times better than baking soda, as the advertiser
claimed. Church & Dwight Co. v. S.C. Johnson & Son., Inc., 873 F.
Supp. 893 (D.N.J. 1994).

In close cases, a court may choose to let a jury determine whether a
statement is literally false or literally true (and thus only actionable
if there's further evidence of actual consumer deception). Where a
product containing mineral seal oil was sold as "wax" for cars, a jury
found the claim literally false, rejecting several experts' testimony
that "wax" could be defined broadly, in favor of the plaintiff's expert
testimony that mineral seal oil was plainly not "wax" because it
lacked the basic characteristics of wax. *See* Hot Wax, Inc. v. S/S Car
Care, 1999 WL 966094 (N.D. Ill. 1999).

3. Implicit Falsity and a New Category: Falsity by Necessary Implication

> A. Introduction (adapted from Rebecca Tushnet, *Running the Gamut from A to B: Federal Trademark and False Advertising Law*, 159 U. PENN. L. REV. 1305 (2010))

In Lanham Act cases, literally true statements must be shown by extrinsic evidence to mislead consumers. The concern is that consumers might not be receiving the same implication as the challenger takes from the ad, so the challenger must first show that a substantial number receive a false message. This requires a consumer survey, which usually adds six figures to the cost of a false advertising case, imposing a significant practical barrier to suit. An explicit claim, in other words, is much easier to challenge than an implicit claim, even when they are the same claim from the consumer's standpoint.

But there are numerous cases in which a claim, though technically implicit, is quite obviously as clearly stated as if it were explicit. This is a feature of ordinary human communication, which regularly relies on implicature (see Chapter 2). Implication is especially useful for advertisers because consumers end up with stronger beliefs when they do some of the persuading for themselves by following implications to their natural conclusions. *See, e.g.*, Alan G. Sawyer, *Can There Be Effective Advertising Without Explicit Conclusions? Decide for Yourself, in* NONVERBAL COMMUNICATION IN ADVERTISING 159–61 (Sidney Hecker & David W. Stewart eds., 1988).

Consumers routinely and automatically draw inferences from ads, because they expect ads, like all forms of communication, to contain implicit information. *See* Julie A. Edell, *Nonverbal Effects in Ads: A Review and Synthesis, in* NONVERBAL COMMUNICATION IN

ADVERTISING 11 (Sidney Hecker & David W. Stewart eds., 1988) (finding that, "when asked to form beliefs about a brand, subjects take whatever data they have been given and make inferences about what those data could mean for that brand"—thus, tissue advertised with a picture of a kitten gets high ratings for softness, even higher than tissue advertised with the words "Brand I Facial Tissues Are Soft"). Consumers even remember implicit claims as if they'd been explicitly presented. *See, e.g.*, Richard J. Harris et al., *Memory for Implied Versus Directly Stated Advertising Claims*, 6 PSYCHOL. & MKTG. 87 (1989).

As a result, advertisers can arbitrage current Lanham Act doctrine, making implicit claims that they could not make explicitly, while still producing the same, or greater, effect on consumers. As Sawyer notes, the research "offers strong evidence that audience members will spontaneously strive to make inferences and conclusions under certain conditions. . . . [A]dvertising audiences are also very likely to 'complete' ambiguous advertising statements or claims. Under conditions [where consumers aren't paying very careful attention], . . . subjects tended to make false conclusions . . . which, if the advertiser could or should be considered as the cause of the incorrect conclusion, would be judged deceptive." Consumers may use ordinary rules of communication to interpret claims as factual that courts dismiss as puffery.

In recent years, courts have reacted to the doctrinal rigidity of the explicit/implicit divide, accepting that some misleading implications are better treated like literally false claims. The resulting doctrine is known as "falsity by necessary implication." The standard is as follows: "A claim is conveyed by necessary implication when, considering the advertisement in its entirety, the audience would recognize the claim as readily as if it had been explicitly stated." Clorox Co. P.R. v. Proctor & Gamble Commercial Co., 228 F.3d 24 (1st Cir. 2000). Thus, an advertisement claiming "longer engine life and better engine protection" without explicitly mentioning what competitors it was "longer" and "better" than, made a comparison to major competitors by necessary implication. Castrol, Inc. v. Pennzoil Co., 987 F.2d 939 (3d Cir. 1993).

The first false advertising case to use the term "necessary implication" involved a claim that a pregnancy test would provide results in "as fast as ten minutes." While some pregnant women would know they were pregnant in ten minutes, others wouldn't, and *all* women who weren't pregnant would have to wait half an hour to be sure. The necessary implication that the test was a "ten-minute" test was false. *See* Tambrands Inc. v. Warner-Lambert Co., 673 F. Supp. 1190 (S.D.N.Y. 1987). The ten-minute claim at issue can also be seen as a run-of-the-mill false claim that certain unusual results are typical. The necessary implication of a ten-minute claim in the context of a pregnancy test is that most women will get such results, just as the necessary implication of an ad focusing on an extremely successful user of another product or service may be that such results are typical or likely.

The Second Circuit adopted the doctrine of necessary implication in *Time Warner Cable, Inc. v. DirecTV, Inc.*, allowing liability without evidence of consumer reaction and without an explicitly false assertion "if the words or images, considered in context, necessarily and unambiguously imply a false message." 497 F.3d 144 (2nd Cir. 2007). DirecTV ran an amusing ad featuring William Shatner as Captain Kirk, who praised the "amazing picture quality" of DirecTV and told viewers, "With what Starfleet just ponied up for this big screen TV, settling for cable would be illogical." Though there was no explicit claim that cable's HD picture quality was worse, in context "illogical" had to mean picture quality. Because cable's HD picture quality was in fact identical, the ads violated the Lanham Act.

In *Southland Sod Farms v. Stover Seed Co.*, 108 F.3d 1134 (9th Cir. 1997), an advertisement claimed superiority for a certain breed of grass, using phrases such as "less mowing," "reduced costs," "less clippings," and "slower growth," and basing its claims and charts on a study of grass growth in springtime. According to a competitor, however, there was no superiority if one took the entire year into account. Although the advertisements always stated that they were based on a springtime study, the Ninth Circuit found that a jury could conclude that the ads were literally false in context, because the claim that the grass saved time and money "would be nonsensical if the bar chart were only intended to represent the turf's growth characteristics during the spring months."

Necessary implication is fundamentally social. It depends on general expectations, not necessarily on what's within the four corners of an ad. In *Playskool, Inc. v. Product Development Group, Inc.*, 699 F. Supp. 1056 (E.D.N.Y. 1988), a toy manufacturer argued that a competitor's claim that its components for play structures "attach[ed]" to the manufacturer's components was false because a structure made from elements of both parties' products would be unstable and unsafe. The court found that the claim might be "literally true" in the sense that "defendant's pieces can in fact be joined or connected to plaintiff's pieces." Nonetheless, the "clear implication" of the claim was that the components would attach *safely*. "On a box of toys for preschool children the statement can have no other reasonable meaning." Background assumptions thus structure interpretation, even when they remain unstated.

The social construction of implied meaning creates difficult problems in certain product areas, such as the area of prescription drugs and supplements. Does the presence of a drug on the market imply that the FDA has found it safe and effective? *See* Mut. Pharm. Co. v. Watson Pharm., Inc., 2010 WL 446132 (D.N.J. 2010) (holding that plaintiff would be allowed a chance to prove this claim). Studies show that consumers expect the FDA to be looking out for them, approving only ads for the safest and most effective drugs, even though a number of drugs are grandfathered out of current safety and efficacy requirements. *See, e.g.*, S.W. Wolfe, *Direct-to-Consumer Advertising-Education or Emotion Promotion?* 346 NEJM 524 (2002).

Falsity by necessary implication is a way for courts to relieve plaintiffs of the burden of an expensive and hotly contested consumer survey, even when a false message in an ad, though obvious, is not stated in full syllogistic form.

B.   Putting the Concept of Falsity by Necessary Implication into Practice

Consider, as you read the following cases, whether the explicit/implicit division and the falsity by necessary implication doctrine are making the appropriate distinctions between types of claims. Would it be better for courts to trust their own judgment, or, given that judges are often from a particular segment of society (not to mention already overconfident of their interpretive prowess), should we perhaps move in the direction of *always* requiring extrinsic evidence of deception? Do Grice's principles of implicature from Chapter 2 provide useful guidance for when courts should find a necessary implication? Are there other alternatives?

In the following two cases, try to identify the assumptions the court makes about how consumers think about the relevant product category, which then affects what statements the court deems ambiguous or unambiguous.

Aussie Nad's U.S. Corp. v. Sivan, 41 Fed. Appx. 977 (9th Cir. 2002)

The district court entered a preliminary injunction prohibiting Aussie Nad's U.S. Corp. ("NADS/USA") from advertising its "No Heat Hair Removal Gel" with the representation that "No Preparation is Required," without a disclosure that the consumer's hair needs to be a minimum 1/8 to 1/4-inch long for the gel to be effective. NADS/USA appeals, contending that the district court erred in concluding that the advertisement is literally false unless reference is made to the minimum hair length. We . . . agree with NADS/USA.

. . . . To find an advertisement "literally false" by "necessary implication," as the district court did here, the claim must be analyzed in its entirety to determine whether "the audience would recognize the claim as readily as if it had been explicitly stated." Here, NADS/USA's claim that its "no heat" hair removal gel requires "no preparation" is at least ambiguous as to whether "no preparation" of the gel is required, as opposed to that required for other hair removal products (such as heating, for wax), or "no preparation" of the person is required. Given that ambiguity, the doctrine of literal falsity is inapplicable and thus cannot sustain the preliminary injunction. . . .

Millennium Import Company v. Sidney Frank Importing Company, Inc., 2004 WL 1447915 (D. Minn. 2004)

Millennium Import Company ("Millennium" or plaintiff), maker of the luxury vodka Belvedere, brought this lawsuit against Sidney Frank Importing Company ("Sidney" or defendant), maker of the luxury vodka, Grey Goose. Millennium accuses Sidney of false and misleading advertisement practices relating to a print advertisement ("print ad") and a "hang tag" advertisement, both of which reference a 1998 taste test in which Grey Goose outscored Belvedere. . . .

BACKGROUND
I. THE VODKAS

Belvedere, introduced in 1996, and Grey Goose, introduced about a year later, are part of a new and fast-growing category of "luxury imported vodka." According to the parties' representations, Belvedere and Grey Goose hold the vast majority of the market share for luxury vodkas. Both types of vodka seem to have done well in the market, though sales of Grey Goose have outpaced those of Belvedere.

II. THE TASTE TEST

In 1998 the privately run Beverage Testing Institute of Chicago ("BTI") conducted a taste test of over 40 vodkas. The BTI is an independent taste-testing organization, which conducts periodic taste tests of wine, beer, and distilled spirits, including vodka. For the 1998 vodka taste test, the BTI tested "luxury" vodkas, as well as the more run-of-the-mill variety. The vodkas were rated on a scale of 1 to 100, according to BTI's regular practices. Points were awarded based on smoothness, nose, and taste. Scores from 100–96 are "superlative;" from 95–90 are "exceptional;" 81–89 are either "recommended" or "highly recommended;" below 80 are "not recommended." Grey Goose came out on top, with a score of 96. Belvedere fared much worse, and scored 74. Although Millennium suggests the test was an anomaly, neither party complains that the 1998 BTI taste test at issue did not follow accepted procedure or was otherwise unreliable.

III. THE AD

Sidney took advantage of Grey Goose's top score, and began to run advertisements touting the 1998 BTI taste-test results. The at-issue print ad has appeared in multiple issues of numerous different magazines, and reads as follows:

471

Rated The # 1 Vodka In The World [in large type]

In 1998, the Beverage Testing Institute of Chicago conducted a blind taste test of more than 40 vodkas. They awarded points based on smoothness, nose, and most importantly, taste. Of all the vodkas, Grey Goose Vodka emerged victorious, receiving 96 points out of a possible 100.

Founded in 1981, the Beverage Testing Institute conducts tests in a specially designed lab that minimizes external factors and maximizes panelists' concentration. The Institute selects judges based on their expertise, and its testing and scoring procedures are widely praised as the best in the industry." [two paragraphs are in a smaller type]

This print ad then lists 31 vodka brands, their countries of origin, and their scores from the 1998 test. In very small print, the ad states that the 31 vodkas are a "sampling" of the 40 vodkas tested. Millennium states that only three "luxury" vodkas are on the list. . . .

[the ad]

Millennium suggests that the 1998 taste test was an anomaly, and points out that in subsequent tests conducted by the BTI, Belvedere consistently has earned "Exceptional" ratings. Millennium reports that Belvedere has attained the following scores in BTI tests: 90 in 1999, 91 in 2001, and 92 in two separate tests in 2002. . . .

1. False by necessary implication

Plaintiff first argues that the ads are "literally false by necessary implication." Plaintiff does not claim that the test was wrong in 1998, or that defendant changed the results. Instead, this "literally false by necessary implication" argument hinges on looking at the overall message of the advertisement, and determining whether "the audience would recognize the claim as readily as if it had been explicitly stated."

. . . . Here, plaintiff's claim is that looking at the overall message of the advertisement, it is clear that Grey Goose is claiming that it is currently ranked the best tasting vodka in the world. Plaintiff also argues that the ad communicates the false message that Belvedere's rating of 74 is the current rating. Plaintiff suggests that even the qualifying words—noting that the tests were conducted in 1998, and the use of the past tense—do not render the ad true. Plaintiff argues that the later tests supersede and contradict the results of the 1998 test.

Defendant responds by arguing that the Grey Goose ad is not "false by necessary implication" because there simply is no implication in the ad. Defendant analogizes to a sporting event, and suggests that advertising a "win" in year one is not false, even if the ad fails to mention that the team "lost" in year two. Defendant also notes the past tense language, and points out that the year of the test is displayed prominently. As a slightly different argument, defendant emphasizes that consumers are accustomed to "taste tests" and understand that taste tests occur with some frequency, and that the results are somewhat subjective. Essentially, defendant argues that consumers know how to read this ad, and consumers are not reading it as putting forth current results of taste tests.

Plaintiff's likelihood of success on the false by necessary implication argument is bolstered somewhat by defendant's alleged violation of the Federal Trade Commission's (FTC) guidelines. Plaintiff argues that according to those guidelines, advertisers should not use outdated third-party endorsements. Some courts have granted FTC guidelines significant weight. . . . [C]ourts, however, also caution against "blur[ring] the distinctions between the FTC and a Lanham Act plaintiff" and note that the Lanham Act plaintiff must "show that the [advertisements] are literally false or misleading to the public," not merely that the advertisements violate FTC guidelines.

The print ad is not literally false, and despite the FTC guidelines, the Court is not persuaded by plaintiff's "false by necessary implication" argument. Given the sheer number of claims by adult beverage makers that theirs is "the best" or "the premier," it is unlikely that the plaintiff will be able to show (and plaintiff has not yet shown) that "the audience would recognize the claim"—that Grey Goose is currently rated the best vodka in the world—"as readily as if it had been explicitly stated."

Plaintiff has not yet persuaded the Court that consumers have no way of knowing that any taste test was ever conducted after 1998, or that it is reasonable to conclude that many consumers would think that the 1998 taste test is the last word on the tastiness of vodkas. The Court notes, however, that at some point, reliance on an outdated test could well render an ad "false by necessary implication" especially where the ad appears to report the most recent taste test results. . . .

NOTES AND QUESTIONS

The NAD Reaches a Different Result. By contrast to the district court's decision, the NARB affirmed the NAD's finding that the ad was misleading and its recommendation that it be withdrawn. Report of NARB Panel #120, June 4, 2003, Appeal of NAD Final Decision Regarding Advertising for Grey Goose Vodka by Sidney Frank Importing Co., Inc. NARB considered the issue to be "straight forward": It was misleading to refer to the 1998 test when at least two subsequent tests gave Belvedere a significantly higher score.

The NARB noted that BTI asserted that its tests were objective and "repeatable," used detailed procedures designed to ensure consistency, and, on its own website, listed vodkas with side-by-side numerical scores from different taste tests conducted over a period of several years. The NARB concluded that, "[i]n the absence of consumer perception evidence, the panel must place itself in the shoes of a reasonable consumer in evaluating the message received from challenged advertising. The panel believes that the challenged advertisement can reasonably be perceived by consumers as reflecting BTI's current assessment of Belvedere Vodka."

The NARB also commented:

> The FTC Guides Concerning Use of Endorsements and Testimonials in Advertising provides some guidance here. . . . The FTC guides provide that an advertiser may use the endorsement of an expert "only as long as it has good reason to believe that the endorser continues to subscribe to the views presented." . . . There is no question that BTI's rating of Belvedere Vodka changed dramatically from 1998 (when BTI's score placed it in the "not recommended" category) to the present (with BTI's currently reported score placing it in the "exceptional" category).

Sidney Frank, however, rejected the NARB's ruling, arguing that BTI does not permit advertisers to make comparisons between different taste tests (and it certainly wasn't about to advertise the more recent results for its own vodka). Since BTI was the expert, Sidney Frank concluded, it would not comply with the NARB.

Which opinion is more persuasive? How do BTI's own standards factor into your analysis?

Individual Words. All words have definitions. A court must therefore interpret the meaning of a word or phrase before it can determine whether that word or phrase is false. In the following case, who has the authority to define the key term?

Cashmere & Camel Hair Manufacturers Institute v. Saks Fifth Avenue, 284 F.3d 302 (1st Cir. 2002)

. . . The Institute is a trade association of cashmere manufacturers dedicated to preserving the name and reputation of cashmere as a specialty fiber. . . .

In 1993, defendant-appellee Harvé Benard, Ltd. ("Harvé Benard") began manufacturing a line of women's blazers that were labeled as containing 70 percent wool, 20 percent nylon, and 10 percent cashmere. Its labels also portrayed the blazers as "A Luxurious Blend of Cashmere and Wool," "Cashmere and Wool," or "Wool and Cashmere." Harvé Benard sold large quantities of these cashmere-blend garments to retail customers, including defendants Saks Fifth Avenue ("Saks") and Filene's Basement.

In 1995, plaintiffs began purchasing random samples of the Harvé Benard garments and giving them to Professor Kenneth Langley and Dr. Franz-Josef Wortmann, experts in the field of cashmere identification and textile analysis. After conducting separate tests on the samples, the experts independently concluded that, despite Harvé Benard's labels to the contrary, the garments contained no cashmere. In addition, Dr. Wortmann found that approximately 10 to 20% of the fibers in the Harvé Benard garments were recycled—that is, reconstituted from the deconstructed and chemically-stripped remnants of previously used or woven garments.

Relying on their experts' findings, plaintiffs filed this suit in district court claiming that defendants falsely advertised their garments in violation of § 43(a) of the Lanham Act, the Massachusetts Unfair and Deceptive Trade Practices Act, Mass. Gen. Laws ch. 93A, and the common law of unfair competition. . . .

[Discussion of the allegations that the garments contained no cashmere at all is omitted.] Whether literal falsity is involved in plaintiffs' claim that defendants improperly labeled their goods as cashmere rather than recycled cashmere . . . is a contentious issue. Defendants argue that this claim is, by definition, one of implied falsity—that is, a representation that is literally true but in context becomes likely to mislead. As further support for their argument, defendants offer a simple syllogism: all suits based on implied messages are implied falsity claims; since plaintiffs assert that the term "cashmere" on the garments' labels implicitly conveys the false message that the garments contain virgin cashmere, their claim must be one of implicit falsity.

We agree with defendants that normally a claim like plaintiffs', in which the representation at issue is literally true (the garments do contain cashmere as the label states) but is misleading in context (defendants failed to disclose that the cashmere is recycled), is evaluated as an implied falsity claim. However, we disagree with defendants' assertion that all claims that rely on implied messages are necessarily implied falsity claims. . . .

After drawing all reasonable inferences in favor of the nonmoving party, a rational factfinder could conclude that plaintiffs' recycled cashmere claim is one of literal falsity. The Wool Products Labeling Act, requires recycled garments and fabrics, including cashmere, to be labeled as such. As a result, whenever a label represents that a garment contains the unqualified term "cashmere," the law requires that the garment contain only virgin cashmere. The Act, then, is essentially telling consumers that garments labeled "cashmere" can be presumed to be virgin cashmere "as if it had been explicitly stated." Plaintiffs also presented evidence demonstrating that experienced retailers, like Saks, were aware of the Act's requirements. Based on this evidence, we conclude that plaintiffs have presented sufficient evidence to demonstrate that consumers would view the term "virgin" as necessarily implicated when a garment was labeled "cashmere." . . .

NOTES AND QUESTIONS

Is the court using necessary implication as a shortcut to accept non-consumer survey evidence about how consumers would likely react to the claims at issue? That is, the court seems to accept testimony from those experienced in the field about the meaning of the otherwise ambiguous term "cashmere." But isn't that the role of consumer survey evidence, according to the formal doctrine? Why can't a plaintiff in an implicit falsity case *always* offer expert testimony about what a contested term means instead of providing a survey?

Images. What about non-verbal claims? An eco-tourism company displayed a picture of a suspension bridge and caves to which it had no right of access, and to which other companies did. The court found false advertising. Though the pictures didn't explicitly say so, they necessarily implied that the bridges and caves were part of the defendant's tour. Veve v. Corporan, 977 F. Supp. 2d 93 (D.P.R., 2013).

Will images often have necessary implications? What might they be (e.g., "this is what the product looks like")?

C.   Putting It All Together in a Lanham Act Case

The following case involves claims of both literal and implied falsity. As you read, pay attention to (1) the role of scientific evidence in establishing underlying facts about the world and (2) the importance of definitions even given those facts. Whose definition of what it means to be "as effective as floss" does the court accept? You should see that the dictionary does not always provide easy answers.

McNeil-PPC, Inc. v. Pfizer Inc., 351 F. Supp. 2d 226 (S.D.N.Y. 2005)

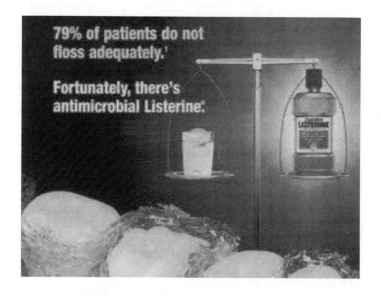

In June 2004, defendant Pfizer Inc. ("Pfizer") launched a consumer advertising campaign for its mouthwash, Listerine Antiseptic Mouthrinse. Print ads and hang tags featured an image of a Listerine bottle balanced on a scale against a white container of dental floss, as shown above.

The campaign also featured a television commercial called the "Big Bang." In its third version, which is still running, the commercial announces that "Listerine's as effective as floss at fighting plaque and gingivitis. Clinical studies prove it." Although the commercial cautions that "[t]here's no replacement for flossing," the commercial repeats two more times the message that Listerine is "as effective as flossing against plaque and gingivitis." . . .

In this case, plaintiff McNeil-PPC, Inc. ("PPC"), the market leader in sales of string dental floss and other interdental cleaning products, alleges that Pfizer has engaged in false advertising in violation of § 43(a) of the Lanham Act, and unfair competition in violation of state law. . . .

A. The Facts

[Plaintiff J&J was the market leader in dental floss.] . . .

2. Oral Hygiene and Oral Diseases

. . . . Plaque build-up may cause gingivitis, an inflammation of the
superficial gum tissues surrounding the tooth. Gingivitis is common,
affecting some two-thirds of the U.S. population. Its symptoms
include red, inflamed, swollen, puffy, or bleeding gums. Periodontitis
is inflammation that develops in deeper tissues . . . . Periodontitis is
less common, affecting some 10–15% (more or less) of the population,
although it becomes more prevalent with age. It is a major cause of
tooth loss.

Gingivitis is generally considered an early form of or precursor to
periodontitis. . . .

The ADA recognizes that "[p]laque is responsible for both tooth decay
and gum disease."

. . . [F]or most people "toothbrushing alone cannot effectively control
interproximal plaque," *i.e.*, the plaque in the hard-to-reach places
between the teeth. As a consequence, removal of plaque from the
interproximal areas by additional methods is particularly important,
for it is in these areas between the teeth that plaque deposits appear
early and become more prevalent. . . .

Flossing provides a number of benefits. . . . As part of a regular oral
hygiene program, flossing helps reduce and prevent not only
gingivitis but also periodontitis and caries.

Some 87% of consumers, however, floss either infrequently or not at
all. Although dentists and dental hygienists regularly tell their

patients to floss, many consumers do not floss or rarely floss because it is a difficult and time-consuming process. . . .

3. The Listerine Studies

Pfizer sponsored two clinical studies involving Listerine and floss. . . . These studies purported to compare the efficacy of Listerine against dental floss in controlling plaque and gingivitis in subjects with mild to moderate gingivitis. [The studies compared daily brushing plus rinsing with Listerine twice a day to daily brushing plus once-daily flossing and to daily brushing plus rinsing with a control. At-home use was unsupervised. The study concluded that both Listerine and flossing were significantly more effective than the control.]

. . . . In general, the Listerine results were better than the floss results.

The authors [of the first study] noted that their study "was designed to simulate actual conditions under which flossing instruction might be employed in dental practice." The results, according to the authors, "indicated" that Listerine was "at least as good as" flossing in reducing interproximal gingivitis and "significantly more effective" than flossing in reducing interproximal plaque over the six-month period.

The authors recognized, however, a potential issue as to compliance. The plaque reductions in the flossing group "appeared to be somewhat lower than would be expected," and there was greater improvement at three months than at six months, suggesting "a deterioration of flossing technique with increased time following instruction." As in real life, the subjects apparently flossed better immediately after they received instruction from a dental hygienist, but the quality of their flossing apparently diminished with the passage of time. . . .

[The second study was substantially identical, and produced consistent results. The authors concluded that Listerine was "at least as good as" dental floss in controlling interproximal gingivitis but concluded: "[W]e do not wish to suggest that the mouthrinse should be used instead of dental floss or any other interproximal cleaning device."] . . .

4. The ADA Approval for Professional Advertising

The ADA requires that all labeling and advertising bearing the ADA seal of acceptance be submitted to the ADA for review and approval prior to use. Listerine carries the ADA seal. . . . Pfizer acknowledged to the ADA that "[w]e recognize that any comparison v. flossing may send an *unintended* message to dental professionals that Listerine can replace flossing," and Pfizer assured the ADA that its advertising was "constructed" to "ensure that this does not happen."

Some consultants to the ADA expressed concerns about the Pfizer studies and the proposed professional advertising. One consultant noted:

> . . . . Because of floss' historically poor compliance record, a replacement for flossing [for] the regimen of daily plaque removal would be most welcome. However, in order for a substitute product to be "as good as" or "better" than flossing it must be compared against the data of a subject group who demonstrates they can and are flossing effectively, which the subjects in the flossing groups [in the two Pfizer studies] were not[,] based on the evidence presented.

. . . . By letter dated June 6, 2002, the ADA approved Pfizer's professional advertisements, as follows:

. . . . The Council concurs with your request for the claim, "Now clinically proven as effective as flossing" for patients with mild to moderate gingivitis. Since study subjects with advanced gingivitis or periodontitis were not included in the studies, no claim can be made about such patients. . . .

The claims were approved for use only with professionals "because of the potential to mislead consumers that they no longer need to floss."

. . . . 6. The ADA Approval for Consumer Advertising

In January 2004, Pfizer sought approval from the ADA to expand its "as effective as flossing" advertising campaign to consumers. Pfizer emphasized in its submission that it had spent the prior eighteen months "educating dental professionals."[10]

. . . . [The ADA approved the following language]:

> "Rinsing with Listerine is as effective as floss at reducing plaque and gingivitis between teeth."
> "Ask your dentist."
> "Floss daily."

---

[10] A number of individual dentists and hygienists complained directly to Pfizer that consumers would get the wrong message. (*See, e.g.,* PX 74 ("I was aghast to read your newsletter wherein you indicate that rinsing with 'Listerine is as effective as floss.' Rinsing with *water* will reduce interproximal plaque. But there is no substitute for flossing. . . . [M]alarkey like this can set back years of progress by the ethical dental profession in convincing patients that flossing is essential for their oral health." (emphasis in original)).

. . . . Prior to the launch of the consumer campaign, the ADA expressed concern about "the concept" that "if consumers don't have the time to floss, they can use Listerine instead." . . . .

7. The Consumer Advertising Campaign

. . . . Pfizer attended a convention of the American Dental Hygienists' Association in Dallas in late June 2004. Its representatives observed:

The hot topic of conversation was the new Listerine commercial. Many professionals voiced concern over the message conveyed. Approximately 85% of professionals said patients would "get the wrong idea" and stop flossing. . . .

8. The Surveys

[The plaintiff's survey concluded that 31% of consumers who saw the TV commercial and 26% of those who saw the label on the bottle's shoulder took away the message that Listerine can replace floss.] . . .

DISCUSSION

. . . To prevail on a Lanham Act false advertising claim, a plaintiff must demonstrate the falsity of the challenged advertisement, by proving that it is either (1) literally false, as a factual matter; or (2) implicitly false, *i.e.*, although literally true, still likely to mislead or confuse consumers.

. . . . In considering the issue of falsity, the court should " 'consider the advertisement in its entirety and not . . . engage in disputatious dissection. The entire mosaic should be viewed rather than each tile separately.' " "[T]ext must yield to context." Finally, the "visual images in a commercial" must also be considered in assessing falsity.

When the challenged statement is literally or explicitly false, the court may grant relief " 'without reference to the advertisement's impact on the buying public.' "

. . . . Where a plaintiff proceeds on a claim of implied falsehood, the plaintiff "must demonstrate, by extrinsic evidence, that the challenged commercials tend to mislead or confuse consumers." As the Second Circuit has explained, the inquiry is: "what does the public perceive the message to be?" The trial judge may not determine whether an advertisement is deceptive "based solely upon his or her own intuitive reaction." The trial judge must first determine "what message was actually conveyed to the viewing audience," and then it must determine the truth or falsity of the message.

Typically, an implied claim is proven through the use of a consumer survey that shows a substantial percentage of consumers are taking away the message that the plaintiff contends the advertising is conveying. Cases have held that 20% would constitute a substantial percentage of consumers. . . .

The plaintiff need not rely on consumer survey evidence to prove an implied falsity claim if the plaintiff " 'adequately demonstrates that a defendant has intentionally set out to deceive the public,' and the defendant's 'deliberate conduct' in this regard is of an 'egregious nature.' " In these circumstances, "a presumption arises 'that consumers are, in fact, being deceived.' "

. . . . 2. The Merits

I conclude that PPC has demonstrated a likelihood of success on both its literal falsity claim and on its implied falsity claim. I address each claim in turn.

a. Literal Falsity

Pfizer's advertisements make the explicit claim that "clinical studies prove that Listerine is as effective as floss against plaque and gingivitis." As Pfizer purports to rely on "clinical studies," this is an "establishment claim" and PPC need only prove that "the [studies] referred to . . . were not sufficiently reliable to permit one to conclude with reasonable certainty that they established the proposition for which they were cited." . . . .

First, [the court found the claim was overbroad, because the studies only covered individuals with mild to moderate gingivitis.] The advertisements do not specify that the "as effective as floss" claim is limited to individuals with mild to moderate gingivitis. Consequently, consumers who suffer from severe gingivitis or periodontitis (including mild periodontitis) may be misled by the ads into believing that Listerine is just as effective as floss in helping them fight plaque and gingivitis, when the studies simply do not stand for that proposition.

Second, the two studies were not sufficiently reliable to permit one to conclude with reasonable certainty that Listerine is as effective as floss in fighting plaque and gingivitis, even in individuals with mild to moderate gingivitis. What the two studies showed was that Listerine is as effective as floss when flossing is not done properly. . . .

Hence, the studies did not "prove" that Listerine is "as effective as floss." Rather, they proved only that Listerine is "as effective as improperly-used floss." . . .

Pfizer and its experts argue that the two studies are reliable, notwithstanding the indications that the participants in the flossing group did not floss properly, because these conditions reflect "real-world settings." But the ads do not say that "in the real world," where most people floss rarely or not at all and even those who do floss have difficulty flossing properly, Listerine is "as effective as floss." Rather, the ads make the blanket assertion that Listerine works just as well as floss, an assertion the two studies simply do not prove. Although it is important to determine how a product works in the real world, it is probably more important to first determine how a product will work when it is used properly. . . .

b. Implied Falsity

In considering the claim of implied falsity, in accordance with Second Circuit law, I determine first the message that consumers take away from the advertisements and second whether that message is false.

(i) The Implicit Message

Pfizer argues that its advertisements do not implicitly send the message that Listerine is a replacement for floss. I disagree. Rather, I find that Pfizer's advertisements do send the message, implicitly, that Listerine is a replacement for floss—that the benefits of flossing may be obtained by rinsing with Listerine, and that, in particular, those consumers who do not have the time or desire to floss can switch to Listerine instead.

First, the words and images used in the advertisements confirm that this is the message being sent. The words ("as effective as floss") and images (a stream of blue liquid tracking floss as it is removed from a floss container and then swirling between and around teeth; a bottle of Listerine balanced equally on a scale against a container of floss) convey the impression that Listerine is the equal to floss.

Second, the [plaintiff's] survey is convincing and was conducted in a generally objective and fair manner. . . .

Fourth, Pfizer's own documents, . . . internal reports of feedback from the dental community (including the overwhelming reactions at the two dental conventions), and internal documents showing that Pfizer anticipated and prepared responses to deal with complaints that it was sending a message that consumers could rinse instead of floss, further confirm that consumers were and are taking away a replacement message.

Pfizer argues that the ads contained cautionary language and disclaimers telling consumers to "floss daily," urging them to consult their dentists, and noting that "[t]here's no replacement for flossing." . . . Notwithstanding the disclaimer language, Pfizer's ads are clearly suggesting to consumers, through its overall words and images, that if they do not have the time or desire to floss, they can rinse with Listerine instead, for Listerine is just "as effective as floss." The few words of disclaimer are lost when the ads are considered as a whole. After all, the point of an implied falsity claim is that even though an advertisement "is literally true it is nevertheless likely to mislead or confuse consumers."[22]

Accordingly, I conclude that the Pfizer ads send an implicit message that Listerine is a replacement for floss. . . .

NOTES AND QUESTIONS

Why was the court convinced that the proper comparison was to flossing "correctly," when everyone agreed that over 80% of consumers don't floss correctly? Did this litigation suppress highly useful information that might have helped consumers' teeth, even if it also made them even less likely to floss correctly? What would Grice's

---

[22] Moreover, when consumers see the words "as effective as floss in fighting plaque and gingivitis," they are not likely to appreciate the distinction between "plaque and gingivitis" and "tooth decay and periodontitis."

Maxims have had to say about the relationship of these ad claims to ordinary conversational implicature?

Did the distinction between explicit and implicit messages make a difference in this case? Given all the other evidence, if the floss replacement message was false, should PPC really have had to spend a substantial amount of time and money proving that consumers received such a message?

Exercise: Pfizer comes to you with the following ad text, to be read by an actor: "Every time I go to the dentist, she tells me I need to floss more. And every time I promise to try. I'm still trying, but I know I'm not perfect. For people who don't floss properly, Listerine is as effective as floss at reducing plaque and gingivitis between the teeth. You should floss—but flossing correctly is hard. Listerine can help."

Would you approve this ad? Would you suggest changes? What would they be? (Keep in mind that your client will not want to have an ad that can't fit in a 30-second TV or internet spot.)

4. Surveys

A.   Survey Evidence

At one time, survey evidence was regarded as hearsay. It is now routinely admitted, generally in conjunction with an expert's opinion. Survey use has substantially increased in scope and importance in false advertising cases over the past two decades.

Properly done surveys are endorsed by the Judicial Conference of the United States. However, courts' theoretical approval may become skepticism when they are confronted with necessarily imperfect surveys or surveys that don't comport with judicial intuitions. *See* MANUAL FOR COMPLEX LITIGATION § 21.493 (3d ed. 1995); Shari

Seidman Diamond, *Reference Guide on Survey Research*, in FEDERAL
JUDICIAL CENTER, REFERENCE MANUAL ON SCIENTIFIC EVIDENCE (2d
ed. 2000).

In Lanham Act cases, surveys are generally needed to show that an
impliedly false message is actually communicated to some practically
significant portion of the commercial audience. Surveys can also form
the basis for substantiating certain types of preference claims. And
they can be used to demonstrate or disprove materiality.

As a practical matter, a survey can be vital to a false advertising case.
Evidence of actual confusion is rare, especially for cheap products
where consumers are unlikely to complain, or when the claims are
hard for consumers to evaluate. One court concluded that "proof of
actual confusion is almost impossible to obtain." Bristol-Myers Squibb
Co. v. McNeil-P.P.C., Inc., 786 F. Supp. 182 (E.D.N.Y.), *aff'd in part*,
vacated in part, 973 F.2d 1033 (2d Cir. 1992). Also, competitors need
to react very quickly to competitive threats to secure a preliminary
injunction, since courts have found that even short delays may be
evidence of a lack of irreparable harm (see Chapter 8 on Remedies).

Thus, survey evidence stands in for actual consumers confused in the
marketplace. A surveyor shows the accused ad to a representative
sample of likely consumers, and usually shows another
representative sample a control ad not alleged to be deceptive, and
asks questions designed to measure whether the ad deceived them.
Courts have deemed this process superior to the alternatives. It's
impractical to get a significant number of the relevant consumers to
testify directly. And even direct testimony from selected consumers,
or expert testimony about them, is less persuasive than "the
justifiable inferences from a scientific survey." Zippo Mfg. Co. v.

Rogers Imps., Inc., 216 F. Supp. 670 (S.D.N.Y. 1963) (trademark case).[*]

That a survey may be a necessity does not mean that presenting a successful one will be easy. Opponents can attack any survey, and courts have disregarded numerous surveys not conducted to their satisfaction. Improperly conducted surveys can be regarded as "junk science." *See, e.g.,* Indianapolis Colts, Inc. v. Metro. Balt. Football Club Ltd. P'ship, 34 F.3d 410 (7th Cir. 1994) (disparaging the "survey researcher's black arts"); L&F Prods. v. Proctor & Gamble, 845 F. Supp. 984 (S.D.N.Y. 1994) ("[Courts are] familiar with the subtle ways surveys are structured. Those who believe they can manipulate the structure of consumer surveys to gain a tactical advantage in the courtroom may actually harm their client's strategic position before the finder of fact."), *aff'd* 45 F.3d 709 (2d Cir. 1995).

To introduce some of the issues that may arise, we will first look at a case involving a hotly contested survey. While you read about the survey, consider how you might criticize it, then compare your criticisms to the defendant's. After this introduction, we will review more general principles courts have developed to evaluate surveys and bring in other examples of contested surveys.

Rocky Brands, Inc. v. Red Wing Shoe Co., 2009 WL 5125475 (S.D. Ohio 2009)

Plaintiffs assert claims of false advertising and false designation of origin under § 43(a)(1) of the Lanham Act, 15 U.S.C. § 1125(a)(1), and the Ohio Deceptive Trade Practices Act ("ODTPA"). Plaintiffs allege, inter alia, that defendants market and advertise their boots in a

---

[*] Because the issues in trademark and false advertising surveys are often similar and courts cite them both without distinction, this section will discuss many trademark survey cases.

manner that falsely suggests the boots are made in the United States, when in fact some lines of defendants' boots are manufactured wholly or partially overseas.

Defendants move to exclude the testimony and survey evidence of plaintiffs' expert The Mantis Group, Inc., arguing that the methodology of the survey is so flawed that the survey lacks any probative value. Plaintiffs contend that the survey's alleged flaws go to the weight of the evidence, not its admissibility. For the reasons that follow, the Court denies defendants' motion to exclude the survey evidence.

I. Background

[The parties compete to sell hunting and work boots. Plaintiff Rocky makes its boots overseas. Defendant Red Wing makes boots in the U.S. and overseas. Sometimes its components are made overseas and then assembled in the U.S.]

B.   The Mantis survey

Rocky's expert, George Mantis . . . states that the purpose of his survey in this case was "to determine whether and if so, to what extent relevant consumers believe that the Irish Setter brand and the Red Wing and Worx brands of footwear are made in the United States." The survey was also "designed to determine consumer choice between two boots that are identical in all respects except country of origin; one made in the USA or one made in another country."

The Mantis survey was conducted at four knife and gun shows in Pennsylvania and Tennessee from July 2007 to October 2007 using three different questionnaires. Respondents were limited to individuals eighteen years old or older who had purchased hunting boots for Questionnaire Version 1 ("V1") and Questionnaire Version 2

("V2"), or hunting or work boots for Questionnaire Version 3 ("V3") or those who were likely to do so in the next twelve months for all three versions. The survey included responses from 383 individuals.

Mantis's survey was conducted by way of face-to-face interviews. For V1, the respondents were shown an Irish Setter boot with labels and tags stating "made in the USA with imported materials." The respondents were then asked, "Where do you think this product is made?" As follow up respondents were asked, "Why do you say that?" and "Anything else?"

For V2, the respondents were shown the same boot as in V1, but with references to "with imported materials" removed from the boot's labels and tags. The respondents were then asked the same questions as in V1.

For V3, the respondents were shown a page from one of Red Wing's catalogs that contained the words "Red Wing Shoe Company, Inc.," "Red Wing Shoes Since 1905," and "WORX by Red Wing Shoes." Respondents were then asked, "Where do you think shoes from this company are made?" Respondents were also asked the same follow-up questions as in V1 and V2: "Why do you say that?" and "Anything else?"

For all three versions, the respondents were asked a third question ("Q3"). Q3 asked respondents to assume that there were two brands of hunting boots (or hunting or work boots for V3) that were the same in every respect except that one was made in the USA and the other was made in another country. Respondents were then shown a card with four statements and asked to select the statement that described the boot they would purchase:

Statement 1: "I would purchase the boot made in the USA."

Statement 2: "I would purchase the boot made in another country."

Statement 3: "I have no preference and would purchase either boot."

Statement 4: "I don't know and have no opinion."

II. Standard of review

To be admissible, a survey should generally satisfy the following requirements:

> (1) the "universe" was properly defined, (2) a representative sample of that universe was selected, (3) the questions to be asked of interviewees were framed in a clear, precise and non-leading manner, (4) sound interview procedures were followed by competent interviewers who had no knowledge of the litigation or the purpose for which the survey was conducted, (5) the data gathered was accurately reported, (6) the data was analyzed in accordance with accepted statistical principles, and (7) objectivity of the process was assured.

" 'Because almost all surveys are subject to some sort of criticism, courts generally hold that flaws in survey methodology go to the evidentiary weight of the survey rather than its admissibility.' " " 'There are limits, however. The court need not and should not respond reflexively to every criticism by saying it merely "goes to the weight" of the survey rather than to its admissibility. If the flaws in the proposed survey are too great, the court may find that the probative value of the survey is substantially outweighed by the prejudice, waste of time, and confusion it will cause at trial.' "

As the proponent of the evidence, Rocky bears the burden of demonstrating admissibility . . . .

III. Discussion

. . .

A.   Alleged flaws

. . . 1.   Survey's universe

Red Wing argues that the survey's universe is overinclusive because it included respondents who were not potential purchasers. . . . In trademark infringement cases, it is well-established that for a consumer confusion survey, the universe must consist only of potential purchasers, not past purchasers. Although there is a dearth of case law on the subject, it appears the same rule may not always apply in a false advertising case.

More importantly, Red Wing will have the opportunity to cross-examine Mantis on the issue of alleged overinclusiveness. Red Wing's expert, Dr. Itmar Simonson, may also address the issue. To the extent the survey's universe is overinclusive as a result of including past purchasers, such overinclusiveness goes to the weight of the evidence rather than its admissibility.

Red Wing also contends that the survey's universe is underinclusive because it was conducted only at gun and knife shows in two states. Red Wing argues that gun and knife show patrons represent only a narrow segment of the relevant market. In addition, Red Wing suggests the survey should have been conducted in states such as California, Florida, Texas, or New York which have larger, more diverse populations. Rocky maintains that Red Wing's arguments go to the weight of the survey evidence, and not its admissibility.

Red Wing's criticisms amount to second-guessing. Red Wing presents no evidence to demonstrate that gun and knife show patrons do not adequately represent likely purchasers of Red Wing's boots. The same is true with the suggestion that the survey should have been conducted in other states. Moreover, to the extent Mantis's choice of venue was deficient, it goes to the weight of the evidence, not its admissibility. . . .

2.   Relevance

. . . Red Wing also contends that the V2 stimuli is irrelevant because it uses a "defaced" product that the respondents would never encounter in the marketplace. The V2 boot is the same as V1 except that any reference to "with imported materials" was removed from the boot's tags and labels. As noted above, comparing the results of V1 with V2 measures the effect of the words "with imported materials" on consumers' perceptions of the country of origin. Hence, V2 is relevant because it measures the difference in response, if any, between shoes labeled "made in USA with imported materials" and "made in USA."

Red Wing argues the stimuli used in V3 is irrelevant because it contains no designation of manufacturing origin and does no more than test the respondents' assumptions about Red Wing and/or WORX. Rocky explains that the purpose of using the catalog page as stimuli for V3 was simply to place before respondents the language "Red Wing Shoe Company, Inc.," "Red Wing Shoes Since 1905," and "WORX by Red Wing Shoes."

V3 tests whether consumers believe that Red Wing and WORX brands of footwear are made in the United States. This issue is "of consequence to the determination of the action." Fed. R. Civ. P. 401. V3 is, therefore, relevant.

Red Wing further asserts that Q3 is irrelevant because it does not test an allegedly false statement and assumes what it seeks to prove—that country of origin is material. . . . [T]he design of Q3 does not force respondents to conclude that country of origin is material because it provides the choices of "no preference" and "no opinion." Whether consumers prefer boots made in the United States over boots made overseas is a central issue in this case. Q3 is relevant. . . .

3.   Market conditions

Red Wing also faults the Mantis survey because it was not conducted in a retail setting, such as a shopping mall. Red Wing suggests the survey should have used a pair of boots, and that respondents should have been given the opportunity to try them on. It maintains that other footwear should have been on hand for comparison, and that a sales staff should have been present to answer questions. . . .

Rocky points out that in V1 and V2 the boot was located on a table. Rocky also notes that respondents were allowed to pick up and examine the boot, and were afforded as much time as they needed to do so. Rocky asserts that the survey therefore adequately approximated market conditions.

. . . Given the purposes for which it was designed, the Mantis survey satisfactorily replicates marketplace conditions. In the alternative, to the extent it does not, the flaw goes to the weight to be given the survey evidence rather than its admissibility.

4.   Leading, ambiguous, and suggestive questions

Red Wing argues that the questions asked in V1 and V2 are both leading and suggestive because the respondents were shown boots with tags that included the words "made in USA." In this sense, Red

Wing contends V1 and V2 shows only that a respondent can read English. . . .

The questions in V1 and V2 are not leading. Nonetheless, the Court agrees with Red Wing that the answer to the first question in V1 and V2 ("Q1") is suggested by the text on the labels and tags of the stimuli boot. Q1 asks the respondent, "Where do you think this product is made?" A boot which is marked "made in USA with imported materials" or "made in USA" suggests that the correct answer to Q1 is the United States. Accordingly, the Court finds that V1 and V2 are suggestive. . . .

Red Wing further asserts that the entire survey is ambiguous because Mantis failed to define the word "made." Rocky argues that the word "made" is not ambiguous because the FTC has determined that "made in USA" means that all or virtually all of a product is made in the United States.

The Court has not yet decided whether it will instruct the jury on the FTC's "all or virtually all" standard for "made in USA." It strikes the Court that the FTC standard is not so much a legal definition as it is a measurement of what the FTC determined consumers believed "made in USA" meant when the FTC conducted its research more than a decade ago. Furthermore, the Court has already determined that the FTC standard is not binding on the Court or the jury. Thus, for purposes of the trial, the FTC standard is simply evidence of a federal commission's opinion on the subject, which the jury may give whatever weight, if any, it deems appropriate in light of all of the other evidence in the case. . . .

Nevertheless, Red Wing's argument concerning the lack of a definition for the word "made" misses the mark. Undoubtedly, if the Mantis survey had attempted to define "made," Red Wing would have asserted the definition was incorrect, since Red Wing has argued from the beginning that the term "made in USA" is subject to varying interpretations. The Mantis survey did not ask respondents what "made in USA" meant to them, so the survey does not provide an answer to that question. That does not, however, render the survey unreliable or inadmissible. The survey is still probative at least to show the difference, if any, between consumers' perceptions of "made in USA" and "made in USA of imported materials."

Lastly, Red Wing argues that Q3 is leading and suffers from demand effects and order bias. Rocky contends that Red Wing's argument improperly suggests that Q3 forced respondents to choose between a boot "made in the United States" and one "made in another country." It points out that Q3 also includes the alternatives "I have no preference and would purchase either boot," and "I don't know and have no opinion."

Given that the first answer to Q3 is "I would purchase the boot made in the USA," the Court tends to agree that Q3 exhibits some degree of order bias. The Court does not view this as a particularly serious flaw, however, and does not render Q3 unreliable. Thus, the flaw goes to the weight of the evidence as opposed to its admissibility. . . .

B.   Admissibility

. . . *Leelanau* [a trademark case] is illustrative. There, the court found three significant flaws in the survey. First, the court found that the survey's universe was substantially overbroad. In addition, the court concluded that the survey failed to approximate actual market conditions, and was " 'little more than a memory test.' " Lastly, the court held that "the entire survey was suggestive." Stating that the case was "close," the court in *Leelanau* ruled that despite "substantial flaws," "the better course is to admit the survey. . . ."

. . . In light of [the court's rulings above], in contrast to *Leelanau*, this is not a close case. . . . The actual flaws are few, and do not so undermine reliability as to render the survey evidence inadmissible. Rather, as Rocky suggests, the flaws go to the weight of the evidence, not its admissibility. Indeed, the Mantis survey's methodology appears to be significantly more reliable than that of the substantially flawed survey admitted into evidence in *Leelanau*. Accordingly, the Court finds that the survey evidence is sufficiently reliable to meet the requirements of Fed. R. Evid. 702 and 703. . . .

NOTES AND QUESTIONS

The court disagreed that the questions were leading, though they were suggestive given the labels and tags. What's wrong with a suggestive question if it's not leading? Is it that it focuses respondents' attention on particular messages? Is that a flaw?

B.   Reliable Survey Design

While no survey is perfect, there are well-recognized flaws that may make a survey entirely unhelpful. Surveys, like other evidence, must be both relevant and reliable. The current standards developed from Daubert v. Merrill Dow Pharmaceuticals, Inc., 509 U.S. 579 (1993), and Kumho Tire Co., Ltd. v. Carmichael, 526 U.S. 137 (1999). A survey expert must show "in the courtroom the same level of intellectual rigor that characterizes the practice of an expert in the relevant field." Kumho, 526 U.S. at 152.

Federal Rule of Evidence 702, which is mirrored by similar rules in many state courts, says a testifying expert must:

> (1) assist the trier of fact to understand the evidence or determine a fact issue;
> (2) base the testimony on sufficient facts or data;

(3) use reliable principles and methods; and

(4) apply those principles and methods reliably to the facts of the case.

The *Rocky Brands* case recites the accepted principle that, applied to surveys, this standard means an expert should be able to show that a survey is trustworthy and probative with evidence that: (1) the population (universe) was properly chosen and defined; (2) the sample chosen was representative of that population; (3) the questions asked were clear and not leading; (4) the survey was conducted by qualified persons following proper interview procedures; (5) the data gathered were accurately reported; (6) the data gathered were analyzed in accordance with accepted statistical principles; and (7) the process was conducted so as to ensure objectivity (which may be lacking if, for example, the survey was conducted by persons who were connected with the parties or counsel or aware of its purpose in the litigation). MANUAL FOR COMPLEX LITIGATION § 21.493 (3d ed. 1995); *see also* Diamond, supra.

The Surveyed Population

The relevant survey universe typically includes prospective purchasers of the *defendant's* product. Surveying the plaintiff's customers ordinarily makes little sense unless they're likely to consider the defendant's goods or services in the future. But how do we know who's a prospective purchaser? Depending on the relevant market, and on circuit precedent, courts have defined prospective purchasers as (1) past purchasers of the defendant's products, Church & Dwight Co., Inc. v. S.C. Johnson & Son, Inc., 873 F. Supp. 893 (D.N.J. 1994) ("past purchasers' behavior provides the most accurate forecast of future behavior"), (2) current users of the product at issue; or, most commonly, (3) people who indicate that they are *likely* to purchase the product in the future.

Sometimes, current users make the most sense. Current antacid users were a proper universe to test an antacid ad "because the primary objective . . . is to convince current users to change brands, not to persuade nonusers to try over-the-counter antacid[s]." Johnson & Johnson-Merck Consumer Pharms. Co. v. Rhone-Poulenc Rorer Pharms., Inc., 19 F.3d 125 (3d Cir. 1994). On the other hand, current wearers of jeans were not an acceptable universe for a jeans survey because the survey "did not inquire as to whether those participants intended to purchase jeans in the future." Jordache Enters., Inc. v. Levi Strauss & Co., 841 F. Supp. 506 (S.D.N.Y. 1993). Other courts have rejected surveys of people who had already leased or bought the video game at issue, Universal City Studios, Inc. v. Nintendo Co. Ltd., 746 F.2d 112 (2d Cir. 1984); who owned hiking boots but "did not necessarily have any present purchase interest" in them, Am. Footware Corp. v. Gen. Footware Co., Ltd., 609 F.2d 655 (2d Cir. 1979); or who were current subscribers of a magazine rather than "contemplating subscribing" in the near future, Inc. Publ'g Corp. v. Manhattan Magazine, Inc., 616 F. Supp. 370 (S.D.N.Y. 1985), aff'd, 788 F.2d 3 (2d Cir. 1986).

A survey universe must be careful to look at prospective purchasers, not just users, when those two groups differ. For instance, a survey of safety razor buyers was found "not reliable" for failing to include women in its universe of prospective purchasers of shaving razors, because market research showed that many women were likely to purchase the advertised razors as gifts for men. Gillette Co. v. Norelco Consumer Prods. Co., 69 F. Supp. 2d 246 (D. Mass. 1999); see also Dannon Co., NAD No. 3129 (July 1, 1994) (since men account for 27% of all yogurt consumption, a survey universe composed entirely of women is flawed).

More generally, surveying an underinclusive universe is a potentially fatal defect, because there is no way of knowing if the unrepresented members would have responded the same way as those who were represented. In one case, the court discounted surveys from both plaintiff Domino's Sugar and defendant Domino's Pizza for selecting underinclusive universes. Domino's Sugar interviewed mainly suburban women shoppers, entirely ignoring "single, male college students," who were likely to be the pizza's primary purchasers. Domino's Pizza company interviewed only walk-in customers at its stores, ignoring the rest of the universe ordering by phone. Amstar Corp. v. Domino's Pizza, Inc., 615 F.2d 252 (5th Cir. 1980).

A survey of the general consumer population may be acceptable for general consumer goods. Light bulbs, lamps, batteries and flashlights, for example, are products "almost anyone would be likely to have." Union Carbide Corp. v. Ever-Ready Inc., 531 F.2d 366 (7th Cir. 1976). In other circumstances, however, the surveyor must be careful to select likely purchasers. So, a universe of frozen food purchasers may be inappropriate for a survey about frozen diet foods. Weight Watchers Int'l, Inc. v. Stouffer Corp., 744 F. Supp. 1259 (S.D.N.Y. 1990). Courts have found surveys unreliable for surveying the general population when the relevant groups were regular restaurant-goers, Frisch's Rest., Inc. v. Elby's Big Boy of Steubenville, Inc., 661 F. Supp. 971 (S.D. Ohio 1987), aff'd, 849 F.2d 1012 (6th Cir. 1988); convenience-and-gasoline store shoppers, Sears, Roebuck & Co. v. Sears Realty Co., Inc., 1990 WL 198712 (N.D.N.Y. 1990); and buyers of financial services, Franklin Res., Inc. v. Franklin Credit Mgmt. Corp., 1997 WL 543086 (S.D.N.Y. 1997).

It should be noted that courts and marketing experts are not necessarily in agreement on the proper universe. Many experts point out that stated intentions are often an extremely poor guide to actual purchasing behavior, so that surveying people who identify themselves as potential purchasers might target the wrong population. See DAVID H. BERNSTEIN & BRUCE P. KELLER, THE LAW OF ADVERTISING, MARKETING AND PROMOTIONS § 5.02[1] at 5–10 (2011).

Nonetheless, where the science and the precedent diverge, lawyers will be tempted to rely on the precedent.

A good advertising lawyer needs some numerical literacy (not just for surveys—substantiation will also often involve being able to understand a chart!). The statistics of surveys may seem intimidating, but the principles are important and well worth learning.

Sampling Techniques

Since a universe consists of all potential purchasers, it can number in the millions. Only a sample can feasibly be surveyed. If the sample is representative, one can fairly project the results from the survey to the entire universe. One way to get a representative sample is to take a "probability sample" by selecting the sample randomly from the entire universe. This technique is often used with telephone surveys, where the numbers can be drawn randomly from a complete list or, for surveys of the general population, randomly generated.*

"Mall intercept" surveys, in which consumers are randomly selected at various shopping malls, are not probability surveys and are thus, strictly speaking, not statistically projectable. Mall intercept surveys are not truly random, because they require that a subject first go to the mall, and some categories of consumers are more likely to go to the mall than others. People in non-probability samples also tend to be more interested in the subject matter, which might skew results, even in the presence of a control (see below).

---

* Even then, lack of randomness can creep into telephone surveys because some categories of consumers may be more likely to answer the telephone from an unknown phone number and engage a telephone surveyor than others. The rise of mobile phones and do-not-call lists further muddies the picture.

Mall intercept surveys have sometimes been criticized for being non-probability samples, Am. Home Prods. Corp. v. Barr Labs., Inc., 656 F. Supp. 1058 (D.N.J.), *aff'd*, 834 F.2d 368 (3d Cir. 1987), or have been given less evidentiary weight than a competing probability-sampling survey, Frank Brunckhorst Co. v. G. Heileman Brewing Co., Inc., 875 F. Supp. 966 (E.D.N.Y. 1994). Furthermore, interviewers in mall intercept surveys, unless instructed otherwise, may be likely to choose friendly looking people or more frequent shoppers. Shari Diamond, *Reference Guide on Survey Research*, in FEDERAL JUDICIAL CENTER, REFERENCE MANUAL ON SCIENTIFIC EVIDENCE 246 (2d ed. 2000). (Can you offer reasons why that might matter?) Surveys can also be criticized for failing to include a proper geographical sampling of malls. *See* Indianapolis Colts, Inc. v. Metro. Balt. Football Club, Ltd. P'ship, 34 F.3d 410 (7th Cir. 1994) (discounting "a survey that consisted of three loaded questions" asked in one Baltimore mall).

Notwithstanding these technical criticisms, mall intercept surveys routinely are admitted as evidence. Courts generally recognize that mall sampling often is "used by major American companies in making decisions of considerable consequence," and, when properly conducted, is probative of responses to be expected from the relevant universe at large. Nat'l Football League Props, Inc. v. N.J. Giants, Inc., 637 F. Supp. 507 (D.N.J. 1986).

An approach accepted in many advertising cases is to ensure that one or two categories of demographics of the sample population closely approximate those of the universe. For example, if one knows the general age and gender demographics for the product or services at issue, as sophisticated marketers often do, the survey researcher can use quotas in a mall intercept survey to ensure that the same demographics (e.g., a certain percentage of women, a certain percentage in the eighteen to thirty-four age bracket, and so on) are reflected in the survey pool.

A mall intercept survey can be further strengthened by surveying in a number of geographically dispersed locations and interviewing at different times of day. If the survey shows similar results across locations and times, it is less likely that the results were obtained as a result of any bias in sample selection. Interviewer bias can be controlled by giving written instructions as to which individuals to approach, e.g., the first person who appears to be of qualified age and sex, the next such person, etc. (As we will see later, Internet surveys, which are becoming increasingly popular, raise their own issues, some similar to those of mall intercepts and some unique.)

Sample size can be a tricky issue. Jacob Jacoby, Amy Handlin and Alex Simonson argue that most contemporary political polls do a good predictive job by sampling 600–2,500 representative voters. *See* Jacob Jacoby, Amy H. Handlin, & Alex Simonson, *Survey Evidence in Deceptive Advertising Cases Under the Lanham Act: An Historical Review of Comments From the Bench*, 84 TRADEMARK REP. 541 (1994). Indeed, they note that the sampling distributions achieve "reasonable stability" with a sample size around 30. A larger sample size doesn't necessarily increase accuracy. It does, however, permit the surveyor to reduce the size of the confidence interval surrounding the estimate.

The confidence interval is an indication of how sure we are that a sampled result reflects the underlying reality of the universe. (Technically, it only applies to probability samples, but it is used with reference to non-probability samples such as mall intercept surveys as well.) It is largest around an estimate of 50%, and decreases as the estimate moves in either direction.

Jacoby et al. illustrate the role of the confidence interval with three sample sizes producing the same estimate of the number of confused consumers, 57.14%:

Sample size	Percentage confused	+/- with 95% confidence*	Range at this confidence level
35	57.14%	16.57%	40.57%–73.71%
350	57.14%	5.24%	51.90%–62.38
3,500	57.14%	1.66%	55.48%–58.80%

In each case, we are 95% confident that the "true" level of deception is somewhere within the range. Nonetheless, in each of the three samples, the *best* estimate is 57.14% deception. Jacoby et al. picked an extreme example, where even the lower bound of the 35-person sample showed significant deception. If a survey instead showed 22% likely deception, reducing the range of the confidence interval might be vital to convincing a court that the true level of deception was high enough to be actionable. As Jacoby et al. conclude, "[w]hen likely deception levels are expected to be in the 15 percent to 25 percent range, the use of larger samples (say, in the order of 300 to 500) not only sounds better, but reduces the size of the confidence interval around the estimate, thereby giving the court more reason for accepting the findings." They recommend using at least 200–300 respondents in each test group, and at least 50 per sub-group when sub-groups of consumers are at issue.

Courts strongly prefer larger samples, regardless of the magnitude of deception found in a survey. In *Ragold, Inc. v. Ferrero U.S.A., Inc.*, 506 F. Supp. 117 (N.D. Ill. 1980), the court found that a 30-person sample was so small as to "cast[] into doubt the general applicability of the results." Accepting a 149-person sample, however, another court reasoned that a small sample size "merely means that the

---

* The 95% confidence interval is often accepted as the standard for reliability.

results cannot be treated as a relatively precise numerical determination which can be reliably extrapolated to the target universe, but only as an indication whether the commercials have the tendency to mislead." McNeilab, Inc. v. Am. Home Prods. Corp., 675 F. Supp. 819 (S.D.N.Y.1987).

Survey Questions, Controls and Procedures

Even with the right group, surveys have to ask the right questions in the right way. Survey questions should be clear and relevant, not leading. Stimuli should be displayed, where possible, in the survey as they would be in the marketplace. Neither interviewers nor consumers should know the survey's sponsor, or the proposition the survey is designed to test; this is known as double-blinding. *See* Pharmacia Corp. v. Alcon Labs., Inc., 201 F. Supp. 2d 335 (D.N.J. 2002) (responses elicited from interviewer who became aware of the lawsuit should have been discarded). Results must be accurately coded and understandably reported. Although these rules appear basic, many surveys have flouted them. A poorly designed survey can even backfire and enhance the court's suspicions about the sponsoring party's case. Sterling Drug Inc. v. Bayer AG, 792 F. Supp. 1357 (S.D.N.Y. 1992) (defendant's survey, although "designed to obfuscate the relevant issues," actually proved that confusion was likely), *aff'd in part*, 14 F.3d 733 (2d Cir. 1994).

Questions

Suggestive or leading questions are one of the most common targets for criticism. One survey seeking to show that defendant's "Donkey Kong" mark for video games infringed the plaintiff's rights in the "King Kong" mark, asked: "To the best of your knowledge, was the Donkey Kong game made with the approval or under the authority of the people who produce the King Kong movies?" Universal City Studios, Inc. v. Nintendo Co., Ltd., 746 F.2d 112 (2d Cir. 1984). The court rejected the question: "The above-mentioned inquiry was an obvious leading question in that it suggested its own answer. The participants were presented with the Donkey Kong–King Kong connection rather than permitted to make their own associations."

One way to avoid suggestive questions is to ask open-ended questions. An open-ended question is not multiple choice and does not require "yes or no" or "true or false" answers. Merial Ltd., NAD No. 3844 (Dec. 18, 2001) ("Open-ended questions are better indicators of how consumers interpret a commercial message because respondents' answers are not colored by the suggestions contained in the questions themselves."). For that reason, surveys often use open-ended questions, such as "What is the main message communicated by the labeling on this product?"

But open-ended questions are more difficult to administer. Interviewers may be unable to ask appropriate follow-up questions. Consumers may have taken many messages away from an ad, and only one of them may be relevant to the case. Without a follow-up, closed-ended question ("Did the ad say anything about X?") it may be impossible to determine whether consumers received the relevant message if it isn't the first thing that comes to their minds. When a response to an open-ended question is ambiguous or incomplete, it is appropriate to instruct the interviewer to probe for a more complete answer. Common probes include asking "Anything else?" or "Can you explain that a little more?"

Relatedly, open-ended questions may result in so many different responses that they are difficult to code and analyze. And even open-ended questions may be leading if they probe too much (e.g., "anything else?" too many times), prompting the respondent to eventually give the "right" answer. One survey asked three times what people thought of aluminum as an antacid ingredient until the third question yielded 45% of people who thought that aluminum was bad for them. The court gave the survey little weight. Johnson & Johnson-Merck Consumer Pharms. Co. v. SmithKline Beecham Corp., 960 F.2d 294 (2d Cir. 1992).

Moreover, precisely because they're so much less likely to elicit a particular message, a defense survey asking only open-ended questions may be criticized as unlikely to identify deception that is in fact present, and an open-ended question can be badly worded or leading in its own way. In *Johnson & Johnson v. Carter-Wallace*, 487 F. Supp. 740 (S.D.N.Y. 1979), *rev'd on other grounds*, 631 F.2d 186 (2d Cir. 1980), the parties disputed whether Carter-Wallace's ads falsely implied that the baby oil in its depilatory smoothed and softened consumers' legs. The key survey question was "What, if anything, is good about having baby oil in the product?" and the court concluded that the question "asks the consumer to speculate as to what benefits, not limited to those claimed in the advertisement, could be attributed to baby oil."

In *American Home Products Corp. v. Abbott Laboratories*, 522 F. Supp. 1035 (S.D.N.Y. 1981), Abbott's ads falsely suggested that its hemorrhoid medication was new. Its survey purported to show that few consumers placed importance on newness. The court was unconvinced because of expert testimony that "consumers cannot, without prompting by specific questions, respond to more than one or two ideas as the most important conveyed by a commercial. Thus, ideas other than those identified as the most important are likely to be perceived and to be given weight by consumers." The court found further support in the "aided-response" portion of the survey, where consumers were asked more specific questions. "No question asked directly about newness; yet, in connection with a question asking whether the defendant's product would live up to its claim that it would stop pain immediately, several respondents stated that they believed the claim because the product was new."

Given all the potential vulnerabilities of surveys, survey experts routinely use questions that are similar to those already approved in other cases to minimize (though never eliminate) admissibility concerns. This is a conventional format:

> [A] well-designed consumer survey first asks 'communication' questions to see what messages the viewer got and to 'filter' or separate those viewers who received certain messages from those who did not. In the next step, the survey asks those who received a particular message . . . "comprehension" questions to determine what the viewers thought the message meant.

Johnson & Johnson-Merck Consumer Pharms. Co. v. Rhone-Poulenc Rorer Pharms., Inc., 19 F.3d 125 (3d Cir. 1994).

The closed-ended question, "Did the ad communicate anything to you about X?" is often considered effective. Another accepted quasi-filter is a clear indication that "I don't know" is an acceptable answer. In fact, courts and the NAD are generally troubled by the absence of a "don't know" option, regardless of whether other filters are present. However, some survey researchers argue that providing "don't know" options produces less accurate results because they allow people who do indeed have relevant opinions to skate through a survey—but given existing precedents favoring "don't know" options, a court would have to be convinced that this cost was worth avoiding. *See* Bernstein & Keller, *supra*, § 5.02[3] at 5–24.

Filter questions can address fears of leading questions. In testing whether an analgesic ad conveyed a message about speedy relief, it might be best to ask first, "Did or didn't the commercial say or suggest anything to you about [various attributes, including 'how fast the product works,' and also an attribute not included in the commercial to serve as a control]?" Then, looking at those people who answered "yes" to the "how fast" question but "no" to the control/s, the surveyor can follow up with "What if anything, did the commercial say or suggest about how fast this product works?" *See* Alex Simonson, *Survey Design in False Advertising Cases*, 1207 PLI/Corp. 309 (2000).

However, this raises another issue: what sort of denominator do we use to calculate the percentage who were deceived? Suppose 30% of the sample responded yes to the "how fast" question, and 60% of those received a (false) superiority message. As Simonson points out, it's intuitive to say that likely deception is 18% (.30 x .60). However, he argues that 60% might be more important. Upon noticing the claim, consumers readily perceived it as a superiority claim. Though courts have generally focused on overall "take away" from ads, Simonson argues that this wrongly privileges level of attention over comprehension. Compare a different scenario, in which 60% of consumers notice a speed claim, and 30% of them interpret it as a superiority claim. The total is again 18%. But, Simonson asks, which variable—attention or comprehension—is more likely to vary between the test setting and the real world? Since attention is based on numerous external factors, he contends, it would be more likely to vary in an artificial survey setting—perhaps in the direction of greater attention because of the lack of distractions, or in the direction of less attention because the respondent isn't actually making a purchasing decision. Either way, given that attention varies, comprehension should be the actual focus of the inquiry. The result would be a conclusion that 60% of relevant respondents in the former example, and only 30% in the latter, were deceived by the claim. Is this argument persuasive?

Where appropriate, the order of questions or advertisements ("stimuli") should be rotated among respondents to reduce "order bias." Respondents to written questions, for instance, are more likely to pick the first choice offered, while telephone respondents tend to

pick the last. Shari Diamond, *Reference Guide on Survey Research*, in
FEDERAL JUDICIAL CENTER, REFERENCE MANUAL ON SCIENTIFIC
EVIDENCE 255 (2d ed. 2000). A consumer is more likely to examine
closely the first jacket handed to him than a second one that closely
resembles it. Winning Ways, Inc. v. Holloway Sportswear, Inc., 913 F.
Supp. 1454 (D. Kan. 1996). Rotation among different respondents
corrects for this bias.

Controls

A control group is not shown the allegedly misleading ad (and is
usually shown some other ad) but is asked the same questions as the
group shown the ad. This can help eliminate "noise" by indicating
whether respondents are (1) reacting to the actual ad or (2) instead
guessing, being led by the survey questions, or replaying their own
preconceptions. In order to determine "net" confusion, that is,
confusion caused by the challenged ad and not by other causes,
researchers subtract the percentage of the control group whose
answers indicated confusion from the percentage reported by the test
group. The importance of a control group has increased substantially
over time, and courts are increasingly likely to exclude surveys
without controls.*

---

* A survey without a control group might have some weight if it has control
questions—usually questions asking about a message clearly not in the ad.
Respondents who say that the message is in the ad can be discounted as
simply "yea-saying" or agreeing to anything in front of them. A very high
level of confusion may also save a survey without a control. Gillette Co.
(Venus ProSkin Moisture Rich Razor), NAD #5473 (2012) ("In cases where
the percentage of confusion is closer to the threshold of approximately 20%
the failure to adequately control might be more troublesome to a claim that
there is consumer confusion. In this case, however, 45.3% of consumers
perceived [the challenged claim], far above the 20% threshold.").

In general, a proper control keeps everything constant except for the aspect or aspects of the ad being challenged. If the control changes too much or too little, it won't be testing the right question. For example, one case rejected a survey where the challenged ad was comparative, but the test ad wasn't. The allegedly false message was that the defendant's nicotine patch produced superior quitting efficacy to the plaintiff's. The control ad just called the defendant's patch the "#1 Doctor Recommended Patch" without mentioning any other patch. The court accepted defendant's expert's testimony that consumers believe that comparative ads make superior efficacy claims by default, and that this preexisting bias must be controlled for in a survey. Pharmacia Corp. v. GlaxoSmithKline Consumer Healthcare, L.P., 292 F. Supp. 2d 594 (D.N.J. 2003). Is this persuasive? If consumers believe that comparative ads make superior efficacy claims by default, why not require a comparative advertiser to disclaim superior efficacy?

How should a proper control ad be identified? Among the alternatives might be no ad at all; a "tombstone" ad with just the name of the product; an edited version of the challenged ad with the allegedly deceptive claim taken out; the challenged ad plus a disclaimer; or another ad for the same product. Because the design of the control ad can affect the percentage of consumers who report a false claim, and because the control results will be subtracted from the results of the test cell, the control may determine whether the survey results fall above or below the threshold for liability. Thus, courts are willing to reject surveys with inappropriate controls. *See, e.g.*, Weight Watchers Int'l, Inc. v. Stouffer Corp., 744 F. Supp. 1259 (S.D.N.Y.1994).

Richard Craswell looked at a study by Cornelia Pechmann, *Do Consumers Overgeneralize One-Sided Comparative Price Claims, and Are More Stringent Regulations Needed?*, 3 J. MKTG. RES. 150 (1996), which tested an actual print ad for United Parcel Services (UPS). The ad stated that the UPS rate for delivering a letter by 10:30 the next morning was $3 less than the Federal Express rate. This was true, but UPS's rate for the class of service used by many customers— delivery by any time before 5 pm the next afternoon—was actually higher than Federal Express's rate. Thirty-seven percent of respondents, however, received the false message that UPS had the lowest rates overall—a fairly high percentage of deception. Pechmann tested a control group exposed to no ad at all, and found that only 16% of respondents believed that UPS had the lowest rates overall. If that had been the control, the net deception would be 21%—likely enough to be actionable. Pechmann also tested a control group with an ad that contained a disclaimer warning consumers that the same rates would not apply to deliveries after 10:30 a.m. Using that ad, 29% of consumers believed that UPS had the lowest rates overall. If that's the proper control, the net deception caused by the original ad is 8%—likely not enough to be actionable. (Was this a good control, or a bad disclaimer? Craswell points out that 29% deceptiveness is probably enough to make the *control* misleading under existing precedent. Richard Craswell, *"Compared to What?": The Use of Control Ads in Deceptive Advertising Litigation*, 65 ANTITRUST L.J. 757 (1997).)

As Craswell concluded, while any control will help with technical issues—leading questions, yea-saying biases, guessing, and so on— defendants would prefer a control ad that produces a small difference between test and control, and plaintiffs would prefer the opposite. The choice of an appropriate control, then, is really a policy issue. While we might initially think that we want the control to reduce deception, we need to take into account truthful information that might be lost as well. To see Craswell's point, imagine a control ad that is merely the name of the product. Unless the product name itself is the problem, this is likely to avoid deception, but at the cost of avoiding useful information as well. Given that in Lanham Act cases surveys will only be relevant when the ad's facial claim is literally true, there is always the risk of suppressing literally truthful information that is useful to some consumers.

In fact, when Pechmann tested the ad with a disclaimer, it turned out to reduce comprehension of the truthful claim that UPS had lower rates for morning delivery from 47% to 33%—so the disclaimer reduced the number of deceived consumers by 8% while reducing the number of correctly informed consumers by 14%, probably not a good tradeoff. This result is not unique. More effective disclaimers often reduce comprehension of truthful claims compared to less effective disclaimers. *See* Richard Craswell, *Regulating Deceptive Advertising: The Role of Cost–Benefit Analysis*, 64 S. CAL. L. REV. 549 (1991).

A good control ad therefore should do its best to strip out the bad and not the good. If that can't be done, that may be good reason to conclude that the accused ad should not be suppressed unless the deception is much more harmful than the truthful information. Craswell proposes that a challenged ad should be illegal if it is sufficiently worse than whichever control ad has the best balance between decreasing deception and preserving truthful information. How easy do you think this will be for surveyors to implement? Should they test multiple control ads in every case?

Presentation

How should stimuli be presented? Ideally, they'd be shown as close as reasonably possible to their marketplace reality. Consumer surveys may not be relevant if they test only a certain claim in isolation without showing consumers the rest of the advertising at issue. *See* Scott's Co. v. United Indus. Corp., 315 F.3d 264 (4th Cir. 2002) (rejecting survey that showed respondents only an isolated portion of the product packaging because "the relevant issue in a false advertising case is the consumer's reaction to the advertisement as a whole and in context.").

Courts have taken different positions on whether an ad or other stimulus should be left in front of consumers during questioning. One strand of cases condemns such procedures as mere reading tests, reasoning that consumers don't study ads that way in real life. *See, e.g.,* Am. Home Prods. Corp. v. Proctor & Gamble Co., 871 F. Supp. 739 (D.N.J. 1994). But other courts dislike removing the stimulus because it turns the survey into a memory test and might not reflect market conditions. *See, e.g.,* Starter Corp. v. Converse, Inc., 170 F.3d 286 (2d Cir. 1999) (survey where stimulus was covered with cloth after respondents briefly examined it was "little more than a memory test"). The best rule is probably that the surveyor should make a reasoned decision about whether keeping or removing the stimulus reflects the particular market conditions at issue. It might not be appropriate, for example, to allow a consumer to replay a TV spot to answer a question. (What about a video internet ad?)

Data Reporting and Analysis

Correct recording of responses and proper coding is the next essential step. Surveys have failed where they aggregated the answers to several questions, or otherwise manipulated the data, to inflate the results. L&F Prods. v. Proctor & Gamble Co., 845 F. Supp. 984 (S.D.N.Y. 1998). In connection with one survey, the expert concluded that a commercial for Maxwell House coffee claiming that "the coffee perking in this pot is America's best-loved coffee" communicated to a substantial percentage of consumers that Maxwell House was the "best-selling" brand of coffee in America. But reference to the underlying responses showed that most consumers understood the claim to be only that Maxwell House was "popular" or a "favorite." Kraft Foods, Inc., NAD No. 3201 (April 24, 1995).

Coding errors or other problems with the underlying survey answers can significantly reduce the weight of a survey. Pharmacia Corp. v.

Alcon Labs., Inc., 201 F. Supp. 2d 335 (D.N.J. 2002) (according survey
little weight because of, inter alia, flaws in the execution of the
survey resulting in anomalous results from one survey interviewer).

Objectivity

As a general rule, surveys should be conducted by an independent
outside party, not the advertiser's market research department. *See*
Aurora Foods, Inc., NAD No. 3658 (June 1, 2000). Relatedly, courts
have repeatedly rejected focus group evidence (from informal
discussion sessions among small groups of consumers generally led by
marketers) in place of surveys. *See, e.g.*, Scotts Co. v. United Indus.
Corp., 315 F.3d 264 (4th Cir. 2002). Focus group moderators are not
objective interviewers.

The lawyer must give the expert leeway to design the survey.
Lawyer-shaped surveys can seem inadmissibly biased, and may open
the surveyor up for discovery and destructive cross-examination. *See,
e.g.*, Greenpoint Financial Corp. v. Sperry & Hutchinson Co., 116 F.
Supp. 2d 405 (S.D.N.Y. 2000) (expressing "serious doubts" about the
validity of survey because of undue influence by the lawyers). As one
federal judge complained:

> It is difficult to believe that it was a mere coincidence that
> when each party retained a supposedly independent and
> objective survey organization, it ended up with survey
> questions which were virtually certain to produce the
> particular results it sought. This strongly suggests that those
> who drafted the survey questions were more likely knaves
> than fools. If they were indeed the former, they must have
> assumed that judges are the latter.

Am. Home Prods. Corp. v. Johnson & Johnson, 654 F. Supp. 568, 582 (S.D.N.Y. 1987).

Sometimes, a good use of an expert is to begin with a pilot study—a cheaper survey of 50 to 100 people that can show the likely results of a full-scale survey. A pilot study may also help reveal flaws in the universe or the questions that can be corrected in the final survey. Though designed by the expert, a pilot study may be conducted by counsel, and if it turns out to be flawed, it may be protected from discovery as lawyer work product. *See* Jewel Cos., Inc. v. Granjewel Jewelers & Distribs., Inc., 185 U.S.P.Q. (BNA) 504 (M.D. Fla. 1975). Federal Rules 26(b)(4)(B) and (C) provide that most communications between the attorney and a testifying expert will be covered by the work-product privilege and will not be subject to broad discovery rights. Parties wouldn't have to disclose a pilot study unless it counts as facts or data the expert considered in forming her opinion. If the advertiser chooses to rely on it, a pilot study might even be useful in obtaining preliminary relief, though it would be unlikely to be sufficient at trial or on summary judgment.

C.   Admitting Surveys as Evidence

Some courts admit surveys under the state-of-mind exception to the hearsay rule, Fed. R. Evid. 803(3), or under the related exception for contemporaneous statements describing or explaining an event or condition, Fed. R. Evid. 803(1). The Second Circuit explained that the great majority of surveys are admitted as Rule 803(3) exceptions because they poll individuals about their presently existing states of mind to establish facts about the respondents' mental impressions. This is particularly appropriate in the false advertising context because "[p]laintiffs alleging an implied falsehood are claiming that a statement, whatever its literal truth, has left an impression on the [consumer] that conflicts with reality. This . . . invites a comparison of the impression, rather than the statement, with the truth." Schering

Corp. v. Pfizer, Inc., 189 F.3d 218 (2d Cir. 1999). Survey evidence has also been admitted under the present sense exception as the basis of expert testimony under Rule 703 and under the residual hearsay exception, Rule 807, provided the methodology used is sound.

As indicated by the *Red Wing* case, absent truly spectacular flaws, a court is more likely to admit a survey and discount it according to its deficiencies. *See, e.g.*, KIS, S.A. v. FOTO Fantasy, Inc., 204 F. Supp. 2d 968 (N.D. Texas 2001) (admitting non-representative sample that failed to replicate market conditions). Jacob Jacoby, Amy Handlin and Alex Simonson studied the treatment of Lanham Act false advertising surveys in 1994. Of the surveys admitted in the cases they reviewed, 55% were accorded "considerable weight," 22% a "moderate amount" of weight, and 23% "little or no weight." Jacob Jacoby et al., *Survey Evidence in Deceptive Advertising Cases under the Lanham Act: An Historical Review of Comments from the Bench*, 84 TRADEMARK REP. 541 (1994).

Cross-examination, even when coupled with criticism of a survey's design or methodology by an opposing expert, is unlikely to win a case by itself. Courts recognize that "[i]t is relatively easy for one expert to criticize a survey done by another." U-Haul Int'l v. Jartran, Inc., 522 F. Supp. 1238 (D. Ariz. 1981), *aff'd*, 681 F.2d 1159 (9th Cir. 1982). Litigants who attack an opposition survey when they do not have their own will often receive little judicial sympathy. Gucci v. Gucci Shops, Inc., 688 F. Supp. 916 (S.D.N.Y. 1988).

However, it is certainly possible for sufficiently flawed surveys to be excluded in their entirety. *See, e.g.*, Arche, Inc. v. Azaleia, U.S.A., Inc., 882 F. Supp. 334 (S.D.N.Y. 1995) (non-representative sample); Simon Prop. Grp. L.P. v. mySimon, Inc., 104 F. Supp. 2d 1033 (S.D. Ind. 2000) (absence of proper control); Nat'l Football League Props., Inc. v. ProStyle, Inc., 57 F. Supp. 2d 665 (E.D. Wisc. 1999) (vague, overbroad question).

Internet Surveys

Internet surveys are becoming more common, and more likely to be accepted by courts than they were initially. Internet surveys can be substantially cheaper and faster than conventional phone or mall intercept surveys, especially if the survey concerns a general consumer product. A fast mall intercept survey takes weeks; a fast Internet survey can be done in ten days. Controls are also cheaper and easier to create and modify on the Internet, where the magic of photo manipulation substitutes for generating physical samples.

Questions of proper universe are quite salient with Internet surveys. College graduates, persons with incomes above $75,000, and persons 18–54 are high Internet users. Non-college graduates, people with incomes below $50,000, and people 55 and older are less likely to use the Internet. Thus, it's important to be sure that the survey can sample relevant and representative consumers. Internet surveys can have trouble obtaining sufficient numbers of respondents in cases involving goods or services restricted geographically, by age or by income. Some survey vendors do try to create a probability sample, but with increased expense and time.

Courts are also concerned with whether an Internet survey can adequately replicate the marketplace and purchase experience. If a consumer would typically be able to pick up or examine the product, an Internet survey will be trickier. Where products or services are sold with brochures and other written information, as insurance often is, they might make good candidates for Internet surveys.

Internet-specific concerns include frequent survey-takers who are compensated for participation. Though a competent survey company will exclude people who've taken a certain number of surveys within a certain period from being further surveyed, a careful survey expert will investigate the details. If the target consumers make up only a small percentage of the general population, but 70% of the survey respondents passed the initial screening by answering the questions as if they were target consumers, further inquiry is required. Relatedly, Internet surveys have fewer checks on the identity of survey respondents. An interviewer's in-person judgments are far from perfect, but in their absence some other sort of validation of identity or qualification is required, such as following up with the respondent later on and cross-checking answers.

Survey responses are also different on the Internet, without an interviewer present to ask clarifying questions. A human interviewer can keep a respondent motivated to answer questions and bring a wandering one back on track. Respondents to web surveys can get lazy answering open-ended questions, and tend to write very short, even unintelligible responses. A survey expert reported that one Internet survey showed no confusion among respondents who answered a question with less than ten words, but substantial confusion among respondents who did the work. This is a problem that has not entirely been worked out, but keeping the survey as short as possible probably helps. Some experts suggest adding an algorithm that will pop up a request for a further explanation if a respondent enters an answer below a certain number of characters. But if the survey does this too often, it will likely trigger profane rants from some respondents!

Another difference is that respondents take very different amounts of time to get through Internet surveys; some blaze through in seconds (and perhaps their answers should be discarded) while others take hours (which means that they walk away and return later, and perhaps also should be excluded). This reinforces the point that information about underlying responses, and not just aggregate numbers, is key to evaluating a survey. To identify respondents who may not be taking the survey seriously, the survey designer can insert fake questions or other clues that the respondent isn't taking enough care reading the survey, and also record the time it took to complete the survey.

One expert concluded, based on sample surveys, that properly designed and conducted Internet surveys can be as reliable as the more traditional telephone and mall intercept surveys. *See* Hal Poret, *A Comparative Empirical Analysis of Online Versus Mall and Phone Methodologies for Trademark Surveys*, 100 TRADEMARK REP. 756 (2010). Poret concluded that Internet surveys can achieve similar if not better response rates and representative samples in terms of age, gender, geographic location, and product/service use. "Negligible" numbers of respondents had trouble viewing the test stimuli, gave nonsense answers, or took the survey extremely fast or extremely slowly. They expressed "no opinion" at about the same rate as respondents in phone and mall surveys. Validation attempts largely bore out the respondents' identity claims. Perhaps of greatest interest, the substantive results of surveys were statistically equivalent across different survey modes. The most important disadvantage of Internet surveys was that respondents provided shorter answers to open-ended questions. This could be troublesome for a plaintiff attempting to show that consumers received certain messages, but conversely helpful for a defendant who'd rather be able to show that consumers *didn't* receive those messages. (Of course, opposing parties can be expected to be well aware of these effects, and criticize the choice of a survey method likely to produce favorable results.)

Internet surveys may even have advantages when answers may be sensitive (respondents are more likely to be honest about their use of Viagra or other intimate personal products when they don't have to confront a human interviewer) or when respondents may need time to process the questions at their own paces. *See* Roger Tourangeau & Shari Seidman Diamond, *Internet Surveys for Evaluating Trademark*

Infringement and Deceptive Advertising, 287, in TRADEMARK AND
DECEPTIVE ADVERTISING SURVEYS: LAW, SCIENCE, AND DESIGN (ed.
Shari Seidman Diamond & Jerre B. Swann, 2012).

How Carefully Should Courts Parse Survey Language?

In *PBM Products, LLC v. Mead Johnson & Co.*, 2010 WL 723750
(E.D. Va. 2010), Mead Johnson, which makes Enfamil infant formula,
claimed that PBM was falsely advertising the equivalence of its store-
brand infant formula with a label such as "Compare to Enfamil Lipil."
Mead Johnson argued that the "compare to" message falsely implied
that the products' performance had been tested and that the formulas
were "identical." Mead Johnson's survey asked a close-ended
question, "Based on [the "compare to"] phrase, which of the following
do you believe?" The potential answer choices were (1) the formulas
had the same ingredients; (2) the formulas had different ingredients;
or (3) don't know or none of the above.

The court rejected Mead Johnson's reliance on the survey because the
survey never defined "same." The evidence showed that the
ingredients of the formulas were very similar, though not identical. In
this context,

> the critical question is whether consumers understand the
> 'compare to' language to make the claim that the formulas are
> indeed "identical," not whether the ingredients are nearly the
> same, substantially the same, or any other gradation one
> could create. Despite that focus, [the] surveys never used the
> word "identical" nor did the surveys probe what respondents
> may have meant when they said the products were the
> "same." Instead, [the expert] assumed that respondents who
> believed the parties' products had all of the same ingredients
> would have selected "the same," while respondents who

believed the products had some or even most of the same ingredients would have selected "different." . . .

Is this a fair criticism? What if the ingredients had been substantially different—would the survey have been acceptable then? Ambiguity in questions has doomed other surveys as well. *See* Scotts Co. v. United Indus. Corp., 315 F.3d 264 (4th Cir. 2002) (where false message was allegedly that defendant's product would kill mature crabgrass, asking respondents whether, based on the ad, they believed that the product would "prevent" crabgrass was fatally ambiguous; problem was worsened by lack of a "not sure" option).

Surveys to Disprove Prior Agency Findings

In *Sanderson Farms, Inc. v. Tyson Foods, Inc.*, 547 F. Supp. 2d 491 (D. Md. 2008), plaintiffs Sanderson and Perdue alleged that Tyson's "Raised Without Antibiotics"/"Raised Without Antibiotics that impact antibiotic resistance in humans" (RWA and qualified RWA) claims constituted false advertising. Tyson used ionophores in its chicken feed, and ionophores are antibiotics. People fear that the rise of antibiotic resistance will create "superbugs." But ionophores are not used in human drugs, so their use for chickens presents only a tiny threat—it is "as close to scientific certainty as possible" that ionophores won't lead to antibiotic resistance in humans. The court noted in a footnote, however, that experts used to think that fluoroquinolones have no impact on human antibiotic resistance, but were removed from the market by the FDA when it turned out that they did. Tyson also injected antibiotics into its eggs 2–3 days before hatching. Tyson defined "Raised Without Antibiotics" to mean "from hatch until slaughter," a definition it didn't provide to the public (or the USDA).

Among the parties' products, only plaintiff Perdue's Harvestland did not use any antibiotics at all. Harvestland was truthfully advertised with the slogan "No Antibiotics Ever." Harvestland chickens were more expensive to produce because, without ionophores, Perdue had to use costly alternative measures to prevent disease. This cost translated to higher retail prices, which some consumers were willing to pay for antibiotic-free chicken. Tyson executives acknowledged that the RWA claims allowed them to raise the price of RWA chicken without losing sales.

The USDA, which has authority over the labels on the chicken itself, revoked its initial approval for the unqualified RWA label, but approved the "Raised Without Antibiotics that impact antibiotic resistance in humans" label on the grounds that this disclosure truthfully disclosed the limits of the claim. Tyson used both qualified and unqualified RWA claims in a multimillion-dollar nationwide ad campaign. "The advertisements uniformly featured smiling children, often accompanied by a parent. Many of the advertisements included a heading in large print declaring 'Chicken your family deserves, raised without antibiotics.'"

The court found plaintiffs' survey compelling as to the deceptiveness of both qualified and unqualified RWA claims. Four cells, each of about 150 shopping mall visitors who were likely chicken purchasers, were shown an unqualified RWA ad, a qualified RWA ad using the USDA-approved language, or a control touting "chicken with great taste, high quality and unmatched variety." Participants were asked "[w]hat is the main idea that the advertisement is trying to communicate?" Respondents who indicated that the advertisement communicated something about Tyson's chicken and antibiotics were then asked, "What does the advertisement imply or state about Tyson and antibiotics?"

The results showed that consumers largely responded to unqualified and qualified RWA claims the same way, and they understood both claims to imply that Tyson's chicken was safer and healthier than competitors' chicken. "In short, consumers believe that there are no antibiotics given to Tyson's chickens." In the unqualified RWA cells, 71.4% and 85.1% reported a "no antibiotics" claim, whereas 63.4% did so in the qualified RWA cell. More than half in the qualified RWA cell, 54.9%, didn't mention resistance, while "9.2% of respondents mentioned 'no antibiotics' and 'antibiotic resistance' as separate but related ideas."

The qualification, to the extent consumers perceived it, generally meant to them that resistance was a *reason* to avoid antibiotics, not an explanation of *which* antibiotics Tyson's chickens didn't get:

> Quite significant to this Court is the fact that only 4.6% of respondents understood the claim to mean what the experts at the USDA understood it to mean—i.e., that Tyson uses antibiotics, but that the antibiotics it uses do not cause antibiotic resistance in humans. . . . [P]articipants appeared to break down the qualified "Raised Without Antibiotics" into two distinct parts. The first part, "Raised Without Antibiotics," was taken literally by participants to mean that Tyson's chicken was not given antibiotics, which is not accurate. The second part of the qualified claim, "that impact antibiotic resistance in humans," was taken by participants to mean that Tyson's chicken does not impact antibiotic resistance in humans because Tyson's chicken has no antibiotics, which is also inaccurate. Taken together, participants largely misunderstood the entire qualified claim to mean that Tyson's chicken had no antibiotics and therefore could not impact antibiotic resistance in humans. Indeed, . . . this Court finds that the qualifying language may actually serve to reinforce the false impression that Tyson's chicken is antibiotic-free.

The court cited a number of specific responses illustrating this point, such as "[t]hat this chicken is raised and fed right, without antibiotics so that people will not become resistant to antibiotics."

Defendant's survey expert made no dent, opining merely that the questions should have been more open-ended. The closed-ended questions, however, made clear that respondents believed that Tyson's chicken was safer and healthier than its competitors', regardless of whether the ads used a qualified or unqualified RWA claim. Subtracting the percentages from the control cell, the net belief that the ads were claiming superior safety and health ranged from 21.9% to 35.7%. The court concluded that all these people were being deceived. The percentage of consumers who reported an unqualified "no antibiotics" message after exposure to the qualified RWA claim was much higher than the 15% or so that is usually sufficient to show likely deception. Plaintiffs received an injunction.

Recall the Smirnoff Ice case, in which the challenger contended that BATF's approval of the label for Smirnoff Ice malt beverage was not dispositive because the agency didn't have access to consumer reaction evidence. Here, USDA allowed the qualified RWA claim as true and not misleading. Should the court have deferred to this determination? If not, then when, if ever, should agency approval of a claim preclude a private party from arguing misleadingness? We will return to this issue when we discuss preemption under the FDA in Chapter 17.

D. Distrust of Surveys and Alternatives

Professor McCarthy has suggested that the credence a judge places in a given survey is more related to the judge's own assessment of the evidence than to a survey's statistical accuracy. *See* 4 J. THOMAS MCCARTHY, TRADEMARKS AND UNFAIR COMPETITION § 32:196 (identifying two categories of survey cases: "[A] survey is accepted and relied upon when the judge already has his or her mind made up in favor of the survey results; and a survey is rejected and torn apart when the judge subjectively disagrees with the survey results.") (citation omitted).

Consider McCarthy's interpretation in light of the following sequence of opinions. Here, it is important to understand the evidence as the district court saw it before you can grasp the full meaning of the court of appeals ruling. What *exactly* do the plaintiff's surveys show in this case?

Mead Johnson & Co. v. Abbott Laboratories, 41 F. Supp. 2d 879 (S.D. Ind. 1999)

Defendant Abbott Laboratories advertises its Similac line of infant formulas under the banner "1st Choice of Doctors." Abbott's chief competitor in the infant formula market is plaintiff Mead Johnson & Company. Mead Johnson contends that the "1st Choice of Doctors" claim is false and/or misleading and thus violates Section 43(a)(1) of the Lanham Act, 15 U.S.C. § 1125(a)(1). Mead Johnson contends the claim is misleading because consumers interpret it to mean that most doctors believe Abbott's product is medically superior to Mead Johnson's product, when in fact most doctors do not have a preference between the two leading brands and there is no evidence that one product is medically superior to the other.

[An example of the product packaging at issue]

. . . As explained below, the court finds that Mead Johnson has shown a substantial likelihood of prevailing on its claim that "1st Choice of Doctors" misleads consumers with respect to Similac in two independent ways. The market research on doctors' views of the competing brands is not consistent with consumers' actual and reasonable interpretations of the "1st Choice of Doctors" claim in two ways. First, consumers reasonably interpret the claim to mean that a majority of doctors choose Abbott products over Mead Johnson products. A fair reading of the many doctor surveys in question shows that Abbott products consistently gain the support of only a plurality of doctors. Second, consumers reasonably interpret the "1st Choice of Doctors" claim to mean that doctors base their choices on professional judgments about the relative quality of the products. The surveys that Abbott offers in support of the claim were not designed to elicit a doctor's exercise of professional judgment as distinct from a "top of the head" product or advertising recall. . . .

Mead Johnson has not tried to frame its case in terms of "literal falsity." As explained in detail below, the claim "1st Choice of Doctors" is deeply—and almost ingeniously—ambiguous. As a result, Mead Johnson must prove first what messages consumers actually receive when they are exposed to the "1st Choice of Doctors" claim. In the advertising business, these received messages are often called the "takeaway." Mead Johnson must prove next that the messages are false or misleading. . . .

Abbott correctly concedes that its "1st Choice of Doctors" claim implies the existence of market research to support the claim. . . . The "1st Choice of Doctors" claim plainly implies the existence of supporting survey data. . . .

1. Infant Formulas: The Market and the Products

. . . [Plaintiff Mead Johnson makes Enfamil; defendant Abbott makes Similac and Isomil.] All witnesses in this case agree that both parties' products are high quality and provide excellent nutrition for infants. . . .

Abbott makes no claim to medical superiority because it could not support such a claim with scientific evidence. There is no scientific evidence showing a clinically significant difference between these products, whether in terms of long-term or short-term health, growth, and development of infants.

. . . . For marketers of each company, proof of such a difference would be professionally equivalent to the discovery of the Holy Grail or the coming of the Apocalypse, depending on which product turned out to be better. Well-financed research teams for both Abbott and Mead Johnson have been trying for years to prove that one product is clinically better than the other. Neither has succeeded to date.

2. The Marketing of Infant Formulas and the Role of Doctors in Marketing

. . . . Abbott and Mead Johnson agree that doctors have significant influence over their patients' brand selections of infant formula. *See, e.g.,* I Tr. 50–51 (doctor recommendation is the strongest advertising message in the market and sells more product than any other message). The infant formulas are treated like medical products, and especially first-time mothers may not be confident that they know enough to make a good decision for their babies. Both Mead Johnson and Abbott view new mothers as emotionally vulnerable, especially with the birth of their first children. *See* III Tr. 85 (doctor's ratification of brand choice relieves consumer of worrying about choice).

. . . In the past, doctors often made specific brand recommendations to their patients. In recent years, however, fewer and fewer doctors have been recommending one particular brand with a high degree of frequency. Most doctors perceive both Abbott and Mead Johnson products as high quality and suitable for infants, which is consistent with the available medical evidence summarized above. Those doctors generally either make no brand recommendation or recommend two or more brands. Mead Johnson and Abbott agree that doctors have become less willing to direct their patients to one specific brand of infant formula. As doctors have become more passive in brand selection, mothers have become more active in the product choice, so both companies have increased their advertising aimed directly at new mothers.

3. Abbott's Use of the "1st Choice of Doctors" Claim

Abbott features the "1st Choice of Doctors" claim prominently in its advertising, marketing, and packaging. Abbott places a blue flag with the words "1st Choice of Doctors" on all its infant formula product labels. That specific phrasing first appeared late in 1995. . . . The uncontradicted testimony of Mead Johnson's McCabe shows that Abbott recently has been increasing the amount of money it spends to promote the "1st Choice of Doctors" claim. . . .

Exhibit 22 is a March 1998 report to Abbott on a test of consumer reactions to several informational advertising pamphlets on Similac. Among six pamphlets, the one stressing the "1st Choice of Doctors" claim scored highest in terms of consumers' likelihood of purchase. The report concluded: "Doctor recommendations and the 'science' behind the formula appeared to drive purchase interest for this concept, as well as the other concepts tested," and use of similar pieces emphasizing the claim was "highly recommended." The advertisement scored very high in terms of convincing consumers that Similac "is the formula doctors prefer."

That market research led to the development and use of Exhibit 39, Abbott's direct consumer advertising piece that leads with the "1st Choice of Doctors" claim. The piece then links the "1st Choice of Doctors" claim directly to a mother's desire for "only the best for your baby," and then emphasizes that "doctors know the science of good nutrition." The message and linkage between doctor preference and superior quality are plain. . . .

4. Consumer Perception of the "1st Choice of Doctors" Claim

. . . (a) Abbott's Evidence on the Message Conveyed

. . . The court does not agree that the meaning of the "1st Choice of Doctors" claim is straightforward or self-evident. . . . How, if at all, does the claim take into account the possibility that many doctors have no "choice" or preference among the top brands? At a more fundamental level, what does the claim mean by "choice?" Does it refer to a doctor's exercise of her professional judgment on behalf of patients, or does it refer to a more superficial brand recognition or top-of-the-head impression about brands?

. . . Why should consumers perceive "trust and confidence" from the "1st Choice of Doctors" claim? Abbott agrees that the claim is one of the most powerful it could use in marketing infant formulas. Why should that be so? One possible answer is that consumers expect doctors to have used their professional judgment in making any "choices" among competing brands. As Dr. McDonald testified, the claim "says to consumers that a professional who is knowledgeable has ratified it [the choice of brand] and, therefore, allows a consumer not to think any more about it." Also, unlike a blander, non-comparative claim such as "trusted by doctors", Abbott's claim to be "1st Choice of Doctors" is an inherently comparative (actually, a superlative) claim. Abbott's assertion that it seeks to communicate trust and confidence simply overlooks the comparative or superlative nature of its claim. . . .

(b) Dr. Ross Survey of Consumers

. . . Dr. Ross supervised a survey of consumers through face-to-face interviews at shopping malls in 16 cities across the United States. Participants were screened so as to be women between the ages of 18 and 44 who either had purchased infant formula in the last three months or intended to purchase infant formula within the next 12 months for one or more of their own children. . . .

For the first question to each participant, the interviewer pointed to the blue flag on the label claiming "1st Choice of Doctors" and then asked: "Please tell me what you understand this part of the label to communicate to you." The interviewer recorded the response verbatim, then continued to probe: "Anything else that communicates to you?" The interviewer was instructed to probe, that is, to repeat the "anything else" question, until the response was "unproductive," meaning the respondent said "no," or "nothing else." Some respondents were asked that question several times. If the respondent answered by essentially repeating or "playing back" the words "first choice," the interviewer was then instructed to ask "what do you mean by that?" or words to that effect.

The second question was a further follow-up: "Although you may already have mentioned this, what do you understand the wording 'first choice' to communicate to you?" The interviewer was again instructed to probe until the response was "unproductive."

The third question asked: "And although you may already have mentioned this, if you have an opinion, what reason or reasons do you think this product was 'first choice of doctors'?" The interviewer was again instructed to probe for additional reasons until the response was "unproductive." The interviewer then asked "why do you say that?" and probed the response once with: "Any other reasons you say that?" The fourth question asked the participants about the types of doctors referred to in the "1st Choice of Doctors" claim.

The survey then probed a central problem posed by doctors' approaches to these competing brands—the fact that a substantial proportion of doctors have no significant preference between them. The fifth question asked: "Now, suppose that a survey of doctors had been conducted by the company which makes this product and that they were relying on the results of that survey to make the statement you see here ["1st Choice of Doctors"]. If you have an opinion, in order for this statement ["1st Choice of Doctors"] to be true, what percent of those doctors would have had to say this product was their first choice?" Interviewers were instructed to probe once: "And why do you say that." Responses were recorded verbatim.

The sixth question went a step farther. The interviewer handed the participant a card showing:

> QUESTION: What brand of infant formula, if any, is your first choice?
> RESULTS: 50% — Said they had no first choice
> 30% — Said Similac was their first choice
> 20% — Said another brand was their first choice
>
> ─────────
>
> 100% — Total doctors surveyed

The interviewer then asked: ". . . If those were the results of the survey, would you say that this statement ["1st Choice of Doctors"] is accurate or would you say that this statement is not accurate, or don't you have an opinion about that one way or the other?"[3] Interviewers probed with "why do you say that?"

. . . In response to the first question about what the claim "1st Choice of Doctors" communicated, 52.6 percent of respondents gave answers that Dr. Ross and his associate coded as a reflection of qualitative superiority: superior, better, best, etc. Abbott's market research expert criticized this calculation because Dr. Ross included answers referring only to doctors' "preferences." The criticism was valid because a consumer perception of doctor "preference" does not necessarily show that the consumer perceived the preference in terms of a view of product quality. In response to the criticism, Dr. Ross did a new calculation showing that if the answers referring only to doctors' "preferences" are subtracted, as they properly should have been, the relevant figure is that 41.3 percent understood the claim as making some claim of superiority.

─────────────────────────

[3] To avoid possible bias resulting from the order of the choices, the questions to half the participants posed "accurate" as the first option and half posed "not accurate" as the first option.

In response to questions about doctors' reasons for choosing Similac, Dr. Ross found that 54.9 percent of participants responded in terms of the quality of the product and/or superiority to other products. The Ross survey did not differentiate between claims of long-term medical superiority defined by clinically proven results, which is the standard Mead Johnson contends is relevant, and less dramatic claims of short-term convenience and tolerance effects.

In response to the fifth question about how many doctors would need to have identified Similac as their "first choice" for the statement to be true, 84 percent of the respondents said it would have to be more than 50 percent of doctors. Only 1.4 percent of respondents gave answers of less than 50 percent as supporting the claim.

The sixth question introduced the hypothetical survey in which 50 percent of doctors had no preference, 30 percent preferred Similac, and 20 percent preferred another brand. That question therefore introduced to participants the problem posed by those doctors having no preference and the possibility of a plurality of doctors preferring Similac. In response to the sixth question, 64.8 percent of respondents said those results would make the "1st Choice of Doctors" statement not accurate, while 19.8 percent said the statement would be accurate, and 15.4 percent had no opinion.

Dr. Ross concluded from the results of his study that more than 80 percent of the consumers understood the "1st Choice of Doctors" claim to convey that a majority of doctors choose or prefer Similac. He also concluded that more than 40 percent understood the claim as making some claim of product superiority. With respect to the issue of doctors' reasons for choosing or preferring Similac, more than half attributed doctors' reasons to the doctors' views of the quality or superiority of the product. More than 90 percent of those respondents who expressed any opinion about doctors' likely reasons for their choices thought that the doctors' opinions would be based on product quality or performance.

Abbott criticizes the Ross consumer survey on several major grounds. Abbott contends that the Ross survey used excessive probing, which can introduce biases into a study by forcing responses from a person who has no meaningful response to give. Second, Abbott criticizes the attempt to ask consumers to speculate about why doctors might choose Similac over other brands. Third, Abbott criticizes the attempt to have consumers quantify the proportion of doctors who would have to choose Similac for the "1st Choice of Doctors" claim to be true. The court is not persuaded by these criticisms.

First, probing was appropriate here because of the ambiguity of the "1st Choice of Doctors" claim. In market surveys probing can be a powerful tool, but it can also introduce biases and produce artificial responses from a participant who has run out of meaningful ideas on a subject. *Compare* L & F Prods. v. Procter & Gamble Co., 845 F. Supp. 984, 996 (S.D.N.Y.1994) (repeating questions "also serves the purpose of clarifying otherwise-ambiguous first responses by probing the implications of previous answers"), *aff'd*, 45 F.3d 709 (2d Cir.1995), *with* Am. Home Prods. Corp. v. Procter & Gamble Co., 871 F. Supp. 739, 748 (D.N.J.1994) (excessive probing undermined credibility of survey evaluating arguably implicit messages). Mead Johnson has the burden of showing what consumers understand that claim to mean. A more directive approach would no doubt have been criticized as introducing other biases into the study. Repeated probing was a fair means of determining the "takeaway" from the claim.

Also, Abbott's criticism of the probing rings a little hollow. An advertiser is responsible for both explicit messages in advertising and implicit messages communicated to a reasonable proportion of the audience. Abbott itself has not undertaken any study of the message or "takeaway" that consumers draw from the "1st Choice of Doctors" claim. . . . Abbott's criticism on this score might have more force if Abbott had offered some conflicting evidence tending to show consumers do not infer something about product quality from the "1st Choice of Doctors" claim. It has offered no such evidence.

Abbott's second criticism—that Dr. Ross invited consumers to speculate about why doctors might prefer Similac—is also unpersuasive. Some doctors may have brand preferences for reasons that have nothing to do with product quality. Perhaps they prefer the service from one brand's sales representative, perhaps they like one company's support for medical research, or perhaps they have any of a variety of other reasons for their preferences. *See, e.g.,* Ex. 456 at PAR00216 (good service and rapport with representative cited by doctors more often than other reasons for preferring Similac).

In the court's view, however, it is perfectly obvious to all the marketing and market research witnesses who testified that the reason the "1st Choice of Doctors" claim is so powerful is that many *consumers* assume that such preferences are based on doctors' professional judgments about product quality. The NAD similarly recognizes that professional recommendations of health-care products are powerful because consumers interpret them as based on professional assessments of product quality. Dr. Ross's questions on the perceived reasons for doctors' choices were less an invitation to speculate than a means of confirming what is common wisdom among those in the business. The strength of that wisdom is confirmed by the fact that, among consumers who offered an opinion on the subject, more than 90 percent answered in terms of product quality or superiority.

Abbott's third principal criticism of Dr. Ross's consumer survey is aimed at the questions about the proportion of doctors who would have to have preferred Similac to support the claim. Abbott argues the questions were "grossly unfair" because they ask lay people difficult problems about statistics and patterns of preferences. As Dr. McDonald observed, the consumers who were surveyed probably do not spend a lot of time thinking about "the base" and the difference between a majority and a plurality.

The court would not hold Abbott to a standard of 90 percent preference simply because one-third or so of the respondents thought that is what "first choice" meant, at least initially, before they were asked about the hypothetical survey of doctors. *See* Ex. 1 at F-13 (total of 32.8% answered 90% or more). The critical difference between a majority and a plurality, however, is well-recognized in the advertising business. When that difference was introduced expressly in the survey, an overwhelming proportion of respondents believed the "1st Choice of Doctors" claim would not be accurate if it were supported by only a plurality. The court agrees with that overwhelming majority.

. . . Thus, the weight of the evidence presented thus far shows that the "1st Choice of Doctors" claim communicates two key messages to consumers: (1) a majority of doctors choose Similac or other Abbott brands over Enfamil and other competitors; and (2) the doctors' choices are the result of the exercise of the doctors' professional judgment about the quality of the products. . . .

5. The Evidence on the Market Research Among Doctors

The central facts affecting all the market research and advertising in dispute in this case are these: surveys of doctors (especially pediatricians) show consistently (a) that a substantial proportion of doctors do not have a professional preference between Mead Johnson's Enfamil brand and Abbott's Similac brand, but (b) that among doctors who do have a brand preference, more favor Abbott's Similac over Mead Johnson's Enfamil brand. . . .

Based on the evidence of consumers' perceptions of the claim, the court reasons that the "1st Choice of Doctors" claim could legitimately be supported only by evidence that a majority, not a plurality, of doctors express a professional "choice" or "preference" for Abbott's products over competitors' products. To be fair and not deceptive or misleading, the base against which the majority is measured must include doctors who do not have a choice or preference for a single brand. *See* Gillette Co. v. Norelco Consumer Prods. Co., 946 F. Supp. 115, 124–125 & n. 7 (D. Mass. 1996) (in evaluating claim of superiority based on consumer test, responses favorable to competitor and "no preference" responses must be combined because all are responses contrary to claim of advertiser's superiority). . . .

Thus, in light of all the evidence presented thus far, the court finds that Mead Johnson has shown a substantial likelihood of prevailing on its claim that Abbott's use of the "1st Choice of Doctors" claim in its advertising is misleading consumers in two independent respects in violation of the Lanham Act. The claim is misleading first in that consumers reasonably understand it to express the choices of a majority of doctors rather than a mere plurality, and second in that consumers reasonably understand it to express doctors' preferences based on the exercise of their professional judgments rather than superficial or "top of the head" brand familiarity. . . .

Mead Johnson & Co. v. Abbott Laboratories, 201 F.3d 883 (7th Cir. 2000)

"1st Choice of Doctors", in a blue ribbon on a product's packaging, conveys the message that more physicians prefer this product than any of its rivals. Does (must?) this phrase mean something more—for example, that a majority of all physicians prefer the product, or that the preference is strong or based on particular grounds? The phrase appears on the packaging of Similac®, an infant formula made by the

Ross Pediatrics division of Abbott Laboratories. More than a score of surveys show that pediatricians prefer Similac over Enfamil®, the second-place formula (made by Mead Johnson), with all other competitors far behind. Many of these surveys show that Similac attracts majority support; most show that two physicians prefer Similac for every one who chooses Enfamil. But the district court nonetheless held that "1st Choice of Doctors" violates § 43(a)(1) of the Lanham Act, because it implies to consumers that a majority of physicians strongly prefer the product for strictly professional reasons. All of the surveys that show majority support are inadequate, the judge concluded, because they were designed to elicit either weak preferences or those based on grounds other than medical judgment about quality. Other surveys, designed to eliminate slight or non-medical preferences, show that Similac enjoys only plurality support among physicians. A regular 2-to-1 margin is not enough to permit Abbott to make the "1st Choice" claim, the court held, and issued a preliminary injunction. In politics this would be a landslide: Bill Clinton was the "1st Choice of Voters" at the 1992 and 1996 Presidential elections even though he received less than half of the popular vote (43% in 1992, 49% in 1996). But in marketing, according to the district court, a product must have majority support to be "first."

In English, "first" is ordinal. It denotes rank in a series. A runner who crosses the finish line ahead of all others is "first" even if the race is slow and ends in a photo finish. A TV series ranks first in its time slot if it has a larger audience than any other series, even though there are so many networks, independent stations, and cable channels that no sitcom or drama attracts an absolute majority of viewers. A political candidate who receives more votes than the next-most-popular candidate finishes first, and for most offices a first-place finish is enough for election. Similac therefore is the "1st Choice of Doctors" according to ordinary usage. Perhaps a truthful claim of this kind could be misleading, and therefore actionable under § 43(a)(1), if both absolute and relative levels of preference were small. Suppose 1.1% of pediatricians preferred Similac, 1% preferred Enfamil, 0.9% preferred some other formula, and 97% thought that all of the infant formulas were functionally identical. But absolute and relative preferences for Similac are substantial. Even if, like the district court, we throw out the surveys finding that a majority of medical professionals recommend Similac, the remaining surveys find that between 25% and 48% of those questioned rank Similac first, while Enfamil is the preference of between 10% and 40% of the respondents and never beats Similac. Surveys designed to elicit weaker preferences show that Similac receives between 51% and 64% support and Enfamil from 29% to 37%, so the roughly two-to-one ratio is not sensitive to methodology. Pediatricians may believe (as Abbott contends) that Similac is better tolerated by infants (*i.e.*, less likely to induce unpleasant side effects such as gas, fussiness, and loose stools) and therefore is better in practice, even though clinical tests do not find nutritional differences and experts agree that both products are of high quality. No matter. When the absolute level of preference for the leading product is high, and the difference in support from the medical profession substantial, it is all but impossible to call the claim of "first choice" misleading.

Unless the meaning of language is itself a question of fact, to be determined by survey evidence. And this is what the district court concluded after a three-day hearing on the request for interlocutory relief. . . .

Everything in the district court's analysis depends on the survey of consumers about their understanding of the phrase "1st Choice of Doctors." It is a problematic exercise, for the survey assumes that "first" is a cardinal number—that is, a count such as "246" or "55" or a ratio of two such numbers, rather than a place in a series. Only if "first" is a ratio of cardinal numbers does it make sense to ask whether its meaning is 90% or 51% or a plurality. Respondents in survey research are suggestible; the form of a question implies an answer, or at least the range of proper answers, and this survey ensured that the answers would be numbers rather than places in a series. Having told the respondents to treat "first" as cardinal, the survey was bound to produce a misleading if not meaningless answer. "First" does not mean 51%, or 90%, or any other ratio, so it is not surprising that the responses were all over the lot. The survey's opening set of questions is less troublesome, but it is hard to get from there to a conclusion that surveys of physicians must attempt to limit the grounds of choice. Many a medical choice depends on ease of use rather than therapeutic effect; think of the enduring debate between champions of oral versus injected polio vaccine. If consumers took away from "1st Choice of Doctors" the implication that Similac is a high-quality product, as the author of the survey concluded, then they were not deceived (this Mead Johnson concedes); we doubt that it is proper to draw more from this survey.

There is a deeper problem: the use of a survey in the first place. Surveys are accepted ways to probe for things such as confusion about the source of goods, for confusion depends on the effect of a phrase or trade dress on the consumer. So far as we can tell, however, never before has survey research been used to determine the meaning of words, or to set the standard to which objectively verifiable claims must be held. Dictionaries themselves are a form of survey; lexicographers determine how words have been used in both scholarly and popular texts. But philologists and others who contribute to dictionaries devote their lives to discovering usage and interpreting nuance. It would be a bad idea to replace the work of these professionals with the first impressions of people on the street, especially because consumers' sketchy understanding of science means that survey results are apt to present firms with unrealistic demands for verification.

Suppose a tube of toothpaste bears this phrase in large type: "SODIUM FLUORIDE ANTICAVITY TOOTHPASTE" immediately above a box with the words "ADA Accepted." These claims could be verified by showing that the American Dental Association had authorized the use of its name and that the dentifrice had "anticavity" effects. To a dentist, the word "anticavity" means that the toothpaste reduces the number of cavities compared with some benchmark (perhaps toothpaste without fluoride, perhaps no toothpaste at all) by a statistically significant amount. Perhaps a group of 1,000 persons using the toothpaste with fluoride for two years had 1,000 cavities, while a control group suffered 1,200 cavities. If the difference satisfies normal tests of significance—meaning that the difference is replicable, rather than the effect of chance—then the claim is true and properly may be made to distinguish this toothpaste from others that are less effective at controlling cavities. It is valuable information to consumers. Imagine, however, a survey administered to shoppers in the toothpaste aisles of drugstores. First the questioner asks consumers "what you understand 'ADA Accepted' to communicate to you." Many are likely to respond that this means that the toothpaste is the best on the market, solves (or at least addresses) all dental problems, or some variation—even though the ADA's rules permit multiple products in the same classification to be "Accepted" if each is medically useful, and the phrase "ADA Accepted" may be applied to a toothpaste that does not have any therapeutic effect against gum disease. *See* AMERICAN DENTAL ASSOCIATION ACCEPTANCE PROGRAM GUIDELINES FOR FLUORIDE-CONTAINING DENTIFRICES (May 1998). Perhaps the survey would continue with a question about what "anticavity" means to the shoppers: does it prevent, say, 90% of all cavities?, a majority of cavities?, and so on. Suppose most of those surveyed thought that "anticavity" means that its use will cut cavities in half. Combining that survey result with the district court's approach to verification would mean that the product could not carry the words "anticavity" or "ADA Accepted" even though these representations help shoppers distinguish toothpaste according to effects that they value.

547

Consumers can't be made better off by removing these words from the product, because then buyers who understand their significance will be deprived of information. The market share of the toothpastes that are most effective in reducing cavities will fall, and the number of cavities will rise.

Section 43(a)(1) forbids misleading as well as false claims, but interpreting "misleading" to include factual propositions that are susceptible to misunderstanding would make consumers as a whole worse off by suppressing truthful statements that will help many of them find superior products. *A "misunderstood" statement is not the same as one designed to mislead.* [Editors' Note: Italics added. See following NOTES AND QUESTIONS for more about this italicized sentence.] Reducing ads and packaging to meaningless puffery can't be the objective of the Lanham Act—though it is a logical (and likely) outcome of Mead Johnson's approach, given the normal level of confusion and misunderstanding reflected in consumer surveys. Asked at oral argument whether a seller of aspirin could label that drug as an anti-inflammatory useful for arthritis (a medically established property of aspirin) if a survey showed that consumers confused palliation of symptoms with a cure for the disease, counsel for Mead Johnson replied that the claim of anti-inflammatory properties would be misleading for the same reason "1st Choice of Doctors" is misleading. This consequence of Mead Johnson's view is so counterproductive that the basic position cannot be accepted. We are not comforted by Mead Johnson's assurance that a seller could overcome consumer misunderstanding and make the claim about anti-inflammatory (or anticavity) benefits if it delivered additional details about the nature and extent of these effects. Requirements along the lines of a package insert with medical details are the province of regulations issued by the Food and Drug Administration, not of litigation under the Lanham Act. What is more, adding details could be so costly and burdensome that sellers might choose to omit all of the information. Anyway, if consumers did not read (or understand) the medical details they would be none the wiser, and on Mead Johnson's view the claim should be enjoined anyway.

By using Mead Johnson's survey to define the meaning of the phrase "1st Choice of Doctors" and then insisting that verification meet the standards thus established, the district court committed a legal error.
. . .

Mead Johnson & Co. v. Abbott Laboratories, 209 F.3d 1032 (7th Cir. 2000)

Mead Johnson . . . has filed a petition for rehearing. In response to that petition, the panel amends its opinion by replacing the paragraph at slip op. 7–8 with this language:

> Section 43(a)(1) forbids misleading as well as false claims, but interpreting "misleading" to include factual propositions that are susceptible to misunderstanding would make consumers as a whole worse off by suppressing truthful statements that will help many of them find superior products. *A statement is misleading when, although literally true, it implies something that is false. "Misleading" is not a synonym for "misunderstood," and this record does not support a conclusion that Abbott's statements implied falsehoods about Similac.* [The "designed to mislead" sentence is omitted, and the balance of the paragraph is the same; the court then adds the following new paragraph:]

> None of this calls into question the understanding, expressed by many decisions, that whether a claim is either "false" or "misleading" is an issue of fact rather than law. Our fundamental conclusion is that a producer cannot make a factual issue just by conducting surveys about how science is done (or, worse, about how surveys should be conducted). The

sort of survey evidence Mead Johnson gathered would not support a conclusion by a reasonable person that Abbott's claim either was false or implied a falsehood.

NOTES AND QUESTIONS

What concerns could have prompted the panel to amend its opinion? Does the amended language fully address those concerns?

Are there some claims that are so straightforward that it just shouldn't matter if consumers misunderstand them? Consider the phenomenon of the "halo effect," where claims about good performance on one attribute leads audiences to believe that the product's performance on other attributes is also good. For example, one study has shown that consumers believe that "fair trade" chocolate is lower in calories than chocolate produced by mistreated laborers. Jonathon P. Schuldt et al., *The "Fair Trade" Effect: Health Halos From Social Ethics Claims*, SOC. PSYCHOL. AND PERSONALITY SCI., Jan. 2012. Should producers of fair trade chocolate really be held responsible for this erroneous belief? What are the regulatory options—leaving the misunderstanding alone, requiring disclosures, or something else? Does it matter how easy it would be to correct the misunderstanding? *See also* Pernod Ricard USA, LLC v. Bacardi U.S.A., Inc., 653 F.3d 241 (3d Cir. 2011) (rejecting survey evidence that 18% of consumers thought that "Havana Club" rum came from Cuba when the label prominently stated that it was "Puerto Rican Rum").

When should courts look to the relevant consumers' definitions of terms used in advertising? In *Energy Four, Inc. v. Dornier Medical Systems, Inc.*, 765 F. Supp. 724 (N.D. Ga. 1991), the defendant's advertisement claimed that the competitor's product was subject to "catastrophic failure." The plaintiff showed that the relevant medical community generally understood catastrophic failure to mean "a failure resulting in serious equipment damage or patient injury." The defendant countered with the definition of catastrophic failure found in an engineering dictionary: a sudden failure not associated with typical wear. The court rejected the dictionary definition because there was "no evidence that the dictionary definition reflected a common understanding among targeted consumers" and found literal falsity. Is this line of reasoning acceptable under *Mead Johnson*? Under *Mead Johnson*, what would it have taken to show that the ad was "misleading" rather than "misunderstood"?

Consider this excerpt from the Listerine/floss case, introduced *supra*, in light of *Mead Johnson*:

McNeil-PPC, Inc. v. Pfizer Inc., 351 F. Supp. 2d 226 (S.D.N.Y. 2005)

[review facts from implicit falsity materials]

. . . . In the first survey, consumers were shown the third version of Big Bang twice and then asked a series of questions about the ideas that were communicated to them by the commercial. The survey found that 50% of the respondents took away the message that "you can replace floss with Listerine." . . .

In the third survey, a control survey, consumers were asked their "pre-existing beliefs" regarding Listerine and floss; the intent was to determine the number of people who did not recall seeing the commercials but who still believed that Listerine could be used instead of floss. A minority of those surveyed did not recall seeing Big Bang, and of those 19% stated the opinion that Listerine could be used in place of floss. . . .

The surveyors then took the three surveys together, subtracted the 19% figure from the 50% . . . figures, . . . and concluded that 31% of

those who saw the commercial . . . took away a replacement message.
. . .

[The court rejects technical criticisms of McNeil's surveys.]

. . . . Finally, Pfizer relies heavily on the Seventh Circuit's decision in
Mead Johnson & Co. v. Abbott Labs., 201 F.3d 883 (7th Cir. 2000).
There, Judge Easterbrook wrote that:

> interpreting "misleading" [in § 43(a)(1) of the Lanham Act] to
> include factual propositions that are susceptible to
> misunderstanding would make consumers as a whole worse
> off by suppressing truthful statements that will help many of
> them find superior products. A "misunderstood" statement is
> not the same as one designed to mislead.

The *Mead Johnson* decision, however, is of little assistance in this
case. The issue there was whether the statement "1st Choice of
Doctors" on infant formula containers was misleading and constituted
false advertisement. The plaintiff argued that "1st" meant more than
50% and that a simple plurality would not suffice.

Understandably, the Seventh Circuit rejected the argument. Here,
the advertised claim is much less nebulous—it is a claim based on
purported proof provided by "clinical tests." Moreover, the court in
Mead Johnson was concerned that surveys were being used in that
case "to determine the meaning of words." . . . In this case, the
Ridgway surveys were used in the manner in which surveys are
traditionally used in false advertisement cases. The *Mead Johnson*
decision does not dictate a different result here.

NOTES AND QUESTIONS

The *Pfizer* court quotes the unamended version of *Mead Johnson*, using language the Seventh Circuit ultimately removed from the opinion. Courts interpreting *Mead Johnson* have done this several times.

Were you convinced by the distinctions the *Pfizer* court made between the survey it confronted and the survey in *Mead Johnson*? The court in *Clorox Co. Puerto Rico v. Proctor & Gamble Commercial Co.*, 228 F.3d 24 (1st Cir. 2000), also declined to extend the *Mead Johnson* holding from printed labels to television commercials. The court held that the claim before it, that people using its detergent would find that "whiter is not possible" for clothes, was "an integral part of a television commercial with substantial text and images. There is a fundamental difference between a slogan on a can label that communicates its meaning to consumers solely through the printed text, and a tag line shown on the screen at the end of a television commercial that communicates its message to consumers through a combination of audio-visual and textual media." Does this distinction make sense? Can't claims on a product label also be affected by their context?

Solvay Pharmaceuticals, Inc. v. Global Pharmaceuticals, 2006 WL 626079 (D. Minn. 2006), involved a lawsuit between two makers of pancreatic enzyme supplements. Defendant Global marketed a (purported) generic alternative to Solvay's supplements, which are used to treat cystic fibrosis patients and others who don't produce the proper enzymes to digest food. Solvay argued that manufacturing differences in formulation, blending, and coating of supplements can lead to different enzyme activity and release rates, resulting in different effects on patients, even if they are truthfully labeled as containing the same enzyme content.

Global worked to have major drug information databases characterize its product Lipram-CR as a generic substitute for Solvay's Creon. Global also told pharmacists that Lipram was "equivalent" to, a "pharmaceutical alternative" to, a "true alternative to," and "the generic form" of Creon. Global argued that it never advertised Lipram as an FDA-approved generic, bioequivalent, "therapeutically equivalent," or "pharmaceutically equivalent" to Creon—all of these terms require extremely stringent standards of equivalence under FDA rules. However, Solvay's surveys of retail pharmacists indicated that 89% of pharmacists agreed that a generic substitute must be therapeutically equivalent to the name-brand product and 93% agreed that the generic must be bioequivalent to the name-brand product. The court denied Global's motion for summary judgment on literal falsity.

Should the surveys be accepted as evidence of what the terms mean? Is this result consistent with *Mead Johnson*? If you were the plaintiff, how would you distinguish *Mead Johnson*?

Getting Rid of a Survey Requirement? Lee Goldman argues that the survey requirement in cases of allegedly misleading advertising should be abandoned. *See* Lee Goldman, *The World's Best Article on Competitor Suits for False Advertising*, 45 FLA. L. REV. 487 (1993). Surveys are expensive, hotly contested, and often not all that high-quality. In many instances, a judge or jury can determine whether an ad makes the allegedly false implied claim. Goldman gives the example of an ad claiming that Extra Strength Maalox Plus was "the strongest antacid there is." This allegedly falsely implied that Maalox was the most effective product on the market. Goldman contends that it's difficult to see why the advertiser would make this strength claim if not to claim superior effectiveness. Because of the current state of Lanham Act doctrine, however, the challenger was required to submit a survey. Because the survey it submitted was flawed, the challenger lost. *See* Johnson & Johnson-Merck Consumer Pharm. Co. v. Rhone-

Poulenc Rorer Pharms., Inc., 19 F.3d 125 (3d Cir. 1994). So, Goldman
argues, the survey requirement is inefficient and leads to
questionable results. The problem is worsened because of the short
timeframe before preliminary relief hearings, which makes it harder
to conduct a good survey. Mistaken rulings at the preliminary
injunction stage are often irreversible, because many if not most
Lanham Act false advertising cases don't proceed past that stage.

Goldman suggests that (properly conducted) surveys should be
considered probative, not mandatory, as they are in the related area
of trademark law. He contends that the survey requirement, while
defended by some as a way to make advertising law more predictable
and avoid chilling advertisers' speech, doesn't in fact make the law
more predictable or accurate. Judges should be considered competent
to interpret ads, as they are competent to interpret other uses of
language such as contracts, and juries should be able to evaluate how
reasonable consumers would understand ad claims even without
surveys. Since we do not live in an ideal world of perfect, cost-free
surveys, he argues, the survey requirement should be made optional.
Given the cases we've read, do you agree?

5. Standing under the Lanham Act

15 U.S.C. § 1125(a) states the following:

> (1)   Any person who, on or in connection with any goods or
> services, or any container for goods, uses in commerce . . . any
> false designation of origin, false or misleading description of
> fact, or false or misleading representation of fact, which—
> (B) in commercial advertising or promotion, misrepresents the
> nature, characteristics, qualities, or geographic origin of his
> or her or another person's goods, services, or commercial
> activities, shall be liable in a civil action by *any person who*

believes that he or she is or is likely to be damaged by such act.
[emphasis added]

Courts have construed standing expansively with respect to the
trademark portions of the Lanham Act—all that is required to bring a
federal trademark claim is ownership of a valid trademark. In some
cases, this merely requires that the plaintiff show it has a commercial
interest to be protected, as opposed to a noncommercial interest (such
as a purely private individual's interest in her reputation for
charitable or creative activities). *See* Stayart v. Yahoo! Inc., 623 F.3d
436 (7th Cir. 2010). When it comes to false advertising, however,
courts applied different standards; the Supreme Court has resolved
one conflict over who can be a Lanham Act plaintiff, but, as you will
see, others remain.

Lexmark Intern., Inc. v. Static Control Components, Inc., 134 S.Ct. 1377 (2014)

Justice SCALIA delivered the opinion of the Court.

This case requires us to decide whether respondent, Static Control
Components, Inc., may sue petitioner, Lexmark International, Inc.,
for false advertising under the Lanham Act, 15 U.S.C. § 1125(a).

I. Background

Lexmark manufactures and sells laser printers. It also sells toner
cartridges for those printers (toner being the powdery ink that laser
printers use to create images on paper). Lexmark designs its printers
to work only with its own style of cartridges, and it therefore
dominates the market for cartridges compatible with its printers.
That market, however, is not devoid of competitors. Other businesses,
called "remanufacturers," acquire used Lexmark toner cartridges,

refurbish them, and sell them in competition with new and refurbished cartridges sold by Lexmark.

Lexmark would prefer that its customers return their empty cartridges to it for refurbishment and resale, rather than sell those cartridges to a remanufacturer. So Lexmark introduced what it called a "Prebate" program, which enabled customers to purchase new toner cartridges at a 20-percent discount if they would agree to return the cartridge to Lexmark once it was empty. Those terms were communicated to consumers through notices printed on the toner-cartridge boxes, which advised the consumer that opening the box would indicate assent to the terms—a practice commonly known as "shrinkwrap licensing." To enforce the Prebate terms, Lexmark included a microchip in each Prebate cartridge that would disable the cartridge after it ran out of toner; for the cartridge to be used again, the microchip would have to be replaced by Lexmark.

Static Control is not itself a manufacturer or remanufacturer of toner cartridges. It is, rather, "the market leader [in] making and selling the components necessary to remanufacture Lexmark cartridges." In addition to supplying remanufacturers with toner and various replacement parts, Static Control developed a microchip that could mimic the microchip in Lexmark's Prebate cartridges. By purchasing Static Control's microchips and using them to replace the Lexmark microchip, remanufacturers were able to refurbish and resell used Prebate cartridges.

Lexmark did not take kindly to that development. In 2002, it sued Static Control, alleging that Static Control's microchips violated both the Copyright Act of 1976, 17 U.S.C. § 101 et seq., and the Digital Millennium Copyright Act, 17 U.S.C. § 1201 et seq. Static Control counterclaimed, alleging, among other things, violations of § 43(a) of the Lanham Act, 60 Stat. 441, codified at 15 U.S.C. § 1125(a). Section 1125(a) provides:

(1) Any person who, on or in connection with any goods or services, or any container for goods, uses in commerce any word, term, name, symbol, or device, or any combination thereof, or any false designation of origin, false or misleading description of fact, or false or misleading representation of fact, which—

(A) is likely to cause confusion, or to cause mistake, or to deceive as to the affiliation, connection, or association of such person with another person, or as to the origin, sponsorship, or approval of his or her goods, services, or commercial activities by another person, or

(B) in commercial advertising or promotion, misrepresents the nature, characteristics, qualities, or geographic origin of his or her or another person's goods, services, or commercial activities,

shall be liable in a civil action by any person who believes that he or she is or is likely to be damaged by such act.

Section 1125(a) thus creates two distinct bases of liability: false association, § 1125(a)(1)(A), and false advertising, § 1125(a)(1)(B). Static Control alleged only false advertising.

As relevant to its Lanham Act claim, Static Control alleged two types of false or misleading conduct by Lexmark. First, it alleged that through its Prebate program Lexmark "purposefully misleads end-users" to believe that they are legally bound by the Prebate terms and are thus required to return the Prebate-labeled cartridge to Lexmark after a single use. Second, it alleged that upon introducing the Prebate program, Lexmark "sent letters to most of the companies in the toner cartridge remanufacturing business" falsely advising those companies that it was illegal to sell refurbished Prebate cartridges and, in particular, that it was illegal to use Static Control's products to refurbish those cartridges. Static Control asserted that by those statements, Lexmark had materially misrepresented "the nature, characteristics, and qualities" of both its own products and Static Control's products. It further maintained that Lexmark's misrepresentations had "proximately caused and [we]re likely to cause injury to [Static Control] by diverting sales from [Static Control] to Lexmark," and had "substantially injured [its] business reputation" by "leading consumers and others in the trade to believe that [Static Control] is engaged in illegal conduct." Static Control sought treble damages, attorney's fees and costs, and injunctive relief.[4]

The District Court granted Lexmark's motion to dismiss Static Control's Lanham Act claim. It held that Static Control lacked "prudential standing" to bring that claim, relying on a multifactor balancing test it attributed to *Associated Gen. Contractors of Cal., Inc. v. Carpenters*, 459 U.S. 519 (1983). The court emphasized that there were "more direct plaintiffs in the form of remanufacturers of Lexmark's cartridges"; that Static Control's injury was "remot[e]" because it was a mere "byproduct of the supposed manipulation of consumers' relationships with remanufacturers"; and that Lexmark's "alleged intent [was] to dry up spent cartridge supplies at the remanufacturing level, rather than at [Static Control]'s supply level, making remanufacturers Lexmark's alleged intended target."

---

[4] Lexmark contends that Static Control's allegations failed to describe "commercial advertising or promotion" within the meaning of 15 U.S.C. § 1125(a)(1)(B). That question is not before us, and we express no view on it. We assume without deciding that the communications alleged by Static Control qualify as commercial advertising or promotion.

The Sixth Circuit reversed the dismissal of Static Control's Lanham Act claim....The Sixth Circuit applied the Second Circuit's reasonable-interest test and concluded that Static Control had standing because it "alleged a cognizable interest in its business reputation and sales to remanufacturers and sufficiently alleged that th[o]se interests were harmed by Lexmark's statements to the remanufacturers that Static Control was engaging in illegal conduct."

We granted certiorari to decide "the appropriate analytical framework for determining a party's standing to maintain an action for false advertising under the Lanham Act."

II. "Prudential Standing"...

In sum, the question this case presents is whether Static Control falls within the class of plaintiffs whom Congress has authorized to sue under § 1125(a). In other words, we ask whether Static Control has a cause of action under the statute. That question requires us to determine the meaning of the congressionally enacted provision creating a cause of action. In doing so, we apply traditional principles of statutory interpretation. We do not ask whether in our judgment Congress should have authorized Static Control's suit, but whether Congress in fact did so. Just as a court cannot apply its independent policy judgment to recognize a cause of action that Congress has denied, it cannot limit a cause of action that Congress has created merely because "prudence" dictates.

III. Static Control's Right To Sue Under § 1125(a)

Thus, this case presents a straightforward question of statutory interpretation: Does the cause of action in § 1125(a) extend to plaintiffs like Static Control? The statute authorizes suit by "any person who believes that he or she is likely to be damaged" by a defendant's false advertising. Read literally, that broad language might suggest that an action is available to anyone who can satisfy the minimum requirements of Article III. No party makes that argument, however, and the "unlikelihood that Congress meant to allow all factually injured plaintiffs to recover persuades us that [§ 1125(a)] should not get such an expansive reading." We reach that conclusion in light of two relevant background principles already mentioned: zone of interests and proximate causality.

A. Zone of Interests

First, we presume that a statutory cause of action extends only to plaintiffs whose interests "fall within the zone of interests protected by the law invoked." . . .

Identifying the interests protected by the Lanham Act . . . requires no guesswork, since the Act includes an "unusual, and extraordinarily helpful," detailed statement of the statute's purposes. Section 45 of the Act, codified at 15 U.S.C. § 1127, provides:

> The intent of this chapter is to regulate commerce within the control of Congress by making actionable the deceptive and misleading use of marks in such commerce; to protect registered marks used in such commerce from interference by State, or territorial legislation; to protect persons engaged in such commerce against unfair competition; to prevent fraud and deception in such commerce by the use of reproductions, copies, counterfeits, or colorable imitations of registered marks; and to provide rights and remedies stipulated by treaties and conventions respecting trademarks, trade names, and unfair competition entered into between the United States and foreign nations.

Most of the enumerated purposes are relevant to false-association cases; a typical false-advertising case will implicate only the Act's

561

goal of "protect[ing] persons engaged in [commerce within the control of Congress] against unfair competition." Although "unfair competition" was a "plastic" concept at common law, it was understood to be concerned with injuries to business reputation and present and future sales.

We thus hold that to come within the zone of interests in a suit for false advertising under § 1125(a), a plaintiff must allege an injury to a commercial interest in reputation or sales. A consumer who is hoodwinked into purchasing a disappointing product may well have an injury-in-fact cognizable under Article III, but he cannot invoke the protection of the Lanham Act—a conclusion reached by every Circuit to consider the question. Even a business misled by a supplier into purchasing an inferior product is, like consumers generally, not under the Act's aegis.

B. Proximate Cause

Second, we generally presume that a statutory cause of action is limited to plaintiffs whose injuries are proximately caused by violations of the statute. For centuries, it has been "a well-established principle of [the common] law, that in all cases of loss, we are to attribute it to the proximate cause, and not to any remote cause." That venerable principle reflects the reality that "the judicial remedy cannot encompass every conceivable harm that can be traced to alleged wrongdoing." Congress, we assume, is familiar with the common-law rule and does not mean to displace it sub silentio. We have thus construed federal causes of action in a variety of contexts to incorporate a requirement of proximate causation. No party disputes that it is proper to read § 1125(a) as containing such a requirement, its broad language notwithstanding.

The proximate-cause inquiry is not easy to define, and over the years it has taken various forms; but courts have a great deal of experience applying it, and there is a wealth of precedent for them to draw upon in doing so. Proximate-cause analysis is controlled by the nature of the statutory cause of action. The question it presents is whether the harm alleged has a sufficiently close connection to the conduct the statute prohibits.

Put differently, the proximate-cause requirement generally bars suits for alleged harm that is "too remote" from the defendant's unlawful conduct. That is ordinarily the case if the harm is purely derivative of "misfortunes visited upon a third person by the defendant's acts." In a sense, of course, all commercial injuries from false advertising are derivative of those suffered by consumers who are deceived by the advertising; but since the Lanham Act authorizes suit only for commercial injuries, the intervening step of consumer deception is not fatal to the showing of proximate causation required by the statute. That is consistent with our recognition that under common-law principles, a plaintiff can be directly injured by a misrepresentation even where "a third party, and not the plaintiff, . . . relied on" it.

We thus hold that a plaintiff suing under § 1125(a) ordinarily must show economic or reputational injury flowing directly from the deception wrought by the defendant's advertising; and that that occurs when deception of consumers causes them to withhold trade from the plaintiff. That showing is generally not made when the deception produces injuries to a fellow commercial actor that in turn affect the plaintiff. For example, while a competitor who is forced out of business by a defendant's false advertising generally will be able to sue for its losses, the same is not true of the competitor's landlord, its electric company, and other commercial parties who suffer merely as a result of the competitor's "inability to meet [its] financial obligations."

C. Proposed Tests

At oral argument, Lexmark agreed that the zone of interests and proximate causation supply the relevant background limitations on suit under § 1125(a). But it urges us to adopt, as the optimal formulation of those principles, a multifactor balancing test derived from *Associated General Contractors*. In the alternative, it asks that we adopt a categorical test permitting only direct competitors to sue for false advertising. And although neither party urges adoption of the "reasonable interest" test applied below, several amici do so. While none of those tests is wholly without merit, we decline to adopt any of them. We hold instead that a direct application of the zone-of-interests test and the proximate-cause requirement supplies the relevant limits on who may sue.

The balancing test Lexmark advocates was first articulated by the Third Circuit in *Conte Bros.* and later adopted by several other Circuits. *Conte Bros.* identified five relevant considerations:

> (1) The nature of the plaintiff's alleged injury: Is the injury of a type that Congress sought to redress in providing a private remedy for violations of the [Lanham Act]?
> (2) The directness or indirectness of the asserted injury.
> (3) The proximity or remoteness of the party to the alleged injurious conduct.
> (4) The speculativeness of the damages claim.
> (5) The risk of duplicative damages or complexity in apportioning damages.

This approach reflects a commendable effort to give content to an otherwise nebulous inquiry, but we think it slightly off the mark. The first factor can be read as requiring that the plaintiff's injury be within the relevant zone of interests and the second and third as requiring (somewhat redundantly) proximate causation; but it is not correct to treat those requirements, which must be met in every case, as mere factors to be weighed in a balance. And the fourth and fifth factors are themselves problematic. "[T]he difficulty that can arise when a court attempts to ascertain the damages caused by some remote action" is a "motivating principle" behind the proximate-cause requirement; but potential difficulty in ascertaining and apportioning damages is not, as *Conte Bros.* might suggest, an independent basis for denying standing where it is adequately alleged that a defendant's conduct has proximately injured an interest of the plaintiff's that the statute protects. Even when a plaintiff cannot quantify its losses with sufficient certainty to recover damages, it may still be entitled to injunctive relief under § 1116(a) (assuming it can prove a likelihood of future injury) or disgorgement of the defendant's ill-gotten profits under § 1117(a). Finally, experience has shown that the *Conte Bros.* approach, like other open-ended balancing tests, can yield unpredictable and at times arbitrary results. *See, e.g.*, Tushnet, *Running the Gamut from A to B: Federal Trademark and False Advertising Law*, 159 U. PA. L. REV. 1305, 1376–1379 (2011).

In contrast to the multifactor balancing approach, the direct-competitor test provides a bright-line rule; but it does so at the expense of distorting the statutory language. To be sure, a plaintiff who does not compete with the defendant will often have a harder time establishing proximate causation. But a rule categorically prohibiting all suits by noncompetitors would read too much into the Act's reference to "unfair competition" in § 1127. By the time the Lanham Act was adopted, the common-law tort of unfair competition was understood not to be limited to actions between competitors. One leading authority in the field wrote that "there need be no competition in unfair competition," just as "[t]here is no soda in soda water, no grapes in grape fruit, no bread in bread fruit, and a clothes horse is not a horse but is good enough to hang things on." It is thus a mistake to infer that because the Lanham Act treats false advertising as a form of unfair competition, it can protect only the false-advertiser's direct competitors.

Finally, there is the "reasonable interest" test applied by the Sixth Circuit in this case. As typically formulated, it requires a commercial plaintiff to "demonstrate '(1) a reasonable interest to be protected against the alleged false advertising and (2) a reasonable basis for believing that the interest is likely to be damaged by the alleged false advertising.' " A purely practical objection to the test is that it lends itself to widely divergent application. Indeed, its vague language can be understood as requiring only the bare minimum of Article III standing. The popularity of the multifactor balancing test reflects its appeal to courts tired of "grappl[ing] with defining" the "reasonable interest" test "with greater precision." The theoretical difficulties with the test are even more substantial: The relevant question is not whether the plaintiff's interest is "reasonable," but whether it is one the Lanham Act protects; and not whether there is a "reasonable basis" for the plaintiff's claim of harm, but whether the harm alleged is proximately tied to the defendant's conduct. In short, we think the principles set forth above will provide clearer and more accurate guidance than the "reasonable interest" test.

IV. Application

Applying those principles to Static Control's false-advertising claim, we conclude that Static Control comes within the class of plaintiffs whom Congress authorized to sue under § 1125(a).

To begin, Static Control's alleged injuries—lost sales and damage to its business reputation—are injuries to precisely the sorts of commercial interests the Act protects. Static Control is suing not as a deceived consumer, but as a "perso[n] engaged in" "commerce within the control of Congress" whose position in the marketplace has been damaged by Lexmark's false advertising. There is no doubt that it is within the zone of interests protected by the statute.

Static Control also sufficiently alleged that its injuries were proximately caused by Lexmark's misrepresentations. This case, it is true, does not present the "classic Lanham Act false-advertising claim" in which " 'one competito[r] directly injur[es] another by making false statements about his own goods [or the competitor's goods] and thus inducing customers to switch.' " But although diversion of sales to a direct competitor may be the paradigmatic direct injury from false advertising, it is not the only type of injury cognizable under § 1125(a). For at least two reasons, Static Control's allegations satisfy the requirement of proximate causation.

First, Static Control alleged that Lexmark disparaged its business and products by asserting that Static Control's business was illegal. When a defendant harms a plaintiff's reputation by casting aspersions on its business, the plaintiff's injury flows directly from the audience's belief in the disparaging statements. Courts have therefore afforded relief under § 1125(a) not only where a defendant denigrates a plaintiff's product by name, but also where the defendant damages the product's reputation by, for example, equating it with an inferior product. Traditional proximate-causation principles support those results: As we have observed, a defendant who " 'seeks to promote his own interests by telling a known falsehood to or about the plaintiff or his product' " may be said to have proximately caused the plaintiff's harm.

The District Court emphasized that Lexmark and Static Control are not direct competitors. But when a party claims reputational injury from disparagement, competition is not required for proximate cause; and that is true even if the defendant's aim was to harm its immediate competitors, and the plaintiff merely suffered collateral damage. Consider two rival carmakers who purchase airbags for their cars from different third-party manufacturers. If the first carmaker, hoping to divert sales from the second, falsely proclaims that the airbags used by the second carmaker are defective, both the second carmaker and its airbag supplier may suffer reputational injury, and their sales may decline as a result. In those circumstances, there is no reason to regard either party's injury as derivative of the other's; each is directly and independently harmed by the attack on its merchandise.

In addition, Static Control adequately alleged proximate causation by alleging that it designed, manufactured, and sold microchips that both (1) were necessary for, and (2) had no other use than, refurbishing Lexmark toner cartridges. It follows from that allegation that any false advertising that reduced the remanufacturers' business necessarily injured Static Control as well. Taking Static Control's assertions at face value, there is likely to be something very close to a 1:1 relationship between the number of refurbished Prebate cartridges sold (or not sold) by the remanufacturers and the number of Prebate microchips sold (or not sold) by Static Control. "Where the injury alleged is so integral an aspect of the [violation] alleged, there can be no question" that proximate cause is satisfied.

To be sure, on this view, the causal chain linking Static Control's injuries to consumer confusion is not direct, but includes the intervening link of injury to the remanufacturers. Static Control's allegations therefore might not support standing under a strict application of the " ' "general tendency" ' " not to stretch proximate causation " ' "beyond the first step." ' " But the reason for that general tendency is that there ordinarily is a "discontinuity" between the injury to the direct victim and the injury to the indirect victim, so that the latter is not surely attributable to the former (and thus also to the defendant's conduct), but might instead have resulted from "any number of [other] reasons." That is not the case here. Static Control's allegations suggest that if the remanufacturers sold 10,000 fewer refurbished cartridges because of Lexmark's false advertising, then it would follow more or less automatically that Static Control sold 10,000 fewer microchips for the same reason, without the need for any "speculative . . . proceedings" or "intricate, uncertain inquiries." In these relatively unique circumstances, the remanufacturers are not "more immediate victim[s]" than Static Control.

Although we conclude that Static Control has alleged an adequate basis to proceed under § 1125(a), it cannot obtain relief without evidence of injury proximately caused by Lexmark's alleged misrepresentations. We hold only that Static Control is entitled to a chance to prove its case.

* * *

To invoke the Lanham Act's cause of action for false advertising, a plaintiff must plead (and ultimately prove) an injury to a commercial interest in sales or business reputation proximately caused by the defendant's misrepresentations. Static Control has adequately pleaded both elements. The judgment of the Court of Appeals is affirmed.

NOTES AND QUESTIONS

Why not allow consumers to have standing? The statutory language clearly includes an intent to protect consumers from "fraud and deception." Some courts inferred from the overall context of the Lanham Act that Congress intended § 43(a)(1) primarily to protect competitors. Others reasoned that competitors would be better plaintiffs than consumers because of their greater resources, and that competitors would be good proxies for consumer interests. In addition, courts pointed to state laws providing consumers with remedies for false advertising and the FTC's jurisdiction to protect consumers as alternatives, showing that consumer standing under the Lanham Act was unnecessary.

Some courts have made explicit the key underlying reason: they don't want a flood of consumer plaintiffs in the federal courts. Jean Wegman Burns has argued that this rule conflicts with the broad language of the statute and invites precisely the wrong plaintiffs: competitors who may be more interested in stifling legitimate competition than in redressing true consumer injury. *See* Jean Wegman Burns, *Confused Jurisprudence: False Advertising under the Lanham Act*, 79 B.U.L. REV. 807 (1999); Jean Wegman Burns, *The Paradox of Antitrust and Lanham Act Standing*, 42 UCLA L. REV. 47 (1994).

After *Lexmark*, is pure disparagement actionable under the Lanham Act? Suppose the defendant is a law firm that, in the course of seeking clients for a personal injury lawsuit against a bank, says that the bank engaged in mortgage fraud, causing the bank to lose sales. Should this suffice for Lanham Act standing? *See* First Mariner Bank v. Resolution Law Grp., P.C., 2014 WL 1652550 (D. Md. 2014) (finding that such a claim "fits snugly within the *Lexmark* framework"). What if, instead, the defendant is a for-profit newspaper that ran a story in its science section about the supposed dangers of the drugs?

Suppose a landlord is entitled to a percentage of its commercial tenant's sales. One of the tenant's competitors disparages the tenant, and the tenant's sales fall. Under *Lexmark*, does the landlord have standing?

What would suffice to plead proximate causation? Suppose the plaintiff is one of four dominant competitors in the market, each with roughly equal market shares. If a new market entrant starts advertising falsely, should we just assume that it will take market share from each of the dominant competitors?

6. Commercial Advertising or Promotion

In order for a claim to be actionable under the Lanham Act, it must also be made in "commercial advertising or promotion." § 43(a)(1)(B). Over the years, courts settled upon a test to define this phrase. The test incorporates concerns for limiting the scope of the law, and currently has three elements: (1) commercial speech; (2) for the purpose of influencing consumers to buy the defendant's goods or services; (3) that is disseminated sufficiently to the relevant purchasing public to constitute advertising or promotion within that industry. Gordon & Breach Sci. Publishers v. Am. Inst. of Physics, 859 F. Supp. 1521 (S.D.N.Y. 1994) (also articulating a fourth prong, competition with the plaintiff, which has generally been recognized in recent cases as supplanted by *Lexmark*); *see also* Grubbs v. Sheakley Gp., Inc., 807 F.3d 785 (6th Cir. 2015) (adopting a definition requiring (1) commercial speech; (2) for the purpose of influencing customers to buy the defendant's goods or services; (3) that is disseminated either widely enough to the relevant purchasing public to constitute advertising or promotion within that industry or to a substantial portion of the plaintiff's or defendant's existing customer or client base).

The second element, that the speech has a purpose of influencing purchases from the defendant, rarely has independent significance. After *Lexmark*, it may provide a hook for certain speech-protective holdings that used to be framed as applications of the "competition" element. *See, e.g.*, Huntingdon Life Scis., Inc. v. Rokke, 978 F. Supp. 662 (E.D. Va. 1997) (rejecting animal testing laboratory's contention that People for the Ethical Treatment of Animals (PETA) was a competitor even though PETA was actively involved in promoting to laboratory's customers methods of testing that did not involve

571

animals; PETA was not itself engaged in testing any consumer products).

Finally, the amount of dissemination sufficient to constitute "advertising or promotion" depends on the size of the underlying market. A statement by a single salesperson to one of thousands of customers will not qualify. But if the relevant market is very small and specialized, a sales pitch to only a few—or even one—potential customer might suffice. *See* Champion Labs v. Parker-Hannifin Corp., 616 F. Supp. 2d 684 (E.D. Mich. 2009) (where parties occupied a niche market for fuel filters intended for a particular engine manufactured by General Motors, representations made to General Motors were in "commercial advertising and promotion" for purposes of avoiding summary judgment).

7. Competitor Suits under State Laws

Many state Unfair and Deceptive Acts and Practices ("UDAP") statutes can be applied to false advertising disputes between business entities. In some jurisdictions, such as Massachusetts and Texas, an express statutory amendment authorizes businesses to bring actions under the UDAP statute. In other states, such as Connecticut and North Carolina, the statute affords any "person" or "aggrieved party" a private right of action, and these terms have often been interpreted to grant standing to one business competitor aggrieved by the deceptive conduct of another. *See, e.g.*, POM Wonderful LLC v. Coca-Cola Co., 679 F.3d 1170 (9th Cir. 2012) (allowing competitor standing under state Unfair Competition Law when competitor is harmed by false advertising).

Several states, including New York, require a "public interest" element. This generally involves a pattern of conduct, a potential for repetition, or other factors suggesting a broader societal interest in the transaction at issue, as opposed to simple private injuries. In these "public interest" states, a business plaintiff asserting that it was *directly* deceived has to show that its harm was suffered in a consumer-type transaction (such as purchasing office supplies) or has the potential to affect consumers generally. A business plaintiff asserting that it was harmed by deception of its potential consumers must likewise show that the harm was more than simple private loss—ordinary trademark infringement, for example, harms the trademark owner, but unless the infringing product poses health or safety risks, it doesn't implicate a sufficient public interest under the state's false advertising law.

Further, whether or not they allow competitors to sue, many state consumer fraud laws limit their scope to transactions involving "consumers," defined as those purchasing for personal, family or household use. Cases involving specialized products purchased only by businesses can therefore not be brought under state law, whether brought by the direct victim or by the false advertiser's competitors. In addition, these consumer-oriented rules exclude claims based on negotiation for personalized products or unique contracts and claims by retailers who bought goods for resale. *See, e.g.*, Abraham v. Penn Mut. Life Ins. Co., 2000 WL 1051845 (S.D.N.Y. 2000) (listing as possible sources of consumer-oriented injury that an insurance policy was sold to the public at large or that the insurer treated an entire class of policies or other policyholders similarly).

Some states choose to limit the reach of the law on the defendant/*seller's* side, covering only practices in the course of a person's business, vocation or occupation. How should a court in a state with a seller-side limitation evaluate whether a person who sells fifteen items a year on eBay is engaged in "business"? *Cf.* Real v. Radir Wheels, Inc., 969 A.2d 1069, 1079 (N.J. 2009) ("[t]here is no doubt that" an individual eBay seller "himself satisfies the statutory definition of 'person'" such that he may be held liable under the NJCFA's general antifraud provision); William J. Diggs, Comment,

Consumer Protection in an eBay Marketplace: An Analysis of the Supreme Court of New Jersey's Radir Wheels Decision to Extend Liability under the New Jersey Consumer Fraud Act to Individual eBay Sellers, 40 SETON HALL L. REV. 811, 813 (2010) ("Notably, eighty-four percent of Internet-auction fraud is committed by a seller who is not engaged in the trade or business of making sales of the type of which he made on eBay . . . ; only the remaining sixteen percent is committed by a seller who is engaged in the trade or business of making sales of the type of which he made on eBay . . . . ") (citation omitted).

Class actions, in which a small number of class representatives bring a claim in the name of a much larger group, alleging common injuries and demanding shared remedies, merit a course of their own. This form of litigation makes lawyers passionate—both on the defense and plaintiff sides. In part, this is because there is a well-defined defense bar (representing advertisers) and a plaintiff's bar (representing consumers) with very few common members. In contrast, in Lanham Act lawsuits, competitors often flip between plaintiff (challenging their rivals) and defense (being challenged), so litigators representing those clients don't view themselves as plaintiff- or defense-oriented.

This chapter attempts to give a sense of the issues that recur specifically in consumer protection class action cases, which make up a large and apparently growing fraction of class actions. We cover key issues in certification, such as choice of law (multi-state or single-state); whether individualized issues of reliance and damages preclude class treatment; and other barriers to certification.

No matter how many obstacles courts and defense counsel put up, a few class actions do survive, at least at the motion to dismiss stage, and sometimes even at the certification stage. Whether this pattern continues indefinitely remains to be seen. As you read through this section, keep an eye on the ever-growing checklist of prerequisites to successfully achieving class certification, especially in a contested case (as opposed to approving a class for settlement purposes only).

For further reading, the National Association of Consumer Advocates has a useful volume that covers important elements of consumer class action practice from both descriptive and normative standpoints. NATIONAL ASSOCIATION OF CONSUMER ADVOCATES, Standards and Guidelines for Litigating and Settling Class Actions (3d ed. 2014). A number of courts have referred to the Guidelines in their own decisions. *See, e.g.,* Figueroa v. Sharper Image Corp., 517 F. Supp. 2d 1292 (S.D. Fla. 2007).

Judge Posner provided an overview of the core dilemma of the class action in *Eubank v. Pella Corp.,* 753 F.3d 718 (7th Cir. 2014):

> The class action is an ingenious procedural innovation that enables persons who have suffered a wrongful injury, but are too numerous for joinder of their claims alleging the same wrong committed by the same defendant or defendants to be feasible, to obtain relief as a group, a class as it is called. The device is especially important when each claim is too small to justify the expense of a separate suit, so that without a class action there would be no relief, however meritorious the claims. Normally only a few of the claimants are named as plaintiffs .... The named plaintiffs are the representatives of the class—fiduciaries of its members—and therefore charged with monitoring the lawyers who prosecute the case on behalf of the class (class counsel). They receive modest compensation, in addition to their damages as class members, for their normally quite limited services—often little more than sitting for a deposition—as class representatives. Invariably they are selected by class counsel, who as a practical matter control the litigation by the class. The selection of the class representatives by class counsel inevitably dilutes their fiduciary commitment.
>
> The class action is a worthwhile supplement to conventional litigation procedure, but it is controversial and embattled, in part because it is frequently abused. The control of the class over its lawyers usually is attenuated, often to the point of nonexistence. Except for the named plaintiffs, the members of the class are more like beneficiaries than like parties; for although they are authorized to appeal from an adverse

judgment, they have no control over class counsel....Class actions are the brainchildren of the lawyers who specialize in prosecuting such actions, and in picking class representatives they have no incentive to select persons capable or desirous of monitoring the lawyers' conduct of the litigation.

A high percentage of lawsuits is settled—but a study of certified class actions in federal court in a two-year period (2005 to 2007) found that all 30 such actions had been settled. The reasons that class actions invariably are settled are twofold. Aggregating a great many claims (sometimes tens or even hundreds of thousands—occasionally millions) often creates a potential liability so great that the defendant is unwilling to bear the risk, even if it is only a small probability, of an adverse judgment. At the same time, class counsel, ungoverned as a practical matter by either the named plaintiffs or the other members of the class, have an opportunity to maximize their attorneys' fees—which (besides other expenses) are all they can get from the class action—at the expense of the class. The defendant cares only about the size of the settlement, not how it is divided between attorneys' fees and compensation for the class. From the selfish standpoint of class counsel and the defendant, therefore, the optimal settlement is one modest in overall amount but heavily tilted toward attorneys' fees....

Fortunately the settlement, including the amount of attorneys' fees to award to class counsel, must be approved by the district judge presiding over the case; unfortunately American judges are accustomed to presiding over adversary proceedings. They expect the clash of the adversaries to generate the information that the judge needs to decide the case. And so when a judge is being urged by both adversaries to approve the class-action settlement that they've negotiated, he's at a disadvantage in evaluating the fairness of the settlement to the class.

Judge Posner goes on to explain that objectors, "[m]embers of the class who smell a rat," can object, and the judge must evaluate those objections. If the objectors succeed and a more favorable settlement is ultimately approved, they receive a cash award. But this dynamic—potentially great risk for defendants, low reward for any given class member, potentially great reward for class attorneys—affects every part of the class action proceeding, not just settlement. Keep these issues in mind as you read the materials that follow.

Increasing Barriers of Many Kinds to Class Actions

Companies can suppress class action litigation by directing consumer litigation into arbitration. Contractual arbitration clauses can contain "no-class-adjudication provisions" that can expressly say that class actions can't be heard in arbitration.

AT&T Mobility v. Concepcion, 563 U.S. 321 (2011), represented the death knell for many consumer class actions. AT&T used a contract that provided for mandatory arbitration of any disputes and prohibited class-wide arbitration (that is, an arbitration on behalf of a class; arbitration could only proceed on an individual-by-individual basis). California followed a rule that a contractual ban on class actions in consumer contracts is inherently unconscionable and thus unenforceable. The Supreme Court reversed, holding that the Federal Arbitration Act preempted this rule as applied to arbitration contracts.

Since *Concepcion*, courts are increasingly upholding mandatory arbitration clauses, including those that block class formation. Companies are also expanding their use of mandatory arbitration clauses. As a result, Myriam Gilles & Gary Friedman, *After Class:*

Aggregate Litigation in the Wake of AT&T Mobility v. Concepcion, 79
U. CHI. L. REV. 623 (2012), have argued that "many—indeed, most—
of the companies that touch consumers' day-to-day lives can and will
now place themselves beyond the reach of aggregate litigation,
including telephone companies, Internet service providers, credit card
issuers, payday lenders, mortgage lenders, health clubs, nursing
homes, retail banks, investment banks, mutual funds and the sellers
of all manner of goods and services."

Because mass-market retailers rarely attempt to impose contract
terms on their customers, the vast majority of current consumer class
actions are for simple products purchased in stores, which generally
don't have class action waivers attached—yet. But if retailers and
consumer products manufacturers could figure out how to impose
class action waivers, they would almost certainly try. For example, in
2014, major food manufacturer General Mills purported to adopt a
class action waiver that would be triggered by using General Mills
coupons downloaded online, using its websites, or "liking" its
Facebook page, but soon retreated in the face of consumer backlash.
See John Aziz, *General Mills Backed Down from Its Controversial
Lawsuit Policy. But the Problem Isn't Over*, TheWeek.com, Apr. 22,
2014. Additional, and presumably more subtle or clever, attempts by
manufacturers to induce consumers to contractually agree to
arbitration are surely coming.

Even without *Concepcion*, the Class Action Fairness Act of 2005
("CAFA"), 28 U.S.C. §§ 1332(d), 1453, and 1711–1715, expanded
federal jurisdiction (and thus allowing removal from state courts) to
include class actions in which the amount in controversy exceeds $5
million, and in which any of the members of a class of plaintiffs is a
citizen of a state different from any defendant, unless at least two-
thirds or more of the members of all proposed plaintiff classes in the
aggregate and the primary defendants are citizens of the state in

which the action was originally filed. CAFA also directed greater scrutiny of class action settlements.

Its aim was to rein in a perceived explosion of class actions against businesses, particularly in certain allegedly overly plaintiff-friendly state courts. As a result, a substantial amount of class action practice shifted to federal courts. Still, some plaintiffs are so determined to stay in state court that it's changed how they plead their cases, such as class actions that voluntarily confine themselves to asking less than $5 million.

Consumer protection class actions are an important subset of class actions, and thus profoundly affected by CAFA. A study by the Federal Judicial Center found a post-CAFA increase in the number of class actions filed in or removed to the federal courts based on diversity jurisdiction, due primarily to increases in consumer class actions. Perhaps surprisingly, many plaintiffs' attorneys are consciously attempting to satisfy the requirements of CAFA, perhaps to avoid a lengthy and expensive fight over removal. *See* Emery G. Lee et al., *The Impact of the Class Action Fairness Act of 2005 on the Federal Courts* (April 2008).

Certification is required for a plaintiff to represent, and potentially bind, an entire class. Federal class actions are governed by FRCP Rule 23, and a consumer class action will essentially always be maintained as a Rule 23(b)(3) class action, which requires a judicial finding that "questions of law or fact common to class members predominate over any questions affecting only individual members, and that a class action is superior to other available methods for fairly and efficiently adjudicating the controversy." Courts break this down into requirements of "commonality," "predominance," and "superiority."

Courts have imposed increasing barriers to certification of class actions, rejecting certification of most non-federal question class actions. *See* Joel S. Feldman, *Class Certification Issues for Non-Federal Question Class Actions—Defense Perspective*, 728 PLI/Lit 221 (2005). The key issue is predominance, both legal and factual. Though federal courts have taken the lead in this reasoning, many state courts have followed suit, as their class action rules generally mimic the federal rules.

The Supreme Court's defendant-favorable decision in *Wal-Mart Stores, Inc. v. Dukes*, 564 U.S. 338 (2011), concerned an employment discrimination class action and a provision of Rule 23 under which consumer class actions are rarely certified. However, it more broadly signaled the Court's discomfort with class actions that put defendants at risk of large damage awards, even when that risk exists simply because the number of people affected is so large. For arguments that the empirical evidence doesn't support the courts' fear of coercive and unjustified class actions, see Joanna C. Schwartz, *The Cost of Suing Business*, 65 DEPAUL L. REV. __ (forthcoming 2016) ("One would expect that, were defendants accepting blackmail settlements, they would do so immediately after certification to avoid the costs of discovery. Instead, it appears that defendants do not generally settle soon after certification and often proceed through discovery. Moreover, settlement and trial rates in class actions are comparable to rates in non-class cases, suggesting that class actions, on the whole, are no more coercive to defendants than any other kind of litigation.").

Initially, many multistate consumer class actions fail due to variations among state laws. Defendants identify different standards of proof, different elements for the cause of action, different statutes of limitation, different definitions of who can sue, different intent requirements, and so on. When legal differences are sufficient, common legal issues don't predominate, and also a class action would be unmanageable—it would be impossible to instruct a jury on all the different laws. *See, e.g.,* Castano v. Am. Tobacco Co., 84 F.3d 734 (5th Cir. 1996).

Some courts even consider the extra pressure a class action puts on defendants as a reason that a class action is not superior to individualized adjudications; the theory is that by raising the stakes for defendants, class actions encourage them to settle even unmeritorious claims—legalized blackmail. Is this an appropriate factor to consider in analyzing superiority? Should courts also consider the extra leverage class actions provide to plaintiffs whose individual claims are too small to justify litigation but whose aggregate losses are large? How should a court determine which consideration is more important in any given case?

Factual variation is another key basis for denying class certification. Where reliance or a reliance-type analysis (such as causation or damages) is at issue, some courts hold that individualized proof would be required for each plaintiff. Thus, common factual issues don't predominate. Factual variation is important because it means that even a single-state class may be impossible to maintain. *See, e.g.,* Peltier Enter., Inc. v. Hilton, 51 S.W.3d 616, 624 (Tex. Ct. App. 2000) (claim under Texas law requires individualized proof because reliance is an essential element).

Other states presume reliance, materiality, or causation based on deceptive acts or practices, allowing a class action to proceed, but state-by-state analysis is essential. *Compare, e.g.,* Sikes v. Teleline, Inc., 281 F.3d 1350 (11th Cir. 2002) (refusing to presume reliance on misrepresentations because presumptions should benefit parties who don't control evidence on an issue, and individual plaintiffs best know the facts of their own reliance), *with, e.g.,* Varacallo v. Mass. Mut. Life Ins. Co., 752 A.2d 807 (N.J. Super. Ct. App. Div. 2000) (ordering certification of a class consisting of all New Jersey residents who purchased certain life insurance policies from defendant during the class period; presuming reliance and fraud where claim was based on insurer's omission of material information with intent that consumers rely on the omission).

Some courts have held that the class action rules contain an implicit requirement of "ascertainability," under which courts in consumer cases have refused to certify classes in the absence of reliable proof of purchase or a knowable list of injured plaintiffs. *See* Carrera v. Bayer Corp., 727 F.3d 300 (3d Cir. 2013) (holding that certification when neither class members nor defendants would have purchase records risks due process violations); *cf., e.g.,* Karhu v. Vital Pharms., Inc., 2014 WL 815253 (S.D. Fla. 2014) (finding class action against dietary supplement maker unmanageable because membership could not be verified without central purchase records or proof of purchase). This requirement, Gilles & Friedman argue, "has sounded a death knell for many (if not most) cases arising from small retail purchases." Cases involving peanut butter, cough medicine, pineapples, cookware, and aspirin have all been dismissed on ascertainability grounds.

Other courts disagree with this conclusion, holding that ascertainability merely requires that an objective definition of the class must be provided, even if class members don't retain receipts. *See* Forcellati v. Hyland's, Inc., 2014 WL 1410264 (C.D. Cal. Apr. 9, 2014) (facilitating small claims is "[t]he policy at the very core of the class action mechanism").

In other variants, courts find that the class isn't ascertainable if the representation at issue was made in an ad instead of the product package or label, since not every purchaser might have seen the ads. (This can also be restated as a commonality problem.) *See* In re POM Wonderful LLC, 2014 WL 1225184 (C.D. Cal. 2014) (decertifying a class for this reason, among others).

Or class certification might be impossible because there's no adequate damages model allowing class compensation. If class action plaintiffs aren't each entitled to a statutory damages award—and in many states they aren't—there needs to be a way of figuring out what they lost (restitution) or what defendants gained (disgorgement). If the product or service at issue wasn't completely worthless, how do we know how much of the price should be attributed to the misrepresentation? What if different people bought for different reasons, and some would have paid just as much without the misrepresentation—are they all entitled to an award regardless? Plaintiffs increasingly allege that a misrepresentation allowed defendants to charge a price premium. While this allegation may survive a motion to dismiss, it may be hard to support sufficiently to achieve certification. *See* In re POM Wonderful LLC, 2014 WL 1225184 (C.D. Cal. 2014) (rejecting a price premium model because it depended on a "fraud on the market" theory; plaintiffs failed to establish why Pom's higher price resulted from its misrepresentations, so damages couldn't be shown on a class-wide basis).

Plaintiffs have tried various workarounds to these problems. Federal courts often reject attempts to apply the law of the defendant's state to a nationwide consumer class. The theory is that choice of law principles and constitutional due process usually require analyzing claims based on plaintiffs' domicile, thus meaning that multiple jurisdictions' laws are implicated. *See* Lyon v. Caterpillar, Inc., 194 F.R.D. 206 (E.D. Pa. 2000) ("All of the relevant jurisdictions have an interest in utilizing the state statute crafted by their state's legislature to protect their consumers and/or residents . . . .").

The Ninth Circuit, where many consumer protection class actions are litigated, has made it almost impossible to certify a nationwide class. Mazza v. Am. Honda Motor Co., 666 F.3d 581 (9th Cir. 2012). A few nationwide classes using a single state's law have, however, been certified. *See, e.g.,* Forcellati v. Hyland's, Inc., 2014 WL 1410264 (C.D. Cal. 2014) (even after *Mazza*, defendants must identify relevant differences in state law; where California-based defendants' homeopathic product was allegedly completely useless and where defendants failed to engage in detailed state-by-state analysis, nationwide class was appropriate). Should it matter to the analysis if defendants can identify another state's laws that are more protective of consumers, if defendants may not face suit in that jurisdiction? *See* Barry A. Weprin, *Plaintiffs' Perspective on Recent Developments in Class Certification of Sales Practice Claims: The Focus Shifts to State Consumer Statutes,* ALI-ABA Conference on Life and Health Insurance Litigation, May 1–2, 2003 ("Courts should treat with healthy skepticism defendant's purported concerns for a consumer's right to litigate under the laws of his or her own state. What such defendants really seek, of course, is to defeat certification so that they need never face the merits of the class claims").

An alternative is subclassing: dividing state laws into types, much as our overview in Chapter 3 did, for issues such as whether reliance is required. Courts have generally rejected subclassing as well, both because it's hard to find exact correspondences between different states' laws and because it's still very difficult to instruct a jury on multiple subclasses.

Still another alternative is partial certification: class treatment for liability or causation, for example, with an individual stage for damages. This too has not proved popular, even though Rule 23(c)(4)(A) specifically provides that "[w]hen appropriate . . . an action may be brought or maintained as a class action with respect to particular issues."

The most successful strategy has been single-state classes, usually filed in large-population states (California, Illinois, Massachusetts and New York are common). In states willing to presume class-wide reliance and deception, a single-state class has some chance of certification.

Amchem Products, Inc. v. Windsor, 521 U.S. 591 (1997), varied the analysis somewhat for a "settlement class," where both parties ask the court for certification so they can settle a claim comprehensively. Manageability isn't an issue for a settlement class; factual and legal variation therefore are less significant problems. *See, e.g.*, O'Keefe v. Mercedes-Benz USA, LLC, 214 F.R.D. 266 (E.D. Pa. 2003) (certifying settlement class based on state consumer fraud statutes). As a result, defendants can decide if they want to defeat class certification based on state-level legal variations, or if they would rather settle and thereby "buy" national resolution of a problem.

Amchem does, however, require that the other portions of Rule 23 designed to protect absentees "demand undiluted, even heightened, attention in the settlement context," so that settlements aren't overbroad or under-compensatory. Courts may conditionally certify a settlement class: if the settlement dissolves, certification must be relitigated. No certification, whether for a litigation class or a settlement class, is final until the court enters judgment approving the settlement after a Rule 23(e) fairness hearing.

Special Rules for California

California has historically had broad consumer protection laws—generally known as the UCL (Unfair Competition Law), FAL (False Advertising Law), and CLRA (Consumer Legal Remedies Act)—and its courts are willing to entertain consumer claims. Combined with the fact that California's economy is, on its own, one of the largest in the world, California is a magnet for consumer class actions. Even a California-only class has the potential to make a defendant very nervous, and, as noted above, California courts occasionally entertain nationwide class actions under California law where the defendant's conduct occurred in California. Though California has cut back, both legislatively and judicially, on the scope of its laws, it remains a vital source of consumer protection law. The UCL Practitioner blog covers California UCL, FAL and related cases.

After *Kasky v. Nike*, discussed in Chapter 2, California residents voted for Proposition 64, a measure that imposed an injury requirement on private plaintiffs: they must have suffered injury in fact and have lost money or property as a result of the unfair practice at issue. The California Supreme Court interpreted Proposition 64 in *In re Tobacco II Cases*, 46 Cal. 4th 298 (Cal. 2009). The court emphasized that California's UCL differed from common law fraud, which requires knowing falsity and reasonable reliance by the victim. Injunctive relief under the UCL requires neither, because it focuses on defendant's conduct, rather than plaintiff's damages, in service of larger consumer protection goals.

The trial court had granted defendants' motion for decertification in *Tobacco II*, a case about cigarette marketing, because it reasoned that absent class members each had to show that they met Proposition 64's standing requirements, and individualized reliance determinations are inconsistent with class actions.

The California Supreme Court reversed. Only the representative plaintiff was required to meet the injury-in-fact/lost-money-or-property requirement. To effectuate the law's purposes, including the ability to grant injunctive relief and to award restitution to those who have been harmed, relief for false advertising under the UCL is available without individualized proof of deception, reliance, and injury.

Given that Proposition 64 was clearly designed to impose limits on private claims under the UCL, it did impose an actual reliance requirement on private plaintiffs suing under the UCL's fraud prong.

CHAPTER 7: CONSUMER CLASS ACTIONS

However, a plaintiff can prove reliance by showing that the defendant's misrepresentation or nondisclosure was an "immediate cause" of her injury; and this can be done by showing that, without the misrepresentation or nondisclosure, the plaintiff "in all reasonable probability" wouldn't have engaged in the injury-producing conduct. She need not show that the misrepresentation was the only cause of the injury-producing conduct, or even the predominant or decisive factor, as long as it played a substantial part in influencing her decision.

Moreover, "a presumption, or at least an inference, of reliance arises wherever there is a showing that a misrepresentation was material." Where a plaintiff alleges exposure to a long-term advertising campaign, "the plaintiff is not required to plead with an unrealistic degree of specificity that the plaintiff relied on particular advertisements or statements." As a California appellate court explained, "Plaintiffs may satisfy their burden of showing causation as to each by showing materiality as to all." *In re* Vioxx Class Cases, 180 Cal. App. 4th 116 (Cal. Ct. App. 2009).

The upshot of *Tobacco II* is that while the named class representatives must meet the new standing requirements, including reliance when the claim involves "fraudulent" conduct, the showing required for unnamed class members has not changed, and individualized proof of deception, reliance and injury are not required for them. The focus of the inquiry is on the reasonable consumer who is a member of the target population.

In *Kwikset Corporation v. The Superior Court of Orange County*, 51 Cal.4th 310 (Cal. 2011), the California Supreme Court further emphasized that "plaintiffs who can truthfully allege they were deceived by a product's label into spending money to purchase the product, and would not have purchased it otherwise, have 'lost money or property' within the meaning of Proposition 64 and have standing to sue." Thus, plausible allegations that, were it not for defendants' misrepresentations, plaintiffs would not have bought a product are sufficient to survive a motion to dismiss, even if the product worked fine and was no more expensive than competing products. (What kind of damages would be appropriate in such a case?)

We will now examine two cases with opposing results. Together, they provide a survey of many of the most common arguments in consumer protection class actions. A defendant-favorable ruling often finds multiple issues blocking certification; when you read *Elations*, keep track of how many of these issues were resolved against the plaintiff as a matter of law and how many were rejected on the facts as alleged. You will see that there are a large number of class action legal issues that divide district courts, without significant guidance yet from the Supreme Court (or indeed from most federal appellate courts).

Algarin v. Maybelline, LLC, 300 F.R.D. 444 (N.D. Cal. 2014)

This action arises out of the allegedly deceptive nature [in which] Defendant Maybelline, LLC, labels and advertises its Superstay 24HR product line. Plaintiffs . . . bring this putative class action pursuant to California's Unfair Competition Law ("UCL") and California's Legal Remedies Act ("CLRA") seeking both monetary and injunctive relief. Presently before the Court is Plaintiffs' motion for class certification. . . . For the following reasons, Plaintiffs' motion is DENIED.

I. BACKGROUND

A. Factual Background

Maybelline manufactures, markets, sells and distributes SuperStay 24HR Lipcolor, a line of lipcolors, and SuperStay 24HR Makeup, a line of skin foundations (collectively the "Class Products"). The Lipcolor features the label "SuperStay 24," "Micro-Flex Formula," "No Transfer," and "Up to 24HR Wear." The Makeup features the Label "SuperStay Makeup 24HR," "Micro-Flex Formula," "ZeroTransfer," and "24HR Wear." . . .

Plaintiff Algarin purchased the SuperStay Lipcolor for $10.00 in reliance on the claimed 24-hour staying power. Plaintiff Murdock purchased the SuperStay Makeup for $12.00 also in reliance on the claimed 24-hour coverage. Both Plaintiffs gave full credence to the claimed 24-hour duration and were thus willing to pay a premium for that purported benefit. Both Plaintiffs used the products as directed and needless to say, were decidedly unimpressed. Plaintiffs were exasperated that the products failed to live up to the representations as "neither the lipcolor nor the foundation lasted 24 hours, or anywhere near 24 hours. . . ." Had the two Plaintiffs known the "truth" about the "premium priced" Class Products, they would have purchased less expensive options. . . .

Maybelline allows dissatisfied consumers to make their complaints known to the company, and in some circumstances will issue a refund, through its Refund Program. . . . Between the Products' launch dates and mid-2013, approximately 2,700 consumers contacted Maybelline regarding the lipcolor and 700 regarding the makeup. Of these communications, 604 were performance complaints about the lipcolor and 97 about the makeup. The median compensation for the lipcolor is $10.00 and for the makeup is $11.00.

. . . Because of the Class Product's deceptive labels and advertisements, Maybelline is able to charge a "hefty price premium." The Lipcolor retails for approximately $10.00–$12.00, which is $1.00–$1.50 higher than other Maybelline products. The Makeup retails for approximately $11.00–$12.00, which is $1.00–$3.00 higher than other

Maybelline foundations. Plaintiffs attribute this price premium solely to the alleged misrepresentations. . . .

II.   LEGAL STANDARD

A.   Class Certification

Federal Rule of Civil Procedure governs class actions. The party seeking certification must provide facts sufficient to satisfy the requirements of Rule 23(a) and (b). "Before certifying a class, the trial court must conduct a 'rigorous analysis' to determine whether the party seeking certification has met the prerequisites of [Rule] 23." Rule 23(a) requires that plaintiffs demonstrate numerosity, commonality, typicality and adequacy of representation in order to maintain a class. If the court finds the action meets the requirements of Rule 23(a), the court then considers whether the class is maintainable under Rule 23(b). In the instant matter, Plaintiffs seek certification under both 23(b)(2) and 23(b)(3).

Rule 23(b)(2) applies when "the party opposing the class has acted or refused to act on grounds that apply generally to the class, so that final injunctive relief or corresponding declaratory relief is appropriate respecting the class as a whole." Claims for monetary relief may not be certified under Rule 23(b)(2), at least where the monetary relief is not incidental to the requested injunctive or declaratory relief. Instead, individualized monetary claims belong in Rule 23(b)(3), "with its procedural protections of predominance, superiority, mandatory notice, and the right to opt out." Rule 23(b)(3) requires the court to find that questions of law or fact common to class members predominate over any questions affecting only individual members, and that a class action is superior to other available methods for fairly and efficiently adjudicating the controversy.

The merits of class members' substantive claims are highly relevant when determining whether to certify a class. It is not correct to say a district court may consider the merits to the extent that they overlap with certification issues; rather, "a district court must consider the merits if they overlap with the Rule 23(a) requirements." Nevertheless, the district court does not conduct a mini-trial to determine if the class "could actually prevail on their claims." . . .

III.   DISCUSSION . . .

Of great importance to the matters in this class certification is the fact Maybelline has introduced unrefuted evidence of who the reasonable consumer in the target audience is and what drives her in making purchasing decisions. As Maybelline contends, the Court does not need to look to the hypothetical reasonable consumer. Similarly, the Court does not need to infer reliance given the evidence presented.

C.   Maybelline's Expert Report

Maybelline's expert, Dr. Eli Seggev, is an expert in the field of marketing. After a thorough review of the Seggev report, the Court finds him qualified, and his opinion to be based on reliable methodologies, relevant to the issues at hand, and useful to the trier of fact. . . .

Dr. Seggev reports that repeat purchasing is a behavioral indicator of customer satisfaction and it follows that repeat purchasers are fully informed as to the duration claims and realities when they decided to purchase the Class Products again. Indeed, with cosmetics such as the ones at issue here, customers can readily discern how well they work and whether they lived up to the claimed representations. Accordingly, repeat purchasers cannot be considered injured in the manner proposed by Plaintiffs. As to the SuperStay lipcolor, Dr.

Seggev's Report indicates that: (1) 45% of purchasers were satisfied with the product based on repeat purchases; (2) duration was not the only motivating factor in making the purchases; (3) over half of purchasers could not recall duration expectations or were satisfied with the duration of the product; (4) 4% of the total sample expected the specific 24-hour duration showing duration expectations varied among purchasers; and (5) only 9% of the total sample were one-time purchasers who expected the product to last 24-hours and thus are "injured" in the manner alleged by Plaintiffs. [The numbers for the makeup were similar though slightly less favorable to Maybelline.] . .
.

D. Ascertainable Class

Though not explicitly stated in Rule 23, courts have held that the class must be adequately defined and clearly ascertainable before a class action may proceed. A class is sufficiently defined and ascertainable if it is "administratively feasible for the court to determine whether a particular individual is a member." . . . "[A]n identifiable class exists if its members can be ascertained by reference to objective criteria, but not if membership is contingent on a prospective member's state of mind."

Maybelline argues the proposed class fails to meet the ascertainability requirement based on two grounds. First, the proposed class is overly broad as it includes uninjured purchasers. Second, membership of the class cannot be readily determined.

Maybelline's first argument is essentially a challenge on the proposed class members' standing. Maybelline presents evidence, in the form of Dr. Seggev's survey and report as well as Maybelline's Early Trier Study, to show the proposed class includes: (1) a large percentage of the potential class of SuperStay purchasers are repeat purchasers who cannot be considered to be misled by the duration representation identified by Plaintiffs and (2) one-time purchases of the Class Products who had no duration expectations and whose purchasing decisions were made without regard to product duration. Because the proposed class includes these "uninjured" purchasers, the class is impermissibly overbroad and thus unascertainable.

As to these arguments regarding the inability of proposed members to show injury, the Court finds them more suitable for analysis under the Rule 23 rubric given the facts of this case. Though it may be true that many purchasers of the Class Products did not rely on the duration claims or were satisfied with the products, and thus "uninjured," these issues would not affect the Court's analysis of ascertainability based on the facts in the instant case.

Consumer action classes that have been found to be overbroad generally include members who were never exposed to the alleged misrepresentations at all. In the instant case, Plaintiffs have alleged a widespread advertising campaign promoting the alleged misrepresentations as well as uniform labeling for each of the Class Products. That the proposed class may include purchasers who did not rely on the misrepresentations and/or were satisfied with the products does not render the class "overbroad" where Maybelline has failed to demonstrate a lack of exposure as to some class members. Maybelline further argues that because the class does not exclude purchasers who have already received refunds through Maybelline's Refund program, it is overbroad and not ascertainable. The Court agrees. As the UCL only permits recovery or restitution/disgorgement, for purchasers who have already received refunds, they have already been compensated well over any potential disgorgement. These purchasers have no claims. However, exclusion of these purchasers from the class definition would still not render certification appropriate.

The Court is satisfied that Plaintiffs' class definition is ascertainable in the sense that class membership can be determined based on an objective criterion. In the instant matter, that criterion will be whether members purchased either the SuperStay lipcolor or the SuperStay makeup. However, the Court is concerned that Plaintiffs have failed to provide a reliable method of determining who the actual members of the class are, indeed as Maybelline contends, such a task may be impossible.

Though the class may be ascertainable in the sense that there are objective criteria for determining who its members are, it is not in the sense that members could actually ever be determined. Plaintiffs have failed to show how it is "administratively feasible to determine whether a particular person is a class member." This inquiry overlaps with the "manageability" prong of Rule 23(b)(3) (D), in which a court assesses whether a class action is superior to other available methods of fairly and efficiently adjudicating the controversy.

Maybelline argues purchasers are unlikely to have documentary proof of purchase and Maybelline does not maintain a purchaser list or other identifying method. In such a situation, the Court and the parties would necessarily rely on class members to self-identify. The Court shares Maybelline's concerns. Indeed there are a number of cases that stand for the proposition that where a court has no way to verify if a purchaser is actually a class member, class certification may be improper.

Cases where self-identification alone has been deemed sufficient generally involve situations where consumers are likely to retain receipts, where the relevant purchase was a memorable "big ticket" item; or where defendant would have access to a master list of consumers or retailers. None of these factors exist in the instant case. The Class Products are small-ticket items that cost between $10.00 to $13.00, it is extremely unlikely the average purchaser would retain receipts and perhaps even remember she purchased the specific SuperStay products versus other similar Maybelline or competitor products. According to deposition testimony taken from named Plaintiffs, even they themselves did not retain receipts and had difficulty recalling many details about their purchases. . . .

However, a lack of ascertainability alone will not defeat class certification. As long as the class definition is sufficiently definite to identify putative class members, "the challenges entailed in the administration of this class are not so burdensome as to defeat certification." Thus, the Court continues to analyze whether the requirements of Rule 23(a) and 23(b) are met.

E. Rule 23(a)

Rule 23(a) provides a class action may proceed only where: (1) the class members are so numerous that joinder is impracticable; (2) common questions of law or fact exist; (3) the claims or defenses of the representative parties are typical of the class; and (4) the representative parties will fairly and adequately protect the interests of the class. Fed.R.Civ.P. 23(a).

1. Numerosity and Adequacy

Maybelline does not dispute that the proposed class meets the numerosity requirement nor do they dispute whether named Plaintiffs and counsel meet the adequacy requirement. Accordingly, the Court . . . finds these two requirements satisfied.

2. Commonality

The commonality factor "requires the plaintiff to demonstrate that the class members have suffered the same injury, which does not mean merely that they have all suffered a violation of the same

596

provision of law." The "claims must depend on a common contention" and "that common contention . . . must be of such a nature that it is capable of class-wide resolution." The existence of shared legal issues with divergent factual predicates is sufficient, as is a common core of salient facts coupled with disparate legal remedies within the class." . . . [F]or purposes of Rule 23(a)(2), even a single common question will suffice.

Plaintiffs have identified several questions of law or fact common to the class: (1) whether the 24-hour/no transfer representation is true, or is misleading, or objectively reasonably likely to receive; (2) whether Maybelline engaged in false or misleading advertising; (3) whether Maybelline's alleged conduct violates public policy; (4) whether Maybelline's alleged conduct constitutes violations of the laws asserted; (5) the proper measure of the loss suffered by Plaintiffs and Class members; and (6) whether Plaintiffs and Class members are entitled to other appropriate remedies, including corrective advertising and injunctive relief. . . .

In light of the objective evidence showing that there was a substantial number of class members who were not misled by the 24-hour claim, whether Maybelline's conduct was false or misleading or likely to deceive is not subject to common proof on a class-wide basis. According to survey results, purchasers had a variety of duration expectations. Indeed, more purchasers expected the product to last less than 24 hours or had no specific duration expectations. Moreover, given the persuasive evidence presented on consumer expectations, the varying factors that influence purchasing decision, and consumer satisfaction, the Court finds that Plaintiffs have also failed to demonstrate that the elements of materiality and reliance are subject to common proof.

Expert evidence shows that materiality and reliance varies from consumer to consumer. Accordingly, the Court finds that these elements are not an issue subject to common proof.

Finally, the existence of economic injury is also not a common question as many purchasers were satisfied with the Class Products. [E.g.,] reviews say "This is the best lipcolor ever . . . I will be back for more," "I love this [lipcolor] . . . I will order more in the future," and "I am so happy I tried this foundation . . . this is my new foundation." As for the other questions of law and fact posed, it is arguable that they may support a finding of commonality under the permissive standards governing this inquiry. As noted above, commonality can be established by the presence of a single significant common issue. However, Plaintiffs meet their downfall with the typicality requirement.

3.   Typicality

Typicality requires a determination as to whether the named plaintiffs' claims are typical of those of the class members they seek to represent. "[R]epresentative claims are 'typical' if they are reasonably co-extensive with those of absent class members; they need not be substantially identical." Typicality, like commonality, is a "permissive standard[ ]." . . . To assess whether or not named Plaintiffs' claims are typical, the Court examines " 'whether other members have the same or similar injury.' " In other words, the inquiry is whether other members have the same or similar injury, whether the action is based on conduct which is not unique to named plaintiffs, and whether other class members have been injured by the same course of conduct.

The Court's analysis of the commonality requirement also informs the analysis for typicality. Based upon the evidence presented, the named

Plaintiffs' reliance on the alleged misrepresentations was not typical of other class members.

. . . The Court further concludes that class certification under either 23(b)(2) or 23(b)(3) is improper.

F. Rule 23(b)(2)

A class is proper under 23(b)(2) where the party opposing the class has acted or refused to act on grounds that apply generally to the class, so that final injunctive relief or corresponding declaratory relief is appropriate respecting the class as a whole. Class certification under Rule 23(b) (2) is appropriate only where the primary relief sought is declaratory or injunctive." For classes certified pursuant to Rule 23(b)(2), monetary damages must be "merely incidental to the primary claim for injunctive relief."

. . . [T]he restitution and disgorgement sought are not "incidental." Named Plaintiffs cannot possibly benefit from injunctive relief as they are now (or at least should be) fully knowledgeable that the Class Products do not last 24 hours. Thus monetary relief is necessarily their "primary concern." Rule 23(b)(2) "does not authorize class certification where each class member would be entitled to an individualized award of monetary damages." . . . Certification is improper where, as here, the request for injunctive and/or declaratory relief is merely a foundational step towards a damages award which requires follow-on individual inquiries to determine each class member's entitlement to damages.

G. Rule 23(b)(3)

Certification pursuant to Rule 23(b)(3) requires Plaintiffs to establish that "the questions of law or fact common to the members of the class predominate over any questions affecting only individual members and that a class action is superior to other available methods for the fair and efficient adjudication of the controversy."

1. Common Questions do not Predominate over Individual Inquiries

Rule 23(b) (3) predominance requires the class to be sufficiently cohesive to warrant adjudication by representation. This inquiry is more stringent than the commonality requirement of Rule 23(a)(2). . .
.

The Court's analysis with regards [sic] to commonality under Rule 23(a) is fully applicable in the analysis of predominance. Given the number of individual purchasing inquiries as well as the evidence showing materiality and reliance varies consumer to consumer, it is evident that common issues do not predominate. Additionally, and of great importance, is the fact that Plaintiffs have failed to demonstrate sufficient evidence showing that any damages claimed to stem from the alleged misconduct.

. . . [A] party seeking certification must offer a class-wide means for calculating damages.

. . . While a court of equity "may exercise its full range of powers in order to accomplish complete justice between the parties," the restitution awarded must be a "quantifiable sum" and must be supported by substantial evidence. The restitution awarded "must correspond to a measurable amount representing the money that the defendant has acquired from each class member by virtue of its unlawful conduct."

Plaintiffs propose the "price premium" method of determining class-wide damage . . . . As Plaintiffs have stated, Maybelline charges

$1.00–$3.00 more for the Class Products than its comparable products that do not bear the 24-hour/no transfer claims.

As an initial matter, it is not intuitively obvious at all that the 24-hour/no transfer claim commands a premium of $1.00–$3.00. Indeed, it is pure speculation on the part of Plaintiffs. The Court can fathom a number of reasons why the Class Products may be priced as they are. For example, perhaps it is due to a higher quality of ingredients, perhaps it is because of the selection of colors offered, or perhaps it reflects the costs Maybelline expended in the research and development of the products. Plaintiffs' method of using comparable products is inconsistent with the law. To establish that any difference in price is attributed solely to the alleged misrepresentation, the Court must use a product, exactly the same but without the 24-hour claim. As Maybelline stated, the Court would have to control and neutralize all other product differences. Such a task is nearly impossible as no two products are completely identical.

. . . Plaintiffs have failed to produce any expert testimony that demonstrate[s] a gap between the market price of the SuperStay 24 HR products and the price they purportedly should have sold at without the 24-hour/no transfer representations. . . .

Moreover, Maybelline contends that the proposed price premium method is inappropriate given the substantial variability in retail prices among the Class Products and competing products. The Court shares this concern. Maybelline does not sell retail and does not set retail prices. Establishing a higher price for a comparable product would be difficult where prices in the retail market differ and are affected by the nature and location of the outlet in which they are sold and/or the use of promotions and coupons. . . .

2.   The Class is Not Superior

Rule 23(b)(3) requires courts to find class litigation is superior to other methods of adjudication before certifying the class. Maybelline argues that its out-of-court Refund Program is a superior alternative. The Court questions the appropriateness of comparing such a private method of resolution.

Based on the language of Rule 23(b)(3) which requires a class action to be "superior to other available methods for . . . adjudicating the controversy," this determination involves a comparison of the class action as a procedural mechanism to available alternatives. In other words, Rule 23(b)(3) asks a court to compare the class action to other types of court action. Although the Court is mindful of cases which have considered whether the class action is superior to other "non judicial" methods of handling the controversy,[5] the Court is wary of stepping outside the text of Rule 23(b)(3).

However, included in the superiority analysis is whether the proposed class action would be manageable. "Courts are 'reluctant to permit action to proceed' where there are 'formidable . . . difficulties of distributing any ultimate recovery to the class members,' because such actions 'are not likely to benefit anyone but the lawyers who bring them.'" The Court has already concluded that the class is unmanageable and that common issues do not predominate, accordingly the class action is not a superior method of adjudicating the controversy. . . .

---

[5] Indeed, these private methods of resolution have a number of appealing attributes, such as affording class members better remedies than a class action and not having to divert a substantial amount of the recovery to line the pockets of attorneys.

NOTES AND QUESTIONS

Consider the court's customer satisfaction rationale. How does it match up with the general prohibition on bait-and-switch advertising? *See* FTC v. Colgate-Palmolive Co., 380 U.S. 374, 389 (1965):

> [A]ll of the above cases, like the present case, deal with methods designed to get a consumer to purchase a product, not with whether the product, when purchased, will perform up to expectations. We find an especially strong similarity between the present case and those cases in which a seller induces the public to purchase an arguably good product by misrepresenting his line of business, by concealing the fact that the product is reprocessed, or by misappropriating another's trademark. In each the seller has used a misrepresentation to break down what he regards to be an annoying or irrational habit of the buying public—the preference for particular manufacturers or known brands regardless of a product's actual qualities, the prejudice against reprocessed goods, and the desire for verification of a product claim. In each case the seller reasons that when the habit is broken the buyer will be satisfied with the performance of the product he receives. Yet, a misrepresentation has been used to break the habit and . . . a misrepresentation for such an end is not permitted.

How would the *Maybelline* court address the following arguments: False claims interfere with consumers' autonomy, which is a harm in itself; they distort the market and make competition harder for producers who can deliver the promised value; and the consumer satisfaction rationale ignores many quirks of human psychology— among other things, once we've made a purchase, we like it more, so as to defend the soundness of our own judgment.

If these arguments are persuasive, should the result in *Maybelline* have been different, or were there still too many fatal problems with the class?

Superiority. Although usually the alternative to a class action is no lawsuit at all, courts have occasionally considered arguments that other forms of relief would be superior. In *Belfiore v. Procter & Gamble Co.*, 311 F.R.D. 29 (E.D.N.Y. 2015), the court found that the FTC was actively investigating the issue at bar—whether defendant's wipes had been falsely advertised as "flushable" when in fact they clogged sewer systems—and stayed six related class actions on the theory that the FTC could probably protect consumers more effectively. Given the risk of inconsistent results on a state by state basis, the FTC was better suited to protect consumers nationally by formulating a uniform definition of "flushable." Although the court merely stayed the cases, it indicated that this reasoning would likely lead it to find a lack of superiority for a damages class if forced to do so. Suppose the FTC closes the investigation without defining "flushable." Should the court certify a damages class?

The following case certifies a class. What's different?

McCrary v. Elations Co., LLC, 2014 WL 1779243 (C.D. Cal. 2014)

[McCrary sued for violation of the CLRA, FAL, and UCL—the usual California statutory consumer protection claims.] Defendant markets, distributes, and sells the Elations dietary joint supplement beverage and promotes it as "clinically proven" to have joint health benefits. However, Plaintiff contends that Elations is not clinically proven to have any impact on joints, and Elations' label was therefore false.

Plaintiff McCrary suffers from arthritic joint pain. While shopping at CVS in August 2011, Plaintiff alleges he reviewed the packaging of

Elations which included the claims that Elations contains a
"clinically-proven formula" and a "clinically-proven combination" of
ingredients. In reliance on these claims, he purchased Defendant's
product, followed all of the instructions, and used it as directed, but
he did not receive the advertised benefits. Plaintiff claims that he
would never have purchased the product had he known of its
ineffectiveness. . . .

The decision to grant or deny a motion for class certification is
committed to the trial court's broad discretion. However, a party
seeking class certification must affirmatively demonstrate compliance
with Rule 23—that is, the party must be prepared to prove that there
are in fact sufficiently numerous parties and common questions of
law or fact. This requires a district court to conduct a "rigorous
analysis" that frequently "will entail some overlap with the merits of
the plaintiff's underlying claim." . . .

B. Class Certification

Plaintiff moves to certify a class pursuant to Rules 23(a) and 23(b)(3)
of "all persons residing in the state of California who purchased
Elations, since January 28, 2009, for personal use and not for resale,
when the following claims were on the packaging and/or labeling of
Elations: 'clinically-proven combination' and/or 'clinically-proven
formula.' " Plaintiff bears the burden of demonstrating that class
certification is proper.

1. Rule 23(a)
a. Ascertainability

A class is ascertainable if it is "administratively feasible for the court
to determine whether a particular individual is a member" using
objective criteria. Plaintiff contends that the class definition

objectively depicts who is bound and proposes that class members self-identify their inclusion via affidavits.

Defendant contends that the class is not ascertainable because there is no objective way to identify the individual members of the class, as it does not have any records identifying consumers of Elations—an over-the-counter supplement sold in retailers throughout the state. Defendant further contends that allowing class members to self-identify violates its due process right to raise individual challenges to class members.

Essentially, Defendant's concern is that class members do not have actual proof that they belong in the class. If Defendant's argument were correct, "there would be no such thing as a consumer class action." The class definition is sufficiently definite so that it is administratively feasible to determine whether a particular person is a class member. "Indeed, the proposed class definition simply identifies purchasers of Defendant's products that included the allegedly material misrepresentations. Because the alleged misrepresentations appeared on the actual packages of the products purchased, there is no concern that the class includes individuals who were not exposed to the misrepresentation."

Defendant's concern that it will be deprived of its due process right to defend against claims of class membership, such as by challenging a class member's actual purchase of the product or their failure to remember the Elations' label, is equally unavailing. . . . In this Circuit, it is enough that the class definition describes "a set of common characteristics sufficient to allow" a prospective plaintiff to "identify himself or herself as having a right to recover based on the description." . . . A prospective plaintiff would have sufficient information to determine whether he or she was an Elations customer who viewed the specified label during the stated time period. "[T]o the extent [Defendant] has individualized defenses, it is free to try those defenses against individual claimants."

Moreover, the fact that particular persons may make false claims of membership does not invalidate the objective criteria used to determine inclusion. Defendant points to the testimony of former Plaintiff Doucette who testified that he purchased Elations, but after further questioning at deposition, it was revealed he purchased another product. Defendant points to Doucette to argue that class members may not remember whether they purchased the product at issue, and the joint supplement market is crowded which may further confuse potential class members. Courts in this district have rejected this argument on the grounds that sufficient notice can cure confusion and these issues may be addressed later in the litigation. . . . [H]ere, Defendant can identify the retailers who sold its product. . . . [O]nce Defendant's "records establish which retailers sold [Elations] during the class period, class notice will further help reveal the class members." In addition, Defendant's contentions regarding a crowded market appear overstated. Defendant's Marketing Director stated that many of the joint supplements which likely competed with Elations were sold "in a pill form," and of the beverage options, many "vary by the additional factor of flavor." The product involved in this action was not available in pill form, nor has it ever been sold or manufactured in flavors. Accordingly, proper notice regarding the form of the product and its characteristics may help reduce consumer confusion regarding class membership.

In addition, Defendant argues that there is no precise time period when all class members purchased Elations with the "clinically-proven" labels. Although the challenged language was on the Elations label from January 28, 2009, through August 26, 2010, Defendant did not recall or re-label existing products once the label change was made. The fact that the allegedly false representation was not on every available product during the class period does not defeat ascertainability. However . . . Elations has a "two year shelf life from the date of bottling," therefore any remaining product should have been removed due to expiration. Accordingly, the Court finds it is necessary to limit the class definition to include purchasers of Elations between May 28, 2009, and December 26, 2012. With this limitation on the class period, the Court finds the class is ascertainable.

b. Numerosity

Rule 23(a)(1) requires the class to be so numerous that joinder of individual class members is impracticable. Here, the proposed California class is sufficiently numerous. During the unamended class period, Defendant shipped 615,623 units of Elations to locations in California. Thus, it is reasonable to estimate that there are thousands of potential class members in California. Defendant does not challenge Plaintiff's calculations, and the unrefuted evidence demonstrates that the numerosity requirement is satisfied.

c. Commonality

"Commonality requires the plaintiff to demonstrate that the class members 'have suffered the same injury,'" which "does not mean merely that they have all suffered a violation of the same provision of law." The "claims must depend on a common contention" and "[t]hat common contention . . . must be of such a nature that it is capable of class-wide resolution—which means that determination of its truth or falsity will resolve an issue that is central to the validity of each one of the claims in one stroke." Commonality is satisfied by "the existence of shared legal issues with divergent factual predicates" or a "common core of salient facts coupled with disparate legal remedies within the class."

Plaintiff has identified legal issues common to the putative class claims, namely whether the claims on Elations' packaging that it contains a "clinically-proven combination" and/or a "clinically-proven formula" are material and false. By definition, class members were exposed to these labeling claims, creating a "common core of salient facts." Defendant does not challenge the commonality requirement under Rule 23(a)(2), and "[c]ourts routinely find commonality in false advertising cases that are materially indistinguishable from this matter."

The Court therefore finds Plaintiff satisfied the commonality requirement under Rule 23(a)(2).

d. Typicality

"The purpose of the typicality requirement is to assure that the interest of the named representative aligns with the interests of the class." "The test of typicality 'is whether other members have the same or similar injury, whether the action is based on conduct which is not unique to the named plaintiffs, and whether other class members have been injured by the same course of conduct.' " Thus, typicality is satisfied if the plaintiff's claims are "reasonably co-extensive with those of absent class members; they need not be substantially identical."

Plaintiff contends his claims are typical of those of the class because he purchased Elations believing it was proven to reduce his joint pain. If Plaintiff had known that Elations was not clinically proven to help with his joint pain, he would not have purchased it. These factual circumstances demonstrate that Plaintiff's claims are "reasonably co-extensive" with unnamed class members. Further, Plaintiff alleges to have suffered the same type of economic injury and seeks the same type of damages as the putative class members, namely a refund of the purchase price. As such, Plaintiff's interests "align[ ] with the interests of the class."

Defendant argues Plaintiff is not typical because he is subject to a unique defense based on his medical history. Specifically, Defendant points out that Plaintiff took Vicodin while he took Elations, which may have interfered with Elations' effectiveness in improving his joints. . . . "In determining whether typicality is met, the focus should be 'on the defendants' conduct and plaintiff's legal theory,' not the injury caused to the plaintiff." Thus, the central focus of the typicality analysis is that Plaintiff and the putative class claim Defendant labeled Elations with a claim of clinical proof knowing it was false. Moreover, the defense raised against Plaintiff is not "[a]typical of the defenses which may be raised against other members of the proposed class," as it is likely many other Elations' users took other medications and/or suffer from other illnesses. Accordingly, this potentially common defense does not render Plaintiff atypical.

In footnotes, Defendant raises the argument that customers who bought Elations online must be excluded from the proposed class. The Court agrees, but for reasons other than those offered. First, the proposed class definition requires that the putative member be exposed to the "packaging and/or labeling of Elations." Most, if not all, online consumers would not have seen the packaging or labeling on the product prior to purchase. This is particularly likely here where the "clinically-proven" claims were printed on "shrink wrap packaging" surrounding the Elations bottles. Thus, online consumers would not share a common injury with members of the class. Even if the websites offering Elations presented similar clinical proof claims in their marketing or description of the product, this would be insufficient because Plaintiff did not view any claims made on the website, nor did he purchase the product online. Therefore, Plaintiff is not typical of putative class members who purchased Elations online. . . .

With the exclusion of online consumers, the typicality requirement is satisfied.

e. Adequacy . . .

[T]he Court concludes that the class representative and class counsel are adequate.

2. Rule 23(b)(3)

Of the three possible bases for certification under Rule 23(b), Plaintiff seeks certification under Rule 23(b)(3) which requires that "the questions of law or fact common to the members of the class predominate over any questions affecting individual members, and that a class action is superior to other available methods for the fair and efficient adjudication of the controversy."

a.   Predominance

Plaintiff moves to certify the class based on Defendant's liability under the UCL, FAL, and CLRA. . . . Class certification under Rule 23(b)(3) is proper when common questions present a significant portion of the case and can be resolved for all members of the class in a single adjudication. *Id.* Defendant argues certification is improper because individual issues predominate over any common issues.

i.   Standing, Materiality, and Reliance

Defendant makes several arguments contending that unnamed class members may lack standing or fail to satisfy elements of the UCL, FAL, or CLRA. Defendant contends that the Court must make individual determinations of whether each member actually viewed the "clinically proven" claim, that such statements were material to the class members' purchase of Elations, and that the consumers actually believed the product was ineffective and caused them damage.

As discussed above, the class definition presupposes exposure to the clinical proof claims. Any person who did not view the claims is not a class member and cannot raise any individualized issues. Moreover, a presumption of exposure is inferred where, as here, the alleged misrepresentations were on the outside of the packaging of every unit for an extended period. The fact that some of the packaging after August 2010 may not have included the clinical proof claims does not alter the presumption of exposure. The case Defendant cites to support its argument that Plaintiff must prove each class member had individualized exposure is distinguishable. In *Mazza v. Am. Honda Motor Co., Inc.*, 666 F.3d 581 (9th Cir. 2012), the Ninth Circuit held that a "presumption of reliance does not arise when class members 'were exposed to quite disparate information from various representatives of the defendant.' " In that case, plaintiff alleged misrepresentations in a brochure and television ads touting the benefits of a technology package available on certain Honda models to which few class members could have been exposed. The Ninth Circuit reasoned that "the limited scope of that advertising makes it unreasonable to assume that all class members viewed it." Defendant does not argue, nor could it, that its clinical proof claims were of limited scope, since it placed them on the packaging of every unit of Elations sold over an 18-month period. The factual dissimilarity of *Mazza* renders it inapplicable.

In the Ninth Circuit, "standing is satisfied [under the UCL and FAL] if at least one named plaintiff meets the requirements. . . . Thus, we consider only whether at least one named plaintiff satisfies the standing requirements." Here, Defendant does not challenge Plaintiff's standing, and thus the Court need not examine whether each putative class member has standing.

Contrary to Defendant's assertion, at the class certification stage
Plaintiff need not prove that the clinical proof claims were material to
all consumers of Elations or that they relied on those claims. " '[A]
presumption, or at least an inference, of reliance arises [under the
UCL and FAL] whenever there is a showing that a misrepresentation
was material.' " Similarly, for a CLRA claim, "[i]f the trial court finds
that material misrepresentations have been made to the entire class,
an inference of reliance arises as to the class.' " The materiality
determination under the FAL, UCL, and CLRA requires an objective
test where plaintiff must "show that members of the public are likely
to be deceived" by the alleged misrepresentations. Therefore, the
determination of materiality, and thus reliance, is determined using
objective criteria that apply to the entire class and do not require
individualized determination.

Defendant contends that such an inference of reliance is unwarranted
here because no evidence supports it. Defendant argues that many
consumers purchase Elations based on the recommendation of a
doctor or friend or for reasons other than the information printed on
the label. However, Plaintiff points to evidence from Defendant's
consumer survey showing that over 75 percent of Elations purchasers
believed that "proven levels" of the active ingredients were worth
paying for. Moreover, Plaintiff's claims of falsity concern the efficacy
of the product and thus go to the heart of a customer's purchasing
decision. Defendant cannot reasonably argue that a putative class
member would purchase a product that does not work, regardless of
who recommended it. Thus, Plaintiff has presented a sufficient
factual basis to warrant an inference of reliance among the putative
class of Elations purchasers.

Moreover, Defendant's concern that some putative class members
were happy with Elations and thus were uninjured is unpersuasive.
"[The requirement of concrete injury is satisfied when the Plaintiffs

and class members in UCL and FAL actions suffer an economic loss caused by the defendant, namely the purchase of defendant's product containing misrepresentations." "The focus of the UCL and FAL is on the actions of the defendants, not on the subjective state of mind of the class members. All of the proposed class members would have purchased the product bearing the alleged misrepresentations. Such a showing of concrete injury under the UCL and FAL is sufficient to establish Article III standing." Accordingly, the Court need not examine whether each putative class member was unsatisfied with the product in order to find that common issues predominate.

In sum, the Court agrees with Plaintiff that common questions predominate over individual questions. Specifically, the predominating common issues include whether Defendant misrepresented that Elations is a "clinically-proven formula" or "clinically-proven combination," and whether the misrepresentations were likely to deceive a reasonable consumer.

ii.   Damages

Defendant also contends that Plaintiff fails to present a viable damages model.

Plaintiff seeks full restitution of the retail price or disgorgement of Elations' net profits. Plaintiff contends that he will be able to prove the proper amount of restitution by relying on documents produced by Defendant relating to net sales, profits, costs, and the retail price of Elations. Defendant counters that return of the full purchase price violates restitutionary principles because Elations provided some value to consumers and that value must be deducted from the price putative members paid. Courts agree with Defendant and hold that "[w]hile Plaintiffs, should they prevail, are likely not entitled to a full refund of the purchase price, having obtained some benefit from the products purchased even if they were not as advertised, Plaintiffs may seek some amount representing the disparity between their expected and received value." This reduction in allowable damages, however, is not fatal to class certification. At this stage, the Court does not require Plaintiff to identify a comparable "clinically-proven" product which could serve to offset damages.

Next, Defendant contends that individual questions of damage would overwhelm the common questions of fact and law. However, "the amount of damages, even if it is an individual question, does not defeat class certification." . . .

Since Plaintiff seeks no remedy that would require an award of damages unique to any particular class member, the Court determines that the potential recovery is not an impediment to the requirement of predominance.

b. Superiority

Rule 23(b)(3) requires the Court to find "a class action is superior to other available methods for fairly and efficiently adjudicating the controversy." Fed.R.Civ.P. 23(b)(3). Considerations pertinent to this finding include:

> (A) the class members' interests in individually controlling the prosecution or defense of separate actions;
> (B) the extent and nature of any litigation concerning the controversy already begun by or against class members;
> (C) the desirability or undesirability of concentrating the litigation of the claims in the particular forum; and
> (D) the likely difficulties in managing a class action."
> Fed.R.Civ.P. 23(b)(3)(A)–(D).

615

The superiority requirement tests whether "class-wide litigation of common issues will reduce litigation costs and promote greater efficiency."

Here, the damages suffered by each putative class member are not large, favoring a class proceeding. It is more efficient to resolve the common questions regarding materiality and scientific substantiation in a single proceeding rather than to have individual courts separately hear these cases. There are no other cases challenging Defendant's advertising claims under California's consumer protection statutes, and the proposed class involves only California purchasers, making this forum desirable for the class. Finally, there is no evidence that this consumer class action will be difficult to manage.

Defendant does not oppose the superiority of a class action for resolving the putative class's claims. Given the large number of potential class members and small amount of the claims, the Court concludes that a class action is a superior method of resolving this case. . . .

NOTES AND QUESTIONS

What is your final count of divergent analyses between the *Maybelline* and *Elations* courts? How much does it matter that one accused product is cosmetics and the other is a nutritional supplement, and why?

The following case differs from the previous two in two key ways: (1) it examines many of the key issues for *multistate* consumer class actions, (2) in the context of a settlement. Pay attention to the issues that give the court the most pause: numerosity is handled quickly, while predominance requires more detailed analysis. Crucially, because this is a settlement class, both sides want to convince the court to approve it. A contested certification would proceed very differently.

In re M3 Power Razor System Marketing & Sales Practice Litigation, 270 F.R.D. 45 (D. Mass. 2010)

This consolidated consumer litigation alleges misrepresentation by the defendant Gillette Company in the marketing of shaving devices. A motion seeking preliminary review and authorization of notice regarding a North American class action settlement raised the challenging question whether and, if so, how class action certification should be made when the governing substantive law is drawn from various North American jurisdictions. . . .

Ultimately, I have been satisfied that where, as here, all the plaintiffs "share[ ] a single, common claim that g[ives] rise to an identical right to recovery under a single state statute for every member of the class," class certification is appropriate in the absence of "variations in state laws . . . so significant as to defeat commonality and predominance, even in a settlement class." Finding no significant variations in other state laws sufficient to defeat the commonality and predominance evident in this case, where all class members have advanced a claim under the Massachusetts Unfair and Deceptive Practices Act, Mass. Gen. Laws ch. 93A, "on the ground that the allegedly deceptive communications originated from [Gillette's Massachusetts-based] headquarters," I certified a single settlement class and authorized publication of the class notice.

I. BACKGROUND . . .

A. Factual Background

[The facts are the same as those recounted in the *Schick v. Gillette* litigation in Chapter 4: Gillette advertised that the M3P could raise hair up and away from the skin with micropulses, allowing a closer shave than other razors.] Plaintiffs allege that the advertising claims were deceptive and materially misleading because Gillette was aware that the M3P did not actually raise facial hair "up and away" from the skin. All of the Representative Plaintiffs claim to have based a decision to purchase the razor on the misleading M3P advertising campaign.

B. Procedural History

. . . Following the issuance of the preliminary injunction in [*Schick v. Gillette*], plaintiffs filed consumer class actions based on the same underlying facts in several United States and Canadian jurisdictions. All actions filed in state courts in the United States were removed to federal court, and all the federal cases in other districts were transferred by the [Joint Panel on Multidistrict Litigation] to this Court. I consolidated the cases and resolved contentious disputes among the several plaintiffs' counsel regarding the appointment of Co-Lead and Liaison counsel.

The parties thereafter commenced formal discovery. . . . [The parties agreed to a settlement, and the court allowed a preliminary notice of settlement, but California Plaintiff Carlos Corrales objected.]

. . . I felt obligated to survey the relevant law on a jurisdiction-by-jurisdiction basis to determine whether material differences, as applied to the proposed settlement, might yield unfair and disproportionate advantages or disadvantages for class members from certain jurisdictions. . . .

II. THE PROPOSED SETTLEMENT

A. Settlement Terms

[Editors' note: The settlement, in brief, provided the option of a $15 refund (including postage and handling) for those class members who chose to return the razor to Gillette or a rebate of up to $10 for Gillette purchases for class members who could produce package codes or receipts from their purchases. If the settlement fund was not exhausted by these claims at the end of the initial claim period, each class member who submitted an approved claim would receive a new Gillette razor, and if that didn't exhaust the settlement fund, each class member who certified that he or she purchased or otherwise obtained an M3P razor during the class period would receive a new Gillette razor. Any leftover funds would be used to distribute free Gillette razors to the general population.]

III. CLASS CERTIFICATION

Federal Rule of Civil Procedure 23 governs class certification in the federal courts. Before certifying a class, "[a] district court must conduct a rigorous analysis of the prerequisites established by Rule 23 . . . " To obtain class certification, plaintiffs must establish each of the four elements of Rule 23(a)—numerosity, commonality, typicality, and adequacy of representation—and one of the elements in Rule 23(b). The fact that class certification is requested only for the purpose of settlement is no barrier to certification. However, considerations stemming from structural concerns about potential collusion and reverse auctions in settlement class actions make it "incumbent on the district court to give heightened scrutiny to the requirements of Rule 23 in order to protect absent class members."

A. Rule 23(a)

Rule 23(a) imposes four prerequisites to class certification:

> (1) the class is so numerous that joinder of all members is impracticable, (2) there are questions of law or fact common to the class, (3) the claims or defenses of the representative parties are typical of the claims or defenses of the class, and (4) the representative parties will fairly and adequately protect the interests of the class.

Fed. R. Civ. P. 23(a). The plaintiffs must demonstrate that each Rule 23(a) requirement is satisfied for class certification to be appropriate.

1.   Numerosity

The numerosity requirement is easily satisfied in this case because Gillette sold over ten million M3P razors across the United States and Canada in the pertinent time periods. No purchaser records were maintained, so there is no possibility of locating, much less joining individually as plaintiffs, all of the potential class members. Given the large number of potential class members, and the relatively small claim each one has for damages, individual lawsuits are clearly impracticable, and Rule 23(a)(1) is satisfied.

2.   Commonality

The threshold for commonality under Rule 23(a)(2) is not high. Because the Rule 23(a)(2) analysis is "[a]imed in part at 'determining whether there is a need for combined treatment and a benefit to be derived therefrom,' the rule requires only that resolution of the common questions affect all or a substantial number of the class members."

Although variations existed in the legal requirements of various state law claims and in the facts necessary to prove such claims, it is beyond dispute that common core questions lie at the heart of this litigation. Stated in their highest degree of generalities, these include: whether Gillette misrepresented the capabilities of the M3P razor to the potential class, whether the potential class members sustained ascertainable damages from such conduct, and, if so, in what amount. These common issues of fact and law are sufficient to meet the threshold of Rule 23(a)(2), and indicate that class certification could be beneficial to the expeditious resolution of this dispute.

3.   Typicality

To establish typicality, the plaintiffs need only demonstrate that "the claims or defenses of the class and the class representative arise from the same event or pattern or practice and are based on the same legal theory." Here, it is clear that the claims of the Representative Plaintiffs are based on the same event (purchase of an M3P razor based on misleading advertisements) as the potential class members. The legal theories of recovery for the Representative Plaintiffs are typical of those of the class as a whole. As reflected in the Amended Consolidated Class Action Complaint, most counts are based on common law causes of action (negligent misrepresentation, intentional misrepresentation, breach of express warranty, breach of implied warranty of fitness of purpose, and unjust enrichment), which will be substantially uniform across the class. The Amended Complaint also alleges violation of various state consumer protection statutes. Although the Representative Plaintiffs are not residents of each of the covered states, the consumer protection statutes in the states in which they reside (Florida, New York, California, Massachusetts, Illinois, Georgia and Canada) appear to be typical of, and generally even more consumer-friendly than, consumer protection laws in the range of jurisdictions that they represent.

Consequently, the Representative Plaintiffs satisfy the typicality requirement of Rule 23(a)(3).

4.   Adequate Representation

Rule 23(a)(4) requires that the proposed class representatives "fairly and adequately protect the interests of the class." This requirement has two parts. The plaintiffs "must show first that the interests of the representative party will not conflict with the interests of any of the class members, and second, that counsel chosen by the representative party is qualified, experienced and able to vigorously conduct the proposed litigation."

As to the former, the Representative Plaintiffs' interests generally align with the class as a whole, because all parties, named and unnamed, are seeking redress from what is essentially the same injury, the purchase of an M3P razor based on misleading advertisements. Indeed, all members of the class share a claim under Chapter 93A of the Massachusetts General Laws. Although some variations exist between potential remedies, depending on the state of residence, these differences do not create the type of intra-class conflicts that often appear in the mass tort context. The problem of differing remedies will be discussed in greater detail below. At this point, it is sufficient to note that the interests of the Representative Plaintiffs and the absent class members are not generally in conflict, and that counsel is adequate. . . .

B.   Rule 23(b)

In addition to satisfying the four elements of Rule 23(a), plaintiffs must demonstrate that at least one subsection of Rule 23(b) applies. I find Rule 23(b)(3) directly applicable, as this subsection allows for class certification if "the court finds that the questions of law or fact common to class members predominate over any questions affecting only individual members, and that a class action is superior to other available methods for fairly and efficiently adjudicating the controversy." Fed. R. Civ. P. 23(b)(3). In short, plaintiffs must demonstrate predominance and superiority.

1.   Predominance

The predominance inquiry overlaps with the commonality requirement of Rule 23(a)(2), but is more demanding. "The Rule 23(b)(3) predominance inquiry tests whether proposed classes are sufficiently cohesive to warrant adjudication by representation." The pertinent legal and factual questions are those that "qualify each class member's case as a genuine controversy," but do not include the fairness or desirability of the proposed settlement in a settlement class action. The predominance standard can be met even if some individual issues arise in the course of litigation, because "Rule 23(b)(3) requires merely that common issues predominate, not that all issues be common to the class." In this connection, some types of cases are uniquely well-suited to class adjudication, and "[p]redominance is a test readily met in certain cases alleging consumer or securities fraud or violations of the antitrust laws."

In this case, it is clear that the issues common to the class predominate over those that are personal to individual class members. The dominant common questions include whether Gillette's advertising was false or misleading, whether the company's conduct violated the statutory and/or common law causes of action delineated in the Amended Complaint, and whether the class members suffered damages as a result of this conduct. Even if state consumer statutes or other state causes of action differ in arguably material ways, common questions, not individual issues, predominate among and within each state's legal regimes. . . . I will address the problem of differences in legal theories in Section III.B.3, *infra*. For now, I note my finding that the predominance requirement of Rule 23(b)(3) appears to be satisfied.

2.   Superiority

Rule 23(b)(3) requires that a class action be "superior to other available methods for fairly and efficiently adjudicating the controversy." Courts must consider:

> (A) the class members' interests in individually controlling the prosecution or defense of separate actions; (B) the extent and nature of any litigation concerning the controversy already begun by or against class members; (C) the desirability or undesirability of concentrating the litigation of the claims in the particular forum; and (D) the likely difficulties in managing a class action.

The predominance and superiority requirements are inherently interrelated, and were added "to cover cases 'in which a class action would achieve economies of time, effort, and expense, and promote . . . uniformity of decision as to persons similarly situated, without sacrificing procedural fairness or bringing about other undesirable results.' " "Rule 23 has to be read to authorize class action in some set of cases where seriatim litigation would promise such modest recoveries as to be economically impracticable."

In this case, involving millions of potential plaintiffs with small individual claims, a class action is the only feasible mechanism for resolving the dispute efficiently. Absent class certification, it is highly unlikely that any individual aggrieved consumer will seek or obtain redress, because the transaction costs of filing and prosecuting a lawsuit individually far exceed the recoverable individual damages, even under the most generous state consumer protection statutes. In short, in the absence of class certification, there would be nothing for an individual class member to control because a separate action would not be prosecuted. . . . Under the circumstances, a class action pursued on a consolidated basis in the District of Massachusetts is superior to any other mechanism for adjudicating the case, and Rule 23(b)(3) is satisfied.

C.   Subclassing

Objecting Plaintiff Corrales opposes certification of the class and authorizing notice of the settlement on the ground that the proposed settlement is insufficiently generous to potential California class members. Corrales argues that the consumer protection statutes in the state of California are so favorable to California consumers, particularly in terms of available remedies, that they should be treated differently from class members of other states. Assuming for the moment that Corrales' objections are valid, one potential mechanism for dealing with differential state remedies is to certify subclasses within the larger class. But this decision must not be made lightly because it inherently reduces the efficiency of the class action mechanism and increases transaction costs (particularly for notice).

Close analysis of a California subclass is a useful means to approach the problems presented by differences in legal theories among the several jurisdictions whose case law is involved by the consolidated complaint. I will consider three related questions to determine whether a California subclass is appropriate. First, what is the significance of variations in state law for purposes of certifying a nationwide class? Second, what is the content of California consumer protection law, and how does it compare to the common claim presented by Mass. Gen. Laws ch. 93A or otherwise differ from laws of other jurisdictions? Third, do any differences rise to a level that would necessitate the certification of a subclass? I will then address the problems more generally to determine what level of additional analysis is necessary given the common factual and legal issues shared by the plaintiff class members.

1.   Variations in State Law

When nationwide class actions are based on state law claims, variations in state law create several potential challenges for certification under Rule 23, quite apart from the trial management issues that illustrate the challenges. State law differences signify "diverse legal standards and a related need for multiple [legal determinations]," and sometimes "multiply the individualized factual determinations" that a court must undertake. Legal variations also undermine the class's ability to satisfy the commonality requirement of Rule 23(a)(2). A related problem raised by state law variations is tension among the plaintiffs: conflicts of interest and allocation dilemmas can become evident and disabling during settlement or judgment. The Supreme Court has made it clear that before certifying a class—even in the settlement context—a court must closely examine potential conflicts of interest, as well as inequality in the strength of claims.

Circuits have required a rigorous analysis of state law variation must precede class certification. . . . Courts must remain sensitive, however, to the "common core" of issues among plaintiffs, even if coupled with "disparate legal remedies within the class."

One solution to the problems of state law variation in a nationwide class is to create a subclass of plaintiffs—a group of claimants from a state (or states) whose legal remedies differ substantially from those of other states. Certification of subclasses, however, must continue to facilitate the operation of the class action. [Klay v. Humana, Inc., 382 F.3d 1241, 1262 (11th Cir. 2004)] (warning that a court "must be careful not to certify too many groups," otherwise instructing the jury on—or otherwise applying—the relevant law would be an "impossible task").

2. Consumer Protection Law as a Basis for Subclassing

Although the Consolidated Amended Complaint presents a multiplicity of causes of action (Negligent Misrepresentation, Intentional Misrepresentation, Express Warranty, Implied Warranty, Unjust Enrichment and Unfair Practices and Consumer Protection Statutes) from a multiplicity of North American jurisdictions, analysis of the relevant questions regarding class certification can be focused by discussion of the California Consumer Protection provisions relied upon by the California plaintiff objector and the Massachusetts claim under Chapter 93A common to all class members.

a. California

. . . As a policy matter, the goal of the California consumer protection statutes is to return ill-gotten gains to consumers, with a secondary purpose of deterring future violations. The restitutionary remedy is not "intended as a punitive provision, though it may fortuitously have that sting when properly applied to restore a victim to wholeness." Before a court may award restitution, the appropriate amount of restitution must be shown by "substantial evidence." . . .

[T]he evidentiary standard for awarding restitution and actual damages is demanding in California state courts. The case before me has . . . valuation difficulties because Gillette has adduced evidence that consumers preferred the M3P razor, even if it did not perform exactly as advertised. The precise value of having one's hair raised "up and away" during a shave is inherently speculative. In this setting, it is not likely that a court applying California law in a California state class action would award restitution. The probability of a large monetary award in the form of restitution or actual damages is by no means the legal certainty Corrales suggests.

The CLRA also allows for punitive damages. . . . [I]t seems highly unlikely that a court applying California law would award such damages in the instant case, where courts around the world divided, at least on an interlocutory basis, over whether Gillette's conduct was even actionable.

It bears emphasizing that after a 2004 referendum, California's procedural and substantive consumer protection law became less consumer-friendly than it once may have been perceived to be. . . .

b.   Massachusetts

The protections for consumers provided by the Massachusetts Unfair and Deceptive Business Practices Act, Mass. Gen. Laws ch. 93A § 9, are quite robust and arguably more consumer-friendly than the California consumer protection regime. Unlike the California UCL cause of action, Chapter 93A does not require reliance, rather the applicable standard for determining whether an act is "deceptive" is whether "it possesses 'a tendency to deceive.'" The Massachusetts Supreme Judicial Court has emphasized that "[u]nlike a traditional common law action for fraud, consumers suing under c. 93A need not prove actual reliance on a false representation. . . . " Materiality and causation are established by a showing that the deceptive representation "could reasonably be found to have caused a person to act differently from the way he [or she] otherwise would have acted."

The consumer may recover compensatory damages under Chapter 93A for misrepresentation whether the misrepresentation is intentional or unintentional. . . . [T]he aggregate of actual damages afforded by a Chapter 93A consumer class action claim necessarily parallels the restitutionary remedy.

c.   Other Jurisdictions

After extended review of the various legal regimes, I find without
reciting the details with particularity, that the Representative
Plaintiffs have demonstrated that, although variations in state law
exist, they do not overcome the common factual and legal issues
shared by the potential class members. The only purported
distinctions actually argued by an objector—those presented by
California consumer protection law—are, to the extent they are
significant at all, differences of degree, not of kind, and are not
substantial and clear-cut enough to require a subclass.[10]

As is apparent from the text of this Memorandum, I have focused on
consumer protection law as dispositive in this litigation. The various
common law and commercial code counts alleged here do evidence
significant differences among jurisdictions. Indeed, consumer
protection statutes were developed principally to ease restrictions on
consumer claims that were perceived to be embedded in common law
and commercial law causes of action consumers might have otherwise
deployed. And among consumer protection statutory schemes, the

---

[10] The similarity between state consumer protection laws was noted by the
California Court of Appeals in a case relied upon by Corrales:

> [e]ven though there may be differences in consumer protection laws
> from state to state, this is not necessarily fatal to a finding that
> there is a predominance of common issues among a nationwide class.
> As the Ninth Circuit has observed, state consumer protection laws
> are relatively homogeneous: "the idiosyncratic differences between
> state consumer protection laws are not sufficiently substantive to
> predominate over the shared claims" and do not preclude
> certification of a nationwide settlement class.

[Editors' note: In *Mazza v. American Honda Motor Co.*, 666 F.3d 581 (9th Cir.
2012), the Ninth Circuit reached the opposite result with a contested
nationwide class, holding that state law variations precluded certification
over the defendant's opposition.]

Massachusetts law under Chapter 93A appears to be in practice as generous as any available to class members in this litigation. . . .

Note the presence of a Canadian class. Should the court give special attention to the treatment of foreign citizens, whose overall legal systems may differ substantially from the American one even if the substantive right to be protected against false advertising looks similar?

How does this case differ from the contested cases above? Does it matter that Gillette had lost an earlier Lanham Act case, and thus might have been estopped on issues such as falsity and materiality if the case had gone to trial? Are there arguments against liability that it could have made against the class that were unavailable to it against a competitor?

Suppose Gillette had decided to oppose certification. What arguments should it have made about legal and factual variation in plaintiffs' claims? Should it have prevailed? Does it make sense to relax the inquiry when the defendant wants to settle? Does that put too much power to control the litigation in the defendant's hands, or does it restore plaintiffs' leverage when without certification they'd likely have to litigate state-by-state, if they could litigate at all?

Alternatives to Class Actions?

As noted earlier, Myriam Gilles & Gary Friedman, *After Class: Aggregate Litigation in the Wake of* AT&T Mobility v. Concepcion, 79 U. CHI. L. REV. 623 (2012), argue that *Concepcion* allows most businesses to force consumers to waive their rights to class actions. The authors identify other barriers to consumer class actions that are also making them almost impossible to win if the defendant decides to fight.

Because consumer class actions are becoming impossible, but deceptive consumer practices are not, Gilles & Friedman recommend outsourcing AGs' consumer enforcement powers to private attorneys, with appropriate limits on maximum fees and scrutiny to avoid "pay-to-play" arrangements. Because the state has its own interests in protecting consumers, consumers' agreement to arbitration will not prevent AGs from suing to protect consumers. But AGs are traditionally underfunded, so Gilles & Friedman argue that states should make greater use of private lawyers with experience in consumer protection cases. AG supervision, they argue, will solve the "agency" problem of uncontrolled private lawyers suing over anything that might make them money in a settlement. However, they note that such partnerships "present especially rich political targets, making it imperative to institute transparent contracting processes and, probably, some measure of fee caps. . . . And AGs will have to be vigilant in their fundraising activities to avoid any element of 'pay-to-play' in the donations they accept from law firms or groups of lawyers."

Gilles & Friedman acknowledge the political risks involved:

> The poster child here is the tobacco litigation, where state AGs hired well-known plaintiffs' lawyers to sue the cigarette manufacturers on a subrogation theory. Although the private lawyers were able to wrest a $246 billion settlement from an industry that had enjoyed total success for decades in fending off any damages liability, critics balked at the $14 billion in aggregate fees paid to outside counsel under contingent fee agreements. Fierce lobbying and popular outcry drove some jurisdictions to place limits on the ability of AGs to hire outside counsel, and led President George W. Bush to ban the

use of contingency fee agreements in federal contracts with outside counsel.

But cooler heads have since prevailed. The Louisiana AG, Buddy Caldwell, recently sought permission from the state legislature to hire private attorneys to handle litigation against BP and others arising out of the Deep Water Horizon disaster. In Caldwell's press release, he noted "We just don't have enough money or enough knowledge to fight this fight as efficiently as the lawyers we want to hire. We think they're going to get the state of Louisiana a damned good settlement and force BP to pay up what it owes to the people it injured. And if we have to pay these lawyers to do that hard work and get us a good deal, I've got no problem with that . . . I think anyone who does have a problem with that just doesn't understand that the state's lawyers can't go up against the fancy firms that BP has hired the same way these private lawyers can." Other AGs have similarly turned to private outside counsel.

In any event, AGs can easily protect themselves from a "tobacco problem" by negotiating to place some sort of limits on fees. Such capping arrangements—often couched as a fee of x% but not to exceed y times the ordinary hourly fees—are not unusual in private contracts, and they need not be particularly draconian to avoid the sort of "windfall" situation that is capable of drawing populist ire.

What do you think of this proposal? Can Gilles & Friedman really achieve the benefits AG-supervised private enforcement without suffering the current problems with class action lawsuits or creating entirely new ones?

Any case must begin with consideration of the plaintiff's desired outcome, which will shape the litigation strategy in multiple ways. We will cover the three major categories of remedies for false advertising violations: injunctions, monetary damages or penalties, and criminal sanctions.

1. Injunctive Relief

In many false advertising cases, the plaintiff's #1 priority is to stop the offending advertising before it causes more harm. As a result, injunctive relief is the remedy most often sought, and both the Lanham Act and the Federal Trade Commission Act grant courts broad authority to fashion appropriate injunctive relief. *See, e.g.,* Porter & Dietsch, Inc. v. FTC, 605 F.2d 294, 304 (7th Cir. 1979) (setting forth standard of review of FTC orders: "[the FTC] has wide latitude for judgment and the courts will not interfere except where the remedy selected has no reasonable relation to the unlawful practices found to exist"). State AGs also may seek injunctive relief to prevent continuing harm to consumers.

Typically, because time is critical in advertising disputes, private competitor-plaintiffs seek provisional relief via a temporary restraining order (TRO) or preliminary injunction. If granted, provisional relief may be converted to permanent relief at the case's conclusion. Since evaluation of the application for a preliminary injunction requires the court to examine the case's merits, however, the resolution of the preliminary injunction motion often gives the litigants enough information to settle the case.

A.   Standard for a TRO or Preliminary Injunction

In cases brought by private litigants, courts traditionally consider four factors in determining whether to grant an application for preliminary relief:

(1) whether the movant has demonstrated a strong likelihood of success on the merits;

(2) whether the movant would suffer irreparable injury in the absence of injunctive relief;

(3) whether the issuance of the injunction would cause substantial harm to the defendant; and

(4) whether the public interest would be served by issuance of an injunction.

(Public enforcers generally do not have to show irreparable injury. *See* FTC v. Affordable Media, LLC, 179 F.3d 1228, 1233 (9th Cir. 1999); FTC v. Warner Commc'ns, Inc., 742 F.2d 1156, 1159 (9th Cir. 1984)).

In all jurisdictions, proof of irreparable harm to the private plaintiff and a likelihood of success on the merits are the key requirements. The various circuits analyze the four factors somewhat differently and give differing weight to each factor. Most significantly, the Second and Ninth Circuits have stated that preliminary injunctions may be appropriate if, instead of likely success on the merits, there is a "sufficiently serious" question going to the merits and a balance of hardships weighing "decidedly" in the plaintiff's favor. *See, e.g.,* Salinger v. Colting, 607 F.3d 68 (2d Cir. 2010).

Irreparable Harm

"Irreparable harm" refers to an injury that cannot be entirely remedied by a later payment of money damages. Such harm traditionally includes damage to a plaintiff's commercial reputation or a loss of goodwill caused by a competitor's false advertising, which will eventually lead to lost sales (but those lost sales will be difficult to measure).

In the past, irreparable harm was typically presumed if an advertisement was shown to be false, "based upon the judgment that it is virtually impossible to ascertain the precise economic consequences of intangible harms." Abbott Labs. v. Mead Johnson & Co., 971 F.2d 6 (7th Cir. 1992).

However, *eBay Inc. v. MercExchange*, L.L.C., 547 U.S. 388 (2006), unsettled the law relating to irreparable harm. *eBay* involved a permanent injunction against patent infringement. Prior to *eBay*, courts had developed a virtually irrebuttable presumption that an injunction was a more appropriate remedy than damages in patent infringement cases. The Supreme Court rejected that presumption, concluding that injunctions in patent cases should be subject to the traditional four-factor test set out above. The Court's language indicated that blanket presumptions favoring injunctive relief were, in general, impermissible.

Some Lanham Act specialists argued that violations of the Lanham Act, with its consumer protection objectives, deserved different treatment than property rights such as copyright and patent, so a presumption in favor of injunctive relief was still appropriate where a plaintiff showed likely success on the merits. *See* David H. Bernstein & Andrew Gilden, *No Trolls Barred: Trademark Injunctions after eBay*, 99 TRADEMARK REP. 1037 (2009).

Courts, however, have increasingly applied *eBay* to Lanham Act cases, and post-*eBay* precedent suggests that any presumptions in favor of injunctions are limited. For example, courts may still presume harm from literally false comparative advertising, or at least intentionally false comparative advertising. *See, e.g.*, Grpe. SEB USA, Inc. v. Euro-Pro Operating LLC, 774 F.3d 192 (3d Cir. 2014) (rejecting presumption of irreparable harm, but accepting lost control of reputation and lost goodwill caused by false comparative advertising as irreparable harm); North American Medical Corp. v. Axiom Worldwide, Inc., 522 F.3d 1211 (11th Cir. 2008) (rejecting presumption of irreparable harm in non-comparative literal falsity case). Other cases stay agnostic on the effect of *eBay* but find case-specific evidence of irreparable harm from, for example, the seriousness of the statements in implicating the fundamental safety of the plaintiff's products. *See, e.g.*, Osmose, Inc. v. Viance, LLC, 612 F.3d 1298 (11th Cir. 2010).

Even if the applicable court isn't likely to embrace *eBay* as precedent, a plaintiff is well advised to submit evidence of actual irreparable harm, both to bolster the appropriateness of the presumption and, even more importantly, to educate the judge on why the equities strongly favor injunctive relief. What evidence would show irreparable harm as opposed to harm that could be redressed with money damages?

As you read the following case, consider what evidence you would want to show irreparable harm, and how you would acquire that evidence.

IDT Telecom, Inc. v. CVT Prepaid Solutions, Inc., 2007 WL 2980181 (3rd Cir. 2007)
[review facts from Materiality section of Chapter 4]

. . . In their Complaint, the Appellants asserted claims for false advertising under the Lanham Act and violations of the consumer protection statutes of New Jersey, New York, California, Illinois, and Florida. All of the parties are engaged in the prepaid calling card business, and the dispute is centered around the advertising of the number of minutes a consumer receives when he or she purchases these calling cards.

Advertising posters and voice prompts are the main sources of information regarding the number of minutes on a particular calling card for calls to a particular destination. The Appellants discovered in 2006 that some of its competitors were offering a higher number of minutes for low-priced calling cards. After testing some of its competitors' calling cards, the Appellants allegedly learned that the cards were not actually providing the number of minutes promised, rather the cards provided fewer minutes than what was advertised. According to the Appellants, unlike their competitors, they provide one-hundred percent of the minutes advertised. The Appellants claim that this "false advertising" by their competitors caused them to lose consumers, which in turn caused distributors to reduce the number of the Appellants' prepaid calling cards they purchase. This loss, according to the Appellants, was a loss of market share, as the Appellees' sales increased during the same time period. They also claim that their distribution network, commercial relations and goodwill have been irreparably harmed.

. . . At the hearing on May 9, 2007, the District Court denied the Appellants' motion for a preliminary injunction. Although the District Court found that a public interest existed in accurate representations to consumers regarding the number of minutes they receive when they purchase a calling card, it determined that the Appellants did not meet their burden of demonstrating that they would suffer irreparable harm. It reached this conclusion because the Appellants failed to show that they would suffer any harm other than just a financial loss or a loss of market share. . . .

"We review the denial of a preliminary injunction for 'an abuse of discretion, an error of law, or a clear mistake in the consideration of proof.' " . . .

As the Appellants argue, we have held that a loss of market share can constitute irreparable harm. However, this does not change the fact that a preliminary injunction should not be granted if the injury suffered by the moving party can be recouped in monetary damages. At the preliminary injunction hearing the Appellants implicitly admitted that the alleged harm they suffered could be calculated in money damages. After explaining that some loss of market share was caused by factors other than the Appellees' alleged false advertising, counsel for the Appellants stated: "We're going to have a real hard time. I'm not saying we won't be able to put forward damage numbers, but our ability to fully capture the damages is going to be severely undermined by the fact that the [Appellees] are going to tell you there may be a number of other factors that may be causing this loss also." As the statement suggests, the Appellants believed that their market losses could be recouped through monetary damages. The only other evidence that IDT points to in support of a potential irreparable injury is its loss of reputation or goodwill. Although we have recognized that such losses may constitute irreparable harm, our case law also indicates that such harm is limited to "the special problem of confusion that exists in cases involving trademark infringement and unfair competition." As the harm claimed by the Appellants is not analogous to the harm caused by consumer confusion, the line of cases recognizing loss of goodwill or reputation as irreparable harm is not applicable. Based on the record we cannot say that the District Court abused its discretion in denying injunctive relief because the Appellants failed to meet their burden of proving irreparable harm. . . .

NOTES AND QUESTIONS

Why is the harm here not analogous to harm that the court has accepted as irreparable in the past? If the plaintiff had claimed its harms weren't quantifiable, would it have risked losing standing?

(See Chapter 6). What should plaintiff have argued, and what evidence would support its claims?

IDT is an outlier. Many courts that find likely success on the merits are likely to accept the argument that, though some measure of damages may ultimately be provable, the actual harm from false advertising is so hard to measure that a finding of irreparable harm is justified. *See, e.g.*, Eastman Chem. Co. v. Plastipure, Inc., 969 F. Supp. 2d 756 (W.D. Tex. 2013), *aff'd*, 775 F.3d 230 (5th Cir. 2014).

Likelihood of Success on the Merits

The evaluation of the likelihood of a plaintiff's success on the merits essentially comes down to whether the plaintiff can show that the advertising claims, as understood by consumers, are false or misleading.

Balancing the Hardships

In evaluating this factor, the court compares the plaintiff's potential injury if an injunction is denied with the defendant's potential injury if an injunction is granted. An injunction that simply prevents the defendant from continuing to advertise falsely is generally not viewed by courts as a hardship for the defendant, as the defendant should be following that practice anyway.

A court may reject a proposed injunction if it would have too harsh an effect on the defendant—for example, if defendant is a small company or a company attempting to enter a new market. In *Abbott Laboratories v. Mead Johnson & Co.*, 971 F.2d 6 (7th Cir. 1992), for example, the parties marketed competing oral rehydration solutions for infants. The court held that the name of the defendant's product, Ricelyte, was misleading because, although it was derived from rice, it did not actually contain rice or rice carbohydrates. The court did not grant plaintiff its requested injunction requiring a recall of any product bearing the misleading labels. The court concluded that forcing the product off the market entirely—which would have been the effect of the proposed injunction—was too harsh a remedy. The Court of Appeals reversed. Although it agreed that a recall would have been too harsh, it directed the district court to fashion a less drastic remedy, such as directing the defendant to cease propounding the false claims and to issue corrective advertising and brochures.

As this example illustrates, a plaintiff should be careful in framing its request for relief to avoid the appearance of overreaching. By the same token, if a defendant cannot defeat preliminary injunctive relief entirely, it may be able to narrow the relief granted by pointing to the hardships that would be imposed if the precise relief requested were granted or by offering less drastic alternatives.

Public Interest

The public interest generally at issue is the public's right not to be deceived or confused by false advertising. This argument can be made by a plaintiff in virtually any case seeking to enjoin false advertising. The public interest factor, however, may be particularly compelling where public health and safety are at stake, especially that of children.

Defendants also can assert a First Amendment-backed public interest in the continued dissemination of advertising that provides consumers with accurate information and legitimate product choices. This factor may also help defendants if granting an injunction would deny the public access to a useful or innovative product. Abbott Labs. v. Mead Johnson & Co., 971 F.2d 6, 18 (7th Cir. 1992) (recalling misleadingly named oral electrolyte solution "would disserve the public interest" because it "is a safe and effective product whose presence in the market has promoted the public welfare by focusing attention upon [oral electrolyte] products and increasing their use").

B.   Permanent Injunctive Relief

The issues involved in permanent injunctive relief are similar to those attending a preliminary injunction, except that by definition a violation of the law has been established—and that makes a big difference. Consider how the court treats the adjudicated false advertiser in the following case.

PBM Products, LLC v. Mead Johnson & Co., 2010 WL 957756 (E.D. Va. 2010)

. . . In April 2009, store-brand infant formula producer PBM Products, LLC and PBM Nutritionals, LLC (collectively "PBM") sued "name-brand" infant formula producer Mead Johnson & Co. over a Mead Johnson advertisement that PBM asserted violated the Lanham Act. During a seven day jury trial, held on November 2–10, 2009, the jury was asked to evaluate whether four specific claims made in the Mead Johnson mailer communicated certain false or misleading messages concerning store-brand infant formulas, such as PBM's. Two of the four claims were express claims—the Mailer stated that (1) "mothers who buy store brand infant formula to save baby expenses are cutting back on nutrition compared to [Mead Johnson's] Enfamil" and (2) "only Enfamil has been clinically proven to improve infants' mental and visual development." Relying on consumer survey evidence, PBM contended that the Mailer also impliedly communicated two false and misleading claims: that (1) "Enfamil contains two important fatty acids, DHA and ARA, and that PBM's store brand infant formulas do not" and (2) "Enfamil has been clinically tested against and shown to be superior to PBM's formula with respect to brain and eye development in infants."

The Jury Verdict Sheet asked, "Has PBM established, by a preponderance of the evidence, that Mead Johnson engaged in false advertising in violation of the Lanham Act?" The jury answered in the affirmative and awarded PBM $13.5 million in damages.

On December 1, 2009, this Court granted the injunctive relief sought by PBM. The Order stated, in relevant part:

> (1) Mead Johnson is immediately enjoined and restrained, directly and indirectly, and whether alone or in concert with others, including any agent, employee, representative, subsidiary, or affiliate of Mead Johnson, from doing any of the following:

>> (A) publishing or circulating any advertisement, promotional material, or other literature that bears any designation, description, or representation concerning PBM's infant formula that is false, including that, "It may be tempting to try a less expensive store brand, but only Enfamil LIPIL is clinically proven to improve brain and eye development," or "There are plenty of other ways to save on baby expenses without cutting back on nutrition," or from implying the same.

>> (B) making any false statement or representation concerning PBM's infant formula that is false, including that, "It may be tempting to try a less expensive store brand, but only Enfamil LIPIL is clinically proven to improve brain and eye development," or "There are plenty of other ways to save on baby expenses without cutting back on nutrition," or from implying the same.

(2) Mead Johnson is DIRECTED to retrieve any and all advertisements, promotional materials or other literature containing the aforementioned assertions, claims, or allegations regarding PBM's store brand formula from the public forum.

(3) This Order shall remain in full force until such time as this Court specifically orders otherwise.

Over the weeks since that injunction was issued, the parties have wrangled over the validity, scope, and effect of the injunction and have filed a number of motions now before the Court. . . .

II. DISCUSSION

Mead Johnson seeks to vacate and amend the injunction because (1) the Court failed to articulate the reasons for issuing the injunction, as is required by *eBay, Inc. v. MercExchange, LLC*, and (2) the scope of the injunction exceeds the bounds of the jury's verdict and the record. For its part, PBM has filed motions to modify and enforce the injunction. These motions create two issues the Court must now address: (1) whether an injunction should be entered at all and (2) if an injunction is entered, what should be its scope. Each issue is addressed below.

A. Propriety of Entering an Injunction

Federal courts have the power to enjoin behavior that is found to be false or misleading under the Lanham Act. 15 U.S.C. § 1116(a). Before an injunction may be issued, the party seeking the injunction must demonstrate that (1) it has suffered an irreparable injury; (2) remedies available at law are inadequate; (3) the balance of the hardships favors the party seeking the injunction; and (4) the public interest would not be disserved by the injunction. A decision to grant or deny a permanent injunction is reviewed for abuse of discretion. Here, each of the required elements favors PBM.

First, the Court observes that "the irreparable harm prong can be satisfied 'upon a demonstration that the competitor's advertising tends to mislead consumers.' " Consequently, the jury's verdict in favor of PBM presumptively satisfies the irreparable injury requirement. Moreover, trial testimony by representatives of both parties established that in addition to lost sales, false advertising also inflicts substantial harm on a company's reputation and goodwill.

Second, "[d]amages to reputation and goodwill are not items that are easily measured by a legal calculation of damages." Thus, while Mead Johnson is correct that it appears the jury awarded PBM some future damages, the Court disagrees with Mead Johnson's conclusion that an award of future damages indicates that monetary damages are an adequate and sufficient award in this case. The monetary judgment against Mead Johnson compensates PBM for harm that flowed from the Mailer, an injunction properly prevents Mead Johnson from infecting the marketplace with the same or similar claims in different advertisements in the future. Mead Johnson asserts, though, that the Mailer is no longer in circulation and it has not made any indication that it will continue to make those claims in future advertisements. It is that uncertainty, however, that makes an injunction all the more appropriate as preventing the necessity of multiple suits is a classic justification for finding common law remedies inadequate.

Third, when faced with the question of whether an injunction should be entered at all, an evaluation of the resulting hardships favors PBM. Mead Johnson simply has no equitable interest in perpetuating the false and misleading claims in the Mailer. Mead Johnson's main contentions concern the nature of injunctive relief, not whether that relief should be granted in the first instance, and therefore do not mandate a different conclusion.

Lastly, the public interest heavily favors injunctive relief in this case. It is self-evident that preventing false or misleading advertising is in the public interest in general. False or misleading messages concerning a matter of public health, such as the nutritional qualities of infant formula, makes that conclusion especially true in this case. Moreover, allowing false or misleading advertising to continue to seep into the public's discourse on the relative benefits of name brand versus store brand formula would undermine, rather than promote, the Lanham Act's goal of protecting consumers. Accordingly, the Court finds that the *eBay* factors each weigh in favor of PBM and therefore an injunction is appropriate in this case.

B. Scope of an Injunction

The parties also disagree over the scope of any available injunctive relief. Mead Johnson claims that because the general verdict entered by the jury did not specify which of the four statements in the Mailer the jury found false or misleading, the injunction must be limited to the entire Mailer or "other advertisements not colorably different from the Mailer." PBM responds by claiming that the Court should enjoin the two express as well as the two implied claims in the Mailer because such a ruling would be supported by the record and not inconsistent with the jury's general verdict.

Rule 65(d) of the Federal Rules of Civil Procedure requires that an injunction "state its terms specifically" and "describe in reasonable detail . . . the act or acts restrained or required." The type of injunctive relief granted "rests within the equitable discretion" of the district court. While that discretion is constrained by a jury's general verdict under the doctrine of collateral estoppel, district courts can nevertheless make factual findings to support equitable relief so long as those findings are not inconsistent with factual findings essential to the jury's verdict.

Based on the parties' arguments and a review of the pleadings and trial transcripts, the Court will enjoin Mead Johnson from distributing the Mailer or any advertisement not colorably different from the Mailer. Although PBM would like the Court to specifically enjoin the implied claims, the Court finds that an injunction applicable to the Mailer or anything similar sufficiently encompasses the implied claims made in the Mailer.

As was done in the original injunction, the Court will also specifically enjoin the two express claims made in the Mailer. Mead Johnson is correct that the general verdict did not specify if the jury concluded that the express claims that (1) store bought brands represent a cut back on nutrition and (2) only Enfamil is clinically proven to improve brain and eye development in infants are false or misleading. But the Court now concludes that the record supports an injunction including the express claims and that such an injunction would not be inconsistent with the jury's verdict. . . .

The original injunction also included a requirement that Mead Johnson retrieve the offending Mailer from the "public forum." PBM and Mead Johnson agree that the Mailer was sent to consumers' homes and thus such a requirement would be futile. PBM, however, requests that the injunction apply to the four claims made in the Mailer and that the retrieval requirement apply to any advertising or promotional material containing those claims. PBM adds that if retrieval is not possible, a sticker should be placed over the offending portions of any label. Mead Johnson has stated the Mailer is no longer distributed and that it is not making three of the claims in the Mailer at all, however, it has continued to make the "only Enfamil Lipil is clinically proven" claim. Mead Johnson, via an affidavit, also notes that this claim is on all of its labels and that retrieving them would cost millions of dollars and would disrupt the entire supply of infant formula in the United States. Placing a sticker, Mead Johnson states, would also cost millions of dollars. A retrieval or stickering requirement would significantly alter the balance of the hardships and thus the Court declines to impose those conditions on Mead Johnson. The injunction does apply, however, to all advertising or promotional material or statements going forward.

Lastly, PBM wants the Court to require Mead Johnson to send corrective advertising to all individuals in Mead Johnson's Enfamil Family Beginnings database stating that the four claims stated in the Mailer are false or misleading. Although the Court acknowledges the reputational harm that false messages can inflict, PBM is not entitled to an order requiring Mead Johnson to issue corrective advertising because it did not seek that remedy in its complaint and has not done any prospective corrective advertising of its own, suggesting that the desire for this remedy arose only after it obtained a favorable verdict. Moreover, the jury's award included damages for future harm from the Mailer, which encompasses the effect the Mailer had on those that received it. Thus, the request for corrective advertising is denied.

NOTES AND QUESTIONS

Why should the court care if it costs the defendant "too much" to remediate the harm it created? After all, those damages are proximately caused by the falsity, and wouldn't they serve as a good deterrent for other advertisers' wrongdoing?

C.   Types of Injunctive Relief

As suggested by the *PBM* case, the types of injunctive relief that may be obtained in a false advertising action fall into three broad categories: (1) prohibition of further dissemination of the false material; (2) a requirement that the offender engage in corrective advertising or consumer education to counter the false message presented; and (3) in extraordinary cases, recall or destruction of the product or advertising.

Prohibition on Further Dissemination

For obvious reasons, an order prohibiting further dissemination of the false advertising is the most commonly sought and granted form of injunctive relief. Such an order typically includes a prohibition on using the particular advertising at issue in all formats in which it appeared, such as television, radio and print, and a requirement that the defendant not make the contested claim in any other advertising.

However, in Lanham Act cases, any such injunction cannot limit a media company if enforcement would interfere with normal publication schedules. The Lanham Act prohibits the issuance of an injunction against the publisher "of a newspaper, magazine, or other similar periodical or an electronic communication containing infringing matter or violating matter" if such an injunction would "delay the delivery of such issue or transmission of such electronic communication after the regular time for such delivery or transmission." 15 U.S.C. § 1114(2)(c).

Fencing-in and Exclusion Orders

A fencing-in order—a remedy available to the FTC, but not to private plaintiffs—restricts the defendant from future conduct that is broader than the defendant's present unlawful conduct. It may cover more claims and/or more products than involved in the litigated case. An exclusion order goes further and bans the defendant from an industry entirely.

Such remedies are prophylactics to prevent future unlawful conduct. Violation of an FTC order can lead to swifter and greater penalties than violation of the FTC Act, even when the covered conduct is the same, which is why the FTC seeks such orders.

In *Telebrands Corp. v. Federal Trade Commission*, 457 F.3d 354 (4th Cir. 2006), the advertiser marketed a wide variety of products, all based on its strategy of free-riding on others' claims. Telebrands violated the FTC Act by advertising a device, the Ab Force; the ads referred to "those fantastic electronic ab belt infomercials on TV" and pointed out that the other belts "promis[e] to get our abs into great shape fast—without exercise." The ads also showed "[f]it, well-muscled models" using the Ab Force, but made no other explicit claims. The ALJ found that Telebrands made unsubstantiated weight-loss and muscle-definition claims. As a remedy, the FTC sought an order governing all claims and products advertised by Telebrands.

The FTC's final order required that Telebrands, "in connection with the manufacturing, labeling, advertising, promotion, offering for sale, sale, or distribution of Ab Force, any other EMS device, or *any food, drug, dietary supplement, device, or any other product, service or program*, shall not make any representation, in any manner, expressly or by implication, about weight, inch, or fat loss, muscle definition, exercise benefits, *or the health benefits, safety, performance, or efficacy of any product, service, or program*, unless, at the time the representation is made, [Telebrands] possess[es] and rel[ies] upon competent and reliable evidence, which when appropriate must be competent and reliable scientific evidence, that substantiates the representation" (emphasis added).

The FTC and reviewing courts consider three factors in determining whether a final order bears a reasonable relationship to the violation it is intended to remedy: (1) the seriousness and deliberateness of the violation; (2) the ease with which the violative claim may be transferred to other products; and (3) whether the respondent has a history of prior violations. This is a sliding scale; not all three factors must be present to uphold a broad remedy.

In the *Telebrands* case, the violations of the FTC Act were serious, not merely overselling a product basically fit for its advertised purpose. Telebrands lacked any substantiation for the core claims at issue. It also mounted a major, successful, nationwide ad campaign, resulting in over $19 million of sales, an additional reason to find that the violation was serious. The violations were also deliberate. Telebrands wanted to capitalize on other ads claiming extensive benefits for abdominal belts. "Telebrands's assertion that, because it did not explicitly make those same claims in the Ab Force advertisements, it did not intend for consumers to believe that the Ab Force provided those same benefits strains credulity. In fact, Telebrands calculatedly fostered such beliefs through its choice of visual images for the television advertisements." These claims were misleading, because regardless of whether the other devices could deliver the promised benefits, Telebrands lacked substantiation for the Ab Force itself.

Moreover, Telebrands's conduct was easily transferable to other products, including many it already marketed. "Compare and save" was one of its standard marketing tools. "Telebrands deliberately selected a popular product category with frequently advertised comparative products. The product category became popular due, at least in part, to the claims that were subsequently the subject of FTC enforcement action." Telebrands controlled the degree of similarity between the Ab Force and the other devices on the market. "Only Telebrands's imagination and budget would limit its ability to use similar tactics in the future." The order didn't bar the compare-and-save strategy, only the use of that strategy to make unsubstantiated claims.

Because of the positive findings on the first two factors, the court found it unnecessary to consider Telebrands's history of prior violations.

Does a fencing-in order raise any First Amendment concerns? What about an exclusion order? *Cf.* POM Wonderful LLC v. FTC, 777 F.3d 478 (D.C. Cir. 2015) (holding that the First Amendment barred a requirement that advertiser possess two randomized clinical trials supporting health claims, but allowing FTC to require at least one randomized clinical trial).

Corrective Advertising/Consumer Education by the Defendant

As indicated above, both courts and the Federal Trade Commission may order offending advertisers to disseminate advertising designed to correct any misperceptions created by the false advertisement. Corrective advertising is particularly appropriate where the offending advertising has contributed to a public perception of a product that is likely to linger in the public's mind even after the false advertising has ceased.

One famous example of corrective advertising ordered by the FTC involves the mouthwash Listerine. In extensive and repeated television commercials and print advertisements, Warner Lambert claimed that its Listerine mouthwash combatted sore throats and other symptoms of the common cold. The FTC determined that the advertisements, which had run in various forms since Listerine was first introduced in 1879, were false, and it ordered Listerine to cease the offending advertising. To help correct the misimpressions created in nearly a century's worth of false ads, the FTC also required Warner Lambert to include the statement "Listerine will not help prevent colds or sore throats or lessen their severity" in the next $10 million of advertising it ran. This was necessary, the FTC concluded, to combat the "widespread reputation" that Listerine had developed "over a period of many years" as a result of the advertisements. *See* Warner-Lambert Co. v. FTC, 562 F.2d 749 (D.C. Cir. 1977).

[Ad: Chicago Tribune, Aug. 26, 1979, w12]

The details of corrective advertising orders vary widely. Normally, such orders will set forth the disclosure required, either in specific wording or by general message, and the time period during which the corrective advertising must run or, as an alternative, the minimum amount of money that must be spent on such advertising. *See, e.g.,* Novartis Corp. v. FTC, 223 F.3d 783, 786 (D.C. Cir. 2000) (ordering that corrective advertising "continue for one year and until respondent has expended on Doan's advertising a sum equal to the average spent annually during the eight years of the challenged campaign"); Gillette Co. v. Norelco Consumer Prods. Co., 946 F. Supp. 115, 140 (D. Mass. 1996) (specifying content, type size, and timing of corrective portion of advertising). Such orders may also require that the advertising be printed in a particular size or font, or mandate other details concerning placement of the corrective advertising. Such specifications are designed to ensure that the corrective disclosures are as effective as possible and are not disseminated in such a way that obscures the intended message.

Orders requiring corrective advertising are less common in Lanham Act cases than in FTC cases; courts often expect Lanham Act plaintiffs to engage in counter-advertising to mitigate its own damages. *See, e.g.,* Eastman Chem. Co. v. Plastipure, Inc., 969 F. Supp. 2d 756 (W.D. Tex. 2013) (declining to order losing defendants to run plaintiff's proposed corrective advertising, given the significant investment plaintiff had already made in correcting the record; "it is unclear what additional effect a digital billboard written by [plaintiff] and posted on Defendants' website will have"), *aff'd,* 775 F.3d 230 (5th Cir. 2014); Irwin Indus. Tool Co. v. Worthington Cylinders Wis., LLC, 747 F. Supp. 2d 568 (W.D.N.C. 2010) (corrective advertising was inappropriate where there was no danger to public health or welfare, plaintiff succeeded on a theory of literal falsity rather than presenting evidence that consumers were actually confused, and the false ads at issue ran a total of four times in one professional publication over two years before trial; plaintiff had already issued multiple press releases and letters to retail customers describing the lawsuit's outcome). When a defendant was found liable for deliberate falsity, never attempted to retract any copies of the false video it made, and continued to encourage its distributors to use the video, however, the court ordered it to send by first-class mail a copy of the jury's findings in this case to each of the vendors or distributors that received the video. *See* Nat'l Prods., Inc. v. Gamber-Johnson LLC, 734 F. Supp. 2d 1160 (W.D. Wash. 2010).

Orders requiring an advertiser to engage in corrective advertising can be challenged on First Amendment grounds, typically because such orders force them to disseminate statements that they would rather not make. In the case of commercial speech, though, courts have held that the First Amendment does not prohibit government or the courts "from insuring that the stream of commercial information flow(s) cleanly as well as freely." *See, e.g.,* Castrol Inc. v. Pennzoil Co., 987 F.2d 939 (3d Cir. 1993). Thus, orders requiring corrective advertising have been upheld against constitutional challenge so long as the "restriction inherent in [the] order is no greater than necessary to serve the interest involved." *See, e.g.*, Novartis Corp. v. FTC, 223 F.3d 783 (2d Cir. 2000) (upholding order requiring corrective advertising as advancing a state interest and tailored to that interest).

Some courts sidestep this issue entirely by adding the plaintiff's cost of responsive advertising to the defendant's damages obligation. This allows the plaintiff to control the content of corrective information, releases the defendant from the burden of unwanted speech, and ensures that the plaintiff is compensated for advertising costs it would not otherwise have incurred. *See, e.g.*, ALPO Petfoods, Inc. v. Ralston Purina Co., 913 F.2d 958 (D.C. Cir. 1990). But is corrective advertising by the injured competitor, which will likely be seen as self-interested, likely to be as effective at educating consumers as corrective advertising by the false advertiser? Consider the likely burden of monitoring the corrective advertising and the advertiser's incentives to downplay the effects of the disclosure when comparing these two choices.

More generally: When an advertiser has caused the consuming public to believe false information, what are the best ways to fix that? Can you think of other options than the advertiser's corrective advertising or a competitor's counter-advertising? Consider the evidence from Chapter 5 about how hard it is to create an appropriate disclosure. Correcting existing misinformation may be even more challenging, since most people resist updating existing beliefs. *See* Stephan Lewandowsky et al., *Misinformation and Its Correction: Continued Influence and Successful Debiasing*, 13 PSYCHOL. SCI. PUB. INT. 106 (2012).

In the following case, the district court ordered a disclaimer, which is not exactly corrective advertising but has some similarities. Given what you know about disclosures and disclaimers, keep an eye on the reaction of the court of appeals—to what extent is the court of appeals making an empirical assessment, and on what evidence is it based?

TrafficSchool.com, Inc. v. Edriver Inc., 653 F.3d 820 (9th Cir. 2011)

[Defendants operated a website at DMV.org offering drivers' education and related services. Many people falsely believed that it was an official DMV site, some going so far as to email sensitive personal information about traffic tickets, credit card numbers, and even Social Security numbers to the site. Even police officers were confused. The district court found both likely and actual confusion.]

. . . By way of a remedy, the district court ordered DMV.org to present every site visitor with a splash screen stating, "YOU ARE ABOUT TO ENTER A PRIVATELY OWNED WEBSITE THAT IS NOT OWNED OR OPERATED BY ANY STATE GOVERNMENT AGENCY." Visitors can't access DMV.org's content without clicking a "CONTINUE" button on the splash screen. Defendants argue that the district court abused its discretion by fashioning a "blanket injunction" that's overbroad—i.e., restrains conduct not at issue in plaintiffs' complaint—and violates the First Amendment.

Overbreadth. The district court reasoned that the splash screen was necessary to: (1) "remedy any confusion that consumers have already developed before visiting DMV.org for the first time," (2) "remedy the public interest concerns associated with [confused visitors'] transfer of sensitive information to Defendants," and (3) "prevent confusion among DMV.org's consumers." Defendants argue that the splash screen doesn't effectuate these stated goals. But their only evidence is a declaration from DMV.org's CEO stating that defendants tested several alternative disclaimers and found them to be more effective than the splash screen in preventing consumers from emailing DMV.org with sensitive personal information. To the extent we credit a self-serving declaration, defendants' evidence doesn't prove that the splash screen is ineffective in this respect, and says nothing about whether the alternative disclaimers serve the other two interests identified by the district court. Defendants haven't carried their "heavy burden" of showing that their alternative disclaimers reduce DMV.org's likelihood of confusing consumers. The scope of an injunction is within the broad discretion of the district court, and the district court here didn't abuse that discretion when it concluded that the splash screen was the optimal means of correcting defendants' false advertising.

First Amendment. Courts routinely grant permanent injunctions prohibiting deceptive advertising. Because false or misleading commercial statements aren't constitutionally protected, such injunctions rarely raise First Amendment concerns.

The permanent injunction here does raise such concerns because it erects a barrier to all content on the DMV.org website, not merely that which is deceptive. Some of the website's content is informational and thus fully protected, such as guides to applying for a driver's license, buying insurance and beating traffic tickets. The informational content is commingled with truthful commercial speech, which is entitled to significant First Amendment protection. The district court was required to tailor the injunction so as to burden no more protected speech than necessary.

The district court does not appear to have considered that its injunction would permanently and unnecessarily burden access to DMV.org's First Amendment-protected content. The splash screen forces potential visitors to take an additional navigational step, deterring some consumers from entering the website altogether. It also precludes defendants from tailoring DMV.org's landing page to make it welcoming to visitors, and interferes with the operation of search engines, making it more difficult for consumers to find the website and its protected content.[6] All of these burdens on protected speech are, under the current injunction, permanent.

The district court premised its injunction on its findings that defendants' "search engine marketing" and "non-sponsored natural listings, including the DMV.org domain name," caused consumers to be confused even before they viewed DMV.org's content [because defendants used terms associated with government entities]. The court also identified specific misleading statements on the website. The splash screen is justified to remedy the harm caused by such practices so long as they continue. But website content and advertising practices can and do change over time. Indeed, the court found that defendants had already "made some changes to DMV.org and how they marketed it."

The splash screen is also justified so long as it helps to remedy lingering confusion caused by defendants' past deception. But the splash screen will continue to burden DMV.org's protected content, even if all remaining harm has dissipated. At that point, the injunction will burden protected speech without justification, thus burdening more speech than necessary.

On remand, the district court shall reconsider the duration of the splash screen in light of any intervening changes in the website's content and marketing practices, as well as the dissipation of the deception resulting from past practices. If the district court continues to require the splash screen, it shall explain the continuing

---

[6] Defendants introduced unrebutted evidence that splash screens commonly interfere with the automated "spiders" that search engines deploy to "crawl" the Internet and compile the indexes of web pages they use to determine every page's search ranking. And splash screens themselves don't have high search rankings: Search engines commonly base these rankings on the web page's content and the number of other pages linking to it, and splash screens lack both content and links.

justification for burdening the website's protected content and what conditions defendants must satisfy in order to remove the splash screen in the future. In the alternative, or in addition, the court may permanently enjoin defendants from engaging in deceptive marketing or placing misleading statements on DMV.org.

NOTES AND QUESTIONS

Examine the splash screen:

Based on what you know about disclosures and disclaimers, is this a good way to prevent consumer confusion? Defendants used to put "Unofficial Guide to the DMV" in their license plate logo, but they removed it. Instead, the disclaimer runs at the very top, a couple of pixels away from the top of the browser window, in grey rather than black text, not near the action invitation to click to continue, and not near the DMV.org logo, both of which are far more prominent to the eye. How would this fare under the FTC's guidelines for online disclosures?

The district court found that the domain name played a key role in the deception. If the splash screen is justified "so long as [the deceptive practices]" continue, won't the splash screen be needed until there is a new domain name?

The remedy of a mandatory splash screen was, as far as your casebook authors are aware, unprecedented. A splash screen can hurt or destroy search engine indexing, effectively rendering the domain name worthless. Therefore, even though the district court didn't award any damages (a ruling affirmed on appeal), the mandatory splash screen was potentially far more detrimental.

Should courts be more willing to order disclaimers? When defendants propose them as alternatives to ceasing a type of advertising entirely, how should courts evaluate them? Despite its concern for the First Amendment, the *Edriver* court also emphasized the undesirability of forcing a successful plaintiff to relitigate every small change, and thus the need to put the burden of showing that a defendant's proposed disclaimer would be effective on the defendant.

Of course, the *court* didn't have to show that its own mandated disclaimer would actually help consumers. Should proof of effectiveness be required before granting any disclaimer remedy? Does it matter that the alternative is to suppress the speech entirely? One argument in favor of complete suppression: if consumers are truly being deceived, and if disclaimers often don't work, then the "compromise" of a disclaimer is likely to be no compromise at all.

Below is the DMV.org landing page as of June 2015. What do you think of this version?

Product Recall / Destruction

In extraordinary cases, recall and destruction of the physical advertising materials may be the only effective remedy. Such cases are rare, however, in part because of the drastic nature of the remedy and the burden inherent in complying with such an order. It can be appropriate, though, in cases of egregious misconduct or other unusual circumstances. *See* Playskool, Inc. v. Product Dev. Grp., Inc., 699 F. Supp. 1056 (E.D.N.Y. 1988) (toy recall ordered because misleading language on packaging created safety hazard for children).

To ensure that the recall is not overly drastic, some courts specifically allow the recalled materials to be preserved. For example, one court ordered a recall of advertising materials including the tags used on garments on which the false claims were made, reasoning that, if the defendant were to succeed on the merits, it could reintroduce the recalled material. In that case, the court cited egregious actions by the defendant as supporting a drastic remedy, noting that the defendant had no evidence to support the claims when it had made them and that the claims were "carelessly or irresponsibly made and that any 'prejudice' which accrues can be considered to be self-inflicted." W.L. Gore & Assoc., Inc. v. Totes, Inc., 788 F. Supp. 800 (D.

Del. 1992). Another alternative where false claims are made on packaging is to order stickers placed over the false claims; this is not cheap, but it is less expensive than a full recall and may be easier for a court to order. *See* Grpe. SEB USA, Inc. v. Euro-Pro Operating LLC, 2014 WL 2002126 (W.D. Pa. May 15, 2014).

As a result of the First Amendment issues that can be implicated, recalls generally are not used when the false claims are made in published materials such as books and magazines.

D.   Defenses to Injunctive Relief

The most common equitable defenses to injunctive relief include delay or laches, acquiescence, mootness, and unclean hands. Invariably, these defenses will fail against a government enforcement action. *But cf.* FTC v. Lane Labs-USA, Inc., 624 F.3d 575 (3d Cir. 2010) (considering FTC's years-long delay in informing defendant that it considered defendant to be in violation of consent decree in evaluating whether defendant was entitled to a defense of substantial compliance, though noting that defendant could still be in violation, regardless of its good faith efforts, if the violations were more than technical or inadvertent).

Delay/Laches

Unreasonable delay by a private plaintiff in challenging a false advertisement, often called "laches," will almost always bar a preliminary injunction. It may also bar relief entirely. However, laches as a total defense is rarely favored.

The Lanham Act itself contains no statute of limitations. As a result, courts typically consider the statute of limitations of analogous state law claims and hold that a claim is entirely barred by laches if the statute has run. See Jarrow Formulas, Inc. v. Nutrition Now, Inc.,

304 F.3d 829 (9th Cir. 2002) (fifteen-year delay in challenging advertising was unreasonable where state false advertising law provided for three-year statute of limitations).

A claim for injunctive relief may be barred by laches where the plaintiff has unreasonably delayed in pursuing a claim and the defendant has suffered prejudice as a result of the delay. In such cases, courts have reasoned that "the 'failure to act sooner undercuts the sense of urgency that ordinarily accompanies a motion for preliminary relief and suggests that there is, in fact, no irreparable injury.'" Tough Traveler, Ltd. v. Outbound Prods., 60 F.3d 964 (2d Cir. 1995).

Even a short delay may be fatal to preliminary relief, especially where a relatively large company is the plaintiff. In *Hansen Beverage Co. v. Innovation Ventures*, LLC, 2008 WL 4492644 (S.D. Cal. 2008), Hansen claimed that 5-Hour Energy's name was false and misleading. Hansen's president indicated that he learned of the claims one month before filing suit. But Hansen's awareness of the energy shot market, in which 5-Hour Energy is a market leader, "must have" predated the lawsuit by "at least several months." This was too much delay.

Courts may, however, grant preliminary relief if a delay is attributable to plaintiff's efforts to investigate the offending activity or settlement negotiations between the parties. W.L. Gore & Assoc., Inc. v. Totes, Inc., 788 F. Supp. 800 (D. Del. 1992) (four-month delay in filing from the discovery of the false claims was not unreasonable, where the plaintiff used that time to investigate the claims and try to negotiate with the defendant). Delay may also be excused if the defendant made representations that lulled the plaintiff into a false sense of security. Similarly, if the defendant has changed its advertising campaign incrementally over time, a court may find that this "progressive encroachment" excuses the delay. For example, where a defendant had incrementally changed its advertising over the course of two years, a court found that the slow process of change did not give the plaintiff adequate notice of the false claims, and thus laches did not bar the issuance of a preliminary injunction. W.L. Gore, *supra*.

Plaintiffs may also avoid a laches defense by showing that their claims weren't complete earlier. *See* Star-Brite Distributing, Inc. v. Gold Eagle Co., 2016 WL 4470093 (S.D. Fla. Jan. 25, 2016).

A successful laches defense to a permanent injunction requires the defendant to show that "assertion [now] of a claim available some time ago would be 'inequitable' in light of the delay in bringing that claim" and that the defendant "has changed his position in a way that would not have occurred if the plaintiff had not delayed." One court thus rejected a false advertising claim brought against Turtle Wax— claiming that the product name was misleading because the product contained no wax—where the plaintiff had "permitted Turtle Wax's advertising and the development of its products to go unchecked for well over a ten- to twenty-year period." The court determined that Turtle Wax had suffered prejudice because, had plaintiff "pressed its claims in a timely manner, Turtle Wax certainly could have invested its time and money in other areas or simply renamed its products." Hot Wax, Inc. v. Turtle Wax, Inc., 191 F.3d 813 (7th Cir. 1999).

Since it is an equitable doctrine, a laches defense may not be available if the equities are against it. For example, if the defendant intentionally committed false advertising or if public health or safety concerns override considerations of equity, courts will be reluctant to bar an otherwise valid claim on laches grounds.

Acquiescence

A defendant may defeat a claim for injunctive relief, and Lanham Act damages, by showing that the plaintiff acquiesced in the advertising in question—that is, the plaintiff provided either an express or implied assurance that plaintiff would not object to the advertising— and those assurances prejudiced the defendant.

For example, where a music publisher expressly allowed the Walt Disney Company to represent to the public for many years in the context of film releases that the rendition of Stravinsky's "The Rite of Spring" in "Fantasia" was "full and accurate," the publisher could not challenge that representation when it was made in connection with release of a videotape of the film. *See* Boosey & Hawkes Music Publications v. Walt Disney Co., 145 F.3d 481 (2d Cir. 1998). Similarly, a court rejected a claim of false advertising where the plaintiff approved the advertisement in question in advance. L.S. Heath & Son, Inc. v. AT&T Information Systems, Inc., 9 F.3d 561 (7th Cir. 1993).

Mootness

An application "for injunctive relief is moot when the offending conduct ceases and the court finds that there is no reasonable expectation that it will resume." In false advertising cases, courts may find the application for injunctive relief moot where, for example, the defendant represents that the allegedly offending advertising has been revised and is no longer being run in its original form or has otherwise been voluntarily withdrawn. *See* American Express Travel Related Servs. Co., Inc. v. Mastercard Int'l Inc., 776 F. Supp. 787 (S.D.N.Y. 1991).

Unclean Hands

An unclean hands defense has three elements: (1) the plaintiff intended to engage in inequitable conduct; (2) the plaintiff was engaged in inequitable conduct when it filed the suit; and (3) that plaintiff's inequitable conduct is substantially related to the issues in the litigation, such as plaintiff's own false advertising concerning a related claim. As an example, unclean hands failed in a lawsuit over an ice cream advertisement suggesting that the product was from Sweden—but was actually domestically produced—where the challenger had engaged in similar advertising tactics, because that wasn't sufficiently related to the advertiser's own allegedly false advertising. Häagen-Dazs, Inc. v. Frusen Glädjé Ltd., 493 F. Supp. 73 (S.D.N.Y. 1980).

However, a court did allow an unclean hands defense to proceed where Pom Wonderful (Pom) sued Coca-Cola for selling a "Pomegranate Blueberry Flavored 100% Juice Blend" with very, very little pomegranate or blueberry juice in it. The court explained that "the relevant inquiry is 'not [whether] the plaintiff's hands are dirty, but [whether] [s]he dirtied them in acquiring the right [s]he now asserts, or [whether] the manner of dirtying renders inequitable the assertion of such rights against the defendants.'" Pom's health claims allegedly created the demand for pomegranate juice. Pom alleged that consumers were confused into thinking they were getting healthy pomegranate-blueberry juice when they were really mostly getting "less healthy" apple and grape juices. Coca-Cola responded that the health benefits were unsubstantiated, which violated the FTCA (a finding that had been recently affirmed by the D.C. Circuit); this was directly related to the conduct Pom alleged had harmed it, even though Coca-Cola wouldn't have been entitled to bring a claim under the FTCA. *See* POM Wonderful LLC v. Coca Cola Co., 166 F. Supp. 3d 1085 (C.D. Cal. 2016).

Balancing Unclean Hands with the Public Interest

TrafficSchool.Com, Inc. v. Edriver, Inc., 653 F.3d 820 (9th Cir. 2011), involved litigants who were not associated with any state's Department of Motor Vehicles (DMV). Defendants owned DMV.org, which carried driver-related information and ads but was not an official DMV site for any state. There was substantial evidence that consumers mistakenly believed the site was an official DMV site, including instances when consumers sent credit card and Social Security numbers to defendants when attempting to renew their licenses. Plaintiffs, who provided traffic school services, sued for false advertising under California state law and the Lanham Act.

Defendants argued that plaintiffs were guilty of unclean hands, because they also registered domain names using "dmv," including dmvlicenserenewal.com. The district court found that those names were confusing in precisely the same way. Moreover, plaintiffs tried to advertise on DMV.org, running test ads on the site and negotiating with defendants for a partnership at precisely the same time as they were also internally planning a campaign of notifying DMVs that DMV.org was causing confusion. Thus, plaintiffs were complicit in the false advertising.

The district court nonetheless reasoned that unclean hands don't necessarily preclude injunctive relief. Injunctions protect the public, and it may be better to remedy one wrong than leave two wrongs unaddressed.

On appeal, the court of appeals held that the finding of unclean hands was clearly erroneous. Plaintiffs' registration of DMV domain names and attempts to advertise on DMV.org was not the required "clear, convincing evidence" that "plaintiff[s'] conduct [wa]s inequitable" and "relate[d] to the subject matter of" their false advertising claims. First, registration of a domain name isn't unclean hands until there's a website that confuses consumers. And plaintiffs' ads on DMV.org ran for just six hours, a de minimis period of time. There was no evidence of actual deception caused by plaintiffs' advertising. Though an internal email from plaintiffs recommended an "[i]f you can't join 'em, shut 'em down approach" to DMV.org, bad intentions that weren't put into effect weren't unclean hands. "[U]sing litigation to shut down a competitor who uses unfair trade practices is precisely what the Lanham Act seeks to encourage."

2. Money Awards

A. Monetary Remedies in FTC Actions

The FTC can seek redress for consumers or disgorgement of the defendant's ill-gotten gains, and it often does so when it finds a violation. (State AGs often proceed similarly). Given that the FTC targets the most exploitative schemes, multimillion-dollar awards are not uncommon. In October 2016, the FTC received the largest judgment in its litigation history, $1.3 billion, based on deceptive payday lending schemes.

When the FTC litigates instead of obtaining a consent decree, it generally seeks monetary redress for consumers as part of a permanent injunction. *See* 15 U.S.C. §53(b). To get the full amount due, it may pursue "relief defendants," people or entities who are in possession of money derived from the §5 violation although they did not participate in it. Banks and spouses are the usual targets, though anyone to whom a gratuitous transfer has been made by a person who did engage in a §5 violation can be a relief defendant. *See* FTC v. LeadClick Media, LLC, 15-1009-cv (2d Cir. Sept. 23, 2016) (holding that a payment of valid intercorporate debt was not a gratuitous transfer and thus that corporate parent was not a valid relief defendant).

Some commentators have questioned the legitimacy of seeking equitable monetary relief for consumers under § 53(b). *See* J. Howard Beales III and Timothy J. Muris, *Striking the Proper Balance: Redress under Section 13(b) of the FTC Act*, 79 ANTITRUST L.J. 1 (2013). In particular, using this tactic avoids § 57(b), which explicitly authorizes consumer redress under the FTCA—but only after extended administrative and then judicial proceedings, and only when the defendant knew or should have known the practices at issue were dishonest or fraudulent.

Still, given the utility of proceeding directly to federal court, especially when immediate asset seizure will prevent fraudsters from taking the money and running, the FTC is unlikely to stop its present practices. Courts have given the FTC wide discretion in determining appropriate remedies, including restitution (redress). *See, e.g.,* Federal Trade Commission v. Ross, 743 F.3d 886 (4th Cir. 2014) (bringing the number of circuits that have allowed monetary redress under §53(b) to six, with zero that have not).

In *Federal Trade Commission v. National Urological Group*, 645 F. Supp. 2d 1167 (N.D. Ga. 2008), the FTC sued the defendants for falsely marketing weight-loss and erectile-performance dietary supplements. The court found injunctive relief and consumer redress appropriate. Defendants made over $15 million in sales. Defendants argued, among other things, that they should get to reduce this amount by sales to customers who reordered the product, who were obviously motivated by actual experience with the product. The court disagreed. There was no evidence of what motivated reordering decisions, and the fact that the consumers' (presumably positive) experience may have contributed to the reorders didn't negate the problems with the ads. *See also* FTC v. Lights of Am., Inc., 2013 WL 5230681 (C.D. Cal. Sept. 17, 2013) (no damages offsets for purported benefits conferred by defendant's falsely advertised lamps; also rejecting argument that low rates of returns showed that there was no need for equitable relief).

The *National Urological Group* defendants proposed to pay redress directly to purchasers, contacting customers and providing or offering a complete refund. The FTC wanted redress to be deposited into a fund in its name. After consumers were redressed, the FTC would use remaining funds for further equitable relief or pay them into the Treasury as disgorgement. The court had "ample discretion" to choose the FTC's proposal, and saw no reason to charge "the purveyors of the deception" with competently and honestly reimbursing consumers. As a result, the court ordered the defendants to pay the entire $15+ million to the FTC.

The FTC also gets more leeway than a private party in establishing the appropriate amounts due, as the following case illustrates. The defendants' gross receipts were much easier to establish than its net profits; defendants wanted the award to reflect significant deductions from gross receipts. The court was not impressed.

Federal Trade Commission v. Direct Marketing Concepts, Inc., 624 F.3d 1 (1st Cir. 2010)

... Turning now to the issue of damages, the Defendants begin by arguing that damages for deceptive advertising are limited to actual profits, not gross receipts. If this were so, then at least part of the district court's damages award would be erroneous. However, the law allows for broad discretion in fashioning a remedy for deceptive advertising; many cases uphold rescission (effectively, restoring the parties to pre-sale status) or restitution (under these facts, the same) as appropriate remedies. Thus, consumer loss, as represented by the Defendants' gross receipts, would appear to be an appropriate measure of damages.

Nevertheless, the Defendants ask us to rely on *FTC v. Verity Int'l, Ltd.*, 443 F.3d 48 (2d Cir. 2006), for the proposition that the FTC's remedy is limited to the Defendants' profits rather than their gross receipts. *Verity*'s limited rule does not apply here.

In *Verity*, a series of unrelated, non-party middlemen partook of the proceeds from the defendants' scheme before the defendants themselves got a bite. The court found this payment structure highly relevant to the issue of damages, noting that "in many cases in which the FTC seeks restitution, the defendant's gain will be equal to the consumer's loss" but casting *Verity*'s facts as an exception limited to the situation "when some middleman not party to the lawsuit takes some of the consumer's money before it reaches a defendant's hands." Here, the Defendants seek to inflate *Verity*'s exception so that it overshadows the rule.

We are not persuaded. Because this set of facts lacks the non-party middleman that gave rise to the exception in *Verity*, we will follow the general rule. Here, the Defendants on appeal took in proceeds directly, except for roughly one year when fellow defendant (but non-appellant) Triad processed Coral Calcium orders. The FTC introduced ample evidence of the overall proceeds from Coral Calcium during this period; however, the parties' financial records were in such disarray that the actual split among the parties could not be determined.[12]

The Defendants on appeal now claim that Triad siphoned off the vast majority of the proceeds, leaving them holding an empty bag, but we cannot tell whether this is the case. Because every entity that had received consumer money was a defendant, the district court held

---

[12] The FTC perhaps ought to have made more of an effort to nail down the details of the parties' finances during discovery. . . . but there is no question that the primary fault lies with the Defendants.

that gross receipts were an appropriate measure of damages; because records were unclear as to how much consumer money each defendant received, the district court evenly split the total receipts between DMC and Triad for the time period when Triad acted as a middleman. This was consistent with *Verity* and within the bounds of the district court's discretion in fashioning an equitable remedy.

Thus, the district court committed no error in resting its damages determination on the Defendants' gross receipts rather than their net profits, and we will proceed to review the court's calculation of what those gross receipts actually were. To determine the appropriate amount of damages in deceptive advertising cases, courts apply a burden-shifting scheme. First, the FTC must provide the court with a reasonable approximation of damages.

Both gross receipts and net customer loss are appropriate measures. Once a reasonable approximation of damages has been provided, the defendant has an opportunity to demonstrate that the figures are inaccurate. Any fuzzy figures due to a defendant's uncertain bookkeeping cannot carry a defendant's burden to show inaccuracy. . . .

NOTES AND QUESTIONS

Is the allocation of burdens between the defendant and the FTC sensible? What are the alternatives? Does the risk of suppressing truthful speech matter at all once a court has determined that the defendant advertised falsely?

Should the defendant be able to deduct the value of the product or service it actually delivered, which will often (though not always) be above zero? *See* FTC v. Lights of Am., Inc., 2013 WL 5230681 (C.D. Cal. Sept. 17, 2013) (no). In a contempt case based on claims made about defendant's calcium supplements in violation of a prior FTC consent order, the FTC sought $15 million in gross sales. But the FTC's own expert agreed that the product was a good form of calcium and the defendant's conduct wasn't willful. The court therefore calculated damages based on the "price premium" commanded by the product. This premium was slightly over 20% of the price; the total price premium was slightly over $800,000, which was ordered refunded to consumers. Is this a better approach than full disgorgement?

B.   Monetary Remedies in Private Actions

Since a decision on a preliminary injunction requires an evaluation of eventual likelihood of success on the merits, false advertising cases often settle after the initial decision granting preliminary relief. Thus, relatively few courts reach the issue of damages in private-competitor false advertising cases.

If the case does proceed beyond the preliminary relief stage, however, the Lanham Act specifically authorizes the award of "(1) defendant's profits, (2) any damages sustained by the plaintiff, and (3) the costs of the action" to a prevailing plaintiff. 15 U.S.C. § 1117(a).

With respect to an award based on defendant's profits, if the court finds the award either inadequate or excessive, the court may in its discretion enter judgment for such sum as the court finds just. An award based on plaintiff's damages, by contrast, permits the court to increase the amount up to three times, in order to achieve a just result, but not to reduce the amount. Recovery must be compensatory and not a penalty. This provision confers broad discretion upon courts in assessing and awarding appropriate damages.

Though rare, damages verdicts can be quite large. *See, e.g.*, Melissa Lipman, *Jury Orders Becton To Pay $114M in Syringe Antitrust Case*, Law360, Sept. 20, 2013 (despite headline, jury awarded entire amount as damages for defendant's false advertising, which was designed to preclude a competitor from gaining a foothold in a medical device market).

Many courts hold that, though literal falsity without evidence of consumer deception can justify an injunction, evidence of consumer deception is required before a damage award is allowed. *See, e.g.,* Bracco Diagnostics, Inc. v. Amersham Health, Inc., 627 F. Supp. 2d 384 (D.N.J. 2009) ("literal falsity, without more, is insufficient to support an award of money damages to compensate for marketplace injury"). Other courts allow presumptions to take the place of specific evidence under certain circumstances, especially willfully false comparative advertising. One court upheld a $19.25 million verdict based on false claims that the plaintiff was a Satanic corporation, using a presumption of actual confusion from the literal falsity of the claims; no further proof of actual confusion was required. Procter & Gamble Co. v. Haugen, 627 F. Supp. 2d 1287 (D. Utah 2008).

In recent years, fact finders have awarded a small but noticeable number of multimillion-dollar verdicts. Damages thus represent a relatively low-probability but high-risk area for defendants.

Defendant's Profits

An award of damages based on profits obtained by the defendant during the period it disseminated the false advertising is generally justified on the grounds that it will deter similar illegal activity and deprive the defendant of the unjust enrichment obtained as a result of the false advertising.

Courts apply varying standards in determining whether an award of such damages is appropriate. Some circuits hold that such damages "may be warranted either by empirical evidence of actual consumer deception or by evidence that the defendant had the intention to deceive the public with false representations," Gillette Co. v. Wilkinson Sword, Inc., 1992 WL 30938 (S.D.N.Y. 1992); other circuits hold that "an award based on a defendant's profits requires proof that the defendant acted willfully or in bad faith." Alpo Petfoods, Inc. v. Ralston Purina Co., 913 F.2d 958 (D.C. Cir. 1990).

The Second Circuit has emphasized that the defendant's profits may be an inappropriate measure of the plaintiff's harm. Relevant factors include: (1) the degree of certainty that the defendant benefited from the unlawful conduct; (2) availability and adequacy of other remedies; (3) the role of a particular defendant in effectuating the wrongful conduct; (4) plaintiff's laches; and (5) plaintiff's unclean hands. *See* Pedinol Pharmacal, Inc. v. Rising Pharms., Inc., 570 F. Supp. 2d 498 (E.D.N.Y. 2008) (when the jury found that both parties engaged in false advertising but awarded the plaintiff only $1 in nominal damages, the defendant/counter-plaintiff's bad behavior didn't bar an award of profits; the plaintiff/counter-defendant was guilty of much worse conduct, and unclean hands requires "truly unconscionable and brazen behavior").

Recently, courts have been receptive to the argument that the 1999 amendments to § 35(a) of the Lanham Act counsel against a bright-line rule making willfulness a prerequisite for an award of defendants' profits. The amendment substituted "a violation under section 43(a) [trademark infringement and false advertising] or (d) [cybersquatting], or a *willful* violation under section 43(c) [trademark dilution]" (emphasis added) for the older language "or a violation under section 43(a)" in setting out the availability of profits.

The potential implication is that willfulness is a prerequisite for a damages award in a trademark dilution action but not in an infringement, false advertising or cybersquatting action. Courts accepting this argument hold that a profits award should be governed by the particular case's equities, including but not limited to the willfulness of defendant's actions. *See, e.g.*, Hipsaver Co., Inc. v. J.T. Posey Co., 497 F. Supp. 2d 96 (D. Mass. 2007) (profits may be awarded in Lanham Act cases not only as a rough measure of harm to the plaintiff, but also to avoid unjust enrichment and to deter a willful bad actor; though willfulness is not required, when the rationale for disgorgement is deterrence and there is no evidence of actual harm, plaintiffs must show willfulness to recover profits). *But see* Pedinol Pharmacal, Inc. v. Rising Pharms., Inc., 570 F. Supp. 2d 498 (E.D.N.Y. 2008) (willfulness is still required to award profits in false advertising cases; the dilution amendment evinced no congressional intent to change the law governing the other damages provisions).

Planned deception and knowledge of significant consumer confusion will qualify as willfulness. TrafficSchool.com, Inc. v. Edriver Inc., 653 F.3d 820 (9th Cir. 2011). Likewise, a jury could reasonably find willfulness when, although the defendants based their statements on a published scientific paper, they didn't stick to the statements in the paper but rather redesigned a bar chart to denigrate a competitor and added in unsupported conclusions; there was evidence that the principal behind the claims had concluded what the results would be even before any tests were carried out; and one employee even testified that he didn't believe in the tests they used. This was enough to indicate knowledge of or indifference to the falsity. Eastman Chem. Co. v. Plastipure, Inc., 969 F. Supp. 2d 756 (W.D. Tex. 2013), *aff'd*, 775 F.3d 230 (5th Cir. 2014).

Courts use a variety of methods to calculate profits. In the most commonly used method, courts calculate defendant's profits as "the sales defendant enjoyed as a result of its violations, less the costs and deductions attributable to those sales." Gillette, *supra*. In such cases, the plaintiff is required to prove defendant's sales; the burden then shifts to defendant to prove any cost or deduction claimed. In evaluating which items of expense or loss may be used as an offset, there is no hard and fast rule, and trial courts are allowed considerable discretion. Examples of possible deductions include losses incurred in separate accounting periods, expenses, salaries, and general overhead/costs of doing business.

In proving or disproving the existence and amount of damages sustained as a result of false advertising, parties often look to expert analysis and testimony. Although courts do not require mathematical precision in fixing such damages, they will require a reasonable basis for calculating profits, which may be difficult to produce without expert testimony establishing acceptable assumptions underlying diverted profits.

In *National Products, Inc. v. Gamber-Johnson LLC*, 734 F. Supp. 2d 1160 (W.D. Wash. 2010), Gamber-Johnson lost a trial over its comparative advertising about the parties' emergency vehicle laptop mounting systems. Though a jury awarded the plaintiff $10 million in defendant's profits, the court reduced the amount to a little under $500,000. A jury verdict will be upheld if supported by substantial evidence, but the district court has discretionary power to modify monetary awards under the Lanham Act, which are "subject to the principles of equity." 15 U.S.C. § 1117(a). Because plaintiff NPI didn't seek actual damages, its recovery was based on unjust enrichment and disgorgement of profits. The court set forth the standard principles that relief is not a matter of right and must be based on the totality of the circumstances, avoiding a windfall to the plaintiff or pure punishment for the defendant. Actual evidence of injury is the touchstone for any award. The court also needed to take into account the jury's finding that Gamber-Johnson deliberately engaged in false advertising.

NPI was entitled to a presumption of actual deception and reliance because Gamber-Johnson's statements were intentionally false or misleading. But that presumption of damages didn't extend to a

676

presumption of sales diversion. NPI had to prove any profits Gamber-Johnson earned that were attributable to the false advertising. At that point, the burden would shift to Gamber-Johnson to prove its expenses and profits attributable to factors other than false advertising. However, there was a dearth of evidence proving that all Gamber-Johnson's sales and profits during the relevant period were attributable to false advertising. After trial, the court requested evidence from NPI connecting the false ad to the profits, but NPI couldn't quantify any connection.

In the end, Gamber-Johnson's own expert testified that the best indication of its profits from sales diverted from NPI was approximately $350,000. Using a higher profit margin estimate as posited by NPI, the court instead calculated that an award of nearly $500,000 "would serve the policy considerations behind the Lanham Act."

NPI argued that its burden was simply to identify the pool of sales attributable or related to the false advertising, and that it had done so by identifying the sales of the falsely advertised goods. The court disagreed. Only some of Gamber-Johnson's customers would have seen the false video, so NPI needed more evidence. *Cf.* Rexall Sundown, Inc. v. Perrigo Co., 707 F. Supp. 2d 357 (E.D.N.Y. 2010) (in a case where the false advertising appeared on the product itself, the court ruled that the plaintiff must establish only the defendant's sales of the product at issue, while the defendant bears the burden of showing all costs and deductions, including any portion of sales that was not due to the allegedly false advertising); Trilink Saw Chain, LLC v. Blount, Inc., 583 F. Supp. 2d 1293 (N.D. Ga. 2008) (when a defendant "specifically disparages a market newcomer through deliberately false advertisements," the plaintiff's burden was only to show gross sales).

An alternative way to calculate the defendant's profits is the cost of defendant's advertising. The Ninth Circuit first deployed this approach on the theory that it is reasonable to assume that the defendant derives a benefit from its false advertising at least equal to the amount it spent on the advertising. U-Haul Int'l, Inc. v. Jartran, Inc., 793 F.2d 1034 (9th Cir. 1986). This methodology, however, has been questioned by other circuits and has not been employed generally. Moreover, the Ninth Circuit itself has recognized that the *U-Haul* methodology is most appropriately applied in situations involving direct comparative advertising. *See* Harper House, Inc. v. Thomas Nelson, Inc., 889 F.2d 197 (9th Cir. 1989).

Plaintiff's Damages

In addition to defendant's profits, courts also may award actual damages sustained by the plaintiff. (There is a rule against double counting, however: plaintiffs can't recover both defendants' profits and their own lost sales from the same sales). Recoverable damages may include any demonstrable damages suffered by plaintiff, including profits lost by the plaintiff on sales actually diverted to the false advertiser; profits lost by the plaintiff on sales made at prices reduced as a result of the false advertising; quantifiable harm to the plaintiff's goodwill; and amounts expended by plaintiff on corrective advertising designed to combat the false message disseminated by defendant. To receive compensation for expenditures for corrective advertising, the plaintiff must normally demonstrate that the corrective advertising was an actual and reasonable response to defendant's activities, which can be hard to do. *See* First Act Inc. v. Brook Mays Music Co., Inc., 429 F. Supp. 2d 429 (D. Mass. 2006).

Most damages disputes are about plaintiff's lost sales and profits. Such cases rely on specialized testimony about the relevant markets, so it is hard to develop generalizable principles from those cases. In determining the amount of actual damages to award, a court may consider "the difficulty of proving an exact amount of damages from false advertising, as well as the maxim that 'the wrongdoer shall bear the risk of the uncertainty which his own wrong has created.'" ALPO Petfoods, Inc. v. Ralston Purina Co., 913 F.2d 958 (D.C. Cir. 1990).

As noted earlier, the Lanham Act further authorizes a court to "enter judgment, according to the circumstances of the case, for any sum above the amount found as actual damages, not exceeding three times such amount." 15 U.S.C. § 1117(a). These enhanced damages are meant to be compensatory in nature, to ensure that the plaintiff is made whole even if it is difficult to prove all damages with specificity. Although enhanced damages are not supposed to be punitive in nature, some courts have required a showing of especially egregious conduct by defendant before enhancing damages awards. In one of the most prominent cases involving trebled damages, the *U-Haul* court awarded double actual damages based on the "publication of deliberately false comparative claims." As a general matter, however, courts rarely exercise their discretion to award treble damages.

Costs

A prevailing plaintiff in a Lanham Act false advertising case also is entitled to an award of costs incurred in prosecuting the claim. 15 U.S.C. § 1117(a). "Costs," though, does not literally mean all costs of the action; rather, it generally refers to the kinds of statutory costs typically available for a prevailing plaintiff.

Costs typically include such items as printing briefs, court reporter fees for depositions actually used in the trial, and filing fees, though the trial court retains discretion in determining what costs will be allowed. In one case, the plaintiff also attempted to recover as costs the expenses of conducting surveys. The court held that these expenses were not recoverable as costs because no "statute explicitly provide[d] for these items" and "Gillette failed to present any authority for awarding the cost of performing consumer surveys." Gillette Co. v. Wilkinson Sword, Inc., 1992 WL 30938 (S.D.N.Y. 1992). The court specified, however, that in future cases it might allow survey costs if the court approved those costs in advance.

Unlike an award of attorneys' fees, willful or bad faith conduct is not necessary to support an award of costs.

Punitive Damages

The Lanham Act specifically prohibits recovery of punitive damages. *See* 15 U.S.C. § 1117(a). In contrast, most state statutes governing unfair competition and false advertising authorize such awards where the defendant's conduct was willful or malicious. This is one reason why many complaints for false advertising assert both federal and parallel state causes of action. In one prominent example, the *U-Haul* district court awarded $20 million in punitive damages under a parallel state claim as an alternative to its finding that damages were warranted under plaintiff's Lanham Act claim. Since the Ninth Circuit affirmed the district court's Lanham Act analysis, it did not reach the issue of punitive damages.

Attorneys' Fees

The Lanham Act authorizes awards of attorneys' fees only in "exceptional cases," and even then, such awards are within the discretion of the court. 15 U.S.C. § 1117(a). The degree of willfulness necessary to support an award of attorneys' fees is generally greater than that necessary to sustain an award of defendants' profits to a prevailing plaintiff. *But see* Nat'l Prods., Inc. v. Gamber-Johnson LLC, 734 F. Supp. 2d 1160 (W.D. Wash. 2010) (a jury's finding that false advertising was deliberate supported a finding of an exceptional case under 15 U.S.C. § 1117(a)); TrafficSchool.com, Inc. v. Edriver Inc., 653 F.3d 820 (9th Cir. 2011) (attorneys' fees may be available even if plaintiff received no damage award; "[i]t would be inequitable to force plaintiffs to bear the entire cost of enjoining defendants' willful deception when the injunction confers substantial benefits on the public"). Courts also are empowered to award attorneys' fees to a prevailing defendant. Attorneys' fee awards are relatively rare in advertising disputes.

One case in which the court did grant attorneys' fees involved a challenge to tax preparer H&R Block's advertising in connection with its "Rapid Refund" program. In prior disputes, H&R Block had agreed in consent orders entered into with state attorneys general to represent a similar program as providing "loans" to consumers, and not as "refunds." In addition, H&R Block had internal studies indicating that the difference between a "refund" and a "loan" was material to the public. Based on this prior history, the court viewed Block's new advertising as an attempt to circumvent consent orders into which it had previously entered and therefore found an award of attorneys' fees warranted. JTH Tax, Inc. v. H&R Block Eastern Tax Servs., 28 Fed. Appx. 207 (4th Cir. 2002).

In an attempt to harmonize the inconsistent language used by the various circuits, Judge Posner articulated a standard for awarding fees in Lanham Act cases. In *Nightingale Home Healthcare, Inc. v. Anodyne Therapy*, LLC, 626 F.3d 958 (7th Cir. 2010), Anodyne successfully defended against Nightingale's false advertising lawsuit, winning summary judgment early in the litigation. Judge Posner noted that some circuits apply different tests depending on whether the plaintiff or defendant prevailed: if the Lanham Act violation was willful or in bad faith, a prevailing plaintiff can get fees, whereas a prevailing defendant can get fees if the lawsuit or its prosecution was groundless or oppressive. Other circuits focus only on the litigation regardless of who the prevailing parties are. In the Seventh Circuit, "vexatious litigation conduct" by any losing party can justify a fee award.

Judge Posner pointed out that businesses may use Lanham Act suits for strategic purposes, to obtain competitive advantages regardless of case outcomes, and that anticompetitive behavior can even occur on the defense side: "a large firm sued for trademark infringement by a small one might mount a scorched-earth defense to a meritorious claim in the hope of imposing prohibitive litigation costs on the plaintiff."

An "exceptional" lawsuit is an anticompetitive one, "for in a battle of equals each contestant can bear his own litigation costs without impairing competition." On the plaintiff's side, "the concept of abuse of process provides a helpful characterization of his conduct." The key is not whether the suit itself is baseless, but whether the plaintiff is using the litigation process for an improper purpose, regardless of whether the claim is colorable. Similarly, "[i]f a defendant's trademark infringement or false advertising is blatant, his insistence on mounting a costly defense is the same misconduct as a plaintiff's bringing a case—frivolous or not—not in order to obtain a favorable judgment but instead to burden the defendant with costs likely to drive it out of the market. Predatory initiation of suit is mirrored in predatory resistance to valid claims."

Thus, a case is exceptional "if the losing party was the plaintiff and was guilty of abuse of process in suing, or if the losing party was the defendant and had no defense, yet persisted in the trademark infringement or false advertising for which he was being sued, in order to impose costs on his opponent." However, a fee proceeding shouldn't be a full tort lawsuit. "[A]n elaborate inquiry into the state of mind of the party from whom reimbursement of attorneys' fees is sought should be avoided. It should be enough to justify the award if the party seeking it can show that his opponent's claim or defense was objectively unreasonable—was a claim or defense that a rational litigant would pursue only because it would impose disproportionate costs on his opponent—in other words only because it was extortionate in character if not necessarily in provable intention."

In the case before the court, Nightingale, a provider of home healthcare services, made the same claims that it accused Anodyne of making falsely and was simply seeking price leverage in its dealings with Anodyne. Thus, the Lanham Act claim was not just meritless but anticompetitive, and a fee award was justified.

More recently, in *Octane Fitness, LLC v. ICON Health & Fitness, Inc.*, 572 U. S. ___ (2014), and *Highmark Inc. v. Allcare Health Management System, Inc.*, 572 U. S. ___ (2014), the Supreme Court held that under the patent statutory provision for the award of attorneys' fees, which has similar statutory language to the Lanham Act, courts have discretion in determining whether to award attorney fees to the prevailing party in "exceptional" cases, and a fee award can't be held to a clear and convincing evidence standard. *Octane* explained that

> [A]n "exceptional" case is simply one that stands out from the others with respect to the substantive strength of a party's litigating position (considering both the governing law and the facts of the case) or the unreasonable manner in which the case was litigated. District courts may determine whether a case is "exceptional" in the case-by-case exercise of their discretion, considering the totality of the circumstances [and without any] precise rule or formula for making these determinations.

Highmark further held that appellate review of such determinations is not de novo, but rather only for abuse of discretion. Thus, fee awards may be litigated more often going forward.

Remedies for Violations of Consumer Protection Law

While class actions involve special considerations to be discussed in the next section, their power is best understood in light of the range of remedies available under consumer protection statutes. These remedies are, in general, similar to the basic remedies available in Lanham Act cases. Injunctive relief has historically been available, but some courts have started to deny it on the ground that a plaintiff who realizes that she's been fooled has no standing to seek injunctive relief, since she won't be fooled again. Some states provide for a set amount of statutory damages per violation; others allow recovery of actual damages. Attorneys' fees are also relatively standard.

California is a particularly plaintiff-favorable jurisdiction in some ways, but since it is such a large state and not entirely unrepresentative of other states, it's worth examining how a California court imposes remedies in an ordinary case.

People v. Sarpas, 225 Cal. App. 4th 1539 (Cal. Ct. App. 2014)

Hakimullah Sarpas and Zulmai Nazarzai operated a scheme by which they promised customers they would obtain loan modifications from lenders and prevent foreclosure of the customers' homes. They operated this scheme through their jointly owned company, Statewide Financial Group, Inc. (SFGI), which did business as U.S. Homeowners Assistance (USHA). Sharon Fasela was, among other things, the office manager of USHA and came up with the key misrepresentation that USHA had a 97 percent success rate. Customers paid USHA over $2 million but received no services in return. There was no credible evidence that USHA obtained a single loan modification, or provided anything of value, for its customers.

The Attorney General, on behalf of the People of the State of California, commenced this action in July 2009 by filing a complaint against SFGI, USHA, Sarpas, Nazarzai, and Fasela (collectively referred to as Defendants), seeking injunctive relief, restitution, and civil penalties under the California unfair competition law (UCL), Business and Professions Code section 17200 et seq., and the California False Advertising Law (FAL), section 17500 et seq. . . .

In July 2012, following a lengthy bench trial, the trial court issued a judgment and a 19-page statement of decision finding against Defendants. The court permanently enjoined USHA, Nazarzai, Sarpas, and Fasela, and ordered restitution be made to every eligible consumer requesting it, up to a maximum amount of $2,047,041.86. The court found USHA, Sarpas, and Nazarzai to be jointly and severally liable for the full amount of restitution, and Fasela to be jointly and severally liable with them for up to $147,869 in restitution. . . .

Sarpas was the 50-percent owner of SFGI, which did business as USHA. Nazarzai owned the other 50 percent. Sarpas and Nazarzai each received 50 percent of the company profits. From March 2008 to April 2009, Sarpas received $490,000 in profits from SFGI. Sarpas also served as operations manager of SFGI and oversaw the company's day-to-day operations.

Fasela worked as the office manager of SFGI for about one year, ending in July 2009. USHA paid Fasela $2,746 in 2007, $135,358 in 2008, and $11,611 in 2009.

. . . [Among other false claims,] USHA represented it had a 97-percent success rate [in modifying mortgages], that it had a success rate of "over 95 percent," or that USHA never had a case in which a loan modification was not approved. Fasela came up with the 97-percent success rate figure "in the beginning." One customer testified the sales representative guaranteed USHA would obtain a loan modification.

In addition, customers were told to stop making their mortgage payments because doing so would make obtaining a loan modification easier. As a result, customers often suffered ruined credit, additional fees, foreclosure proceedings, and even loss of the home USHA had promised to save.

No credible evidence was presented at trial that USHA ever obtained a loan modification, or did anything of value, for any customer. USHA made no refunds to customers, despite its promises, and despite customer demands. Not only did USHA not have a legal team, it had no attorneys whatsoever working on loan modifications.

Section 17203 authorizes an order of restitution as a remedy for violations of section 17200. In part, section 17203 reads: "The court may make such orders or judgments, . . . as may be necessary to restore to any person in interest any money or property, real or personal, which may have been acquired by means of such unfair competition." Section 17535 likewise authorizes an order of restitution for a violation of section 17500. "The restitutionary remedies of section 17203 and 17535 . . . are identical and are construed in the same manner." . . .

Restitution under the UCL and FAL may be ordered without individualized proof of harm. (In re Tobacco II Cases (2009) 46 Cal.4th 298, 326, 93 Cal.Rptr.3d 559, 207 P.3d 20 [" 'California courts have repeatedly held that relief under the UCL [(including restitution)] is available without individualized proof of deception, reliance and injury' "].)

Because individualized proof of harm was unnecessary, the Attorney General was not required to present testimony from each and every USHA customer for whom restitution and civil penalties were being sought. . . . The Attorney General presented evidence sufficient to support a reasonable inference of deception and harm as to all USHA customers, and, therefore, the restitution and civil penalties as to all USHA customers were lawful.

B. Restitution Is Not Limited to Direct Payment from Victims.

. . . Sarpas and Fasela argue they cannot be ordered to pay restitution absent evidence either one received money directly from USHA customers. Although the trial court found that USHA received over $2 million from customers, Sarpas and Fasela argue neither of them personally received money directly, and "[l]egally, under California law, a defendant who has violated the UCL, cannot be made to restore to a consumer that which he or she never directly received from the consumer." This argument is legally incorrect.

. . . Sarpas and Fasela received money indirectly from customers by having them pay USHA. The customers parted with property in which they had an ownership interest and are entitled to its return. The rule urged by Sarpas and Fasela would allow UCL and FAL violators to escape restitution by structuring their schemes to avoid receiving direct payment from their victims.

Sarpas and Fasela argue that, if Sarpas can be ordered to pay restitution, his share of restitution must be limited to the net profits he received from USHA. We disagree. "Where restitution is ordered as a means of redressing a statutory violation, the courts are not concerned with restoring the violator to the status quo ante. The focus instead is on the victim. 'The status quo ante to be achieved by the restitution order was to again place the victim in possession of that money.'" . . .

Sarpas and Nazarzai "drained substantial amounts of money from the corporation" and there was no evidence that either of them put funds into the corporation. Sarpas and Fasela do not challenge those findings. Based on those findings and the evidence presented at trial, the trial court could exercise its equitable discretion to conclude USHA, Sarpas, and Nazarzai acted as a single enterprise for the purpose of ordering restitution under the UCL and the FAL. . .

Pursuant to sections 17206 and 17536, the trial court imposed civil penalties against USHA, Sarpas, and Nazarzai, jointly and severally, in the amount of $2,047,041, and imposed additional civil penalties against Fasela, USHA, Sarpas, and Nazarzai, jointly and severally, in the amount of $360,540. In setting the amount of civil penalties, the court considered (1) the purpose of civil penalties to punish and deter; (2) Defendants' targeting of the elderly and the disabled; (3) the "enormous" number of UCL and FAL violations committed by Defendants; and (4) evidence establishing there were 1,259 "payors" checks deposited into USHA accounts.

Section 17206, subdivision (a) states in part that "[a]ny person who engages, has engaged, or proposes to engage in unfair competition shall be liable for a civil penalty not to exceed two thousand five hundred dollars ($2,500) for each violation." Section 17536, subdivision (a) states in part that "[a]ny person who violates any provision of this chapter shall be liable for a civil penalty not to exceed two thousand five hundred dollars ($2,500) for each violation." UCL penalties may be increased by up to $2,500 per violation if the victim is elderly or disabled. Under both section 17206, subdivision (b) and section 17536, subdivision (b), the court should consider, in assessing the amount of civil penalties, one or more of the following: "the nature and seriousness of the misconduct, the number of violations, the persistence of the misconduct, the length of time over which the misconduct occurred, the willfulness of the defendant's misconduct, and the defendant's assets, liabilities, and net worth." . . .

As we have emphasized, individualized proof of each and every UCL and FAL violation is not required; from the evidence presented at trial, the trial court could draw the reasonable inference Sarpas and Fasela committed hundreds, if not thousands, of UCL and FAL violations. In this regard, the trial court found: "Defendants made false and misleading statements to each and every consumer who entered into a contract with Defendants. . . . "

Sarpas and Fasela argue the amount of civil penalties is excessive in light of their respective financial situations. A court should consider a defendant's assets, liabilities, and net worth in calculating the amount of civil penalties. But, "evidence of a defendant's financial condition, although relevant, is not essential to the imposition of the statutory penalties, making the issue of a defendant's financial inability a matter for the defendant to raise in mitigation." Sarpas did not testify at trial. Fasela testified some about her financial situation, but she presented no documentary evidence in support, and the trial court found her testimony on the subject was not credible. As to Sarpas, all the civil penalties are affirmed.

. . . The trial court offered no explanation or computation for coming up with $360,540, despite requests from Fasela to make factual findings. . . . We therefore will strike the civil penalties awarded against Fasela only and remand with directions to recalculate the amount of civil penalties under sections 17206 and 17536.

NOTES AND QUESTIONS

Is it fair to order restitution for every consumer without individualized proof of harm? In fraud cases like this one where consumers received nothing of value, the answer seems easy: of course. But what if consumers had received a product or service worth less than they paid for it, but still perhaps worth something? What if some of them were satisfied with the product or service?

The case here was brought by the attorney general. Should statutory damages also be available to private plaintiffs? This is an area where states diverge.

Class Action Settlements under Consumer Protection Laws

As noted in previous chapters, class actions provide leverage against practices that would otherwise go unchallenged because of the minimal harm done to any individual consumer. This makes determination of appropriate remedies challenging, since the transaction costs of finding deceived consumers and redressing the harm can far outweigh any actual restitution. Concern over settlements that provide millions for the lawyers and virtually nothing for the consumers allegedly being protected have led to greater scrutiny of proposed settlements. The following case shows how a court that has already determined that class treatment is appropriate is likely to analyze the terms of a proposed settlement.

In re M3 Power Razor System Marketing & Sales Practice Litigation, 270 F.R.D. 45 (D. Mass. 2010)

. . . The revised proposed Settlement Agreement as Amended obligates Gillette to establish a Settlement Fund of $7.5 million for the distribution of cash and other benefits to class members. Up to $2.45 million of the Settlement Fund is available to provide notice to potential class members. Any notice costs over this amount, including the potential costs of providing additional notice if the settlement is not approved at the Final Fairness Hearing, will be borne solely by Gillette.

[Editors' note: Details of the settlement are discussed in Chapter 7. Recall the provision that any leftover funds would be used to distribute free Gillette razors to the general population. Was this provision appropriate, given its apparent distance from the harm

Gillette allegedly caused and the potential for Gillette to build brand goodwill from this aspect of the settlement? Coupon settlements and other non-monetary redress provisions have been criticized on the grounds that they are marketing tools, not penalties.*]

The proposed Settlement Agreement contains no reverter clause, and the full $7.5 million, including up to $2.45 million for notice, will be distributed for the benefit of class members. Potential class members have the right to opt out, if written notice is postmarked at least 21 days prior to the date of the Final Fairness Hearing. In addition to the $7.5 million Settlement Fund, Gillette has agreed to pay up to $1,850,000, subject to Court approval, for attorneys' fees, costs, and expenses, as well as incentive awards to the Representative and named Plaintiffs in amounts of $500 (or the prevailing Canadian dollar equivalent) to $1,000 each.

In *Colgan*, a California Court of Appeals reversed a lower court decision to award $13,012,255.50 in total restitution under the FAL, UCL, and CLRA, finding that the restitution order was not supported by sufficient evidence. The plaintiffs presented evidence regarding the market value and retail price of the Leatherman tools at issue, and the market price of similar tools made in China. The trial court refused to consider this evidence, however, finding it unreliable. The

---

* For a particularly entertaining version of this criticism, see the objector's brief filed by William Chamberlain, then a Georgetown Law student, objecting to a proposed settlement of claims against Muscle Milk, where amounts remaining after distribution to class claimants would be distributed to charitable athletic events—in the form of free Muscle Milk for participants, valued for settlement purposes at retail value instead of at the producer's cost. Chamberlain notes that this "remedy" not only has promotional value to the advertiser, but also is somewhat ironic given that the underlying allegations involved false claims that Muscle Milk was a healthy product. *Objection To Proposed Settlement and Fee Request and Notice of Appearance,* Delacruz v. Cytosport Inc., No. 4:11-cv-03532 (N.D. Cal. filed Mar. 5, 2014).

trial court also refused to consider Leatherman's gross profits on the items as a measure of damages, rejecting this approach as "inequitable"; because "although the purchasers did not receive entirely what they bargained for . . . these Class members did benefit from the quality, usefulness, and safety of these multi-purpose tools," and it would be unfair to return to them the entire purchase price. Expert testimony was introduced on the advantages Leatherman obtained through false advertising, but the Court of Appeals rejected this testimony as a basis for a damage calculation, finding that "the expert did not attempt to quantify either the dollar value of the consumer impact or the advantage realized by Leatherman."

IV. STANDARDS FOR CLASS ACTION SETTLEMENT APPROVAL

Federal Rule of Civil Procedure 23(e) requires judicial approval of all class action settlements. Before approving a class action settlement, I must find that it is "fair, reasonable, and adequate." When asked to review a class action settlement preliminarily, I examine the proposed settlement for obvious deficiencies before determining whether it is in the range of fair, reasonable, and adequate. . . . Ultimately, the more fully informed examination required for final approval will occur in connection with the Final Fairness Hearing, where arguments for and against the proposed settlement will be presented after notice and an opportunity to consider any response provided by the potential class members.

It is inherently difficult to determine the fairness and adequacy of a proposed settlement in the preliminary review context where the parties have advanced a settlement in lieu of litigation. Courts and commentators, nevertheless, have developed a presumption that the settlement is within the range of reasonableness when certain procedural guidelines have been followed. These guidelines include whether: "(1) the negotiations occurred at arm's length; (2) there was sufficient discovery; (3) the proponents of the settlement are experienced in similar litigation; and (4) only a small fraction of the class objected."

I am satisfied that the negotiations in this case occurred at arm's length, and that the revised proposed settlement is more favorable to the potential class members than was Gillette's original response to pre-suit demand letters under state consumer protection statutes. Gillette originally offered to provide a $12 refund, or the actual amount paid if documented to be higher, to any consumer who purchased an M3P razor on or before July 1, 2005 and wished to return the razor. Postage was to be reimbursed based on the actual postage cost, and participating consumers would receive a coupon for $1 off a future purchase. The offer was limited to two razors per household, and there was no minimum floor on recovery.

The revised and then amended Settlement Agreement has improved on the original offer in several ways. First, it establishes a minimum Settlement Fund of $7.5 million, and provides for notice with 80-percent reach to inform consumers of their rights as class members.[12] Second, the Settlement Class Period was extended from July 1, 2005 to either September 30 or October 31, 2005, depending on the class member's country of residence. Third, the refund amount was increased from $12 to $13, and the reimbursement for shipping and handling was increased from the actual cost of postage, which necessarily omitted any handling costs, to $2. Fourth, consumers are no longer required to return the M3P razor to obtain a benefit. Fifth, the Gillette shaving product available for rebate includes, as a result of the Amended Settlement Agreement, the newest offering in the Gillette product line. Sixth, the number of permitted claims per

---

[12] Corrales argues that the original offer contained no ceiling either, but all parties recognize that consumer redemption rates in cases such as this are likely to be low, so it is highly unlikely that the request for refunds under the original offer would come close to the $7.5 million allocated to the proposed settlement.

household was increased from two to three. Seventh, assuming money is left over from the Settlement Fund after the Initial Claim Period, members of the class will receive free Settlement Razors, along with coupons valued at $4.

The Objecting Plaintiff Corrales has not offered evidence that the negotiations were not at arm's length or were collusive in any way, and I see no reason to find otherwise. . . .

I am also satisfied that sufficient discovery has been undertaken to provide the parties with adequate information about their respective litigation positions. Gillette produced over 100,000 pages of documents from the District of Connecticut litigation against Schick, allowing the parties to acquire enough information rapidly to make serious settlement negotiations feasible. Gillette also produced pertinent financial information as part of confirmatory discovery, and Co-Lead counsel deposed a Gillette representative who was familiar with the relevant financial information. Having reviewed this information, I find it is sufficient to make an informed preliminary review of the fairness of the proposed settlement. Finally, the only practical way to ascertain the overall level of objection to the proposed settlement is for notice to go forward, and to see how many potential class members choose to opt out of the settlement class or object to its terms at the Final Fairness Hearing.

I do impose one additional requirement upon the Representative Plaintiffs as they proceed with the notice of the class action. In the notice to class members on the website created for this proposed settlement, the "Joint Submission by the Proponents of the Proposed Settlement Comparing the Relevant Laws of Applicable Jurisdiction for Settlement Class Certification" must be posted together with a copy of this Memorandum and Order alerting class members to the issues presented by the varying state law causes of action and remedies available to the class members. In this way, class members who may wish to learn more about those alternatives and consider their implications will have a foundation for doing so.

. . . On the present state of the record, I have found sufficient basis to permit notice of the proposed Settlement Agreement to go forward and to certify a class, without subclasses, solely for the purpose of settlement.

I believe this certification is consistent with the directions provided by the First Circuit, which has taken a practical and common sense approach toward class settlements. Recently, in *In re* Pharmaceutical Industry Average Wholesale Price Litigation, 588 F.3d 24 (1st Cir. 2009), the court observed that while Judge Saris, after detailed and rigorous analysis of the diverse legal regimes implicated, had originally excluded nine states from a nationwide litigation class, "since their consumer-protection statutes differed," she thereafter expanded the settlement class to reincorporate them. In affirming the settlement class order, the First Circuit explained that it was "perfectly clear why the district court expanded the settlement class . . . [The defendant] bargained for 'total peace' to resolve all remaining claims against it."

More recently, the First Circuit has observed that "[a]lthough in class actions there is a preference for individually proved damages," nevertheless, "it is well accepted that in some cases an approximation of damages or a uniform figure for the class is the best that can be done." After extended reflection, I am satisfied on the basis of the record before me, and subject to reconsideration or refinement in connection with the Final Fairness Hearing, that the proposed settlement represents an acceptable resolution of this dispute. . . .

NOTES AND QUESTIONS

An option in the settlement included a new Gillette razor, the product that allegedly deceived the class members to begin with. How is receiving another razor returning the ill-gotten gain to the consumer? Does this remedy suggest that skepticism over class actions is justified?

Concerns for protecting both class plaintiffs and defendants recur in consumer protection class actions. While the concern for defendants essentially involves blackmail—the idea that defendants will make nuisance payments to lawyers to get a lawsuit to go away—the concern for plaintiffs is that those who are truly harmed will be ignored in low-value settlements. Where there are multiple plaintiffs' attorneys competing to represent a class, as is often the case when the claims are disseminated nationwide, the defendant can conduct a "reverse auction" among rival plaintiffs' groups. There is an incentive for the plaintiffs' lawyers to settle for low amounts, given that the lawyers who lose the auction usually get nothing because their compensation is on a contingency basis. As the *MP3 Power* decision suggests, courts are supposed to scrutinize a settlement for its fairness to both sides—in a situation where both litigants will be jointly urging the judge to approve the settlement.

Because claim rates in class actions are so low, when the defendant reserves a pool of money for settlement, it's usually the case that this pool is much larger than the actual total claims. But because of concerns over making sure that settlements serve some real deterrence function, and to avoid the manipulation of the nominal size of the pool in order to increase attorneys' fees, settling parties will provide that the defendant will pay some minimum amount of money. (The FTC does the same thing when it agrees on redress provisions). But if the settlement money does not go to consumers who submit claims, then to whom? The practice in false advertising cases had been to choose some inoffensive charity related to the defendant's products or services, using a rationale drawn from trust law known as *cy pres* (Law French for "as close as possible"). The theory was that giving to the charity was as close as possible to compensating harmed consumers.

In *Dennis v. Kellogg Co.*, 697 F.3d 858 (9th Cir. 2012), however, the Ninth Circuit raised significant objections to a settlement heavily premised on *cy pres* payments. If we were serious about *cy pres*, the court reasoned, the residual amount in the pool wouldn't go to a product-related charity—in the Kellogg case, it was charities that provided food to hungry people. But "[t]his noble goal . . . has little or nothing to do with the purposes of the underlying lawsuit or the class of plaintiffs involved." Kellogg wasn't being sued for failing to feed people. As a matter of fact, it was being sued for deceiving people about how healthy its food was. To get "as close as possible" to benefiting consumers whose harm came from being deceived, some consumer protection-related charity would be far more appropriate as the residual charity.

While Kellogg likely has less philosophical objection to giving to a food bank than to Consumers Union or some other charity that often takes policy positions opposed to Kellogg, most large companies behave rationally once a case is in a settlement posture. Thus, on remand, the parties renegotiated, including by dropping plaintiffs' attorneys' fee request substantially in response to other concerns expressed by the Ninth Circuit. The final cash fund was $4 million, and Kellogg agreed to give the amount remaining after class members filed their claims to Consumers Union, Consumer Watchdog, and the Center for Science in the Public Interest.

The district court approved the renegotiated settlement. Given the risks to both sides to pursuing the case through trial, and the nontrivial relief afforded to the class, in which claimants would receive at least $5 and up to $45, the court was satisfied that the settlement was fair, adequate, and free of collusion. Dennis v. Kellogg Co., 2013 WL 6055326 (S.D. Cal. Sept. 10, 2013).

Why should we worry so much about the residual charity, or about low consumer recoveries? Consider the following argument from Professor Brian Wolfman (formerly of Public Citizen):

> [I]n 2012, the Vermont Attorney General sued a company called Vermints under Vermont's consumer protection law alleging that Vermints had mislabeled its mints "*Vermont's* All-Natural Mints" (my emphasis). . . . According to the suit, the company is Massachusetts-based and the mints were manufactured in Canada, using mostly non-Vermont ingredients. . . . Vermints has settled the case by agreeing to remove the offending labels, paying Vermont $30,000, and giving $35,000 to the Vermont Foodbank, the state's largest anti-hunger organization. . . .
>
> If private lawyers (acting as so-called private attorneys general) had brought the suit on behalf of consumers of Vermints, the same settlement might have raised eyebrows. A class-action critic might have said the case bordered on the frivolous. Who cares about the label on a tin of mints? . . . In settling the suit [the AG] said:
>
>> Use of the term "Vermont" has great economic value, and many businesses go to the expense of sourcing their ingredients and processing within the state in order to market their products as Vermont products. We need to maintain a level playing field when it comes to claims of geographic origin, and to ensure that consumers who care about where their food

comes from get accurate information in the marketplace.

. . . [I]f the case had been filed by private plaintiffs, objectors might say that a cy pres award to the Foodbank was impermissible because of the lack of nexus between the underlying claim (misleading labeling of candy) and the mission of the cy pres recipient (alleviation of hunger in Vermont). They might even express concern that the plaintiffs themselves got no monetary relief. How can it be right to settle a case, they might say, where the lawyers and a charity, but not the class members, walk away with all the goodies?

That concern makes little sense in many small-claims consumer cases, as the Vermont AG recognized in settling the Vermints case without providing a dime to consumers. It would have been economically irrational to provide money to a class of people who had purchased mislabeled Vermints. Strictly speaking, some consumers may have been injured. But what would individualized relief look like? A buck for each class member who swore under oath on a claim form that she was duped by the faulty label into buying a tin of mints? Some class-action settlements actually seek to provide very small amounts of money to claiming class members. (I was once sent a three-cent class-action settlement check via first-class mail). But that's often a waste because most of the money the defendant has agreed to cough up goes for claims processing, check-writing, and postage. Generally, the best type of relief in small-harm cases is aggregated relief: injunctive-like benefits, such the label change the AG obtained, and lump-sum payments to help offset the costs of litigation and to promote deterrence, such as the payments to the state and to the Vermont Foodbank.

. . . [I[f a state's consumer protection laws authorize members of the public to act as private attorneys general, as most of them do to one degree or another, aren't private lawyers' suits, like AG suits, carrying out the legislature's intent— particularly given that consumer protection laws generally encourage suit by requiring the defendant to pay a successful plaintiff's attorney's fees? So, why shouldn't those suits be viewed as consistent with democratic ideals? After all, if a legislature decides it no longer likes private suits to enforce its consumer protection laws, because it thinks that private lawyers don't exercise the type of enforcement restraint that the political process imposes on AGs, it can amend those laws to eliminate or narrow private enforcement (as legislatures have done on occasion).

How do you think a critic of class actions would respond to Professor Wolfman? Consider the findings of a recent study. In fifteen lawsuits against large banks, between 1% and 70% of class members received compensation in these settlements, and the average payout ranged from $13 to $90, representing between 6% and 69% of average class member damages as claimed. The high participation rates generally came when the parties were able to use information from the defendants to automatically deposit settlement proceeds into class members' accounts or mail checks to them. Many class members deposited checks mailed to them even when the checks were for less than $5, sometimes as often as 80% of the time. Brian T. Fitzpatrick & Robert C. Gilbert, *An Empirical Look at Compensation in Consumer Class Actions*, 11 N.Y.U. J. L. & BUS. 767 (2015). But what are the implications of the fact that a substantial number of checks were never deposited, even when sent automatically?

Insurance Coverage

Standard commercial liability policies often include coverage for
"advertising injury." *See generally* Kyle Lambrecht, Note, *The
Evolution of the Advertising Injury Exclusion in the Insurance Service
Office, Inc.'s Comprehensive General Liability Insurance Policy
Forms*, 19 CONN. INS. L.J. 185 (2012).The advertiser's insurance
coverage may determine the course of litigation, since the insurer is
likely to have deeper pockets but also a greater willingness to settle if
it takes over the defense.

Though insurance policies define advertising injury in various ways
and often contain various exclusions, generally they provide
insurance coverage for a non-publisher defendant who might
allegedly disparage, invade the privacy of, "misappropriate . . .
advertising ideas" of, or otherwise harm someone else through
advertising. (Publishers generally secure a "media" policy for the
business of publishing). Standard exclusions include intentional acts
and for trademark infringement, but each policy must be read
carefully.

Insurance law varies by state, but in general, an insurance policy is
read broadly in favor of the insured, and the insurer has a duty to
defend if the underlying complaint could be read to state a covered
claim, even if the facts might ultimately not support that claim. The
duty to defend thus is much broader than the duty to indemnify. This
is important when, for example, the underlying complaint alleges a
willful violation of the Lanham Act. Since the Lanham Act does not
require intent, the exclusion for intentional acts does not excuse the
insurer of its duty to defend (if the policy otherwise covers a claim),
even though the insurer has no duty to indemnify if the advertiser is
ultimately found liable for a willful violation.

Nonetheless, insurers routinely deny coverage and any duty to defend, and so there is a fair amount of litigation about what constitutes "advertising injury." One issue that has come up repeatedly is whether allegedly false comparative advertising constitutes covered "disparagement." Usually, false positive things said about the advertiser's product will not be considered to have disparaged other parties by implication. *See, e.g.*, Skylink Technologies v. Assurance Company of America, 400 F.3d 982 (7th Cir. 2005) (an insured's allegedly false claim that its garage door openers are compatible with underlying plaintiff's garage door openers was not covered "disparagement"). However, false advertising claims based on direct comparisons that claim superiority to a competitor may trigger advertising injury coverage, even if the underlying complaint doesn't contain a cause of action styled "disparagement." *See, e.g.*, Winklevoss Consultants v. Fed. Ins. Co., 11 F. Supp. 2d 995 (N.D. Ill. 1998); *cf.* E.piphany v. St. Paul Fire & Marine Ins., 590 F. Supp. 2d 1244 (N.D. Cal. 2008) (disparagement can exist even without directly mentioning the underlying plaintiff negatively but instead through "clear implication," as when ad claims that underlying defendant has the "only" product suitable for certain use).

Hyundai Motor America v. National Union Fire Insurance Co., 600 F.3d 1092 (9th Cir. 2010), found that "advertising injury" included a patent infringement suit based on a patented method of advertising. Hyundai's "build your own" online tool let car buyers customize features like color, trim and model to see what the resulting car would look like. Hyundai prevailed against its insurer because the patents covered a marketing method, and thus the alleged patent infringement constituted covered "misappropriation of advertising ideas." By contrast, advertising injury coverage would not help where the insured advertised an infringing product, because there the foundation of liability is the product and not the advertising.

Defendants Against Whom Relief May Be Sought

States and state agencies cannot be sued for false advertising unless they waive their sovereign immunity. College Sav. Bank v. Florida Prepaid Postsecondary Educ. Expense Fund, 527 U.S. 666 (1999).

In addition to ad agencies (discussed in Chapter 16), proper defendants can sometimes include the advertiser's officers, Donsco, Inc. v. Casper Corp., 587 F.2d 602 (3d Cir. 1978), and research agencies assisting the advertiser, Grant Airmass Corp. v. Gaymar Indus., Inc., 645 F. Supp. 1507 (S.D.N.Y. 1986).

The FTC is more likely to pursue related parties, particularly corporate officers, than private litigants are. For employees, directors, and the like, liability is appropriate "when the defendant participated directly in the violative conduct or had authority to control it," and had or should have had knowledge of it.

"Authority to control can be evidenced by active involvement in business affairs and the making of corporate policy," and such active involvement may also establish the requisite knowledge. FTC v. Lights of Am., Inc., 2013 WL 5230681 (C.D. Cal. Sept. 17, 2013). The knowledge standard includes people who are recklessly indifferent to or intentionally avoid the truth. Thus, even if an individual personally doesn't perceive or believe that ads are deceptive, her knowledge of multiple complaints about those ads can suffice for the knowledge requirement. FTC v. Ross, 743 F.3d 886 (4th Cir. 2014).

In addition, final yes-or-no authority over advertising isn't required for liability. A person who participated directly in meetings about advertising concepts and content, reviewed and edited ad copy, managed the day-to-day affairs of the marketing team, and possessed hiring and firing authority over the head of the marketing department was therefore held individually liable for false advertising. POM Wonderful, LLC v. FTC, 777 F.3d 478 (D.C. Cir. 2015).

In some cases, vicarious liability—liability that doesn't require knowledge or fault—may also be imposed. *Proctor & Gamble Co. v. Haugen*, 222 F. 3d 1262 (10th Cir. 2000), concerned Amway's liability for false statements disseminated by its distributors:

> Vicarious liability may arise either from an employment or agency relationship. In the present case, the district court found P & G had failed to show that either kind of relationship existed between Amway and its distributors so as to give rise to a genuine issue of material fact regarding vicarious liability.

> With regard to the distributors' employment status vis-à-vis Amway, the Utah Supreme Court has drawn a distinction between an employee and an independent contractor. In general,

>> [a]n employee is one who is hired and paid a salary, a wage, or at a fixed rate, to perform the employer's work as directed by the employer and who is subject to a comparatively high degree of control in performing those duties. In contrast, an independent contractor is one who is engaged to do some particular project or piece of work, usually for a set total sum, who may do the job in his own way, subject to only minimal restrictions or controls and is responsible only for its satisfactory completion.

> Factors a court may consider in determining the nature of the relationship include: "(1) whatever covenants or agreements exist concerning the right of direction and control over the

employee, whether express or implied; (2) the right to hire and fire; (3) the method of payment, i.e., whether in wages or fees, as compared to payment for a complete job or project; and (4) the furnishing of the equipment."

In the present case, although Amway sets parameters within which its distributors function, those distributors and Amway stand in relation to one another essentially as wholesaler and retailer and at the same time retailer and consumer. The record indicates that Amway sets certain rules, and provides certain resources like the AmVox voice message system (in the same way a wholesaler might provide factory warranty service and require a certain standard of behavior from its distributors), but Amway distributors, like retailers, act virtually autonomously in determining in what manner to sell (or consume) Amway products. Based on the undisputed evidence in the record before us, we conclude Amway does not exercise a "comparatively high degree of control" over them. Therefore, the distributors are more analogous to independent contractors than to employees under Utah law.

The evidence also fails to create a genuine issue of material fact as to whether the distributors were Amway's agents. An agent is "a person authorized by another to act on his behalf and under his control." "The existence of an agency relationship is determined from all the facts and circumstances in the case."

> Under agency law, an agent cannot make its principal responsible for the agent's actions unless the agent is acting pursuant to either actual or apparent authority. Actual authority incorporates the concepts of express and implied authority. Express authority exists whenever the principal directly states that its

agent has the authority to perform a particular act on the principal's behalf. Implied authority, on the other hand, embraces authority to do those acts which are incidental to, or are necessary, usual, and proper to accomplish or perform, the main authority expressly delegated to the agent. Implied authority is actual authority based upon the premise that whenever the performance of certain business is confided to an agent, such authority carries with it by implication authority to do collateral acts which are the natural and ordinary incidents of the main act or business authorized. This authority may be implied from the words and conduct of the parties and the facts and circumstances attending the transaction in question.

In the present case, P & G cites no facts to show that Amway told the distributors to spread the subject message. The distributors' authority is therefore not "express" . . . . Nor did the distributors who spread the subject message act with implicit authority. Nothing in the record supports the conclusion that spreading the subject message, and indeed satanic rumors regarding P & G generally, was "natural[ly] and ordinar[ily]" incident to Amway's business.

Some states' consumer protection laws may not recognize vicarious liability, but they can still penalize anyone who aids and abets a violation. For example, a corporate officer or employee who knows that conduct is wrongful and provides substantial assistance or encouragement to it may be liable. *See* People v. Sarpas, 225 Cal. App. 4th 1539 (Cal. Ct. App. 2014) (discussed *supra*).

3. Criminal Liability

Criminal prosecutions for violations of the FTC Act or state consumer protection statutes are rare—but not unheard of.

The FTC Act provides that a violation committed with the intent to defraud or mislead is criminal. 15 U.S.C. § 54. The maximum penalty is a $10,000 fine or up to one year in prison. However, the FTC relies on the Department of Justice to prosecute criminal violations, and this rarely occurs. The FTC can—and does—prosecute criminal cases under CAN-SPAM, which, as its acronym indicates, governs deceptive commercial email schemes. *See FTC Announces First CAN-SPAM Cases.*

In addition, federal district court orders may be enforced through civil or criminal contempt actions filed in district court. In 1997, the FTC implemented Project Scofflaw, which involved both criminal and civil enforcement against violators of FTC-obtained district court orders. Results included a 125-month sentence for six counts of criminal contempt arising from violation of a court order barring violations of the FTC's Franchise Rule, United States v. Ferrara, 334 F.3d 774 (8th Cir. 2003), along with other prison sentences.

The FTC also established a Criminal Liaison Unit ("CLU") in 2003 to encourage criminal prosecution of consumer fraud by enhancing coordination with criminal law enforcement authorities interested in pursuing such cases. The number of concurrent or subsequent criminal prosecutions in the past two decades is only in the dozens, but it remains a possibility for particularly egregious frauds. Multiple defendants may be indicted in a single fraud. *See* Frank Gorman, *How the FTC Can Help Local Prosecutors with Cases of Criminal Fraud*, THE PROSECUTOR, Oct./Nov./Dec. 2008, at 28.

The CLU works with state AGs or local prosecutors. State attorneys general's authority over consumer fraud is exclusively civil in some jurisdictions, but criminal sanctions are authorized in others, sometimes for specific types of fraud such as mortgage or insurance fraud. *See, e.g.*, Ohio Rev. Code Ann. § 1345.02(E)(3) (authorizing the Ohio attorney general to initiate criminal prosecutions for consumer law violations if the local prosecuting attorney declines to prosecute or requests the attorney general to bring the case); Okla. Stat. tit. 15, § 762(B) (2001) (establishing that the Oklahoma attorney general has "powers of a district attorney to investigate and prosecute suspected violations of consumer laws"); *see also* Ga. Code Ann. § 16-8-104 (2007) (authorizing the Georgia attorney general and district attorneys to prosecute cases of residential mortgage fraud); Idaho Code Ann. § 41-213(3) (2010) (establishing that the Idaho attorney general has concurrent authority with county attorneys over insurance fraud). Some states, such as New Jersey, have units dedicated to prosecuting fraud, including consumer fraud. Division of Criminal Justice, St. N.J. Off. Att'y Gen., http://www.njdcj.org/fincab.htm.

Given the general scienter requirements of criminal law, criminal prosecutions for consumer protection violations require the prosecution to prove the defendant's knowledge of falsity, rather than mere falsity. For this and other reasons, such prosecutions are the least common means of enforcing consumer protection law. DEE PRIDGEN & RICHARD M. ALDERMAN, CONSUMER PROTECTION AND THE LAW § 7.22 (2009).

This chapter doesn't cover the full range of business torts. Instead, it focuses on those most closely connected to false advertising claims, specifically the common law claims of *defamation* and *disparagement*: saying nasty things about the competition or about the competition's goods or services. These claims implicate the First Amendment, but over time the jurisprudence has become more tolerant of critical remarks and comparative advertising.

The torts we'll consider in this chapter can be brought alongside Lanham Act and state consumer protection claims; or occasionally on their own when the plaintiff wouldn't have standing to bring those core claims. They mostly involve statements about competitors' products—not statements about an advertiser's own products. Tortious interference with existing or prospective economic advantage is a potential exception, though that usually is alleged when there's some sort of comparative statement being made.

1. Defamation and Disparagement

Though the Lanham Act and state consumer protection laws generally offer commercial plaintiffs greater prospects of success than defamation and product disparagement, the latter claims are still regularly pled and litigated. As you go through the sometimes bewildering variety of common law claims, often with state-by-state variations in the way elements are described, keep in mind that the core differences between the common law causes of action in this chapter and statutory claims under the Lanham Act, the FTCA, and state consumer protection laws revolve around (1) scienter (sufficient knowledge of falsity, usually called "malice" in disparagement cases), (2) intent to harm, and (3) circumstances in which harm to the plaintiff can be presumed for purposes of awarding damages.

In addition, these torts cover all speech, not just commercial speech. Because the causes of action are available to anyone—not just government regulators, competitors or consumers—higher standards with respect to awareness of falsity, intent to harm and proof of damages limit the torts.

Thus, saying something mistaken and negative about a business doesn't automatically lead to liability. Consider, for example, a talk show host who runs a story about the hidden dangers of apples or beef; without heightened standards for knowing falsity and intent to harm, sellers could deter speech about important health issues.

Given the increased First Amendment constraints on the common law claims, it was only a matter of time before a plaintiff bringing both Lanham Act and defamation claims would face the argument that the First Amendment also barred liability without fault under the Lanham Act. As you read the following case, pay attention to the remaining differences between defamation (which targets the plaintiff) and disparagement (which targets the plaintiff's goods or services). Can you identify differences that will be important in practice?

U.S. Healthcare, Inc. v. Blue Cross of Greater Philadelphia, 898 F.2d 914 (3d Cir. 1990)

. . . FACTS AND PROCEDURAL HISTORY

These cross appeals arise from a comparative advertising war between giants of the health care industry in the Delaware Valley— U.S. Healthcare on the one side and Blue Cross/Blue Shield on the other. The thrust of these claims is that each side asserts the other's advertising misrepresented both parties' products.

710

For over fifty years, Blue Cross/Blue Shield operated as the largest
health insurer in Southeastern Pennsylvania by offering "traditional"
medical insurance coverage. Traditional insurance protects the
subscriber from "major" medical expenses, with the insurer paying a
negotiated amount based upon the services rendered, and the
subscriber generally paying a deductible or some other amount. The
subscriber has freedom in choosing hospitals and health care
providers (i.e., doctors).

In the early 1970's, U.S. Healthcare began providing an alternative to
traditional insurance in the form of a health maintenance
organization, generically known as an "HMO." An HMO acts as both
an insurer and a provider of specified services that are more
comprehensive than those offered by traditional insurance. Generally,
HMO subscribers choose a primary health care provider from the
HMO network who coordinates their health care services and
determines when hospital admission or treatment from a specialist is
required. Usually, subscribers are not covered for services obtained
without this permission or from providers outside this network. By
1986, U.S. Healthcare was the largest HMO in the area, claiming
almost 600,000 members. During the same period, Blue Cross/Blue
Shield experienced a loss in enrollment of over 1% per year, with a
large number of those subscribers choosing HMO coverage over
traditional insurance, and a majority of those defectors choosing a
U.S. Healthcare company.

. . . In late 1985, in an admitted attempt to compete with HMO, Blue
Cross/Blue Shield introduced a new product that it called "Personal
Choice," known generically as a preferred provider organization or
"PPO." PPO insurance provides subscribers with a "network" of
health care providers and hospitals, and generally "covers"
subscribers only for services obtained from the network providers and
administered at the network hospitals. Subscribers must obtain

permission to receive treatment from providers outside the network, and in such instances receive at most only partial coverage.

Thereafter, Blue Cross/Blue Shield consulted with two separate advertising agencies before arriving at a marketing strategy for its new product. In July 1986, Blue Cross/Blue Shield launched what it termed a deliberately "aggressive and provocative" comparative advertising campaign calculated "to introduce and increase the attractiveness of its products"—in particular, Personal Choice—at the expense of HMO products. Blue Cross/Blue Shield's campaign, which included direct mailings, as well as television, radio and print advertisements, ran for about six months at a total cost of approximately $2.175 million. According to a Blue Cross memorandum that purported to reflect the directions of Markson, the campaign was designed specifically to "reduce the attractiveness of [HMO]."

The Blue Cross/Blue Shield advertising campaign consisted of eight different advertisements for the print media, seven different advertisements for television, three different advertisements for radio, and a direct mailing including a folding brochure. . . . After describing HMO's referral procedure, . . . three of the eight print advertisements—as well as the brochure—say the following:

> You should also know that through a series of financial incentives, HMO encourages this doctor to handle as many patients as possible without referring to a specialist. When an HMO doctor does make a specialist referral, it could take money directly out of his pocket. Make too many referrals, and he could find himself in trouble with HMO.

One of the print advertisements and the brochure also feature a senior citizen under the banner heading "Your money or your life," juxtaposed with Blue Cross/Blue Shield's description of "The high cost of HMO Medicare."

Of the seven television advertisements run by Blue Cross/Blue Shield, four are innocuous, mentioning HMO only in the closing slogan common to all seven of the ads: "Personal Choice. Better than HMO. So good, it's Blue Cross and Blue Shield." The fifth features an indignant every man, who simply states "I resent having to ask my HMO doctor for permission to see a specialist," before a spokesperson extols the benefits of Personal Choice without reference to HMO until, again, the closing slogan. The sixth features a cab driver who says, "I don't like those HMO health plans. You get one doctor, no choice of hospitals," before a shopper tells him about the virtues of Personal Choice—again, without reference to HMO until the closing slogan. The seventh television advertisement used by Blue Cross/Blue Shield, while following the same general format, seems to us a dramatic departure from the others in that it appears consciously designed to play upon the fears of the consuming public. The commercial features a grief-stricken woman who says, "The hospital my HMO sent me to just wasn't enough. It's my fault." The implication of the advertisement is that some tragedy has befallen the woman because of her choice of health care.

. . . [U.S. Healthcare's] responsive advertising campaign, which began sometime after the Blue Cross/Blue Shield campaign and ran until late February 1987, cost $1.255 million. . . .

U.S. Healthcare's responsive campaign did not just highlight the positive characteristics in its own product, but also featured "anti-Blue Cross" advertisements. Of the three remaining print advertisements, one simply shows a comparative list of the features available under HMO and Personal Choice, with a banner heading that reads "It's your choice." The other two explain that under Personal Choice, the number of hospitals available to the subscriber is limited and, moreover, that many Personal Choice doctors do not have admitting privileges at even those few. One of these advertisements ran under a banner heading of "When it Comes to Being Admitted to a Hospital, There's Something Personal Choice May Not Be Willing to Admit"; the other ran under a banner heading of "If You Really Look Into 'Personal Choice,' You Might Have a Better Name For It."

. . . The final television commercial was U.S. Healthcare's own attempt to play upon the fears of the consuming public. As solemn music plays, the narrator lists the shortcomings of Personal Choice while the camera pans from a Personal Choice brochure resting on the pillow of a hospital bed to distraught family members standing at bedside. The advertisement closes with a pair of hands pulling a sheet over the Personal Choice brochure.

. . . After a fourteen-day trial, followed by eight days of deliberations, the jury announced it was deadlocked on all issues of liability and damages. . . .

The [district] court held that because the objects of the advertisements are "public figures," and because the matters in the advertisements are "community health issues of public concern," heightened constitutional protections attach to this speech. [The district court then held that, under the First Amendment, the Lanham Act claims as well as the commercial disparagement, defamation and tortious interference claims required proof by clear and convincing evidence of knowledge or reckless disregard of falsity, and that neither party could satisfy that standard.] . . .

II. The Actionable Claims and Counterclaims under Applicable
Substantive Federal and State Law. . .

A. Applicable Federal and Pennsylvania Common Law.

. . . 2. Defamation.

Under Pennsylvania law, a defamatory statement is one that " 'tends
so to harm the reputation of another as to lower him in the
estimation of the community or to deter third persons from
associating or dealing with him.' " It is for the court to determine, in
the first instance, whether the statement of which the plaintiff
complained is capable of a defamatory meaning; if the court decides
that it is capable of a defamatory meaning, then it is for the jury to
decide if the statement was so understood by the reader or listener.
To ascertain the meaning of an allegedly defamatory statement, the
statement must be examined in context.

> The test is the effect the [statement] is fairly calculated to
> produce, the impression it would naturally engender, in the
> minds of the average persons among whom it is intended to
> circulate. The words must be given by judges and juries the
> same signification that other people are likely to attribute to
> them.

Opinion that fails to imply underlying defamatory facts cannot
support the cause of action.

In an action for defamation, the plaintiff has the burden of proving 1)
the defamatory character of the communication; 2) its publication by
the defendant; 3) its application to the plaintiff; 4) an understanding
by the reader or listener of its defamatory meaning; and 5) an
understanding by the reader or listener of an intent by the defendant

that the statement refer to the plaintiff. Additionally, in order to recover damages, the plaintiff must demonstrate that the statement results from fault, amounting at least to negligence, on the part of the defendant. Finally, the plaintiff has the burden of proving any special harm resulting from the statement. . . .

3. Commercial Disparagement.

A commercially disparaging statement—in contrast to a defamatory statement—is one "which is intended by its publisher to be understood or which is reasonably understood to cast doubt upon the existence or extent of another's property in land, chattels or intangible things, or upon their quality, . . . if the matter is so understood by its recipient." In order to maintain an action for disparagement, the plaintiff must prove 1) that the disparaging statement of fact is untrue or that the disparaging statement of opinion is incorrect; 2) that no privilege attaches to the statement; and 3) that the plaintiff suffered a direct pecuniary loss as the result of the disparagement.

The distinction between actions for defamation and disparagement turns on the harm towards which each is directed. An action for commercial disparagement is meant to compensate a vendor for pecuniary loss suffered because statements attacking the quality of his goods have reduced their marketability, while defamation is meant protect an entity's interest in character and reputation. . . .

Given the similar elements of the two torts, deciding which cause of action lies in a given situation can be difficult. The Court of Appeals for the Eighth Circuit gave the following time-honored explanation of when impugnation of the quality of goods crosses the line from disparagement of products to defamation of vendors:

[W]here the publication on its face is directed against the goods or product of a corporate vendor or manufacturer, it will not be held libelous per se as to the corporation, unless by fair construction and without the aid of extrinsic evidence it imputes to the corporation fraud, deceit, dishonesty, or reprehensible conduct in its business in relation to said goods or product. . . .

B. The Actionable Construction of the Advertisements

. . . [W]e consider as a group the bulk of the advertisements, which either compare the competing health plans on one or more points, or simply criticize the competitor's health plan without detailed exposition of the advertiser's own competing plan. Because they may contain misrepresentations beyond puffing, a cause of action may lie under the Lanham Act, even for those advertisements that focus exclusively on the competitor's health plan. In addition, as these advertisements all make representations about the competitor's product, a cause of action may lie for commercial disparagement with respect to any of them. None of these, however, could be said to impute to the competitor by fair construction any "fraud, deceit, dishonesty, or reprehensible conduct." Consequently, no cause of action for defamation will lie with regard to these. . . .

We believe [certain] advertisements are capable of defamatory meaning. These include, first, the Blue Cross/Blue Shield advertisements that suggest HMO primary care physicians have a financial interest in not referring patients to specialists and, indeed, that HMO makes reprisals against those primary care physicians who make too many referrals. These advertisements imply that U.S. Healthcare, the people who run it, and the doctors who are employed by it, all place personal profit above adequate health care. Such an implication goes beyond the comparative quality of HMO health care

717

to suggest reprehensible conduct by U.S. Healthcare and its employees in the conduct of their business.

Also capable of defamatory meaning is Blue Cross/Blue Shield's "Distraught Woman" advertisement. Her statement that "The hospital my HMO sent me to just wasn't enough," matched with her grief-stricken demeanor, suggests she has suffered some tragedy because of HMO's substandard care. The suggestion that U.S. Healthcare chose to send her to a hospital that could not adequately treat her problem goes beyond the product itself to impute reprehensible conduct to the corporation. Indeed, the scare tactic is the point of the commercial.

Finally, we find U.S. Healthcare's "Critical Condition" television commercial to be capable of a defamatory construction as well. As a dirge plays, the narrator lists the shortcomings of Personal Choice while the camera pans from a Personal Choice brochure resting on the pillow of a hospital bed to distraught family members standing around the bed. At the end of the advertisement, a pair of hands pulls a sheet over the Personal Choice brochure. We do not believe the depiction of a distressing death scene in a health insurance commercial is an uncalculated association. Again, we believe a scare tactic was the intent and, more to the point, a jury could find the commercial suggests Blue Cross/Blue Shield knowingly provides health care so substandard as to be dangerous.

As to this final group of advertisements, no action for commercial disparagement will lie because the statements are directed at the vendor, not his goods. Nonetheless, Lanham Act claims may lie. . . .

III. First Amendment Principles and the Standard of Proof in Claims Arising from a Comparative Advertising Campaign

Having determined that some of the advertisements may be actionable under federal and state law, we must now consider whether the First Amendment affects the standard of proof. . . . [The district court] rejected U.S. Healthcare's argument that the advertisements were commercial speech and thereby entitled to less constitutional protection. The district court viewed the comparative advertising campaign giving rise to this litigation as a "dispute . . . about how best to deal with spiraling medical costs," and concluded that, "[t]o characterize the advertisements in this case as mere commercial speech ignores the fact that, at their core, they are instruments in a debate between two providers of public health care 'intimately involved in the resolution of important public questions.' " . . .

A. Background

Distinguishing the Supreme Court's First Amendment jurisprudence is an express intention to "lay down broad rules of general application," rather than to allow balancing between competing values on a case-by-case basis, an approach that the Court fears would "lead to unpredictable results and uncertain expectations, and . . . render [its] duty to supervise the lower courts unmanageable." In delineating the limits placed on state authority by the First Amendment, the Court has articulated two distinct lines of cases, one involving defamation and the other involving government regulation of commercial speech. We have found no decision by the Court considering a defamation action involving expression properly characterized as commercial speech.

Despite its intention to enunciate general rules, the Court has implicitly recognized the need for balancing when a novel issue arises. Given the unique issue presented here, we believe it is necessary to evaluate the competing state and First Amendment

719

interests. In taking this approach, we are mindful of the Supreme Court's admonition that nothing in *Gertz* "indicated that [the] same balance would be struck regardless of the type of speech involved."

Our approach will proceed in light of the analytical framework of the defamation cases. We have found no comparable case, and the parties cite none. In what we believe is a matter of first impression, we are presented with the unique circumstance of allegedly defamatory statements made in the context of a comparative advertising campaign.

B. Rules and Conceptual Framework

. . . In evaluating these competing interests, the Court has determined that the state has only a "limited" interest in compensating public persons for injury to reputation by defamatory statements, but has a "strong and legitimate" interest in compensating private persons for the same injury. The Court has provided a two-fold explanation for the discrepancy in the extent of the state interests. First, because public officials and public figures enjoy "greater access to the channels of effective communication and hence have a more realistic opportunity to counteract false statements than private individuals," the states have a greater interest in protecting private persons whose relative lack of "self-help" remedies render them "more vulnerable to injury." Second, the state has a stronger interest in protecting the reputations of private individuals because, unlike public persons, they have not voluntarily placed themselves in the public eye.

On the other side of the coin, the "type of speech involved" also affects the way in which the "balance is struck," by varying the weight of the First Amendment interest. "[S]peech on 'matters of public concern' . . . is 'at the heart of the First Amendment's protection.'" The Court has determined that "speech of private concern," such as a credit report for business, is of less First Amendment importance, in the same way that utterances labeled "commercial speech" are "less central to the interests of the First Amendment."

C. Application of the Rules and Conceptual Framework

. . . We next turn to assessing the relative weight of the First Amendment interests in this case. We recognize that traditional defamation analysis usually begins with an examination of the status of the plaintiff. Because of the facts presented, however, we shall first consider the content of the speech involved. Nor do we believe that such inverted analysis is improper.

Similarly, traditional defamation analysis would have us consider the public or private nature of the speech in assessing the weight of the First Amendment interests. We believe, however, that the novel facts here require a different approach. Our appraisal of these interests depends on whether the speech at issue can properly be characterized as commercial speech. "There is no longer any room to doubt that what has come to be known as 'commercial speech' is entitled to the protection of the First Amendment, albeit to protection somewhat less extensive than that afforded 'noncommercial speech.' " If the speech here is commercial speech, then it likely does not mandate heightened constitutional protection.

We recognize that the Supreme Court cases creating the commercial speech doctrine all involve some form of government regulation of speech and that none involve defamation actions. Further, the focus in the commercial speech cases is on First Amendment protection itself, not the heightened protection afforded by the actual malice standard. However, we believe the subordinate valuation of commercial speech is not confined to the government regulation line of cases.

In *Dun & Bradstreet*, the Court held that speech on matters of private concern, such as a credit report for business, receives less First Amendment protection than speech on matters of public concern. More significantly for our purposes, the Court justified its decision to allow less protection for speech of private concern by drawing an analogy to the reduced First Amendment protection afforded commercial speech:

> This Court on many occasions has recognized that certain kinds of speech are less central to the interests of the First Amendment than others. . . . In the area of protected speech, the most prominent example of reduced protection for certain kinds of speech concerns commercial speech. Such speech, we have noted, occupies a "subordinate position in the scale of First Amendment values." It also is more easily verifiable and less likely to be deterred by proper regulation. Accordingly, it may be regulated in ways that might be impermissible in the realm of noncommercial expression.

. . . [T]he statements here are commercial in nature. First, there is no question that they are advertisements; they were disseminated as part of an expensive, professionally run promotional campaign. Second, the speech specifically refers to a product; it touts the relative merits of Personal Choice (or U.S. Healthcare's HMO) over competing products. Third, the desire for revenue motivated the speech; the record contains abundant evidence that Blue Cross/Blue Shield launched the promotional campaign in order to recoup its share of the health insurance market. . . . Similarly, protection of its new market share motivated U.S. Healthcare's speech. In short, "common sense" informs us that the statements here propose a commercial transaction, and thus differ from other types of speech.

Even more importantly, we find it significant that the advertisements have all of the characteristics that the Supreme Court has identified in the commercial speech cases as making speech durable, not susceptible to "chill." Consequently, they do not require the heightened protection we extend to our most valuable forms of speech. Because the thrust of all of the advertisements is to convince the consuming public to bring its business to one of these health care giants rather than the other, there is no doubt that the advertisements were motivated by economic self-interest. Furthermore, given the size of the health care market in the Delaware Valley—Blue Shield virtually shouts about the hundreds of millions of dollars at stake—we believe it would have to be a cold day before these corporations would be chilled from speaking about the comparative merits of their products. *Cf. Dun & Bradstreet*, 472 U.S. at 762–63 (because credit report was solely motivated by profit "any incremental 'chilling' effect of libel suits would be of decreased significance").

In addition, these are advertisements for products and services in markets in which U.S. Healthcare and Blue Cross/Blue Shield deal—and, presumably, know more about than anyone else. The facts upon which the advertisements are based—comparative price, procedures, and services offered—are readily objectifiable. These advertisements were precisely calculated, developed over time and published only when the corporate speakers were ready. Consequently, the advertisements were unusually verifiable.

Finally, while the speech here does discuss costs and consequences of competing health insurance and health care delivery programs, some of the advertisements capable of defamatory meaning here add little information and even fewer ideas to the marketplace of health care thought.[26] The expression in these advertisements "differs markedly

---

[26] We believe one such advertisement implicates important health care concerns. This advertisement suggests that HMO primary care physicians have a financial incentive to deny referrals to specialists. On the other hand, we believe the other advertisements capable of defamatory meaning make no

from ideological expression because it is confined to the promotion of specific . . . services." *Cf. Zauderer*, 471 U.S. at 637 & n. 77 (advertisement containing information that, in another context would be fully protected, nonetheless commercial speech, as it proposed commercial transaction in advertiser's self-interest). And to the extent that the advertisements are false statements of fact, of course, the speech has no constitutional value at all. . . .

Despite these conclusive indications that the speech here is commercial in nature, Blue Cross/Blue Shield argues that the speech should be accorded heightened constitutional protection. Relying on *Bigelow v. Virginia*, 421 U.S. 809 (1975), it argues that speech which does more than "simply propose a commercial transaction" constitutes something more than commercial speech. Furthermore, it maintains that the "*Bigelow* standard" is applicable when the products are not merely linked to a public debate but are themselves "at the center of the public debate."[27] Blue Cross/Blue Shield concludes that its own advertisements "educate[d] the public about the substantial differences among the[ ] available means for financing and delivering

---

such contribution. One portrays a woman grieving that the hospital to which HMO sent her was inadequate. The second, a "death" scene, shows a pair of hands pulling a hospital sheet over a personal choice brochure as a dirge plays. "There is simply no credible argument that this type of [advertisement] requires special protection to ensure that 'debate on public issues [will] be uninhibited, robust, and wide-open.' "

[27] In *Bigelow*, a newspaper editor published an abortion clinic's advertisement, which the state court determined violated a state criminal statute prohibiting dissemination of publications encouraging the processing of an abortion. The Supreme Court struck down the statute on First Amendment grounds, stating that the advertisement could not be regulated as commercial speech because, "[v]iewed in its entirety, [it] conveyed information of potential interest and value to a diverse audience—not only to readers possibly in need of the services offered . . . ."

health care, thereby ensuring informed purchasing decisions" and
rendering the advertisements non-commercial.

. . . [T]he *Central Hudson* decision, in which the Supreme Court
expressly rejected such attempts to "blur further the line the Court
has sought to draw in commercial speech cases," represents the
proper approach. *Central Hudson* prevents an advertiser from
immunizing, in effect, otherwise defamatory speech—behind the
actual malice standard afforded to core speech by the First
Amendment—simply by reference to an issue of public concern.

. . . Therefore, while the speech here is protected by the First
Amendment, we hold that the First Amendment requires no higher
standard of liability than that mandated by the substantive law for
each claim. The heightened protection of the actual malice standard
is not "necessary to give adequate 'breathing space' to the freedoms
protected by the First Amendment."

. . . [T]raditional defamation analysis is not well suited to strike the
proper balance between the state and federal interests and First
Amendment values in the context of commercial speech.

In weighing the state interest, we must look to the status of the
claimants. As we have noted, the Court has determined that the state
has only a "limited" interest in compensating public persons for injury
to reputation but has a "strong and legitimate" interest in
compensating private persons for the same injury. Contending that
the actual malice standard applies because a public figure is
implicated, Blue Cross/Blue Shield argues that the following factors
render U.S. Healthcare a "public figure": it has voluntarily exposed
itself to public comment on the issues involved in this dispute; it is a
contributor to the ongoing debate concerning health care insurance; it
is among the nation's largest providers of HMO-type insurance
coverage; it markets its products extensively and aggressively, and

has a substantial annual advertising budget; and it frequently and consistently asserts the advantages of its method of health care financing and delivery, and has done so in advertisements, press releases, professional journals, newspapers, magazines and speeches before public assemblies. These activities, Blue Cross/Blue Shield submits, "constitute a voluntary effort to influence the consuming public." Similar statements can be made regarding Blue Cross/Blue Shield.

Gertz identified three classes of public figures: those who achieve such stature or notoriety that they are considered public figures in all contexts; those who become public figures involuntarily, but these are "exceedingly rare"; and those who are deemed public figures only within the context of a particular public dispute. The Court defined the last group, limited purpose public figures, as individuals who voluntarily "thrust themselves to the forefront of particular public controversies in order to influence the resolution of the issues involved."

. . . The first factor indicative of a claimant's status is his relative access to the media. Clearly, both parties have access to the media. Moreover, the magnitude of the advertising campaigns shows their ability to utilize it on a vast scale. While access to the media does not always make one a public figure for purposes of First Amendment analysis, the tremendous ability of these parties to advertise, indicating their lack of vulnerability, would support a finding that both are public figures.

The second factor is the manner in which the risk of defamation came upon them. Both companies, attempting to influence consumers' decisions, have thrust themselves into the controversy of who provides better value in health care delivery and insurance. Blue Cross/Blue Shield began the comparative advertising war with its pointed attacks on HMO. U.S. Healthcare, even before responding with its own comparative advertising, had used advertising to help establish itself as a leading provider of health care in the Delaware Valley. Consequently, by inviting comment and assuming the risk of unfair comment, both claimants resemble public figures. *See* Steaks Unlimited, Inc. v. Deaner, 623 F.2d 264, 274 (3d Cir. 1980) ("In short, through its advertising blitz, [the plaintiff corporation] invited public attention, comment and criticism.").

Under traditional defamation analysis, the parties' considerable access to the media and their voluntary entry into a controversy are strong indicia that they are limited purpose public figures. Indeed, inflexible application of these factors would warrant a finding of public figure status and facilitate a finding of heightened constitutional protection. Nonetheless, we hold that these corporations are not public figures for the limited purpose of commenting on health care in this case.

As noted, *Gertz* defines the limited purpose public figure as one who has "thrust [himself] to the forefront of particular public controversies in order to influence the resolution of the issues involved." Although some of the advertisements touch on matters of public concern, their central thrust is commercial. Thus, the parties have acted primarily to generate revenue by influencing customers, not to resolve "the issues involved."

While discerning motivations of the speaker is often difficult, we have a more fundamental reason for declining to find limited purpose public figure status in this case. The express analysis in *Gertz* is not helpful in the context of a comparative advertising war. Most products can be linked to a public issue. And most advertisers—including both claimants here—seek out the media. Thus, it will always be true that such advertisers have voluntarily placed themselves in the public eye. It will be equally true that such advertisers have access to the media. Therefore, under the *Gertz* rationale, speech of public concern that implicates corporate advertisers—i.e., typical comparative advertising—will always be insulated behind the actual malice standard. We believe a corporation must do more than the claimants have done here to become a limited purpose public figure under *Gertz*.

In summary, we conclude that the speech at issue does not receive heightened protection under the First Amendment. Because this speech is chill-resistant, the *New York Times* standard is not, as we have noted, "necessary to give adequate 'breathing space' to the freedoms protected by the First Amendment." Therefore, the standard of proof needed to establish the substantive claims is that applicable under federal and state law. . . .

NOTES AND QUESTIONS

Revisiting Advertising Theory. Consider the search/experience/credence qualities framework from Chapter 4. The quality of medical services is a classic credence attribute. How does that predict consumer reactions to claims that a competitor's medical services are inferior? Arguably, the court used the standard of proof to calibrate what kinds of claims will be tolerated in comparative advertising.

Malice Is a Term of Art. A speaker acts with "malice" if it knows of the falsity of a statement or acts with reckless disregard toward its truth or falsity. Some states are also permit a malice finding if the defendant acts with ill will or intent to interfere with the plaintiff's economic interest in an unprivileged fashion. The Restatement (Second) of Torts takes no position on whether such a rule is appropriate, in part because the First Amendment implications of such a rule are unclear.

Kinetic Concepts, Inc. v. Bluesky Medical Corporation, 2005 WL 3068209 (W.D. Tex. 2005), found a genuine issue of material fact on malice when the defendant "described his marketing plan . . . as an effort to 'contract[ ] the market from $400 million per year to $40 million per year and therefore sow[ ] the seeds of chaos and contraction into the marketplace." The letter went on to state that the defendant wished to "reduce and change the profit vector of the competition from Black to a glowing deep red hue." That is, the defendant really wanted to harm the plaintiff. Does that indicate the defendant acted maliciously? Is it appropriate to find malice if the defendant was negligently mistaken, but not reckless in its disregard for the truth? What if the defendant was not negligent, but simply mistaken—should its ill will or intent to interfere with the plaintiff's economic interest still count as malice? Recall that modern consumer protection statutes often don't require negligence or any fault at all, nor does the Lanham Act.

Convergence in the Torts

As the *Blue Cross/Blue Shield* case indicates, First Amendment constraints on defamation have made it more similar to the product disparagement tort. The differences between the classic causes of action for product disparagement, trade libel, and defamation, though highly technical and subject to judicial nitpicking, are often not practically significant in the context of claims brought by commercial entities, especially claims against other commercial entities.

In fact, the Restatement (Second) of Torts §623A subsumes the concept of trade libel within injurious falsehood, which is why we haven't used the term "trade libel" here, though some states still have a tort called that. The Restatement says that "[o]ne who publishes a false statement harmful to the interests of another is subject to liability for pecuniary loss resulting to the other if (a) he intends for publication of the statement to result in harm to interests of the other

729

having a pecuniary value, or either recognizes or should recognize that it is likely to do so, and (b) he knows that the statement is false or acts in reckless disregard of its truth or falsity." Then §626, Disparagement of Quality—Trade Libel, says that the injurious falsehood rules apply to statements "disparaging the quality of another's land, chattels or intangible things." "Trade libel" is simply the old term for this type of injurious falsehood.

Defamation law is aimed at protecting the personal reputation of the plaintiff, while the injurious falsehood tort is designed to protect economic interests. Before *New York Times v. Sullivan*, the general rule was that damaging statements were presumed false in defamation cases, and liability for falsity was strict, neither of which were true for injurious falsehood. These differences between the torts have been swept away by modern First Amendment jurisprudence. Likewise, defamation used to allow presumptions of damage, while injurious falsehood always required proof. Presumptions of damage in defamation have been cut back substantially in many instances. However, the presumptions may still be significant in some cases, especially in allowing a claim to survive dismissal at the pleading stage, as we will discuss below.

The Line between Defamation and Product Disparagement

The *Blue Cross/Blue Shield* court applied the rule that only ads that impute "fraud, deceit, dishonesty, or reprehensible conduct" to the other party could be defamatory, while product disparagement (or "commercial disparagement") covered a broader range of statements.

The remaining significance of this distinction involves pleading or presuming harm. Product disparagement requires proof of special damages—that is, specific harms such as specific lost customers. Courts often require plaintiffs to plead the names of lost customers or potential customers. Pleading only "lost sales" is insufficient to survive a motion to dismiss.

As a plaintiff's attorney, how would you find evidence of special damages for disparagement in the case of a large-scale, widely disseminated ad campaign? Is the special damages requirement an indication that the tort not meant to govern large-scale advertising campaigns?

In defamation, by contrast, damages may generally be presumed if the statements are per se defamatory—if they're the kind of statements that naturally would be expected to injure a party's reputation.

In *Dorman Products, Inc. v. Dayco Products, LLC*, 2010 WL 4342014 (E.D. Mich. 2010), the court held that statements about the inferiority of Dorman's products didn't create a defamation claim. Allegations of inferiority are "par for the course" and "the most innocuous kind of puffing," generally not capable of misleading the public. However, statements that arguably suggested that Dorman misrepresented product quality were actionable as defamation, not just as trade disparagement. The potentially actionable statements included suggestions that Dorman's products were defective and that Dorman misled the public into believing that its products conformed to industry standards. Asserting that Dorman infringed Dayco's trade dress, that the similarity was non-coincidental, and that Dorman misled consumers, "ha[d] the potential" to impute an intent to mislead to Dorman, which was enough to survive a motion to dismiss.

Given this result, when can an advertiser be confident that its negative statements about a competitor will be judged by trade disparagement standards and not defamation standards? *See also* Cohen v. Hansen, 2015 WL 3609689 (D. Nev. June 9, 2015) (statements alleging that executive had been convicted of fraud and that business was organized to perpetrate illegal activities constituted defamation per se, not business disparagement, so actual damages need not be proved).

Procter & Gamble Co. v. Haugen, 222 F. 3d 1262 (10th Cir. 2000), involved false claims by Amway distributors that P&G was a corporate agent of Satan.

horn

horn

Inverted 666!

The devil's two horns and Antichrist's number 666

[Procter & Gamble's old logo with critiques]

Though the court of appeals held that P&G alleged a violation of the Lanham Act's prohibition on false statements about "commercial activities," it affirmed dismissal of P&G's state-law defamation claims:

> With regard to summary judgment on P & G's state law claims, under Utah law the subject message would be actionable as slander per se if "the defamatory words fall into

732

one of four categories: (1) charge of criminal conduct, (2) charge of a loathsome disease, (3) charge of conduct that is incompatible with the exercise of a lawful business, trade, profession or office; and (4) charge of the unchastity of a woman." Slander per se . . . permits a finding of liability without the need to prove special harm. On appeal, P & G challenges the district court's conclusion that the satanic rumor was "not incompatible with conducting a lawful business." It argues the representations that it "financially supports the Church of Satan and places the Devil's mark on its products are incompatible with P & G's lawful business of selling popular products for personal care and hygiene and for the home."

The false statements contained in the subject message are not the kind of allegations that constitute slander per se. As P & G notes, the question is whether the alleged behavior is incompatible with its business of selling household consumer goods, not whether the alleged behavior is lawful. . . . P & G's business is clearly lawful. However, allegations that it directs a percentage of its profits to the church of Satan are not incompatible with that business in the manner necessary to be actionable as slander per se.

> Disparaging words, to be actionable per se . . . must affect the plaintiff in some way that is peculiarly harmful to one engaged in [the plaintiff's] trade or profession. Disparagement of a general character, equally discreditable to all persons, is not enough unless the particular quality disparaged is of such a character that it is peculiarly valuable in the plaintiff's business or profession.

733

For example, "charges against a clergyman of drunkenness and other moral misconduct affect his fitness for the performance of the duties of his profession, although the same charges against a business man or tradesman do not so affect him." Although offensive to many, an allegation of Devil worship, like drunkenness, is "[d]isparagement of a general character, equally discreditable to all persons" and does not pertain to a quality that is peculiarly valuable in plaintiffs' professional activities of manufacturing and selling household consumer goods. We therefore hold that the district court properly granted summary judgment as to this claim. . . .

Would a statement that a business was routinely late in paying its bills be "disparagement of a general character, equally discreditable to all persons"? Could an accusation that a company's products come from China, not from America, be defamatory? *See* AvePoint, Inc. v. Power Tools, Inc., 981 F. Supp. 2d 496 (W.D. Va. 2013) (defendant's accusation that plaintiff's software was developed and maintained in China and India, not the U.S. as advertised, stated a claim for defamation).

2. Commercial Speech in an Age of Convergence

The Third Circuit set forth a clear line dividing ads from non-ads. But as advertising methods have changed and the lines between advertising and editorial content blur, can its distinction be preserved?

In *Edward B. Beharry & Co., Ltd. v. Bedessee Imports Inc.*, 2010 WL 1223590 (E.D.N.Y. 2010), Beharry sold various spices under the Indi brand, including Special Madras Curry Power. Bedessee was a competitor.

In 2008, *The Caribbean New Yorker*, read by the parties' customer base, ran an article, "FDA warns of filthy 'Special Madras Curry Powder.'" The article stated that Beharry's Special Madras Curry Powder posed a threat to the public, given that the FDA had rejected a June 2008 shipment because it was "filthy." The article then explained that FDA guidelines define an item as "filthy" if it "appears to consist in whole or in part of a filthy, putrid or decomposed substance or to be otherwise unfit for food." The article continued, "Contradicting Beharry's claim of pride in providing its customers with high quality products and services, its 'famous' Indi brand curry was denied entry to the United States." Further, it stated that the FDA had rejected entry to shipments of Indi curry powder repeatedly during the mid-1980s on similar grounds. Moreover, the FDA had issued a warning on Beharry custard powder for containing "non-permitted and undeclared tartrazine." The article concluded that "[t]he West-Indian community must be made aware of repeated adverse FDA actions regarding Beharry's food products and any corollary health risks," and provided (broken) links to the FDA announcements.

Beharry sued for defamation, alleging that Bedessee "contributed to, authored, conceived, submitted and/or otherwise caused" the piece to be published. Beharry alleged that individual defendant Invor Bedessee circulated the full article by email to distributors and the customer base.

The court denied Bedessee's motion to dismiss. Bedessee's denial of any connection to the publication merely created a factual dispute. Beharry noted that the publication didn't contain a byline, and claimed that the piece was a paid ad rather than a news article. Bedessee's email could raise additional suspicion, because when he forwarded it, he expressly characterized it in quotation marks as a "'public article.'" The court further found that the parties' prior history of litigation against each other supported the allegation of a connection with the article. What should the result be if Bedessee is "connected" to the article in the sense of convincing the magazine that it was a worthwhile story to run, but didn't pay for it to appear?

Beharry also claimed violation of the Lanham Act. Bedessee argued that the Lanham Act claim failed because the article wasn't commercial speech. The court agreed. "No named defendant appears anywhere in the publication, nor do any of defendants' products, prices, or business contacts. As the public would have no reason to associate the publication with defendants, it cannot possibly propose a commercial transaction between defendants and readers of *The Caribbean New Yorker*. Even if defendants paid to run the piece with a motivation toward indirectly influencing customers to buy their goods, such a motivation does not transform the piece into commercial speech."

Is attribution required for this article to be commercial speech? If failing to label an ad as an ad moves content from commercial speech to noncommercial speech, how are advertisers likely to respond, and is this a good idea? Is this holding consistent with the court's ruling on defamation?

Consider the following case of speech to a news organization. It was by a competitor, but not in a traditional advertising context. What standard should regulate it?

Boulé v. Hutton, 328 F.3d 84 (2d Cir. 2003)

Plaintiffs-appellants René and Claude Boulé ("the Boulés") appeal from the decisions of the district court (1) granting partial summary judgment to defendants-appellees Ingrid Hutton ("Hutton"), the Leonard Hutton Galleries, Inc. ("the Gallery"), Mark Khidekel ("Mark") and Regina Khidekel ("Regina"), (2) finding for defendants on certain of plaintiffs' claims after a bench trial, and (3) denying plaintiffs' motion for relief from judgment under Fed. R. Civ. P. 60(b). For the reasons set forth below, we affirm in part, and vacate in part the decisions of the district court.

At its heart, this is a dispute about the authenticity of works of art (the "Paintings") owned by the Boulés. While the Boulés believe the Paintings to be early works of the Russian Suprematist artist Lazar Khidekel ("Lazar"), Lazar's son Mark and daughter-in-law Regina (collectively, "Khidekels") claim that they are not. The Khidekels are selling their own collection of Lazar's art through Hutton and her Gallery.

The Boulés brought suit under the Lanham Act and state law causes of action to recover for the damage to the value of the Paintings that they assert occurred because of statements made by the defendants. The Honorable Miriam Goldman Cedarbaum held, inter alia, that the Boulés had not carried their burden of showing that the Paintings were authentic, that is, painted by Lazar. On the other hand, she found that the Khidekels had falsely and in bad faith denied that Mark had given the Boulés certificates acknowledging that at least some of the Paintings were indeed his father's. Applying the special damage rules that pertain to the law of defamation, the district court awarded the Boulés nominal damages. Each of these rulings and others entered by Judge Cedarbaum in her three opinions have been challenged on appeal.

BACKGROUND

Lazar was born in 1904 in Vitebsk, Russia, and joined the Suprematist school of Russian avant-garde artists in the years following the Russian Revolution. In his youth, Lazar studied with two of the better-known artists of the period, Marc Chagall and Kazmir Malevich, and later in life became a prominent architect. The artworks in his possession upon his death in 1986 became the property of Mark and Regina.

The Boulés are Parisian art collectors who own a number of works from the Russian avant-garde period; in addition, Claude has published a scholarly work on Russian Constructivism. By the late 1980s, the Boulés had acquired 176 works attributed to Lazar. As it was both illegal and dangerous to acquire Russian avant-garde art prior to the fall of the Soviet Union, the majority of the Boulé's pieces were acquired through non-traditional channels.

The Boulés and the Khidekels first encountered each other in Paris in 1988. Over the next few years, the Khidekels and the Boulés developed a friendship, as the Khidekels were pleased to find admirers of Lazar's work in the West, and the Boulés were happy to show their collection to them. They made (ultimately unrealized) plans to pool their collections of Lazar's work for an exhibition in Canada, and, in 1991, in exchange for approximately $8,000, Mark signed certificates of authenticity in Paris for sixteen of the Paintings he selected from the Boulés' collection. The certificates stated: "I, Mark Khidekel, having examined the artwork shown to me . . . hereby confirm that it is the work of my father, Lazar Khidekel, and that it can be identified as a study."

During this period, although the Khidekels were surprised that a collection of Lazar's work existed in Paris, and told the Boulés that some of the pieces they owned were different from those of Lazar's works that the Khidekels possessed, Mark and Regina never expressed to the Boulés any reservations about the legitimacy of the collection. As the district court found at trial, "Mark noted some differences between the Boulés' collection and his collection, and commented that the bulk of the Boulés' collection was created when Lazar Khidekel was a very young student—possibly as early as 1920."

The Boulés exhibited the Paintings at the Joliette Museum of Art in Montreal, Canada in 1992, and galleries in Canada over the course of the months that followed. Although Mark expressed an interest in lecturing at the Joliette Museum in conjunction with the exhibition of the Paintings, the Khidekels ultimately did not participate.

The Khidekels began an association with Hutton in 1992, and moved to New York in 1993. Hutton is a prominent dealer of art of the Russian avant-garde, which has a small but global market. The Khidekels soon entered into a consignment agreement with Hutton to facilitate the sale of their collection of Lazar's work. In 1995, the Gallery exhibited works from the Khidekel's collection. The exhibition catalogue noted that it represented the first-ever display of Lazar's work, despite the earlier show at the Joliette Museum in Canada that had included works from the Boulés' collection. In late 1995 and early 1996, the Khidekels and Hutton sent a jointly-signed letter to at least twenty-five art galleries around the world (the "Repudiation Letter"), repudiating the Paintings that had been loaned by the Boulés and attributed to Lazar in the Canadian exhibition.

In 1996, after being approached by a reporter, Hutton arranged for the Khidekels to be interviewed for an article in *ARTnews*, a leading industry publication, entitled "The Betrayal of the Russian Avant-Garde." The article discussed the entry of "thousands" of fraudulent artworks into galleries, museums and private collections. The Khidekels were quoted in the article as stating that the Paintings were not Lazar's work, and as so advising the Boulés when they had initially viewed the Boulés' collection.[3] An article that appeared

---

[3] The *ARTnews* article contained the following passages:

[Lazar] never had a solo show during his lifetime, nor did he or his family ever sell or part with any of his works, according to his son and daughter-in-law, Mark and Regina Khidekel. On this point, they were adamant. . . .

shortly thereafter in Le Devoir, a Montreal publication, contained a quotation from Regina specifically denying that she or Mark had ever authenticated any portion of the Boulés' collection.[4]

The Boulés brought suit in 1997, alleging that defendants' statements in the Gallery catalogue, the Repudiation Letter, *ARTnews*, and in *Le Devoir*, and other statements to art dealers and journalists violated the Lanham Act. They further alleged that the statements violated the New York General Business Law, and state law causes of action against disparagement, defamation, tortious interference with business relationships, unfair competition, unjust enrichment and breach of contract.

A. The summary judgment rulings

. . . . The district court found that the statements in the Repudiation Letter were not actionable because they could not be considered a "representation of fact" within the meaning of the Lanham Act. The claim pertaining to the statements to *ARTnews* was dismissed because the district court held that a response to an unsolicited inquiry from a reporter on a topic of public concern—fraud in the Russian avant-garde art market—was not a statement made "in commercial advertising or promotion."

Mark and Regina say that they told the Boulés the works were not Khidekels. . . . What makes Mark and Regina most indignant is that the catalogue [for the Joliette Museum exhibition] gives the impression that they endorse the Boulé collection, which they most emphatically do not.

[4] In the February 23, 1996 *Le Devoir* article, Regina is quoted as saying that "neither she nor her husband ever 'authenticated' anything and the fake certificates were forged."

B. The trial

. . . . Judge Cedarbaum did find for plaintiffs on part of their defamation claim. The district court found that the statements published in *Le Devoir* to the effect that Mark had never signed the certificates of authenticity, and in *ARTnews* representing that Mark and Regina had told the Boulés that the Paintings were not authentic, were false and defamatory, but that plaintiffs had not proved special damages. The district court found, however, that the *ARTnews* statements constituted libel per se with regard to Claude Boulé in her capacity as an art historian, but declined to award any more than nominal damages. The plaintiffs also received judgment on their breach of contract claim, as the district court found that Mark had breached the implied covenant of good faith and fair dealing by repudiating the certificates. On this basis, plaintiffs were awarded restitution, but not expectation damages. The remaining state law causes of action were dismissed. . . .

DISCUSSION

[The court concluded that the plaintiffs could not bring Lanham Act claims based on the *ARTnews* statements because they were not commercial speech, and the Lanham Act covers only commercial speech.]

. . . ii. State law claims

The Boulés appeal from the denial at trial of their claims under Section 349 of New York's General Business Law and the New York common law of unfair competition by disparagement. The district court denied these claims based on its conclusion that the plaintiffs had failed to carry their burden to show that the Paintings were authentic. While most of the state law claims were based on statements about the authenticity of the Paintings, some were not.

The *Le Devoir* and *ARTnews* statements addressed the certificates that Mark had provided to the Boulés and the conversations between the Boulés and Khidekels about the Paintings. As the district court held that plaintiffs proved by a preponderance of the evidence the falsity of the statements in *Le Devoir* and *ARTnews*, we remand for further proceedings to determine whether these false statements constitute a violation of Section 349 and the claim of unfair competition by disparagement. In addition, because Section 349 requires proof of a deceptive practice, and does not require proof that a statement is false, we remand for further proceedings on all of plaintiffs' claims under Section 349.

A few additional observations about these two causes of action may prove of assistance on remand. Section 349 prohibits "[d]eceptive acts or practices in the conduct of any business, trade or commerce." N.Y. Gen. Bus. Law. § 349(a). To establish a claim under Section 349, the plaintiff must show "a material deceptive act or practice directed to consumers that caused actual harm." We have not yet decided whether false statements are likely to be deceptive. "Deceptive acts" are defined objectively, as acts "likely to mislead a reasonable consumer acting reasonably under the circumstances." Further, a deceptive practice "need not reach the level of common-law fraud to be actionable under section 349."

The district court expressed reservations as to whether plaintiffs are within the class of persons, namely, consumers, for whose protection Section 349 was enacted. Section 349, however, allows recovery not only by consumers, but also by competitors if there is "some harm to the public at large." Although a Section 349 plaintiff is not required to show justifiable reliance by consumers, "[a]n act is deceptive within the meaning of the New York statute only if it is likely to mislead a reasonable consumer."

On appeal, the Boulés describe their claim of "unfair competition by disparagement" as a claim for defamation of another's business.[8] Where a statement impugns "the basic integrity" of a business, an action for defamation per se lies, and general damages are presumed. Nonetheless, actual damages must be proved with competent evidence of the injury. . . .

CALABRESI, Circuit Judge, concurring.

. . . . Congress did not wish to extend federal Lanham Act liability to speech that is subject to broader general First Amendment protection than is commercial speech. Such noncommercial speech, however, may well remain the grounds of recovery under state laws. In other words, as the opinion notes, even noncommercial speech may, in appropriate cases, be actionable. Today's holding means only that Congress chose not to make that kind of speech federally actionable under the Lanham Act. It is for these reasons that the opinion is able to remand the speech here discussed for consideration of whether it (a) violates section 349 of New York's General Business Law or (b) may be the basis for recovery under the New York common law of unfair competition by disparagement.

NOTES AND QUESTIONS

Given the First Amendment, how far does New York's General Business Law go in making noncommercial speech actionable? As applied to commercial speech, the law clearly covers false speech even when made without fault, but how could it constitutionally apply the

---

[8] . . . On appeal, [the Boulés] press only the claim for defamation of their business presumably because of the difference in the standard for an award of damages. A claim for defamation of another's business is distinct from a claim for product disparagement. Among other things, special damages must be proven for a product disparagement claim. . . .

same rule to noncommercial speech? Should a court refuse to apply the GBL to such speech at all, or should it imply special constraints on a GBL cause of action against noncommercial speech?

Were the Khidekels' statements about authenticity statements of fact or statements of opinion? How can we tell? The next case revisits the fact/opinion line. Consider whether this is the same type of analysis you saw in the Lanham Act cases in Chapter 4.

Cuba's United Ready Mix, Inc. v. Bock Concrete Foundations, Inc., 785 S.W.2d 649 (Mo. Ct. App. 1990)

. . . Plaintiff [a seller of concrete] alleged that defendant Ben Bock, in his capacity as an "officer, director agent and employee of Defendant corporation, Bock Concrete Foundations, Inc. [a contractor that used concrete in construction], . . . made the statement to many persons, other than the Plaintiff's officers and employees, . . . that 'Cuba United Ready Mix, Inc. was delivering inferior material and that he would not be a part of the fraud.' "

. . . The dispositive question here is whether defendants are correct that Bock's statements were opinion, for which there is no liability. . . . " '[A] defamatory communication may consist of a statement in the form of an opinion, but a statement of this nature is actionable only if it implies the allegation of undisclosed defamatory facts as the basis for the opinion.' " . . .

Whether the alleged statements of Bock are fact or opinion, we conclude that they imply that he has knowledge of undisclosed defamatory facts. . . . Such a statement indicates that Bock knew facts establishing that the material of plaintiff was inferior and plaintiff knew it and concealed it. As such, it may constitute actionable defamation.

NOTES AND QUESTIONS

Note the different positions in the sales chain occupied by the parties. Why do you think Bock might have had incentives to say negative things about Cuba's United? After *Lexmark*, could a Lanham Act claim be brought against defendants?

Now consider the court's holding about whether the statements were actionable. Was it Bock's position as a user of concrete that made it plausible to think that he had knowledge of undisclosed defamatory facts supporting his opinion? What if he'd posted the same statement as an anonymous comment on a blog about the plaintiff—would the statement still be potentially defamatory?

Bock's statements were of the kind one might expect an individual to make in the course of soliciting specific customers. Historically, the business torts developed to address that kind of situation. Consider how well these torts fit with a modern, mass advertising campaign. (Hint: maybe not that well?)

In *Verizon Directories Corp. v. Yellow Book USA, Inc.*, 309 F. Supp. 2d 401 (E.D.N.Y 2004), Verizon sued Yellow Book over TV ads that used humor to suggest that Yellow Book was superior. According to Verizon, the ads falsely represented that more people used the Yellow Book than Verizon's offering; the number of users is relevant to the prices a directory can command from advertisers. One ad, for example, showed a "Senior Focus Group" in which everyone claimed to use the Yellow Book and no one had heard of the alternative (Verizon). In another ad, a wind tunnel easily blew Verizon's directory away, while the Yellow Book proved more substantial because it had "the right stuff." Verizon alleged Lanham Act claims, violation of New York's statutory false advertising law (§§ 349–350, discussed above), and product disparagement.

Yellow Book argued that its ads were merely puffery. The court, applying the same analysis to the Lanham Act claims as to the state law claims, found that it could not determine puffery as a matter of law. Though the ads were literally "playful and absurd," in context, consumers might interpret the ads to mean that more people used the Yellow Book than the Verizon directory. The ads were "skillfully crafted and shown at great expense to subtly but firmly communicate an idea—that the Yellow Book is preferred by users to Verizon's book and that, more to the point, advertisers will reach more potential consumers if they put their names and money in the former rather than the latter." The judge's background was very different from ordinary viewers', and the judge declined to resolve the meaning of the ad to them, an issue requiring "surveys, expert testimony, and other evidence of what is happening in the real world of television watchers and advertisers in yellow pages."

In applying the Lanham Act puffery standards to the state law disparagement claims, was the *Verizon* court doing something different than what the court did in the *Bock* case with respect to the line between opinion and fact? Historically, defamation and product disparagement cases didn't involve expert testimony or consumer surveys—juries were left to their own interpretation of the accused materials. Why isn't that still the right rule for a defamation/disparagement claim, given the other barriers to bringing such a claim? Is there something different about mass media campaigns that would justify different treatment?

3. Why All These Negative Ads?: Public Policy and Comparative Advertising

Historically, comparative advertising was regarded with suspicion (and still is in the European Union; see Chapter 11). A few decades ago, however, impelled by concerns that advertising restrictions were suppressing competition and raising prices, the FTC made a major push to encourage such advertising.

Federal Trade Commission, Statement of Policy Regarding Comparative Advertising, August 13, 1979

. . .(b) Policy Statement

The Federal Trade Commission has determined that it would be of benefit to advertisers, advertising agencies, broadcasters, and self-regulation entities to restate its current policy concerning comparative advertising.[6] Commission policy in the area of comparative advertising encourages the naming of, or reference to competitors, but requires clarity, and, if necessary, disclosure to avoid deception of the consumer. Additionally, the use of truthful comparative advertising should not be restrained by broadcasters or self-regulation entities.

(c) The Commission has supported the use of brand comparisons where the bases of comparison are clearly identified. Comparative advertising, when truthful and non-deceptive, is a source of important information to consumers and assists them in making rational purchase decisions. Comparative advertising encourages product improvement and innovation, and can lead to lower prices in the marketplace. For these reasons, the Commission will continue to scrutinize carefully restraints upon its use.

---

[6] For purposes of this Policy Statement, comparative advertising is defined as advertising that compares alternative brands on objectively measurable attributes or price, and identifies the alternative brand by name, illustration or other distinctive information.

(1) Disparagement

Some industry codes which prohibit practices such as "disparagement," "disparagement of competitors," "improper disparagement," "unfairly attacking," "discrediting," may operate as a restriction on comparative advertising. The Commission has previously held that disparaging advertising is permissible so long as it is truthful and not deceptive. In *Carter Products, Inc.*, 323 F.2d 523 (5th Cir. 1963), the Commission narrowed an order recommended by the hearing examiner which would have prohibited respondents from disparaging competing products through the use of false or misleading pictures, depictions, or demonstrations, "or otherwise" disparaging such products. In explaining why it eliminated "or otherwise" from the final order, the Commission observed that the phrase would have prevented:

> respondents from making truthful and nondeceptive statements that a product has certain desirable properties or qualities which a competing product or products do not possess. Such a comparison may have the effect of disparaging the competing product, but we know of no rule of law which prevents a seller from honestly informing the public of the advantages of its products as opposed to those of competing products.

Industry codes which restrain comparative advertising in this manner are subject to challenge by the Federal Trade Commission.

(2) Substantiation

On occasion, a higher standard of substantiation by advertisers using comparative advertising has been required by self-regulation entities. . . . However, industry codes and interpretations that impose a higher standard of substantiation for comparative claims than for unilateral claims are inappropriate and should be revised.

Effect of the FTC Statement

The FTC's statement focused on consumer information and antitrust concerns: an agreement to refrain from saying nasty things about the competition could have anticompetitive effects. Comparative advertising became quite widespread in the U.S. By some measures, one-third of U.S. ads are comparative, and comparative ads may be more persuasive and memorable than non-comparative ads. *See* Jenna D. Beller, Comment, *The Law of Comparative Advertising in the United States and Around the World: A Practical Guide for U.S. Lawyers and Their Clients*, 29 INT'L LAW. 917 (1995).

A separate question is raised by comparative advertising: what happens when an ad doesn't name the competition? *Kinetic Concepts, Inc. v. Bluesky Medical Corporation*, 2005 WL 3068209 (W.D. Tex. 2005), applied the general defamation rule that "it is not necessary that the individual referred to be named if those who knew and were acquainted with the plaintiff understand from reading the publication that it referred to the plaintiff." The plaintiff in *Kinetic* conducted a study showing that 33.3% of physicians and 95% of nurses in its sample believed that the relevant ads were comparing the parties' products. This created a genuine issue of material fact on the element that a defamatory statement must be "of and concerning" the plaintiff to be actionable.

4. A Final Business Tort: Tortious Interference

Tortious interference with contract or with prospective contractual relations is often alleged alongside various other advertising-related torts. There are substantial state-law variations in the elements of the tort, which we will not detail. It is rarely successful in the advertising and marketing law context. The following case against Google, which makes its money from advertisers who often bid against their competitors even for their own trademarks, illustrates that the tort is not well-suited for a modern, large-scale advertising practice.

Google Inc. v. American Blind & Wallpaper Factory, Inc., 74 U.S.P.Q.2d 1385 (N.D. Cal. 2005)

[This is a keyword advertising case, as described in Chapter 11: Google sells the plaintiff's trademark and domain name as keywords in its AdWords program so that competitors' ads appear as sponsored links in response to a search for "American Blind." The court refused to dismiss American Blind's trademark claims for failure to state a claim.]

. . . C. Tortious Interference with Prospective Business Advantage

Defendants move to dismiss American Blind's state law claim of tortious interference with prospective business advantage.[31] The

---

[31] American Blind alleges that (1) "[m]any" of its customers are "repeat customers" and "regularly" purchase products from its Web site, (2) it is probable that "such customers and others" will "continue to seek to visit" the Web site and purchase products and services "in the future," (3) Defendants were aware of American Blind's "reasonable expectation of future transactions" with its "returning customers," as well as with customers who "may be attracted" to its goods and services because of its goodwill, advertising, and promotion, (4) "[a]bsent Defendants' intentional and improper interference through their deceptive and manipulated search engine 'results,' it is reasonably certain that American Blind would realize additional sales from existing customers and/or new customers," (5) Defendants "intentionally and improperly interfered with American Blind's future and prospective sales," and (6) American Blind has suffered and will continue to suffer irreparable injury as a result of Defendants' actions.

elements of tortious interference with prospective business advantage are as follows: (1) an economic relationship between the plaintiff and some third party, with the probability of future economic benefit to the plaintiff, (2) the defendant's knowledge of the relationship, (3) intentional acts on the part of the defendant designed to disrupt the relationship, which acts are wrongful by some legal measure other than the fact of interference itself,[32] (4) actual disruption of the relationship, and (5) economic harm to the plaintiff proximately caused by the defendant's acts. Defendants argue that American Blind fails to allege an independently wrongful act, as required by the third element, or probability of future economic benefit from existing economic relationships, as required by the first element.

. . . . As American Blind's claims of trademark violations, unfair competition, false representation, and injury to business reputation will proceed past the motion-to-dismiss stage, so too can those claims serve, for present purposes, as allegations that satisfy the pleading requirements for the third element of tortious interference with prospective business advantage.

However, the Court agrees with Defendants that American Blind's allegations with respect to the first element of the claim are insufficient. The tort of interference with prospective business advantage applies to "interference with existing noncontractual relations which hold the promise of future economic advantage. In other words, it protects the expectation that the relationship eventually will yield the desired benefit, not necessarily the more speculative expectation that a potentially beneficial relationship will eventually arise." Allegations that amount to a mere "hope for an

---

[32] An act is independently wrongful if it is "unlawful, that is, if it is proscribed by some constitutional, statutory, regulatory, common law, or other determinable legal standard."

economic relationship and a desire for future benefit" are inadequate to satisfy the pleading requirements of the first element of the tort.

Even though American Blind has alleged relationships with "repeat customers" who "probabl[y]" will "continue to seek to visit" its Web site and purchase its goods and services, American Blind's alleged expectation of "future and prospective sales" to these customers, with which Defendants are alleged to have interfered, is too speculative to support this claim. It does not rise to the level of the requisite "promise of future economic advantage," instead expressing merely a "hope . . . and a desire" for unspecified future sales to unspecified returning customers, in the form of a legal conclusion. Moreover, it goes without saying that American Blind's even more speculative allegations regarding "new" customers with whom it cannot claim any past or present interactions, however insubstantial, also are inadequate to support this claim. American Blind has failed to point to any case law suggesting that its allegations regarding the probability of future economic benefit from its existing economic relationships with third parties are sufficient. Accordingly, Defendants' motions to dismiss American Blind's claim of tortious interference with prospective business advantage are GRANTED.

Made in the USA
San Bernardino,
CA